THE HORROR READER

Horror has been one of the more spectacular and controversial genres in both cinema and fiction – its wild excesses relished by some, vilified by many others. Often defiantly marginal, it nevertheless inhabits the very fabric of everyday life, providing us with ways of imagining and classifying our world: what is evil and what is good; what is monstrous and what is 'normal'; what can be seen and what should remain hidden.

The Horror Reader brings together twenty-nine key articles to examine the enduring resonance of horror across culture. Spanning the history of horror in literature and film, and discussing texts from Britain, the United States, Europe, the Caribbean and Hong Kong, it explores a diversity of horror forms from classic gothic literature like *Frankenstein* and *Dr Jekyll and Mr Hyde*, to contemporary serial killers, horror film fanzines and low-budget movies such as *The Leech Woman* and *The Texas Chainsaw Massacre*.

The *Reader* opens with an introduction to 'the field of horror' by Ken Gelder, and each thematic section includes an introductory preface. There is also a comprehensive bibliography of horror literature.

Themes addressed include: the fantastic, horror and psychoanalysis, monstrosities, different Frankensteins, vampires, queer horror, American gothic, stalker and slasher films, race and ethnicity, lowbrow and low-budget horror, and new regional horror.

Editor: **Ken Gelder** is Reader in English at the University of Melbourne. His books include *Reading the Vampire* (Routledge 1994) and, as co-editor, *The Subcultures Reader* (Routledge 1997).

THE HORROR READER

Edited by

Ken Gelder

London and New York

First published 2000
by Routledge
11 New Fetter Lane, London EC4P 4EE

Simultaneously published in the USA and Canada
by Routledge
29 West 35th Street, New York, NY 10001

Reprinted 2001

Routledge is an imprint of the Taylor & Francis Group

Typeset in Perpetua by
Florence Production Ltd, Stoodleigh, Devon
Printed and bound in Great Britain by
TJ International, Padstow

British Library Cataloguing in Publication Data
A catalogue record for this book is available from the British Library

Library of Congress Cataloging-in-Publication Data
The horror reader / edited by Ken Gelder.
    p.   cm.
  Includes bibliographical references and index.
  1. Horror tales—History and criticism.   2. Horror films—
History and criticism.   I. Gelder, Ken, 1955–
PN3435 .H69 2000
809.3'8738–dc21   99–087412

ISBN 0–415–21355–X (hbk)
ISBN 0–415–21356–8 (pbk)

Contents

Illustrations

Acknowledgements

Special thanks go to the contributors to this Reader, who gave their kind permission to be reprinted – often in substantially (but always sensitively!) edited form – and offered encouragement along the way. Thanks also go to Rebecca Barden and Alistair Daniel from Routledge for their support for this project. I am grateful to Audrey Yue for help with new Asian horror resources, and to Annamarie Jagose and Ken Ruthven for some useful suggestions. Finally, I am indebted as always to Hannah, Christian and Julian for putting up with the whole thing: bedtime reading one day, perhaps.

Chapter 1   Tzvetan Todorov, 'Definition of the Fantastic', in *The Fantastic* (Cornell University Press, 1975). Reprinted by permission of Georges Borchardt Inc.

Chapter 2   José B. Monleon, '1848: The Assault on Reason' in *A Specter is Haunting Europe*. © 1990 Princeton University Press. Reprinted by permission of Princeton University Press.

Chapter 3   Terry Castle, 'Phantasmagoria and the Metaphorics of Modern Reverie' in *Critical Inquiry* 15 (Autumn 1988). © 1988 by The University of Chicago. All rights reserved. Reprinted by permission of The University of Chicago.

Chapter 4   Joan Copjec, 'Vampires, Breast-Feeding and Anxiety' in *October*, no.58 (1991/2). © Joan Copjec.

Chapter 5   Barbara Creed, 'Kristeva, Femininity, Abjection' in *The Monstrous Feminine* (Routledge 1993).

Chapter 6   Slavoj Žižek, 'In his Bold Gaze My Ruin is Writ Large' in
             *Everything you wanted to know about Lacan (but were afraid to
             ask Hitchcock)* (London: Verso, 1995). Reprinted by permission
             of Verso.

Chapter 7   Reprinted by permission of the publisher from *Monstrous
             Imagination* by Marie-Hélène Huet, Cambridge, Mass.: Harvard
             University Press. © 1993 by the President and Fellows of Harvard
             College.

Chapter 8   Mary Russo, 'Freaks', in *The Female Grotesque* (New York:
             Routledge Inc, 1994). Reproduced by permission of Routledge, Inc.

Chapter 9   Mark Seltzer, 'The Serial Killer as a Type of Person' in *Serial
             Killers* (New York Routledge Inc., 1998). Reprinted by permission
             of Routledge, Inc.

Chapter 10   Paul O'Flinn, 'Production and Reproduction: The Case of
             Frankenstein' in *Popular Fictions* (London: Methuen, 1986).
             © Routledge.

Chapter 11   Elizabeth Young, 'Here Comes the Bride: Wedding Gender and
             Race in *Bride of Frankenstein*' in *Feminist Studies,* Vol 17. no. 3
             (Fall 1991): 403–437, by permission of the publisher, Feminist
             Studies, Inc.

Chapter 12   Franco Moretti, 'Dialectic of Fear' in *Signs Taken for Wonders*
             (London: Verso, 1995). Reprinted by permission of Verso.

Chapter 13   Stephen D. Arata, 'The Occidental Tourist' in *Victorian Studies,*
             Vol. 33, no.4 (Summer 1990). Reprinted by permission of Indiana
             University Press.

Chapter 14   Jennifer Wicke, 'Vampiric Typewriting' in *English Literary History*,
             no. 59 (1992) pp.467–493. © 1992 The Johns Hopkins University
             Press.

Chapter 15   Elaine Showalter, 'Dr Jekyll's Closet' in *Sexual Anarchy*
             (Penguin 1990). © Elaine Showalter. Reprinted by permission of
             the author.

Chapter 16   Sue-Ellen Case, 'Tracking the Vampire' in *differences,* Vol.3, no.2
             (Summer 1991) Reprinted by permission of the publisher, Indiana
             University Press.

Chapter 17   Patricia White, 'Female Spectator, Lesbian Spectator: The
             Haunting' in *Inside/Out* (New York: Routledge, Inc., 1991).
             Reprinted by permission of Routledge, Inc.

Chapter 18   Ken Gelder, 'Vampires in Greece' in *Reading the Vampire* (London:
             Routledge, 1994). © Routledge.

Chapter 19   Fatimah Tobing Rony, '*King Kong* and the Monster in Ethnographic
             Cinema' in *The Third Eye: Race, Cinema and Ethnographic
             Spectacle.* © 1996 Duke University Press. All rights reserved.
             Reprinted with permission.

Chapter 20   Gregory A. Waller, 'Introduction' from *American Horrors*
             (University of Illinois Press 1987) pp.1–13. © 1987 by Board of

Trustees of the University of Illinois. Used with permission of the University of Illinois Press.

Chapter 21   Teresa A. Goddu, 'Introduction' from *Gothic America* (Columbia University Press 1997). © 1997 Columbia University Press. Reprinted with the permission of the publisher.

Chapter 22   Philip Brophy, 'Horrality – the Textuality of Contemporary Horror Films' in *Screen* Vol.27, no.1 (1986). Reprinted by permission of the publisher.

Chapter 23   Tania Modleski, 'The Terror of Pleasure' in *Studies in Entertainment* (1986) Indiana University Press, Bloomington. Reprinted by permission of the publisher.

Chapter 24   Carol J. Clover, 'Her Body, Himself' in *Men, Women and Chainsaws.* © 1992 Princeton University Press. Reprinted by permission of Princeton University Press.

Chapter 25   David Sanjek, 'Fans Notes: The Horror Film Fanzine' in *Literature/Film Quarterly*, Vol.18, no.3 (1990). © 1990 Literature/Film Quarterly.

Chapter 26   Leon Hunt, 'A (Sadistic) Night at the *Opera*' in *The Velvet Light Trap* no.30 (Fall 1992), pp.65–75. © 1992 by the University of Texas Press. All rights reserved.

Chapter 27   Vivian Sobchack, 'Revenge of the Leech Woman' in *Uncontrollable Bodies* (Bay Press 1994). Reprinted by permission of the author.

Chapter 28   Huggan, Graham 'Ghost Stories, Bone Flutes, Cannibal Countermemory' in *Cannibalism and the Colonial World* (Cambridge University Press 1998). Reprinted by permission of the publisher.

INTRODUCTION
The field of horror

■   Ken Gelder

THIS READER BRINGS TOGETHER the best academic essays on horror from over the last twenty-five years, with the aim both of giving 'the field of horror' some definition and of affirming that this field is worth studying. I take the notion of a 'field', somewhat loosely, from Pierre Bourdieu, who has developed ways of conceptualizing the broader 'field of cultural production' (Bourdieu: 1993). Horror is one of many forms of cultural production, represented in this Reader primarily through film and fiction – horror texts – but also through the everyday deployment of what might be called the rhetorics of horror. Obviously, much attention has been given to horror *as* a form of cultural production in society by media commentators, philosophers, various government authorities, and so on. Some people are anxious about it, others defend it, even relish it; a great deal has been said about it one way or the other. Horror texts thus have real socio-cultural effects, making available (to draw on Bourdieu again) a range of positions and dispositions; they have their own 'politics', in the sense that they are never represented to the world in a neutral way. But the rhetorics of horror circulate more broadly still. They provide ways of defining, for example, what is evil (and what is good) in societies, what is monstrous (and what is 'normal'), what should be seen (and what should remain hidden), and so on. These rhetorics are put to use routinely not just in horror texts themselves, but in the very same socio-political system that can find itself worrying about their proliferation. We can probably agree that horror, its rhetorics, its narratives, the paradigms and discourses it provides for imagining and classifying the world, inhabits that system – our system – for better or worse. Braver souls might even suggest that the socio-political system *needs* these rhetorics, narratives and so on – that is, it needs horror itself – in order to be what it is and do what it does.

Take the question of evil, as one example. For Joan Copjec, whose essay on vampires, breast-feeding and anxiety is represented in this Reader, Kant's belated acknowledgement of 'radical evil' at the end of the eighteenth century turned the Enlightenment's advocacy of 'moral improvement' into nothing less than a wild fantasy (Copjec: 1996, ix). Evil was identified as 'a positive fact, firmly rooted in reality', at the very moment at which modernity secured its faith in 'infinite progress' and a free humanity (ibid., xi). For others, of course, evil has mysteriously been with us since time immemorial; it may indeed be figured as modern and archaic simultaneously. Nevertheless, the view that certain *kinds* of evil – the kinds that produce horror (from the Latin *horrere*, to shudder) – are inextricably entwined with post-Enlightenment civilization, born (again) out of its very aspirations, has become increasingly commonplace in the modern world. In his book *Literature and Evil* (1957), the French novelist and philosopher Georges Bataille notes that evil is thus 'always the object of an ambiguous condemnation' (Bataille: 1997, 29). An advocate of passionate excess and 'intoxication', Bataille saw Emily Brontë's novel *Wuthering Heights* (1847) as a striking expression of this ambiguity: both utterly 'humane' and an example of evil in 'its most perfect form' (ibid., 17). Evil may these days be thought of as peripheral to society, like a kind of distant, dark relative (Heathcliff) who turns up only intermittently. Yet as the high priest of postmodernism, Jean Baudrillard, remarks, it can at the same time appear to be 'everywhere'. Influenced by Bataille, Baudrillard nevertheless sees the task of western modernity as one of diminishing evil, 'minimizing' its effects, smoothing away its various accompanying 'negativities' (Baudrillard: 1993, 86) – in which case good always becomes a reactive condition, made to signify austerity and restraint. The west may find itself resting comfortably in the knowledge that it can no longer be assaulted by evil dressed up as a 'barbarian' Other. For Baudrillard, however, the result is a certain loss of power, whereby the west now paradoxically becomes vulnerable 'even to the mildest of viral attacks' (ibid., 82). His example is the Ayotollah's *fatwa* against the novelist, Salman Rushdie: a viral attack which 'consists in subtly injecting archaic elements into a modern context' (ibid., 84); an act of violence against the west which is primarily symbolic and discursive, but no less effective for all that.

These various claims for evil can help us to situate horror itself, both in terms of its rhetorical deployments in society and as a form of cultural production (film, fiction; horror texts). There is certainly an argument to be made for seeing horror, too, as a modern phenomenon arising out of the Enlightenment: the contributions to Part One of this Reader, particularly from José B. Monleon and Terry Castle, turn back to the eighteenth and nineteenth centuries to make precisely this point. Once, horror was condemned to be otherwordly; but now, as Mark Seltzer and others show in this Reader, it inhabits the very fabric of ordinary life, daily picking away at the limits of reason and the aspirations underpinning 'moral improvement', and gaining new identities along the way. Horror as a form of cultural production is also routinely linked to excess, to a *lack* of restraint; horror texts can thus appear to delight in the very 'negativities' that, for Baudrillard, the west would otherwise wish to downplay. In doing so, horror may itself become the object of 'ambiguous condemnation'. Linda Ruth Williams makes exactly this point in a short essay on a cluster of body-horror films which throw the 'struggling moral subject' and the 'frenzied subject of excess' together, raising the important question: with which are we meant to sympathize (Williams: 1993, 33)? Body-horror films – the cinema of David Cronenberg, for example – give expression to the kind of preoccupation with 'viral attacks' that Baudrillard identifies as symptomatic of the modern west. So do possession films, vampire films, zombie films, werewolf films, and so on, all of which show one kind of body mutating wildly into another: the struggling moral subject actually becoming the frenzied subject of excess. Moreover, the mutation turns away from 'infinite progress', 'moral improvement' and human freedom often to foreground their opposites: enslavement, degradation and a level of *regression* that can seem to take us out of modernity altogether and into something much more 'primal'. In this way, horror in fact pre-empts the Ayotollah's strategy of injecting (subtly or otherwise) 'archaic elements into a modern context'. Indeed, the contributions to Part Two in particular, on horror and psychoanalysis, see this entanglement as central to horror's capacity to disorient and disturb. Horror is where the archaic (the 'primal', the 'primitive', the 'frenzied subject of excess') and the modern (the 'struggling moral subject', rational, technological) suddenly find themselves occupying the same territory.

Horror texts may very well represent this entanglement; how they resolve it is another question. Horror can sometimes find itself championed as a genre because the disturbance it wilfully produces is in fact a disturbance of cultural and ideological categories we may have taken for granted. Indeed, a number of contributions to this Reader examine horror texts and images precisely in terms of their ability to call conventional representations of temporal, sexual, cultural and national identities into question. For the American film critic Robin Wood, the most 'authentic' horror launched a traumatic assault on those categories, its monsters signifying what he famously termed a 'return of the repressed' (Wood *et al.*: 1979). But Wood was also alert to a conservative streak in some horror cinema, identifying its reactionary potential. In José B. Monleon's contribution to this Reader, the rhetorics of horror developing through the eighteenth and nineteenth centuries were ultimately in the service of the Enlightenment, ensuring its survival. In Barbara Creed's, horror enables the monstrous to *remain* monstrous, keeping cultural categories intact; her work on the maternal woman as a site for deployment of rhetorics of horror is echoed in the contribution to Part Three from Marie-Hélene Huet. Fatimah Tobing Rony's contribution reads the film *King Kong* (1933) in the same way, throwing the archaic (the 'savage') into the frame of the civilized only to confirm their absolute incommensurability. Horror may indeed visualize the Other simply in order to consolidate its Otherness. Mary Russo's account of 'freaks' in Part Three, however, calls for a certain *recovery* of Otherness, lending some support to Baudrillard's point that the west has righteously tended to 'minimize' what it has regarded as 'negativities'.

Various critics in this Reader and elsewhere have noted that horror texts can disturb in some ways, and console in others – leading them to cultivate a certain ambivalence (much like Bataille's 'ambiguous condemnation') towards the form.

Noël Carroll, for example, notes that the events dramatized in horror texts may well exceed 'ideological accounts' of the world, yet they are by no means 'emancipatory' (Carroll: 1990, 197). Drawing on the work of Mary Douglas, Carroll links this critical ambivalence towards horror with what he diagnoses as its 'paradox', its definitive capacity both to disgust and fascinate. The problem with Carroll's analysis is that — perhaps like this introduction thus far — it tends to homogenize horror, seeing all horror texts as performing much the same kind of task. But 'the field of horror' is a fractured, many-faceted thing, and critical dispositions not only depend on what is being looked at, and when, but will *determine* what is being looked at (and what is deemed inappropriate, irrelevant, and so on) in the first place. Like the broader field of cultural production, for example, horror has its high and low cultural components — and these may themselves be seen as absolutely incommensurable with one another. Horror texts at the bottom end of the market, for example, can send the more discerning member of the audience scuttling off to other, more accommodating points in the field. Feeling swamped by a mass of 'neurotically compulsive' horror films, Lizzie Francke (as if bearing out Baudrillard's claim about the west) turns with relief back to the 'minimalist' horror cinema of Val Lewton which, for her, encourages audiences to 'let loose their own imagination' (Francke: 1993, 12). The schlock-horror film-maker Brian Yuzna unexpectedly confesses his admiration for Robert Wise's film, *The Haunting* (1963): 'It is all about sensitivity and vulnerability', he suggests (Yuzna: 1994, 43). Jeremy Dyson is also in flight from contemporary graphic horror films, yearning for the 'greatness' of early black-and-white horror cinema — a disposition which enables him to find *The Haunting* 'more fascinating with each screening' (Dyson: 1997, xii). One critic may declare his preference for earlier 'aesthetically shaped' horror films over contemporary 'sensationalist' ones (Prawer: 1980, 48). Another may even moralistically reject the contemporary field altogether, finding his own brand of 'authentic' horror in late eighteenth and nineteenth century gothic literature — and writing elegiacally of its passing (Edmundson, 1997).

The preference for subtle or incomplete forms of horror over a more confronting, sensationalist horror text that shows everything (or, shows 'too much') is certainly one way of dividing up the field — although Robin Wood has been one critic who has paid tribute to both ends of the spectrum, praising the excesses of Tobe Hooper's *The Texas Chainsaw Massacre* (1974) as much as subtleties of the Val Lewton film, directed by Jacques Tourneur, *I Walked with a Zombie* (1943) (see Wood *et al.*: 1979; and Wood: 1976). Another way has been through dividing commercial horror films from low-budget or independent horror, with 'authenticity' (registered as an important criterion in so many critical accounts of the field) assigned to the latter at the former's expense. As David Sanjek notes in his contribution to Part Ten, this is a strategy commonly found in horror fanzines which provide lovingly detailed cartographies of the lower depths of the horror field. Graphic, sensationalist features are usually celebrated rather than disavowed, privileged rather than 'minimized': the more 'primal' a horror text seems to be, the more it is enjoyed. Other essays in this Reader, from Carol J. Clover and Vivian Sobchack, draw particular value from low-budget, no-nonsense horror films. But commercial horror texts can often, in turn, be too easily demonized. For Joseph Grixti, for instance, contemporary horror fiction fails to deal with the 'uncertainties' of present-day realities (Grixti: 1989, 182); the novels of Stephen King and others, in his view, are not ambivalent *enough*. However, the requirement that horror texts themselves be as ambivalent as the world around us rules out commercial forms pretty much altogether, because they are generally unconcerned with presenting their narratives realistically. Moreover, it condemns those commercial forms, and their audiences, to be seen only in derisive terms, as 'dumb', merely thrill-seeking, uncritical, escapist – rhetorics which are analysed in *relation* to horror by Jennifer Wicke and Tania Modleski in this Reader. A different view to Grixti's, however, is taken elsewhere by Jeffrey Sconce, who contrasts the teen-oriented *Nightmare on Elm Street* series with the low-budget film, *Henry: Portrait of a Serial Killer* (1987). For Sconce, the 'visual stimulation' of the one is incompatible with the critically provocative realism of the other, reminding us that the field of horror is arranged primarily in terms of a politics of taste (Sconce: 1993, 114). And this is not just true of contemporary horror, of course, as – for example – Robert Morrison and Chris Baldick make clear in their study of the commercial, sensationalist 'terror tales' published in magazines such as *Blackwood's* during the early part of the nineteenth century (Polidori: 1997).

It is not the purpose of this Reader fully to legitimize the study of horror, which has of course so often staked out its place in the broader field of cultural production in terms of *illegitimacy*: as an often shocking, spectacular, sensationalist and 'immoral' (or amoral) form which can seem to take pleasure from the fact that so many people find it disturbing, distasteful or even downright unacceptable. The 'minimizing' of the impact of horror texts happens most directly through censorship, of course: William Friedkin's *The Exorcist* (1973) had long been denied a video certificate in Britain, for example, and was said at the time to produce 'lasting negative or disturbing effects' (Kermode: 1998, 8). The scapegoating of so-called 'video nasties' in the early 1980s was also aimed primarily at horror films. The 'negative effects' of horror, real or imagined, keep the genre downtrodden and free from complexities: as if a horror text, like pornography (to which it is often compared), is a simple matter of cause and effect, arousing, nauseating or inciting, as the case may be. Outside of this sensual equation horror may, to some, be entirely bereft of meaning. The academic readings included in this Reader, however, take the opposite view. They see horror texts as signifying systems: their approach is primarily semiotic. A number of contributions draw on the 'revealing', decoding methodologies of psychoanalysis. These and other essays thus provide 'deep' readings of a genre that may, to the unsympathetic, seem either superficial or incomprehensible. We might contrast this kind of reading to the practice of horror fanzines and genre guides, which instead lay out the field of horror 'horizontally': processing vast numbers of films and novels, often providing the most minor or idiosyncratic particulars about directors, writers, stars, special effects, and so on. But this Reader also draws attention to academic work that develops a not dissimilar 'horizontal' approach to the field: from the contribution by Terry Castle, excavating details about late eighteenth and early nineteenth century ghost shows, through to essays by Leon Hunt, Carol J. Clover, Philip Brophy, Vivian Sobchack, Gregory A. Waller and others, which demonstrate an extensive knowledge of horror genealogies and networks.

The close readings of specific horror texts, however, do raise the question: how much significance can horror take? In some cases – as in Teresa A. Goddu's account of 'American Gothic', my own extract on vampires in Greece, Graham Huggan's essay on Caribbean ghost stories and Audrey Yue's reading of two 'preposterous' Hong Kong horror films – a marginal form is made significant enough to speak to a national predicament. The various monsters mobilized in horror texts can find themselves right at the centre of semiotic attention: as Judith Halberstam has noted, 'Monsters are meaning machines' (Halberstam: 1995, 21). Part Three in this Reader is precisely about monstrosity and its meanings, while the essays in Parts Four and Five look closely at two of the foundational monsters of modernity. A section devoted to queer approaches to horror draws out the often hidden or impacted significances of horror texts – as if horror is somehow 'haunted' by its *own* ghosts. The essays by Carol J. Clover and Audrey Yue in other sections of this Reader return to the topic of queerness, undercutting straight(forward) gendered readings of audience/monster or audience/victim identification. Yet the approaches here *remain* semiotic: almost no ethnographic work of any consequence on actual horror audiences has been done, although the occasional pious reminder that horror audiences are as 'diverse' as the field of horror itself (see, for example, Tudor: 1997) may be of as little help to analysis as the weary dismissal of horror as a genre that performs the same task over and over again.

The primary task of a Reader is to organize a field of study, identifying key terms and key interests, and representing the best work in that field to date. Horror *aficionados* who come here expecting every horror text to be accounted for will be disappointed, and in fact there are real gaps in the academic analysis of horror that have indeed placed some limits on its reach. It *has* neglected audiences; its range of inquiry can be curtailed by what it identifies as canonical in the field; and it is certainly striking that the analysis of contemporary forms has focused mostly on cinema, ignoring horror novelists altogether (with one or two exceptions), and rarely noticing horror on television or in other media. Academics, of course, both develop and are constrained by their *own* politics of taste. Nevertheless, this Reader – while avoiding the cliché that horror and its audiences are 'diverse' – covers a great many horror forms, and reflects a range of critical approaches. It begins with a section on 'the fantastic', a term which gives expression to horror's modern inhabitation of everyday life. Part Two focuses on psychoanalytical approaches to horror, with readings of vampires, Hitchcock's *Psycho* (1960), and the 'monstrous-feminine' in contemporary popular horror cinema. Part Three examines the ways in which monsters, or monstrosities, are shaped and signified in culture, covering monstrous births, freaks and freakiness, and the rhetorics which assemble around the serial killer. Parts Four and Five are built around canonical nineteenth century horror texts, with readings of some of the many adaptations of Mary Shelley's novel *Frankenstein* (1818), as well as detailed analyses of Bram Stoker's vampire novel, *Dracula* (1897). Part Six brings horror into the realm of queer theory, which attends to its often fraught representations of sexuality – and mounts an argument with feminist approaches to horror in the process. In Part Seven, the focus is on ethnicity, with essays examining the links between horror and early ethnographic cinema, and the Greekness of vampires. Part Eight turns to American horror, covering the 'American Gothic', and the post-1968 horror film. It is a short step from the latter to Part Nine, with essays on slasher and splatter films from the 1970s and early 1980s. Part Ten then turns directly to lowbrow, low-budget horror, examining the critical dispositions of horror fanzines, the art/lowbrow crossover of Italian horror cinema, and low-budget films about ageing women. Finally, in Part Eleven, the focus is on another neglected area of analysis, namely, horror outside of Britain, Europe and America – in this case, ghost stories from the Caribbean and ghost films from Hong Kong. Each section has its own introduction, drawing the contributions together, providing contexts for them, and detailing important themes and issues.

Part One

THE FANTASTIC

Introduction to Part One

■   Ken Gelder

THIS SECTION BEGINS WITH the Bulgarian-born critic Tzvetan
Todorov's famous recovery of the fantastic as a literary term. We may need
to remember that the fantastic was a term long used in derogatory fashion, linked
to tasteless excess, irresponsibility, delusion, even mental derangement. The
Elizabethan poet Edmund Spenser typically spoke against it in *The Fairie Queene*
(1590) through his character Phantastes, who dwells alone, idle and 'melancholy',
in a 'dispainted', fly-blown chamber (Book ii, Canto ix, 49–52). In *The Teares of
the Muses* (1591), Spenser saw bad poetry as the 'fruitfull spawne of ranke
fantasies', resembling nothing less than 'a monster' (ll.322, 558). Fantasy here
and elsewhere was hardly seen as literary at all. Fantasy writers themselves, of
course, came tenaciously to defend the genre, usually giving its sensationalist,
otherworldly features a positive spin. In 1945 H. P. Lovecraft, for instance, spoke
of the 'weird tale's' capacity to excite in the reader 'a profound sense of dread',
calling up the oldest and most primal of emotions, fear (Lovecraft: 1973, 16).
But this was precisely why the fantastic was refused entry into the respectable
literary field: it was seen as a throwback to premodern times, utterly sensual,
without intellectual content.

   For Todorov, the fantastic is not primal and premodern at all, but in fact
sophisticated enough to stand for the nature of literature itself. Its project involves
not the arousal of primal emotions, but the production of an epistemological, and
very modern, problem. The fantastic was defined by the fact that it produced a
'hesitation' about the truth or falsehood of phantoms or apparitions. It raised the
question: is my ghost imagined by me, or is it something real? And in doing so,
it shifted away from conventional views of fantasy as an 'escape' from, or an
'alternative' to or idealization of, the world, because it showed the world and the

otherwordly – the real and the imagination – to be inextricably entwined. The fantastic, far from being located in some otherworldly chamber, situates its inexplicable and terrifying visions in the very midst of ordinary life. And the effect of this is to blur the boundaries between the two: one 'hesitates' to choose between them simply because they so completely inhabit each other.

This mutual inhabitation makes the fantastic both a modern and a fragile genre. For Todorov, a character's (or a reader's) 'hesitation' could be resolved in two ways: by producing a worldly or familiar explanation for the apparition, which he referred to as the 'uncanny'; or by preserving the inexplicable supernaturalism of the event, which he called the 'marvellous'. The fantastic, on the other hand, refuses to resolve itself, maintaining the kind of ambiguity of effect more commonly associated with literature itself. At the same time, its sensational, sensual features remain: the 'hesitation' may be intellectual, but it derives (as we see in Todorov's literary examples) from experiences that are both terrifying and erotically arousing.

Todorov's essay concentrates on the form of the fantastic; he has nothing much to say about the *history* of that form. The extracts from José B. Monleon's *A Specter is Haunting Europe* and Terry Castle's *The Female Thermometer* turn to this topic, drawing on Todorov's account of the fantastic as a genre which entwines the real and the spectral and developing his implied suggestion that the fantastic is a modern (not a premodern or 'primal') genre. Monleon in fact sees the fantastic as coincidental with the rise of capitalism in newly industrialized countries. The fear it arouses is an articulation of ideological crises specific to an increasingly powerful, but anxious, bourgeoisie – beset by revolutions and a faltering faith in the grand narratives of progress and rationality. The fantastic in this account is not marginal any longer, but profoundly significant: the extract included here begins by placing modern séances alongside Marx and Engels' *The Communist Manifesto* (1848), as if they speak to a similar predicament. A new kind of inhabitation becomes apparent during the late eighteenth and nineteenth centuries. Once the poor had been confined or banished; now they are all too 'proximate'. Once the spectral was condemned to the irrational realms of an otherworld; now the irrational spectralizes reason itself.

Monleon's extract comes from a meditation on the fantastic as a precise expression of the internalization of unreason during and after the Enlightenment. Todorov's 'hesitation' over whether something is real or spectral is now broadly registered as modernity's loss of confidence over the difference between reason and unreason, good and evil, humanness and monstrosity, norms and deviances, self and other, inside and outside. Yet Monleon does not see the fantastic as a subversive genre, as, say, Rosemary Jackson (1981) had. For Jackson, the fantastic revealed the otherness within – this was its own form of enlightenment – and so challenged the dominant order. For Monleon, however, the fantastic remains a bourgeois invention, troubling the dominant order only in order to enable it to survive.

Terry Castle also turns back to the Enlightenment to draw out its dark dreams. She traces the history of the word 'phantasmagoria', 'the most delirious-sounding of English words', as she puts it. It turns out to have been originally associated with so-called 'ghost shows' or magic lantern shows during the late eighteenth and early nineteenth centuries: optical machines that produced phantasmagorical effects as an externalized spectacle for the public. These ghost shows were certainly sensational, yet they were nonetheless 'fraught with symbolic potential'. Castle reads them, in fact, as providing a 'master trope' in Romantic writing, with phantasmagoria working both as spectacle and yet increasingly coming to signify something *internal* to the mind: the very workings of the imagination itself. The task of the Enlightenment (in the wake of Spenser and others) was to demystify, to scoff at superstitions, expose frauds and relegate spirits and phantoms to the otherworld of an excitable mind. But the latter, in particular, had the paradoxical effect of making ghosts seem, as Castle says, 'more real than ever before', confusing external images and internal imaginings. Castle discusses the tales of Edgar Allan Poe in the light of this, making him an important figure in the ongoing 'spectralization' of the mind – as he is for Monleon, too. Her work also contributes to the prehistory of modern cinema.

Both Castle and Monleon turn to the darker side of the Enlightenment, showing it to be always inhabited by its own otherness. For Castle, one key modern text gives this inhabitation its fullest expression: Sigmund Freud's 'The "Uncanny"' (1919). This essay is itself a meditation on enlightenment, that is, on the various fears and terrors the 'spectralized' mind can 'bring to light'. We shall see other contributors to this Reader drawing on Freud's seminal essay in various ways. Here, however, Castle gives it some historical grounding in the phantasmagorical interests of the eighteenth century. Freud's essay itself had turned to the eighteenth century writer E.T.A. Hoffman for some of its inspiration. Interestingly, his analysis – like Castle's, with her magic lantern shows – had focused on a technological invention, the beautiful mechanical doll Olympia in Hoffman's tale of the Sandman. The doll produces a fantastic effect, blurring the boundaries between the machine and life itself. But it reminds us of the fantastic's erotic potential, too, allowing a further 'hesitation' over the differences between thought process and sensual excitement – and producing an anxiety built upon the entwining of arousal and terror. We shall see this theme developed in the next section, on horror and psychoanalysis.

Chapter 1

TZVETAN TODOROV

DEFINITION OF THE FANTASTIC

ALVARO, THE MAIN CHARACTER of [Jacques] Cazotte's tale *Le Diable Amoureux* (1772), lives for two months with a female being whom he believes to be an evil spirit: the devil or one of his henchmen. The way this being first appeared clearly suggests that she is a representative of the other world. But her specifically human (and, what is more, feminine) behavior, and the real wounds she receives, seem, on the contrary, to prove that she is simply a woman, and a woman in love. When Alvaro asks where she comes from, Biondetta replies: 'I am a sylphide by birth, and one of the most powerful among them. . . .' But do sylphides exist? ('I could make nothing of these words,' Alvaro continues. 'But what could I make of my entire adventure? It all seems a dream, I kept telling myself; but what else is human life? I am dreaming more extravagantly than other men, that is all. . . . What is possible? What is impossible?')

Thus Alvaro hesitates, wonders (and the reader with him) whether what is happening to him is real, if what surrounds him is indeed reality (in which case sylphides exist), or whether it is no more than an illusion, which here assumes the form of a dream. Alvaro is later induced to sleep with this very woman who *may* be the devil; and, alarmed by this eventuality, he questions himself once more: 'Have I been asleep? Is it my fortune that all this has been no more than a dream?' His mother will reflect in the same fashion: 'You have dreamed this farm and all its inhabitants.' The ambiguity is sustained to the very end of the adventure: reality or dream? truth or illusion?

Which brings us to the very heart of the fantastic. In a world which is indeed our world, the one we know, a world without devils, sylphides, or vampires, there occurs an event which cannot be explained by the laws of this same familiar world. The person who experiences the event must opt for one of two possible solutions: either he is the victim of an illusion of the senses, of a product of the imagination – and laws of the world then remain what they are; or else the event has indeed taken place, it is an integral part of reality – but then this reality is controlled by laws unknown to us. Either the devil is an illusion, an imaginary being; or else he really exists, precisely like other living beings – with this reservation, that we encounter him infrequently.

The fantastic occupies the duration of this uncertainty. Once we choose one answer or the other, we leave the fantastic for a neighboring genre, the uncanny, or the marvelous. The fantastic is that hesitation experienced by a person who knows only the laws of nature, confronting an apparently supernatural event.

[. . .]

Is such a definition at least an original one? We may find it, though formulated differently, in the nineteenth century. First of all, in the work of the Russian philosopher and mystic Vladimir Solovyov: 'In the genuine fantastic, there is always the external and formal possibility of a simple explanation of phenomena, but at the same time this explanation is completely stripped of internal probability.' There is an uncanny phenomenon which we can explain in two fashions, by types of natural causes and supernatural causes. The possibility of a hesitation between the two creates the fantastic effect.

Some years later, M. R. James, a British author specializing in ghost stories, adopted virtually the same terms: 'It is sometimes necessary to keep a loophole for a natural explanation, but I might add that this hole should be small enough to be unusable.' Once again, then, two solutions are possible.

Here is a more recent German example: 'The hero continually and distinctly feels the contradiction between two worlds, that of the real and that of the fantastic, and is himself amazed by the extraordinary phenomena which surround him' (Olga Riemann). We might extend this list indefinitely. Yet let us note a difference between the first two definitions and the third: in the former, it is the reader who hesitates between the two possibilities; in the latter, it is the character; we shall return to this difference.

It must further be noted that recent French definitions of the fantastic, if they are not identical with ours, do not on the other hand contradict it. We shall give a few examples drawn from the 'canonical' texts on the subject. [Pierre-Georges] Castex, in *Le Conte Fantastique en France* (1951), writes: 'The fantastic . . . is characterized . . . by a brutal intrusion of mystery into the context of real life.' Louis Vax, in *L'Art et la Littérature Fantastiques* (1960): 'The fantastic narrative generally describes men like ourselves, inhabiting the real world, suddenly confronted by the inexplicable.' Roger Caillois, in *Au Cœur du Fantastique* (1965): 'The fantastic is always a break in the acknowledged order, an irruption of the inadmissible within the changeless everyday legality.'

These definitions are all included within the one proposed by the first authors quoted, which already implied the existence of events of two orders, those of the natural world and those of the supernatural world. But the definitions of Solovyov, James, *et al.* indicated further the possibility of supplying two explanations of the supernatural event and, consequently, the fact that *someone* must choose between them. It was therefore more suggestive, richer; and the one we ourselves have given is derived from it. It further emphasizes the differential character of the fantastic (as a dividing line between the uncanny and the marvelous), instead of making it a substance (as Castex, Caillois, *et al.* do). As a rule, moreover, a genre is always defined in relation to the genres adjacent to it.

But the definition still lacks distinctness, and it is here that we must go further than our predecessors. As has already been noted, they do not specify whether it is the reader or the character who hesitates, nor do they elucidate the nuances of the hesitation. *Le Diable Amoureux* offers insufficient substance for a more extended analysis: here the hesitation occupies us only a moment. We shall therefore turn to another book, written some twenty years later, which permits us to raise more questions; a book which magisterially inaugurates the period of the fantastic narrative, Jan Potocki's *Saragossa Manuscript* (1797–1815).

A series of events is initially related, none of which in isolation contradicts the laws of nature as experience has taught us to recognize them; but their accumulation raises a problem. Alfonso van Worden, the work's hero and narrator, is crossing the mountains of the Sierra Morena. Suddenly his *zagal* (valet) Moschite vanishes; some hours later, the other valet, Lopez, vanishes as well. The local inhabitants assert that the region is haunted by ghosts, those of two bandits who had recently been hanged. Alfonso reaches an abandoned inn and prepares to go to sleep, but at the first stroke of midnight 'a beautiful negress, half naked and bearing a torch in each hand,' enters his room and invites him to follow her. She leads him to an underground chamber where he is received by two young sisters, both lovely and very scantily clad. They offer him food and drink. Alfonso experiences strange sensations, and a doubt is born in his mind: 'I no longer knew whether they were women or insidious succubae.' They then tell him their story, revealing themselves to be his own cousins. But as the first cock crows, the narrative is broken off; and Alfonso recalls that 'as everyone knows, ghosts have power only from midnight till cockcrow.'

All this, of course, does not transcend the laws of nature as we know them. At most, one might say that they are strange events, unexpected coincidences. The next development is the decisive one: an event occurs which reason can no longer explain. Alfonso goes to bed, the two sisters join him (or perhaps he only dreams they do), but one thing is certain: when he awakes, he is no longer in a bed, he is no longer in an underground chamber. 'I saw the sky. I saw that I was in the open air. . . . I was lying under the gallows of Los Hermanos, and beside me – the bodies of Zoto's two brothers!' Here then is a first supernatural event: two lovely girls have turned into two rotting corpses.

Alfonso is not yet convinced of the existence of supernatural forces: a conviction which would have suppressed all hesitation (and put an end to the fantastic). He looks for a place to spend the night, and comes upon a hermit's cottage; here he encounters a man possessed by the devil, Pascheco, who tells his story, a story which strangely resembles Alfonso's own: Pascheco had slept in the same inn; he had entered an underground chamber and spent the night in a bed with two sisters; the next morning *he* had wakened under the gallows, between two corpses. This similarity puts Alfonso on his guard. Hence he later explains to the hermit that he does not believe in ghosts, and he gives a 'natural' explanation of Pascheco's misfortunes. He similarly interprets his own adventures:

> I did not doubt that my cousins were women of flesh and blood. I was convinced of this by some emotion more powerful than all I had been told as to the power of the demons. As to the trick that had been played upon me of placing me under the gallows – I was greatly incensed by it.

So be it – until new developments rekindle Alfonso's doubts. He again encounters his cousins in a cave, and one night, they come to his bed. They are about to remove their chastity belts, but first Alfonso himself must remove the Christian relic he wears around his neck; in place of this object, one of the sisters bestows a braid of her hair. No sooner are the first transports of love over, than the stroke of midnight is heard. . . . Someone enters the cave, drives out the sisters and threatens Alfonso with death, obliging him to drink a cup of some unknown liquid. The next morning Alfonso wakens, of course, under the gallows, beside the corpses; around his neck there is no longer the braid of hair, but in its place a noose. Returning to the inn where he had spent the first night, he suddenly discovers, between the floorboards, the relic taken from him in the cave. 'I no longer knew what I was doing. . . . I began to imagine that I had never really left this wretched inn, and that the hermit, the inquisitor [see below] and Zoto's brothers were so many phantoms produced by magic spells.' As though to weigh the scale more heavily, he soon meets Pascheco, whom he had glimpsed during his last nocturnal adventure, and who gives him an entirely different version of the incident:

> These two young persons, after bestowing certain caresses upon him, removed from around his neck a relic which had encircled it, and from that moment, they lost their beauty in my eyes, and I recognized in them the two hanged men of the valley of Los Hermanos. But the young horseman, still taking them for charming persons, lavished the tenderest endearments upon them. Then one of the hanged men removed the noose from around his neck and placed it around that of the horseman, who thanked him for it by renewed caresses. Finally they closed their curtain, and I do not know what they did then, but I believe it was some hideous sin.

What are we to believe? Alfonso knows for sure that he has spent the night with two lascivious women – but what to make of the awakening under the gallows, what of the rope around his neck, what of the relic in the inn, and what of Pascheco's narrative? Uncertainty and hesitation are at their height, reinforced by the fact that other characters suggest to Alfonso a supernatural explanation of the events. For example, the inquisitor, who will arrest Alfonso and threaten him with torture, asks him: 'Do you know two Tunisian princesses? Or, rather, two infamous witches, execrable vampires and demons incarnate?' And later on Rebecca, Alfonso's hostess, will tell him: 'We know that they are two female demons whose names are Emina and Zibeddé.'

Alone for several days, Alfonso once again finds the forces of reason returning. He seeks a 'realistic' explanation for these incidents.

I then recalled the words which had escaped Don Emmanuel de Sa, governor of this city, which made me think that he was not altogether alien to the mysterious existence of the Gomélez creatures. It was the governor who had given me my two valets, Lopez and Moschite. I took it into my head that it was upon his orders that they had left me at the disastrous valley of Los Hermanos. My cousins, and Rebecca herself, had often led me to believe that I was being tested. Perhaps at the inn I had been given some drug to put me to sleep, and subsequently nothing was easier than to transport me, in my unconscious state, beneath the fatal gallows. Pascheco might have lost an eye through some other accident than his amorous relations with the two hanged men, and his hideous story might well have been an invention. The hermit who had constantly sought to pluck out the heart of my mystery was doubtless an agent of the Gomélez, who wished to test my discretion. Finally Rebecca, her brother, Zoto, and the leader of the Gypsies – perhaps all these people were in league to put my courage to the test.

The uncertainty is not thereby settled: minor incidents will once again incline Alfonso toward a supernatural solution. Outside his window, he sees two women who appear to be the famous sisters; but when he approaches them, he finds their faces utterly unknown to him. He then reads a satanic tale which so resembles his own story that he admits: 'I nearly reached the point of believing that fiends, in order to deceive me, had animated the bodies of the hanged men.'

'*I nearly reached the point of believing*': that is the formula which sums up the spirit of the fantastic. Either total faith or total incredulity would lead us beyond the fantastic: it is hesitation which sustains its life.

Who hesitates in this story? As we see at once, it is Alfonso – in other words, the hero, the central character. It is Alfonso who, throughout the plot, must choose between two interpretations. But if the reader were informed of the 'truth,' if he knew which solution to choose, the situation would be quite different. The fantastic therefore implies an integration of the reader into the world of the characters; that world is defined by the reader's own ambiguous perception of the events narrated. It must be noted that we have in mind no actual reader, but the role of the reader is implicit in the text (just as the narrator's function is implicit in the text). The perception of this implicit reader is given in the text, with the same precision as the movements of the characters.

The reader's hesitation is therefore the first condition of the fantastic. But is it necessary that the reader identify with a particular character, as in *Le Diable Amoureux* and in *The Saragossa Manuscript*? In other words, is it necessary that the hesitation be *represented* within the work? Most works which fulfill the first condition also satisfy the second. Nonetheless there exist exceptions: for example in Villiers de l'Isle-Adam's 'Véra.' Here the reader may question the resurrection of the count's wife, a phenomenon which contradicts the laws of nature but seems to be confirmed by a series of secondary indications. Yet none of the characters shares this hesitation: neither Count d'Athol, who firmly believes in Véra's second life, nor the old servant Raymond. The reader therefore does not identify with any character, and his hesitation is not represented within the text. We may say that this rule of identification involves an optional condition of the fantastic: the fantastic *may* exist without satisfying this condition; but it will be found that most works of fantastic literature are subject to it.

When the reader emerges from the world of the characters and returns to his own *praxis* (that of a reader) a new danger threatens the fantastic: a danger located on the level of the interpretation of the text. There exist narratives which contain supernatural elements without the reader's ever questioning their nature, for he realizes that he is not to take them literally. If animals speak in a fable, doubt does not trouble the reader's mind: he knows that the words of the text are to be taken in another sense, which we call *allegorical*. The converse situation applies to *poetry*. The poetic text might often be judged fantastic, provided we required poetry to be representative. But the question does not come up. If it is said, for instance, that the 'poetic I' soars into space, this is no more than a verbal sequence, to be taken as such, without there being any attempt to go beyond the words to images.

The fantastic implies, then, not only the existence of an uncanny event, which provokes a hesitation in the reader and the hero; but also a kind of reading, which we may for the moment define negatively: it must be neither 'poetic' nor 'allegorical.' If we return now to *The Saragossa Manuscript*, we see that this requirement is fulfilled in both respects. On the one hand, nothing permits us to give, immediately, an allegorical interpretation to the supernatural events described; on the other hand, these events are actually given as such, we are to represent them to ourselves, and not to consider the words which designate them as merely a combination of linguistic units. A remark by Roger Caillois gives us a clue as to this property of the fantastic text:

> This kind of image is located at the very heart of the fantastic, halfway between what I have chosen to call infinite images and limited images. . . . The former seek incoherence as a principle and reject any signification; the latter translate specific texts into symbols for which an appropriate lexicon permits a term-by-term reconversion into corresponding utterances.

We are now in a position to focus and complete our definition of the fantastic. The fantastic requires the fulfillment of three conditions. First, the text must oblige the reader to consider the world of the characters as a world of living persons and to hesitate between a natural and a supernatural explanation of the events described. Second, this hesitation may also be experienced by a character; thus the reader's role is so to speak entrusted to a character, and at the same time the hesitation is represented, it becomes one of the themes of the work — in the case of naive reading, the actual reader identifies himself with the character. Third, the reader must adopt a certain attitude with regard to the text: he will reject allegorical as well as 'poetic' interpretations. These three requirements do not have an equal value. The first and the third actually constitute the genre; the second may not be fulfilled. Nonetheless, most examples satisfy all three conditions.

[. . .]

Chapter 2

JOSÉ B. MONLEÓN

1848: THE ASSAULT ON REASON
(extract)

IN 1848, AT FOX FARM in the state of New York, the first séances of modern spiritualism were conducted. That same year, across the Atlantic, Marx and Engels published the *Communist Manifesto*, with the now famous introductory sentence, 'A spectre is haunting Europe – the spectre of Communism.' The language of esotericism connects two apparently unrelated events. When Marx adopted an image of the fantastic to depict a concrete political phenomenon, he was both using dominant discourse as well as deconstructing a cultural metaphor; he was referring to a new attitude in bourgeois culture as well as pointing out the ultimate source of this posture. In this sense, then, the introductory sentence of the *Communist Manifesto* reveals the extent to which the imagery of the fantastic was shaped by and gave form to concrete problems. Marx and Engels endowed unreason, as far as it implied a negation of bourgeois order, with a definite political name; they assigned to those specters which populated the imagination a concrete space and time. The phantom was *hic et nunc* [here and now], in contemporary times and within the geographic boundaries of the 'advanced' European societies. Suddenly, the marginality with which otherness had engaged its first incursions dissipated in the words of a program that openly proclaimed the true identity of the monster. Prince Prospero, in Edgar Allan Poe's *The Red Death* (1842), protects himself from the plague that surrounds his palace by erecting walls lined with armed guards and camouflaging his guests with smiles of diversion. Prince Prospero might have perpetuated the Gothic belief in peripheral threats and acted accordingly; and yet at the end, not only would he discern amidst his guests the unpleasant presence of a death mask, but he would also discover that behind the disguise of that red death stood, in effect, the red death.

However, even if the *Manifesto* depicted without any disguise the terms of the conflict, even if Prospero proved that adopting the mask of unreason was a sign of unreason, bourgeois culture continued to attempt to postpone the unveiling of naked truth, relegating to the other side of a reinforced ideological barrier all the elements that haunted its existence. Throughout the nineteenth century, Europe portrayed itself as plagued by vague fears that tinged the imagination with colorful but imprecise menaces. [. . .]

What all these fears ultimately shared was the suggestion that the social order was in danger, even though daily experience did not indicate the presence of a threat. The empirical 'testing' of social reality was not sufficient to dissipate the beliefs ingrained in bourgeois culture. It was not important whether there existed, in the Rhineland as in England, a concrete and direct possibility of the destruction of order, because at this stage in the development of the industrial society, danger revealed an attitude toward order itself more than a reaction to immediate threats: 'Just as the European middle classes of the 1840's thought they recognized the shape of their future social problems in the rain and smoke of Lancashire, so they thought they recognized another shape of the future behind the barricades of Paris, that great anticipator and exporter of revolutions' (Hobsbawm: 1975, 11). Attached to the system as an ontological part of it, destruction could manifest itself in unreliable or unbelievable forms, but it would always be there, casting a shadow over the future and the prosperity announced by the comfortable universe of the bourgeoisie.

In opposition to the perception of the classical age, the seeds of destruction – which the Gothic had always portrayed as coming from the margins of order – were accepted by the new industrial epoch as sown within its premises. *The Fall of the House of Usher* (1839), by Edgar Allan Poe, has been frequently read as a representation of the decline of reason (see, for instance, Peithman: 1981, 60). But Usher's house is a place as well as the embodiment of a dynasty, Roderick and Madeline being the last two representatives: '[the] appellation of the "House of Usher" – an appellation which seemed to include, in the minds of the peasantry who used it, both the family and the family mansion' (ibid., 63). From the very beginning, then, the text establishes an identification between the house and its owners; thus, the crack along the walls that the narrator notices upon his arrival parallels the fissure in Roderick's mind and anticipates the double final collapse of mansion and protagonists. As the narrator soon discovers, the causes of Usher's troubles form an intrinsic part of his being: '[Roderick Usher] entered, at some length, into what he conceived to be the nature of his malady. It was, he said, a constitutional and a family evil' (ibid., 66). The house is, then, the palace of reason inhabited by unreason as well as the individual's rational mind demolished by madness.

This genetic determination offers the possibility of exploring at least two roads of interpretation. On the one hand, the descent into madness unearths a journey into primitiveness, discovering insanity at the root of 'man's' psyche. In this sense, it implies a voyage back in time to a precivilized state. On the other hand, by identifying person with house Poe endows the mansion with a symbolic value: it is reason overpowered by unreason. Hence it also suggests the collapse of the reasonable premises of bourgeois epistemology. In this sense it alludes to the role of unreason in shaping society's future, thus uncovering a social and political issue. As with the Gothic production, the recall of primitiveness, of 'backwardness,' announced the form of things to come. The problem now resided precisely in locating and determining those forms, in assigning an appropriate imagery.

Unreason during the eighteenth century moved around the urban periphery, overtaking the nonproductive sectors, touching the rural immigration, caressing in general the poor population — a population whose members were considered to be foreigners and regarded, as [Louis] Chevalier affirms, 'as not belonging to the city, as suspect of all the crimes, all the evils, all the epidemics and all the violence' (Chevalier: 1973, 365) in a kind of tautological argument that made of crime an external threat, and of every alien a potential criminal. The street people of the nineteenth century were different: if they still represented barbarism, they now belonged to the city. Eugène Sue opened his *Mystères de Paris* (1842–1843) by calling the reader's attention to the fact that the barbarians and the savages he would be introducing did not belong to remote countries but were to be found 'among ourselves.' Reynolds's *The Mysteries of London* (1845–1848) would follow a similar pattern with a savage depiction of the English 'low' life. In fact, just as the Gothic's tendency was to reproduce medieval and 'backward' settings, the new scenery in popular literature became, especially after 1848, the 'unknown country' of the bas-fonds.

This internalization of monstrosity by the dominant culture would still maintain, during the major part of the nineteenth century, a certain ambivalence, as if the social imagination hesitated and was incapable of deciding what image to assign to unreason: either to completely mask otherness or to blur the lines of separation between the self and the other. For Thomas Plint, in his *Crime in England* (1851), there was no doubt that the metaphors of danger referred to an inner origin spreading like a cancer through society: 'The criminal class live amongst, and are dove-tailed in, so to speak, with the operative classes. . . . They constitute a pestiferous canker in the heart of every locality where they congregate' (Himmelfarb: 1985, 387). For Saint-Marc Girardin, on the other hand, the image of suburb was still present. As he wrote in the *Journal des débats* of December 8, 1831, 'Every manufacturer lives in his factory like the colonial planters in the midst of their slaves, one against a hundred, and the subversion of Lyons is a sort of insurrection of San Domingo. . . . The barbarians who menace society are neither in the Caucasus nor in the steppes of Tartary; they are in the suburbs of our industrial cities' (Hobsbawm: 1962, 238). Whatever the preferred image, heart or suburb, two common elements emerged as depicting the new social representation of threat: first, emphasis was placed upon the proximity and internal character of unreason; second, a definite association was established between danger and the working classes.

[. . .]

The dream of reason definitely produced monsters. This paradox, which at the end of the eighteenth century represented only a blurring of bourgeois vision, now announced the real possibility of an eclipse. The new industrial age created its own negation. Marx and Engels developed an entire political program from this premise, elaborating on the material conditions as well as on the imagery of contradiction: 'The development of Modern Industry, therefore, cuts from under its feet the very foundation on which the bourgeoisie produces and appropriates products. What the bourgeoisie, therefore, produces, above all, is its own grave-diggers' (Marx and Engels: 1968, 46).

Frankenstein's creature is thus not only a psychological projection but also, as

Franco Moretti (1983) has shown, the embodiment of industrial production: he was built, literally, as a result of scientific and material advances. Movies have given us a monster tailored to a proletarian image which does not correspond with the novel's depiction. Such a transformation – which is in itself revealing about the perception of monstrosity during the first decades of the twentieth century – was possible in part because Shelley's book already alluded to this question. Frankenstein's monster traveled through the European countryside not only retracing the Napoleonic invasions but also incarnating the incursions of industrialism into the 'harmonic' universe of peasants and fishermen, inspiring fear and chaos by his mere presence. The response that the monster's intrusion elicits from the people is reminiscent of certain attitudes toward industrialization, in particular that of the Luddite movement, which reached its apogee during the first decade of the nineteenth century. The 'obscure and Satanic' mills of the industrial revolution, as Richard Astle points out, silently gravitate in Shelley's novel (Astle: 1977, 71).

For S. L. Varnado, 'Mary Shelley suggests, in fact, that some of the evil nature of the monster is the result of economic and moral dislocations in society' (Varnado: 1981, 65). If reason produced monsters, then it is easily understandable that a sense of culpability would arise among those of the dominant culture. [Henry] Mayhew insisted upon this: 'If the London costers belong especially to the "dangerous classes", the danger of such a body is assuredly an evil of our own creation. . . . I am anxious to make others feel, as I do myself, that *we* are the culpable parties in these matters' (Himmelfarb: 1985, 327; my italics). Such an affirmation had already been formulated prior to Mayhew's work and actually formed part of the generalized belief. On April 12, 1836, the *New York Herald* addressed the famous Robinson Jewett murder with the following editorial: ' "The question now before the public involves more than the guilt of one person": it involves the guilt of a system of society – the wickedness of a state of morals – the atrocity of permitting establishments of such infamy [brothels] to be erected in every public and fashionable place in our city' (Schiller: 1981, 59). Victor Frankenstein discovered an identical truth. If Shelley's novel, on the one hand, leaves no doubt as to the criminality of the monster, since he kills innocent people, his monstrosity, on the other hand, could no longer be neatly attributed to external causes and had to be shared by Frankenstein himself: 'How they would, each and all, abhor me and hunt me from the world did they know my unhallowed acts and the crimes which had their source in me!' (Shelley: 1965, 176).

This definite internalization of otherness, this final inclusion of unreason within the parameters of reason, implied not only that monstrosity was 'real,' but that it actually formed part of reason. The monsters were possible because 'we' were the monsters. Victor and his creature, the representation of science and progress, and the projection of crime and destruction were all part of a single unit standing in a precarious equilibrium. The final elimination of the monster would inevitably mean the death of the doctor. They represented a single system in which evil and good intermingled, in which the separation of characteristics was difficult to grasp: 'I [Victor] wandered like an evil spirit, for I had committed deeds of mischief beyond description horrible, and more, much more (I persuaded myself) was yet behind. Yet my heart overflowed with kindness and the love of virtue. I had begun life with benevolent intentions. . . . Now all was blasted' (ibid., 86). 'When I [the monster] run over the frightful catalogue of my sins, I cannot believe that I am the same creature whose thoughts were once filled with sublime and transcendent visions of the beauty and the majesty of goodness. But it is even so; the fallen angel becomes a malignant devil' (ibid., 209–10). Satan is a fallen angel; human beings are at the same time virtuous and vicious, magnificent and abject. Such a portrayal of unreason, after its banishment from history, necessarily created a sense of confusion and ambiguity. The old polarization between good and evil that had been effective in the Gothic tales disappeared with the progressive internalization of the demonic. As a result of this process, an epistemological uncertainty arose in bourgeois thought, a crisis that was articulated through and tamed by the fantastic, and that, as Rosemary Jackson (1981) shows, very often appeared in artistic representation in the form of madness, hallucinations, or multiple divisions of the subject. This uncertainty gave expression to the dichotomy that confronted the representatives of the epoch. They, as Victor, were forced to choose between the happiness of their creations and the protection of their own species – that is, between accepting the consequences of their philosophical principles and defending their class interests.

This choice affected the entire bourgeois political spectrum. Even liberalism did not have clear theoretical defenses with which to face this contingency. For Hobsbawm, all the 1848 revolutions 'were, in fact or immediate anticipation, social revolutions of the labouring poor. They therefore frightened the moderate liberals whom they pushed into power and prominence – and even some of the more radical politicians – at least as much as the supporters of the old regimes' (Hobsbawm: 1975, 10). Thus, the implantation of peace and order through 'unreasonable' repressive measures would be preferred to the ultimate development of democratic theories when these meant an assault on the socioeconomic organization of the bourgeoisie.

If confinement had been the gesture characterizing preindustrial society, it was now uncertainty which defined the attitude toward unreason. Undoubtedly, the space of unreason had become more difficult to delimit, spreading as it had from confinement to the sewers, undermining the foundations of order. But what definitely blurred bourgeois perception was the fact that unreason had acquired a discourse – a fact that in itself was contradictory, since discourse implied, by definition, the discourse of reason. 'The most effective and powerful critique of bourgeois society,' claims Hobsbawm, 'was to come not from those who rejected it (and with it the traditions of classic seventeenth-century science and rationalism) in toto and *a priori*, but from those who pushed the traditions of its classical thought to their anti-bourgeois conclusions' (Hobsbawm: 1962, 310). Marx and Engels spelled it out in writing and claimed the support of science. In 1848, with the *Communist Manifesto*, an 'unreasonable' political program coincided with a revolutionary movement to foredoom, through an expropriated voice of reason, the end of reason: 'The weapons with which the bourgeoisie felled feudalism to the ground are now turned against the bourgeoisie itself. But not only has the bourgeoisie forged the weapons that bring death to itself; it has also called into existence the men who are to wield those weapons – the modern working class – the proletarians' (Marx and Engels: 1968, 41). The battles in the streets were now framed by another struggle: a philosophical challenge had arisen from within the frame-work of the dominant discourse. In the course of a few decades, what had been secluded broke its silence and managed to create its own voice from within. Reason, then, found itself in the locus previously assigned to unreason. 'Je est un autre,' Rimbaud would affirm later in the century, expressing an identity crisis that would progressively exacerbate the difficulty in distinguishing the double from its referent.

[. . .]

The process of internalization that I have been underlining shaped the charac-teristics of the fantastic during the first two thirds of the nineteenth century. At the beginning of the twentieth century, it would culminate in a cultural production in which unreason would be indistinguishable from reason, and in which reality would be presented as nonapprehensible. In the meantime, the two systems coexisted and overlapped, drawing diffused contours at the line of suture, ques-tioning each other's validity, but remaining ultimately distinguishable. Unreason had infiltrated the space of order and offered itself as an alternative.

The paradox of representation that dominated the early fantastic acquired now the full status of an epistemological antinomy. Reality, as defined by preindustrial relations of production, saw its arrogant affirmation of supremacy undermined by the shadows implicit in its own assertion of progress. The fantastic articulated this paradox and offered to the public the disquieting possibility that reality was a problematic entity with several, and even contradictory, layers of signification.

Jean Baptiste Baronian defines the fantastic of this period as *le fantastique réaliste* because supernatural manifestations were presented within the coordinates of reality and as having an internal origin. In Mérimée, rational explanations were just as valid as irrational ones; in Balzac, the supernatural was always rooted and always appeared in a realistic framework. Even Eugène Sue shared these premises; his novelty, his art, according to Baronian, resided in the fact that he managed 'to create an equilibrium between the fantastic myth and reality – a concrete, tangible and ordinary reality' (Baronian: 1978, 88). In other words, Baronian alludes to an artistic expression that presented as equally acceptable two sets of opposing worldviews. This dichotomy produced an inquiry into the self, at both the social and individual levels, that revealed the complexity and difficulty of knowing the 'I.' Once the vestiges of the old economic system promoted by the ancien régime had been demolished, once the traditional depository of other-ness had been eliminated, any contradiction, any questioning of the new terms of reality had to lead necessarily to a self-questioning. How to reconcile the image of the Restoration with the egalitarian vision of the Enlightenment? The pages of the fantastic, with their diffuse contours, shadows, and uncertainties, would be traversed precisely by a problem of vision, of recognition.

Poe was probably the most significant representative of this period of the fantastic. His production, characterized by a struggle between polarized forces, alternated between different universes, reproducing the signs of confinement and the open streets, mythical settings and contemporary backgrounds. In Poe, reason did not appear as the supreme ruler of truth, and the return to order was not, as in the Gothic, guaranteed. The American writer used accepted cognitive models to parody the reliance on the rational mind as the creator ex nihilo, in [Carol] Becker's words (1975), of the universe: unreliable or mad narrators, thematic incongruences, and similar uncertainties populate Poe's stories, undermining what was considered the clearest representation of the discourse of reason – writing itself. In *The Black Cat* this self-undermining of authoritative discourse is clearly expounded: 'For the most wild, yet most homely narrative which I am about to pen, I neither expect nor solicit belief. Mad indeed would I be to expect it, in a case where my very senses reject their own evidence. Yet, mad I am not – and very surely do I not dream. . . . Hereafter, perhaps, some intellect may be found which will reduce my phantasm to the common place – some intellect more calm, more logical, and far less excitable than my own' (Peithman: 1981, 140). As the narration unfolds, however, the temperate and reasonable depiction of unreasonable events inverts these postulates, and the reader is cornered into acknowledging the possibility of their occurrence. The end result of these subterfuges is a difficulty in recognizing and separating two systems that appear not (as in the Gothic) tangential to each other but overlapping.

The monster in the Gothic tale always maintained a recognizable profile. True, at times there were shadows that, instead of displaying monstrosity, suggested it; but ultimately, all the fleeing figures found a concreteness, a definition that rooted them either in this world or in the other. Not so during this period of the fantastic, where monstrosity exchanged places and bodies without clearly affixing its image: Who was the true monster, Victor or his creature? In *Usher*, Madeline, the strange and vague white figure at the very heart of the mansion, is Roderick's twin sister, thus projecting once again, as in *Frankenstein*, the idea of the double. Given this confusion, this doubling of identities, how was monstrosity portrayed? What were its features?

The monster assumed two tendencies. On the one hand, it emerged in the literary imagination as an imprecise figure. Very little is known about Frankenstein's creature, except that he is too big, too ugly, and dressed in clothes (the doctor's) too small for him. On the other hand, it was presented as a normal human being. Polidori's vampire, for instance, did not deviate in looks, language, or dress from the standard gentleman. Carmilla, and many of Le Fanu's monsters, were indistinguishable from other members of society except for slight deviations, such as paleness or sharp teeth. Yet their behavior and morals revealed their monstrosity. In general, the monster was offered as a simple perversion of the human image, as a physical or psychological distortion of the bourgeois norm. In this sense the image of the monster did not differ much from the conception that dominant culture imposed upon the lower classes. As Arthur Harding would ironically comment apropos of his life in the East End underworld, 'the whole thing was having your poverty well known to the people who had the giving of charity. . . . If you wasn't poor you had to look poor. The clothes you wore had to be something that didn't fit. . . . But you had to be clean' (Samuel: 1981, 24). After all, normality and even humanity were defined by male bourgeois standards. Thus, street folk were considered 'parodies of bourgeois man' (Himmelfarb: 1985, 391) and the poor in general 'were talked of as though they were not properly human at all' (Hobsbawm: 1962, 236).

When William Drew visited a ragged school [in London in 1851] he was impressed by its inhabitants: 'Most of the pupils were children from six to fifteen years of age; but some, I noticed, were gray headed men and women – objects almost too frightful to approach as if they were human beings' (Drew: 1852, 171). The alienation and reification of the worker were problems openly addressed during the nineteenth century. By losing his humanity, the proletarian entered the universe of unreason; from there, he became a threat. The paradox arose from the nature of social and economic organization. 'I am malicious because I am miserable,' said Frankenstein's monster. And those *misérables* were the direct product of society. Proudhon continually repeated this idea in his speeches: 'When the worker has been stupefied by the fragmentary division of labor, by serving machines, by obscurantist education; when he has been discouraged by low wages, demoralized by unemployment and starved by monopoly . . . then he begs, he filches, he cheats, he robs, he murders' (Chevalier: 1973, 269).

The two positions within the dominant class were then reconciled. Either by nature or by nurture, for conservatives as well as progressives, either to condemn or to justify, the 'lower' classes formed a monstrous category (comprising beggars, murderers, and workers) intrinsically attached to the bourgeois society and indispensable to its subsistence. This category, created by reason in its own image, and in the negation of its own image, inhabited the world as the concave reflection of bourgeois order. Such were the paradoxes that the revolutions of 1848 unmasked.

But this concave reflection – the poor-as-caricature, as Harding implied – also showed the ultimate resemblance of the poor and the rich. Dominant culture thus singled out traits that could define and, at the same time, justify social difference. During the second part of the nineteenth century, Cesare Lombroso, in his studies of criminological psychology, recognized the criminal type by certain characteristics that very often alluded to racial distinctions. Lombroso may have limited his 'scientific' findings to the criminal; yet, as [Carlton] Hayes indicates (Hayes: 1963, 116), those characteristics were also applied, in daily use and in reports and articles, to the worker. These were features that would also appear in the portrayal of fantastic monsters: frequent gesticulations and ape-like agility (Frankenstein's monster, in spite of having been created several decades before, was described in these same terms; and an ape was the murderer of the Rue Morgue!), sharply pointed ears and sharp teeth (vampires), hairy bodies (wolf-men), and so on.

Distortion was thus a new mechanism in the fantastic by which the frontiers between the real and the unreal became definitively blurred. And yet, by its essence, distortion served not only to portray monstrosity but also to reveal the familiarity of those images of unreason. Just as the contours of norm were recognized in 'the other,' so too could the signs of monstrosity be discovered in 'the self.' Therefore, it is not strange that fantastic representations adopted some introspective tendencies. As Rosemary Jackson affirms, fantastic literature 'progressively turned inwards to concern itself with psychological problems, used to dramatize uncertainty and conflicts of the individual subject in relation to a difficult social situation' (Jackson: 1981, 97). In this light, the intrusion into Usher's internal world acquires all the characteristics of an exploration of the subconscious: the narrator enters the house and descends through its labyrinthine hallways until the image of tension is finally located – it is the ghostly figure of Madeline. Of course, a systematic and scientific study of the psyche would not be formulated until the latter part of the century, but the grounds for the discovery of the sources of unreason within the self were already laid out.

Once the internal, endemic nature of monstrosity had been acknowledged, not even the house (the home) could serve as a secure shelter. Prince Prospero had not been able to keep death from striking while the constant sound of the ticking of a clock served as a reminder of an inevitable future. The assault on reason ran through the entire spectrum of bourgeois life, reaching its far corners as it questioned the self and the images of affirmation that served to displace the ancien régime. From banishment and confinement to ambiguity and uncertainty; from marginality to distortion; from acknowledgment to alternative: unreason was internalized and, in the process, a transformation in dominant epistemology began to unfold.

TERRY CASTLE

PHANTASMAGORIA AND THE METAPHORICS OF MODERN REVERIE
(extract)

WHAT DOES IT MEAN to speak of phantasmagoria? In his *French Revolution* Thomas Carlyle, we find, obsessively figures the bloody spectacle of civil insurrection as a kind of spectral drama – a nightmarish magic-lantern show playing on without respite in the feverish, ghostly confines of the 'Historical Imagination.' Witness, for example, his description of the storming of the Bastille, as seen through the eyes of the Jacobin leader Thuriot: 'But outwards, behold, O Thuriot, how the multitude flows on, welling through every street: tocsin furiously pealing, all drums beating the *générale*: the Suburb Saint-Antoine rolling hither-ward wholly, as one man! Such vision (spectral yet real) thou, O Thuriot, as from thy Mount of Vision, beholdest in this moment: prophetic of what other Phantasmagories, and loud-gibbering Spectral Realities, which thou yet beholdest not, but shalt' (Carlyle: 1837, 1:165). The same phantasmic imagery occurs again in the account of the September massacres. While the ghastly figure of Murder stalks through 'murky-simmering Paris,' her 'snaky-sparkling head' raised in grim anticipation of the Terror, the narrator warns us that 'the Reader, who looks earnestly through this dim Phantasmagory of the Pit, will discern few fixed certain objects' (ibid., 3:22–4). 'Most spectral, pandemonial!' he observes, describing a subsequent scene in which the Convention, led by the austere Jacobin faction, finally condemns Louis XVI to death: 'Figures rise, like phantoms, pale in the dusky lamp-light; utter from this Tribune, only one word: Death. "*Tout est optique*," says Mercier, "The world is all an optical shadow"' (ibid., 3:88–9). And once again, as the frightful climax of the Terror draws near, the figures of phantom-show proliferate: Robespierre's 'Feast of Pikes' is a 'Scenic Phantasmagory unexampled' (ibid., 3:155), while in the terrible days of Prairial, the red-shirted crown of condemned 'flit' toward the guillotine – a 'red baleful Phantasmagory, towards the land of Phantoms' (ibid., 3:229).

A phantasmagoric effect indeed: the most delirious-sounding of English words has come to stand, in Carlyle's heightened, expressionistic rhetoric, for the delirium of history itself. But what does this fantastical word *phantasmagoria* really mean? We are familiar, of course, with its late romantic denotation, as in the third entry under the term in the *Oxford English Dictionary*: 'a shifting series or succession of phantasms or imaginary figures, as seen in a dream or fevered condition, as called up by the imagination, or as created by literary description.' But few people, I imagine, know the word's original technical application to the so-called ghost-shows of late eighteenth-century and early nineteenth-century Europe – illusionistic exhibitions and public entertainments in which 'spectres' were produced through the use of a magic lantern. Hence the first OED entry: 'A name invented for an exhibition of optical illusions produced chiefly by means of the magic lantern, first exhibited in London in 1802.' An appended note continues: 'In Philipstal's "phantasmagoria" the figures were made to increase and decrease in size, to advance and retreat, dissolve, vanish, and pass into each other, in a manner then considered marvellous.' These 'dark rooms, where spectres from the dead they raise,' wrote a poet in the pages of *Gentleman's Magazine* in June 1802 –

> What's the Greek word for all this *Goblinstoria*?
> I have it pat – It is *Phantasmagoria*.
> (Sulivan: 1802, 544)

Yet it is precisely this literal meaning – and the connection with post-Enlightenment technology and popular spectacle – that has been lost.

In what follows I would like to uncover part of this history, not just as an exercise in romantic etymology (or for the sake of a certain Carlylean local color) but as a way of approaching a larger topic, namely, the history of the imagination. For since its invention, the term *phantasmagoria*, like one of Freud's ambiguous primary words, has shifted meaning in an interesting way. From an initial connection with something external and public (an artificially produced 'spectral' illusion), the word has now come to refer to something wholly internal or subjective: the phantasmic imagery of the mind. This metaphoric shift bespeaks, I think, a very significant transformation in human consciousness over the past two centuries – what I [call] the spectralization or 'ghostifying' of mental space. By spectralization (another nonce word!) I mean simply [. . .] the absorption of ghosts into the world of thought. Even as we have come to discount the spirit-world of our ancestors and to equate seeing ghosts and apparitions with having 'too much' imagination, we have also come increasingly to believe, as if through a kind of epistemological recoil, in the spectral nature of our own thoughts – to figure imaginative activity itself, paradoxically, as a kind of ghost-seeing. Thus in everyday conversation we affirm that our brains are filled with ghostly shapes and images, that we 'see' figures and scenes in our minds, that we are 'haunted' by our thoughts, that our thoughts can, as it were, materialize before us, like phantoms, in moments of hallucination, waking dream, or reverie.

We consider such beliefs to be rational; and indeed in an important sense they provide a conceptual foundation for the rationalist point of view. Ghosts are of course only things 'of the mind' – or so we learn at an early age. Whether or not we recall, each of us was once taught that to see things no one else could see, to

Figure 3.1 Frontispiece from *Phantasmagoria; or, The Development of Magical Deception* (London, printed for Tegg and Castleman, 1803). Courtesy of the University of Virginia Library, Sadleir-Black Gothic Collection of Novels.

envision monsters or phantoms or strange figures at the foot of the bed, was really but to *imagine* – to engage in a certain intensified form of thought itself. The rationalist attitude, it might be argued, inevitably depends on this primal internalization of the spectral. For as long as the external world is populated by spirits – whether benign or maleficent – the mind remains unconscious of itself, focused elsewhere, and unable to assert either its autonomy or its creative claim on the world.

What I would like to explore by examining the history of phantasmagoria, however, is the latent irrationalism haunting, so to speak, this rationalist conception of mind. How comprehensible is it, after all, to say that thoughts have a power to 'haunt' us? The post-Enlightenment language of mental experience is suffused with a displaced supernaturalism that we seldom stop to examine. Ironically, it is precisely the modern attempt to annul the supernatural – to humanize the daemonic element in human life – that has produced this strange rhetorical recoil. In the very act of denying the spirit-world of our ancestors, we have been forced to relocate it in our theory of the imagination.

The ambiguity of the phantasmagoria captures the paradox neatly. The spectre-shows of the late eighteenth and early nineteenth centuries [. . .] mediated oddly between rational and irrational imperatives. Producers of phantasmagoria often claimed, somewhat disingenuously, that the new entertainment would serve the cause of public enlightenment by exposing the frauds of charlatans and supposed ghost-seers. Ancient superstition would be eradicated when everyone realized that so-called apparitions were in fact only optical illusions. The early magic-lantern shows developed as mock exercises in scientific demystification, complete with preliminary lectures on the fallacy of ghost-belief and the various cheats perpetrated by conjurers and necromancers over the centuries. But the pretense of pedagogy quickly gave way when the phantasmagoria itself began, for clever illusionists were careful never to reveal exactly how their own bizarre, sometimes frightening apparitions were produced. Everything was done, quite shamelessly, to intensify the supernatural effect. Plunged in darkness and assailed by unearthly sounds, spectators were subjected to an eerie, estranging, and ultimately baffling spectral parade. The illusion was apparently so convincing that surprised audience members sometimes tried to fend off the moving 'phantoms' with their hands or fled the room in terror. Thus even as it supposedly explained apparitions away, the spectral technology of the phantasmagoria mysteriously recreated the emotional aura of the supernatural. One knew ghosts did not exist, yet one saw them anyway, without knowing precisely how.

Translated into a metaphor for the imagery produced by the mind, the phantasmagoria retained this paradoxical aspect. It was never a simple mechanistic model of the mind's workings. Technically speaking, of course, the image did fit nicely with post-Lockean notions of mental experience; nineteenth-century empiricists frequently figured the mind as a kind of magic lantern, capable of projecting the image-traces of past sensation onto the internal 'screen' or backcloth of the memory. But the word phantasmagoria, like the magic lantern itself, inevitably carried with it powerful atavistic associations with magic and the supernatural. To invoke the supposedly mechanistic analogy was subliminally to import the language of the uncanny into the realm of mental function. The mind became a phantom-zone – given over, at least potentially, to spectral presences and haunting obsessions. A new kind of daemonic possession became possible. And in the end, not so surprisingly, the original technological meaning of the term seemed to drop away altogether. 'Je suis maître en fantasmagories,' wrote Arthur Rimbaud in *Un Saison en enfer* (1873). By the end of the nineteenth century, ghosts had disappeared from everyday life, but as the poets intimated, human experience had become more ghost-ridden than ever. Through a strange process of rhetorical displacement, thought itself had become phantasmagorical.

How then, amid such metaphoric fantasia, do we recover the world of the 'real' phantasmagoria? We need to return, interestingly enough, to the French

Revolution. In Germinal Year VI (March 1798) a Belgian inventor, physicist, and student of optics named Étienne-Gaspard Robertson presented what he called the first 'fantasmagorie' at the Pavillon de l'Échiquier in Paris. [. . .] Robertson's phantasmagoria grew out of an interest in magic, conjuring, and optical effects. As he recalled in his *Mémoires récréatifs, scientifiques et anecdotiques* of 1830–34, he had been fascinated in youth with the conjuring device known as the magic lantern, invented by Athanasius Kircher in the seventeenth century. Kircher's device, from which all of our modern instruments for slide and cinematic projection derive, consisted of a lantern containing a candle and a concave mirror. A tube with a convex lens at each end was fitted into an opening in the side of the lantern, while a groove in the middle of the tube held a small image painted on glass. When candlelight was reflected by the concave mirror onto the first lens, the lens concentrated the light on the image on the glass slide. The second lens in turn magnified the illuminated image and projected it onto a wall or gauze screen. In darkness, with the screen itself invisible, images could be made to appear like fantastic luminous shapes, floating inexplicably in the air. In the 1770s a showman named François Séraphin produced what he called Shadow Plays, or 'Ombres Chinoises,' using a magic lantern at Versailles; another inventor, Guyot, demonstrated how apparitions might be projected onto smoke. Robertson began experimenting in the 1780s with similar techniques for producing 'fantômes artificiels.' He soon devised several improvements for the magic lantern, including a method for increasing and decreasing the size of the projected image by setting the whole apparatus on rollers. Thus the 'ghost' could be made to grow or shrink in front of the viewer's eyes.

Robertson recognized the uncanny illusionistic potential of the new technology and exploited the magic lantern's pseudonecromantic power with characteristic flamboyance. He staged his first 'fantasmagorie' as a Gothic extravaganza, complete with fashionably Radcliffean decor.

[. . .]

When he returned to Paris he began producing even more elaborate and bizarre spectacles in the crypt of an abandoned Capuchin convent near the Place Vendôme. Here, amid ancient tombs and effigies, Robertson found the perfect setting for his optical spectre-show – a kind of sepulchral theatre, suffused with gloom, cut off from the surrounding city streets, and pervaded by (as he put it) the silent aura of 'des mystères d'Isis.' His memoirs, along with a surviving 'Programme Instructif' from the early 1800s, provide a picture of a typical night in the charnel house. At seven o'clock in the evening spectators entered through the main rooms of the convent, where they were entertained with a preliminary show of optical illusions, trompe l'oeil effects, panorama scenes, and scientific oddities. After passing through the 'Galerie de la Femme Invisible' (a ventriloquism and speaking-tube display orchestrated by Robertson's assistant 'Citoyen Fitz-James'), one descended at last to the 'Salle de la Fantasmagorie.' Here, the single, guttering candle was quickly extinguished, and muffled sounds of wind and thunder (produced by 'les sons lugubres de *Tamtam*') filled the crypt. Unearthly music emanated from an invisible glass harmonica. Robertson then began a somber, incoherent speech on death, immortality, and the unsettling power of superstition and fear to create terrifying illusions. He asked the audience to imagine the feelings of an ancient Egyptian maiden attempting to raise, through necromancy, the ghost of her dead lover in a ghastly catacomb: 'There, surrounded by images of death, alone with the night and her imagination, she awaits the apparition of the object she cherishes. What must be the illusion for an imagination thus prepared!' (Robertson: 1885, 1, 163). At last, when the mood of terror and apprehension had been raised to a pitch, the spectre-show itself began. One by one, out of the darkness, mysterious luminous shapes – some seemingly close enough to touch – began to surge and flit over the heads of the spectators.

In a 'Petit Répertoire Fantasmagorique' Robertson listed some of the complex apparitions he produced on these occasions. Several, we notice, specifically involved a metamorphosis, or one shape rapidly changing into another – an effect easily achieved by doubling two glass slides in the tube of the magic lantern over one another in a quick, deft manner. Thus the image of 'The Three Graces, turning into skeletons.' But in a sense the entire phantasmagoria was founded on discontinuity and transformation. Ghostly vignettes followed upon one another in a crazy, rapid succession. The only links were thematic: each image bore some supernatural, exotic, or morbid association. In selecting his spectral program pieces Robertson drew frequently on the 'graveyard' and Gothic iconography popular in the 1790s. Thus the apparition of 'The Nightmare,' adapted from Henry Fuseli, depicted a young woman dreaming amid fantastic tableaux; a demon pressing on her chest held a dagger suspended over her heart. In 'The Death of Lord Lyttelton,' the hapless peer was shown confronting his famous phantom and expiring. Other scenes included 'Macbeth and the Ghost of Banquo,' 'The Bleeding Nun,' 'A Witches' Sabbath,' 'Young Interring his Daughter,' 'Proserpine and Pluto on their Throne,' 'The Witch of Endor,' 'The Head of Medusa,' 'A Gravedigger,' 'The Agony of Ugolino,' 'The Opening of Pandora's Box.' Interspersed among these were single apparitions familiar from the earlier phantasmagoria shows – often the bloody 'revolutionary' spectres of Rousseau, Voltaire, Robespierre, and Marat. Robertson concluded his shows with a parting speech and a macabre coup de théâtre. 'I have shown you the most occult things natural philosophy has to offer, effects that seemed supernatural to the ages of credulity,' he told the audience; 'but now see the only real horror . . . see what is in store for all of you, what each of you will become one day: remember the phantasmagoria.' And with that, he relit the torch in the crypt, suddenly illuminating the skeleton of a young woman on a pedestal (ibid., 1, 165).

I shall return in a moment to the symbolic aspects of the phantasmagoria and the various philosophical and psychological themes with which it quickly became associated. It is enough to note here that the show itself was an immediate, overwhelming success. Robertson himself continued to produce spectre-shows for six years and acknowledged later that they had made his fortune. But he soon had imitators at home and abroad. In the course of a lawsuit in 1799 against two former assistants who had started their own 'fantasmagorie,' Robertson was forced to reveal many of his technical secrets to the public. From then on, he recalled afterwards, magic-lantern exhibitions sprang up everywhere. So popular were such shows, he wrote, Paris itself came to resemble the Elysian Fields: 'It only took a slightly metaphorical imagination to transform the Seine into the river Lethe; because the phantasmagoria were principally located on its banks, there was not one quai . . . which did not offer you a little phantom at the end of a dark corridor or at the top of a tortuous staircase' (ibid., 1, 183).

The phantasmagoria soon travelled across the Channel, where it met with – if possible – an even more enthusiastic reception. Given the indigenous mania for things Gothic, England indeed seemed the natural home for phantasmagoria. [. . .] Phantasmagoria shows rapidly became a staple of London popular entertainment. Mark Lonsdale presented a 'Spectrographia' at the Lyceum in 1802; Meeson offered a phantasmagoria modeled on Philipstal's at Bartholomew Fair in 1803 (Mayes: 1959, 49). A series of 'Optical eidothaumata' featuring 'some surprising Capnophoric Phantoms' materialized at the Lyceum in 1804. In the same year the German conjuror Moritz opened a phantasmagoria and magic show at the King's Arms in Change Alley, Cornhill, and in the following year, again at the Lyceum, the famous comedian and harlequin Jack Bologna exhibited his 'Phantoscopia.' Two 'Professors of Physic,' Schirmer and Scholl, quickly followed suit with an 'Ergascopia' (Altick: 1978, 218). In 1807, Moritz opened another phantasmagoria show at the Temple of Apollo in the Strand, this one featuring a representation of the raising of Samuel by the Witch of Endor, the ghost scene from *Hamlet*, and the transformation of Louis XVI into a skeleton (Frost: 1881, 170). In 1812 Henry Crabb Robinson saw a 'gratifying' show of spectres – their 'eyes &c' all moving – at the Royal Mechanical and Optical Exhibition in Cathcrine Street (Robinson: 1966, 47). In De Berar's 'Optikali Illusio,' displayed at Bartholomew Fair in 1833, Death appeared on a pale horse accompanied by a luminous skeleton (Frost: 1881, 311).

How realistic were the 'ghosts'? Strange as it now seems, most contemporary observers stressed the convincing nature of phantasmagoric apparitions and their power to surprise the unwary. Robertson described a man striking at one of his phantoms with a stick; a contributor to the *Ami des Lois* worried that pregnant women might be so frightened by the phantasmagoria they would miscarry (Robertson: 1885, 1, 129). One should not underestimate, by any means, the powerful effect of magic-lantern illusionism on eyes untrained by photography and cinematography. Still, not everybody was satisfied. As early as 1802 Nicholson had complained of the 'poorly drawn' figures on Philipstal's lantern slides, and the scientist Sir David Brewster, in his *Letters on Natural Magic* from 1833, observed that 'even Michael Angelo would have failed in executing a figure an inch long with transparent varnishes, when all its imperfections were to be magnified' (Brewster: 1833, 85). Better images and a more complex technology were required. Brewster's own solution was the 'catadioptrical phantasmagoria' – an apparatus of mirrors and lenses capable of projecting the illuminated image of a living human being. 'In place of chalky ill-drawn figures, mimicking humanity by the most absurd gesticulations,' he wrote, 'we shall have phantasms of the most perfect delineation, clothed in real drapery, and displaying all the movements of life' (ibid., 86). In the renowned show of 'Pepper's Ghost,' exhibited at the Royal Polytechnic Institution in London in the 1860s, just such an apparatus was used to great effect. Wraithlike actors and actresses, reflected from below the stage, mingled with onstage counterparts in a phantasmagorical version of Dickens' *The Haunted Man* on Christmas Eve, 1862. 'The apparitions,' wrote Thomas Frost, 'not only moved about the stage, looking as tangible as the actors who passed through them, and from whose proffered embrace or threatened attack they vanished in an instant, but spoke or sang with voices of unmistakable reality' (Frost: 1881, 315).

But the desire for more compelling illusions also produced momentous changes in the magic lantern itself. Lime ball, hydrogen, and magnesium gaslight replaced the candle inside the apparatus, thus giving a more powerful illumination to the phantasmagoric image. Photographic transparencies – as in the modern slide projector – gradually took the place of painted glass slides. Ultimately, of course, the technology of phantasmagoric illusion, like that of the panorama, the bioscope, stereoscopic projection, and related nineteenth-century image-reproduction techniques, provided the inspiration for early cinematography. A desire to give lifelike movement to the ghostly images of the magic lantern prompted Eadweard Muybridge, for example, to construct a 'Zoopraxiscope,' which projected some of the world's first moving pictures in 1882 (see Quigley: 1948, 115–38). In the end the phantasmagoria gave way to new kinds of mechanical representation. Yet amid all the technological breakthroughs and the refinements in cinematic technique, the ghost-connection, interestingly enough, never entirely disappeared. Well into the twentieth century motion-picture shows continued to be advertised in the manner of the old ghost-shows, and many early films, such as Georges Méliès's, featured explicitly phantasmagorical illusions. In various ways the new medium of motion pictures continued to acknowledge and reflect on its 'spectral' nature and origins.

We cannot conclude this brief history of the phantasmagoria without noting one final development – the popularization of do-it-yourself magic-lantern shows in the later decades of the nineteenth century. At the same time that staged phantasmagoria became more and more elaborate, the basic technology of the magic lantern became increasingly accessible to ordinary people. Middle-class Victorians began purchasing magic lanterns as toys and tabletop curiosities in the middle part of the century; books like *The Magic Lantern: How to Buy and How to Use It*, by 'A Mere Phantom' (1866), containing a section on 'How to Raise a Ghost,' offered simple instructions for making 'Parlour or Drawing-Room Phantasmagoria.' Promoters liked to argue that the device 'charmed away' the monotony of home life and brought parents and children together. 'How delightful,' wrote 'A Mere Phantom,' 'is one of those gatherings! where youth, infancy, and maturity are, for different reasons, equally interested in the mimic scenes so vividly presented; infancy charmed with the rapid change of form and colour and grotesque fun, and its infectious laughter echoed by young and old' ('A Mere Phantom': 1866, 7). A less sentimental – and more evocative – response to the new technology appears, however, in the opening pages of *À la recherche du temps perdu* (1913):

> At Combray, as every afternoon ended, long before the time when I should have to go to bed and lie there, unsleeping, far from my mother and grandmother, my bedroom became the fixed point on which my melancholy and anxious thoughts were centred. Someone had indeed had the happy idea of giving me, to distract me on evenings when I seemed abnormally wretched, a magic lantern, which used to be set on top of my lamp while we waited for dinner-time to come; and, after the fashion of the master-builders and glass-painters of gothic days, it substituted for the opaqueness of my walls an impalpable iridescence, supernatural phenomena of many colours, in which legends were depicted as on a shifting and transitory window. But my sorrows were

only increased thereby, because this mere change of lighting was enough to destroy the familiar impression I had of my room, thanks to which, save for the torture of going to bed, it had become quite endurable. Now I no longer recognised it, and felt uneasy in it, as in a room in some hotel or chalet, in a place where I had just arrived by train for the first time. . . . The anaesthetic effect of habit being destroyed, I would begin to think — and to feel — such melancholy things.

(Proust: 1981, 9–11).

Here, ironically, the magic lantern produces nothing but estrangement — by plunging the child Marcel into a world of solitary reverie. Under its flickering, uncanny influence, he becomes obsessed, as it were, with the 'supernatural pheno-mena' of his own mind. What the Proustian anecdote encapsulates, while also infusing with pathos, is the classic nineteenth-century connection between phantas-magoria and the alienating power of the imagination. To this complex metaphoric formulation we may now turn.

From the start phantasmagorical spectacle had seemed fraught with symbolic poten-tial. The bizarre, claustrophobic surroundings, the mood of Gothic strangeness and terror, the rapid phantom-train of images, the disorientation and powerlessness of the spectator — every aspect of the occasion seemed rich in metaphoric possibility. Given its sensational nature, it is not surprising the phantasmagoria should become a kind of master trope in nineteenth-century romantic writing. This is not to say that every contemporary use of the term was elaborately figurative: in many nineteenth-century writings the simple referential power of the word is still very much present — as in Honoré de Balzac's description [in *Un Episode sous la Terreux* (1846)] of one of his characters disappearing with 'une rapidité fantasmagorique,' or Victor Hugo's image, in *Notre-Dame de Paris* (1831), of wavering objects on the Seine at night making 'une sorte de fantasmagorie.' In the spectral context of *The Vision of Judgment* (1822), Byron's comic description of the ghostly George III as 'a phantasmagoria in himself' seems hardly metaphorical at all:

> The more intently the ghosts gazed, the less
> Could they distinguish whose the features were;
> The Devil himself seem'd puzzled even to guess;
> They varied like a dream — now here, now there;
> And several people swore from out the press,
> They knew him perfectly; and one could swear
> He was his father; upon which another
> Was sure he was his mother's cousin's brother:
>
> Another, that he was a duke, or knight,
> An orator, a lawyer, or a priest,
> A nabob, a man-midwife; but the wight
> Mysterious changed his countenance at least
> As oft as they their minds: though in full sight
> He stood, the puzzle was only increased;

> The man was a phantasmagoria in
>   Himself – he was so volatile and thin!
>   (Byron: 1986, 961)

The term also made a number of straightforward, if anachronistic appearances in contemporary writings on ancient necromancy and magical deception. Sir Walter Scott, in his *Letters on Demonology and Witchcraft* (1830), described the mysterious apparition raised by the Witch of Endor in the Book of Samuel as a 'phantasmagoria'; and Eusèbe Salverte, in *Sciences occultes* (1837), spoke of the spirit-illusions manufactured by ancient Egyptian and Mesopotamian magicians as 'similar to those exhibited in the modern Dioramas and Phantasmagorias.' [. . .] But the general tendency in nineteenth-century writing was toward metaphoric displacement. The crucial connection between phantasmagoria and the so-called ghosts of the mind seems to have been made very early on. Even before Robertson's first spectre-shows opened in Paris, Goethe, for example, anticipated the paradoxical imagery of the nineteenth century in several influential passages in *The Sorrows of Young Werther* (1774)). 'Wilhelm,' exclaims Werther at one point, 'what would the world mean to our hearts without love! What is a magic lantern without its lamp! As soon as you insert the little lamp, then the most colorful pictures are thrown on your white wall. And even though they are nothing but fleeting phantoms, they make us happy as we stand before them like little boys, delighted at the miraculous visions' (Goethe: 1971, 47–8). Desire, like Kircher's amazing invention, produces marvelous 'phantoms' in the mind's eye. Thus Werther, overwhelmed by his passion for Lotte, speaks of seeing her inside his head – 'in my forehead, at the focus of my inner vision' – like a kind of apparition: 'How her image haunts me!' Compared with the impressive *noumena* of the imagination, the everyday world looks, ironically, like a mere 'optical illusion' (ibid., 124, 84).

[. . .]

The first writer to offer a metaphoric gloss on the actual phantasmagoria itself, however, seems to have been Henry Lemoine, the editor and bookseller, who published a poem called 'Phantasmagoria' in *Gentleman's Magazine* in June 1802, undoubtedly to capitalize on the popularity of Philipstal's recently installed exhibition at the Lyceum. Lemoine turned his poetic account of the new spectacle into a meditation on the delusional nature of reverie. The poem begins with an Addisonian reflection, reminiscent of *Spectator* no. 12, on the power of darkness and imagination to create terrifying illusions, even in the minds of brave men:

> How sweep the forms which magic fears impart,
> Dismay and trembling to the doubtful heart!
> Ah! e'en to those whom Death could ne'er appall,
> Before the polish'd steel or cannon ball.
> Nocturnal fear, we know, has cowards made
> Of heroes that no dread had e'er betrayed.

Similar forms, he continues, rise up at the spectre-show, where hideous demons 'swim in array and crowd the pictur'd plain' and sepulchral figures hover in the gloom:

> Down from her head the mournful shroud depends,
> Beneath her feet the winding garment ends;
> Her lucid form a ghastly paleness wears,
> Her trembling hand a livid taper bears. . . .

Yet such 'mimic scenes' merely remind us, he concludes, that supposedly real ghosts and apparitions are but the 'motley visions' of an overwrought imagination. Only by despising such 'wild fantastic forms' can one avoid the fate of the 'lonely dame' who nods 'delirious o'er the expiring flame' and 'faints with the haunted notions of her mind.'

Lemoine's poem preserves the facetious tone of eighteenth-century satire, but nonetheless makes a powerful protoromantic discovery: the true 'Phantasmagoria' is the human brain itself. By the second decade of the nineteenth century this notion had become a poetic and philosophical commonplace. Thus Byron in *Don Juan* (1819) could speak of fears and nightmares spreading 'their loathsome phantasmagoria o'er the Mind.' Similarly, Thomas De Quincey, in *Confessions of an English Opium-Eater* (1822), described the multifarious 'phantasmagoria' playing in the brain of the philosophical opium-fiend. 'We sit as in a boundless Phantasmagoria and Dream-grotto,' Carlyle affirmed in *Sartor Resartus* (1833–4); the phenomenal world is but 'the reflex of our own inward Force, the "phantasy of our Dream"' (Carlyle: 1973, 39). [. . .]

The emotional valence of the metaphor fluctuated. Some writers, to be sure, used the phantasmagorical image fairly lightheartedly, to evoke pleasurable or whimsical states of imaginative experience. [. . .] More common, however, was the application of the word to disturbing and frightening mental phenomena — states of delirium and psychic alienation, hallucination, the sensation of being pursued or possessed by horrifying thoughts — as in Bulwer-Lytton's melodramatic novel of mesmeric possession, *A Strange Story* (1862). The narrator is obsessed with the mysterious figure of Margrave, a young man who seems to have diabolical powers: 'To my astonishment now succeeded shame and indignation — shame that I, who had scoffed at the possibility of the comparatively credible influences of mesmeric action, should have been so helpless a puppet under the hand of the slight fellow-man beside me, and so morbidly impressed by phantasmagorical illusions; indignation that, by some fumes which had special potency over the brain, I had thus been, as it were, conjured out of my senses' (Bulwer-Lytton: 1862, 154). He has dreadful visions of Margrave surrounded by snakes and scorpions: 'the phantasmagoria of the naturalist's collection revived'. Still later Margrave's 'Luminous Shadow' seems to lead him in his sleep to a ruined mausoleum. But the whole excursion is strangely hallucinatory: 'How I got into my own room I can remember not — I know not; I have a vague reminiscence of some intervening wanderings, of giant trees, of shroud-like moonlight, of the Shining Shadow and its angry aspect, of the blind walls and the iron door of the House of the Dead, of spectral images — a confused and dreary phantasmagoria' (ibid., 162, 263–4).

   [. . .]

This association with delirium, loss of control, the terrifying yet sublime overthrow of ordinary experience, made the phantasmagoria a perfect emblem, obviously, of the nineteenth-century poetic imagination. Especially among the later romantic and symbolist writers – Poe, Baudelaire, Rimbaud, the Goncourt brothers, Loti, Lautréamont, Nerval, and later still, Yeats, Pound, Apollinaire, Eliot, and Artaud – the phantasmagoria was a favorite metaphor for the heightened sensitivities and often-tormented awareness of the romantic visionary. It conveyed exquisitely the notion of the *bouleversement de tous les sens*: that state of neurasthenic excitement in which images whirled chaotically before the inward eye, impressing on the seer an overwhelming sense of their vividness and spiritual truth. As Yeats put it, 'there is always a phantasmagoria' in the mind of the poet (Yeats: 1961, 509). The word has persisted in this context in critical writing to this day.

The figure of the inward spectre-show was not, however, as straightforward, conceptually speaking, as its popular exploitation might lead us to assume. Indeed, it concealed a profound epistemological confusion. The confusion derived from the ambiguous notion of the ghost. What did it mean, after all, the 'see ghosts'? Were ghosts themselves real or illusory? Inside the mind or outside it? Actual phantasmagoric spectacle, we recall, had enforced on its audience a peculiar kind of split consciousness on exactly this point. Promoters like Robertson prefaced their shows with popular rationalist arguments: real spectres did not exist, they said; supposed apparitions were merely 'l'effet bizarre de l'imagination' (Robertson: 1885, 1, 162). Nonetheless, the phantoms they subsequently produced had a strangely objective presence. They floated before the eye just like real ghosts. And in a crazy way they *were* real ghosts. That is to say, they were not mere effects of imagination: they were indisputably there; one saw them as clearly as any other object of sense. The subliminal power of the phantasmagoria lay in the fact that it induced in the spectator a kind of maddening, contradictory perception: one might believe ghosts to be illusions, present 'in the mind's eye' alone, but one experienced them here as real entities, existing outside the boundary of the psyche. The overall effect was unsettling – like seeing a real ghost.

Some nineteenth-century writers, to be sure, sensed an epistemological abyss at the heart of the metaphor. Edgar Allan Poe, for example, in his supernatural tales, used the phantasmagoria figure precisely as a way of destabilizing the ordinary boundaries between inside and outside, mind and world, illusion and reality. Poe was well aware, of course, of the technical meaning of *phantasmagoria*. He often uses the word near the beginning of a tale specifically to describe an eerie optical effect – as in *The Fall of the House of Usher* (1839), when the narrator returns to the ancestral hall of his friend Roderick Usher and finds himself strangely disturbed by the once familiar surroundings: 'the carvings of the ceilings, the sombre tapestries of the walls, the ebon blackness of the floors, and the phantasmagoric armorial trophies which rattled as I strode' (Poe: 1978, 2, 400). Similarly in *Ligeia* (1838), the word first appears in a description of the bizarre chamber filled with Egyptian carvings, rugs in 'Bedlam patterns,' and 'gorgeous and fantastic draperies' in which the narrator lives with his bride Rowena: 'The phantasmagoric effect was vastly heightened by the artificial introduction of a strong continual current of wind behind the draperies – giving a hideous and uneasy animation to the whole' (ibid., 2, 321–2).

But Poe's references, predictably enough, soon become psychological in nature. The narrator of *The Fall of the House of Usher* learns that his sickly friend Usher suffers from 'phantasmagoric conceptions' (ibid., 2, 405) and is obsessed, to the point of madness, with thoughts of phantoms and apparitions, Rowena, in *Ligeia*, gives way to the 'phantasmagoric influences' of the cryptlike chamber and falls victim to terrifying fancies:

> She partly arose, and spoke, in an earnest low whisper, of sounds which she *then* heard, but which I could not hear — of motions which she *then* saw, but which I could not perceive. The wind was rushing hurriedly behind the tapestries, and I wished to show her (what, let me confess it, I could not *all* believe) that those almost inarticulate breathings, and those very gentle variations of the figures upon the wall, were but the natural effects of that customary rushing of the wind. But a deadly pallor, over-spreading her face, had proved to me that my exertions to reassure her would be fruitless.
>
> (ibid., 2, 324–5).

In such passages Poe seems to evoke a simple environmental determinism: to dwell in 'phantasmagoric space' (the decaying House of Usher, the tomblike chamber) is to become vulnerable to the maddening 'phantoms' of the mind. The familiar metaphor enforces a pervasive sense of the *illusory*: just as we take artificially produced effects of light and shadow for apparitions, or see figures in moving draperies, Poe implies, so we mistake the images in our heads for realities.

Disturbing this relatively coherent structure of meaning, however, is the uncanny horror at the end of each story. In *Usher* one of Roderick Usher's most powerfully 'phantasmagoric' notions — his belief that his dead sister is really alive — far from being illusory, is grotesquely realized when Madeline Usher indeed returns, spectrelike, from the crypt in which she has been interred. A similar fantasy is realized in *Ligeia*. After the death of Rowena (who has yielded to her insanity), the narrator has 'passionate waking visions' over her corpse (ibid., 2, 327). Gazing with 'unquiet eye' on 'the varying figures of the drapery,' he begins to think obsessively of his first love, the dead Lady Ligeia. And gruesomely enough, each time he imagines her, the corpse of Rowena seems to shift under its shroud. This 'hideous drama of revivification' reaches its terrible climax when Rowena's corpse slowly rises from its bier, and letting its 'ghastly cerements' fall away, reveals itself — as the Lady Ligeia herself (ibid., 2, 326, 328, 330).

In each case a mental image appears to come to life, fantastically, *in the flesh*. The phantom becomes a reality. Granted, hints of illusionism remain: Madeline Usher's 'lofty and enshrouded figure' comes through a doorway in a 'rushing gust' of air (ibid., 2, 416), like one of Robertson's luminous deceptions; the corpse of Rowena seems to grow 'taller' than itself, even as the narrator gazes at it, like a spectrum projected from a moving magic lantern. The entire Rowena/Ligeia transformation is very much like the phantasmagorical effect known as the transmutation, achieved by shifting two magic-lantern slides together. But even as we recognize these signs of artifice, we also succumb — along with the narrator in each tale — to the incontrovertible reality of that which is *seen*. It is the real Madeline Usher, we are led to believe, who returns from the crypt; the real Lady Ligeia who rises from the bier.

How to account for this uncanny movement from mental image to spectral reality? To answer this we need to gain some historical distance – to relate the ambiguous metaphor of the phantasmagoria to the larger problem of ghost belief in post-Enlightenment Western culture. In particular we need to look at the powerful modern theme of demystification and the highly paradoxical arguments by which scientists and philosophers in the late eighteenth and early nineteenth centuries attempted to do away with the old theological world of apparitions and gave voice to a new and explicitly psychological theory of supernatural phenomena. What we find, it seems to me, is that the demystifying project was peculiarly compromised from the start. The rationalists did not so much negate the traditional spirit world as displace it into the realm of psychology. Ghosts were not exorcized – only internalized and reinterpreted as hallucinatory thoughts. Yet this internalization of apparitions introduced a latent irrationalism into the realm of mental experience. If ghosts were thoughts, then thoughts themselves took on – at least notionally – the haunting reality of ghosts. The mind became subject to spectral presences. The epistemologically unstable, potentially fantastic metaphor of the phantasmagoria simply condensed the historical paradox: by relocating the world of ghosts in the closed space of the imagination, one ended up supernaturalizing the mind itself.

The phantasmagoria was invented, it turns out, at a crucial epoch in the history of Western ghost belief – at precisely that moment when traditional credulity had begun to give way, more or less definitively, to the arguments of scientific rationalism. This is not to say that ghost belief simply vanished at the end of the eighteenth century: orthodox religious opinion had always supported the idea of a transcendental spirit world, and popular faith in apparitions weakened only gradually. In England, for example, spectacular episodes like the Cock Lane Ghost in the 1760s, Lord Lyttelton's Ghost in 1779, and the Hammersmith Ghost of 1804 testified to the vestigial power of traditional beliefs. But the forces of secularization had also been at work for some time. Renaissance skepticism had called into question the nature of many supposedly supernatural phenomena, and the successes of Enlightenment science reinforced the rationalist view. In 1751 the writers of the *Encyclopédie* ridiculed 'les esprits timides & crédules' who mistook everything they saw for apparitions. By 1800 similar attitudes had more or less triumphed among the educated classes across Western Europe. When Scott, quoting Crabbe, mockingly described the belief in spirits as ' "the last lingering fiction of the brain," ' he illustrated how profoundly received opinion had altered since the days of Lavater, Glanvill, Baxter, Beaumont, Mather and other renowned defenders of the 'invisible world' (Scott: 1831, 342).

How had such a remarkable cognitive reorientation come about? Without attempting to speculate here on ultimate causes, we can nonetheless characterize the basic shift in thought. The age-old philosophical problem had always been how to account for the many sightings of ghosts reported by reputable witnesses throughout the centuries. Rather than resort to the theological notion of a spirit world, the rationalists proposed two new modes of explanation. The first line of argument held that apparitions were the result of simple deception. Writers since Reginald Scot had argued that many apparitions were in fact the products of legerdemain or trickery – conjurers' illusions (like the Witch of Endor's famous 'raising' of Samuel in the Bible, or Cagliostro's fake crystal-ball apparitions) or simple cheats perpetrated by those out to intimidate or manipulate the credulous. The spread of popular scientific knowledge in the eighteenth century supported this kind of explanation; recent developments in optics, the new technology of mirrors and lenses, and the refinement of inventions like the magic lantern itself gave would-be skeptics a technical language with which to debunk, retroactively, many reported spectral appearances, including the notorious spirit-raisings performed by ancient pythonesses and necromancers.

But the second line of argument (not always in perfect accord with the first) ultimately came to dominate modern thinking on the apparition problem. According to this hypothesis, spectres came somehow from within, originating in the disordered brain or sensorium of the ghost-seer himself or herself. Earlier writers, again, had propounded a crude version of the idea. Those suffering from a surplus of melancholy humours, wrote Robert Burton in his *Anatomy of Melancholy* (1621), were especially likely to see spectres. Thomas Hobbes, in *Leviathan* (1651), argued that it was not God's doing, but the 'distemper of some of the inward parts of the Body' that brought on dreams and apparitions. At the end of the eighteenth century, however, thanks to the emergence of the new scientific theory of mind, the projective argument took on a conceptual sophistication and an ideological urgency unmatched in previous epochs.

A host of polemical treatises on apparitions appeared in England, France, and Germany beginning around 1800. The authors were usually medical men, concerned to eradicate superstition and place all seemingly supernatural phenomena on a solid psychological footing. Their arguments were resolutely Lockean and mechanistic in nature. Thus, in one of the first and most influential of such works, *An Essay Towards a Theory of Apparitions* (1813), the Manchester physician John Ferriar invoked the new mentalist concept of the hallucination to explain spectral occurrences. Poor digestion, a diseased state of the nerves, irregular circulation, or some other 'peculiar condition of the sensorium,' he argued, all served to enflame the brain and 'renew' visual or auditory impressions imprinted in the past. A 'renewed' impression then manifested itself upon the brain as if it were an external object – to the surprise or terror of the perceiver. The images most likely to be revived in this delusional way, Ferriar deduced, were precisely those originally accompanied by a strong sense of fear or horror: thus the prevalence of corpses and bloody sights and other grotesque images in popular ghost visions. Religious mania, poetic frenzy, or an overburdening sense of guilt, he added, might intensify the power of the spectral illusion (Ferriar: 1813, 95, 15, 16–20, 63, 99–100, 109–10).

Something of Ferriar's influence can be felt in a comic essay in *Blackwood's Magazine* from 1818 (significantly entitled 'Phantasmagoriana'), which celebrated the 'decisive victory of the genius of physiology over the Prince of Darkness.' Thanks to '*ferriarism*,' its author averred, one no longer had to cross a dark churchyard with 'any *worse* apprehension than that of mere mortal rheumatism or asthma' – all phantom-fear having been annihilated by the new 'principle of *hallucination*' (Anon: 1818, 590). But other important debunking texts quickly followed: Joseph Taylor's *Apparitions; or, The Mystery of Ghosts, Hobgoblins, and Haunted Houses, Developed*

(1815), Samuel Hibbert's *Philosophy of Apparitions* (1825), John Abercrombie's *Inquiries Concerning the Intellectual Powers* (1830), William Newnham's *Essay on Superstition* (1830), Brewster's *Letters on Natural Magic* (1833), Walter Cooper Dendy's *The Philosophy of Mystery* (1841), and Charles Ollier's *The Fallacy of Ghosts, Dreams, and Omens* (1848). In France the most significant book on the subject (and indeed one of the most influential works of nineteenth-century psychology before Freud) was undoubtedly Alexandre Brierre de Boismont's *Des Hallucinations: ou, Histoire raisonnée des apparitions, des visions, des songes, de l'extase, des rêves, du magnétisme et du somnambulisme* (1845), translated into English in 1850.

Allowing for certain variations in emphasis, the basic argument in each of these works was the same: spectres were products of the imagination. Yet herein lay an unforeseen epistemological pitfall. The paradoxical effect of the psychological argument was to subvert the boundary between ghost-seeing and ordinary thought. Of course some apparitions could be attributed, quite simply, to specific pathological causes – fevers, head injuries, inhaling or imbibing stimulants. But the rationalists, at the same time, could not forebear reaching after a seemingly more universal or totalizing explanation: that thought itself was a spectral process, and, as such, easily modulated into hallucination. Ferriar led the way by confusing the distinction between simple recollection and the 'faculty of spectral representation.' 'From recalling images by an art of memory,' he wrote, 'the transition is direct to beholding spectral objects, which have been floating in the imagination' (Ferriar: 1813, 100). But others soon enlarged on the spectral nature of contemplation. It was possible for the mind to become so absorbed by an idea, wrote William Newnham, that the idea 'then haunts its waking and its sleeping moments' (Newnham: 1830, 41). 'The objects of mental contemplation,' Samuel Hibbert observed, 'may be seen as distinctly as external objects' (Hibbert: 1825, 251). Describing 'Ghosts of the Mind's Eye, or Phantasma' in his philosophical dialogue *The Philosophy of Mystery* (1841), Walter Cooper Dendy, senior surgeon at the Royal Infirmary for Children, concluded that a ghost was 'nothing more than an *intense idea*' and that seeing a phantom was 'an act of thinking.' Yet if ghosts were thoughts, it was not far to go, through a kind of symbolic recoil, to a perception that thoughts were ghosts:

> It is as easy to believe the power of mind in conjuring up a spectre as in entertaining a simple thought; it is not strange that this thought may appear *embodied*, especially if the external senses be shut: if we think of a distant friend, do we not *see* a form in our mind's eye, and if this idea be intensely defined, does it not become a phantom?

Between an idea and a phantom, wrote Dendy, 'there is only a difference in degree; their essence is the same as between the simple and transient thought of a child, and the intense and beautiful idea of a Shakespeare, a Milton, or a Dante' (Dendy: 1841, 55–6).

In the end, it seemed, one could no longer distinguish between the specialized psychic act of seeing a ghost and the everyday business of remembering or imagining. Brierre de Boismont made this indeterminacy strikingly obvious when he argued for the existence of what he called 'normal hallucinations' – the 'delirious conceptions . . . forever flitting around man, similar to those insects that are seen whirling around by thousands on a fine summer evening' (de Boismont: 1855, 354, 359). And in a crucial passage on the etiology of illusion, he found an even more suggestive metaphor:

> Sufficient attention has not been bestowed on this misty phantasmagoria in which we live. Those undecided forms, which approach and retire unceasingly, with a thousand tantalizing smiles, and after which we run with so much ardor, travel through our brains, emerge from their clouds, and become clearer and clearer; then the moral or physical point is reached; thought revived, colored, and represented, suddenly appears in a material form, and is transformed into an hallucination.
>
> (ibid., 287)

What such statements articulated, at bottom, was a new conception of the daemonic or irrational nature of thought. There was now a potential danger in the act of reflection – a danger in paying too much attention to mental images or in 'thinking too hard.' One's inmost thoughts might at any moment assume the strangely externalized shape of phantoms. The antiapparition writers often attacked the activity they referred to as reverie – the habit of indulging in erotic or poetic fancies, dwelling too long on things one had read, or brooding over obscure intellectual problems. Like a supernatural impulsion, reverie had the power to lead one out of oneself into madness. Given the spectral nature of thought, anyone theoretically could become like that 'monomaniac of a cultivated and ardent mind,' mentioned by Brierre de Boismont, who, through too great a delight in the creations of his imagination, saw waking dreams as realities:

> One day . . . we found him with eyes fixed, a smiling mouth, and in the act of clapping his hands in sign of applause. He did not hear us open the door of his room. To our question: 'What does this mean? What are you doing?' 'I am,' he replied, 'like the fool that Horace speaks of: I am seeing an imaginary play. I was wearied by my fireside; I am fond of the beauties of the opera, and have been playing to myself the ballet of *The Sylphide*; and when you touched me on the shoulder, I was applauding Taglioni, with whose graceful and noble dancing I had never before been so much charmed.'
>
> (ibid., 369)

We can see how the metaphor of the phantasmagoria mediated perfectly between the two contradictory perceptions inherent in the rationalist position. Ghosts were unreal, according to the skeptics, in the sense that they were artificial – the product of certain internal mechanistic processes. The magic lantern was the obvious mechanical analogue of the human brain, in that it 'made' illusionary forms and projected them outward. But in another highly paradoxical sense, ghosts now seemed *more real than ever before* – in that they now occupied (indeed preoccupied) the intimate space of the mind itself. The paradox was exactly like that achieved at the real phantasmagoria: ghosts did not exist, but one saw them anyway. Indeed, one could hardly escape them, for they were one's own thoughts bizarrely externalized.

[. . .]

Part Two

HORROR AND
PSYCHOANALYSIS

Introduction to Part Two

■   Ken Gelder

W E   H A V E   A L R E A D Y   N O T E D the importance of Sigmund Freud's 1919 essay 'The "Uncanny"'' in analyses of horror. The basic perception of psycho-analysis – that one's consciousness is not whole but constituted through a 'lack' (or perhaps a 'surplus') which it represses and yet which inevitably returns to it – was linked in this essay to the production of fear and anxiety. The uncanny effect occurs when something returns to consciousness that has long been forgotten. It is, Freud says, 'that class of the frightening which leads back to what is known of old and long familiar' (Freud: 1985, 340). When it returns, the 'old and long familiar' can now seem disturbingly *unfamiliar*. However, Freud also showed that these two terms – familiar and unfamiliar, or in German, *heimlich* (homely) and *unheimlich* (unhomely) – seem somehow to 'coincide', as if inhabiting each other. The uncanny effect is thus an example of misrecognition, when what is familiar has been so forgotten that it seems strange, or estranging, when it suddenly 'comes to light'. Freud's examples are often to do with primitive beliefs and super-stitions that may, incredibly, achieve some realization in modern times. But he also speaks of the maternal woman in this context, with the mother's body and genitals as similarly both familiar and estranging. Here, the uncanny effect combines fear or anxiety with psychoanalysis's favourite topic, desire.

The three extracts in this section are influenced by the more recent psycho-analytical work of Jacques Lacan and Julia Kristeva. Nevertheless, they all have something to say about the maternal woman and invoke in one way or another Freud's uncanny. Joan Copjec, in an extract from an article first published in *October*, looks at the importance placed on nursing mothers and breastfeeding at the end of the eighteenth century. She focuses on a key moment in psychoanalytic criticism: the separation of the subject from the mother, the end of the maternal breast as 'object-cause of desire', and its transformation into a 'lack' from which the subject must maintain a certain distance. The vampire also sucks, of course, and in doing so it 'menaces the breast as object-cause of desire', making us feel *unheimlich* (unhomely, estranged) in our own bodies.

Copjec's essay is thus also about anxiety, which she reads as functioning like the Lacanian real, a preOedipal or primal life-force. For Lacanians, the subject's entry into the symbolic order requires a negation of the real. But to negate the real means that one is also compelled to signify it – and to recognize the impossibility of its signification. All this means that one is in flight from it and stuck to it simultaneously – rather like the predicament outlined in Mary Shelley's *Frankenstein* (1818), which Copjec takes as a foundational modern text. The subject's encounter with the real is not unlike civilization's encounter with the 'primitive' – which is then diagnosed, integrated, authorized, and so on. Copjec also talks of 'doubt' as a 'defense against the real', in a way that perhaps recalls Todorov's view that the fantastic produces a certain 'hesitation'. Her essay, in common with many horror texts, is in fact partly a meditation on belief itself. Psychoanalysis is presented (not immodestly!) as the exemplary human science in this respect, neither sceptical nor believing but rather a 'belief without belief', a belief in something 'whose very existence is dependent on our lack of knowledge'. It *also* diagnoses, integrates, authorizes; yet it ceaselessly comes up against the real which is beyond its grasp. Like horror, psychoanalysis is thus a true child of the Enlightenment. Indeed, for Copjec anxiety itself proliferated at precisely the moment at which the modern subject itself was born.

Slavoj Žižek is the most productive and exhilarating of contemporary readers of Lacan, often using popular culture – including horror texts – to clarify the teachings of this opaque psychoanalyst. His contribution to this section, on *Psycho* (1960), comes from a much longer essay on the films of Alfred Hitchcock – a Master who might compare here with Lacan himself. This essay turns on the viewer's relationship to a cinema that seems utterly 'indifferent'. Yet such indifference paradoxically ensures the viewer's complicity in the films' moral universes. Film theory from the 1970s had often focused on the gaze (and desires) of the viewing subject. *Psycho* ends, however, with the psychotic Norman looking back into the camera, as a character who himself seems indifferent to humanity – 'blind' in this sense – and yet who also appears to 'watch us all the time'. This indifferent returning of the knowing gaze is a mark of his monstrosity.

The notorious shower scene in *Psycho* marks the point where the viewer's identification is radically shifted from Marion to Norman. For Žižek, this abruptly transfers the viewer from the 'hysteria' of everyday American life to the 'psychotic' world of pathological crime. It also takes us from the mobile realm of perpetually-unsatisfied desire to the enclosed, static world of the always-already-satisfied drive (Norman is without desire). The film itself is 'monstrous' through its yoking together of these two realms – which Žižek also represents as the modern (the car, the motel) and the traditional (the old house). Again, the paradigm is one of inhabitation, or perhaps we might say 'embodiment'. Žižek in fact compares this yoking together of opposites with the attempt in the final scene to place the mother's voice in the son's body. Voice and body inhabit each other and yet remain estranged, again producing an uncanny effect.

The mother–son relationship in *Psycho* supplies one of the paradigms for Barbara Creed's work on the 'monstrous-feminine'. The psychoanalytical inspiration for Creed, however, comes from Julia Kristeva's influential study, *Powers of Horror: An Essay on Abjection* (1982). For Kristeva, abjection refers to that improper, unclean Other which disturbs the identity of the subject I. It 'precedes and possesses' the subject, as an 'archaic' thing which is expelled through what Kristeva calls 'primal repression' (Kristeva: 1982, 10, 12). When it returns, it threatens the subject with dissolution, blurring the boundaries which are conventionally and often ritualistically drawn between human and inhuman, clean and defiled. The result may provoke disgust, as well as fascination. Kristeva had turned mostly to Biblical texts and modern literature, Louis-Ferdinand Céline especially, for themes of abjection. But Creed turns to the contemporary popular horror film, which – think of *The Exorcist* (1973), for example – routinely stages this return as a spectacular event, often literally dissolving the subject's identity in the process through mutilation, pollution, possession, body-melt, and so on.

For Creed and Kristeva, women have a 'special relationship' to the abject through menstruation and the maternal function. The 'proper' subject is fully integrated into the symbolic order; but the maternal woman, in this account, remains tied to nature and is thus still at least in part 'archaic'. Rituals and rites of passage give expression to the child's movement away from the latter and into the former. But the archaic mother may be reluctant to release the child: like Norman's mother in *Psycho*, she might even wilfully obstruct the child's capacity for separation and symbolic integration. For Creed, this is where the 'monstrous-feminine' resides. The maternal woman's authority is primal and functions without guilt or shame, in which case it is destined for conflict with the law of the father. She may even, like Jennifer in *I Spit on Your Grave* (1977), become what Creed calls a '*femme castratice*', sadistic and vengeful. But Creed sees the horror film much as José B. Monleon had seen the fantastic, that is, as in service to the symbolic order that it ultimately helps to preserve – not least by ensuring that the 'monstrous-feminine' *remains* monstrous.

Chapter 4

JOAN COPJEC

VAMPIRES, BREAST-FEEDING,
AND ANXIETY
(extract)

Jean-Jacques Rousseau, *Emile* (1762):

> Do you wish to bring everyone back to his first duties? Begin with
> mothers. You will surprised by the changes you will produce. Everything
> follows successively from this first depravity [i.e., mothers who despise
> their first duty and no longer want to feed their children]. The whole
> moral order degenerates. . . . But let mothers deign to nurse their
> children, morals will reform themselves, nature's sentiments will be
> awakened in every heart, the state will be repeopled. This first point,
> this point alone, will bring everything back together.
>
> (Rousseau: 1979, 46)

Mary Wollstonecraft, *Thoughts on the Education of Daughters with Reflections on Female
Conduct in the more important Duties of Life* (1787):

> I conceive it to be the duty of every rational creature to attend to its
> offspring. . . . The mother (if there are not very weighty reasons to
> prevent her) ought to suckle her children. Her milk is their proper
> nutriment, and for some time quite sufficient.
>
> (Wollstonecraft: 1972, 3)

LET THESE TWO – PROBABLY the most prominent – examples stand as
indications of a phenomenon that was widespread in the eighteenth century,
an insignia, we might even say, of Enlightenment thought: the advocacy of breast-
feeding. This phenomenon is currently the subject of much speculation by
historically informed literary theorists intent on establishing its links with the
political, philosophical, and literary themes of the period. While I, too, will urge

a consideration of these links, I do not propose to attempt an explication of either the external causes or the meaning of the phenomenon. For to do so would be to ignore its most essential aspect: *the aura of anxiety that surrounds it*. It is this aspect that allows us to observe the historical coincidence and close correspondence between this phenomenon and a form of literature which emerged in the eighteenth century. I am speaking, of course, of vampire fiction, in all its Gothic forms. I will argue that the political advocacy of breast-feeding cannot be properly understood unless one sees it for what it is: the precise equivalent of vampire fiction.

It is necessary, first of all, to say something about anxiety. If its cause cannot be determined, this is because it is the most primitive of phenomena. It is that which nothing precedes. One could also say, conversely, that that which nothing precedes, that which follows from nothing, is what awakens anxiety. Anxiety registers the non sequitur, a gap in the causal chain. It was the difficulty of trying to think this very priority of anxiety that made *Inhibitions, Symptoms and Anxiety* (1926) the confused text that it is, with Freud switching from his 'first theory' (in which repression precedes anxiety) to this 'second theory' (in which anxiety precedes repression) and back – several times – and quarrelling with Otto Rank about whether or not birth can be the occasion of anxiety. Freud says that it cannot, but he also seems to incorporate Rank's arguments at points.

And yet a definition does clearly emerge from Freud's text: anxiety is a signal of danger. This signal is extraordinary because it works without the use of any signifiers. Since a signifier can always be negated, the message it sends can always be doubted. Rather than a signifier, then, anxiety is an affect – a special sort of affect – and as such it cannot be doubted. Common usage notwithstanding, anxiety is connected to certitude rather than doubt. This is also a way of saying that what anxiety signals is real. As we have just remarked, Freud – like Kant, who gave both respect, the signal of moral law, and terror, the signal of the sublime, a special status – sets anxiety apart from all the other affects, feelings, sentiments that are caused by objects acting on the subject. If anxiety can be considered a presentiment, it is only in the etymological sense of that term; it appears *prior* to any sentiment in the 'normal,' 'pathological' sense. (The pun on *presentiment* is made by Lacan in his unpublished seminar on anxiety [1962–3].)

Anxiety – again, like respect and terror – is not only not caused by any object, it is not even caused by any loss/lack of object (which is why anxiety can be distinguished from disappointment, say, or grief). Rather than an object or its lack, anxiety signals a lack of lack, a failure of the symbolic reality wherein all alienable objects, objects which can be given or taken away, lost and refound, are constituted and circulate. Somewhat perversely, however, Lacan does refer to this encounter with a 'lack of lack' as an encounter with an *object*: object small *a*. But this object is unique; it has neither an essence nor a signification. It cannot be communicated or exchanged. It has, in short, no *objectivity*. The danger that anxiety signals is the overproximity of this object *a*, this object so *inalienable* that like Dracula and all the other vampires of Gothic and Romantic fiction it cannot even be cast as a shadow or reflected as a mirror image, and yet so *insubstantial* that like Murnau's Nosferatu it can disappear in a puff of smoke.

Now, if the signal of anxiety cannot lie, if we cannot be misled as to its message, it stands to reason that any *interpretation* of anxiety is superfluous and inappropriate. But if interpretation is not the proper response, what is? The best way to answer this question is to look once again at that overinterpreted anxiety dream, the dream of Irma's injection. Lacan's commentary on this dream is designed to demonstrate how we must act – and how we must not act – in the face of anxiety (see Lacan: 1988, 146–71). The dream is divided by Lacan into two parts, each of which is marked by its own climax. In the first part, Freud appears as a man free of any 'Oedipus complex'; his research is driven entirely by his desire to know, whatever the cost. Propelled by this desire, he stalks his party guest, Irma, and struggling against her resistances, peers curiously down her throat, only to make his truly horrible discovery. What he witnesses is the very 'origin of the world,' the equivalent of the female genitals. It is clear that the uncanny appearance of what ought to have remained hidden is a sickening, noxious sight. But what is it, really? 'A large white spot . . . curled structures . . . white-gray scabs.' Almost nothing. This is the climax of the first part of the dream, the anxiety-filled encounter with the object *a*.

After this encounter the dream abruptly switches into another mode. The dream space becomes fantasmatically populated with Freud's doctor friends: Dr. M., Otto, Leopold; in other words, the space becomes 'Oedipalized.' By this I mean, first of all, that the second part of the dream is defined by a *turning away from* the object *a* which erupted in the first part. In the second part, Freud no longer wants to know; his primary desire is a desire *not* to know anything of the real that provoked in him so much anxiety. The abruptness of the transition indicates that Freud *flees* from the real – Irma, her white scabs, the unconscious – into the symbolic community of his fellow doctors.

So, the proper response to anxiety is, according to this dream, flight. But is it not the height of absurdity to say that the founder of psychoanalysis, of the study of the unconscious, based the whole of this discipline (recall how proudly Freud thought of a future commemoration of this dream, as though it were the cornerstone of the edifice of psychoanalysis) on a turning away from the unconscious? On a desire to know nothing about it? Some further clarification of the character of the consequent, Oedipalized space is necessary before this suspicion can be allayed. Filled with paternal figures, this space is infused with an air of interdiction, of rules, regulations, and prescriptions, and yet it offers relief from the constricted, asphyxiating space that *zusammenschnüren*, that chokes, Freud as well as Irma. In what, then, does this relief consist, and how is it secured? Most simply put, it consists in the setting up of the symbolic as rampart against the real; the symbolic *shields* us from the terrifying real. The climax of the second part, the triumphant pronouncement of the word *trimethylamine*, indicates that it is the word itself, or the symbolic itself, which is our salvation.

But in order for the symbolic to evict the real and thereby establish itself, a judgment of existence is required, i.e., it is necessary to *say* that the real is absented, to *declare* its impossibility. The symbolic, in other words, must include the negation of what it is not. This requirement is not without its paradoxical effects, for it means ultimately that the symbolic will not be filled with only itself, since it will also contain this surplus element of negation. According to this reasoning – which is to be found in Freud's 1919 essay 'Negation' – *that which is impossible must also be prohibited.*

It should be evident right away that this negation of the real by the symbolic presents a special problem. The real that is to be negated cannot be represented by a signifier, since the real is, by definition, that which *has* no adequate signifier. How, then, can this negation take place *within* the symbolic as the requirement demands? The answer is: through repetition, through the signifier's repeated attempt – and failure – to designate itself. The signifier's difference from itself, its radical inability to signify itself, causes it to turn in circles around the real that is lacking in it. It is in this way – in the circumscription of the real – that its nonexistence or its negation is signified *within* the symbolic.

This is also the explanation of the Lacanian thesis that *doubt is a defense against the real*. Doubt – which emerges from the signifier's noncoincidence with itself, its incapacity to guarantee itself – registers the impossibility of the real and thereby defends us against its intrusion into the symbolic. Dr. M., Otto, Leopold, the three sorry figures of authority in the dream of Irma's injection, will illustrate this argument. Their supposedly professional probings and pronouncements are simply ridiculous. Whatever principle of diagnosis one may represent is quickly transgressed by the other, who proposes a different and contradictory principle. These fellows are simply not credible as standard-bearers of their profession. But have we not entered here into that place so often evoked by Lacan, the place where tracks are made *in order to be taken as false*? As so many, including Foucault, have noted, laws are made to be broken, prohibitions to be transgressed, but through its very violability the law simply binds us closer to it. The law has an irrefutably *positive* force to which every transgression, which defines itself in terms of the law while dreaming itself beyond it, attests. It is wrong to assume, however, as so many, including Foucault, have, that the fundamentally *negative* character of the law is in this way refuted. For the transgression of the law's interdiction of specific, named acts in no way violates the law's other, more basic interdiction – of the real. This interdiction, unlike the first type, is never *named* by the law, but is inscribed in it nevertheless: in the law's very inability to authorize itself. The Foucauldians have simplified the Freudian thesis about negation by rendering it as 'that which is negated must be named' and by failing to realize that that which is impossible must be negated *without being named*.

In the psychoanalytic version, the symbolic order defends against the real by substantifying its negation in the interdictions and doubts that define symbolicity as such. We have thus described the space of the second half of Freud's dream as an Oedipalized space both because it instantiates an avoidance of the real, a desire not to know anything about it, and because this avoidance necessitates an important, violable (i.e., Oedipal) law. It is now necessary to confess a considerable complication of this argument. We have called that from which Freud takes flight the object *a*, but though we have refrained until now from saying so, that which marks his avoidance of this traumatic point, the absence of the real, is also called object *a*. The object *a* is both real and a positivization of the symbolic's failure to say the real; it is both real and imaginary. What is the explanation for this terminological conundrum? If the symbolic must inscribe its lack of foundation in the real, the inaccessibility to it of some knowledge of this real, then, we are obliged to admit that it also thereby inscribes the real itself, since it is precisely there where we do *not* know, that enjoyment, *jouissance* (a pleasure in the real), arises.

Jouissance is a kind of 'secondary gain' obtained where knowledge fails. As Lacan says at the beginning of *Television*, 'Saying it all is literally impossible: words fail. Yet it's through this very impossibility that the truth holds onto the real' (Lacan: 1990, 3). This statement demonstrates a Möbius strip kind of logic, for in the last analysis it means that the real *is* its own negation, its own prohibition. The real encounters itself in its own lack, its exclusion from the system of signifiers.

In his dream of Irma's injection, then, Freud does not simply flee from the unconscious or from the real of Irma's desire: *he holds onto them*. This is the reason psychoanalysis can claim to found itself on the unconscious and on the desire of the woman, precisely because it so rigorously registers their inaccessibility. We could say, then, using the Lacanian definition of sublimation, that psychoanalysis 'raises' the unconscious and the woman's desire 'to the dignity of the Thing.' It is in its refusal to interpret them that psychoanalysis maintains them, for there where they are interpreted they cease to be.

But if in order to preserve itself psychoanalysis has to register its own radical inability to know, does it not consign itself to scepticism? Must we place Freud among his foolish mentors, equal to them in his ignorance of the truth? No, psycho-analysis is not a scepticism. By not declaring merely that the good (which would be a standard of our actions) *cannot* be known, but insisting further that it *must* not be known, psychoanalysis commits itself to what Lacan refers to as a 'belief without belief,' to a belief in an Other whose very existence is dependent on our lack of knowledge.

'It's because we cannot be content with the idea that some good person is able to dictate man's obligations that the problem of evil is worth raising. The exalted representation of evil will safeguard the greatest revolutionary value' (Lacan: 1986, 85). It's because radical doubt undermines the position of every would-be master that the problem of radical evil must be raised. Psychoanalysis shares this position with a certain strain of Enlightenment thought, which cele-brated evil while attempting to secure the individual subject's freedom from authority. For both psychoanalysis and this mode of thinking that originated in the eighteenth century, the exalted evil referred to is synonymous with the subject itself, since it is the subject that seems to pose the greatest threat to the estab-lished social order. But one should not be too quick to equate this conception with the standard reading of the Romantic opposition between the individual and society. Romantic notions are fundamentally recast by this conception, which neither sees the subject as the external cause of society's corruption, nor society as the corrupter of the pure, innocent subject. Instead of an external opposition between the subject and society, we must learn to think their necessary interrelation: the very existence of the subject is simultaneous with society's failure to integrate it, to represent it.

It is its rendering of this peculiar interrelation that makes *Frankenstein* (1818) such an exemplary text and Frankenstein's monster such a paradigmatic example of the modern subject. While it gives reign to the fantasy that things might have turned out otherwise, that society would have been spared the monster's maleficence if only it had treated him with more kindness, if only the young De Lacey had not burst into the cottage just as the monster was about to reveal his true character to the old, blind De Lacey, *Frankenstein* also exposes the truth on which this fantasy depends: the monster is, constitutionally, he whose character cannot be revealed. He, like the modern subject in general, is located there where knowledge of him is omitted. His monstrosity is therefore structural, not accidental.

This is why the common belief that Victor Frankenstein invented the monster is in error. If the monster were, in fact, the product of a scientific invention, he would have awakened at the end of chapter four, but he does not; it is only at the very beginning of chapter five that the baleful yellow eye first opens. If Frankenstein had succeeded in his scientific project, this success would have been recorded as the climax of a series of steps and discoveries, as the end product of a causal chain of effort and effect. But at the end of the chapter in which these discoveries are recorded, the invention remains uninvented. That Frankenstein has failed is apparent in the opening of the following chapter where the thing that he strove to animate lies lifeless at his feet. It is only *then* and in the absence of any indication or sense of agency on Frankenstein's part – the inventor is described as a passive witness of the event – that the monster comes to life. There seems to be only one reading of this narrative pacing: Frankenstein's invention did not go awry, as the standard reading claims, it *failed*. It is only insofar as it failed, only inasmuch as Frankenstein's scientific efforts fell short of their goal, that the monster appears, the embodiment of this failure. It is therefore misleading to call the creature 'Frankenstein's monster,' as though it were not precisely the *lack* of that 'belong to me aspect so reminiscent of property' (in Lacan's phrase) which provided the creature with its essential definition – and made him so uncanny.

In response to anxiety's signal of danger, one flees or avoids the real. But one flees into a symbolic whose hedge against the real is secured only through its negation of the real, i.e., through its failure to coincide with itself, to guarantee itself. The subject – like the Frankenstein monster – *is* the failure that maintains the symbolic, prevents it from collapse. But we claimed earlier that in his discussion of the dream of Irma's injection, Lacan made clear not only the proper but also the improper manner of accomplishing this avoidance. Despite the many insights with which Lacan credits him, Erik Erikson is, to some extent, used to illustrate an improper response, a certain deafness, to the signal sounded by the dream. There is, of course, a major difference between Erikson and Freud regarding the characterization of the second space of the dream. Lacan's understanding of this space as symbolic reality in its function as shield against the traumatic real, as being simultaneously salutary for the subject and the place of its *nonintegration*, would make no sense at all to Erikson, for whom reality is that into which the healthy ego is integrated. He therefore comprehends this space differently: as the place of the regression of the ego. Rather than focus on all the broad and basic differences between Lacanian psychoanalysis and ego psychology, however, let us note that Lacan chose to derogate Erikson's *interpretation* of Freud's dream with the term *culturalist*. What most disturbs Lacan is Erikson's digging into Freud's life and culture in the hopes of finding some additional facts that will push the interpretation beyond the limit demarcated by Freud. Against this endless ransacking of the archives, Lacan maintains not that history is unimportant, but that historicism can only bring about the destruction of history: that some limits are meant to be observed. In the middle of his making this point, something wonderful happens: a member of the audience intervenes to make the point for him, *a contrario*. At the very moment Lacan asks us to confront the horrifying real which threatens to choke Irma and Freud, the moment Lacan points to the suffocation, the gasping for breath that evidences the overwhelming presence of the real, Mme. X – we can give her a more descriptive name, Mme. Culturalist, or Mme. Historicist – interjects the following observation: 'In the old days, three or four people were needed to pull on the laces of a corset to tighten it' (Lacan: 1988, 153).

Here we have a clear example of an avoidance of the real, but not of the sort at which we have been aiming. In place of a negative judgment of existence (the establishment of a second symbolic space which would announce its nonreal status: 'I am no longer anything,' is the way Lacan phrases it), Mme. Historicist offers *no judgment* on the real's existence. She *forecloses* rather than repudiates it. No anxiety disquiets her, nothing signals the danger that faces Irma and Freud. What Freud confronts in his moment of anxiety is a gap in symbolic reality, a point which interpretation, the logic of cause and effect, cannot bridge. In response, he does not bridge it; he records its unbridgeability and in this way circumscribes it. Mme. Historicist does not come up against a gap; she sees only an uninterrupted chain of signifiers which she interprets by assigning them a place in another causal chain.

The drying up of the breast

Now, it is precisely this sort of historicist interpretation that we must guard against while considering the eighteenth-century advocacy of breast-feeding. For there is ample evidence that this advocacy expressed a profound anxiety, that it situated itself at the very limit of interpretation. If we return to the Rousseau and Wollstonecraft texts previously cited, we will find that each utters its plea for the maternal breast as a safeguard against what? Against the suffocation, the strangulation the child will suffer without it. Rousseau thus rails against the child's 'being prevented from breathing,' its being more cramped, more constrained, more compressed than 'in the amnion,' its being 'garroted' – all as a result of its being deprived of its mother's breast (Rousseau: 1979, 43–4). And Wollstonecraft speaks of such a child as being 'overloaded,' as being in a state of unalleviated bodily pain, and later contends that 'it is easy to distinguish the child of a well-bred person [i.e., of a mother who honors her duty to breast-feed her child] if it is not left entirely to the nurse's care. These women are of course ignorant, and to keep a child quiet for the moment, they humor all its little caprices. Very soon does it begin to be perverse, and eager to be gratified in everything' (Wollstonecraft: 1972, 3, 5). Both Rousseau and Wollstonecraft understand the deprivation resulting from the mother's neglect of her 'duty to breast-feed' as a *deprivation of deprivation*. This understanding is then reiterated in their subsequent warnings against the *excesses* of motherly devotion. It is a 'cruel' mother, Rousseau warns, who 'plunge[s] her] children in softness.' The encouragement of breast-feeding seeks to submit the child not to the mother, but – quite the contrary – to social law.

But we have promised to come to terms with this phenomenon by establishing its corollary in vampire fiction. That the encounter with the vampire is always anxiety-ridden would seem to be undebatable. And yet even this seemingly obvious fact is in danger of being lost by those analyses that attempt to define the Gothic depiction of this encounter as a form of either sentimental or sensation fiction. As we argued earlier, anxiety is not an affect or a sentiment like others; it has, for the reasons stated, an exceptional status. The Gothic world is, in fact, only conceivable as the elimination of sentiment. If vampirism makes our hearts pound, our pulses race, and our breathing come in troubled bursts, this is not because it puts us in contact with objects and persons – others – who affect us, but because it confronts us with an absence of absence – an Other – who threatens to asphyxiate us. And rather than making us more at home in our bodies, rather than anchoring us to bodies conceived as the agents of our intelligence, the makers of sense, vampirism presents us with a bodily double that we can neither make sense of nor recognize as our own.

In what, essentially, does the phenomenon of vampirism consist? The first thing to note is that it is a matter of an *oral relation*, of a *jouissance* attained through sucking. One might spontaneously think of the child in its oral-parasitic relation to its mother as the image of vampirism. But as Lacan – along with all the narratives and iconography of vampirism – makes clear, it is not the child who is the vampire. (Lacan's passing remarks on vampirism as an anxiety that profiles the 'drying up of the breast' are found in his seminar on anxiety, May 15, 1963.) The image of the child at the mother's breast is not one that elicits anxiety. Vampirism is located beyond this point where the child maintains itself in relation to a partial object, an object of desire. It is only at the point where the fantasy enabling this relation to the partial object no longer holds that the anxiety-ridden phenomenon of vampirism takes over, signaling, then, *the drying up of the breast as object-cause of desire*, the disappearance of the fantasy support of desire. The drying up of desire is the danger against which vampirism warns us, sending up a cry for the breast which would deliver us from this horror.

The breast – like the gaze, the voice, the phallus, and the feces – is an object, an appendage of the body, from which we separate ourselves in order to constitute ourselves as subjects. To constitute ourselves, we must, in other words, throw out, reject our nonselves. Our discussion of the Freudian concept of negation has taught us, however, that this rejection can only be accomplished through the inclusion within ourselves of this negation of what we are not – within our being, this lack-of-being. These Freudian objects are, then, not only rejected from, but also internal to the subject. In brief, they are *extimate*, which means they are in us that which is not us.

It is precisely because the subject is defined in this way – or, as we will argue later, *when* the subject is defined in this way – that it stumbles into the dimension of the uncanny. The special feeling of uncanniness is a feeling of anxiety that befalls us whenever we too closely approach the extimate object in ourselves. In his theorization of the uncanny, Freud, influenced by the literary works on which he drew, underlined the privileged relation uncanniness maintained with the gaze. But as vampire fiction demonstrates, the uncanny can also manifest itself as an over-proximity to the 'extimate' breast.

Normally, when we are at some remove from it, the extimate object *a* appears as a lost part of ourselves, whose absence prevents us from becoming whole; it is then that it functions as the object-cause of our desire. But when our distance from it is reduced, it no longer appears as a partial object, but – on the contrary

– as a complete body, an almost exact double of our own, except for the fact that this double is endowed with the object which we sacrificed in order to become subjects. This would mean that the vampire is not only a creature that menaces the breast as object-cause of desire, but that it is also a double of the victim, whose distorted bodily form indicates its possession of a certain excess object: the breast once again, but this time as source of *jouissance*. The most vivid confirmation of this thesis concerning the double is given in Bram Stoker's *Dracula* (1897), in that horrifyingly obscene moment when we are startled to witness Mina Harker *drinking from the breast of Dracula*. Desire, society itself, is endangered by Mina's intimacy with this extimate object. But it is Alfred Hitchcock's *Rebecca* (1940) – a twentieth-century version of an eighteenth-century form, the 'female Gothic' (see Doane: 1987, 123–75; Kahane: 1980, 43–64) – which best illustrates the fact that the object which 'completes' the subject, filling in its lack, is also always a disfiguring surplus. In this film the paradox functions as a plot device when the baby with which Rebecca is supposed to have been pregnant when she died is revealed to have been instead a fatal cancer.

[. . .]

Breast-feeding and freedom

In *Architecture civile*, a portfolio of drawings by the eighteenth-century 'visionary' architect Jean Jacques Lequeu (1757–1825), we find the famous image of a rather robust woman lying on her back under an archway. The angle of the drawing is designed to profile her breasts; a bird in flight is visible at the top of the arch. The drawing, whose title is *He is free*, turns the image of vampirism inside out – replacing the terrifying vampire with the simple bird and the horror of the drying up of the breast with these full breasts – and returns us to our main concern: the relation between the advocacy of breast-feeding and a new, revolutionary definition of the subject as free. We have been arguing that this advocacy must be viewed as a manifestation of anxiety, especially similar to that expressed in vampire fiction. We have also argued that anxiety must not be interpreted, that we must not seek an external cause for it. This does not prevent us, however, from asking why there seems to have been so much anxiety in the late eighteenth and early nineteenth centuries, for we can answer this question without recourse to any external phenomenon. It was the very definition of the subject *as* free that insured this increase of anxiety. That is, the eighteenth century detached a double of the subject which it made inaccessible to annihilation (to paraphrase Lacan's description of the function of suffering in Sade: Lacan: 1986, 303); this double, unlike older notions of the immortal soul, allowed the subject to become detached from the world without becoming attached to some other-worldly principle – the unfortunate consequence of the conception of the double as soul. Rather than as another principle, the Enlightenment double was conceived as nothing, nothing but the negation of the subject's attachment to the world. This double, then, guaranteed the *autonomy* of the subject, its freedom from a pathetic existence in which it could be manipulated by other things, persons, or traditions. But once this double was thus detached, once it was set loose in the world, it was inevitable that the subject would occasionally 'run into it,' approach it a little too closely. Whenever this happens, anxiety signals us to take our distance once again.

This suggests that there are times when the real overtakes us *without* warning, that we are sometimes not provided with an opportunity to protect ourselves from it. Freud himself makes this suggestion: there are occasions, he says, when anxiety is omitted, when it does not arise to prepare us from the real's overproximity. In these cases, the results are always catastrophic. We would argue that anxiety increases with the emergence of the modern subject, that it is this inclusion of the real *within* the symbolic, this negation within reality that sounds the warning which not only unsettles society but also allows it to take steps against a more catastrophic confrontation.

The steps we must take have also already been spelled out: we must not stop writing the impossibility of the real, the impossibility of 'saying it all.' As Lacan pointed out in *L'éthique de la psychanalyse*, it is Kant's conception of the beautiful that writes this impossibility most eloquently. The symbolic world – the second space of Freud's dream of Irma's injection – is strictly parallel to the Kantian conception of the aesthetics of the beautiful. The question of aesthetics, as we know, assumed a priority during the eighteenth century. In the widespread investigations of this topic an important shift is discernible: the aesthetic field is regularly conceived as *excluding* the subject. Think, for example, of Diderot's influential dictum: 'Act as though the curtain never rose,' that is, subtract the subject from the aesthetic field and focus on establishing the field's unity and homogeneity. But while others excluded the subject in order the better to *affect* him/her, in order to attain the maximum emotional effect, Kant completely revolutionized aesthetic theory by excluding the subject in order to *protect* him/her – in order to hold onto the subject as free. This he did by defining the beautiful object as one that could not be subsumed under any determinate concept, as one about which we could not say all. Kant thus made the beautiful the signifier of a limit, a barrier against the real. With this the object *a*, the nothing that guarantees the subject's freedom, was prohibited from being spoken – and thus from being lost.

Before the Kantian revolution, as we know, the question of rights was determined 'vertically'; rights were assigned and assured by a power beyond man. With the Kantian revolution, some have argued, this question was determined 'horizontally'; it was assumed that the rights of one individual were only curtailed by those of another. This made one subject the limit of his neighbor, that which prevented him from achieving all that he might. The problem with this conception of rights – which is, admittedly, *a* modern although not *the* modern conception, and certainly *not* the one that issues from the Kantian theorization of the subject – is that it perceives rights only as a series of *demands*, fully expressible in language and fully known to the subject who insists on them. This notion of rights pits one subject, one consciousness, against another and decides all conflicts by determining which demand will best benefit the *general will*. What this reduction of rights to demands results in is the elimination of the question of the subject's desire. It eliminates the question of the subject's attachment to what language cannot say, to the unspeakable double which is the indestructible support of our freedom. For it is only if the 'lonely hour' of the S_2, the final signifier that retroactively determines our meaning, 'does *not* arrive' that our actions can be determined by anything other than self-interest.

So, if the advocacy of breast-feeding, as I have argued, is not to be understood as a demand, but as a cry for the object-cause of desire, then it could only have been properly answered by assurances of the subject's freedom. It would be naive to suppose, however, that the historicism which turns a deaf ear to anxiety is only a current danger; it is clear that this same historicist response was a possibility contemporaneous with the anxiety-filled cry itself. It is certain that there were many who understood this anxiety before the drying up of the breast as a demand that the woman be subsumed under the category of the mother, that the biological family become the primary cell of society, even though these demands – that the woman cede her desire, that one place one's faith in the sexual relation – are absolutely antithetical to the political project whose possibilities had only just been opened up.

Victor Frankenstein is probably one of the most instructive illustrations of this sort of contemporary historicist reaction to the celebration of breast-feeding. As many critics have pointed out, *Frankenstein* is a novel about motherhood in which Frankenstein plays the role of an extremely bad mother. But what is it that makes him so bad? Not the fact that he refuses the demand of 'his child,' but that he interprets his cry as a demand. Earlier we asked, rhetorically, if the monster's attempt to justify his existence wouldn't entail the destruction of that existence – knowing well that it would. Now we must note that it is no coincidence that it is to Frankenstein that this justification is offered; it is he alone who hears the monster's long speech, the whole of which is set out in quotes, since it is from Frankenstein (and not the monster) that *we* (along with Walton) hear it. If Frankenstein is able to quote this long tale verbatim, we can only imagine that this is because *he takes the monster literally*; he refuses to question the words of the monster in order to tease out what he *wants* to say, what he desires.

In other words, to Frankenstein the monster is *not* the uncanny being we have taken him to be; to Frankenstein, the scientist, there is no pure being without sense, no desire. After the initial shock of seeing this monstrous embodiment of his failure, Frankenstein treats the creature as just another being whose rights threaten to abridge his own. It is no wonder, then, that he interprets the monster's cry as a demand, and of a very specific sort: a demand for a sexual relation. If he refuses to grant this demand, it is not because he doubts its validity or attainability. In fact we can surmise that he believes in this relation, that he believes that one subject must complement the other or engage him in a battle to the death. This last is the only relation he can imagine having with the monster, and so he refuses him, thinking the monster's profit can only mean his loss.

Under the circumstances, the novel could only have ended as it did – with Frankenstein's melancholy journeying to the ends of the earth. For, deprived of the ballast of the object *a* – the object-cause of desire which lends things their only value, their desirability – the subject is condemned to wander in pursuit of one thing after another, without any hope of freedom, that is, without any hope of choosing a path that is not dictated by the objects themselves. At one point Frankenstein refers to the monster as 'my own vampire.' We know that what he had in mind was closer to the vulgar image of the child sapping its mother's strength with its demands than to the horrifying Gothic image of the menacing double. We now see that he would have been better off had he felt some of the anxiety that vampires aroused in many of his contemporaries.

Chapter 5

BARBARA CREED

KRISTEVA, FEMININITY, ABJECTION

We may call it a border; abjection is above all ambiguity. Because, while releasing a hold, it does not radically cut off the subject from what threatens it — on the contrary, abjection acknowledges it to be in perpetual danger.

Julia Kristeva, *Powers of Horror* (1982)

JULIA KRISTEVA'S *POWERS OF HORROR* provides us with a preliminary hypothesis for an analysis of the representation of woman as monstrous in the horror film. Although her study is concerned with psychoanalysis and literature, it nevertheless suggests a way of situating the monstrous-feminine in the horror film in relation to the maternal figure and what Kristeva terms 'abjection', that which does not 'respect borders, positions, rules', that which 'disturbs identity, system, order' (Kristeva: 1982, 4). In general terms, Kristeva is attempting to explore the different ways in which abjection works within human societies, as a means of separating out the human from the non-human and the fully constituted subject from the partially formed subject. Ritual becomes a means by which societies both renew their initial contact with the abject element and then exclude that element. Through ritual, the demarcation lines between the human and non-human are drawn up anew and presumably made all the stronger for that process.
[. . .]
A full examination of this theory is outside the scope of this project; I propose to draw mainly on Kristeva's discussion of the construction of abjection in the human subject in relation to her notion of (a) the 'border' (b) the mother-child relationship and (c) the feminine body. At crucial points, I shall also refer to her writings on the abject in relation to religious discourses. This area cannot be ignored, for what becomes apparent in reading her work is that definitions of the

monstrous as constructed in the modern horror text are grounded in ancient religious and historical notions of abjection – particularly in relation to the following religious 'abominations': sexual immorality and perversion; corporeal alteration, decay and death; human sacrifice; murder; the corpse; bodily wastes; the feminine body and incest. These forms of abjection are also central to the construction of the monstrous in the modern horror film.

The place of the abject is 'the place where meaning collapses', the place where 'I' am not. The abject threatens life; it must be 'radically excluded' (ibid., 2) from the place of the living subject, propelled away from the body and deposited on the other side of an imaginary border which separates the self from that which threatens the self. Although the subject must exclude the abject, the abject must, nevertheless, be tolerated for that which threatens to destroy life also helps to define life. Further, the activity of exclusion is necessary to guarantee that the subject take up his/her proper place in relation to the symbolic.

The abject can be experienced in various ways – one of which relates to biological bodily functions, the other of which has been inscribed in a symbolic (religious) economy. For instance, Kristeva claims that food loathing is 'perhaps the most elementary and archaic form of abjection' (ibid.). Food, however, only becomes abject if it signifies a border 'between two distinct entities or territories' (ibid., 75). Kristeva describes how, for her, the skin on the top of milk, which is offered to her by her father and mother, is a 'sign of their desire', a sign separating her world from their world, a sign which she does not want. 'But since the food is not an "other" for "me," who am only in their desire, I expel myself, I spit myself out, I abject myself within the same motion through which "I" claim to establish myself' (ibid., 3). In relation to the horror film, it is relevant to note that food loathing is frequently represented as a major source of abjection, particularly the eating of human flesh (*Blood Feast* (1963), *Motel Hell* (1980), *Blood Diner* (1987), *The Hills Have Eyes* (1977), *The Corpse Grinders* (1971)).

The ultimate in abjection is the corpse. The body protects itself from bodily wastes such as shit, blood, urine and pus by ejecting these things from the body just as it expels food that, for whatever reason, the subject finds loathsome. The body ejects these substances, at the same time extricating itself from them and from the place where they fall, so that it might continue to live:

> Such wastes drop so that I might live, until, from loss to loss, nothing remains in me and my entire body falls beyond the limit – *cadere*, cadaver. If dung signifies the other side of the border, the place where I am not and which permits me to be, the corpse, the most sickening of wastes, is a border that has encroached upon everything. It is no longer I who expel. 'I' is expelled.
>
> (ibid., 3–4)

Within a biblical context, the corpse is also utterly abject. It signifies one of the most basic forms of pollution – the body without a soul. As a form of waste it represents the opposite of the spiritual, the religious symbolic. In relation to the horror film, it is relevant to note that several of the most popular horrific figures are 'bodies without souls' (the vampire), the 'living corpse' (the zombie), corpse-eater (the ghoul) and the robot or android. What is also interesting is that such ancient figures of abjection as the vampire, the ghoul, the zombie and the witch (one of her many crimes was that she used corpses for her rites of magic) continue to provide some of the most compelling images of horror in the modern cinema. Were creatures, whose bodies signify a collapse of the boundaries between human and animal, also belong to this category.

Abjection also occurs where the individual is a hypocrite, a liar. Abject things are those that highlight the 'fragility of the law' and that exist on the other side of the border which separates out the living subject from that which threatens its extinction. But abjection is not something of which the subject can ever feel free – it is always there, beckoning the self to take up the place of abjection, the place where meaning collapses. The subject, constructed in/through language, through a desire for meaning, is also spoken by the abject, the place of meaninglessness – thus, the subject is constantly beset by abjection which fascinates desire but which must be repelled for fear of self-annihilation. A crucial point is that abjection is always ambiguous. Like Bataille, Kristeva emphasizes the attraction, as well as the horror, of the undifferentiated.

Abjection and the horror film

The horror film would appear to be, in at least three ways, an illustration of the work of abjection. First, the horror film abounds in images of abjection, foremost of which is the corpse, whole and mutilated, followed by an array of bodily wastes such as blood, vomit, saliva, sweat, tears and putrefying flesh. In terms of Kristeva's notion of the border, when we say such-and-such a horror film 'made me sick' or 'scared the shit out of me', we are actually foregrounding that specific horror film as a 'work of abjection' or 'abjection at work' – almost in a literal sense. Viewing the horror film signifies a desire not only for perverse pleasure (confronting sickening, horrific images/being filled with terror/desire for the undifferentiated) but also a desire, once having been filled with perversity, taken pleasure in perversity, to throw up, throw out, eject the abject (from the safety of the spectator's seat). In Kristeva's view, woman is specifically related to polluting objects which fall into two categories: excremental and menstrual. This in turn gives woman a special relationship to the abject – a crucial point which I will discuss shortly.

Second, the concept of a border is central to the construction of the monstrous in the horror film; that which crosses or threatens to cross the 'border' is abject. Although the specific nature of the border changes from film to film, the function of the monstrous remains the same – to bring about an encounter between the symbolic order and that which threatens its stability. In some horror films the monstrous is produced at the border between human and inhuman, man and beast (*Dr Jekyll and Mr Hyde*, *Creature from the Black Lagoon*, *King Kong*); in others the border is between the normal and the supernatural, good and evil (*Carrie*, *The Exorcist*, *The Omen*, *Rosemary's Baby*); or the monstrous is produced at the border which separates those who take up their proper gender roles from those who do not (*Psycho*, *Dressed to Kill*, *A Reflection of Fear*); or the border is between normal and abnormal sexual desire (*The Hunger*, *Cat People*). Most horror films also construct a border between what Kristeva refers to as 'the clean and proper body' and the abject body, or the body which has lost its form and integrity. The fully symbolic body must bear no indication of its debt to nature. In Kristeva's view the image of woman's body, because of its maternal functions, acknowledges its 'debt to nature' and consequently is more likely to signify the abject (ibid., 102). The notion of the material female body is central to the construction of the border in the horror film. [. . .]

Interestingly, various sub-genres of the horror film seem to correspond to religious categories of abjection. For instance, cannibalism, a religious abomination, is central to the 'meat' movie (*Night of the Living Dead*, *The Hills Have Eyes*); the corpse as abomination becomes the abject of ghoul and zombie movies (*The Evil Dead*; *Zombie Flesheaters*); blood is central to the vampire film (*The Hunger*) as well as the horror film in general (*Bloodsucking Freaks*); the corpse is constructed as the abject of virtually all horror film; and bodily disfigurement as a religious abomination is also central to the slasher movie, particularly those in which woman is slashed, the mark a sign of her 'difference', her impurity (*Dressed to Kill*, *Psycho*).

The third way in which the horror film illustrates the work of abjection is in the construction of the maternal figure as abject. Kristeva argues that all individuals experience abjection at the time of their earliest attempts to break away from the mother. She sees the mother-child relation as one marked by conflict: the child struggles to break free but the mother is reluctant to release it. Because of the 'instability of the symbolic function' in relation to this most crucial area – 'the prohibition placed on the maternal body (as a defense against autoeroticism and incest taboo)' – Kristeva argues that the maternal body becomes a site of conflicting desires. 'Here, drives hold sway and constitute a strange space that I shall name, after Plato (*Timaeus*, 48–53), a *chora*, a receptacle' (ibid., 14). The position of the child is rendered even more unstable because, while the mother retains a close hold over the child, it can serve to authenticate her existence – an existence which needs validation because of her problematic relation to the symbolic realm.

In the child's attempts to break away, the mother becomes an 'abject'; thus, in this context, where the child struggles to become a separate subject, abjection become '*a precondition of narcissism*' (ibid.). Once again we can see abjection at work in the horror text where the child struggles to break away from the mother, representative of the archaic maternal figure, in a context in which the father is invariably absent (*Psycho* (1960), *Carrie* (1976), *The Birds* (1963)). In these films the maternal figure is constructed as the monstrous-feminine. By refusing to relinquish her hold on her child, she prevents it from taking up its proper place in relation to the symbolic. Partly consumed by the desire to remain locked in a blissful relationship with the mother and partly terrified of separation, the child finds it easy to succumb to the comforting pleasure of the dyadic relationship. Kristeva argues that a whole area of religion has assumed the function of tackling this danger:

> This is precisely where we encounter the rituals of defilement and their derivatives, which, based on the feeling of abjection and all converging

on the maternal, attempt to symbolize the other threat to the subject: that of being swamped by the dual relationship, thereby risking the loss not of a part (castration) but of the totality of his living being. The function of these religious rituals is to ward off the subject's fear of his very own identity sinking irretrievably into the mother.

(ibid., 64)

How, then, are prohibitions against contact with the mother enacted and enforced? In answering this question, Kristeva links the universal practices of rituals of defilement to the mother. She argues that within the practices of all rituals of defilement, polluting objects fall into two categories: excremental, which threatens identity from the outside; and menstrual, which threatens from within. Both categories of polluting objects relate to the mother. The relation of menstrual blood is self-evident: the association of excremental objects with the maternal figure is brought about because of the mother's role in sphincteral training. Here, Kristeva argues that the subject's first contact with 'authority' is with the maternal authority when the child learns, through interaction with the mother, about its body: the shape of the body, the clean and the unclean, the proper and improper areas of the body. It is the concept of the 'maternal authority' that, in my analysis of the monstrous-feminine in horror, I will expand and extend into the symbolic in relation to castration. Kristeva refers to the processes of toilet training as a 'primal mapping of the body' which she calls 'semiotic'. She distinguishes between maternal 'authority' and 'paternal laws': 'Maternal authority is the trustee of that mapping of the self's clean and proper body; it is distinguished from paternal laws within which, with the phallic phase and acquisition of language, the destiny of man will take shape' (ibid., 72). In her discussion of rituals of defilement in relation to the Indian caste system, Kristeva draws a distinction between maternal authority and paternal law. She argues that the period of the 'mapping of the self's clean and proper body' (ibid.) is characterized by the exercise of 'authority without guilt', a time when there is a 'fusion between mother and nature' (ibid., 74). However, the symbolic ushers in a 'totally different universe of socially signifying performances where embarrassment, shame, guilt, desire etc. come into play – the order of the phallus'. In the Indian context, these two worlds exist harmoniously side by side because of the working of defilement rites. Here Kristeva is referring to the practice of public defecation in India. Kristeva argues that this split between the world of the mother (a universe without shame) and the world of the father (a universe of shame) would in other social contexts produce psychosis; in India it finds a 'perfect socialization': 'This may be because the setting up of the rite of defilement takes on the function of the hyphen, the virgule, allowing the two universes of *filth* and *prohibition* to brush lightly against each other without necessarily being identified as such, as *object* and as *law*' (ibid.).

Virtually all horror texts represent the monstrous-feminine in relation to Kristeva's notion of maternal authority and the mapping of the self's clean and proper body. Images of blood, vomit, pus, shit, etc., are central to our culturally/socially constructed notions of the horrific. They signify a split between two orders: the maternal authority and the law of the father. On the one hand, these images of bodily wastes threaten a subject that is already constituted, in relation to the symbolic, as 'whole and proper'. Consequently, they fill the subject – both the protagonist in the text and the spectator in the cinema – with disgust and loathing. On the other hand they also point back to a time when a 'fusion between mother and nature' existed; when bodily wastes, while set apart from the body, were not seen as objects of embarrassment and shame. Their presence in the horror film may invoke a response of disgust from the audience situated as it is within the social symbolic; but at a more archaic level the representation of bodily wastes may invoke pleasure in breaking the taboo on filth – sometimes described as a pleasure in perversity – and a pleasure in returning to that time when the mother-child relationship was marked by an untrammelled pleasure in 'playing' with the body and its wastes.

The modern horror film often 'plays' with its audience, saturating it with scenes of blood and gore, deliberately pointing to the fragility of the symbolic order in the domain of the body where the body never ceases to signal the repressed world of the mother. In *The Exorcist* (1973) the world of the symbolic, represented by the priest-as-father, and the world of the pre-symbolic, represented by a pubescent girl aligned with the devil, clashed head on in scenes where the foulness of woman was signified by her putrid, filthy body covered in blood, urine, excrement and bile. Significantly, the possessed girl is also about to menstruate – in one scene, blood from her wounded genitals mingles with menstrual blood to provide one of the film's key images of horror. [. . .] In *Carrie* (1976), the film's most monstrous act occurs when the couple are drenched in pig's blood, which symbolizes menstrual blood in the terms set up by the film: women are referred to in the film as 'pigs', women 'bleed like pigs', and the pig's blood runs down Carrie's body at a moment of intense pleasure, just as her own menstrual blood ran down her legs during a similar pleasurable moment when she enjoyed her body in the shower. Here, women's blood and pig's blood flow together, signifying horror, shame and humiliation. In this film, however, the mother speaks for the symbolic, identifying with an order which has defined women's sexuality as the source of all evil and menstruation as the sign of sin. [. . .]

Kristeva'a semiotic posits a pre-verbal dimension of language which relates to sounds and tone of the voice and to direct expression of the drives and physical contact with the maternal figure: 'it is dependent upon meaning, but in a way that is not that of *linguistic* signs nor of the *symbolic* order they found' (ibid., 72). With the subject's entry into the symbolic, which separates the child from the mother, the maternal figure and the authority she signifies are repressed. Kristeva then argues that it is the function of defilement rites, particularly those relating to menstrual and excremental objects/substances, to point to the 'boundary' between the maternal semiotic authority and the paternal symbolic law.

Kristeva argues that, historically, it has been the function of religion to purify the abject, but with the disintegration of these 'historical forms' of religion, the work of purification now rests solely with 'that catharsis *par excellence* called art' (ibid., 17). This, I would argue, is also the central ideological project of the popular horror film – purification of the abject through a 'descent into the foundations of the symbolic construct'. The horror film attempts to bring about a confrontation with the abject (the corpse, bodily wastes, the monstrous-feminine) in order finally to eject the abject and redraw the boundaries between the human and non-human.

As a form of modern defilement rite, the horror film attempts to separate out the symbolic order from all that threatens its stability, particularly the mother and all that her universe signifies. In this sense, signifying horror involves a representation of, and a reconciliation with, the maternal body. Kristeva's theory of abjection provides us with an important theoretical framework for analysing, in the horror film, the representation of the monstrous-feminine, in relation to woman's reproductive and mothering functions. However, abjection by its very nature is ambiguous; it both repels and attracts. Separating out the mother and her universe from the symbolic order is not an easy task – perhaps it is, finally, not even possible.

   [. . .]

Chapter 6

SLAVOJ ZIZEK

'IN HIS BOLD GAZE MY RUIN IS WRIT LARGE'
(extract)

Psycho's Moebius band

PSYCHO (1960) CARRIES TH[E] Hitchcockian subversion of the viewer's identification to its utmost, forcing him/her to *identify with the abyss beyond identification*. That is to say, the key that enables us to penetrate the film's mystery is to be sought in the rupture, in the change of modality, that separates the first third from the last two-thirds [. . .]. During the first third of the film we identify with Marion, we experience the story from her perspective, which is why her murder derails us, causing us to lose the ground from under our feet – up to the end of the film, we are in search of a new footing, clinging to the point of view of the detective Arbogast, of Sam and Lila . . . yet all these secondary identifications are 'empty' or, more precisely, supplementary: in them, we identify not with subjects but with a pure, flat, investigative machine on which we rely in our effort to reveal the mystery of Norman, the 'hero' who replaces Marion as the film's focal point and dominates the last part, and who is in a sense nothing but her mirror-negative (as is indicated by the very mirror-relationship of their respective names: Marion – Norman). In short: after the murder of Marion, identification with the personality who dominates the diegetic space becomes impossible. Where does this impossibility of identification come from? In other words, wherein consists the change of modality generated by the passage from Marion to Norman? At its most obvious, Marion's world is the world of contemporary American everyday life, whereas Norman's world is its nocturnal reverse:

> Car, motel, policeman, road, office, money, detective, etc. – these are
> signs of the present, actual positivity and renunciation; villa (= haunted
> castle), stuffed animals, mummy, stairs, knife, false clothes – these are

signs from the stock of terrifying figurations of the forbidden past. It is only the dialogue of the two sign-systems, their mutual relationship brought about not by analogies but by contradictions, which creates the visual tension of this thriller.

(Seesslen: 1980, 173)

We are therefore a long way from the usual Hitchcockian subversion of the idyllic everyday surface with its dark reverse: the 'surface' subverted, literally turned inside out, in *Psycho* is not the idyllic image one encounters at the outset of *Rear Window* (1954), or *The Trouble with Harry* (1955), but a dreary, grey 'leaden time', full of 'banal' worries and anxieties. This American alienation (financial insecurity, fear of the police, desperate pursuit of a piece of happiness – in short, the *hysteria* of everyday capitalist life) is confronted with its *psychotic* reverse: the nightmarish world of pathological crime.

The relationship between these two worlds eludes the simple oppositions of surface and depth, reality and fantasy, and so on – the only topology that suits it is that of the two surfaces of the Moebius band: if we progress far enough on one surface, all of a sudden we find ourselves on its reverse. This moment of passage from one surface to its reverse, from the register of hysterical desire to that of psychotic drive, can be located very precisely: the fade-in, after the murder of Marion, of the close-up of the drain which swallows water and blood, into the close-up of her dead eye. Here, the spiral first *enters* the drain, then *exits* the eye (see Wood: 1977, 112), as if passing through the zero-point of an eclipse of time, a 'night of the world', to quote Hegel – in terms of science fiction, one can say that we 'pass the doors of time' and enter another temporal modality. A comparison with *Vertigo* (1958) is revealing here: in *Psycho*, we enter precisely that abyss which draws Scottie in *Vertigo*, yet which he is still able to resist.

As a result, it is not difficult to discern Lacanian names for the two surfaces of this Moebius band – to propose an elementary formula which regulates Marion's and Norman's universe:

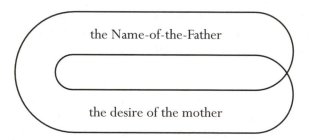

Marion stands under the sign of the Father – that is, of the symbolic desire constituted by the Name-of-the-Father; Norman is entrapped into the mother's desire not yet submitted to the paternal Law (and as such not yet a desire *stricto sensu*, but rather a pre-symbolic drive): the hysterical feminine position addresses the Name-of-the-Father, whereas the psychotic clings to the mother's desire. In short, the passage from Marion to Norman epitomizes the 'regression' from the register of *desire* to that of *drive*. In what does their opposition consist?

Desire is a metonymic sliding propelled by a lack, striving to capture the elusive lure: it is always, by definition, 'unsatisfied', susceptible to every possible interpretation, since it ultimately coincides with its own interpretation: it is *nothing but* the movement of interpretation, the passage from one signifier to another, the eternal production of new signifiers which, retroactively, give sense to the preceding chain. In opposition to this pursuit of the lost object which remains for ever 'else-where', drive is in a sense *always-already satisfied*: contained in its closed circuit, it 'encircles' its object – as Lacan puts it – and finds satisfaction in its own pulsa-tion, in its repeated failure to attain the object. In this precise sense, drive – in contrast to symbolic desire – appertains to the Real-Impossible, defined by Lacan as that which 'always returns to its place'. And it is precisely for this reason that identification with it is not possible: one can identify with the other only as desiring subject; this identification is even *constitutive* of desire which, according to Lacan, is by definition a 'desire of the Other' – that is to say intersubjective, mediated by the other: in contrast to the 'autistic' drive, contained in its circuit.

Norman thus eludes identification in so far as he remains prisoner of the psychotic drive, in so far as access to desire is denied him: what he lacks is the effectuation of the 'primordial metaphor' by means of which the symbolic Other (the structural Law epitomized by the Name-of-the-Father) supplants *jouissance* – the closed circuit of drive. The ultimate function of the Law is to confine desire – *not the subject's own, but the desire of his/her (M)Other*. Norman Bates is therefore a kind of anti-Oedipus *avant la lettre*: his desire is alienated in the maternal Other, at the mercy of its cruel caprice.

This opposition of desire and drive determines the contrasted symbolic economy of *Psycho*'s two great murder scenes, the shower-murder of Marion and the staircase-slaughter of the detective Arbogast. The shower-murder scene has always been a *pièce de résistance* for interpreters, its power of fascination diverting attention from the second murder, the film's truly traumatic point – a textbook case of what Freud called 'displacement'. Marion's violent death comes as an absolute surprise, a shock with no foundation in the narrative line which abruptly cuts off its 'normal' deployment; it is shot in a very 'filmic' way, its effect is brought about by editing: one never sees the murderer or Marion's entire body; the act of murder is 'dismembered' into a multitude of fragmentary close-ups which succeed one another in frenetic rhythm (the rising dark hand; the knife's edge close to the belly; the scream of the open mouth . . .) – as if the repeated strikes of the knife have contaminated the reel itself and caused the tearing-up of the continuous filmic gaze (or, rather, the opposite: as if the murderous shadow stands in, within the diegetic space, for the power of editing itself . . .).

How, then, is it possible to surpass this shock of the intrusion of the Real? Hitchcock found a solution: he succeeded in intensifying the effect by presenting the second murder as something *expected* – the rhythm of the scene is calm and continuous, long shots prevail, everything that precedes the act of murder seems to announce it: when Arbogast enters the 'mother's house', stops at the base of the empty staircase – this crucial Hitchcockian leitmotiv – and casts an inquisitive glance upwards, we immediately know that 'something is in the air'; when, seconds later, during Arbogast's ascent of the stairs, we see in close-up the crack in the second-floor door, our premonition is further confirmed. What follows then is the famous overhead shot which gives us a clear – so to speak geometrical – ground-plan of the entire scene, as if to prepare us for what finally arrives: the appearance of the 'mother'-figure which stabs Arbogast to death. . . . The lesson of this murder scene is that we endure the most brutal shock when we witness the exact real-ization of what we were looking forward to – as if, at this point, *tuche* and *automaton* paradoxically coincide: the most terrifying irruption of *tuche* which wholly perturbs the symbolic structure – the smooth running of *automaton* – takes place when a structural necessity simply realizes itself with blind automatism.

This paradox reminds one of the well-known sophism which proves the impos-sibility of a surprise: the pupils in a class know they will have to pass a written test within the next week, so how can the teacher effectively surprise them? The pupils reason as follows: Friday, the last day, is out, since on Thursday evening everybody would know that the test will have to take place the next day, so there would be no surprise; Thursday is also out, since on Wednesday evening, every-body would know that – Friday already being ruled out – the only possible day is Thursday, and so on. . . . What Lacan calls the Real is precisely the fact that, despite the irrefutable accuracy of this reasoning, *any day except Friday will still constitute a surprise*.

Behind its apparent simplicity, Arbogast's murder thus relies on a refined dialectic of expected and unexpected – in short, of (the viewer's) desire: the only way to explain this paradoxical economy, where the greatest surprise is caused by the complete fulfilment of our expectations, is to assume the hypothesis of a subject who is split, desiring – whose expectation is cathected by desire. What we have here is, of course, the logic of the fetishistic split: 'I know very well that event X will take place (that Arbogast will be murdered), yet I do not fully believe it (so I'm none the less surprised when the murder actually takes place).' Where, exactly, does the desire reside here, in the knowledge or in the belief?

Contrary to the obvious answer (in the belief – 'I know that X will take place, but I refuse to believe it since it runs against my desire . . .'), the Lacanian answer here is quite unambiguous: in the knowledge. The horrifying reality that one refuses to 'believe in', to accept, to integrate into one's symbolic universe, is none other than the Real of one's desire, and the unconscious belief (that X could not actu-ally happen) is ultimately a defence against the Real of desire: as viewers of *Psycho*, we desire the death of Arbogast, and the function of our belief that Arbogast will not be attacked by the 'mother'-figure is precisely to enable us to avoid the confrontation with the Real of our desire. And what Freud calls 'drive' – in its opposition to desire, whose nature is by definition split – is perhaps precisely a name for the absolute 'closure' where what actually happens corresponds perfectly to what one knows exactly will happen. . . .

Aristophanes reversed

What one should be attentive to in *Psycho* is how this opposition of desire and drive is far from being simply an abstract conceptual couple: a fundamental *histor-ical* tension is invested in it, indicated by the different scenery of the two murders which relates to the way Norman is divided between the two locales. That is to say, the architectural locale of the two murders is by no means neutral; the first takes place in a motel which epitomizes anonymous American *modernity*, whereas the second takes place in a Gothic house which epitomizes the American *tradition*; it is not by accident that both haunted the imagination of Edward Hopper, an American painter if ever there was one – 'Western Motel' and 'House by the Railroad', for example (according to [Stephen] Rebello's *Alfred Hitchcock and the Making of 'Psycho'* [1980], 'House by the Railroad' actually served as the model for the 'mother's house').

This opposition (whose visual correlative is the contrast between the horizontal – the lines of the motel – and the vertical – the lines of the house) not only introduces into *Psycho* an unexpected historical tension between tradition and modernity; it simultaneously enables us to locate *spatially* the figure of Norman Bates, his notorious psychotic split, by conceiving his figure as a kind of impossible 'mediator' between tradition and modernity, condemned to circulate endlessly between the two locales. Norman's split thereby epitomizes the incapacity of American ideology to locate the experience of the present, actual society into a context of historical tradition, to effectuate a symbolic mediation between the two levels. It is on account of this split that *Psycho* is still a 'modernist' film: in postmodernism, the dialectical tension between history and present is lost (in a postmodern *Psycho*, the motel itself would be rebuilt as an imitation of old family houses).

In consequence, the very duality of desire and drive can be conceived as the libidinal correlative of the duality of modern and traditional society: the matrix of traditional society is that of a 'drive', of a circular movement around the Same, whereas in modern society, repetitious circulation is supplanted by linear progress. The embodiment of the metonymic object-cause of desire which propels this endless progress is none other than *money* (one should recall that it is precisely money – 40,000 dollars – which disrupts Marion's everyday circuit and sets her on her fateful journey).

Psycho is thus a kind of hybrid of two heterogeneous parts: it is easy to imagine *two* 'rounded-off' stories, quite consistent in themselves, glued together in *Psycho* to form a monstrous whole. The first part (Marion's story) could well stand alone: it is easy to perform a mental experiment and to imagine it as a thirty-minute TV story, a kind of morality play in which the heroine gives way to temptation and enters the path of damnation, only to be cured by the encounter with Norman, who confronts her with the abyss that awaits her at the end of the road – in him, she sees a mirror-image of her own future; sobered, she decides to return to normal life. From her standpoint, the conversation with Norman in the room with stuffed birds is therefore an exemplary case of a successful communication in the Lacanian sense of the term: she gets back from her partner her own message (the truth about the catastrophe that lurks) in a reversed form. So when Marion takes her shower, her story is – as far as the narrative closure goes – strictly speaking over: the shower clearly serves as a metaphor of purification, since she has already made a decision to return and to repay her debt to society: that is, assume again her place in the community. Her murder does not occur as a totally unexpected shock which cuts into the midst of the narrative development: it strikes during the interval, the intermediate time, when the decision, although already taken, is not yet realized, inscribed into the public, intersubjective space – in the time which the traditional narrative can easily leave out (many films actually end with the moment of 'inner' decision).

The ideological presupposition behind it is, of course, that of a pre-stabilized harmony between Inside and Outside: once the subject really 'makes up his/her mind', the implementation of his/her inner decision in social reality ensues automatically. The timing of Marion's murder relies, therefore, on a carefully chosen ideologico-critical jest: it reminds us that we live in a world in which an insurmountable abyss separates the 'inner decision' from its social actualization: that is, where – in contrast to the prevailing American ideology – it is decidedly *not* possible to accomplish everything, even if one really resolves to do so.

The film's second part, Norman's story, is also easy to imagine as a closed whole, a rather traditional unravelling of the mystery of a pathological serial killer – the entire subversive effect of *Psycho* hinges on putting together the two heterogeneous, inconsistent pieces. In this respect, the structure of *Psycho* mockingly reverses Aristophanes' myth from Plato's *Symposium* (the split of the original androgynous entity into a masculine and a feminine half): the two constituents, taken in themselves, are fully consistent and harmonious – *it is their fusion into a larger Whole which denaturalizes them*. In contrast to the abrupt ending of Marion's story, the second part seems to accord perfectly with the rules of 'narrative closure': at the end, everything is explained, put in its proper place. . . . Yet on a closer look, the denouement proves far more ambiguous.

As Michel Chion has pointed out (Chion: 1992, 195–207), *Psycho* is ultimately the story of a Voice ('mother's voice') in search of its bearer, of a body to whom it could stick; the status of this Voice is what Chion calls *acousmatic* – a voice without a bearer, without an assignable place, floating in an intermediate space, and as such all-pervasive, the very image of the ultimate Threat. The film ends with the moment of 'embodiment' when we finally behold the body in which the Voice originates – yet at this precise moment, things get mixed up: within the traditional narration, the moment of 'embodiment' demystifies the terrifying phantom-like Voice, it dispels its power of fascination by enabling us – the viewers – to *identify* with its bearer. (This reversal whereby the unfathomable Phantom assumes shape and body – is reduced to a common measure – is far from being limited to horror movies: in *The Wizard of Oz* (1939), for example, the Wizard's voice is 'embodied' when the little dog who follows the smell behind the curtain uncovers the helpless old man who creates the spectacle of the Wizard by means of a complicated apparatus of machinery).

While *Psycho* also 'embodies' the Voice, the effect of it here is the exact opposite of 'gentrification' which renders possible our – the viewer's – identification: it is only now that we confront an 'absolute Otherness' which precludes any identification. The Voice has attached itself to the wrong body, so that what we get is a true zombie, a pure creature of the Superego, totally powerless in itself (Norman–mother 'wouldn't even hurt a fly'), yet for that very reason all the more uncanny.

The crucial feature with regard to the allegorical functioning of *Psycho* is that at this precise moment when, finally, the Voice finds its body, Norman – in the penultimate shot of the film which immediately precedes 'The End' – raises his gaze and looks directly into the camera (i.e. into us, the viewers) with a mocking expression which displays his awareness of our complicity: what is accomplished thereby is the reversal of our gaze from I to a, from the neutral gaze of the Ego-Ideal to the object. We look for the 'secret behind the curtain' (who is the shadow which pulls off the curtain and slaughters Marion?), and what we obtain at the end is a Hegelian answer: we always-already partake in the absolute Otherness which returns the gaze.

[. . .]

Part Three

MONSTROSITIES

Introduction to Part Three

■   Ken Gelder

TWO OF THE CONTRIBUTORS to this section note that the word *monster* is linked to the word *demonstrate*: to show, to reveal. This link reminds us that monsters signify, that they function as meaningful signs. In this respect, their role may not have changed much since the Renaissance, where monstrosity often served as a portent, a warning. Monsters were seen as a peculiar, even 'accidental' kind of abnormality, but they also carried a message that was central to the culture that gazed upon it. Their function was, and still is, critical: they always brought bad tidings.

Several essays in this Reader use the word *teratology*, meaning tales about, or the study of, monstrosities (from the Greek word *teras*, monster). *Teratogeny* refers to the production of monstrosity, and some cultures may indeed be more teratogenic than others. If monsters signify something about culture, then culture can (at least to a degree) be read through the monster. Its revelatory capacity need not be taken for granted, however. Sometimes the monster might well work to obscure certain features that make a culture what it is; a monster's inscrutability may point to a certain *blindness* culture has about itself. Monstrosity most often resides at (or is relegated to) the edge of culture, where categories blur and classificatory structures begin to break down. Mary Douglas, in her important study *Purity and Danger* (1966), draws attention to cultural fears about 'pollution', where forms that are ordinarily distinct from one another now inhabit the same space. Monsters can also be generic hybrids, combining different features (like the Ravenna monster mentioned by Marie-Hélene Huet in the first extract in this section) not to produce some new whole but to show up the disjunction between each conjoined part. Or, they might be either formally incomplete or grotesquely excessive. Monsters can exaggerate difference itself, sitting outside 'normal', socially-accepted definitions – especially definitions of what counts as 'human'.

These days, scholars in the humanities and social sciences spend much time recovering the various 'deviant' or 'hybrid' identities relegated to this edge-of-culture position. Mary Shelley's *Frankenstein* (1818) may be one of the first novels to invite sympathy for the monster, and the post-Romantic interests of much Parisian-influenced criticism (following the work of Jacques Derrida, Julia Kristeva, Michel Foucault, Deleuze and Guattari) continue in this vein. Sympathy for deviant and hybrid identities underwrites much recent scholarly work on horror in particular, which this Reader reflects. Certainly there are contemporary instances where the monstrous is over-enthusiastically romanticized, as a means of deconstructing the 'human' in order to think 'beyond' it, standing 'at the threshold ... of becoming' (Cohen: 1996, 20), inducing the kind of delirium imagined to be appropriate to the end of the millennium (Grunenberg: 1997), and so on. Even so, whether one offers sympathy or withdraws it, whether one is fascinated or repelled, it is generally taken for granted these days that monsters at least deserve our understanding.

Who imagines monsters? Marie-Hélene Huet's extract from the introduction to *Monstrous Imagination* answers this question by returning to the maternal woman and the Renaissance idea that 'monstrous progeny' resulted from desires and traumas experienced by the mother during pregnancy. The monstrous child was one who did not resemble its parents, and the mother was to blame. Offering a different version of the 'monstrous-feminine' to Barbara Creed's, Huet argues that women were thus credited with enough imaginative power to 'repress' paternal influences altogether – but only in the production of monstrosity. The Romantics later inverted this by turning the monstrous imagination over to the male artist-(pro)creator, a predicament Mary Shelley literalized in *Frankenstein*. Huet's book investigates other forms of monstrous birth which don't always rely on the mother, such as a modern version of the Jewish legend of the golem, an artificial man without a soul, born out of language itself – a narrative that frees the mother of blame, but only by removing her entirely from the picture.

Mary Russo's extract, from her book *The Female Grotesque*, notes the downside to the contemporary romanticization of (in this case) the 'freak'. In 1960s America, 'freakiness' became a sign of dissent, worn with pride by a relatively open and expansive community of people. Freakiness was celebrated and one expressed solidarity with it; later on, it attracted a certain nostalgia. The interest in the humanities in the work of the Russian critic Mikhail Bakhtin is symptomatic of this: his work on 'carnival' as a countercultural space and on the genre of 'grotesque realism' is useful to Russo, but she is also wary of its utopian sentiments. In the meantime, the 'real freak' was left behind, losing its spectacularity to a culture that righteously refused to stare at the Other. Her extract, part of a longer reading of Tod Browning's notorious film *Freaks* (1932) – itself rediscovered in the 1960s (see Skal: 1993, 21) – expresses solidarity with this more authentic kind of freakishness and notes the need for culture to retain the estranging capacities of the freakish (self-)image.

Mark Seltzer's extract concerns the creation of a permanently stigmatized 'species of person': the serial killer. This particular monster was born around the end of the nineteenth century and, in contrast to the declining popularity of the 'real freak', soon became a key figure in the infrastructure of modern culture's ongoing fascination with bodily violence. Seltzer's remarkable book *Serial Killers* looks at the entanglement of the serial killer with culture at large, particularly through information technologies and mass media. In America, the serial killer may even stand for culture itself, spreading indiscriminately and 'inhumanely' across space, addicted to media images, a hybrid conflation of the celebrity seeker and the relentlessly banal. The serial killer is 'abnormally normal', an uncanny figure who epitomizes the breakdown of distinctions between self and society, 'private desire and public fantasy', compulsive drive and an 'utterly dispassionate rationality'. Seltzer thus suggests that culture is closer to the serial killer than it might otherwise imagine. The public sphere itself is 'pathological' and traumatized, a 'wound culture' obsessed with 'torn and open bodies'. The serial killer is thus rather like the golem or Frankenstein's creation, not born but culturally (and meticulously) constructed – out of expert opinions, media representations, statistics, psychological 'profiles'. In the process, his own individuality is 'largely extinguished'. But this itself is a cultural construction: the serial killer's monstrous difference paradoxically lies in the fact that he copies, simulates, over-identifies with others just like 'us'.

Chapter 7

MARIE-HÉLÈNE HUET

INTRODUCTION TO *MONSTROUS IMAGINATION*

WHERE DO MONSTERS COME from, and what do they really look like? In the Renaissance, answers to these puzzles were as numerous and varied as the physiological prodigies they sought to elucidate. Monsters came from God and the Devil, they were caused by stars and comets, they resulted from copulation with other species and from flaws in their parents' anatomies. The cosmic range of speculations also tried to account for the physical aspect of the marvellous beings observed in nature. Some monsters lacked an essential part of the body, others claimed an extra member, some looked like mythical animals, and a few were born with hermetic symbols imprinted on their strange physiology. Thus the much-discussed Ravenna monster was born without arms, but with a beautiful pair of wings, a fish tail, and mysterious markings on his chest: a Greek letter, a cross, and, in some accounts, a half-moon as well. But a remarkably persistent line of thought argued that monstrous progeny resulted from the disorder of the maternal imagination. Instead of reproducing the father's image, as nature commands, the monstrous child bore witness to the violent desires that moved the mother at the time of conception or during pregnancy. The resulting offspring carried the marks of her whims and fancy rather than the recognizable features of its legitimate genitor. The monster thus erased paternity and proclaimed the dangerous power of the female imagination. The theory that credited imagination with a deceiving but dominant role in procreation continued to be the object of heated discussions until the beginning of the nineteenth century.

Around the same time, literature reappropriated the complex relationship between imagination and resemblances, between unfulfilled desires and the act of generation. By assigning to the artist as monstrous father the power once attributed to the mother to create singular progeny, the Romantic metaphor of procreation restaged in its own terms the ideology of misguided desires that spawned aberrant offspring. Imagination, already rehabilitated in the 1777

Figure 7.1   The Ravenna monster, after Boaistuau, from Ambroise Paré, *Des monstres et prodiges* (1573).

Supplement to Diderot's *Encylopédie* as a powerful creative agent that 'belongs to genius' and spurs poetic 'fecundity,' played a privileged role in the conception of the Romantic *oeuvre*. [. . .]

In the fourth book of *Generation of Animals*, Aristotle wrote: 'Anyone who does not take after his parents is really in a way a monstrosity, since in these cases Nature has in a way strayed from the generic type. The first beginning of this deviation is when a female is formed instead of a male, though this indeed is a necessity required by Nature, since the race of creatures which are separated into male and female has got to be kept in being; . . . As for monstrosities, they are not necessary so far as the purposive or final cause is concerned, yet *per accidens*' (Aristotle: 1963, IV, 401–3). These lines make a decisive association between the monstrous and the female as two departures from the norm, as two exceptions to another tenet of Aristotelian doctrine, namely, that 'like produces like.' The monster and the woman thus find themselves on the same side, the side of *dissimilarity*. 'The female is as it were a deformed male,' Aristotle also pointed out (ibid., II, 175). Since she herself is on the side of the dissimilar, it was argued, the female appears to be destined by nature to contribute more figures of dissimilarity, if not creatures even more monstrous.

But the female is a necessary departure from the norm, noted Aristotle, a useful deformity; the monster is gratuitous and useless for future generations. Aristotle's thoughts on generation offered a definition of monstrosity that was primarily linked not to physical imperfections but rather to a deficiency in the natural and visible link between genitors and their progeny. 'Monstrosities,' he repeated, 'come under the class of offspring which is unlike its parents' (ibid., IV, 425). But the monster is also monstrous in another important way, one that Aristotle described as a 'false resemblance' to another species.

> It is not easy, by stating a single mode of cause, to explain . . . why sometimes the offspring is a human being yet bears no resemblance to any ancestor, sometimes it has reached such a point that in the end it no longer has the appearance of a human being at all, but that of an animal only – it belongs to the class of monstrosities, as they are called. And indeed this is what comes next to be treated . . . the causes of monstrosities, for in the end, when the movements (that came from the male) relapse and the material (that came from the female) does not get mastered, what remains is that which is most 'general,' and this is the (merely) 'animal.' People say that the offspring which is formed has the head of a ram or an ox; and similarly with other creatures, that one has the head of another, e.g., a calf has a child's head or a sheep an ox's head. The occurrence of all these things is due to the causes I have named; at the same time, *in no case are they what they are alleged to be, but resemblances only*, and this of course comes about even when there is no deformation involved.
>
> (ibid., IV, 417–19, emphasis added)

Monstrosities are thus doubly deceptive. Their strange appearance – a misleading likeness to another species, for example – belies the otherwise rigorous law that offspring should resemble their parents. By presenting similarities to categories of being to which they are not related, monsters blur the differences between genres and disrupt the strict order of Nature. Thus, though the monster was first defined as that which did not resemble him who engendered it, it nevertheless displayed some sort of resemblance, albeit a *false* resemblance, to an object external to its conception.

The genesis of that false resemblance played a crucial role in one of the most ancient and enduring theories of generation, namely, the tradition that credited the mother's imagination with the shape of her progeny. A lost text, attributed to Empedocles, first suggested what was to become one of the most popular beliefs in the study of procreation. Empedocles was said to have stated that 'progeny can be modified by the statues and paintings that the mother gazes upon during her pregnancy' (Rostand: 1930, 38). Far from being discarded by medical thought when discoveries on generation redefined the respective roles of the father and mother in procreation, the view that the maternal imagination was responsible for the shape of progeny gained a growing number of followers in seventeenth- and eighteenth-century Europe. In 1621, Maître André du Laurens, the chancellor at the University of Montpellier as well as first physician to the king of France, expanded on Empedocles' suggestion as follows:

Empedocles the Pythagorician links [resemblance] to imagination alone, whose power is so great that, just as it often changes the body of one who has some deep thought, so it inscribes its form on the fertilized seed. The Arabs granted imagination so much power that, through it, they thought the soul could act not only on its own body, but on that of another. It seems that Aristotle recognized the imagination's power in the act of conception, when he asked why individuals of the human species are so different from each other, and answered that the quickness and activity of human thought and the variety of the human mind leave different marks of several kinds upon the seed.

(Laurens: 1634, 409–10)

As late as 1788, Benjamin Bablot reminded his readers that 'the philosopher Empedocles, from Agrigenta in Sicily, who, according to received opinion, died at a very old age when he fell into the sea and drowned in 440 B.C., acknowledged no other cause for dissemblance between children and their parents than the imagination of pregnant women. According to Amyot, Plutarch's naive translator, Empedocles held that it was through the woman's imagination during conception that children were formed, 'for often women have been in love with images and statues and have given birth to children resembling them' (cited in Bablot: 1788, 10). Thus, following Empedocles' theory, it was long believed that monsters, inasmuch as they did not resemble their parents, could well be the result of a mother's fevered and passionate consideration of images. More specifically, monsters were the offspring of an imagination that literally imprinted on progeny a deformed, misshapen resemblance to an object that had not participated in their creation. They were products of art rather than nature, as it were. Of course, during the Middle Ages and the Renaissance, the mother's imagination was only one of several elements believed to cause monstrous births: others included sex with the devil or animals, as well as defective sperm or a deformed womb. Yet no theory was more debated, more passionately attacked or defended, than the power of the maternal imagination over the formation of the fetus.

Several traditions linked the word *monster* to the idea of showing or warning. One belief, following Augustine's *City of God*, held that the word *monster* derived from the Latin *monstrare*: to show, to display (*montrer* in French). *Monster*, then, belongs to the etymological family that spawned the word *demonstrate* as well. For Renaissance readers, this tradition confirmed the idea that monsters were signs sent by God, messages showing his will or his wrath, though Fortunio Liceti gave it a simpler meaning in 1616: 'Monsters are thus named, not because they are signs of things to come, as Cicero and the Vulgate believed . . . but because they are such that their new and incredible appearance stirs admiration and surprise in the beholders, and startles them so much that everyone wants to show them to others [se les *monstre* réciproquement]' (Liceti: 1708, 2). Another tradition, the one adopted by current etymological dictionaries, derived the word *monster* from *monere*, to warn, associating even more closely the abnormal birth with the prophetic vision of impending disasters. These etymologies gave monstrosity a pre-inscribed interpretation. They also justified its existence by including the monster within the larger order of things. Monstrous births were understood as warnings and public testimony; they were thought to be 'demonstrations' of the mother's unfulfilled desires. The monster was then seen as a visible image of the mother's hidden passions. This theory gained a greater audience in the seventeenth century and culminated in the hotly debated Quarrel of Imaginationism, which lasted through the eighteenth century.

Although the mother's imagination was never considered the *only* possible cause of monstrosity, and did not receive exclusive medical attention at any time in the history of thought on the process of generation, it nevertheless haunted centuries of medical research. In fact, the theory that the mother could be responsible for monstrous births persisted despite all possible evidence to the contrary. In the nineteenth century, discoveries in the fields of embryology and heredity provided scientists with new ways of explaining resemblances. But if the mother's imagination was no longer perceived by the medical field to be a factor in resemblances, its role as the shaper of progeny was never totally forgotten. The idea that imagination could give life and form to passive matter became a central theme of Romantic aesthetics, and to this day popular beliefs still attribute birthmarks to maternal desires during pregnancy.

The theory that confers on the maternal imagination the power to shape progeny also suggests a complex relationship between procreation and art, for imagination is moved by passion and works in a mimetic way. 'Nature,' wrote Claude de Tesserant in 1567 in *Histoires prodigieuses*, 'portrays after a living model, just as a painter would, and tries to make children resemble their parents as much as possible' (see Céard: 1977, 320). For Paracelsus, 'By virtue of her imagination the woman is the artist and the child the canvas on which to raise the work' (Pagel: 1958, 122). In 1731, François-Marie-Pompée Colonna noted: 'It is true that the semen is the visible agent, but we can also say that like the Painter, the Sculptor, and other Artisans who use certain instruments to fashion their materials into desired shape, similarly this invisible workman uses the male's seminal matter as the instrument that leads the female to generate an animal' (Colonna: 1731, 230). In 1812 in *Tableau de l'amour conjugal*, Dubuisson added, 'The semen is to generation what the sculptor is to marble; the male semen is the sculptor who gives shape, the female liquor is the marble or matter, and the sculpture is the fetus or the product of generation' (Darmon: 1981, 249). From this point of view, the mother could be said to have taken over the male role of the artist when, overwhelmed by gazing at images or by unchecked desires, she let her imagination interfere with the creative process and reproduce strange figures, or monstrosities. If Art must imitate Nature, in cases of monstrous procreation Nature imitates Art. Treatises on the role of the mother's imagination received very little attention after the theory was set aside by the medical world in the early 1800's. Yet these texts offer a striking reassessment of the maternal role in procreation and at the same time elucidate the relationship between imagination and art, nature and mimesis.

Thus when the thesis that the maternal imagination played an important role in the formation of monstrosities was finally abandoned toward the beginning of the nineteenth century, it remained an important part of literary aesthetics. In many texts, we find explicit reference to the power of imagination in procreation.

In *Elective Affinities* (1809), for example, Goethe describes the birth of a child who displayed the effects of his parents' imagination, thereby betraying their moral adultery. Charlotte and Edward's son is the striking image not of his parents, but of those they love secretly: 'People saw in it a wonderful, indeed a miraculous child . . . what surprised them more . . . [was] the double resemblance, which became more and more conspicuous. In figure and in the features of the face, it was like the Captain; the eyes every day it was less easy to distinguish from the eyes of Ottilie' (Goethe: 1962, 224). E. T. A. Hoffmann's Cardillac, the monster of his short story 'Mademoiselle de Scudéry' (1819–21), attributes his fateful passion for jewels to 'the strange impressions which afflict pregnant women, and . . . the strange influence these impressions from outside can have on the child' (Hoffmann: 1982, 63). 'What vision of a tiger haunted my mother when she was carrying me?' asks [Alfred de] Musset's dramatic hero Lorenzaccio (1834). Oliver Wendell Holmes, in his best-known novel, *Elsie Venner* (1859), describes his heroine as the monstrous result of her mother's imagination, the mother having been terrorized by an encounter with a deadly snake, 'an antenatal impression which had mingled an alien element in her nature' (Holmes: 1861, 434).

But if many nineteenth-century writers explicitly referred to this all-but-discarded theory of monstrosity, their implicit reappropriation of the idea of the monstrous imagination was more striking still. In theories of monstrosity the maternal element repressed the legitimate father. The maternal imagination erased the legitimate father's image from his offspring and thus created a monster. In the constitution of the modern *episteme*, the silent father regains his place. Romantic aesthetic theory sketched out a model genealogy for the work of art and the procreative role of the artist (see Abrams: 1958). In so doing, Romanticism reassigned the *vis imaginativa* to the father alone. Romantic aesthetics reaffirmed the seductive power of the monstrous as aberration, and the creative role of the scientist, or the artist, as visible father. Imagination was reclaimed as a masculine attribute, and just as theories of generation had long been theories of Art, Romantic Art became a theory of generation. For the Romantics, imagination was no longer the faculty to reproduce images, but the power to create them. Imagination did not imitate, it generated, and in doing so, it also produced monstrous art. The notion of monstrosity that emerged shifted its emphasis from the maternal to the paternal but kept intact the key elements of singular progeny. The act of artistic creation thus appeared as an imitation of a monstrous genetic process: as painted models, fatal passions, striking resemblances, and creatures that were as frightening for their deformities as for their perfection. The erasure of the maternal role in procreation and new forms of mechanical engendering were also echoed in the myth of the Romantic artist as lone genitor in awe of his own creation. If the theory that credited the maternal imagination with the birth of unnatural progeny implied a theory of art as imitation, Romanticism, in turn, reinterpreted art as teratology. The vision of the Romantic artist as creator borrowed a metaphor of creation from the theory that long ascribed the birth of monstrous progeny to the maternal imagination.

[. . .]

Chapter 8

MARY RUSSO

FREAKS

WHAT IS NOW CALLED 'identity politics' may be traced to the 1960's identification of and with the 'freak.' Radically democratic and open to the most individualistic self-appropriations of class, race, ethnicity, gender, and sexuality, 'freakiness' is a distinctly U.S. style of dissent. Although the tradition of the freak as monster – literally, the de-*monstrater* of the marvelous power of the divine – has a long history in European culture, the demonstrations of the sixties in the United States were characterized by a new articulation of hetero-geneous social groups, and by a mixing of external and internal demands for dramatic visibility. Being a freak was, and remains, an individual choice for some and an oppressive assignment for others, as in Jimi Hendrix's famous 'If 6 was 9': the 'white plastic finger' pointed at Black men like Hendrix, but other, self-designated freaks, pointed at themselves. Strikingly, no particular quality seemed to exclude one definitively from the imaginary community of freaks. For even the 'white-collared conservative flashing down the street' or his suburban wife could, and did, 'freak out,' and the narratives of their rage and mental illnesses were often allegories of conversion to new, better families or communities. The freak ethos required an identification with otherness within the secret self. It also demanded a certain openness to recruits and volunteers. Anyone could march in some guise under the freak flag.

The appropriation of the term 'freak' in the 1960s in rock music and street culture as a marker of life-style and identity parallels the powerful, historic detours of words like 'black,' or more recently 'queer,' away from their stigmatizing func-tion in the hands of dominant culture, a trajectory that is often described as moving from shame to pride. Only the smallest space is left in these 'meaning maps' for ambivalence. 'Real Freaks' or 'freaks of nature,' as the sideshow 'curiosities' ([P. T.] Barnum's term) were called, had alternately rejected the term in reaction to the intense ostracism and display of human anomalies as scientific spectacle, and reclaimed it as properly theirs in the face of market extinction as the popular entertainment venues which had featured their bodies as exhibitions began to die out. Threatened with invisibility, the professional freak would often prefer the risk and blame associated with an intensely marked body and identity to the disregard and neglect which had always characterized one particularly hypocritical aspect of bourgeois Anglo-American culture which admonished its children, 'Don't stare.' In Stalinist Russia and in Nazi Germany, freak shows were banned by the state, displacing the containment of the freak within fairs and circuses to encampments for socially designated anomalies. In the United States, an individualistic culture tended increasingly to ignore 'real freaks' and to steal the magic of their spectacularity.

There are many fictional and historical anecdotes which figure freaks as either resisting or taking up the names and stereotypes of dominant culture. In 'La patente' (The License), a short story by Luigi Pirandello typifying the Sicilian grotesque, a hunchback with the 'evil eye' demands a license to certify his status as a dangerous presence so that he can be paid for avoiding certain public and commercial areas in the village. More recently, in Katherine Dunn's novel, *Geek Love* (1990), a woman who has begun her career as a geek biting off the heads of chickens (though she had a secret wish to be in an aerial act) is persuaded to breed freak children through the ingestion of drugs and insecticides in order to save the family carnival. In other contexts, lines were drawn by communities and subcultures reclaiming the representations of their bodily identities as their own. Towards the end of her life, Diane Arbus, whose photographs of freaks and urban subculture made her a cult figure in her own right, was devastated to receive a letter from the organizers of a convention of midgets in Florida who wrote: 'We have our own little person to photograph us' (Bosworth: 1985, 365).

Leslie Fiedler wrote his important work on this topic, *Freaks: Myths and Images of the Secret Self*, in the wake of the counterculture in 1978. At once a deeply personal and expansive study of freaks and freak culture, Fiedler's chronicle narrates the popular history of freaks from carnivals, circuses and fairs into science fiction and film. Fiedler dedicates his book to 'my brother who has no brother' and to 'all my brothers who have no brothers,' suggesting the alienation and community (or at least fraternity) of freakdom for him. He also acknowledges, preliminarily, that the adoption of the word 'freak' by technical non-freaks and the injunction to 'Join the United Mutations' (Mothers of Invention) implies 'as radical an alteration of consciousness as underlies the politics of black power or neofeminism or gay liberation' (Fiedler: 1978, 14–15). Fiedler, in other words, acknowledges here and sporadically throughout his book the shadow presence of those social movements whose programs included a politics of style and counterproduction.

Fiedler's book was written as a 'belated tribute' to the director Tod Browning whose film, *Freaks* (1932) was almost as inspirational as Frank Zappa and the Mothers of Invention in advancing the mythology of contemporary freaks. Arbus' biographer, Patricia Bosworth, for instance, reports that the photographer attended repeated showings of the film, often stoned, and 'was enthralled because the freaks in the film were not imaginary monsters, but *real*' (Bosworth: 1985, 189). Like Arbus and many others who flocked to the revival of the cult which had been banned and then ignored in its own time, Fiedler found the film most remarkable in its use of

well-known sideshow performers like Harry Earles and his sister Daisy, who play
the dwarfs whose romance is ruined by a 'normal' female aerial performer called
Cleopatra, and Daisy and Violet Hilton, famous Siamese twins who were making
their film debut after a legal fight to win their freedom from the family that bought
them as infants. There are very different levels of performance in the film. As Fiedler
notes, Harry Earles had other roles in cinema, and here plays a melodramatic
role as a rich and betrayed husband. Other performers like Joseph/Josephine (the
Half-Man, Half-Woman), Slitzie (the Pin-Head), and Olga Roderick (the Bearded
Lady) seemed indistinguishable in their film roles from their 'real' parts in sideshows.
This documentary aspect of Browning's project has been seen variously as daring,
exploitative, and authentic. The conflation of the authentic with the unconventional
in the bodies of the freaks in a prevalent (and in my view greatly romanticized)
reception of the film tends to ignore the meaning of the film's most spectacularized
image: the apparently mutilated body of the 'normal woman,' Cleopatra, after she
has been literally cut down to size for violating the code of the freaks.

Before elaborating on this point, some clarification of the relationship between
the freak and the grotesque is necessary. If we follow [Mikhail] Bakhtin on this
point, the distinction is clear. The grotesque body of carnival festivity was not
distanced or objectified in relation to an audience. Audiences and performers were
the interchangeable parts of an incomplete but imaginable wholeness. The grotesque
body was exuberantly and democratically open and inclusive of all possibilities.
Boundaries between individuals and society, between genders, between species,
and between classes were blurred or brought into crisis in the inversions and hyper-
bole of carnivalesque representation. Grotesque realism presented a dynamic,
materialist, and unflinching view of human bodies in all stages and contours of
growth, degeneration, anomaly, excess, loss, and prosthesis. The grotesque body
had nothing to do with 'modern canons' of the body, drawn from science, bourgeois psychology, or nineteenth and twentieth century fictional realism: 'The fact
is that the new concept of realism has a different way of drawing the boundaries
between bodies and objects' (Bakhtin: 1984, 53).

> The new bodily canon, in all its historic variations and different genres,
> presents an entirely finished, completed, strictly limited body, which
> is shown from the outside as something individual. That which
> protrudes, bulges, sprouts, or branches off (when a body transgresses
> its limits and a new one begins) is eliminated, hidden or moderated.
> All orifices of the body are closed. The basis of the image is the indi-
> vidual, strictly limited mass, the impenetrable facade.
>
> (ibid., 320)

For Bahktin, the new bodily canon extends to codes of speech: 'There is a sharp
line of division between familiar speech and "correct" language' (ibid.).

The freak and the grotesque overlap as bodily categories. Susan Stewart, in
her wonderful study of culture and scale, has pointed out that 'the physiological
freak represents the problems of the boundary between self and other (Siamese
twins), between male and female (the hermaphrodite), between the body and the
world outside the body (the *monstre* par excès), and between the animal and

the human (feral and wild men).' Of course, the 'physiological freak,' like the grotesque, is produced through discursive formations including, but not restricted to, empiricism. 'Often referred to as a "freak of nature," the freak, it must be emphasized, is a freak of culture' (Stewart: 1993, 109). As a cultural representation in the late nineteenth century, the freak belongs to the increasingly codified world of spectacle, appearing in culturally varied venues. Within the confines of spectacle, the freak appears only as a particular image which may appear, reproduce, or simulate the earlier carnivalesque body described and idealized by Bakhtin, but also and more importantly as a bodily construct produced within different social relations. More than merely an image or collection of images, the spectacle is a way of looking, 'a world vision which has become objectified' (Debord: 1983, 1).

A spectacle, by definition, requires sight lines and distance. Audiences do not meet up face to face or mask to mask with the spectacle of freaks. Freaks are, by definition, apart, as beings to be viewed. In the traditional sideshow, they are often caged and most often they are silent while a barker narrates their exotic lives. Also, given the history of freaks in the nineteenth and twentieth century (as medical discoveries and exhibitions defined the limits of the normal), it must be remembered that it was the discourse of biology which constituted their status as performers of the objective bodily 'truth.' Modern biology and empirical social science constituted them as 'real.' This biological 'realness,' of course, separates the freak from an earlier, archaic history which viewed them as divine monsters who mediated the natural and cosmic world. This is not to say that freaks are born freaks, only that they are made to seem like 'real, living breathing monsters' in the intersection between their presentation in freak shows, photography, cinema, the discourses of biology, and, increasingly, eugenics, all of which supported this illusionism.

Stewart makes an important historical distinction between the grotesque body in earlier times as described by Bakhtin and the grotesque spectacle of the freak show in pointing out that the freak is doubly marked as object and other within the world of spectacle:

> We find the freak inextricably tied to the cultural other – the Little Black Man, the Turkish horse, the Siamese twins (Chang and Eng were, however, the children of Chinese parents living in Siam), the Irish giants . . . The body of the cultural other is by means of this metaphor both naturalized and domesticated in a process we might consider to be characteristic of colonization in general. For all colonization involves the taming of the beast by bestial methods and hence the conversion and projection of the animal and human, difference and identity. On display, the freak represents the naming of the frontier and the assurance that the wilderness, the outside, is now territory.
>
> (Stewart: 1993, 109–10)

Produced historically in the same field of vision, freaks shared the same distancing, scrutiny, classification and exchange value as other colonial and domestic booty as the discourses of medicine, criminology, tourism, advertising, and entertainment converged. In the twentieth century, the discourses of medicine (particularly eugenics) contributed increasingly to the ways in which freaks were presented. Robert Bogdan, in a study of the social history of freak shows, distinguishes between the 'exotic' and the 'aggrandizing' modes of presenting freaks, the difference, in his example, between presenting the same giant as a Zulu and as a military figure (Bogdan: 1988, 97). The most famous instance of the aggrandized model was the aristocratic General Tom Thumb, born Charles Stratton. In Bogdan's chronology of freak shows, he charts an increasing tendency to medicalize the freak so that 'by the early twentieth century the audience was learning to view freaks as people who were sick – who had various genetic and endocrine disorders – and the exotic hype lost its appeal' (ibid., 94–116). As his own study indicates, however, the hype around freaks never entirely lost its appeal, and exoticism exists in even in the continuing lore of 'aliens' and extraterrestrials as monsters to be conquered or adopted. The freak show has always been something of a hybrid production, existing in proximity to other acts in carnival and circus contexts, and within various visual media.

Outside 'show business,' the role of the freak converged with the social roles available to the racially marked and underclasses – despite the aristocratic and exotic pretensions of their acts. Sometimes the freak was literally a slave. The 'North Carolina Twins,' Millie and Christine, were born into slavery in 1851, kidnapped, and taken to England where they became 'The United African Twins,' visiting and delighting, as did so many freaks of the period, Queen Victoria. Later, they returned to the United States through the efforts of their original owner, who reunited them with their family. Eng and Chang, the original Siamese twins, were 'discovered' by a Scottish merchant and brought to America by his trading partner. Chang and Eng enjoyed relative prosperity and supported twenty-two children when they retired to the rural South. In an unusual turn, the Siamese twins, like other North Carolina farmers, were said to rely on slave labor themselves.

Violet and Daisy Hilton, who appear in Browning's film, while not literally slaves, were sold by their mother to Mary Hilton, whose family and associates exploited them until they obtained legal representation at twenty-three years of age. Like Millie and Christine, they were multitalented performers and worked in various entertainment venues, joining the ranks of not quite respectable popular performers who lived very modest, if not impoverished, lives after they dropped out of sight.

Although Bakhtin's model of carnival was surely nostalgic and utopian in its portrayal of the social relations of carnival, it more importantly did not consider the complexities of twentieth century popular entertainments, advertising, and media. He provides, as Stewart shows, a very useful model of contrast for considering freaks in the nineteenth and twentieth century as grotesque spectacles. The question is not whether or not these modern grotesques are produced in very different conditions of visibility, but whether, on the one hand, there is still a model of community available to them which internally produced that 'reciprocal democracy' imagined by Bakhtin, or, on the other hand, whether that spectacularity embodied by the freak can be reworked or counterproduced as distinctly twentieth century grotesque representations, available not only as the post-Freudian 'creature features' of the individual psyche gone underground, but as a means of connection to existing social groups and to new socialities.

Any critical viewer of these materials intent upon keeping things in their place might simply see the freak as 'ruined' by spectacle and commodification. Fiedler, writing in the seventies, saw in the new reception of the movie *Freaks* a latter-day tribute, if not worship, of lost 'sacred' monsters by the enchanted youth of the counterculture. Comparing his own generation with theirs, he writes:

> We all firmly believed in those days that 'science' which had failed to deliver us from poverty but was already providing us with weapons for the next Great War, had desacralized human monsters forever. Three decades later, however, Browning's *Freaks* was to be revived for a new audience capable of recognizing in the Bearded Lady, the Human Caterpillar, and the Dancing Pinhead, Slitzie, the last creatures capable of providing the thrill our forebears felt in the presence of an equi- vocal and sacred unity we have since learned to secularize and divide.
> (Fiedler: 1978, 19).

Fiedler's comment here, and his book generally, is as nostalgic and idealizing in its way as are aspects of Bakhtin's writings on carnival in early modern Europe, although it reads much more autobiographically. The sense of a Romantic belat- edness and lost unity in relation to the sacred world of earlier monsters is prefaced by Fiedler's recollections of his lost youth: '. . . his movie has played and replayed in my troubled head so often that merely recalling it, I call up again not only its images, but the response of my then fifteen-year-old self' (ibid., 18–19). The thrills and wonderment of seeing 'actual' freaks, or imagining oneself as, or in solidarity with, the freaks, is a function, in part, of the recollection of the fantasies of youth. It is an instance, if you will, of the Freudian sublime in renewed proximity to the primitive and the archaic as stand-ins for 'the presence of an equivocal and sacred unity we have since learned to secularize and divide.'

It could be said that the countercultural production of the freak to which Fiedler refers was an unanticipated expression of the carnivalesque as an historic and imaginative possibility, what Wini Breines has called a 'prefigurative politics' (Breines: 1982, 6). In my view, however, this attitude can only be understood in relation to grotesque spectacle, not as the ruination of a lost, truer, or more complete world, but in full acknowledgement of the extent to which spectacle, the body, and politics are by now inseparable as distorted and hyperbolized aspects of media culture, which is to say the world we have now. Freak bodies appear not as collections of weird images assembled somewhere else, but as events and experiences, as is said of news events, 'blown out of proportion.' The freak embodies the most capacious aspects of media culture, taking in and consolidating otherwise lost or fragile identities. The freak can be read as a trope not only of the 'secret self,' but of the most externalized, 'out there,' hypervisible, and exposed aspects of contemporary culture and of the phantasmatic experience of that culture by social subjects.

Social movements in the United States in the last thirty years have all been acutely aware of the importance of producing and controlling images. Sheila

Rowbotham has described what has become the dominant allegory of political progress as a coming into visibility in the midst of false images:

> The vast majority of human beings have always been mainly invisible to themselves while a tiny minority have exhausted themselves in the isolation of observing their own reflections. Every mass political movement of the oppressed necessarily brings its own vision of itself into sight . . . In order to create an alternative an oppressed group must at once shatter the self-reflecting world which encircles it and, at the same time, project its own image onto history.
>
> (Rowbotham: 1973, 27)

She compares the media to a 'prism which refracts reality' and a 'hall of mirrors' which 'turns itself into a fun house.' Much effort has gone into straightening out the grotesque images of the fun house variety and in establishing 'real' histories and normalizing and neutralizing representations of women, sexual and racial minorities, and the disabled (ibid., 29). A riskier gambit by far lies in the strange mimesis of counterproducing such stretched and stunted caricatures, of posing and parading in these fun house mirrors, of surrendering one's identity as no longer possibly correct, recognizable, or selfsame, but inevitably bound to other bodies and strange selves.

[. . .]

Chapter 9

MARK SELTZER

THE SERIAL KILLER AS
A TYPE OF PERSON
(extract)

WHAT COUNTS AS SERIAL killing? Or, to put it a bit differently, how did the particular kind of person called the serial killer come into being and into view? The answers to these questions are by no means simple, even in what might appear to be the most self-evident of cases.

The new face of evil

Here is something approaching a personal confession, part of an anonymous letter received by the Ohio newspaper the *Martin's Ferry Times Leader* in November 1991:

> I've killed people. . . . Technically I meet the definition of a serial killer (three or more victims with a cooling-off period in between) but I'm an average-looking person with a family, job, and home just like yourself.
>
> (Methvin: 1995, 34)

There is nothing extraordinary about such communications to the mass media. Interactions between the serial killer and public media (or, in some cases, circulation-boosting simulations of that interaction) have formed part of the profile of serial murder, from the inaugural Jack the Ripper case on; for serial murder is bound up through and through with a drive to make sex and violence visible in public. Nor is there anything extraordinary about the 'technical' self-definition of the serial killer that centers this confession, although there is some disagreement as to the baseline qualifying number. (One recent and comprehensive study of the governing views on serial homicide simply defines the serial murder case 'as involving an offender associated with the killing of at least four victims, over a period greater than seventy-two hours' [Jenkins: 1994, 23–5].) And the 'cooling-off period' – distributing the murders repetitively and serially over time – has come to provide the working distinction between serial and mass murder (with 'spree killing' falling somewhere in between [see Holmes and De Burger: 1988, 18–23; Norris: 1988, 7–46; Masters: 1993, 231–89]).

Yet if there is then nothing extraordinary in the technical definition cited by the killer, there is perhaps something uncanny, even horrifying, in the sheer ordin-ariness – in the abnormally normal form – this confession takes. For if this is a personal confession, it is, on several counts, strangely *im*personal. I am referring not merely to the utterly *average* and *generic* self-description provided by the killer ('average-looking person with *a* family, job, and home') but also to the way in which his identity seems to melt away in his absolute identification with others ('just like yourself'). Both this *abnormal normality* and this compulsive *over-identification* are crucial to the understanding of the serial killer.

But the style of over-identification in such cases remains to be clarified. For if the anonymous writer of the letter here defines himself by way of the working definition of the serial killer, how then do such definitions or characterizations of the subject of repetitive violence enter into the 'inner' experience of that subject, seeming in effect to fill – or, better, to replace or to evacuate – his interior?

Here again are the words of the Ohio killer, ultimately identified as Thomas Dillon (a civil servant who confessed to five 'motiveless' killings):

> I knew when I left my house that day that someone would die. . . .
> This compulsion started with just thoughts about murder and progressed from thoughts to action. I've thought about getting professional help but how can I ever approach a mental-health professional? I can't just blurt out in an interview that I've killed people.
>
> (Methvin: 1995, 34–44)

The sheer banality these statements contain is perhaps their point. And this is not merely because, as everyone knows, modern, repetitive, systematic, anonymous, machine-like, psycho-dispassionate evil can scarcely be separated from banality.

The killer, for one thing, notes his compulsive drive to repetitive bodily violence with an utterly dispassionate rationality. Anything like a 'private' iden-tity or psychology has vanished, disintegrated 'into the two poles of expert knowledge and psychotic "private" truth,' with all the links between public know-ledge and 'private' or hidden truth of desire cut off (Žižek: 1992, 262). Or, rather, private truth has become thoroughly identified with expert knowledge, but as if without subjective force or conviction. The drive to kill is immediately referred to the 'psy' sciences – in the form of a client 'interview' with the 'mental-health professionals.' This is, as it were, just one step from a twelve-step outlook on addictive killing. And this is, as it were, one version of the modern replacement of the sense of interior states with information: the replacement of the soul and, in this case, the soul of evil, with knowledge systems, expert and scientific.

The killer's experience of his own identity is directly absorbed in an identifi-cation with the personality type called 'the serial killer': absorbed into the case-likeness of his own case. On one level, this points to the manner in which the serial killer *internalizes* the public (popular and journalistic) and expert (criminological and psychological) definitions of his kind of person: 'serial killers are influenced by the media as well as by academic psychology, and many make a specific study of earlier offenders' (Jenkins: 1994, 224; O'Reilly-Fleming: 1992, 3–4, 14). Such observations have by now become routine in accounts of the type of person called the serial killer. But the larger implications have perhaps, for that very reason, not quite been registered.

One detects, in the serial killer's identification with his type of person, the empty circularity by which the serial killer typifies typicality. One detects, that is, what has recently been called the 'looping-effect' by which 'systems of knowledge about kinds of people interact with the people who are known about,' affecting the 'way in which individual human beings come to conceive of themselves.' The concepts of kinds of persons, such as the concept of the serial killer, tend to lift themselves up by their own bootstraps: feeding on the representations and identifications that thus become inseparable from that concept (Hacking: 1995, 6).

The style of this interaction, in the case of the serial killer, assumes extreme, even terminal, form. What disappears – in the thorough self-identification with others and with expert systems of knowledge – is anything like a discrete interiority or individual motive. As Dillon described the attraction of serial killing to the friend who eventually gave him up: 'There is no motive' (Methvin: 1995, 34).

The 'technical' definition of the serial killer as a kind of person became available in the mid-1970s, with what FBI agent Robert Ressler called a 'naming event': the coining of the term 'serial killer.' A naming event is more complex than a simple nominalism; it is not that the concept or category is simply 'made up,' but that the make-up of such concepts has its own internal 'torque.' It involves the positing of a category or type of person as a sort of point of attraction around which a range of acts, effects, fantasies, and representations then begin to orbit. But it involves too the empty circularity by which the social construction of a kind of person becomes the point of attraction of the kind of person who traumatically experiences himself as nothing 'deeper' than a social construction.

It is this empty circularity – at the level of social construction and at the level of self construction – to which I want to return here. From the take-off point of the mid-1970s, large quantities of information about the serial killer have accumulated: in the form of criminological and psychological investigations; feminist, gender, and cultural studies; journalistic, fictional, and cinematic representations. A good deal of this material, professional and popular, rehearses a body of confident, if uncertainly reliable, general knowledge about serial murder (see, for instance, Norris: 1988, 21–49; Masters: 1993, 230–89). But a good deal more has taken the form of lurid, purely descriptive case histories, which often resemble nothing more than collections of evil kitsch (see, for instance, Newton: 1990, 1992).

But even the more interpretive studies of the serial killer have faltered at the impasse we have begun to detect. On the one side, there is the avowed failure, in these accounts, to locate a point of contact between private compulsion and public accounting; on the other, one sees the uncanny intimation that the killer's private compulsion is nothing but these public accountings of the subject, turned outside in.

Recent accounts of the serial killer routinely turn to the *social constructions* of 'the serial killer problem,' of the malady called serial killing, and of the type of person called the serial killer (serial killing and serial killers as the 'symptoms' or 'reflections' of social crises and anxieties [see Jenkins: 1994, 2–7, 225–9]). It is perhaps possible to invert this perspective: to consider not only the social construction of the malady called serial killing but also serial killing at least in part as a malady of social construction, experienced at the level of the subject.

The social construction assumption, at the level of the social, is that there is nothing deeper to the social order than its structuring of itself by itself, nothing deeper than its strictly immanent and 'indwelling network of relations of power and knowledge.' The social construction assumption, at the level of the subject, is that there is nothing deeper to the subject than his formation from the outside in. On this view, interior states become merely 'the subjective synonym of the objective fact of the subject's construction,' and thus 'pleasure becomes a redundant concept and the need to theorize it is largely extinguished' (Copjec: 1994, 6–7, 153–4; 227–43). The subject itself, that is, becomes a redundant, and largely extinguished, concept.

It may then be possible to understand the pleasure-killer as one version of the largely extinguished subject: the 'devoided' and predead subject, for whom pleasure has become bound to the endless persecution of pleasure and to the endless emptying or voiding of interiors, in himself and in others. This kind of subject may then be one version of the person in whom the 'social ego' has replaced the agency pertaining to the person: agency replaced with the merely 'personalized' form of a social determination painfully and traumatically drilled into and fused onto the individual. For this reason, there are affinities between what Klaus Theweleit (1989) identifies as the soldier-male's regimen of killing for pleasure and the careers of some serial killers. But there are also basic differences, and it is necessary at this point to specify further the social ego of the serial killer and the sort of social order into which it melts into place.

Psychology as public culture

Compulsive killing has its place in a public culture in which addictive violence has become not merely a collective spectacle but also one of the crucial sites where private desire and public culture cross. The convening of the public around scenes of violence has come to make up a *wound culture*: the public fascination with torn and opened private bodies and torn and opened psyches, a public gathering around the wound and the trauma. One of the preconditions of our contemporary wound culture is the emergence of psychology as public culture.

Stranger-intimacy, that is, is bound up not merely with the conditions of urban proximity in anonymity but also with its counterpart: the emergence of intimacy in public (see Giddens: 1992). Roughly stated, the late nineteenth century in the United States – the period of the first wave of sexual serial killing and the first wave of feminism – was also the period of the rise of a therapeutic culture of self-realization (see, for example, Lears: 1983, 3–38). And roughly stated, the post-World War II era – the period of the second wave of sexual serial killing and second wave of feminism – was the period in which 'subjectivity and its management' was renovated as a growth industry: the industry of growing persons as both expert professional and popular culture (Herman: 1995, 14–16). As C. Wright Mills observed in 1951, 'We need to characterize American society of the mid-twentieth century in more psychological terms, for now the problems that concern us most border on the psychiatric' (Mills: 1951, 7).

The bordering of the social on the psychiatric became visible on several fronts in the post war decades: in the spreading of the mental health profession and in the abnormal normality of psychic pain ('psychological help was defined so broadly that everyone needed it'); in the transformation of patient into 'client' and 'mental health' into something that could be mass produced and purchased; in the rise of sociologistic psychologies of self-actualization (the work of Carl Rogers and Abraham Maslow, among others); in the appearance of psychologistic sociologies of collective and national psychopathology (from the inaugural diagnosis of 'American nervousness' to 'future shock' and 'the culture of narcissism,' to 'Prozac nation' and the 'trauma culture' of the 1990s). There appears an insatiable public demand – in the print media, drama, films, and television – for accessible, entertaining information on psychological disturbances and psychiatric experts: 'private ordeals' become 'a matter of great public curiosity and untiring investigation' (see Herman: 1995, 12–15, 262, 311, et passim).

Stranger-intimacy and its maladies have become public culture: part of a pathological public sphere. Consider, for example, the talking cure as mass-media event: talk radio. The serial killer Ted Bundy described himself as 'a radio freak' who 'in my younger years . . . depended a lot on the radio.' From about the sixth grade on, one of his favorite programs was a San Francisco radio talk show: 'I'd really get into it. It was a call-in show. . . . I'd listen to talk shows all day. . . . I genuinely derived pleasure from listening to people talk at that age. It gave me comfort . . . a lot of the affection I had for programs of that type came not because of their content, but because it was people talking! And I was eavesdropping on their conversations' (Michaud and Aynesworth: 1989, 10–11).

This version of stranger-intimacy on the air was taken a step further in the psychology student's university work-study job at a crisis hot line. Bundy's biographer, or thanographer, Ann Rule recounted, 'The two of us were all alone in the building, connected to the outside world only by the phone lines. . . . We were locked in a boiler room of other people's crises . . . constantly talking to people about their most intimate problems' (Rule: 1980, 25). Stranger-intimacy and stranger-killing seem uncertainly alternatives and substitutes. The 'Russian Ripper,' the sex-killer Chikitilo, simply observed: 'I never had sexual relations with a woman and I had no concept of a sex life. I always preferred to listen to the radio' (Cullen: 1993, 234).

There is, it has recently been observed, a certain 'paradox of radio: a universally public transmission is heard in the most private of circumstances' (Weiss: 1995, 6). One might easily reverse the terms of this paradox: the paradox of talk radio is that a private communication is heard in the most public of circumstances. But it is precisely the reversibility, or opening, of the boundaries between public and private that makes up at least in part the appeal of talk radio (and now confession TV). The 'pleasure' of these paradoxically open secrets thus goes beyond voyeurism or 'eavesdropping': it intimates a collective gathering around private ordeals.

'A hundred years earlier,' Stephen Singular remarks in *Talked to Death* (the basis of the film *Talk Radio*), 'Walt Whitman had listened to his countrymen speak and written that he could America singing. Talk radio became the sound of America singing, arguing, whining, bitching, confessing, and letting raw feelings, private problems, and political or social opinions hang in the air for everyone with a radio to absorb' (Laufer: 1995, 43). This popular version of the national body electric, this suspension in the air of 'the private' and 'the social' – raw feelings and political opinions, the psychological and the national – seems at once a virtual, popular town meeting and its pop-simulation – a version of the consumerist pop-superego. 'Pop' may be 'popular,' but it is also 'Dad,' the Master's Voice. 'My father had gone over to the radio in about 1970,' the neo-Nazi Ingo Hasselbach recently recalled: 'It was like this disembodied voice that I knew was my father, trying to brainwash all the kids in the nation. . . . My father's voice *was* the state' (Hasselbach: 1996, 39).

The bordering of the social on the psychiatric

This superegotistical voice of the state might be understood in terms of the peculiar formation of the social ego: the depsychologized ego unremittingly dependent on external support, as a sort of insectoid exoskeleton. It is uncertainly the command of the superego as 'the "spirit of community" at its purest,' and, at the same time, the 'traumatic dimension of the Voice, which functions as a kind of foreign body perturbing the balance of our lives' (Žižek: 1994, 54, 117). It may be seen in terms of the advent of a mass psychology that voids individual psychology: the direct enlisting of the subject in the service of the social order, the mass pleasure-drills of a 'repressive desublimation' that amounts to 'a direct "socialization" of the unconscious' (see Adorno: 1991, Jacoby: 1977; Žižek: 1994).

On this view, the direct socialization of the unconscious, the replacement of the psychical by the social ego, amounts to the formation of the subject from the outside in: to 'psychology' as implant. Something like this notion of a social ego grounds the sociologistic psychology and psychologistic sociology that proliferated in the post war decades. But this work scarcely moves beyond the jargon of authenticity and inauthenticity, the psychologism and sociologism, it deplores. It thus stands as the 'paramnesic' symptom of its culture: that is, its image and its disavowal.

A brief sampling must suffice here. One discovers again and again in this work a grim diagnosis of unrestrained self-inflation in the cult of self-actualization ('the culture of narcissism'). This is self-realization as the realization of the merely personalized person – what David Riesman in his best-seller of the early '60s, *The Lonely Crowd*, called the formation of the 'psuedo-personalized' subject. Riesman's diagnosis of the fall into stranger-intimacy in the lonely crowd devolves on a basic distinction between the 'inner-directed' subject and the 'other-directed' pseudo-subject. The inner-directed subject displays, for Riesman, 'that endoskeletal quality and hardness, which makes many inner-directed individuals into "characters" in the colloquial sense.' By implication, the other-directed subject displays that exoskeletal, or insectoid, quality that is one refrain in the understanding of the pleasure-killer (Riesman: 1989, 14–20, 21, xxxvii–xxxviii).

But there is something deceptive in this simple opposition between inner and outer directedness. For inner directedness is ' "inner" in the sense that it is implanted early in life . . . and directed toward generalized but nonetheless inescapably destined goals.' This amounts to the implantation of a 'psychological mechanism' that Riesman describes as the internalization of a 'psychological gyroscope.' In the other-directed person, this version of the influencing machine is replaced by another. The other-directed person is an endlessly attuned 'receiver' of 'signals from near and far' 'whose relations with the outer world and with oneself are mediated by the flow of mass communication' and by the 'anonymous voices of the mass media.' His 'control equipment' is not like the gyroscope, but instead 'like a radar' (ibid., 15–16, 22, 25).

In both cases, then, control is implanted from the outside: an outside control experienced, in the first case (inner directedness), as control from within and, in the second (other-directedness), as control from without. In both cases, one discovers the formation of what the psychoanalytic theorist Jean Laplanche has called 'an internal alien entity' – or what Ted Bundy, radio freak, simply called 'the entity.' 'Everything comes from without in Freudian theory, it might be maintained,' Laplanche observes, 'but at the same time every effect – in its efficacy – comes from within, from an isolated and encysted interior' (Laplanche: 1976, 42–3). The psychoanalytic account holds visible the radical uncertainty that Riesman's psychologistic account registers only in the form of a tacit contradiction: the insecurity as to where the subject of machine culture comes from, its feeling of inner-directedness and its intimations of other-directedness, the internal otherness of the subject.

There is a basic uncertainty, too, as to the status of such an other-directedness: as one way of understanding the subject *tout court* (a primary extimacy) or as a way of understanding a particular kind of subject (the other-directed subject of mass culture, influencing machines, and stranger-intimacy). This coming down of the boundaries between inside and outside, between the psychological and the social, between public and private orders, is crucial. It may provide one way of understanding the foundational status of trauma in psychoanalysis (trauma as a failure of distinction between inside and outside, private and public registers) and, in turn, may provide one way of understanding how private trauma itself has emerged as public culture on the contemporary scene: how the psychopathologies of shock, trauma, and the wound have emerged as the very model of the public sphere.

In the psychologistic sociology of the postwar years (particularly in its cultural-conservative variants), this breakdown of the distinctions between inside and outside and between private and public – this bordering of the social on the psychiatric – is the malady itself. The very 'opening' of the borders between the psychical and the social, the private and the public, is condemned as pathological. As Daniel Bell expresses it: 'The private realm – in morals and economics – is one where consenting parties make their own decisions, so long as the spillover effects (porno-graphy in one instance, pollution in the other) do not upset the public realm' (Bell: 1976, xiv). The 'spillover' of the private into the public, the overflowing of inside into outside, is itself pornography (sex in public) and pollution (shit in public).

Hence, the culture of narcissism – the empty circularity of self-seeking – is also, on this account, the narcissism of culture – the empty circularity of a culture seeking only itself. As Bell summarizes it, 'Culture has become supreme . . . given a "blank check."' Since 'the cultural realm is one of self-expression and self-gratification,' sheer culturalism and sheer narcissism become two ways of saying the same thing. The self-made man's fantasies of self-origination give way to self-originating fantasies. For this reason, the modern emphasis on 'self-expression' amounts to 'the erasure of the distinction between art and life.' Whatever Bell means by 'life,' what he means by 'art' is the 'acting out of impulse,' putting the realm of the imagination and fantasy in place of reality: 'The greater price was exacted when the distinction between art and life became blurred so that what was once permitted in the *imagination* (the novels of murder, lust, perversity) has often passed over into *fantasy*, and is acted out by individuals who want to make their "lives" a work of art' (ibid., 35, xvii, xv, xxii–xxiii).

The transformation of lives into 'lives' – the simulations of life – is the erup-tion of art into life, private into public, interior states into acts: reality and fantasy have changed places. The panic about representations come to life and taking life; about the yielding of 'real life' to the image; about the traumatic replacement of perception by representation: all have become familiar enough in accounts of the 'fall' into 'post-industrial' or 'information' society. They have become one way of understanding a culture of narcissism and self-inflation and also its more recent mutation into a culture of trauma and self-evacuation. And they have become one way in which the question of violence and its causes have come to devolve on the question of a failure of distance with respect to representation [. . .].

The indictment of a general yielding of the social and psychological orders to pop-sociology and pop-psychology became a general refrain in the postwar decades – and not least as a refrain *within* a burgeoning pop-sociology and pop-psychology. One approaches here what Barbara Ehrenreich has called 'the nightmare anomie of the pop psychologists' vision: a world where other people are objects of consumption, or the chance encounters of a "self" propelled by impulse alone' (Ehrenreich: 1983, 51, 182). A strange turn takes place here in the notion of the 'pop-psychologists' vision' reduplicating itself in the world. Reality and fantasy change places again, this time as an *effect* of the pop-psychologists' vision of the replacement of real psychology and real sociology by pop-psychology and pop-sociology.

In popular serial-killer fiction, such as Thomas Harris's *Red Dragon* (1981), the killer's career is nothing but an acting out of the drive to self-actualization (what the killer Dolarhyde calls 'The Becoming'). It is nothing but the transformation of art into life; the killer experiences pure identification with reproductions of Blake's image 'The Red Dragon' and with mass reproduction generally. He liter-alizes the cannibalistic devouring of other people as objects of consumption (Dolarhyde as 'Dollar Hide,' bodily flows and money flows referring back to each at every point). That career, in other words, is nothing but a realization in pop-fiction of the pop-psychologist's nightmare vision.

Serial killers read many books about serial killing, and the pop-psychologists' visions make up part of their curriculum. What is the Unabom Manifesto other than a crash-course in these popular diagnoses? What are psychology student Ted Bundy's conversations in the third person other than personalized pop-psychology and pop-sociology? What is Thomas Dillon's 'confession' in the papers other than the inhabiting of the popular understanding of the serial killer as a self-understanding?

'There is some evidence that actual serial killers may pattern themselves on fictional accounts.' There is evidence too that these fictional accounts are often based on official accounts, which in turn often draw on fictional accounts: 'It is difficult to know whether the bureaucratic law enforcement attitudes toward serial murder preceded or followed changes in popular culture. . . . In turn, the invest-igative priorities of bureaucratic agencies are formed by public and legislative expectations, which are derived from popular culture and the news media . . . [I]n coverage of serial murder, the boundaries between fiction and real life were often blurred to the point of nondistinction' (Jenkins: 1994, 15, 81, 223). The Seattle area serial killer, George Russell Jr., a middle-class black male and self-described 'Bundy man,' 'thought he could pull off the perfect crime if he just read enough. . . . He's always talked and read about the hillside stranglers and John Wayne Gacy and Bundy and [popular media misconceptions about] the lack of black serial murderers. . . . He borrowed my books on Ted Bundy and Charles Manson and didn't return them. The things he read ["my books"] – *ugh!*' (Olsen: 1994, 119, 297, 216).

It is in this context that we may reconsider the 'empty circularity' of the serial killer: his hyperidentification with place, context, or situation, and his psychas-thenic way of melting into place. That is, we may now consider the matters of the 'self-construction' or 'social construction' of the serial killer from a somewhat different perspective: the becoming abstract and general of the individuality of the individual. In the serial killer – Thomas Dillon, for example – this typicality becomes indistinguishable from self-identity: he takes the FBI profile as a self-portrait. The point is not then that the serial killer problem is a 'social construction,' nor that the malady called the serial killer is 'socially constructed,' nor quite that the serial killer is a terminal instance of the self-made or self-constructed man. All these are elements in serial killing. But these intricated notions of construc-tion – social construction and self-construction and the relations between them – indicate something more.

Obey your thirst!

There is an empty circularity in the notion of the kind of person called the serial killer lifting itself by its own bootstraps: the conception that there is nothing more to the subject than what he makes of himself. There is an empty circularity, too, in the notion of the social construction of the social: the strictly 'historicist' concep-tion that there is nothing more to the social order than its structuring of itself by itself. These two notions are not merely parallel constructions: they are at once radically inseparable and radically incompatible. The experience of social construction at the level of the subject – to the very extent that it is experienced as a social mandate: 'be your self' – in effect evacuates the subject it mandates. The law of self-realization is a law that aborts itself. The injunction to realize yourself, to desire yourself into being – to enjoy your self – is at the same time imposed as an injunction from without. If the formula of the first is 'be yourself,' the formula of the second is 'Obey your thirst!' (Sprite) or 'Enjoy your symptom!' ([Slavoj] Žižek). 'Lifting oneself up by one's own bootstraps' is the logic of the self-made man and the logic of addiction both. The thirst of the self-made man to realize himself is at the same time his obedience to the command: 'thirst.' On the addictive loop of user and used, substance-abuse and self-abuse, the self-made subject is subjected to an endless drill in self-making that becomes indistinguishable from a repeated self-evacuation.

Tocqueville anticipated this drill in enjoyment of the self-made man (the man who gives birth to himself) in the self-legitimated democratic state (the nation that gives birth to itself) in *Democracy in America* (1835–40):

> The type of oppression which threatens democracies is different from anything there has ever been in the world before. . . . It likes to see its citizens enjoy themselves, provided they think of nothing but this enjoyment. It gladly works for their happiness but wants to be the sole agent and judge of it. It provides for their security, foresees and supplies their necessities, facilitates their pleasures, manages their principal concerns, directs their industry, makes rules for their testaments, and divides their inheritances. Why should it not entirely relieve them from the trouble of thinking and all the cares of living?

The threat of a totalitarian conformity of desire and thought in mass culture (oppressive enjoyment, repressive desublimation) has by now become one of the commonplaces of mass culture (the emperor reveals that he has no clothes – so much for demystification!).

It is possible provisionally to set out a basic implication of this bordering of the social on the psychiatric, this sociality bound to pathology. In the most general terms, we can detect here one of the constitutive 'psycho-social' paradoxes of liberal society: a paradoxical situatedness within power (social construction) that is at the same time a requirement of radical autonomy (self-construction). It is the unrelieved inhabiting of this paradox that casts the liberal subject into failure: 'the failure to make itself in the context of a discourse in which self-making is assumed, indeed, is its assumed nature.' This failure intensifies in 'late modern secular society, in which individuals are buffeted and controlled by global configurations of disciplinary and capitalist power of extraordinary proportions, and are at the same time nakedly individuated, stripped of reprieve from relentless exposure and accountability for themselves' (Bacon: 1995, 67).

It is the suffering of this failure, the avenging of this pain through the redistribution of this pain, that Nietzsche identified early on as the production of the 'slave morality' of *ressentiment*. *Ressentiment*, in short, seeks to deaden the pain of relentless self-exposure and failed self-accountability in two directions: by *externalizing* it (locating a site, or another, on which to revenge one's wound) and by *generalizing* it (remaking the world in the image of the wound, an injury landscape and a wound culture). The 'sovereign subordinated subject' thus achieves its revenge through the imposition of suffering and through the predication of a culture of suffering. In this way, the subject as victim seeks his victims. Here is Nietzsche's description of the psychophysiology of this traumatic violence:

> For every sufferer instinctively seeks a cause for his suffering, more exactly, an agent; still more specifically, a *guilty* agent who is susceptible to suffering – in short, some living thing which he can, on some pretext or other, vent his affects. . . . This . . . constitutes the actual physiological cause of *ressentiment*, vengefulness, and the like: a desire to *deaden pain by means of affects* [e.g., turning pain to rage] . . . to *deaden*, by means of a more violent emotion of any kind, a tormenting secret pain that is becoming unendurable, and to drive it out of consciousness at least for the moment: for that one requires an affect, as savage an affect as possible, and, in order to excite that, any pretext at all [e.g., the guilty agent, who will be wounded and deadened in turn].
>
> (Nietzsche: 1969, 127)

[. . .] The yielding of autonomy to generality, subject to situation, persons to conditions, individuality to state numbers (statistics) – all are hard wired to the very notion of the 'statistical picture' or composite 'profile' of the serial killer.

   [. . .]

Part Four

MANY FRANKENSTEINS

Introduction to Part Four

■ Ken Gelder

As **PAUL O'FLINN POINTS** out in his extract in this section, Mary Shelley's *Frankenstein* (1818) was once barely credited with any literary value at all. In the 1970s, however, the novel was forthrightly moved into the canon, thanks mostly to the interests of feminist Romantic scholars. In 1987, Harold Bloom, the great father of modern literary canon-formation, edited the Modern Critical Interpretation volume on Shelley's novel and secured its centrality — although his introduction had nothing to say at all about the various feminist approaches proliferating around him. In the meantime, the work of Ellen Moers (1977), Sandra Gilbert and Susan Gubar (1979), Mary Poovey (1984), Margaret Homans (1986) and Anne Mellor (1988) produced a complicated fabric of relations between the novel, its author, her circle, her literary and parental influences, and her immediate historical context. The thematic focus was invariably on Shelley's representations of motherhood, childbirth, reproduction and monstrosity.

Around the same time, studies were beginning to look at reproductions of the novel itself, particularly through theatre and film adaptations. There are certainly no shortage of examples, beginning with Richard Brinsley Peake's stage melodrama of 1823, *Presumption: or, The Fate of Frankenstein*, which had played at the English Opera House. Mary Shelley attended a performance and it may have influenced some revisions she later made to the 1831 edition of her novel (including Victor Frankenstein's new description of the monster as a 'living monument of presumption': see Baldick: 1987, 61). In the Author's Introduction to this edition, she famously 'bid my hideous progeny go forth and prosper', which it did with a vengeance. *Frankenstein* is one of only a dozen or so novels whose protagonists, and their predicaments, have long since slipped out of the restricted realm of the literary field to swamp the popular imagination. The monster and his creator may have lost the plot in the process, but – to draw from the study of another popular literary hero – they have gained a 'career' (Bennett and Woollacott, 1987).

George Levine and U.C. Knoepflmacher's collection, *The Endurance of Frankenstein* (1979), is the key text in the coming-together of these two zones of inquiry, compiled, as the editors say, in the wake of films such as Paul Morrissey's *Flesh for Frankenstein* (1974) and Mel Brooks's comedy *Young Frankenstein* (1974). The word 'endurance' reflects the transitional aspect of this book: it pays glowing tribute to Shelley's source-novel, but it also wants seriously to consider the various modern popular adaptations. *Frankenstein's* new-found centrality in the canon, however, means that the latter are always found wanting: the novel remains, say the editors, 'larger, infinitely more complicated and suggestive than any of its progeny' (Levine and Knoepflamacher: 1979, xiii). In fact, it provides the paradigms for their analysis. Contributors are asked, like Victor Frankenstein, to 'create something new' (ibid., xiv). The editors even imagine themselves back at the moment of *Frankenstein's* conception, the result of a story-telling game with Byron, Percy Shelley, Mary and Dr Polidori while vacationing in Switzerland in 1816: 'we suggested, half-jokingly', they say, 'that a book might be written in which each contributor-contestant might try to account for the persistent hold that *Frankenstein* continues to exert on the popular imagination' (ibid., xi–xii).

The novel has since provided the very language with which to talk about the adaptations that have followed, as 'stitched together' like the monster from various constituent parts, and so on. This imagery, of course, would suggest that the conventional view of an adaptation – that it should be faithful to its source – no longer holds. In his contribution, Paul O'Flinn notes that great works of literature (a Jane Austen novel, for example) usually *require* an adaptation to honour them, much in the fashion of a tribute. But the horror novel is not usually so demanding. As we see even with Peake's 1823 melodrama, there is no obligation for subsequent adaptations of *Frankenstein* to, in O'Flinn's words, 'get it right'. O'Flinn's extract begins with the acknowledgement that Shelley's 'hideous progeny' has indeed gone forth and prospered: 'There is no such thing as *Frankenstein*', he says, 'there are only *Frankensteins* . . .'. But he does not wish to slide over to the other end of fidelity by celebrating an 'endless plurality of meanings' in these various texts. His extract in fact places the novel, as well as two cinematic adaptations, securely in their historical and political contexts. Looking at Universal's 1931 film of *Frankenstein*, directed by James Whale, and Hammer Studios' 1957 film, *The Curse of Frankenstein*, directed by Terence Fisher, O'Flinn traces the ways in which changing historical and political circumstances produce new kinds of monsters, each with their own ideological significance.

Like José B. Monleon, O'Flinn sees horror as emerging out of times of political turbulence. Indeed, as Chris Baldick has shown in his book, *In Frankenstein's Shadow* (1987), Shelley's monster came to speak for a number of different kinds of political crises through the remainder of the nineteenth century and beyond. The second extract in this section from Elizabeth Young also focuses on political contexts, but entangles this with issues of gender and sexuality. She turns to James Whale's 1935 sequel for Universal, *Bride of Frankenstein*, a film which seemed to relish its camp humour and bombastic pronouncements – the most famous of these, Dr Praetorius's gleeful toast to 'a new world of gods and monsters', providing the title for a biography of Whale and a film about his life.

In *Bride*, as well as Whale's *Frankenstein* (but not in Shelley's novel), the monster is continually chased by angry townspeople brandishing torches and home-made weapons. Young accordingly places events in the context of US race relations at the time, turning especially to official anxieties about the lynching of black Americans. The monster is racially coded here, and his predicament is presented sympathetically. On the other hand, it is also represented as a sexual threat to vulnerable characters like Elizabeth, Frankenstein's fiancée – linking up to rape anxieties involving black men and white women. Sympathy for the monster in these terms now seems to be withdrawn. The creation of a Bride for the monster (a job Frankenstein had refused in the original novel) may be an attempt to settle some of these contradictory features. Yet *Bride of Frankenstein* ends with her piercing screams of rejection and the inconsolable monster's suicide, taking the Bride and Praetorius with him.

Young notes that the actress playing the Bride, Elsa Lanchester, also plays Mary Shelley in an opening tableau in the film. Here, she sits demurely between two powerful, egocentric men, the poets Percy Shelley and Byron. Mary Shelley and the Bride seem to become 'doubles', the closing screams functioning as a kind of Other to Lanchester's angelic demeanour at the beginning. In the meantime, two more men, Frankenstein and Dr Praetorius, bond with each other over their new creation. The latter, as an ageing, flamboyant dandy, tips the film over into high camp and turns the frantic relationship with Frankenstein into something approaching the homoerotic. Whale himself had lived openly as a homosexual and it is usually agreed that his homosexuality found some expression in his films, this one especially. Women, on the other hand, seem to be 'erased' from *Bride of Frankenstein*, returning only at the end to bring it all to a traumatic and despairing finale. With the closing introduction of the Bride, then, the film seems to split its monsters down the middle, unable to bring them together without imploding. They seem here to be both monstrously powerful and surprisingly fragile.

Chapter 10

PAUL O'FLINN

PRODUCTION AND REPRODUCTION
The case of *Frankenstein*
(extract)

M ARY SHELLEY'S GOTHIC NOVEL *Frankenstein* was published anonymously in 1818. In the same year, a couple of other novels — Peacock's *Nightmare Abbey* and Jane Austen's *Northanger Abbey* — also appeared and their derisive use of Gothic conventions suggested that the form, fashionable for fifty years, was sliding into decline and disrepute. There seemed good reason to suppose that *Frankenstein*, an adolescent's first effort at fiction, would fade from view before its print run was sold out.

Yet several generations later Mary Shelley's monster, having resisted his creator's attempts to eliminate him in the book, is able to reproduce himself with the variety and fertility that Frankenstein had feared. Apart from steady sales in Penguin, Everyman and OUP editions, there have been over a hundred film adaptations and there have been the Charles Addams cartoons in the *New Yorker*; Frankie Stein blunders about in the pages of *Whoopee* and *Monster Fun* comics, and approximate versions of the monster glare out from chewing gum wrappers and crisp bags. In the USA he forged a chain of restaurants; in South Africa in 1955 the work was banned as indecent and objectionable.

None of these facts is new and some of them are obvious to anyone walking into a newsagent's with one eye open. They are worth setting out briefly here because *Frankenstein* seems to me to be a case where some recent debates in critical theory about cultural production and reproduction might usefully be centred, a work whose history can be used to test the claims that theory makes (see, for instance, Bennett: 1979; Belsey: 1980; Eagleton: 1981). That history demonstrates clearly the futility of a search for the 'real', 'true' meaning of a work. There is no such thing as *Frankenstein*, there are only *Frankensteins*, as the text is ceaselessly rewritten, reproduced, refilmed and redesigned. The fact that many people call the monster Frankenstein and thus confuse the pair betrays the extent of that restructuring. What I would like to offer is neither a naive deconstructionist delight at the endless plurality of meanings the text has been able to afford nor a gesture of cultural despair at the failure of the philistines to read the original and get it right. Instead I'd like to argue that at its moment of production *Frankenstein*, in an oblique way, was in touch with central tensions and contradictions in industrial society and only by seeing it in those terms can the prodigious efforts made over the last century and a half to alter and realign the work and its meanings be understood [. . .].

Frankenstein is a particularly good example of three of the major ways in which alteration and realignment of this sort happens: first, through the operations of criticism; second, as a function of the shift from one medium to another; and third, as a result of the unfolding of history itself. The operations of criticism on this text are at present more vigorous than usual. When I was a student twenty years ago I picked up the *Pelican Guide to English Literature* to find the novel more or less wiped out in a direly condescending half-sentence as 'one of those second-rate works, written under the influence of more distinguished minds, that sometimes display in conveniently simple form the preoccupations of a coterie' (Harding: 1957, 45). *Frankenstein* may have been on TV but it wasn't on the syllabus. A generation and a lot of feminist criticism later and Mary Shelley is no longer a kind of half-witted secretary to Byron and Shelley but a woman writer whose text articulates and has been convincingly shown to articulate elements of woman's experience of patriarchy, the family and the trauma of giving birth (see, for example, Moers: 1974; Ellis: 1979; Gilbert and Gubar: 1979).

The second instance – the way a text's meaning alters as it moves from one medium to another – is something I'd like to look at in more detail later in this essay by examining the two classic screen versions: Universal's movie directed in 1931 by James Whale and starring Boris Karloff, and Terence Fisher's picture for Hammer Films in 1957 with Peter Cushing. Literary criticism only metaphorically rewrites texts: the words on the page remain the same but the meanings they are encouraged to release differ. But a shift of medium means the literal rewriting of a text as novel becomes script becomes film. Scope for the ideological wrenching and reversing of a work and its way of seeing is here therefore even larger. [. . .] The third category is one I suggested earlier – namely the way in which the movement of history itself refocuses a text and reorders its elements. *Frankenstein*, I would like to argue, meant certain things in 1818, but meant and could be made to mean different things in 1931 and 1957, irrespective of authorial 'intention'. [. . .]

Mary Shelley's monster, in short, is ripped apart by one or more of at least three processes in each generation and then put together again as crudely as Victor Frankenstein constructed the original in his apartment. Faced with these processes, traditional literary criticism can either, with a familiar gesture, pretend not to notice and insist instead that *Frankenstein* 'spanned time' with 'timeless and universal themes' that 'live beyond literary fashion' (Dunn: 1978, 131, 134). Or it can pay attention to those changes but slip past the power and the politics that they imply, so that shifts in the work's presentation become a plain mirror of human evolution: 'the Monster . . . is no longer separate, he is quite simply ourselves' (Small:

1972, 331); 'it is a magnified image of ourselves' (Tropp: 1976, 156). Capitalism creates and re-creates monsters; capitalist ideology then invites us to behold ourselves. I'd like to try to do something else.

First I would like to argue that much of the text's strength that continues to be released derives from certain issues in the decade of its composition, issues that the text addresses itself to in oblique, imaginative terms and that remain central and unresolved in industrial society. In that decade those issues erupted more turbulently than ever before: they were, briefly, the impact of technological developments on people's lives and the possibility of working-class revolution. Those issues fuel the Luddite disturbances of 1811–17 and the Pentridge rising of 1817.

There had been instances of machine-breaking before in British history but never with the same frequency and intensity. The size of the army marshalled to squash the Luddites – six times as big as any used previously for internal conflicts in the estimate of one historian (Thomis: 1970, 144) – is a measure of the extent to which the new technologies, in the first generation of the industrial revolution, threatened traditional livelihoods and provoked violent resistance. There is the same sort of new and disruptive energy evident in the Pentridge rising of June 1817, when 300 men marched towards Nottingham on the expectation of similar marches, designed to overthrow the Government, occurring across the country. The group was soon rounded up by Hussars and three of its leaders executed in November. The revolt ended in shambles and failure but its significance for E. P. Thompson is epochal – it was 'one of the first attempts in history to mount a wholly proletarian insurrection, without any middle-class support' (Thompson: 1968, 733).

The composition of *Frankenstein* needs to be seen in the context of these deep changes in the nature of British society. Mary began work on the novel in June 1816 at the Maison Chapuis, Montalègre, near Geneva, where she was living with Shelley. Byron lived nearby at the villa Diodati and the book's impetus came from Byron's challenge – 'We will each write a ghost story' – during one of their regular evening visits. The point is that as Mary set about writing her first novel she was working alongside two men who had responded publicly and politically to the Luddite crisis. Byron's magnificent maiden speech in the House of Lords in February 1812 had attacked Tory proposals to extend the death penalty for machine-breaking, denouncing a process whereby men were 'sacrificed to improvements in mechanism'. And then in January 1813, when fourteen men were executed at York for Luddite activities, Harriet Shelley had written to the radical London bookseller Thomas Hookham on Shelley's behalf: 'I see by the Papers that those poor men who were executed at York have left a great many children. Do you think a subscription would be attended to for their relief? If you think it would, pray put down our names and advertise it in the Papers' (Jones: 1964, 351). Mary and Percy returned to England from Geneva in September 1816 and Luddites were still being hanged in April 1817 as Mary made the last revisions to her manuscript. Before *Frankenstein*'s publication in March 1818, Shelley reacted to the execution of the leaders of the Pentridge rising with *An Address to the People on the Death of Princess Charlotte*, a forceful political pamphlet published in November 1817 and eagerly read by Mary, as she noted in her journal. The pamphlet lamented the

'national calamity' of a country torn between abortive revolt and despotic revenge
– 'the alternatives of anarchy and oppression' (Ingpen and Peck: 1965, 81).

What was Mary Shelley's own response to these events and reactions? To try
to pass *Frankenstein* off as a conservative riposte to the politics of Godwin and
Shelley, as Muriel Spark has done (Spark: 1951), is to ignore the book's brave
dedication to the unpopular Godwin as well as Mary's own correct anticipation
that a 'courtly bookseller' like John Murray would refuse to publish it when the
manuscript was offered to him (Bennett: 1980, 36). (It is also, as we shall see in
a moment, to ignore most of the book's contents.) Similarly, to describe her politics at the time she wrote *Frankenstein* as 'innately conservative', as Jane Dunn does
(Dunn: 1978, 134), is to muddle her views in middle age with those she held at
eighteen – often a mistake with Romantic writers and particularly so in Mary
Shelley's case. Her letters around the time of *Frankenstein* reveal a woman who
shared the radicalism of Byron and Shelley. The result was a politics shaped by a
passion for reform, a powerful hatred of Tory despotism with its 'grinding &
pounding & hanging and taxing' and a nervousness about the chance of the revolutionary violence such despotism might provoke. Thus, for example, she wrote to
Shelley in September 1817 between the completion of *Frankenstein* in May and its
publication the following March:

> Have you seen Cobbett's 23 No. to the Borough mongers – Why he
> appears to be making out a list for proscription – I actually shudder to
> read it – a revolution in this country would (not?) be *bloodless* if that
> man has any power in it. . . . He encourages in the multitude the worst
> possible human passion *revenge* or as he would probably give it that
> abominable *Christian* name retribution.
>
> (Bennett: 1980, 138, 49)

Her politics here in short are those of a radical liberal agonizing in the face of the
apparent alternatives of 'anarchy and oppression', to use the phrase which, as we
have already seen, Shelley was to deploy six weeks later in his *Princess Charlotte*
pamphlet. That politics also addressed itself to contemporary scientific and technological developments and their social implications. Discussion and speculation at
the Villa Diodati ranged across galvanism and Darwin's experiments, as Mary carefully notes in her 1831 introduction to the novel. In the autumn of 1816, as she
completed her manuscript, she read Davy's *Elements of Chemical Philosophy*.

It is out of these politics and this way of seeing that *Frankenstein* emerges.
[. . .]
The monster describes a crucial part of his education as follows:

> Every conversation of the cottagers now opened new wonders to me.
> When I listened to the instructions which Felix bestowed upon the
> Arabian, the strange system of human society was explained to me. I
> heard of the division of property, of immense wealth and squalid
> poverty; of rank, descent, and noble blood.
>
> The words induced me to turn towards myself. I learned that the
> possessions most esteemed by your fellow-creatures were high and

unsullied descent united with riches. A man might be respected with
only one of these advantages; but, without either, he was considered,
except in very rare instances, as a vagabond and a slave, doomed to
waste his powers for the profits of the chosen few! And what was I?
Of my creation and creator I was absolutely ignorant; but I knew that
I possessed no money, no friends, no kind of property.

(Shelley: 1969, 119–20)

Looking at that passage, it is perhaps worth remembering that the first person to
offer the text as a straightforward allegory of the class struggle is not some vulgar
Marxist in the twentieth century but one of the book's protagonists. Read as the
monster suggests, the novel argues that, just as Frankenstein's creation drives him
through exhausting and unstinting conflicts to his death, so too a class called into
being by the bourgeoisie and yet rejected and frustrated by it will in the end turn
on that class in fury and vengeance and destroy it.

This way of seeing the work, as well as being overtly stated by the work
itself, is rendered more likely if we look again for a moment at the text's context.
Lee Sterrenburg has documented the extent to which the populace as a monster,
bent on the destruction of the ruling class and its property, figures as a standard
trope in conservative journalism in the generation after the French Revolution
(Sterrenburg: 1979, 143–71). During the Luddite years, the monster appeared to
some to be on the loose. Factories in Yorkshire were fired in January and April
1812 and in March and April in Lancashire; there were murders, attempted assas-
sinations and executions again and again between 1812 and 1817. During the most
famous attack, on Rawfolds mill in the Spen Valley in April 1812, two of the
Luddites were killed and 'Vengeance for the Blood of the Innocent' appeared
chalked on walls and doors in Halifax after one of the funerals.

In the midst of this crisis, Mary Shelley picks up a way of seeing – the populace as a destructive monster – provided by Tory journalism and tries to re-think
it in her own radical-liberal terms. And so in the novel the monster remains a
monster – alien, frightening, violent – but is drenched with middle-class sympathy
and given central space in the text to exercise the primary liberal right of free
speech which he uses to appeal for the reader's pity and understanding. The caricatured people-monster that haunts the dominant ideology is reproduced through
Mary Shelley's politics and becomes a contradictory figure, still ugly, vengeful and
terrifying but now also human and intelligent and abused.

[. . .]

To see the text in these terms is not, as I have argued already, a daft left-
wing distortion but a reading suggested by the text itself and one that is also
apparent if we turn to the way the text was taken up in the nineteenth century.
In 1848, for example, the year of revolutions and of the *Communist Manifesto*,
Elizabeth Gaskell published *Mary Barton*, the first English novel with a Communist
as its protagonist. Describing John Barton she writes at one point:

And so on into the problems and mysteries of life, until, bewildered
and lost, unhappy and suffering, the only feeling that remained clear

and undisturbed in the tumult of his heart, was hatred to the one class, and keen sympathy with the other.

But what availed his sympathy. No education had given him wisdom; and without wisdom, even love, with all its effects, too often works but harm. He acted to the best of his judgment, but it was a widely-erring judgment.

The actions of the uneducated seem to me typified in those of Frankenstein, that monster of many human qualities, ungifted with a soul, a knowledge of the difference between good and evil.

The people rise up to life; they irritate us, they terrify us, and we become their enemies. Then, in the sorrowful moment of our triumphant power, their eyes gaze on us with mute reproach. Why have we made them what they are; a powerful monster, yet without the inner means for peace and happiness?

(Gaskell: 1970, 219–20)

What is intriguing about this reference is that Elizabeth Gaskell obviously hasn't read the book – she confuses Frankenstein with the monster and she doesn't know that the monster has a very clear knowledge of the difference between good and evil. What she has absorbed instead and passes on is the dominant political reading of the text, the sense that the middle classes are threatened by a monster of their own making. That monster, as we have seen, was manufactured out of the violence and anxieties of the Luddite decade; a generation later, at the peak of the Chartist decade, Elizabeth Gaskell reaches into cultural mythology to find the imaginative terms for her own predicament and that of her class.

It is significant that this political reproduction of the text persists and tends to surface at times of sharpening conflict. The 1961 Supplement to the *Oxford English Dictionary* notes Sidney Webb's use in *Fabian Essays*, published in 1889 at the height of the socialist revival: 'The landlord and the capitalist are both finding that the steam engine is a Frankenstein which they had better not have raised.' And the 1972 Supplement quotes the *Daily Telegraph*, 3 May 1971: 'There are now growing indications that the Nationalists in South Africa have created a political Frankenstein which is pointing the way to a non-white political revival.' Again, in both cases, monster and Frankenstein are muddled, indicating a level in ideology at which the text itself has ceased to exist but a myth and a metaphor torn and twisted from it is being strenuously put to work.

This separating of myth and metaphor from text and constructing something entirely new in ideology begins very early. In September 1823, Mary Shelley wrote to Leigh Hunt that she found herself famous – not for her novel but for a stage adaptation of it called *Presumption, or the Fate of Frankenstein* by Richard Brinsley Peake that was having a successful run in London. The title betrays the way the work is already being realigned as one idea in the complex structure is pulled out and foregrounded, and this foregrounding is underscored by a statement on the playbills for the opening performance on 28 July at the English Opera House. 'The striking moral exhibited in this story is the fatal consequence of that presumption which attempts to penetrate, beyond prescribed depths, into the mysteries of nature' (Nitchie: 1953, 221). Frankenstein certainly concludes from his own experience that the pursuit of knowledge ought to be prohibited, but the text does not endorse that kind of obscurantist morality [. . .]. But the later, more conservative and religious Mary Shelley slides towards this position, so that we find her insisting in the 1831 introduction: 'supremely frightful would be the effect of any human endeavour to mock the stupendous mechanism of the Creator of the world'. She herself, in fact, is among the first to nudge the text into the space occupied by the dominant ideology, and we can also see that nudging going on in some of the revisions she makes for this third 1831 edition; for example, Elizabeth Lavenza is no longer Frankenstein's cousin, so that the potentially offensive hint of incest is deleted, while the orthodox notion of the family as moral and emotional sanctuary is boosted by the addition of several passages in the early chapters idealizing the domestic harmony of Frankenstein's childhood. If ideology has taken hold of *Frankenstein* and remade it for its own purposes, Mary Shelley led with her own suggestions about how it might be done.

What I would like to do in the rest of this essay is to look at the two most famous reproductions of *Frankenstein* in the twentieth century, namely Universal's *Frankenstein* directed in 1931 by James Whale and starring Boris Karloff as the monster, and Hammer Films' *The Curse of Frankenstein* (1957) directed by Terence Fisher with Peter Cushing as Baron Frankenstein. The constructions and the operations of ideology are complex, and within the scope of an essay I cannot hope to do more than gesture at what seem to me to be the implications of the content of those two versions; wider questions about, for example, the precise relationship within the movie industry between honest popular entertainment, calculated profit-seeking, capitalist propaganda and painstaking aesthetic practice must inevitably be left to one side. [. . .]

That said, there seem to me to be at least three different types of shift that need to be borne in mind when looking at the gap between Mary Shelley's book and twentieth-century films; those shifts concern medium, audience and content. In the case of *Frankenstein*, the shift of medium is particularly important because it must inevitably obliterate and replace what is central to the novel's meaning and structure – namely the patterned movement through three narrators as the reader is taken by way of Walton's letters into Frankenstein's tale and on to the monster's autobiography before backing out through Frankenstein's conclusions to be left with Walton's last notes. That process cannot be filmed and so the very medium demands changes even before politics and ideology come into play.

The turning of the novel into film also involves a change in the nature of the work's audience. David Punter has convincingly argued that the Gothic novel is pre-eminently a middle-class form in terms of authors and values as well as readership (Punter: 1980). The films in question are middle-class in none of these senses, produced as they are by large businesses in search of mass audiences. That different site of production and area of distribution will again bear down on the work, pulling, stretching and clipping it to fit new needs and priorities.

Where this pulling, stretching and clipping appears most obviously is in the alterations in the third category mentioned earlier, namely the work's content, and I would like to detail some of those in a moment. What needs emphasizing here is that the radical change in the class nature of producer and audience hacks away at the content of the original, so that the book is reduced to no more than an approximate skeleton, fleshed out in entirely and deliberately new ways. This makes it quite different from, for example, a BBC serial of a Jane Austen novel, where some attempt is made at a reasonably faithful reproduction of the text [. . .] – not least because there are no immutable fears in human nature to which horror stories always speak in the same terms. There is not, for all David Punter's strenuous arguing, 'some inner social and cultural dynamic which makes it necessary for those images to be kept alive' (ibid., 424); rather, those images need to be repeatedly broken up and reconstituted if they are to continue to touch people, which is one of the reasons why horror films that are 30 or 40 years old can often seem simply boring or preposterous to a later audience.

The Universal movie was calculated quite precisely to touch the audiences of 1931. At that time Universal was not one of the front-rank Hollywood studios; its rather cautious and unimaginative policies had left it some distance adrift of the giants of the industry at the end of the 1920s, namely Famous Players, Loews and First National. But a way out of the second rank seemed to offer itself with the huge box office success of Universal's *Dracula*, starring Bela Lugosi, which opened in February 1931 and soon grossed half a million dollars. In April Universal bought the rights of Peggy Webling's *Frankenstein: An Adventure in the Macabre*. The play had run in London in 1930 and its title already suggests a tilting of the work away from Mary Shelley's complex scientific and political statement towards those conventional terror terms for which *Dracula* had indicated a market. *Frankenstein*, filmed in August and September 1931, was an even bigger profit-maker than *Dracula*. Costing a quarter of a million dollars to make, it eventually earned Universal 12 million dollars, was voted one of the films of 1931 by the *New York Times* and confirmed a fashion for horror movies that was soon to include Paramount's *Dr Jekyll and Mr Hyde* and Universal's *The Murders in the Rue Morgue*. In looking at the content of this movie I'd like to confine my comments to [some] areas where the shifts from the novel seem to me most important in terms of the ideological and political re-jigging that they betray. [. . .]

On the question of the nature of the monster, the most important revision here concerns the creature's brain. The film adds a new episode in which an extra character called Fritz, Frankenstein's assistant, is sent to a laboratory to steal a brain for the monster. In that laboratory are two such pickled organs, in large jars boldly labelled NORMAL BRAIN and ABNORMAL BRAIN. Before the theft, the audience hears an anatomy lecture from Professor Waldman in which he draws attention to various features of the normal brain, 'the most perfect specimen', and contrasts them with the abnormal brain whose defects drive its owner to a life of 'brutality, of violence and murder' because of 'degenerate characteristics'. Its original owner was, in fact, 'a criminal'. The lecture over, Fritz creeps in, grabs the normal brain and then lets it slip so that jar and contents are smashed on the floor. He is forced to take the abnormal brain instead.

The implications for the monster and his story are immense. A central part of Mary Shelley's thesis is to insist that the monster's eventual life of violence and revenge is the direct product of his social circumstances. The monster summarizes his own life in terms that the text endorses: 'Every where I see bliss, from which I alone am irrevocably excluded. I was benevolent and good; misery made me a fiend. Make me happy, and I shall again be virtuous' (Shelley: 1969, 100). The film deletes this reading of the story through its insistence that the monster's behaviour is not a reaction to its experience but biologically determined, a result of nature, not nurture.

Most commentators on the film are bewildered by this change, one not found in Peggy Webling's play. It has been variously dismissed as an 'absurd and unnecessary sequence . . . a cumbersome attempt at establishing motivation', 'ridiculous' and 'the main weakness' (see Tropp: 1976, 87, 90; Pirie: 1973: 69; Jensen: 1974, 30). If seen from Mary Shelley's stance, these comments are true; seen in terms of the film's ideological project, they miss the point. At one level in the text, Mary Shelley was concerned to suggest, in the imaginative terms of fiction, that Luddite violence was not the result of some brute characteristics of the nascent English working class but an understandable response to intolerable treatment. The Universal film, consciously or unconsciously, destroys the grounds for such a way of seeing with its radical political implications and instead sees violence as rooted in personal deficiencies, to be viewed with horror and to be labelled, literally, ABNORMAL and so sub-human. Bashing the monster ceases to be the problem but becomes instead the only way that the problem can be met and solved. So it is that Mary Shelley is stood on her head and *Frankenstein* is forced to produce new meanings for 1931.

This upending of Mary Shelley's book and its meaning explains two other profound changes in the monster's presentation that the film introduces. In the text, the monster spends chapters 11 to 16 describing his life – a huge speech that is placed right in the centre of the novel and fills over 20 per cent of its pages. In the film the monster can't speak. Again, in the novel, the monster saves a child from drowning in chapter 16; in the film, the monster drowns a child. Both reversals are of a piece with the Abnormal Brain scene and flow from it in that both deliberately seek to suppress audience sympathy for the monster. [. . .]

The way the film ends flows directly from the drowning of the child. [. . .] In the novel, Frankenstein dies in his pursuit of the monster across the icy Arctic while the latter, in the final sentence, is 'borne away by the waves, and lost in darkness and distance'. In the film, the drowning of the child provokes the villagers to pursue the brute and trap it in an old windmill which is then burnt down; a brief, single-shot coda shows a recovered Frankenstein happily reunited with his fiancée Elizabeth. The politics of the mill-burning scene are overt: as the blaze engulfs the blades they form a gigantic fiery cross that deliberately suggests the Ku Klux Klan, virulently active at the time, and so, as Tropp crudely puts it, 'points up the mob violence that does the monster in' (Tropp: 1976, 97). Similarly, another observer sees the film ending 'with what Whale called "the pagan sport of a mountain man-hunt"; at the finale, the film's sympathies are with the monster rather than with the lynch mob' (Jensen: 1974, 41).

These may have been Whale's intentions but there is a wide gap between director's aims and the movie as distributed. In Whale's original version, in the drowning scene, the girl dies because the monster innocently tries to make her float on the water like the flowers they are playing with and then searches frantically for her when she sinks. But these moments were chopped from the print of the film put out for general release: there we simply see the monster reaching out towards the girl and then cut to a grief-stricken father carrying her corpse. Child rape and murder are the obvious assumptions, so that the immediate response of the community in organizing itself to eliminate the savage culprit comes across as a kind of ritual cleansing of that community, the prompt removal of an inhuman threat to civilized life which is comfortably justifiable within routine populist politics and at the same time provides the firm basis for and so receives its sanction from the conventionally romantic final scene of hero and heroine at last happy and free from danger. If Mary Shelley's monster alludes indirectly to working-class insurrection, one answer to that canvassed in the 1930s was counter-revolutionary mob violence.

Political readings of the film tend to see it either in simple reflectionist terms (Tropp, for example, regards the monster as 'a creature of the '30s shaped by shadowy forces beyond its control, wandering the countryside like some disfigured veteran or hideous tramp' (Tropp: 1976, 93), while another finds 'a world in which manipulations of the stock-market had recoiled on the manipulators; in which human creatures seemed to be abandoned by those who had called them in being and those who might have been thought responsible for their welfare' [Prawer: 1980, 22]) or as escapist – 'Large sections of the public, having difficulty in dealing with the Depression, were glad to spend some time in the company of a monster that could more easily be defeated' (Jensen: 1974, 44). Readings of that sort can only be more or a lot less inspired speculation. I'd prefer to look within the film and see it as a *practice*, as an intervention in its world rather than just a picture of it or a retreat from it, a practice whose extent is marked out by the reconstruction of the text that I have indicated. Certainly it was released in the depths of the Depression, depths which can shock even when seen from Thatcherite Britain. The value of manufactured goods and services produced in the USA in 1929 had stood at 81 billion dollars and output at 119 (1923 = 100); as the film criss-crossed the nation in 1932, the value of goods and services had more than halved to 40 billion dollars and output was down to 64. There were 14 million unemployed. How the film reflects that catastrophe or seeks to escape from it is less important than what it says to it. As we saw earlier, it is historically at precisely such moments of crisis that Frankenstein's monster tends to be summoned by ideology and have its arm brutally twisted till it blurts out the statements that ideology demands. What Universal's *Frankenstein* seeks to say specifically to the mass audience at whom it is aimed concerns above all mass activity in times of crisis: where that activity [. . .] is traditional and reactionary (the mill-burning), it is ambiguously endorsed. The extent to which the film powerfully articulates those familiar stances of the dominant ideology in the 1930s is measured by its box-office success.

The fact that Frankenstein's monster is most urgently hailed at times of crisis perhaps accounts for the fact that, with the jokey exception of Universal's *Abbott and Costello Meet Frankenstein* in 1948, the English-speaking movie industry left the brute alone between 1945 (Universal's *House of Dracula*) and 1957 (Hammer's *The Curse of Frankenstein*) as the long post-war boom slowly built up. The Hammer film marked the end of the lengthiest break in Frankenstein pictures in the past fifty years and was the first attempt by a British studio to reproduce the story.

The relationship between, say, *Roderick Random* (1748) and early capitalism are complex and highly mediated. The links between Hammer Films and late capitalism are less obscure; the executive producer of *The Curse of Frankenstein*, Michael Carreras, whose family founded Hammer Film Productions in 1947 and have run it for three generations, has put it simply enough: 'The best film is the one that makes money. Our job is to entertain and promote something that is really exploitable. Exploitation is the thing' (Prawer: 1980, 241). Hammer's policy proceeded directly from this philosophy and has been well analysed by David Pirie (1973, 26). It specialized in stories that were already 'pre-sold' to the public by tradition or by radio or television so that public recognition of the product was not a problem – hence early films like *PC 49*, *The Man in Black*, *Robin Hood* and so on. At the same time, it sought for itself an area of the market left untouched by the dimpled complacencies of Rank and Ealing Studios. These two strands of policy combined to push it towards horror films, first with *The Quatermass Experiment* in 1955, a spin-off from the 1953 BBC serial *Quatermass*. The success of both serial and film prompted Hammer to explore the genre further, and the filming of *The Curse of Frankenstein* began in November 1956.

The result was a cultural phenomenon whose scale and importance has certainly been noted but whose significance has not really been investigated. *The Curse of Frankenstein* is, it has been claimed, 'the biggest grossing film in the history of the British cinema in relation to cost' (Eyles *et al.*: 1973, 16). When it opened in the West End in May 1957 it at once started breaking box-office records and it did the same across the USA that summer. One consequence was that the connections that Hammer had with the American market were rapidly reinforced: in September, for example, Columbia Pictures put Hammer under contract to make three films a year and by 1968 Hammer found itself a recipient of the Queen's Award to Industry after three years in which they had brought a total of £4.5 million in dollars into Britain – this at a time, of course, when most of the rest of the British film industry was in a state of vigorous collapse. In the decade and a half after the success of *The Curse of Frankenstein* Hammer made six sequels, all starring Peter Cushing as the eponymous hero.

In looking at the first of this series, it's Cushing and the part he plays that I would like to focus on, because it is there that the efforts of ideology in putting the myth to work for fresh purposes are most strenuous. [. . .]

The singularity of Cushing's role has been spotted by several observers without much attempt being made to see why this should be so (Pirie: 1973, 69ff; Tropp: 1974, 125ff). The fact that the film is centred on creator rather than monster in this version is signposted by the way that Boris Karloff, the monster in the Universal movie, at once became a star while Colin Clive, who was Frankenstein, remained obscure; conversely, in the Hammer picture, it was Peter Cushing who featured in the sequels, whereas Christopher Lee never took the part of the monster again.

Central to the specificity of Cushing's part is the way he makes Frankenstein unambiguously the villain of the story and this shift is produced by at least three major changes in his presentation. First and most obviously there are the crimes he commits which have no basis in the text or in previous film versions: to get a brain for his creature he murders a colleague, Professor Bernstein, and later on he sets up the killing of his servant Justine to conceal from his fiancée Elizabeth the fact that he has got her pregnant. Second, there is a marked class mutation that takes a tendency that is apparent in earlier versions several stages further. Mary Shelley's hero is a student, the son of a magistrate; in the Universal movie he becomes the son of a baron; in the Hammer film for the first time he himself is styled Baron Frankenstein and is given decadent aristocratic trappings to go with his title – he becomes, in Pirie's eyes, 'a dandy'. And then thirdly there is the change in age: Mary Shelley's youthful student is turned into Peter Cushing's middle-aged professor. The relevance of that emerges if we remember that 70 per cent of the audience for horror movies in the 1950s were aged twelve to twenty-five, a fact of which the commercially alert Hammer were well aware. A film pitched largely at adolescents could evoke hostility towards the protagonist more easily by transforming him from one of their own kind into a standard adult authority figure.

In short, the ambiguity of earlier readings of the story is removed by these revisions and we are given a Frankenstein to hate – a Frankenstein who, as Martin Tropp points out, is the real monster, a villain who ends the film facing the guillotine and straightforwardly enacting Terence Fisher's own way of seeing: 'If my films reflect my own personal view of the world . . . it is in their showing of the ultimate victory of good over evil, in which I do believe' (Eyles *et al*.: 1973, 15). Peter Cushing's Baron Frankenstein is a lethal nutter, an archetypal mad scientist.

It is here that the break with the Universal version is sharpest. James Whale had worked specifically to avoid a mad scientist reading of the story and had written to actor Colin Clive insisting that Frankenstein is 'an intensely sane person . . . a sane and lovable person' (Jensen: 1974, 35). And the one moment in Whale's film when this analysis wavers – namely Frankenstein's megalomaniac cry of 'Now I know what it feels like to be God' as his creature moves for the first time – was chopped by pious censors before anybody else got to see it.

What I'd like to argue is that close to the root of this transformation in the reading and reproduction of *Frankenstein* is a shift in the structure of fears within the dominant ideology. The possibility of working-class insurrection that had concerned Mary Shelley and terrified Universal was no longer a prime source of anxiety in 1956. To take one crude statistical indicator of working-class discontent: the number of working days lost, or rather won, in strikes in Britain in the 1940s and 1950s was the lowest in the twentieth century. But on the other hand the development of atomic and hydrogen bombs created a new and dire nightmare of the risk of world destruction flowing from a single, deranged individual – a cultural neurosis that the James Bond novels and films, for instance, were to run and run again through the 1960s and beyond. To imagine a universal catastrophe initiated by one mad scientist was a fear that was simply unavailable to Mary Shelley granted the level of scientific capacities in 1818; indeed, the very word 'scientist' was not coined until 1834. *The Curse of Frankenstein*, by contrast, was made at a time when the processes of science seemed to threaten human survival. As David Pirie points out, six months before filming began, a headline in *The Times* on 21 May 1956 had read: 'Giant H-Bomb Dropped, Luminosity More Than 500 Suns.' Equally importantly, we need to remember events in the very week that filming began. The cameras turned for the first time on 19

November; two days earlier, the first Hungarian refugees had arrived in Britain driven out by the Russian tanks that smashed their revolution; a fortnight earlier, on 5 November, Anglo-French airborne troops had landed at Port Said at the depths of the fiasco of the Suez invasion.

The Curse of Frankenstein was therefore made at a unique and overdetermined conjuncture in world history when, for the first time, both the technology and the crises existed to threaten the very survival of the planet. Once again Mary Shelley's novel was pulled off the shelf and ransacked for the terms to articulate cultural hysteria. In one sense, of course, the movie represents a flight from the politics of Eden and the Kremlin into a spot of escapist Gothic knockabout; but to see it and then dismiss it as no more is to wipe out a series of factors including Fisher's ideology, Hammer's business sense, American investment and contemporary critical responses, all of which mark out the seriousness of the project at one level. To put it baldly, at a time of genuine and multi-layered public fears, *The Curse of Frankenstein* addresses itself to a predominantly young audience and locates the source of anxiety in a deranged individual, focuses it down to the point where its basis is seen as one man's psychological problem. Wider systematic and social readings [. . .] are repressed, as a structure whose values go unquestioned is presented as threatened by a loony rather than as being itself at the root of instability. Responsibility for imminent catastrophe is limited to a single intellectual standing outside both ordinary lives and the political establishment, so that the film can flow from and then feed back into a populist politics and a scrubby anti-intellectualism frustrated by its own impotence. *The Curse of Frankenstein* is the curse of blocked democracy looking for a scapegoat and being sidetracked from an analysis.

What I have tried to show is that there is no eternal facet of our psyche that horror stories address themselves to. The reworkings of Frankenstein's story in the last century and a half prove that if there are, in Mary Shelley's phrase in the 1831 introduction, 'mysterious fears of our nature' to which her tale seeks to speak, those fears, like our nature itself, are produced and reproduced by the processes of history itself. Elsewhere in the same introduction Mary Shelley insists that 'invention, it must be humbly admitted, does not consist in creating out of void, but out of chaos; the materials must, in the first place, be afforded; it can give form to dark, shapeless substances but cannot bring into being the substance itself'. To look for those materials, that chaos, that substance, elsewhere in literature alone and so to read *Frankenstein* simply as shuffling round the themes and structures of earlier Romantic and Gothic texts is to fail to account for the way the novel, ceaselessly reconstituted, vigorously survives while those other fictions are long forgotten – forgotten, indeed, even by Mary Shelley herself by 1831 (see Rieger: 1963, 461–72). I suggest that the chaos and the materials were there in the struggles of the Luddite decade, just as other materials and other kinds of chaos were there first in the 1930s and then in the 1950s to produce new meanings in a process that continues. [. . .]

What conclusions can we draw from all this? First, surely, we need to see that here as in any text there is no 'real', 'true' reading waiting for a sharp academic to nail it down for ever in the pages of a monograph; even for its own ostensible creator, *Frankenstein* meant certain things in 1818 and began to mean other things by 1831. A historically informed criticism needs to see those meanings, not abolish them. And then what, in the face of those meanings? S.S. Prawer concludes his study of horror movies by calling for 'standards' that will enable us to distinguish the work of the likes of James Whale from those mindlessly misusing the conventions of horror 'for the sake of profit' (Prawer: 1980, 279). Such a search is likely to prove futile, especially if it begins with the odd assumption that somehow Universal weren't trying to make a lot of money. The standards that will distinguish between meanings – that will struggle for some and that will detect but resist others – are politically informed ones; standards that are based on a politics that knows where meanings come from and where they lead and is not afraid to fight on the grounds of that knowledge.

Chapter 11

ELIZABETH YOUNG

HERE COMES THE BRIDE
Wedding gender and race in *Bride of Frankenstein*

(extract)

JAMES WHALE'S 1935 FILM, *Bride of Frankenstein*, is such a fixture in American popular culture that its most memorable image – of a woman in a long white dress with a wacked-out, white-streaked Nefertiti hairdo and wild, glazed eyes – has become the standard currency, requiring no explanation, for parodies ranging from *The Rocky Horror Picture Show* to *Far Side* cartoons. Enshrined in popular culture, it ranks, too, as a favorite with film critics (see Glut: 1973; Glut: 1984; Levine and Knoepflmacher: 1979; Everson: 1974; Forry: 1990). Devotees of the horror film term it 'a masterpiece,' 'a nearly perfect feature,' and 'the last word in monster movies; glittering and intelligent, frightening and humorous, with the right touches of both whimsy and the Gothic macabre' (Glut: 1973, 132; Florescu: 1975, 193; Steinbrunner and Goldblatt: 1972, 106). Recent film historians praise its formal construction, asserting that the film is 'close to flawless' in its 'acting, direction, photography, set design, editing and overall presentation' (Brunas *et al.*: 1990, 120). And a third strand of criticism focuses on the film's comic possibilities, celebrating it as 'one of the world's first camp classics' (Norden: 1986, 150).

What these various accolades leave untouched, however, is the way in which this very funny horror film is about some very serious issues. For even as it appears to escape into a genre of fantasy – in this case, Gothic horror – *Bride of Frankenstein* refracts a series of social anxieties involving gender, sexuality, and race. Feminist criticism and social history enable us to locate in the film a series of complex, and at times contradictory, narratives of historically situated power relations. To begin with, the film's complex gender dynamics, which consistently take the form of a triangle involving two men and a woman, seem at first to enact the exchange and erasure of women, whether this triangle is configured Oedipally or – in a more capacious explanatory frame – as an instance of the 'traffic in women.' But the film also challenges the static parameters of such triangular models, both by trans-

Figure 11.1   Still from *Bride of Frankenstein* (Universal Pictures 1935). Courtesy of the
Ronald Grant Archive.

forming the competitive force of male rivalry into a subversive mode of male
homoeroticism and by undermining its apparent demonization of women with a
final, fleeting moment of female power. The film's gender triangles, that is, inter-
rogate even as they illuminate explanatory frames of feminist theory, emerging as
highly unstable structures in terms of both gender and sexuality.

We can evaluate the film's potentially transgressive treatment of gender,
however, only through a more precise assessment of its relation to its historical
moment, the 1930s. In *Bride of Frankenstein*, I will argue, the monster appears as
a marker of racial difference, and his sexualized advances to the film's women
encode racist American discourse of the 1930s on masculinity, femininity, rape,
and lynching. This focus on race radically revises an initial feminist reading of the
film's discordant gender moments – and the limited explanatory paradigms on
which they rest. The film stands, in other words, as one complex instance of the
relationship between race and gender in Depression-era U.S. culture and as a
testing ground for the feminist theory that would seek to explain such relationships.

The complexity of these relations, moreover, both responds to and comments
critically upon directions in feminist film theory. Recent feminist criticism of the
horror film, like feminist film theory generally, has developed powerful psychoanalytic interpretations, focusing, for example, on the explanatory force of male
anxieties about castration and about the maternal body (see, for example, Hollinger:

1989; Creed: 1989; Williams: 1984). Although such readings are useful, they often lack historical specificity, and can be inattentive to what Paula Rabinowitz has recently termed 'the relationship between the intrapsychic process of subjectivity and the social formations of sex, gender, class, and race' (Rabinowitz: 1990, 168). The following reading of *Bride of Frankenstein* takes as its central contention the interdependence of these social formations and, in so doing, attempts to dislodge feminist film theory's myopic focus upon the white male gaze and spectator. For the axes of gender and race crosscut each other by the film's end, suggesting an ideological complexity with important implications for our understanding of both film and feminism.

Given the many versions of the Frankenstein story, it may be useful to begin with a discussion of *Bride of Frankenstein* and its textual parents. In Mary Shelley's 1818 novel *Frankenstein*, several speakers relate the disastrous relationship between an ambitious young scientist, Victor Frankenstein, and his unnamed, monstrous creation. After a series of murders by the monster, the book ends with the death of Frankenstein, and possibly of the monster, near the North Pole. Whale's first Frankenstein film (*Frankenstein*, Universal Studios, 1931) simplifies this plot, focusing on the moment of the monster's creation, his murder of a child, his attack upon the scientist's bride, Elizabeth, and his death in a fire; in contrast to the ending of the book, here the scientist and his bride emerge unscathed.

A sequel to the earlier film, *Bride of Frankenstein* draws upon another episode in the Shelley novel, that of the creation of a female mate for the monster. *Bride of Frankenstein* opens with a framing device, a discussion among Lord Byron, Percy Bysshe Shelley, and Mary Shelley about the Frankenstein story. To orient new viewers, the character of Mary Shelley summarizes the plot of the first film, but with an important revision: rather than perishing in the mill burning that concluded the previous film, the monster (Boris Karloff), it seems, is still alive. The film then segues into its new story, in which the monster wanders the countryside. Pursued by a group of angry townspeople, he is caught and imprisoned. Escaping, he finds solace with a blind hermit who plays music and teaches him to speak, but he is again discovered and must flee for his life.

Meanwhile, Dr. Frankenstein (Colin Clive), happily reunited with Elizabeth (Valerie Hobson), falls under the spell of his former teacher, Dr. Praetorius (Ernest Thesiger), who wants to create a female mate for the monster but needs the expertise of Frankenstein (now renamed Henry). The two stories intersect when Dr. Praetorius encounters the monster in a crypt, where the doctor is grave robbing for his experiments, and the monster is hiding from the crowd. Praetorius instructs the monster to abduct Elizabeth, after which Henry, fearing for her safety, lends his skills to the scientific project. The climax of the film is a creation scene in which the two men bring a female form to life. After animation, however, the bride (Elsa Lanchester) recoils from the monster's advances; he, in rage and despair, blows up the castle, himself, Dr. Praetorius, and the bride. Alone among the film's characters, Henry and Elizabeth escape, and they look tearfully back upon the exploding castle in the film's final moment.

What gender arrangements underlie this plot? Its original source, Mary Shelley's *Frankenstein*, has been one of the proof-texts for contemporary feminist literary criticism, with various interpretations focusing, for example, on the novel's complex thematics of maternity, its self-reflexive commentary upon female language and authorship, and its implicit evocation of the relation between gender and imperialism (see, for example, Moers: 1974; Gilbert and Gubar: 1979; Spivak: 1985; Gallagher and Young: 1991). We may begin to untangle the role of gender in Whale's film by turning to one of the many feminist approaches to the novel, Mary Jacobus's 'Is There a Woman in This Text?' which concentrates on the moment in Shelley's *Frankenstein* in which the male scientist and his male creature argue over the creation of a female monster. Jacobus reads this scene – from which the plot of *Bride of Frankenstein* will emerge and expand – as dependent on an asymmetrical gender triangle constituted by a woman and two rivalrous men. Locating this triangular model in relation to Freud, as both an evocation and a critique of Oedipal rivalry, she suggests that it 'characteristically invokes its third (female) term only in the interests of the original rivalry and works finally to get rid of the woman' (Jacobus: 1982, 119).

An initial look at *Bride of Frankenstein* confirms the salience of this model, for the film – which Jacobus touches on briefly – repeatedly stages gender as a disappearing act, whereby once two men are together, the lady vanishes. From the first, Praetorius acts as the elder figure of authority to whom Henry is involuntarily drawn, in a rivalrous relation which is founded, and continually dependent on, the exclusion of Elizabeth. When Praetorius first arrives at the Frankenstein manor, Henry and Elizabeth are tearfully huddled together on Henry's bed; Henry asks Elizabeth to leave the room, and a long shot charts her disappearance from the frame as the two men embark on their conversation. In the next scene, the two men retire to Praetorius's chambers – 'You must see *my* creation,' Praetorius exhorts – leaving Elizabeth behind entirely. Once they are there, women become merely the hypothetical term of a future undertaking, as Praetorius urges that 'together, we create his mate.' Later, after Elizabeth has been kidnapped at Praetorius's instructions, he allows Henry to telephone her. Again, Elizabeth only appears in order to disappear, for what the camera marks as salient about the scene is the two men clustered together at the mouthpiece.

Disembodying women metaphorically, the film also dismembers them literally, as the narrative of the bride's creation graphically demonstrates. When Dr. Praetorius and his ghoulish assistant go grave robbing, the camera shows two male figures suspended above a female corpse; later, Praetorius and Frankenstein begin their experiment by conversing over a female heart in a jar. All this is preparation for the film's climactic scene, in which the two scientists animate the female monster; at this moment, the camera frames them in medium shot on opposite sides of her mute, bandaged form. Reading this moment against the first scene between Henry and Praetorius, we can see that the bride's appearance fills the same function, structurally, as Elizabeth's earlier disappearance. Both are silent catalysts for the furthering of relations between the film's male protagonists, with the bride providing a more visceral example, different in degree but not in kind, of the treatment of Elizabeth.

Indeed, for all the apparent contrast between them, Elizabeth and the monster's mate are two of the film's female doubles – a twinning that the very title of the film ambiguously encodes. For just who is the bride of Frankenstein? Frankenstein, of course, is Henry's surname, and *his* bride is Elizabeth; indeed, because it is not clear exactly when in the film the two marry, Elizabeth is perpetually Frankenstein's bride. Yet in the creation scene, Praetorius triumphantly baptizes the female monster as 'the Bride of Frankenstein.' There are, then, not one but two brides of Frankenstein — or perhaps even more than two, for the film's title phrase, 'bride of Frankenstein,' omits the definite article, as if to suggest the endless repeatability of this most common female role.

The relation between Elizabeth and the bride in turn forms part of a broader circulation of female roles in *Bride of Frankenstein*, because, as the film's audience was well aware, the actress Elsa Lanchester plays both bride and Mary Shelley. In the film's first scene, Lanchester as Mary Shelley sits demurely on a drawing-room couch, embroidering carefully, dressed in a long, white gown, and flanked by her husband, Percy Shelley, and Lord Byron. Her angelic persona serves contradictorily both to promote and to defuse her narrating powers; she occupies the important position of author, but here only as the conduit for a story passing between two men. Lanchester's later appearance extends the assumption of powerlessness that underlies this position, as the bride lies mute between a second pair of men, Praetorius and Frankenstein. She who seemed ostensibly to be the creator, Mary Shelley, is, at the end, reduced to man's creation; she, too, is 'of Frankenstein,' if not his wifely property then his artistic and scientific achievement. In the film's gender system, Mary Shelley, Elsa Lanchester, Elizabeth Frankenstein, and the monster's mate are all Mrs. Frankenstein. And as the maleness of the marital patronymic suggests, this is a role in which women become not only interchangeable but no one at all.

This analysis of the film's gender dynamics considerably expands the explanatory rubric of Oedipal rivalry with which we began, for it suggests that *Bride of Frankenstein* offers not only a psychoanalytic paradigm of male rivalry and female erasure but also the performance of a more capacious and complex system of gender exchange. Indeed, the film's gender triangles as we have traced them suggest the continuing relevance of a founding model of contemporary gender theory, Gayle Rubin's formulation of the 'traffic in women,' in which the exchange of women, which is enacted in psychoanalytic modes, serves fundamentally to consolidate gendered social structures (Rubin: 1975, 157–210). As we have seen, *Bride of Frankenstein* encodes such circulation on a variety of registers: the women within its plots pass between a series of husbands and monsters, disappearing and reappearing as they spill beyond the confines of an Oedipal triangle. As the film's title highlights, in a system of male exchange, women's identity is most fully marked by their value as commodities, their status as property — marital, scientific, creative, authorial — passing between men.

Yet *Bride of Frankenstein* also suggests the stresses under which the 'traffic of women' itself operates. For although the film triangulates and traffics in its women, its narrative also gestures toward a series of challenges implicit within this gender paradigm. We may begin to locate these sites of contradiction by returning to the film's title, which not only marks the instability of the term 'bride' but also highlights the ambiguity of *male* identity within the film, for 'Frankenstein' — in Shelley's novel, the name of the doctor — here signifies both scientist and monster. If this slippage among male names suggests generally that male identity in the story is unfixed, then a second look at the film's opening tableau provides a fuller set of clues to the complexities of the film's presentation of men. At times during this scene, the camera frames Mary Shelley between her husband and Lord Byron, enacting in visual terms her intermediate status between them. Yet at other moments the triangle is reconfigured visually, when the camera separates Mary Shelley off to one side, and focuses on the two men; in these shots, Lord Byron leans against Percy Shelley with his arm draped over the other man's shoulder. This opening sequence offers a suggestive frame for the workings of the film's gender triangles, as it oscillates between an overt mode of female exchange and the implicit homoerotic connections that, with a new focus of the camera lens, can be seen to underlie it. The scene suggests, in short, that in order to assess the contradictions within the film's presentation of gender, we will need to attend more closely to what it is that might pass sexually between men.

In work that builds on Gayle Rubin's, Eve Kosofsky Sedgwick (1985) has argued that in patriarchal culture, sexual ideology must negotiate uneasily between two very similar arrangements: homosociality, the constant affirmation of shared interests between men, which, in a patriarchal society, works to consolidate male power; and homosexuality, the overt, erotic expression of sexual desire between men, which is of great subversive potential within such a system and therefore must, by its logic, be brutally suppressed. Women serve, then, not merely as a medium of exchange in the homosocial system but also as a desperate cover-up, a means of channeling suspicion of homosexuality into heterosexual appearances. In such a homophobic culture, any threat of exposing the potential homoeroticism that underlies male homosociality constitutes a challenge to the whole system of exchange.

If *Bride of Frankenstein*'s opening presentation of Byron and Percy Shelley helps to highlight this threat, within the film's Frankenstein plot, each successive gender triangle is even less stable, and suggests a progressive falling away from an 'acceptable' homosociality into an overt homosexuality. We have already seen how Dr. Praetorius's arrival activates a scene of male rivalry with Dr. Frankenstein. But the moment also serves to consolidate a sexualized relation between the two men: Praetorius is, after all, enticing Henry away from his marital bed and inviting him to his own apartment. If Praetorius is Henry's rival as scientist, that is, he is also Elizabeth's rival as lover. Moreover, Praetorius's physical appearance and behavior are ambiguously marked; film historian Vito Russo argues that the character appears 'odd, sissified,' and carries connotations of homosexuality (Russo: 1981, 51). We may locate this 'oddness' more precisely in the stereotypically gay attributes of a later scene, when Praetorius is shown dining alone in a crypt with a skull set before him, a bottle of wine next to him, a long cigarette in his hand, and an insouciant expression on his face. At this moment, the doctor appears in the visually coded form, here rendered campily, of the homosexual as decadent aristocrat.

Like Praetorius, the monster stands outside of normative male sexuality, but his form of male sexual 'confusion' has far more serious consequences for the film's gender triangles. The monster, like the cultural stereotype of the homosexual man, is an 'unnatural' creation, an analogy to which the film gives form in significant ways (see ibid., 49; Wood: 1984, 172). When the monster learns to speak, for example, he indiscriminately links the word 'friend' – his only term for an affective bond – with the hermit who first befriends him; then, in the scene just discussed, with Dr. Praetorius; and finally with his future female mate. He has no innate understanding that the male-female bond he is to forge with the bride is assumed to be primary or that it carries a different sexual valence from his relationships with the two men: all affective relationships, with women and men, are as easily 'friendships' as 'marriages.'

In the face of such sexual instability, the film struggles to reassert heterosexual ideology anew, most pointedly in the final creation scene. The imagery of this birth scene is specifically and hyperbolically phallic, from the long shaft that elevates the bride to the roof, where she will receive lightning conducted from the storm raging outside; to the men's excited shouts of 'It's coming up' as she is raised; and finally to the orgasmic quality of the lightning hitting the bed. The camera work, which Albert J. LaValley terms 'extravagant, almost unhinged,' lends an air of manic instability to the proceedings (LaValley: 1979, 272). For the first time, Praetorius and Frankenstein are framed not with a level camera but in diagonal medium-shots; rapid crosscutting from shaft to body to men further disorients the eye, as if to confirm formally the volatility of the film's presentation of gender. At this point, in short, the creation of the female form is essential to quiet what are increasingly unfixed gender designations.

In this context, the bride's rejection of the monster has disastrous repercussions. When the bride first comes to life, she stands neatly flanked by the two men: the covertly homosocial, rather than overtly homosexual, order seems restored, and she need only acquiesce to the monster's (heterosexual) invitation. But instead, she recoils from his advances, shrieking not once but twice. At the bride's second rejection, she actually falls out of the left-hand side of the frame, as if her act is so chaotic as to destabilize the camera itself. Given this catastrophic rejection, the monster's insistence that he and Praetorius die together marks the recognition that at least two of the male identities in the film cannot be reconstituted for normative heterosexuality. To be sure, order is nominally restored at the film's end: it is the heterosexual couple, Elizabeth and Henry, who remain alive. But given the instability that has preceded their happy coupling, it is doubtful that the system as a whole now looks so smooth; at the very least, the violence with which such eruptions must be suppressed has been exposed. As D.A. Miller argues in reference to the sensation novel: 'Reconstituted in a "sensational" account of its genesis, [a heterosexual] norm risks appearing *monstrous*: as aberrant as any of the abnormal conditions that determine its realization' (Miller: 1986, 119).

If the bride's rejection of the monster forms the climax to the film's narrative of homosociality, it also signals a key reversal in *Bride of Frankenstein*'s presentation of female powerlessness. At first glance, the female monster seems to behave in a manner fully congruent with the female passivity that the 'traffic in women' demands. As Karen F. Hollinger describes, 'She clings submissively to Henry Frankenstein, is terrified of the male monster . . . and seems created only to act as the ultimate victim for the male monster's final demonstration of power' (Hollinger: 1989, 40). Yet the bride's apparent passivity is, in fact, a compensatory behavioral cover for what her very presence suggests: that she stands as an index of male anxiety about, rather than indifference to, women and their bodies. After all, the bride's composite female form translates the idea of the social construction of woman into an essentialist nightmare, whereby women are *literally* constructed, assembled horrifically from female body parts. The violence of this process suggests that beneath the film's fantasy of male parthenogenesis, there is something in whole female bodies to be feared, which Hollinger identifies as 'the underlying threat of female sexuality and of the power of sexual difference that shapes it' (ibid., 45). Despite her secondary status as a creature of male fantasy, the monster betrays the fear that all female bodies are in fact unspeakably monstrous — and in this monstrosity, unspeakably powerful.

If such an analysis provides the bride with only the most indirect agency, as a demonized figure of repressed sexual power, then the moment when she first refuses the monster stands as a more overt instance of female authority. As Jacobus notes, this moment is one of sexual autonomy, as the bride refuses 'to mate in the image in which she was made' (Jacobus: 1982, 135). Moreover, in the film's imagery of doubling, whereby the bride consistently represents a more extreme version of Elizabeth, her shrieks enact an inchoate refusal of the female coming-of-age narrative that the other woman has assumed — a narrative conveniently telescoped, in the bride's case, to the only two events deemed essential for women: birth and marriage. Finally, we should note that when the bride just says no to being the monster's first lady, her rejection is significant specifically as an act of speech — one whose authority is implicitly twinned, via the double casting of Elsa Lanchester, with the authorship of Mary Shelley. After all, Shelley, who not only speaks but writes, sets the story in motion with a female signature. Reading backward, we can see Mary's opening words as forming the story that gives voice to the bride's scream; reading forward, we can see the bride's scream as the most visceral and impassioned version of the 'angelic' Mary's story. Together, that is, the bride's scream and Mary's speech offer a rejection of the systems of circulation that would disembody, dismember, exchange, and erase them, in a moment — suggested only to be suppressed — when the female goods get together and refuse to go to market (see Luce Irigaray: 1985, 196).

Gender relations in *Bride of Frankenstein*, I have argued thus far, are simultaneously conventional and disruptive. The film at first seems to stress a rigidly restrictive paradigm in which women pass interchangeably between men. At the same time, however, the narrative hints at two implicit fissures in this theoretical ground, through its presentation of the homoeroticism that guides its male characters and of the monstrous power that informs the bride's shriek of refusal. This reading of the film renders dynamic certain features of feminist theory, suggesting the inter-relation between psychic and structuralist models of gender exchange, between issues of gender and sexuality, and between female powerlessness and female agency. What we now need to ask, however, is how these theoretical paradigms operate in precise relation to *Bride of Frankenstein*'s particular cultural moment of the mid-1930s. How can we read this film historically — and how, in turn, will a historical reading of *Bride of Frankenstein* revise our initial assessment of the film?

First, recent assessments of the 1930s suggest that the era resists any easy initial charcterization in terms of both gender and sexuality. On the one hand, despite the massive social effects of the Depression, the period seems not to have brought significant disruptions of conventional gender arrangements; as Susan Ware suggests, the roots of the Feminine Mystique of the 1940s and 1950s are clearly visible in the preceding decade (Ware: 1982, 199). [. . .] Yet if relations between genders were fundamentally unchanging during the era, relations within genders were slowly altering, in terms of the ideological construction of same-sex desire. John D'Emilio and Estelle Freedman (1988) suggest that in the 1920s and 1930s, discussion of homosexuality was taking new, and newly anxious, forms. In this period, a variety of discursive forms – books like *The Well of Loneliness* (1928), blues songs like 'Sissy Man' and 'Bull Dagger Woman,' the psychiatric language of 'inversion' – brought the newly 'invented' category of 'the homosexual' to the public eye, from a variety of perspectives. Even as scientific definitions codified homosexuality in strictly negative and punitive terms, other modes, like the blues song, offered a more diverse sexual vocabulary. As D'Emilio and Freedman put it, 'the resources for naming homosexual desire slowly expanded' (D'Emilio and Freedman: 1988, 288–9).

What was the relation of film to this ambiguous social matrix of gender and sexuality? The 1930s were famously a 'golden age' for Hollywood, not only in film's new formal sophistication or its popularity with Depression audiences but also, for women, in its on-screen presentation of strong female actresses like Katharine Hepburn, Bette Davis, and Rosalind Russell. As Ware interprets it, such stars and the roles they played both reflected and fostered new images of women in the culture at large, in a constitutive model of culture that we may apply similarly to *Bride of Frankenstein*, despite its apparent distance from lived gender relations (Ware: 1982, 173). Reading allegorically, we can see the film's systems of exchange as schematic, if parodic, representations of the most conventional workings of gender in the era; its almost – but not quite – total suppression of female agency, meanwhile, acts as commentary upon very real anxieties about the role of women in the 1930s. Finally, the homoeroticism of the film's plots similarly echoes and shapes contemporary images of masculinity, with the male creature literally incarnating the monstrous connotations of homosexual 'inversion.'

If such an interpretation can only proceed metaphorically, with the film allegorizing the tensions of its era, then the history of *Bride of Frankenstein* as an artifact of mass culture offers more specific connections between the work and its cultural moment. *Bride of Frankenstein* was made five years after the establishment of the infamous Hollywood Production Code and less than a year after Will Hays, responding to public pressure, created the Production Code Administration to enforce it. Because the first *Frankenstein* had already been the subject of a bitter censorship battle over its goriness (Brunas *et al*.: 1990, 27), the makers of *Bride of Frankenstein* were undoubtedly aware of the need to restrain overt displays of brutality and violence – as well as of sexuality, adultery, and anything that threatened the so-called sanctity of marriage and the home. In this context, then, we can understand the film to be battling against a specific and highly publicized set of constraints that sharply delimited representational possibilities for both horror and gender.

As the film is in tension with the overt gender prescriptions of the Production Code, so too the history of *Bride of Frankenstein*'s prerelease editing hints at its negotiation of contemporary gender norms. In addition to customary editing, the film went through a substantial last-minute cut after being shown briefly in previews.

It was trimmed at this point from ninety to seventy-five minutes, and among the later changes was the omission of a grim scene in which Praetorius experiments on a live woman, dissecting her until she awakens and screams for mercy. The ending was also altered at the last minute to omit the suggestion, present in the film's final shooting script, that the female monster's heart might be that of Elizabeth (Glut: 1973, 127, 131). The question of the filmmakers' intentions in making such changes aside, we may infer that the omitted material would have made too explicit the brutal asymmetry of power relations between the sexes. Had the film even briefly suggested that the bride's heart came from Elizabeth, for example, it might have exposed the fragility of the romantic fiction cloaking the 'traffic in women.' Indeed, such a suggestion would have implied that the customary emotional danger of romance – a woman's broken heart – might be the visceral, literal result of association with men.

If we turn from the history of the film's production to that of its consumption, a related series of social concerns, involving normative masculinity, come into view. *The New Republic*, for example, in favorably comparing *Bride of Frankenstein* with *The Cabinet of Dr. Caligari* (1919), praised its art as the kind

> that gives the healthy feeling of men with their sleeves rolled up and working, worrying only about how to put the thing over in the best manner of the medium – no time for nonsense and attitudes and long hair.
>
> (Ferguson: 1935, 75)

Here, the film's art is ostensibly rescued from an effeminized realm – obliquely rendered as 'attitudes and long hair' – and reclaimed, strenuously, for the terrain of real men, those who work 'with their sleeves rolled up.' Yet in the light of the film's homoeroticism – and particularly, given Praetorius, its aesthetics of decadence – this assertion of normative masculinity appears rather anxious, as though the review claims the film's 'maleness' not in spite of but because of considerable evidence to the contrary. A second example, from *Time*'s 29 April 1935 review of the film, further emphasizes the link between *Bride of Frankenstein* and contemporary sexual ideology as it affected both women and men: 'In private life also Miss Lanchester is the wife of Henry VIII (Charles Laughton). Although he is known for his plump effeminacy, she is mannish in dress.' Here, a compulsion to spot real-life 'inversions' (the effeminate man, the mannish woman) coincides with commentary upon a film about monstrous creatures with 'unnatural' desires. In fact, we need only look at the story of James Whale to note the proximity of the film's themes to its era, for according to Vito Russo, Whale was ostracized professionally for being openly gay in homophobic Hollywood. Whale's directorial signature reminds us not only of the historical link between camp sensibility and gay male culture but also of the explicit social consequences of being perceived as sexually 'unnatural' (Russo: 1981, 50). In the film's negotiation of contemporary sexual ideologies, the realities of the Gothic could be as distant as its parodically Romantic, Mitteleuropa setting – or as close as the editor's scissors, the reviewer's pen, or the director's chair.

This reading of *Bride of Frankenstein*'s historicity, which suggests the film's mediation of gender norms and anxieties in the 1930s, is, however, itself incomplete, for it treats gender in isolation from other social phenomena of the 1930s, particularly the volatile and contested ground of U.S. race relations. If gender and sexuality were only implicitly in flux during this era, the Depression's impact on race relations was immediately felt in at least one arena – that of lynching. The first half of the decade saw an increase in the lynching of Black men. The well-known Scottsboro case (1931), in which an all-white Southern jury sentenced a group of young Black men to death for allegedly raping two white women, offered a legally sanctioned version of the tradition in which Black men were brutally murdered for their supposed crimes against whites. Antilynching activist Jessie Daniel Ames suggested in a 1942 report that lynching in the early 1930s was distinguished not only by its frequency but also by the barbaric nature of the individual crimes. Although such crimes were vigorously protested by Black activists, as well as by some white liberals, such protests were often thwarted. In 1934, for example, the NAACP renewed its long-term lobbying for a national antilynching bill, but the bill was defeated the following year, 1935 – the year, that is, of *Bride of Frankenstein*'s release (see Ames: 1973, 2; Zangrando: 1980, 98–138).

Moreover, the representation of race in film was itself a highly contested issue throughout the 1930s. The decade was framed by the release of films that featured Black characters in demeaning stereotypes, from *Hearts of Dixie* (1929), which introduced the figure of Stepin Fetchit, to *Gone with the Wind* (1939), whose Black characters formed a nostalgic romanticization of 'happy slaves' in the antebellum South. Other films with Black characters – *Hallelujah* (1929), *Imitation of Life* (1934), *So Red the Rose* (1935), *Green Pastures* (1936), *Prisoner of Staten Island* (1936) – also caricatured Black life, and the period as a whole has been characterized as the era offering only servant roles for Black actors (Bogle: 1989, 36). But Black writers and activists consistently fought against such images, not only challenging the showing of overtly racist films – like D.W. Griffith's epic, *The Birth of a Nation* (1915), which underwent a mid-decade revival – but also influencing the production of films. The NAACP was able to temper some of the more egregious racial content of *Gone with the Wind* during filming; the film also met with Black protest upon its release. Hollywood filmmakers also nervously accommodated conservative standards for the representation of race: battle scenes between Blacks and whites in *Rhodes of Africa* (1935), for example, were cut so as to minimize direct racial confrontations, and the liberalism of the antilynching film, *Fury*, was tempered by a focus on a white victim (see Archer: 1973; Leab: 1975). Such self-censorship against both Left and Right suggests that the apparent uniformity of Black servant roles on screen in fact served as an ideological screen for the volatility of Depression-era race relations.

Given this contemporary struggle over both lived and filmic race relations, *Bride of Frankenstein*'s monster takes on new significance, as a creature marked not only by an undifferentiated 'otherness' but also specifically by behavioral and visual codes associated with Blackness. In a 1944 article on images of Black men in film, Lawrence Reddick cited the stereotypes of irresponsible citizen, social delinquent, vicious criminal, and mental inferior (Reddick: 1975, 4). Within this cluster of stereotypes, one – that of the Black 'brute' – carried particular force, perhaps because it exposed the fears domesticated by valorizing the figure of the Black servant. From *Birth of a Nation* onward, as Donald F. Bogle describes, Black men were depicted as 'subhuman and feral . . . nameless characters setting out on a rampage full of black rage' (Bogle: 1989, 13). Delinquency, criminality, inferiority, subhumanity: these attributes fully converge in *Bride of Frankenstein*'s monster. Indeed, in an era when Hollywood hesitated to depict Black characters committing violence, the film's monster – for all his apparent distance from 'reality' – may more fully emblematize the iconography of U.S. racism than any other film, more openly mimetic, could have in this era.

If the monster's behavior implicitly links criminality with contemporary images of Black violence, so too does his physical appearance gather force from racist stereotypes. His large, black-clad, awkward form embodies the racist association of Blackness with subhumanity, as does his facial appearance, which makeup artist Jack Pierce apparently designed to 'give the monster a primitive, Neanderthal appearance' by sloping 'the brow of the eyes in a pronounced ape-like ridge of bone' (Glut: 1973, 100). This confluence of racist stereotypes appears elsewhere in films of this era, for we might think of the monster as cousin to that most famous of demonized movie characters, the one who not only appears 'ape-like,' but in the form of an actual ape: King Kong, who became, as Thomas Cripps puts it, 'a mythic figure, part "bad nigger" and part universal victim of exploitation' (Cripps: 1977, 278).

In *Bride of Frankenstein*, too, the monster appears as victim, in this case as a fugitive whose repeated escapes from mob pursuit resonate with contemporary accounts of lynching. The first Whale *Frankenstein* film concludes with an extended sequence about the monster's flight from a crowd of angry townspeople, whose pursuit of him is figured with all the visual markers – barking dogs, fiery torches, angry shouts – of a lynch mob (see O'Flinn: 1986, 212). *Bride of Frankenstein* confirms and extends the force of this imagery, presenting the monster in a condition of continual flight from a murderous mob. Captured partway into the film, he is strung up on a tree as an angry cluster of men surrounds him. This visual moment is so shockingly reminiscent of the imagery of lynching that, as with the monster's 'Blackness,' the film here radically rewrites boundaries between the 'fantasy' of horror film and the 'realism' of other cinematic genres. Indeed, *Bride of Frankenstein* is able to take up contemporary racism not despite its Gothicism but by virtue of it. In contrast to films like *Fury* (1936), whose obvious topicality set sharp limits on their content, it may be that *Bride of Frankenstein* could articulate a lynching plot more vividly through fantasy than could be represented through realism.

The generic conventions of film horror in fact provide unusual insight into lynching, as the film suggests in its presentation of the metaphorics of monstrosity. Not only does the pursuit of the monster suggest a lynching narrative, but the very composition of his body offers a grisly echo of the consequences of lynching. Composed of the mutilated and dismembered parts of corpses, the monster emblematizes the frequent mutilation and dismemberment of lynching victims. That the monster's parts were stolen from graves emphasizes this connection, for the corpses of lynching victims were similarly desecrated, as in the case of George Armwood who 'was mauled and mutilated before he was lynched . . . and whose body was then burned and further desecrated.' Continuing with the news that 'whatever fragments of his corpse remained in his coffin may have been dug up,' this newspaper story offers a plot whose ending – dismemberment – is the monster's own beginning (see Ginzburg: 1962, 203).

Finally, another newspaper report of lynching from the same era suggests an uncomfortable circulation between horror films and acts of lynching as viewer 'spectacles': 'The lynching site was located across the street from a picture show where a horror film was playing. A number of women emerging from the theater saw the Negro hanging from the tree and fainted' (ibid., 220). This account literalizes the close connection between the movie theater and the setting for lynching, which physically neighbor each other as they offer similar sights of terror. In its evocation of the connection between U.S. racism and Gothic monstrosity, *Bride of Frankenstein* manifestly participates in this representational slippage. Even as it dilutes its horror with comedy and situates it in a zone of apparent 'fantasy,' the film yet more strongly invokes – indeed, has more license to invoke – the imagery, narrative, and formal conventions of contemporary U.S. lynching.

Keeping in mind this link between the horror of lynching and the horror of the monster movie, we can read *Bride of Frankenstein* initially as intervening in lynching discourse in order to present the plight of the monster sympathetically. Counterposed to the unjust pursuit by the frightening lynch mob are the actions of the kind hermit, blind to the monster's appearance, who teaches him language, literally enacting 'color-blind' liberalism. Such sympathy further emerges in the iconography of Christian martyrdom that surrounds the monster throughout the film. When the old man comforts the monster to sleep, a crucifix remains brightly lit above their heads even after the camera fades to black. With the monster recognizably coded as a Black fugitive, this religious symbolism translates, via *Uncle Tom's Cabin*, into the Christian abolitionist narrative of slave humanity, misery, and redemption.

If the monster is figured sympathetically as a martyred Black fugitive, he is also, however, a *male* fugitive, a gendering that transforms both his character and the film as a whole. In the history of U.S. race relations, lynching was commonly connected with fraudulent rape charges, a false charge that formed, in Angela Davis's words, 'one of the most formidable artifices invented by racism' (Davis: 1981, 173). In the racist iconography that sustained such accusations, the most common cultural image was that of a Black man, 'a monstrous beast, crazed with lust,' assaulting a white woman (Hall: 1983, 333). As Jacqueline Dowd Hall has shown, such accusations not only imprisoned white and Black women in sexual stereotypes but also served as a powerful means of controlling Black men, who were mutilated and killed in the thousands of lynchings following the end of the Civil War (ibid., 335).

By the 1930s, the myth of the Black rapist so permeated Hollywood film that the explicit representation of rape – something the Production Code in any case severely restricted – was not required in order for its ideological threat to be registered. Again, *King Kong* (1933) provides one version of this overdetermined racist cultural fantasy, in the film's memorable image of the fair, blonde Fay Wray dangling helplessly in the brutish paw of the dark male gorilla. In the logic of racial representation, the very explicitness of this image seems enabled by the film's extreme distance from mimesis, its adherence to the safely nonrealist fantasy of science fiction. By contrast, in films set closer to home, the proximity of U.S.

racism presumably proscribed such explicitness, even as it made the imagery of interracial rape yet more available on the slimmest of connotations. In *Gone with the Wind*, for example, as Eve Kosofsky Sedgwick has noted, the scene in which an ex-slave attempts to rob Scarlett depends for its effect on the imagery of rape (Sedgwick: 1985, 10).

Bridging the ideologically explicit fantasies of *King Kong* and the more muted historical 'realism' of *Gone with the Wind*, both *Bride of Frankenstein* and its predecessor, Whale's *Frankenstein*, bear the traces of the racist connection in U.S. culture between race and rape. In one sequence in the earlier film, the monster enters Elizabeth's room on her wedding night and corners her behind the locked door; the camera cuts away to other people in the house hearing her screams. When they break into her room, her white dress is disheveled and she lies across one corner of the rumpled bed moaning desperately, 'Don't let it come here.' Although the monster's crime is officially the penetration of the room, not the woman, his actions are framed precisely according to the stereotype of interracial rape. The next scene of the film implicitly realizes the disastrous consequences of such rape, when an angry young father displays to the crowd the body of his little girl, whom the monster has killed by accident. Reading these two scenes together, it is as though the body of the girl, utterly victimized and now dead, metaphorizes the fatal effects for white women of contact with Black men. By the end of this sequence, the Black man has become the archetypal rapist. If not actually dead, the white woman is, as Hall puts it, 'the quintessential Woman as Victim: polluted, "ruined for life," the object of fantasy and secret contempt' (Hall: 1983, 335).

Bride of Frankenstein deploys this powerful stereotype of interracial rape throughout its narrative. The monster's resuscitation of a drowning girl appears, to the two men who come upon him, as an imminent sexual violation, as does his abduction of Elizabeth while she is resting in her bedroom. Again, the scenes do not require explicit sexual content for the overdetermined imagery of interracial rape to take hold, for as Valerie Smith notes, 'the fiction of a black male perpetrator automatically [sexualizes] a nonsexual crime' (Smith: 1990, 276). But the perpetrator, in this case, is also a victim, in an overlay of iconographic forms – rapist and martyr – that sets the film in conflict with itself. Indeed, in both Frankenstein films, the monster embodies a paradox, the sympathetic lynch-mob target who is also, possibly, a demonic rapist. But because the monster's status as innocent victim is transformed if he seems to pose a 'genuine' sexual threat, ultimately the force of this second, gendered metaphoric persona – Black male rapist – is so great that it overrides the first, undercutting any claims to compassion.

In this context, relations between the monster and other men, and between the bride and the monster, require rereading. Because cultural stereotypes of interracial rape presumed female victims and male attackers, the film's insistence upon the monster as would-be rapist serves to highlight his heterosexuality and consequently to alter the terms of his involvement in the film's homoeroticism. As male, the monster is allowed into some of the homoerotic bonds that are determined through the exclusion of women, particularly those with Praetorius; indeed, with his indiscriminate 'friends,' his inability to grasp normative gender codes, the monster manifests this homoeroticism too overtly for the stability of the film's sexual plots. As a *Black* man, however, the monster is also, contradictorily, defined against these same men, as a figure of monstrous heterosexuality. And having incarnated both these threats – the excessively homoerotic white man and the excessively heterosexual Black man – the monster's presence is too explosive for him to survive. Hence he effects the explosion that closes the film, a suicidal act which literalizes the self-cancelling effects of embodying sexual and racial contradictions.

The racial coding of the bride as white victim works similarly to undermine previous interpretations, for it recasts what incipient subjectivity we might have identified in her – as monstrous, sexual nay-sayer – in racial terms. She seems clearly to be figured as 'white': her skin is very fair, she is dressed in a long white gown similar to those worn by both Mary Shelley and Elizabeth, and her physical gestures echo visually the repulsion felt by Elizabeth in both films' protorape scenes. Given this racial costuming, the bride's shrieks take on new meaning. Not simply a plea for female subjectivity, or a revelation of a homosocial dynamic, they metaphorically encode a rejection by the white woman of the Black man's sexual advances. That is, in questioning the coercive power of the white man – and the homosocial bonds that ratify it – the bride also defines and flees the heterosexuality of the Black man. In this context, moreover, the bride's death at the end of the film not only recalls but brings to fruition the sequence in the first *Frankenstein* film in which the monster's attack on Elizabeth herself is followed by the death of the little girl. For if Elizabeth herself survives, the fate of the monster's mate, like that of the little girl, more pointedly signals the underlying consequences for a white woman of being sullied – indeed, beneath the white dress, 'blackened' – by contact with the Black man: a degradation so great that it must lead to death.

A reading of *Bride of Frankenstein* through multiple historical frames, then, helps us to see that gender, sexuality, and race inextricably implicate one another in this film. Attention to the interdependent historical paradigms of race and gender relations shows that bonds between men in the film are located on two axes, sexual and racial, which contradict each other. Similarly, interracial rape here acts, as Smith has theorized, as a 'border case' that splits potential allegiances between race and gender (ibid., 272), a splitting that means that the film's model of female identity can gain its authority only through a racist assertion of whiteness. In their very interdependence, moreover, the film's narratives of power relations are indelibly marked by contradiction rather than closure. Even though Henry and Elizabeth survive and the monsters die at the end of *Bride of Frankenstein*, this ending hardly resolves the film's knot of contradictions. Rather, in a film in which death is the precondition for life, we might take the destruction of the monster and his mate as a sign that they – like the ideological fears they incarnate – will have been dismembered here only to be remembered elsewhere, reanimated in life and animated on screen.

[. . .]

Part Five

READING THE
KING VAMPIRE

Introduction to Part Five

■   Ken Gelder

LIKE *FRANKENSTEIN*, BRAM STOKER'S *Dracula* (1897) has also become a canonical text in recent years, attracting the kind of close critical attention usually devoted solely to works of high literature. This novel is now a 'classic', a foundational work of horror, continually re-energized by the readings it seems only too willing to accommodate. Like *Frankenstein* again, it has spawned hundreds of adaptations, rewrites, sequels and variations – beginning, it is generally agreed, with F.W. Murnau's silent German film, *Nosferatu* (1922), an 'unauthorized' version of Stoker's novel which set the agenda by deviating significantly from its source. At the same time, critical interest in *Dracula* has also established it as the definitive novel of the 1890s, speaking to just about all this decade's trends and concerns: the rise of the 'New Woman' (through Lucy and Mina), anxieties about Darwinian notions of human evolution, the proliferation of discourses of decay and 'degeneration' (see Pick: 1989), the impact of psychoanalysis, the advocacy of late imperialist values, the emergence of new technologies, the influence of eugenics, and so on. *Dracula* is seen as a vibrant, bustling, 'sensationalist' novel, almost bursting at the seams with issues and themes – some glaringly obvious, some needing to be teased out or unpacked by the diligent reader.

There has been particular interest amongst contemporary critics in the novel's treatment of sexuality and desire. The sex scenes in *Dracula* are striking indeed: Jonathan Harker's breathless seduction by three mysterious vampire women; the frantic transfusing of various men's blood into Lucy's ailing body, as well as the later 'phallic' staking of Lucy which produces her 'orgasmic' writhing; and, stranger still, the scene (a 'horrifyingly obscene moment' for Joan Copjec: see Chapter 4) which has Mina kneeling on the bed before Dracula and swallowing the blood which pours from an open wound in his chest. The sexuality of the vampire has been exploited in many of the later adaptations, of course: this often highly attractive monster may combine terror with an erotic awakening, drawing out latent inner desires. Dracula himself is coded as promiscuous, perverse, sexually fluid (heterosexual, yet homoerotic), insatiable, queer (see, for example, Craft: 1984) – all in the frame of a late Victorian novel.

Dracula thus seems to literalize internal (and hence 'unspeakable') desires. But he may also be seen only as an *external* threat. Stephen Arata's extract in this section, from a longer article reprinted in his book, *Fictions of Loss in the Victorian Fin de Siècle*, turns back to the 1890s to read *Dracula* as a 'narrative of reverse colonization'. Here, the usual imperialist journey out to the 'heart of darkness' is mirrored through the colonized Other's unexpected arrival in the heart of the colonizer's metropolis. Such a narrative has, of course, been wonderfully ripe for exploitation by late- or post-colonial horror texts, from Sir Arthur Conan Doyle's mummy stories to contemporary films such as Peter Jackson's *Braindead* (1992) or Peter Hyams' *The Relic* (1997). *Dracula's* 'heart of darkness' is Transylvania in Eastern Europe, a real place made fantastic by Stoker's novel. British Victorian travellers – and Jonathan Harker is one of them – had made occasional forays into Transylvania and its environs, seeing it as both 'picturesque' and racially volatile. A suitable distance is maintained, with the traveller refusing to allow his British national identity to 'dissolve' away into Otherness. But Dracula turns out to be an 'accomplished Occidentalist' who is able to walk through the streets of London unhindered. Jonathan Harker's glimpse of Otherness thus also provides him with a 'shock of recognition', an uncanny effect which results from seeing the Other make himself perfectly at home.

Before the nineteenth century, the vampire was found mostly in collections of folk tales, a localized figure who pretty much kept to the same spot. Picked up by the novel later on, however, the vampire began to circulate, moving through nations and across borders, a marauding, 'incorporeal' figure. Franco Moretti's important early reading of *Dracula*, from his book *Signs Taken for Wonders*, takes up this feature, drawing attention to descriptions already available in nineteenth century culture of the vampire as a 'metaphor'. He focuses on Karl Marx's famous account of capital as 'vampire-like', a circulating thing which gains its energy only by preying upon 'living labour'. But how can Stoker's Dracula be a metaphor for capital if he is also presented as a foreign threat? For Moretti, Dracula provides capital's bad image, a 'true monopolist, solitary and despotic'. I have noted elsewhere that in this respect he resembles the figure of the 'Jew' as it was for Marx – providing good reason to read Stoker's novel as anti-Semitic (Gelder: 1994, 20–3; see also Sue-Ellen Case, Chapter 16). To kill the vampire is to 'purify' capital, to make it more acceptable to British liberal-bourgeois interests, so earnestly represented by the Crew of Light. The novel thus serves a fairly straightforward ideological function for Moretti, working to secure the reader's 'assent' in this process through fear.

Moretti's extract also offers a psychoanalytical reading of *Dracula*, seeing the vampire as an example of 'the return of the repressed' – in fact, as an image of the primal mother, rather like Barbara Creed's 'monstrous-feminine'. These two accounts of Dracula, as a metaphor for monopoly capital and one's fear of the returning mother, are, as he admits, difficult to integrate into one 'harmonious' reading. The third extract in this section, by Jennifer Wicke, attempts to do exactly this, however, by drawing economic and sexual readings of the vampire together through the processes of 'consumption'. Wicke looks at the novel's entanglement with the newly invented processing technologies of mass culture: Harker's Kodak camera, Dr Seward's phonograph and its wax cylinders, Mina's Traveller's type-writer. Snippets from newspapers are scattered through the text; Mina collates and copies documents; Harker himself writes in shorthand. The novel seems colon-ized, or 'vampirized' as Wicke suggests, by 'mass mediation'; it brings the 'sexy act of vamping' and the 'prosaic labour on the typewriter' together. Mass culture is thus, as Andreas Huyssen (1986) put it, like a woman – to whom the vampire is inexorably drawn. But the later shift in the novel from Lucy to Mina turns consumption into something more productive, a form of 'knowledge'. Mina's hypnosis allows her to pinpoint Dracula's whereabouts accurately, like a radar, drawing her in turn towards him but only to bring about his destruction.

All the extracts in this section note the way *Dracula* sends the Gothic tumbling into the modern world. Wicke even sees it as 'the first great modern novel in British literature', using an ancient monster to speak to the emergent technologies of the information age. We have seen monstrosity and technology linked before; here, it seems to produce what Mark Seltzer has called 'a sort of *techno-primi-tivism*' (Seltzer: 1998, 81). Seltzer draws on Friedrich A. Kittler's important book, *Discourse Networks 1800/1900* (1990), which reads *Dracula* as a novel saturated with multimedia technologies. The new hero in this and other recent accounts is thus not Van Helsing or any member of the Crew of Light, but Mina, 'the central relay station of an immense information network' (Kittler: 1990, 354). From this point of view, *Dracula* may have its fatal vampire but it also unveils, as Wicke puts it, 'the more banal terrors of modern life'.

Chapter 12

FRANCO MORETTI

DIALECTIC OF FEAR
(extract)

Dracula

COUNT DRACULA IS AN ARISTOCRAT only in manner of speaking. Jonathan Harker – the London estate agent who stays in his castle, and whose diary opens Stoker's novel – observes with astonishment that Dracula lacks precisely what makes a man 'noble': servants. Dracula stoops to driving the carriage, cooking the meals, making the beds, cleaning the castle. The Count has read Adam Smith: he knows that servants are unproductive workers who diminish the income of the person who keeps them. Dracula also lacks the aristocrat's conspicuous consumption: he does not eat, he does not drink, he does not make love, he does not like showy clothes, he does not go to the theatre and he does not go hunting, he does not hold receptions and does not build stately homes. Not even his violence has pleasure as its goal. Dracula (unlike Vlad the Impaler, the historical Dracula, and all other vampires before him) does not *like* spilling blood: he *needs* blood. He sucks just as much as is necessary and never wastes a drop. His ultimate aim is not to destroy the lives of others according to whim, to waste them, but to *use* them. Dracula, in other words, is a saver, an ascetic, an upholder of the Protestant ethic. And in fact he has no body, or rather, he has no shadow. His body admittedly exists, but it is 'incorporeal' – 'sensibly supersensible' as Marx wrote of the commodity, 'impossible as a physical fact', as Mary Shelley defines the monster in the first lines of her preface [to *Frankenstein*]. In fact it is impossible, 'physically', to estrange a man from himself, to de-humanize him. But alienated labour, as a *social* relation, makes it possible. So too there really exists a social product which has no body, which has exchange-value but no use-value. This product, we know, is money. And when Harker explores the castle, he finds just one thing: 'a great heap of gold . . . – gold of all kinds, Roman, and British, and Austrian, and Hungarian, and Greek and Turkish money, covered with a film of dust, as though it had lain long in the ground.' The money that had been buried comes back to life, becomes capital and embarks on the conquest of the world: this and none other is the story of Dracula the vampire.

'Capital is dead labour which, vampire-like, lives only by sucking living labour, and lives the more, the more labour it sucks' (Marx: 1976a, 342). Marx's analogy unravels the vampire metaphor. As everyone knows, the vampire is dead and yet not dead: he is an Un-Dead, a 'dead' person who yet manages to live thanks to the blood he sucks from the living. *Their* strength becomes *his* strength. The *stronger* the vampire becomes, the *weaker* the living become: 'the capitalist gets rich, not, like the miser, in proportion to his personal labour and restricted consumption, but at the same rate as he squeezes out labour-power from others, and compels the worker to renounce all the enjoyments of life.' Like capital, Dracula is impelled towards a continuous growth, an unlimited expansion of his domain: accumulation is inherent in his nature. 'This', Harker exclaims, 'was the being I was helping to transfer to London, where perhaps for centuries to come, he might, amongst its teeming millions, satiate his lust for blood, and create a *new and ever widening* circle of semi-demons to batten on the helpless' (my italics). 'And so the circle goes on *ever widening*', Van Helsing says later on; and Seward describes Dracula as 'the father or furtherer of a *new* order of beings' (my italics). All Dracula's actions really have as their final goal the creation of this 'new order of beings' which finds its most fertile soil, logically enough, in England. And finally, just as the capitalist is 'capital personified' and must subordinate his private existence to the abstract and incessant movement of accumulation, so Dracula is not impelled by the *desire* for power but by the *curse* of power, by an obligation he cannot escape. 'When they (the Un-Dead) become such', Van Helsing explains, 'there comes with the change the curse of immortality; they cannot die, but must go on age after age adding new victims and multiplying the evils of the world.' It is remarked later of the vampire that he 'can do all these things, *yet he is not free*' (my italics). His curse compels him to make ever more victims, just as the capitalist is compelled to accumulate. His nature forces him to struggle to be unlimited, to subjugate *the whole of society*. For this reason, one cannot 'coexist' with the vampire. One must either succumb to him or kill him, thereby freeing the world of his presence and him of his curse. When the knife plunges into Dracula's heart, in the moment before his dissolution, 'there was in the face a look of peace, such as I would never have imagined might have rested there.' There flashes forth here the idea, to which we shall return, of the *purification* of capital.

If the vampire is a metaphor for capital, then Stoker's vampire, who is of 1897, must be the capital of 1897. The capital which, after lying 'buried' for twenty long years of recession, rises again to set out on the irreversible road of concentration and monopoly. And Dracula is a true monopolist: solitary and despotic, he will not brook competition. Like monopoly capital, his ambition is to subjugate the last vestiges of the liberal era and destroy all forms of economic independence. He no longer restricts himself to incorporating (in a literal sense) the physical and moral strength of his victims. He intends to make them his *for ever*. Hence the horror, for the bourgeois mind. One is bound to Dracula, as to the devil, for *life*, no longer 'for a fixed period', as the classic bourgeois contract stipulated with the intention of maintaining the freedom of the contracting parties. The vampire, like monopoly, destroys the hope that one's independence can one day be brought back. He threatens the idea of individual liberty. For this reason the nineteenth-century bourgeois is able to imagine monopoly only in the guise of Count Dracula, the aristocrat, the figure of the past, the relic of distant lands and dark ages. Because the nineteeth-century bourgeois believes in free trade, and he knows that in order to become established, free competition had to destroy the tyranny of feudal monopoly. For him, then, monopoly and free competition are irreconcilable concepts. Monopoly is the *past* of competition, the middle ages. He cannot believe it can be its *future*, that competition itself can *generate* monopoly in new forms. And yet 'modern monopoly is . . . the true synthesis . . . the negation of feudal monopoly insofar as it implies the system of competition, and the negation of competition insofar as it is monopoly' (Marx: 1976b, 195).

Dracula is thus at once the final product of the bourgeois century and its negation. In Stoker's novel only this second aspect – the negative and destructive one – appears. There are very good reasons for this. In Britain at the end of the nineteenth century, monopolistic concentration was far less developed (for various economic and political reasons) than in the other advanced capitalist societies. Monopoly could thus be perceived as something extraneous to British history: as a *foreign threat*. This is why Dracula is not British, while his antagonists (with one exception, as we shall see, and with the addition of Van Helsing, born in that other classic homeland of free trade, Holland) are British through and through. Nationalism – the defence to the death of British civilization – has a central role in *Dracula*. The idea of the nation is central because it is collective: it coordinates individual energies and enables them to resist the threat. For while Dracula threatens the freedom of the individual, the latter alone lacks the power to resist or defeat him. Indeed the followers of pure economic individualism, those who pursue their own profit, are, without knowing it, the vampire's best allies. Individualism is not the weapon with which Dracula can be beaten. Other things are needed – in effect two: money and religion. These are considered as a single whole, which must not be separated: in other words, money at the service of religion and vice versa. The money of Dracula's enemies is money that *refuses to become capital*, that wants not to obey the profane economic laws of capitalism but to be used *to do good*. Towards the end of the novel, Mina Harker thinks of her friends' financial commitment: 'it made me think of the wonderful power of money! What can it not do when it is properly applied; and what might it do when basely used!' This is the point: money should be used according to justice. Money must not have its end *in itself*, in its continuous accumulation. It must have, rather, a *moral*, anti-economic end to the point where colossal expenditures and losses can be calmly accepted. This idea of money is, for the capitalist, something inadmissable. But it is also the great ideological lie of Victorian capitalism, a capitalism which is ashamed of itself and which hides factories and stations beneath cumbrous Gothic superstructures; which prolongs and extols aristocratic models of life; which exalts the holiness of the family as the latter begins secretly to break up. Dracula's enemies are precisely the exponents of *this* capitalism. They are the militant version of Dickens's benefactors. They find their fulfilment in religious superstition, whereas the vampire is paralysed by it. And yet the crucifixes, holy wafers, garlic, magic flowers, and so on, are not important for their *intrinsic* religious meaning but for a subtler reason. Their true function consists in setting impassable limits to the vampire's activity. They prevent him from entering this or that house, conquering this or that person, carrying out this or that metamorphosis. But setting limits to the vampire-capital means attacking his very raison d'être: he must by his nature be able to expand without limit, to destroy every restraint upon his action. Religious superstition imposes the same limits on Dracula that Victorian capitalism declares itself to accept spontaneously. But Dracula — who is capital that is not ashamed of itself, true to its own nature, an end in itself — cannot survive in these conditions. And so this symbol of a cruel historical development falls victim to a handful of whited sepulchres, a bunch of fanatics who want to arrest the course of history. It is they who are the relics of the dark ages.

At the end of *Dracula* the vampire's defeat is complete. Dracula and his lovers are destroyed, Mina Harker is saved at the last moment. Only one cloud darkens the happy ending. In killing Dracula, Quincy P. Morris, the American who has been helping his British friends to save their nation, dies too, almost by accident. The occurrence seems inexplicable, extraneous to the logic of the narrative, yet it fits perfectly into Stoker's sociological design. The American, Morris, *must* die, because Morris is a vampire. From his first appearance he is shrouded in mystery (a friendly sort of mystery, it is true — but isn't Count Dracula himself likeable, at the beginning?). 'He is such a nice fellow, an American from Texas, and he looks so young and so fresh [he *looks*: like Dracula, who looks it but isn't] that it seems almost impossible that he has been to so many places and has had such adventures.' What places? What adventures? Where does all his money come from? What does Mr Morris do? Where does he live? Nobody knows any of this. But nobody suspects. Nobody suspects even when Lucy dies — and then turns into a vampire — immediately after receiving a blood transfusion from Morris. Nobody suspects when Morris, shortly afterwards, tells the story of his mare, sucked dry of blood in the Pampas (like Dracula, Morris has been round the world) by 'one of those big bats that they call vampires'. It is the first time that the name 'vampire' is mentioned in the novel: but there is no reaction. And there is no reaction a few lines further on when Morris, 'coming close to me, . . . spoke in a fierce half-whisper: "What took it [the blood] out?"' But Dr Seward shakes his head; he hasn't the slightest idea. And Morris, reassured, promises to help. Nobody, finally, suspects when, in the course of the meeting to plan the vampire hunt, Morris leaves the room to take a shot — missing, naturally — at the big bat on the window-ledge listening to the preparations; or when, after Dracula bursts into the household, Morris hides among the trees, the only effect of which is that he loses sight of Dracula and invites the others to call off the hunt for the night. This is pretty well all Morris does in *Dracula*. He would be a totally superfluous character if, unlike the others, he were not characterized by this mysterious connivance with the world of the vampires. So long as things go well for Dracula, Morris acts like an accomplice. As soon as there is a reversal of fortunes, he turns into his staunchest enemy. Morris enters into competition with Dracula; he would like to replace him in the conquest of the Old World. He does not succeed in the novel but he will succeed, in 'real' history, a few years afterwards.

While it is interesting to understand that Morris is connected with the vampires — because America will end up by subjugating Britain in reality and Britain is, albeit unconsciously, afraid of it – the decisive thing is to understand why Stoker does *not* portray him as a vampire. The answer lies in the bourgeois conception of monopoly described earlier. For Stoker, monopoly *must* be feudal, oriental, tyrannical. It cannot be the product of that very society he wants to defend. And Morris, naturally, is by contrast a product of Western civilization, just as America is a rib of Britain and American capitalism a consequence of British capitalism. To make Morris a vampire would mean accusing capitalism directly: or rather accusing Britain, admitting that it is Britain herself that has given birth to the monster. This cannot be. For the good of Britain, then, Morris must be sacrificed. But Britain must be kept out of a crime whose legitimacy she cannot recognize. He will be killed by the chance knife-thrust of a gypsy (whom the British will allow to escape unpunished). And at the moment when Morris dies, and the threat disappears, old England grants its blessing to this excessively pushy and unscrupulous financier, and raises him to the dignity of a Bengal Lancer: 'And, to our bitter grief, with a smile and in silence, he died, a gallant gentleman.' (the sentence significantly abounds in the clichés of heroic-imperial English literature). These, it should be noted, are the *last* words of the novel, whose true ending does not lie – as is clear by now – in the death of the Romanian count, but in the killing of the American financier.

One of the most striking aspects of *Dracula* – as of *Frankenstein* before it – is its system of narrative senders. To begin with, there is the fact that in this network of letters, diaries, notes, telegrams, notices, phonograph recordings and articles, the narrative function proper, namely the description and ordering of events, is reserved for the British alone. We never have access to Van Helsing's point of view, or to Morris's, and still less to Dracula's. The string of events exists only in the form and with the meaning stamped upon it by British Victorian culture. It is those cultural categories, those moral values, those forms of expression that are endangered by the vampire: it is those same categories, forms and values that reassert themselves and emerge triumphant. It is a victory of convention over exception, of the present over the possible future, of standard British English over any kind of linguistic transgression. In *Dracula* we have, transparently, the perfect and immutable English of the narrators on the one hand, and Morris's American 'dialect', Dracula's schoolbook English and Van Helsing's bloomers on the other. As Dracula is a danger because he constitutes an unforeseen variation from the British cultural code, so the maximum threat on the plane of content coincides with the maximum inefficiency and dislocation of the English language. Half way through the novel, when Dracula seems to be in control of the situation, the frequency of Van Helsing's speeches increases enormously, and his perverse English dominates the stage. It becomes dominant because although the English language possesses the word 'vampire', it is unable to ascribe a meaning to it, in the same way that British society considers 'capitalist monopoly' a meaningless expression. Van Helsing has to explain, in his approximate and mangled English, what a vampire is. Only then, when these notions have been translated into the linguistic and cultural code of the English, and the code has been reorganized and reinforced, can the narrative return to its previous fluidity, the hunt begin and victory appear secure. It is entirely logical that the last sentence should be, as we saw, a veritable procession of literary English.

In *Dracula* there is no omniscient narrator, only individual and mutually separate points of view. The first-person account is a clear expression of the desire to keep hold of one's individuality, which the vampire threatens to subjugate. Yet so long as the conflict is one between human 'individualism' and vampirical 'totalization', things do not go at all well for the humans. Just as a system of perfect competition cannot do other than give way to monopoly, so a handful of isolated individuals cannot oppose the concentrated force of the vampire. It is a problem we have already witnessed on the plane of content: here it re-emerges on the plane of narrative forms. The individuality of the narration must be preserved and at the same time its negative aspect – the doubt, impotence, ignorance and even mutual distrust and hostility of the protagonists – must be eliminated. Stoker's solution is brilliant. It is to collate, to make a systematic integration of the different points of view. In the second half of *Dracula*, that of the hunt (which begins, it should be noted, only *after* the collation), it is more accurate to speak of a 'collective' narrator than of different narrators. There are no longer, as there were at the beginning, *different* versions of a single episode, a procedure which expressed the uncertainty and error of the individual account. The narrative now expresses the *general* point of view, the official version of events. Even the style loses its initial idiosyncrasies, be they professional or individual, and is amalgamated into Standard British English. This collation is, in other words, the Victorian compromise in the field of narrative technique. It unifies the different interests and cultural paradigms of the dominant class (law, commerce, the land, science) under the banner of the common good. It restores the narrative equilibrium, giving this dark episode a form and a meaning which are finally clear, communicable and universal.

The return of the repressed

A sociological analysis of *Frankenstein* and *Dracula* reveals that one of the institutions most threatened by the monsters is the family. Yet this fear cannot be explained wholly in historical and economic terms. On the contrary, it is very likely that its deepest root is to be found elsewhere: in the eros, above all in sex. 'Dracula', David Pirie has written, ' . . . can be seen as the great submerged force of Victorian libido breaking out to punish the repressive society which had imprisoned it; one of the most appalling things Dracula does to the matronly women of his Victorian enemies (in the novel as in the film) is to make them sensual' (Pirie: 1973, 84). It is true. For confirmation one only has to reread the episode of Lucy. Lucy is the only protagonist who falls victim to Dracula. She is punished, because she is the only one who shows some kind of *desire*. Stoker is inflexible on this point: all the other characters are immune to the temptations of the flesh, or capable of rigorous sublimations. Van Helsing, Morris, Seward and Holmwood are all single. Mina and Jonathan get married in hospital, when Jonathan is in a state of prostration and impotence; and they marry in order to mend, to forget the terrible experience (which was also sexual) undergone by Jonathan in Transylvania: 'Share my ignorance' is what he asks of his wife. Not so Lucy, who awaits her wedding day with impatience. It is on this restlessness – on her 'somnambulism'

– that Dracula exerts leverage to win her. And the more he takes possession of Lucy, the more he brings out her sexual side. A few moments before her death, 'She opened her eyes, which were now dull and hard at once, and said in a soft voluptuous voice, such as I had never heard from her lips: . . .'. And Lucy as a 'vampire' is even more seductive: 'The sweetness was turned to adamantine, heartless cruelty, and the purity to voluptuous wantonness . . . the face became wreathed with a voluptuous smile . . . she advanced to him with outstretched arms and a wanton smile . . . and with a langorous, voluptuous grace, said: – "Come to me, Arthur. Leave these others and come to me. My arms are hungry for you. Come, and we can rest together. Come, my husband, come!"' The seduction is about to work, but Van Helsing breaks its spell. They proceed to Lucy's execution. Lucy dies in a very unusual way: in the throes of what, to the 'public' mind of the Victorians, must have seemed like an orgasm: 'The Thing in the coffin writhed; and a hideous, blood-curdling screech came from the opened red lips. The body shook and quivered and twisted in wild contortions; the sharp white teeth champed together till the lips were cut and the mouth was smeared with a crimson foam.' Surrounded by his friends who goad him on with their cries, Arthur Holmwood Lord Godalming purges the world of this fearful Thing; not without deriving, in distorted but transparent forms, enormous sexual satisfaction: 'He looked like a figure of Thor as his untrembling arm rose and fell, driving deeper and deeper the mercy-bearing stake, whilst the blood from the pierced heart welled and spurted up from around it.'

Dracula, then, liberates and exalts sexual desire. And this desire *attracts* but – at the same time – frightens. Lucy is beautiful, but dangerous. Fear and attraction are one and the same: and not just in Stoker. Much of nineteenth-century bourgeois high culture had already treated eros and sex as *ambivalent* phenomena. Their rhetorical figure is the oxymoron, the contradiction in terms, through which Baudelaire sings the ambiguity of amorous relations. Among the condemned poems of *Les Fleurs du Mal* (1857) – a title which is itself an oxymoron – is 'Les métamorphoses du vampire', where the irresistible female seducer is described 'writhing like a snake over charcoal.' And Stendhal noted in the margin of the first page of *De l'Amour* (1822): 'I undertake to trace with a mathematical precision and (if I can) truth, the history of the illness called *love*.' Love is an illness: it entails the renunciation of man's *individuality* and *reason*. For Stendhal, the devotee of enlightenment, this means denying one's very reason for existing: love becomes a *mortal* danger, and only a *greater* danger (Dracula!) can cure the person who falls victim to it: 'The leap from Leucates was a fine image in antiquity. In fact, the remedy for love is almost impossible. It requires not only that danger which sharply recalls a man's attention to his own preservation; it also requires – something far more difficult – the continuity of an enticing danger' (Stendhal: 1957, 118). *An enticing danger*, just as that of love is a *dangerous enticement*: fear and desire incessantly overturn into one another. They are indivisible. We find this confirmed in Sade, in Keats's Lamia, in Poe's Ligeia, in Baudelaire's women, in Hoffmann's woman vampire. Why is this?

Vampirism is an excellent example of the identity of desire and fear: let us therefore put it at the centre of the analysis. And let us take the psychoanalytic interpretation of this phenomenon, advanced for example by Marie Bonaparte in her study of Poe. Commenting on Baudelaire's remark that all Poe's women are 'strikingly delineated as though by an adorer', Marie Bonaparte adds: 'An adorer . . . who dare not approach the object of his adoration, since he feels it surrounded by some fearful, dangerous mystery' (Bonaparte: 1949, 209–10). This mystery is none other than vampirism:

> the danger of sexuality, the punishment that threatens all who yield, is shown, as in *Berenice*, by the manner in which Egaeus is obsessed by her teeth. And indeed, in psychoanalysis, many cases of male impotence reveal, though more or less buried in the unconscious – strange as it may seem to many a reader – the notion of the female vagina being furnished with teeth, and thus a source of danger in being able to bite and castrate . . . Mouth and vagina are equated in the unconscious and, when Egaeus yields to the morbid impulse to draw Berenice's teeth, he yields both to the yearning for the mother's organ and to be revenged upon it, since the dangers that hedge it about make him sexually avoid all women as too menacing. His act is therefore a sort of retributive castration inflicted on the mother whom he loves, and yet hates, because obdurate to his sex-love for her in infancy. . . . This concept of the *vagina dentata* and its consequent menace is, however, also a displacement (in this case downwards) of a factor with roots deep in infantile experience. We know that babes which, while toothless, are content to suck the breast, no sooner cut their first teeth than they use them to bite the same breast. This, in each of us, is the first manifestation of the aggressive instinct, . . . later, when the sense of what 'one should not do' has been instilled by ever severer and more numerous moral injunctions . . . the memory, or rather the phantasy of biting the mother's breast must have become charged, in the unconscious, with past feelings of wickedness. And the child, having learnt by experience what is meant by the law of retaliation when he infringes the code . . . begins, in his turn, to fear that the bites he wished to give his mother will be visited on him: namely, retaliation for his 'cannibalism'.
>
> (ibid., 218–19)

This passage identifies with precision the *ambivalent* root, interweaving hate and love, that underlies vampirism. An analogous ambivalence had already been described by Freud [in *Totem* and *Taboo*, 1913] in relation to the taboo on the dead (and the vampire is, as we know, also a dead person who comes back to life to destroy those who remain): 'this hostility, distressingly felt in the unconscious as satisfaction over the death . . . [is displaced] on to the object of the hostility, on to the dead themselves. Once again . . . we find that the taboo has grown up on the basis of an ambivalent emotional attitude. The taboo upon the dead arises, like the others, from the contrast between conscious pain and unconscious satisfaction over the death that has occurred. Since such is the origin of the ghost's resentment, it follows naturally that the survivors who have the most to fear will be those who were formerly its nearest and dearest' (Freud: 1955a, 61).

Freud's text leaves no doubt: the ambivalence exists *within the psyche of the person suffering from the fear*. In order to heal this state of tension one is forced to *repress*, unconsciously, one of the two affective states in conflict, the one that is socially more illicit. From the repression arises fear: 'every affect belonging to an emotional impulse, whatever its kind, is transformed, if it is repressed, into anxiety'. (Freud, 1955b, 241). And fear breaks out when – for whatever reason – this repressed impulse returns and thrusts itself upon the mind: 'an uncanny experience occurs either when infantile complexes which have been repressed are once more revived by some impression, or when primitive beliefs which have been surmounted seem once again to be confirmed' (ibid., 249). Fear, in other words, coincides with the 'return of the repressed'. And this brings us perhaps to the heart of the matter.

The literature of terror is studded with passages where the protagonists brush against the awareness – described by Freud – that the perturbing element is *within them*: that it is they themselves that produce the monsters they fear. Their first fear is – inevitably – that of *going mad*. [. . .] 'God preserve my sanity . . . there is but one thing to hope for: that I may not go mad, if, indeed, I be not mad already' (*Dracula*, Harker's words). '[Dr Seward] says that I afford him a curious psychological study' (*Dracula*, Lucy). 'I have come to the conclusion that it must be something mental' (*Dracula*, Seward, who is also the director of a mental hospital). [. . .] In these novels, reality tends to work according to the laws that govern dreams – 'I wasn't dreaming', 'as in a dream', 'as if I had gone through a long nightmare'. This is the return of the repressed. But *how* does it return? Not as madness, or only marginally so. The lesson these books wish to impart is that one need not be afraid of going mad; that is one need not fear one's own repressions, the splitting of one's own psyche. No, one should be afraid of the *monster*, of something *material*, something *external*: '"Dr Van Helsing, are you mad?" . . . "Would I were!" he said. "Madness were easy to bear compared with truth like this."' *Would I were*: this is the key. Madness is nothing in comparison with the vampire. Madness does not present a problem. Or rather: madness, in itself, *does not exist*: it is the vampire, the monster, the potion that creates it. *Dracula*, written in the same year that saw Freud begin his self-analysis, is a refined attempt by the nineteenth-century mind not to recognize itself. This is symbolized by the character who – already in the grip of fear – finds himself by chance in front of a mirror. He looks at it and jumps: in the mirror is a reflection of his face. Bu the reader's attention is immediately distracted: the fear does not come from his having seen his *own* image, but from the fact that the *vampire* is not reflected in the mirror. Finding himself face to face with the simple, terrible truth, the author – and with him the character and the reader – draws back in horror.

The repressed returns, then, but disguised as a monster. For a psychoanalytic study, the main fact is precisely this metamorphosis. As Francesco Orlando has remarked of his analysis of Racine's *Phèdre* (1677), 'the relationship between the unconscious and literature was not postulated according to the presence of contents, whatever their nature, in the literary work . . . perverse desire could not have been acceptable as content in the literary work without the latter's also accepting *the formal model capable of filtering it*' (Orlando: 1978, 138, 140; my italics). This formal model is the monster metaphor, the vampire metaphor. It 'filters', makes bearable to the conscious mind those desires and fears which the latter has judged to be unacceptable and has thus been forced to repress, and whose existence it consequently cannot recognize. The literary formalization, the rhetorical figure, therefore has a double function: it *expresses* the unconscious content and at the same time *hides* it. Literature always contains *both* these functions. Taking away one or the other would mean eliminating either the problem of the unconscious (by asserting that everything in literature is transparent and manifest) or the problem of literary communication (by asserting that literature serves *only* to hide certain contents). Yet while these two functions are always present in the literary metaphor, the relationship between them can nevertheless change. One can stand out more than the other and win a dominant position within the overall signification of the work. These observations have a direct bearing on our argument, because the metaphor of the vampire is a splendid example of how the equilibrium of literary functions can vary. The problem can be posed thus: what is the sex – in literature, naturally, not in reality – of vampires? Vampires, unlike angels, do have sex. But it changes. In one set of works (Poe, Hoffmann, Baudelaire: 'elite' culture) they are women. In another (Polidori, Stoker, the cinema: 'mass' culture) they are men. The metamorphosis is by no means accidental. At the root of vampirism, as we have seen, lies an ambivalent impulse of the child towards its mother. To present the vampire as a *woman* therefore means to make relatively little distortion of the unconscious content. The literary figure still retains the essential element – the sex – of that which is at the source of the perturbation. The defences that literature puts up to protect the conscious mind are relatively elastic: D. H. Lawrence (as Baudelaire, implicitly, before him) passes with ease from the vampire theme back to Poe's perverse erotic desires (see Lawrence: 1924, chapter 6). But if the vampire becomes a man, the unconscious source of the perturbation is hidden by a further layer of signifieds. The link becomes more tenuous. The conscious mind can rest easy: all that remains of the original fear is a word, 'Dracula': that splendid and inexplicable feminine name. The metamorphosis, in other words, serves to protect the conscious mind, or more precisely to keep it in a state of greater unawareness. The vampire is transformed into a man by mass culture, which has to promote spontaneous certainties and cannot let itself plumb the unconscious too deeply. Yet at the same time and for precisely this reason, the repressed content, which has remained unconscious, produces an irresistible fear. Spurious certainties and terror support each other.

The strategy of terror

Marxist analysis and psychoanalytic analysis have permitted us to isolate two prominent groups of signifieds which come together in the literature of terror and which render it, so to speak, necessary. They are, clearly, different signifieds, and it is hard to unite them harmoniously. I do not propose here to reconstruct the many missing links that might connect socio-economic structures and sexual-psychological structures in a single conceptual chain. Nor can I say whether this undertaking – attempted many times and in many different ways – is really possible: whether, that is, it is permissible to 'integrate' Marxism and psychoanalysis into a much broader and much more solid science of modern society. It is a highly complicated scientific problem, and I do not intend to broach its general aspects. I would merely like to explain the two reasons that – in this specific case – persuaded me to use two such different methodologies. The first is rather obvious. The central characters of this literature – the monster [in *Frankenstein*], the vampire – are *metaphors*, rhetorical figures built on the analogy between *different semantic fields*. Wishing to incarnate Fear as such, they must of necessity combine fears *that have different causes*: economic, ideological, psychical, sexual (and others should be added, beginning with religious fear). This fact seems to me to make it possible, if not obligatory, to use different tools in order to reconstruct the multiform roots of the terrorizing metaphor. But the monster and the vampire are metaphors for another reason too. Not only in order to synthesize phenomena of different natures, but also to *transform them*: to change their form, and with it their meaning. In Dracula there is monopoly capital and the fear of the mother: but these meanings are *subordinated* to the literal presence of the murderous count. They can be expressed only if they are hidden (or at least transformed) by his black cloak. Only in this way can the social consciousness admit its own fears without laying itself open to stigma. Marxism and psychoanalysis thus converge in defining the function of this literature: to take up within itself determinate fears in order to present them *in a form different from their real one*: to transform them into *other* fears, so that readers do not have to face up to what might really frighten them. It is a 'negative' function: it distorts reality. It is a work of 'mystification'. But it is also a work of 'production'. The more these great symbols of mass culture depart from reality the more, of necessity, they must expand and enrich the structures of false consciousness: which is nothing other than the dominant culture. They are not confined to distortion and falsification: they form, affirm, convince. And this process is automatic and self-propelling. Mary Shelley and Bram Stoker do not have the slightest intention of 'mystifying' reality: they interpret and express it in a spontaneously mendacious manner. This becomes clearer if we go back once again to the fact that monsters are metaphors. Now generally, in literature, metaphors are constructed (by the author) and perceived (by the reader) precisely as metaphors. But in the literature of terror this rule no longer applies. The metaphor is no longer a metaphor: it is a character as real as the others. 'The supernatural', Todorov has written, 'often appears because we take a figurative sense literally' (Todorov: 1975, 76–7). Taking the figurative sense literally means considering the metaphor as an *element of reality*. It means, in other words, that a particular intellectual construction – the metaphor and the ideology expressed within it – really has become a 'material force', an independent entity, that escapes the rational control of its user. The intellectual no longer builds the cultural universe; rather, this universe speaks through the intellectual's mouth. After all, this is a familiar story: it is the story of Dr Frankenstein. In Mary Shelley's novel, the monster, the metaphor, still appears, at least in part, as something constructed, as a product. The monster, she warns us, is something 'impossible as a physical fact': it is something metaphorical. Yet the monster *lives*. Frankenstein's first moment of terror arises precisely in the face of this fact: a metaphor gets up and walks. Once this has happened, he knows that he will never be able to regain control of it. From now on, the metaphor of the monster will lead an autonomous existence: it will no longer be a product, a consequence, but the very origin of the literature of terror. By the time of *Dracula* – which carries the logic of this literature to its farthest consequences – the vampire has existed since time immemorial, uncreated and inexplicable.

There is another point on which the works of Shelley and Stoker diverge radically from one another: the *effect* they mean to produce on the reader. The difference, to paraphrase Benjamin, can be put like this: a description of fear and a frightening description are by no means the same thing. *Frankenstein* [. . .] does not want to *scare* readers, but to *convince* them. It appeals to their reason. It wants to make them reflect on a number of important problems (the development of science, the ethic of the family, respect for tradition) and agree – rationally – that these are threatened by powerful and hidden forces. In other words it wants to get the readers' assent to the 'philosophical' arguments expounded in black and white by the author in the course of the narration. Fear is made subordinate to this design: it is one of the means used to convince, but not the only one, nor the main one. The person who is frightened is not the *reader*, but the *protagonist*. The fear is resolved within the text, without penetrating the text's relationship with its addressee. Mary Shelley uses two stylistic expedients to achieve this effect. She fixes the narrative time in *the past*: and the past attenuates every fear, because the intervening time enables one not to remain a prisoner of events. Chance is replaced by order, shock by reflection, doubt by certainty – all the more completely in that (the second expedient) the monster has nothing *unknown* about him: we watch Frankenstein assemble him piece by piece, and we know from the start what characteristics he will have. He is threatening because he is alive and because he is big, not because he is beyond rational comprehension. For fear to arise, reason must be made insecure. As Barthes puts it: '"suspense" grips you in the "mind", not in the "guts"' (Barthes: 1977, 119).

The narrative structure of *Dracula*, the real masterpiece of the literature of terror, is different. Here the narrative time is always the present, and the narrative order – always paratactic – never establishes causal connections. Like the narrators, the readers have only clues: they see the effects, but do not know the causes. It is precisely this situation that generates suspense. And this, in its turn, reinforces the readers' identification with the story being narrated. They are dragged forcibly *into* the text; the characters' fear is also theirs. Between text and reader there no longer exists that distance which in *Frankenstein* stimulated reflection. Stoker does not want a thinking reader, but a frightened one. Of course, fear is not an end in itself: it is a means to obtain consent to the ideological values we have examined. But this time, fear is the *only* means. In other words the conviction is no longer in the least rational: it is just as unconscious as the terror that produces it. And thus, while professing to save a reason threatened by hidden forces, the literature of terror merely enslaves it more securely. The restoration of a logical order coincides with unconscious and irrational adherence to a system of values beyond dispute. Professing to save the individual, it in fact annuls him. It presents society – whether the feudal idyll of *Frankenstein* or the Victorian England of *Dracula* – as a great corporation: whoever breaks its bonds is done for. To think for oneself, to follow one's own interests: these are the real dangers that this literature wants to exorcise. Illiberal in a deep sense, it mirrors and promotes the desire for an integrated society, a capitalism that manages to be 'organic'. This is the literature of *dialectical* relations, in which the opposites, instead of separating and entering into conflict, exist in function of one another, reinforce one another. Such, for Marx, is the relation between capital and wage labour. Such, for Freud, is the relation between super-ego and unconscious. [. . .] Such is the relationship that binds Frankenstein to the monster and Lucy to Dracula. Such, finally, is the bond between the reader and the literature of terror. The more a work frightens, the more it edifies. The more it humiliates, the more it uplifts. The more it hides, the more it gives the illusion of revealing. It is a fear one *needs*: the price one pays for coming contentedly to terms with a social body based on irrationality and menace. Who says it is escapist?

Chapter 13

STEPHEN D. ARATA

THE OCCIDENTAL TOURIST

Dracula and the anxiety of reverse colonization

(extract)

Joseph Conrad, 'Turgenev' (1917):

Fashions in monsters do change.

(Conrad: 1921, 62)

BRAM STOKER'S *DRACULA* participates in that 'modernizing' of Gothic which occurs at the close of the nineteenth century. Like Stevenson's *Dr. Jekyll and Mr. Hyde* (1886) and Wilde's *Picture of Dorian Gray* (1891), Stoker's novel achieves its effects by bringing the terror of the Gothic home. While Gothic novelists had traditionally displaced their stories in time or locale, these later writers root their action firmly in the modern world. Yet critics have until recently ignored the historical context in which these works were written and originally read. Most notably, criticism has persistently undervalued *Dracula*'s extensive and highly visible contacts with a series of cultural issues, particularly those involving race, specific to the 1890s. This neglect has in part resulted from the various psycho-analytic approaches taken by most critics of Gothic. While such approaches have greatly enriched our understanding of *Dracula*, and while nothing in psychoanalytic critical theory precludes a 'historicist' reading of literary texts, that theory has in practice been used almost exclusively to demonstrate, as Stoker's most recent critic puts it, that *Dracula* is a 'representation of fears that are more universal than a specific focus on the Victorian background would allow' (Stevenson: 1988, 139–49). Yet the novel's very attachment to the 'Victorian background' – what *The Spectator* [on 31 July] 1897 called its 'up-to-dateness' – is a primary source of Stoker's continuing power. Late-Victorian Gothic in general, and *Dracula* in particular, continually calls our attention to the cultural context surrounding and informing the text, and insists that we take that context into account.

In the case of *Dracula*, the context includes the decline of Britain as a world power at the close of the nineteenth century; or rather, the way the perception of that decline was articulated by contemporary writers. *Dracula* appeared in a

Jubilee year, but one marked by considerably more introspection and less self-congratulation than the celebration of a decade earlier. The decay of British global influence, the loss of overseas markets for British goods, the economic and political rise of Germany and the United States, the increasing unrest in British colonies and possessions, the growing domestic uneasiness over the morality of imperialism – all combined to erode Victorian confidence in the inevitability of British progress and hegemony. Late-Victorian fiction in particular is saturated with the sense that the entire nation – as a race of people, as a political and imperial force, as a social and cultural power – was in irretrievable decline. What I will be examining is how that perception is transformed into narrative, into stories which the culture tells itself not only to articulate and account for its troubles, but also to defend against and even to assuage the anxiety attendant upon cultural decay.

Dracula enacts the period's most important and pervasive narrative of decline, a narrative of reverse colonization. Versions of this story recur with remarkable frequency in both fiction and nonfiction texts throughout the last decades of the century. In whatever guise, this narrative expresses both fear and guilt. The fear is that what has been represented as the 'civilized' world is on the point of being colonized by 'primitive' forces. These forces can originate outside the civilized world (in Rider Haggard's *She* [1887], Queen Ayesha plans to sack London and depose Queen Victoria) or they can inhere in the civilized itself (as in Kurtz's emblematic heart of darkness). Fantasies of reverse colonization are particularly prevalent in late-Victorian popular fiction. They occur not just in Haggard's novels, but in Rudyard Kipling's early fiction ('The Mark of the Beast,' 'At the End of the Passage,' *The Light that Failed* [1891]), in Conan Doyle's Sherlock Holmes stories (*The Sign of Four* [1890], 'The Crooked Man' [1893]), in H. G. Wells's science fiction tales (*The Time Machine* [1895], *The War of the Worlds* [1898]), and in many of the numerous adventure novels of G. A. Hope, Henry S. Merriman, and John Buchan. In each case, a terrifying reversal has occurred: the colonizer finds himself in the position of the colonized, the exploiter becomes exploited, the victimizer victimized. Such fears are linked to a perceived decline – racial, moral, spiritual – which makes the nation vulnerable to attack from more vigorous, 'primitive' peoples.

But fantasies of reverse colonization are more than products of geopolitical fears. They are also responses to cultural guilt. In the marauding, invasive Other, British culture sees its own imperial practices mirrored back in monstrous forms. H. G. Wells located the germ of his *War of the Worlds* in a discussion with his brother Frank over the extermination of the indigenous Tasmanian population under British rule (see Bergonzi: 1961, 124). Reverse colonization narratives thus contain the potential for powerful critiques of imperialist ideologies, even if that potential usually remains unrealized. As fantasies, these narratives provide an opportunity to atone for imperial sins, since reverse colonization is often represented as deserved punishment.

Fantasies of reverse colonization sprang from the same font of cultural anxiety that produced the innumerable 'invasion scare' and 'dynamite' novels of the 1880s and '90s. *The Invasion of England*, Sir W. F. Butler's title for his 1892 novel, describes the subject matter, overt or displaced, of hundreds of late-Victorian fictions, all of them concerned with the potential overthrow of the nation by

outsiders. There are distinctions between these subgenres and the reverse colonization narratives I am discussing, however. Invasion-scare novels focus on the
threat posed to Britain by other industrial nations, particularly Germany, France,
and the United States. As I. F. Clarke demonstrates, changes in international power
relationships were mirrored in these novels, as different foreign powers were in
turn perceived as the most likely invader (Clarke: 1966, 107–61). Dynamite novels,
with their emphasis on anarchist or nihilist activities, originated partly in the
Victorian fascination with the 'criminal element,' especially as it was thought to
exist among the growing urban underclass. These novels articulate a middle-class
fear both of foreign revolutionaries (like the mysterious Hoffendahl of Henry
James's *The Princess Casamassima* [1886]) and of an industrial underclass that was
itself becoming increasingly politicized.

By contrast, reverse colonization narratives are obsessed with the spectacle of
the primitive and the atavistic. The 'savagery' of Haggard's Amahaggers and Wells's
Morlocks both repels and captivates; their proximity to elemental instincts and
energies, energies seen as dissipated by modern life, makes them dangerous but
also deeply attractive. Patrick Brantlinger has linked this interest in the primitive
to the late-Victorian fascination with the occult and the paranormal, and by extension to the Gothic. The primitive and the occultist alike operated beyond or beneath
the threshold of the 'civilized' rational mind, tapping into primal energies and
unconscious resources as well as into deep-rooted anxieties and fears. Brantlinger
identifies a body of fiction he terms 'imperial Gothic' in which the conjunction of
imperialist ideology, primitivism, and occultism produces narratives that are at
once self-divided and deeply 'symptomatic of the anxieties that attended the climax
of the British Empire.' The 'atavistic descents into the primitive' characteristic of
imperial Gothic 'seem often to be allegories of the larger regressive movement
of civilization' and of the ease with which it could be overcome by the forces of
barbarism (Brantlinger: 1988, 228–79). What Brantlinger finally shows is how,
in late-Victorian Britain, political and cultural concerns about empire become goth-
icized. The novel of empire and the adventure story especially become saturated
with Gothic motifs: Kipling's 'The Phantom Rickshaw' and 'At the End of the
Passage,' Conan Doyle's 'The Brown Hand,' Edgar Wallace's *Sanders of the River*
(1911), and Haggard's *She* are representative in this respect. Unlike dynamite or
invasion-scare narratives, which generally aim at a documentary-like realism, turn-
of-the-century fictions involving the empire often inhabit the regions of romance
and the supernatural.

A concern with questions of empire and colonization can be found in nearly
all of Stoker's fiction. His quite extensive body of work shows how imperial issues
can permeate and inform disparate types of fiction. Stoker's oeuvre apart from
Dracula can be roughly divided into two categories in its handling of imperial
themes. First, there are works such as 'Under the Sunset' (1882), *The Snake's Pass*
(1890), *The Mystery of the Sea* (1902), and *The Man* (1905) in which narratives of
invasion and colonization, while not central to the plot, intrude continually upon
the main action of the story. Legends of French invasions of Ireland in *The Snake's
Pass*; attacks by the Children of Death on the Land Under the Sunset in the fairy
tales; accounts of the Spanish Armada, Sir Francis Drake, and in a more contemporary vein, the 1898 Spanish-American War, in *The Mystery of the Sea*; allusions

to the Norman invasion of Saxon England in *The Man* – in each work, seemingly unrelated narratives of imperial expansion and disruption themselves disrupt the primary story, as if Stoker were grappling with issues he could not wholly articulate through his main plot. And, as his references to the Armada and to Norman and French invasions suggest, Stoker is everywhere concerned with attacks directed specifically against the British Isles.

The second category comprises Stoker's more overtly Gothic fictions: *The Jewel of Seven Stars* (1903), *The Lady of the Shroud* (1909), and *The Lair of the White Worm* (1911). These works fit Brantlinger's paradigm of imperial Gothic, with its emphasis on atavism, demonism and the supernatural, and psychic regression. Each of the 'heroines' in these novels – Queen Tera, Princess Teuta, Lady Arabella – represents the eruption of archaic and ultimately dangerous forces in modern life. (That Stoker associates these eruptions with women is worth noting; fear of women is never far from the surface of his novels.) Equally important is the fact that each of these Gothic fantasies intersects with narratives of imperial decline and fall: the decay of the Egyptian dynasties in *Jewel*, the defeat of the Turkish empire in *Shroud*, the collapse of the Roman empire in *Lair*. The conjunction of Gothic and empire brings Stoker's later novels thematically close to *Dracula*. If they cannot match *Dracula's* power and sophistication, this is in part because Stoker became increasingly unwilling or simply unable to address the complex connections between his fictions and the late-Victorian imperial crisis. Only in *Dracula* is Stoker's career-long interest in the decline of empire explicitly an interest in the decline of the *British* empire. Only in this novel does he manage to imbricate Gothic fantasy and contemporary politics.

[. . .]

Stoker maps his story not simply onto the Gothic but also onto a second, equally popular late-Victorian genre, the travel narrative. By examining how and to what extent *Dracula* participates in these two genres, we can illuminate the underlying fear and guilt characteristic of reverse colonization narratives. Like late-century Gothic, the travel narrative clearly displays aspects of imperial ideology. Like Gothic, too, the travel narrative concerns itself with boundaries – both with maintaining and with transgressing them. The blurring of psychic and sexual boundaries that occurs in Gothic is certainly evident in *Dracula* (and is one reason the novel is so accessible to psychoanalytic interpretation), but for Stoker the collapse of boundaries resonates culturally and politically as well. The Count's transgressions and aggressions are placed in the context, provided by innumerable travel narratives, of late-Victorian forays into the 'East.' For Stoker, the Gothic and the travel narrative problematize, separately and together, the very boundaries on which British imperial hegemony depended: between civilized and primitive, colonizer and colonized, victimizer (either imperialist or vampire) and victim. By problematizing those boundaries, Stoker probes the heart of the culture's sense of itself, its ways of defining and distinguishing itself from other peoples, other cultures, in its hour of perceived decline.

In many respects, *Dracula* represents a break from the Gothic tradition of vampires. It is easy, for instance, to forget that the 'natural' association of vampires with Transylvania begins with, rather than predates, *Dracula*. The site of Castle

Dracula was in fact not determined until well after Stoker had begun to write. As Joseph Bierman points out, Stoker originally signalled his debt to his countryman Le Fanu's *Carmilla* (1872) by locating the castle in 'Styria,' the scene of the earlier Gothic novella (Bierman: 1977, 39–41). In rewriting the novel's opening chapters, however, Stoker moved *his* Gothic story to a place that, for readers in 1897, resonated in ways Styria did not. Transylvania was known primarily as part of the vexed 'Eastern Question' that so obsessed British foreign policy in the 1880s and '90s. The region was first and foremost the site, not of superstition and Gothic romance, but of political turbulence and racial strife. Victorian readers knew the Carpathians largely for its endemic cultural upheaval and its fostering of a dizzying succession of empires. By moving Castle Dracula there, Stoker gives distinctly political overtones to his Gothic narrative. In Stoker's version of the myth, vampires are intimately linked to military conquest and to the rise and fall of empires. According to Dr. Van Helsing, the vampire is the unavoidable consequence of any invasion: 'He have follow the wake of the berserker Icelander, the devil-begotten Hun, the Slav, the Saxon, the Magyar' (Stoker: 1984, 286).

Nowhere else in the Europe of 1897 could provide a more fertile breeding ground for the undead than the Count's homeland. The Western accounts of the region that Stoker consulted invariably stress the ceaseless clash of antagonistic cultures in the Carpathians (see, for example, Paget: 1855; Noyes: 1857; Boner: 1865; Johnson: 1885; Gerard: 1888; Bates: n.d.; Crosse: 1878). The cycle of empire – rise, decay, collapse, displacement – was there displayed in a particularly compressed and vivid manner. 'Greeks, Romans, Huns, Avars, Magyars, Turks, Slavs, French and Germans, all have come and seen and gone, seeking conquest one over the other,' opens one late-century account (Bates: n.d., 3). The Count himself confirms that his homeland has been the scene of perpetual invasion: 'there is hardly a foot of soil in all this region that has not been enriched by the blood of men, patriots or invaders,' he tells Harker (Stoker: 1984, 33). His subsequent question is thus largely rhetorical: 'Is it a wonder that we were a conquering race?' (ibid., 41).

[. . .]

For Stoker, the vampire 'race' is simply the most virulent and threatening of the numerous warrior races – Berserker, Hun, Turk, Saxon, Slovak, Magyar, Szekely – inhabiting the area. Nineteeth-century accounts of the Carpathians repeatedly stress its polyracial character. The standard Victorian work on the region, Charles Boner's *Transylvania* (1865), begins by marvelling at this spectacle of variety:

> The diversity of character which the various physiognomies present that meet you at every step, also tell of the many nations which are here brought together. . . . The slim, lithe Hungarian . . . the more oriental Wallachian, with softer, sensuous air, – in her style of dress and even in her carriage unlike a dweller in the West; a Moldavian princess, wrapped in a Turkish shawl. . . . And now a Serb marches proudly past, his countenance calm as a Turk's; or a Constantinople merchant sweeps along in his loose robes and snowy turban. There are, too, Greeks, Dalmatians, and Croats, all different in feature: there is no end to the variety.
>
> (Boner: 1865, 1–2)

Transylvania is what Dracula calls the 'whirlpool of European races' (Stoker: 1984, 41), but within that whirlpool racial interaction usually involved conflict, not accommodation. Racial violence could in fact reach appalling proportions, as in the wholesale massacres, widely reported by the British press, of Armenians by Turks in 1894 and 1896, the years in which *Dracula* was being written. For Western writers and readers, these characteristics – racial heterogeneity combined with racial intolerance considered barbaric in its intensity – defined the area east and south of the Danube, with the Carpathians at the imaginative center of the turmoil.

By situating Dracula in the Carpathians, and by continually blurring the lines between the Count's vampiric and warrior activities, Stoker forges seemingly 'natural' links among three of his principal concerns: racial strife, the collapse of empire, and vampirism. It is important too to note the sequence of events. As Van Helsing says, vampires follow 'in [the] wake of' imperial decay (ibid., 286). Vampires are generated by racial enervation and the decline of empire, not vice versa. They are produced, in other words, by the very conditions characterizing late-Victorian Britain.

Stoker thus transforms the materials of the vampire myth, making them bear the weight of the culture's fears over its declining status. The appearance of vampires becomes the sign of profound trouble. With vampirism marking the intersection of racial strife, political upheaval, and the fall of empire, Dracula's move to London indicates that Great Britain, rather than the Carpathians, is now the scene of these connected struggles. The Count has penetrated to the heart of modern Europe's largest empire, and his very presence seems to presage its doom:

> This was the being I was helping to transfer to London [Harker writes
> in anguish] where, perhaps for centuries to come, he might, amongst
> its teeming millions, satiate his lust for blood, and create a new and
> ever widening circle of semi-demons to batten on the helpless.
>
> (ibid., 67)

The late-Victorian nightmare of reverse colonization is expressed succinctly here: Harker envisions semi-demons spreading through the realm, colonizing bodies and land indiscriminately.

[. . .]

Through the vampire myth, Stoker gothicizes the political threats to Britain caused by the enervation of the Anglo-Saxon 'race.' These threats also operate independently of the Count's vampirism, however, for the vampire was not considered alone in its ability to deracinate. Stoker learned from Emily Gerard that the Roumanians were themselves notable for the way they could 'dissolve' the identities of those they came in contact with:

> The Hungarian woman who weds a Roumanian husband will neces-
> sarily adopt the dress and manners of his people, and her children will
> be as good Roumanians as though they had no drop of Magyar blood
> in their veins; while the Magyar who takes a Roumanian girl for his
> wife will not only fail to convert her to his ideas, but himself, subdued
> by her influence, will imperceptibly begin to lose his nationality. This

> is a fact well known and much lamented by the Hungarians themselves, who live in anticipated apprehension of seeing their people ultimately dissolving into Roumanians.
>
> (Gerard: 1888, 304–5)

Gerard's account of the 'imperceptible' but inevitable loss of identity – national, cultural, racial – sounds remarkably like the transformations that Lucy and Mina suffer under Dracula's 'influence.' In life Dracula was a Roumanian (Gerard designates the Szekelys as a branch of the Roumanian race); his ability to deracinate could thus derive as easily from his Roumanian as from his vampire nature.

The 'anticipated apprehension' of deracination – of seeing Britons 'ultimately dissolving into Roumanians' or vampires or savages – is at the heart of the reverse colonization narrative. For both Gerard and Stoker, the Roumanians' dominance can be traced to kind of racial puissance that overwhelms its weaker victims. This racial context helps account for what critics routinely note about Dracula: that he is by his very nature vigorous, masterful, energetic, robust. Such attributes are conspicuously absent among the novel's British characters, particularly the men. All the novel's vampires are distinguished by their robust health and their equally robust fertility. The vampire serves, then, to highlight the alarming decline among the British, since the undead are, paradoxically, both 'healthier' and more 'fertile' than the living. Perversely, a vampiric attack can serve to invigorate its victim. 'The adventure of the night does not seem to have harmed her,' Mina notes after Lucy's first encounter with Dracula; 'on the contrary, it has benefited her, for she looks better this morning than she has done in weeks' (Stoker: 1984, 115). Indeed, after his attack, Lucy's body initially appears stronger, her eyes brighter, her cheeks rosier. The corresponding enervation that marks the British men is most clearly visible in Harker (he is 'pale,' 'weak-looking,' 'exhausted,' 'nervous,' 'a wreck'), but it can be seen in the other male British characters as well. Harker and Dracula in fact switch places during the novel; Harker becomes tired and white-haired as the action proceeds, while Dracula, whose white hair grows progressively darker, becomes more vigorous.

The vampire's vigor is in turn closely connected with its virility, its ability to produce literally endless numbers of offspring. Van Helsing's concern that the earth in Dracula's boxes be 'sterilized' (ibid., 347, 355) underlines the connection between the Count's threat and his fecundity. In marked contrast, the nonvampires in the novel seem unable to reproduce themselves. Fathers in particular are in short supply: most are either dead (Mr. Westenra, Mr. Harker, Mr. Murray, Mr. Canon), dying (Mr. Hawkins, Lord Godalming, Mr. Swales), or missing (Mr. Seward, Mr. Morris), while the younger men, being unmarried, cannot father legitimately. Even Harker, the novel's only married man, is prohibited from touching Mina after she has been made 'unclean.' In *Dracula's* lexicon, uncleanliness is closely related to fertility, but it is the wrong kind of fertility; Mina, the men fear, is perfectly capable of producing 'offspring,' but not with Jonathan. The prohibition regarding Mina is linked to the fear of vampiric fecundity, a fecundity that threatens to overwhelm the far less prolific British men. Thus, as many critics have pointed out, the arrival of little Quincey Harker at the story's close signals the final triumph over Dracula, since the Harkers' ability to secure an heir – an heir whose racial credentials are seemingly impeccable – is the surest indication that the vampire's threat has been mastered. Even this triumph is precarious, however. Harker proudly notes that his son is named after each of the men in the novel, making them all figurative fathers (ibid., 449), yet Quincey's multiple parentage only underscores the original problem. How secure is any racial line when five fathers are needed to produce one son?

[. . .]

Jonathan Harker's initial journey to Castle Dracula constitutes a travel narrative in miniature, and the opening entries in his journal reproduce the conventions of this popular Victorian genre. Critics have occasionally noted the travel motifs in *Dracula*, but have not pursued the implications of Stoker's mixing of genres. To be sure, Gothic has always contained a strong travel component. The restless roaming found in many Gothic fictions – Victor Frankenstein's pursuit of his monster, Melmoth's wanderings, Mr. Hyde's perambulations of London – suggests that an affinity between the two genres has always existed. Stoker's use of travel conventions is new, however. Earlier Gothic writers were interested primarily in the psychological dimensions of travel; the landscape traversed by the Gothic protagonist was chiefly psychological. Stoker on the other hand is interested in the ideological dimensions of travel. Harker's early journal entries clearly reveal his Orientalist perspective, which structures what he sees and what he misses as he travels through the Carpathians. This perspective is embedded in the generic conventions that Harker deploys, conventions familiar to late-Victorian readers. Stoker's disruption of Harker's tourist perspective at Castle Dracula also calls into question the entire Orientalist outlook. Stoker thus expresses a telling critique of the Orientalist enterprise through the very structure of his novel.

Early in his stay at Castle Dracula, Harker to his great surprise finds his host stretched upon the library sofa reading, 'of all things in the world,' an English *Bradshaw's Guide* (ibid., 34). We probably share Harker's puzzlement at the Count's choice of reading material, though like Harker we are apt to forget this brief interlude amid ensuing horrors. Why is Dracula interested in English train schedules? The Count's absorption in *Bradshaw's* echoes Harker's own obsessive interest in trains. (Later we discover that Mina, attempting to secure Harker's affections, has herself become a 'train fiend,' memorizing whole sections of *Bradshaw's* for his convenience.) Harker's journal opens with the terse note: 'should have arrived at 6.46, but train was an hour late' (ibid., 9). The next morning, more delays give him further cause to grumble: 'It seems to me that the further East you go the more unpunctual are the trains. What ought they to be in China?' (ibid., 10–11).

An obsession with trains – or, as in Harker's case, an obsession with trains running on time – characterizes Victorian narratives of travel in Eastern Europe. Even Emily Gerard, whose enthusiasm for all things Transylvanian seldom flagged, had little patience with its trains. 'The railway communications were very badly managed,' she writes of one journey, 'so that it was only on the evening of the second day (fully forty-eight hours) that we arrived at Klausenberg . . . It would hardly have taken longer to go from Lemberg to London' (Gerard: 1888, I, 30). Harker immediately invokes a second convention of the travel genre when, having crossed the Danube at Buda-Pesth, he invests the river with symbolic significance. 'The impression I had was that we were leaving the West and entering the East;

the most Western of splendid bridges over the Danube . . . took us among the traditions of Turkish rule' (Stoker: 1984, 9). In crossing the Danube, Harker maintains, he leaves 'Europe' behind, geographically and imaginatively, and approaches the first outpost of the 'Orient.'

Harker's first two acts – noting that his train is late, and then traversing a boundary he considers symbolic – function as a kind of shorthand, alerting readers that Harker's journal is to be set against the background of late-Victorian travel narratives. Once the travel genre is established, there is an inevitability about Harker's subsequent gestures. Not only does he continue to gripe about the trains, he also searches for quaint hotels, samples the native cuisine, ogles the indigenous folk, marvels at the breathtaking scenery, wonders at local customs, and, interspersed throughout, provides pertinent facts about the region's geography, history, and population. Harker's first three journal entries (chapter 1 of the novel) are so thoroughly conventional as to parody the travel genre. Such conventions constitute what Wolfgang Iser calls the 'repertoire of the familiar' that readers can be expected to bring to texts (Iser: 1974, 34). Indeed, Harker is so adept an imitator of travel narratives in part because he has been such an assiduous reader of them. Like Stoker himself, Harker 'had visited the British Museum, and made search among the books and maps in the library regarding Transylvania' in order to gain 'some foreknowledge of the country' (Stoker: 1984, 9).

This foreknowledge – the textual knowledge gathered before the fact, the same knowledge that any casual reader of contemporary travel narratives would also possess – structures Harker's subsequent experiences. In assuming the role of the Victorian traveller in the East, Harker also assumes the Orientalist perspective that allows him to 'make sense' of his experiences there. For Harker, as for most Victorian travel writers, that 'sense' begins with the assumption that an unbridgeable gap separates the Western traveller from Eastern peoples. The contrast between British punctuality and Transylvanian tardiness stands, in Harker's view, as a concrete instance of more fundamental and wide-ranging oppositions: between Western progress and Eastern stasis, between Western science and Eastern superstition, between Western reason and Easter emotion, between Western civilization and Eastern barbarism. The 'backwardness' of the Carpathian races displayed itself most surely in what one traveller called their inability to '[settle] themselves down to the inexorable limits of timetables' (Crosse: 1878, 342). As Harker moves further east toward Castle Dracula, he leaves even the railroads behind and is forced to travel by stagecoach. Simultaneously, he leaves Western rationality behind: 'I read that every known superstition in the world is gathered into the horseshoe of the Carpathians' (Stoker: 1984, 10).

Harker may marvel and wonder at this strange world he has entered, but he does not expect to be disconcerted. He trades extensively on his 'foreknowledge,' which allows him to retain a comfortable distance from the scene. He views it simply as a diverting spectacle, imagining the 'barbarian' Slovaks he sees by the roadside as 'an Oriental band of brigands' performing 'on the stage' (ibid., 11). At first, Harker's descent into the dark heart of the Carpathians serves only to titillate, not to unsettle. His favorite word in this first section is 'picturesque,' that stock term of the travel genre. Throughout his journey, he is able to reduce everything he encounters to an example of the picturesque or the poetic.

Until he reaches Castle Dracula, that is. There, everything is disrupted. Stoker undermines the conventions of the travel narrative, just as Dracula undermines all the stable oppositions structuring Harker's – and his readers' – foreknowledge of Eastern and Western races. For the fact is, by Harker's own criteria, Dracula is the most 'Western' character in the novel. No one is more rational, more intelligent, more organized, or even more punctual than the Count. No one plans more carefully or researches more thoroughly. No one is more learned within his own spheres of expertise or more receptive to new knowledge. A reading that emphasizes only the archaic, anarchic, 'primitive' forces embodied by Dracula misses half the point. When Harker arrives at the end of his journey East, he finds, not some epitome of irrationality, but a most accomplished Occidentalist. If Harker has been diligently combing the library stacks, so too has the Count. Harker writes: 'In the library I found, to my great delight, a vast number of English books, whole shelves full of them, and bound volumes of magazines and newspapers. . . . The books were of the most varied kind – history, geography, politics, political economy, botany, geology, law – all relating to England and English life and customs and manners' (ibid., 30). Displacing an epistemophilia to rival Harker's own, Dracula says: '"These friends" – and he laid his hand on some of the books – "have been good friends to me, and for some years past, ever since I had the idea of going to London, have given me many, many hours of pleasure. Through them I have come to know your great England"' (ibid., 31).

The novel thus sets up an equivalence between Harker and Dracula: one can be seen as an Orientalist travelling East, the other – unsettling thought for Stoker's Victorian readers – as an Occidentalist travelling West. Dracula's absorption in *Bradshaw's* timetables echoes Harker's fetish for punctual trains, just as the Count's posture – reclining comfortably on a sofa – recalls the attitude of the casual Western reader absorbed in a late-Victorian account of the exotic.

But of course Dracula's preoccupation with English culture is not motivated by a disinterested desire for knowledge; instead, his Occidentalism represents the essence of bad faith, since it both promotes and masks the Count's sinister plan to invade and exploit Britain and her people. By insisting on the connections between Dracula's growing knowledge and his power to exploit, Stoker also forces us to acknowledge how Western imperial practices are implicated in certain forms of knowledge. Stoker continually draws our attention to the affinities between Harker and Dracula, as in the oft-cited scene where Harker looks for Dracula's reflection in the mirror and sees only himself (ibid., 37). The text's insistence that these characters are capable of substituting for one another becomes most pressing when Dracula twice dons Harker's clothes to leave the Castle. Since on both occasions the Count's mission is to plunder the town, we are encouraged to see a correspondence between the vampire's actions and those of the travelling Westerner. The equivalence between these two sets of actions is underlined by the reaction of the townspeople, who have no trouble believing that it really is Harker, the visiting Englishman, who is stealing their goods, their money, their children. The peasant woman's anguished cry – 'Monster, give me my child!' (ibid., 60) – is directed at him, not Dracula.

The shock of recognition that overtakes Harker, and presumably the British reader, when he sees Dracula comfortably decked out in Victorian garb is, however, only part of the terror of this scene. The truly disturbing notion is not that Dracula impersonates Harker, but that he does it so well. Here indeed is the nub: Dracula can 'pass.' To impersonate an Englishman, and do it convincingly, is the goal of Dracula's painstaking research into 'English life and customs and manners,' a goal Dracula himself freely, if rather disingenuously, acknowledges. When Harker compliments him on his command of English, Dracula demurs:

> Well I know that, did I move and speak in your London, none there are who would not know me for a stranger. That is not enough for me. Here I am noble . . . I am master . . . [in London] I am content if I am like the rest, so that no man stops if he sees me, or pause in his speaking if he hear my words, to say 'Ha, ha! a stranger!' I have been so long master that I would be master still — or at least that none other should be master of me.
>
> (ibid., 31)

To understand fully how disquieting Dracula's talents are, we have only to remember that in Victorian texts non-Western 'natives' are seldom — I am tempted to say never, since I have not come up with another example — permitted to 'pass' successfully. Those who try, as for instance some of Kipling's natives do, become the occasion for low comedy or ridicule, since Kipling never allows the possibility that their attempts could succeed to be seriously entertained. Grish Chunder De in 'The Head of the District' (1890) and Huree Babu, the comic devotee of Herbert Spencer, in *Kim* (1901) are two examples. Kipling voices a common assumption, one that structures British accounts of non-Western cultures from Richard Burton to T. E. Lawrence. The ability to 'pass' works in only one direction: Westerners can impersonate Easterners, never vice versa.

Dracula is different, however. A large part of the terror he inspires originates in his ability to stroll, unrecognized and unhindered, through the streets of London. As he tells Harker, his status as 'master' resides in this ability. So long as no one recognizes him as a 'stranger,' he is able to work his will unhampered. Like Richard Burton travelling disguised among the Arabs, or like Kipling's ubiquitous policeman Strickland passing himself off as a Hindu, Dracula gains power, becomes 'master,' by striving 'to know as much about the natives as the natives themselves' (Kipling: 1987, 24). The crucial difference is that in this case the natives are English.

[. . .]

Chapter 14

JENNIFER WICKE

VAMPIRIC TYPEWRITING
Dracula and its media
(extract)

IN THE INTRODUCTION TO the *Grundrisse* (1857–8) Marx asks, thinking about the relation of Greek art to the present day: 'What chance has Vulcan against Roberts & Co., Jupiter against the lightning-rod and Hermes against the Credit-Mobilier? All mythology overcomes and dominates and shapes the forces of nature . . . it therefore vanishes with the advent of real mastery over them. What becomes of Fama alongside Printing House Square?' (Marx: 1973, 110). The incongruity – and mastery – of *Dracula* lies in its willingness to set the mythological, Gothic, medieval mystery of Count Dracula squarely in the midst of Printing House Square. The *Grundrisse* is Marx's complex meditation on the intertwined fates of production, consumption and distribution, prefaced by these worries about the place of the aesthetic in the modern socioeconomic landscape. Within its novelistic form, *Dracula* too could be said to pose and to enact the occultation of those three processes, by its privileging of consumption, which subsumes the other two. This engorgement is staged by the collision of ancient mythologies with contemporary modes of production.

Miss Mina Murray writes to Miss Lucy Westenra about her current preoccupations: 'I have been working very hard lately, because I want to keep up with Jonathan's studies, and I have been practicing shorthand very assiduously. When we are married I shall be able to be very useful to Jonathan, and if I can stenograph well enough I can take down what he wants to say in this way and write it out for him on the typewriter, which I am also practicing very hard. He and I sometimes write letters in shorthand, and he is keeping a stenographic journal of his travels abroad' (Stoker: 1981, 57). While such girlish pursuits, if slavishly dutiful, scarcely seem ominous, it is Mina's very prowess with the typewriter that brings down Dracula on unsuspecting British necks, even including her very own. In what follows I want to propose that as radically different as the sexy act of vamping and such prosaic labor on the typewriter appear, there are underlying ties between them that can ultimately make sense of the oxymoron of vampiric typewriting. The argument will turn attention to the technologies that underpin vampirism, making for the dizzy contradictions of this book, and permitting it to be read as the first great *modern* novel in British literature. In doing so, I will be concentrating on the shabby, dusty corners of *Dracula*, inspecting its pockets for lint rather than examining its more delicious excesses, and putting pressure on the aspects of *Dracula* that have received less attention because they, like practicing shorthand, don't immediately seem as pleasurable. *Dracula* cannot help but be a heady cocktail, even under inauspiciously stringent critical circumstances, and part of what I hope to show in so pursuing its media are its connections to the everyday life of typewriters, neon, advertisement and neoimperialism we are still living today. To drain *Dracula* of some of its obvious terrors may help to highlight the more banal terrors of modern life.

Franco Moretti bifurcates his stimulating analysis of *Dracula*: one strand follows a Marxist allegorical path, examining the abstract fears aroused by the specter of monopoly capital rising up in Britain's free trade society, and centering on Count Dracula as the metaphoric instantiation of monopoly capital gone wild in its eerie global perambulations; his second appraisal locates Dracula's terror, rather unsurprisingly, in the realm of eros, and advances the notion that the root fear vampirism expresses is the child's ambivalent relation to its mother, and the psychosexual repressions that ambivalence exacts. Both vectors are vigorously and excellently argued, but my concern here is with Moretti's ultimate acknowledgement that these are discrete analyses: 'I do not propose here to reconstruct the many missing links that might connect socio-economic structures and sexual-psychological structures in a single conceptual chain. Nor can I say whether this undertaking . . . is really possible. I would merely like to explain the two reasons that – in this specific case – persuaded me to use such different methodologies . . . Marxism and psychoanalysis thus converge in defining the function of this literature: to take up within itself determinate fears in order to present them in a form different from their real one . . .' (Moretti: 1983, 105) These are two disparate fears, then, with only overdetermination to account for their co-presence. The theoretical split Moretti chooses to elide is just as fraught as he describes it to be; I think it is possible, however, to find a way of addressing this text without accepting such hermetically sealed compartments of analysis. There can been more traffic across these divides; my choice of *Dracula* rests on a desire to investigate the uncoupled chain of materialist and psychosexual readings, because I see *Dracula* lodged at the site of that difficulty, at a crux that marks the modernist divide for both theory and literature. It is necessary to juggle several balls in the air at once, to force a collision between these vocabularies. What causes Moretti's economic and sexual allegories to diverge so thoroughly, in my view, is the paradoxical absence of the category of consumption; what I will work through here is the uneasy status of consumption as it is poised between two seemingly exclusionary vocabularies that nonetheless intersect (often invisibly) precisely there.

In considering *Dracula*, I am turning the text to face forward into the twentieth century, rather than assessing its status as Victorian mythography, since what I want to give is a reading that opens up into a thesis about the modernity we can then read off the wildly voluptuous, and even Medusan, *volte face* thereby revealed. This is not to discount the probing and incisive readings that do annex *Dracula* to its very real Victorian contexts (see Auerbach: 1982; Stevenson: 1988, 139–49; Pick: 1988, 71–87), but rather to shift the agenda in critical terms to the work that the text can do as a liminal modernist artifact, an exemplary text that then lies hauntingly behind the uncanny creations of modernism, at the borders of what is accepted as 'high modernism,' the high art tradition of its literature. The vampirism this text articulates is crucial to the dynamics of modernity, as well as to giving a name to our current theoretical predicaments. *Dracula* is not a coherent text; it refracts hysterical images of modernity. One could call it a chaotic reaction-formation in advance of modernism, wildly taking on the imprintings of mass culture.

To begin by eliminating all the suspense of my own theoretical trajectory: the social force most analogous to Count Dracula's as depicted in the novel is none other than mass culture, the developing technologies of the media in its many forms, as mass transport, tourism, photography and lithography in image production, and mass-produced narrative. To take seriously the status of mass culture in an incipiently mass cultural artifact is to have privileged vantage on the dislocations and transformations it occasions, especially because *Dracula* has been so successful in hiding the pervasiveness of the mass cultural within itself, foregrounding instead its exotic otherness.

What has been little remarked about the structure of *Dracula* is precisely how its narrative is ostensibly produced, its means of production. A narrative patchwork made up out of the combined journal entries, letters, professional records and newspaper clippings that the doughty band of vampire hunters had separately written or collected, it is then collated and typed by the industrious Mina, wife of the first vampire target and ultimately a quasi-vampire herself (see Seed: 1985, 61–75). The multiplicity of narrative viewpoints has been well discussed, but the crucial fact is that all of these narrative pieces eventually comprising the manuscript we are said to have in our hands emanate from radically dissimilar and even state-of-the-art media forms. *Dracula*, draped in all its feudalism and medieval gore, is textually completely *au courant*. Nineteenth-century diaristic and epistolary effusion is invaded by cutting edge technology, in a transformation of the generic materials of the text into a motley fusion of speech and writing, recording and transcribing, image and typography.

Dr. Seward, for example, the young alienist who operates the private insane asylum so fortuitously located next to Count Dracula's London property, produces his voluminous journal not by writing it, but by recording his own words on gramophone records, which then must be transcribed. Since the gramophone is in 1897 an extremely recently invented device, even Dr. Seward is confused by some of its properties: his worst realization is that in order to find some important gem of recorded insight, he will have to listen to all the records again. Never fear, since the incomparable Madame Mina offers to transcribe all the cylinders to typewritten form after she has listened to them, realizing their value as part of the puzzle of tracking the vampire. 'I put the forked metal to my ears and listened,' she writes. And later, 'that is a wonderful machine, but it is cruelly true . . . No one must hear them (his words) spoken ever again! I have copied out the words on my typewriter.' Despite the apparent loss of 'aura,' in [Walter] Benjamin's sense, ostensibly found in the mechanical reproduction of Seward's diary, what

Mina is struck by is the latent emotional power of the recorded voice, whose spectacular emotion the typewriter can strip away. Her transcription of Dr. Seward's wax cylinders occurs mid-way in the text, when the search for Dracula in London is begun in earnest. What that timing implies is that all Dr. Seward's previous entries, and there are many, are recordings, as it were, voicings coded in the most up-to-date inscription, speaking to us from out of the text. There is ample textual confusion swirling about this point, and much inconsistency, since Dr. Seward's diary includes abbreviations and chemical formulas that do not have meaning 'orally'; moreover, when the machine is used by others, there is a vampiric exchange involved – a chapter title tells us, 'Dr. Seward's Phonograph Diary, spoken by Van Helsing.' The burden this mode of production puts on narration is expressed when Dr. Seward reacts to hearing the burial service read over Mina, a prophylactic act in case they have to kill her. 'I – I cannot go on – words – and – v-voice – fail m-me!' (Stoker: 1981, 352). Such doughty sentimentality cannot mask the fact that Seward's diary constitutes the immaterialization of a voice, a technologized zone of the novel, inserted at a historical point where phonography was not widespread, because still quite expensive, but indicative of things to come. We are not dealing here with pure speech in opposition to writing, but instead with speech already colonized, or vampirized, by mass mediation.

The other materials forming the narrative's typed body are equally mass-culturally produced. Jonathan Harker's journal, which begins the novel and recounts the fateful discovery of Count Dracula as a vampire, only to have the memory of this insupportable revelation wiped out by a bout of brain fever, is 'actually' a document in stenographic form, later itself uncoded by Mina's act of typewriting. Stenography is a fortuitous code for Jonathan, since Dracula, who seems to know everything else, does not take shorthand, and doesn't confiscate the journal, an act that would deprive us of the first-hand frisson of narrative in progress. We as readers don't see on the page the little swirls and abbreviations we might expect from a manuscript in shorthand, since that would keep us from reading; it would produce cognitive dissonance for readers to be reminded that the terrifying narrative his diary unfolds is meant to be inscribed in that elliptical, bureaucratized form of writing known as shorthand. What, after all, is the stenographic version of 'kiss me with those red lips,' Jonathan's hot inner monologue as he lies swooning on the couch surrounded by his version of Dracula's angels? Shorthand may seem to fall innocently outside the sphere of mass cultural media, but in fact it participates in one of the most thoroughgoing transformations of cultural labor of the twentieth-century, the rationalization (in Weber's sense) of the procedures of bureaucracy and business, the feminization of the clerical work force, the standardization of mass business writing. The modern office is very far afield from Transylvania, the doomed castle, and the ghastly doings Jonathan experiences there, but shorthand is utterly material to the ramifications of vampirism. Vampirism springs up, or takes command, at the behest of shorthand. Although the pages we open to start our reading of the book look like any printed pages, there is a crucial sense in which we are inducted into Count Dracula lore by the insinuation of this invisible, or translated, stenography. This submerged writing is the modern, or mass cultural, cryptogram; the linkage of this mode of abbreviated writing with the consumption process is made apparent by our willingness to invest these abbreviations with the fully-fleshed body of typed and printed writing. Shorthand flows through us, as readers, to be transubstantiated as modern, indeterminate, writing.

Jonathan has begun his journey to that foreboding place as a tourist of sorts; the impressions he jots down with most relish initially are the recipes for strange foods he would like Mina to try – the 'national dishes,' as he calls them: '(*Mem.*, get recipe for Mina)'. He first tastes a chicken dish made with red pepper that, insidiously enough, makes him thirsty; even the red peppers are suspicious in a text with such a fixed color scheme of red and white. Count Dracula, of course, has a national dish as well, only it is comprised of the bodies not yet belonging to his nation, and Mina, who was going to get the chance to whip up the national dish of the Carpathians, is to become his food for thought. The local color Jonathan drinks in, as recipes and customs and costumes, has the form of regularized tourism; Dracula's castle becomes an unwonted departure from the Transylvanian Baedeker. This may be the point at which to broach the larger argument that will dog the more local one I am making. I am trying to give a reading of the society of consumption and its refraction in *Dracula*, but that society rests on, is impossible without, the imperial economy. It is overly glib to talk about commodity culture without this insistent awareness; what particularly draws me to *Dracula*, and what makes it a modern text, is the embeddedness there of consumption, gender, and empire. Jonathan's travels are made not to a specific British colonial or imperial possession, but to a place with a dense history of conquest and appropriation. He is funneled into this history by means of the accoutrements of modern travel and leisure; Jonathan, who is on business, is nonetheless a tourist *manqué*. In this instance too, Count Dracula and his extraordinary logic of production are encountered through the lens of mass cultural preoccupations and techniques.

Jonathan bears a gift of sorts for Dracula, a set of Kodak pictures of the British house the latter is interested in purchasing, although Dracula in fact has another motive for having brought the rather drab young law clerk so far from England: he wants to borrow his speech, to learn English perfectly from his captive, Harker Jonathan, as he occasionally slips in addressing him. The presence of the Kodak camera in the midst of such goings on is unexpected and yet far from accidental. Photography joins the list of new cultural techniques or processes juxtaposed with the story of the medieval aristocratic vampire, but the Kodak snapshot camera so many people were wielding at the time is really also a celluloid analog of vampirism in action, the extraction out of an essence in an act of consumption. For a time at the turn of the century, 'kodak' meant eye-witness proof; a testimony to the accuracy of Joseph Conrad's portrayal of circumstances in the Belgian Congo was headed 'A Kodak on the Congo.' The photographic evidence Jonathan brings to Count Dracula is also a talismanic offering, a simulacrum of the communion wafer Professor Van Helsing will put to Mina's forehead with such disastrously scarring results. In the latter case, the alembic contamination of vampire blood produces the 'image' of vampirism as a red mark on white skin; photography makes its images in a similarly alchemical, if less liturgical, fashion. Jonathan Harker and Count Dracula come into a relation of exchange with one another through the mediation of the photographic image; more than that, the untoward aspects of vampirism are first signaled by the mention of the Kodak, which precedes the Count's version of vampirism by several pages. Both the history of photography as a domestic practice, as well as photography's connection to ethnography and travel, are summoned up textually by Jonathan's kodaks. Even the subsequent descriptions of what the Count looks like are altered by these initial references to photography, since his frightful looks bear such resemblance to the photographically cataloged 'deviants' of Lombroso and others, and his quaint alterity seems to cry out for immortalization by the National Geographic (that is, photographic) touch. It is possible to speculate that if a vampire's image cannot be captured in a mirror, photographs of a vampire might prove equally disappointing. That scary absence from the sphere of the photographable shunts the anxiety back onto vampirism itself: vampirism as a stand-in for the uncanny procedures of modern life.

[. . .]

When Madame Mina, 'pearl among women,' provides the typescript that resolves the incommensurabilities of the assorted documents, phonographic records and so on, she is able to do this because, as she tells Dr. Seward with rightful pride, her typewriter has a function called 'Manifold' that allows it to make multiple copies in threes. This function is positively vampiric, even to the name it has been given, reverberating with the multiplicity of men Dracula is, the manifold guises of the vampire, and the copying procedure which itself produces vampires, each of which is in a sense a replica of all the others. Here we step into the age of mechanical reproduction with a vengeance, since the reproductive process that makes vampires is so closely allied to the mechanical replication of culture. The perverse reversals of human reproduction that vampirism entails, making a crazy salad of gender roles and even of anatomical destiny, have been well discussed, and assuredly impinge on the terrors of *Dracula*. The ties to cultural reproduction and to cultural consumption need to be acknowledged as well, to place the book in its genuine context of modernity. Because Mina operates the manifold function her relation to Dracula is as close as it is later perverse. Typewriting itself partakes of the vampiric, although paradoxically in this text it can serve also as an instrument used to destroy it (see Benjamin: 1969, 212–51).

The gender division of labor in consumption strongly pervades the representation of this mass cultural vampire and helps to situate Dracula unmistakably as a figure for consumption. Dracula cannot enter your home and molest you unless invited in; that same invitation is the one extended to the mass cultural, in the sense that it is its seductive invasion of the home that allows the domestic to become the site, the opening puncture wound, for all the techniques of mass culture. Mass culture or consumption can be said to transform culture from within the home, despite the obvious fact that many of its cultural technologies are encountered elsewhere, in the department store, on the billboard, in the nickelodeon parlor, at the newsstand or the telegraph office. The book is obsessed with all these technological and cultural modalities, with the newest of the new cultural phenomena, and yet it is they that shatter the fixed and circumscribed world the novel seems designed to protect through those very means, as the home is opened up to the instabilities of authority and the pleasures that lie outside the family as a unit of social reproduction. The same science, rationality and technologies of social control relied on to defend against the encroachments of Dracula are the source of the vampiric powers of the mass cultural with which Dracula, in my reading, is allied. Homes are the most permeable membrane possible for this trans-fusion, since by installing the middle-class and even the lower-class woman in economic isolation there by the end of the nineteenth century, a captive audience for the vampiric ministrations of commoditized culture, consumption and so-called 'leisure,' in the case of upper-class women, is thereby created (see Huyssen: 1987; Modleski: 1991, 23–4). Women are the ones who ineluctably let Dracula in.

It may seem that I accept the text's ambivalence about mass cultural trans-formation in connecting Dracula to it, but what I want to propose is a very different spin on the notion of consumption – the need to see it as, as Pierre Bourdieu calls it, 'the production that is consumption.' These changes are extraordinary and have powerful political effects: they are also, as I have claimed, premised on a canni-balization of resources from invisible places 'elsewhere,' in global economic terms. The contradictions of consumption run like fault lines through this text, and corres-pondingly in our own contemporary theory. It should be underscored, however, that consumption is always a labor – I don't at all mean the work of shopping, but a form of cultural labor, including the producing of meanings. Because *Dracula* focuses on the entry into mass culture, it becomes one of our primary cultural expressions of that swooning relation and thus has needed to be revived inces-santly, in films, books, and other cultural forms. The vampiric embrace is now a primary locus for our culture's self-reflexive assessment of its cultural being, since that being is fixed in the embrace of material consumption.

[. . .]

The vampiric consumption of blood in *Dracula* is simultaneously and complexly a sexual act, as commentators like Nina Auerbach, Christopher Craft and John Stevenson have variously shown, and its process holds both victim and perpetrator in a version of sexual thrall or ecstasy. I want to comment on the sexual thrust of *Dracula's* dynamic, if you will, but first I want to trace out the implications of seeing these exchanges also in sumptuary terms.

Dracula takes blood, but he also gives something, that intangible but quite ineluctable gift of vampirism, which enters invisibly into victims during their act of expenditure. A model of the consumptive paradigm is enacted in their bloody congress; something is interiorized in the giving over to Dracula. Once the mass cultural makes its appearance it unleashes pleasure, it transforms attention, it mobilizes energies outside the norms of authority. I'm not giving this a utopian cast, simply remarking on the rearrangements of the social and the psychic consump-tion exacts, nowhere more specifically than in the realm of sexuality. The modern discourse of sexuality is indeed based on consumption, as Foucault's work has demonstrated, and recently Lawrence Birken's book has annexed sexology to the epistemic shift of consumption (Birken: 1988). *Dracula* bears this out. The history of mass culture is at least in part the history of regaining and reasserting control over sexuality; in *Dracula*, this battle is still so new that the enemy is us.

The vampire yokes himself to the feminine because the mass cultural creeps in on little female feet, invades the home and turns it inside out, making it a palace of consumption. Dracula consumes but thereby turns his victims into consumers; he sucks their blood and renders them momentarily compliant and passive and then wild, powerful and voluptuous. What the text can't decide, nor can we, is how to determine which of these is likely, and then, which of these is preferable. This may help us to understand why Dracula, unlike, say, Jack the Ripper, feasts exclusively on British middle-class women, when, it would seem, the rest of the population, female and even male, is more readily available for his delectation. Lucy, for example, directs her vampire attentions to children of the lower orders; there is some evidence in the text that female vampires do tend to subsist on children, unless particularly enticing erotic possibilities present themselves. In this way the three vampire ladies of Dracula's castle are thrown little children in sacks, but hunger for Jonathan Harker when he is within their spectral chambers; Lucy hunts the parks, but turns to her fiancé Arthur when she hopes to consummate her vampirism with an erotic meal. The connection between mass culture and the feminine has been made since its beginnings, and is arrestingly refigured in *Dracula*, since mass culture is appraised as feminizing, passive, voluptuous, carnal and anti-imperial, in the case of Lucy, and labor-intensive, productive and properly imperial where Mina is involved.

Lucy and Mina have shown themselves to be appetitive even before the attacks Dracula makes on them. The very day of Lucy's vamping by Dracula, who as a secret stowaway on the ship that has wrecked against the coast has just arrived at the seaside town of Whitby where the two are staying, the women go out to share that very British meal of 'tea,' a meal defined as a beverage. Mina says: 'I believe we should have shocked the New Women with our appetites. Men are more tolerant, God bless them.' The tea that they devour so sensually, in defiance of the putative austerity of the New Women, is a foreshadowing of their exposure to vampiric lust, but also an index of their placement in the chain of consumption. Another striking detail of the text attests to the propriety and discipline of Mina, yet also hints at unexplored depths of commodity desire. She rescues Lucy, although too late, from her vamping by Dracula as she sits in a zombie state by the sea. Since Lucy has walked out to meet Dracula in a somnambulant trance, she has neglected to put on shoes, so Mina gives hers over to Lucy upon hastening to her side. This leaves Mina with an awkward predicament: if she is seen by any townspeople on the midnight trip back to the relative safety of bourgeois girlhood's boudoir, they will draw inferences from her lack of footgear. Mina hits upon a startling trick, but one in keeping with her plucky pragmatism. She daubs her feet with mud, so that no reflection of white foot or ankle twinkling in the night can alert any sleepy voyeur who might be looking out a window. So Mina makes the trip back with her feet coated in mud; that expedient is a brilliant one, but also presents us subliminally with the image of a Mina thoroughly earth-bound, enmired. The scandal occurs for the reader's eyes alone, so that Mina's earthiness will be underscored even in her hour of intense decorum. The text's surface establishes the two women's purity and asexuality, yet slips in a glimpse of their susceptibility to consumption – a consumption that also demarcates them favorably in opposition to the New Women who eschew marriage and home. You're damned if you do, and damned if you don't consume.

[. . .]

The textual investment [in Lucy] shifts when Mina is vamped. For one thing, as Van Helsing has already pointed out, Madame Mina 'has man-brain,' so her relation to the equilibration of consumption and empire alters. Mina is an anomaly in evolutionary terms, and as such is affiliated to Dracula; her brain is not a female one, but instead is white, male and European, according to the brain science not merely of this book but of Western racial science generally until it peters out in the 1930s, to persist in Schockley and the sociobiologies. On that evolutionary scale the female brain, the criminal brain and the so-called savage or primitive brain are on a par; the adult white male brain is the evolutionary summit (see Gould: 1981; McWhir: 1987, 31–40). By leaping over this divide Mina occupies unclear territory, and one way of reading what happens to her is to assume that she is set up as Dracula's next victim as a means of establishing her femininity. With lavish abandon and extravagant bad faith her so-called protectors leave her alone in the insane asylum to spend the night, and congratulate themselves at every turn on having shielded her from unbearably painful knowledge; this, of the woman who has typed all the previous vampire documents, and is therefore the most fully in the know.

Having been imprinted with vampirism in a uniquely mediated way, by nursing from and fellating Dracula at the same moment, as she is forced to suck his blood from a wound in his breast, Mina becomes his telepathic double. There's a kinky notion of cerebral sex involved in this, to be sure; at the same time, it begins to make perfect sense that Dracula would have this intimate cognitive relationship with Mina. If it is the case that at least part of *Dracula's* marshaling of fear has to do with assigning a status to the mass cultural, and working through the anxieties it evokes, then the gender slippage that surrounds the characterization of Mina helps account for this. Consumption is psychosexual, yet also socioeconomic. Mina occupies a strange niche between these two, since she is consumed by Dracula, who banquets on her, and also consumes him, but without longing, without desire, and with all her cognitive faculties intact. She could be said to be a perfect replica of the labor of consumption in this regard: she is always doing something with it, always is consciously co-present with the act, unlike Lucy's white zombiedom. The text wants to protect itself from Mina's brain, from her knowledge. After her vamping, the men alternately need to tell her everything, and want to tell her nothing. Oscillating back and forth between these positions, Mina becomes more and more the author of the text; she takes over huge stretches of its narration, she is responsible for giving her vampire-hunting colleagues all information on Dracula's whereabouts, and she is still the one who coordinates and collates the manuscripts, although she has pledged the men to kill her if she becomes too vampiric in the course of time. Her act of collation is by no means strictly secretarial, either; Mina is the one who has the idea of looking back over the assembled manuscripts for clues to Dracula's habits and his future plans. Despite the continual attempts both consciously by the characters and unconsciously by the text itself to view Mina as a medium of transmission, it continually emerges that there is no such thing as passive transmission – invariably, intelligent knowledge is involved, and Mina goes to the heart of things analytically and structurally.

Mina is treated as a medium when Professor Van Helsing hypnotizes her repeatedly to allow her to reveal Dracula's whereabouts; of course we recognize in this a version of the psychoanalytic 'cures' beginning to be effected through hypnotism, by Freud and others (see Greenway: 1986, 212–30). The woman is placed in a state where she does not know her own knowledge, she simply relates it as it is drawn from her by a man who knows what to make of it. All the reverberations to Freud's Dora are in place; the mesmeric and hypnotic world of Charcot is an open intertext of the novel. On all these grounds, including the professional activities of Dr. Seward and the psychoanalytic mutterings of Van Helsing as he repudiates surface meanings for deeper trance states and hysterical body signs, psychoanalysis does a duet with *Dracula*. This should point us to Dracula's role in making vivid the split nature of consciousness and the predatory energies of the libidinal unconscious, and yet it should also be an alert that psychoanalysis and the novel *Dracula* are up against the same problematic: describing or figuring a process that is both productive and consumptive, contradictorily placed both psychically and socially. Mina does tell what her shared or double consciousness is up to, as if she were in the enviable and dangerous position of having her unconscious, which she has in a sense swallowed, speak to her with an audible voice, absent the condensations and displacements of lesser mortals. And yet she is not a controllable medium for Van Helsing, nor just a transparent recording device of the id within, Count Dracula. She is productive in her consumptive possession: Mina essentially becomes the detective of the final segment of the story.

The situation has gotten desperate in London; the men have found all but one of the Count's magic boxes and consecrated them, but he only needs one, and he has obviously departed in it from London. As the men fall prostrate in one or another ways, Mina sends them to lie down and vigorously applies herself to deducing the precise route Dracula must take to get himself carried back in his box to the Castle. For the first time an entry reads 'Mina's Memorandum' (Stoker: 1981, 371). With relentless logic, the keen use of maps, geometrical calculations and brilliant speculation, she provides them all with a plan of attack, deciding which river Dracula will need to use to get home and how he can best be countered. 'Once again Madame Mina is our teacher,' Van Helsing cries out. 'Her eyes have been where ours were blinded' (ibid., 374). In a text that claims again and again that women need to be shielded from the reality of vampirism, a woman is responsible for seeing the way out. Yet Mina's prescience and logical ability are predicated on her proximity to the mass cultural forms she has mastered: for example, her hobby is memorizing the train schedule, since she is, in her own words, 'a train fiend,' which allows her to recreate Dracula's line of escape. Additionally, she is a typist with a portfolio. 'I feel so grateful to the man who invented the "Traveller's" typewriter,' she testifies in eerie simulation of the traveling count (ibid., 371). Mina is that hybrid creature, the consumed woman whose consumption is a mode of knowledge, as Georg Simmel predicted.

[. . .]

As Van Helsing sees it, Dracula's appetite is not for blood, but for a kind of knowledge and power he has become aware of as the attributes of modern, consumer capitalist culture. His 'desire is keen' surely not just to enlarge the vampire dominions, but to transform vampire-dom, to take it to the heart of the metropolis, where it feeds on the forces already set in motion by technological development. 'What more may he not do when the greater world of thought is open to him,' the professor muses, imagining Dracula's feelings as he lies on the periphery in his moldy Carpathian tomb. This should make it clear that it is not merely the atavism of Dracula that makes his appearance in England so frightful; it is his relative modernity, his attempt to be more British than the British in consolidating his goals. Franco Moretti interestingly hypothesizes Dracula as the figure for the circulation of money in late capitalism; Dracula does have a vivid scene where coins shower out of his clothes. Nonetheless, that symbology may take too literally the meaning of the 'economic,' since Dracula's economy is so mediated by its relation to consumption and to the forces of empire.

Understandably, *Dracula* concludes haltingly, and can only end by letting the modern, urban world of technology and consumption recede altogether. The final confrontation with the vampire takes place on horseback in the countryside, Dracula's coffin protected by a group of gypsy cart drivers. This low-tech ending allows the religiosity the text nervously relies on to resurface with less apparent anachronism, but the ancient and the modern cannot be made to converge. They each move on separate curves, asymptotically, never coalescing. Mina, the typist, has lost all her office equipment by the end, although she does narrate Dracula's death and records his last look of peace — a far cry from the orgasmic turbulence that passes over Lucy's visage. Mina's vampire mark, the red scar burned into her forehead by its contact with a holy wafer, recedes with the setting sun, and Mina is free to become a mother, to reproduce what she has heretofore only copied.

The novel doesn't forget its complex relation to the techniques of modernity, however; the religious apotheosis is not its last gasp. *Dracula* is an unstable brew, because it is made up out of mass cultural forms, and yet tries to use this loose collection to mount a retrogressive search and destroy mission against itself. Only the Bible seems to be a text with enough authority to confront Count Dracula — a text that seems (although it is not) to be unscathed by the market forces of commodity culture, a written assemblage of the spoken holy word, as composite and palimpsestic as the textual production this novel itself claims. It would appear that Mina's sudden unscarring would be proof of those powers, but the novel has already shown us again and again that these sacred words are not powerful enough, do not address the conditions of modern life, are not sufficiently passed through the crucible of mass culture to answer the problems of foreignness, otherness, and the unstable self. The baptismal font of language in this book has to be the type-writer, and it seems blasphemous to direct attention to the printed nature of the Bible, its role as the first printed book of Western culture, by Gutenberg's hand.

As a final proof of the divisions within the text, divisions that fruitfully and fearfully show us the dislocations in cultural authority that prompt its new world of language, consider the last and then the first words of the text. The group gets together years later, huddling around the boy who is, through Lucy's transfusions and the passage of her blood to Dracula, and hence to Mina, the putative son of all of the men and all the women, the 'sexual history' going back to Dracula and his three brides; and 'we were struck with the fact that, in all the masses of material of which the record is composed, there is hardly one authentic document: nothing but a mass of typewriting' (ibid., 400). The only proof of the ravages of Dracula is the existence of the boy, young Quincey, named after the gallant Texan who gave his life for Mina's unvamping, and while he may constitute bodily proof for the friends, his unmarked state would represent the opposite to most people. But the first thing we read as we begin the text is this: 'How these papers have been placed in sequence will be made manifest in the reading of them . . . there is throughout no statement of past things wherein memory may err, for all the records chosen are exactly contemporary, given from the standpoints and within the range of knowledge of those who made them.' Which is it, truth, origin, the authority of knowledge, or a 'mass of typewriting'? What makes this text so modern, not to say modernist, is that it knows that it will be consumed – it stages the very act of its own consumption, and problematizes it. The energies of modernity flow out of these same ineluctable wounds, and the undecidable nature of consumption. Most of all, the modernist text follows *Dracula* in acknowledging, however repressedly, the necessary relation of the modern world to its dialectical other, the rest of the globe. In that encounter, which *Dracula* enacts, a modernist writing begins.

The reading of the mass of typewriting is the labor of consumption the text requires of us. This mass is vampiric typewriting, this vampire is mass typewriting, this typewriting mass vampirism. Under the sign of modernity we are vampires at a banquet of ourselves, we are Dracula and Madame Mina, the one who bites and the one who is bitten, the one who types and the one who is typewritten.

Part Six

QUEER HORROR

Introduction to Part Six

■   Ken Gelder

IT IS SOMETIMES SUGGESTED that the figure of the homosexual 'haunts' heterosexuality. The latter earnestly goes about exorcising the former from its domain, even though the achievement of its self-definition depends upon the homosexual's unceasing presence. Its 'tolerant' declaration of indifference to homosexuality only masks (barely) the fact that it has always been utterly pre-occupied with it. Diana Fuss puts the relationship this way: 'Heterosexuality can never fully ignore the close psychical proximity of its terrifying (homo)sexual other, any more than homosexuality can entirely escape the equally insistent social pressures of (hetero)sexual conformity. Each is haunted by the other . . . ' (Fuss: 1991, 3). And Harry M. Benshoff, in his major study of homosexuality and horror films, begins by noting that even the most heterosexual of horror films can exchange 'conjunctural moments' with queerness (Benshoff: 1997, 24).

Queer theory's readings are always about sex relations. It teases out the proximity of one sexuality to another, to the extent that a haunting can seem like an inhabitation or even a possession. Gaining expression through the work of Judith Butler, especially her book *Gender Trouble* (1990), it draws liberally on psycho-analysis and poststructuralist semiotics and acknowledges its debt to Michel Foucault's writings on the history of sexuality. It argues with feminism's tendency to take women as a group with common, fixed characteristics, since this simply reinforces a heterosexual gender binary – men are one thing, women another – which patriarchal culture has already installed. Queerness dislodges gender from its normative 'essence' and turns it into something more fluid, more perfor-mative, more the result of the position in which one finds (or puts) oneself. It celebrates aberrations, relishing the spectral power of the sexually non-normative. Heterosexuality may well have made the homosexual into a monster defined by lack; but queer theory embraces this feature and returns it as a visitation of poltergeistian proportions.

Elaine Showalter's extract, on R. L. Stevenson's horror classic *The Strange Case of Dr Jekyll and Mr Hyde* (1886), comes from her book *Sexual Anarchy*, a major study of fin-de-siecle nineteenth century literature. 'Sexual anarchy' is itself an expression of queerness, a recognition of the ever-permeable nature of conventionally-drawn sexual boundaries. Showalter reads the fin-de-siècle, however, as a 'backlash' against this threat and a reassertion of normative gender definitions: a regressive, rather than progressive, time. Richard von Krafft-Ebing's *Psychopathia Sexualis* (1889) had identified male homosexuality and lesbianism as perversions (on relations between this text and Stevenson's novel, see Heath: 1988). Homosexuality became 'pathologized', treated as a medical problem; and the Labouchère Amendment to the Criminal Law Amendment Act of 1885 made all homosexual acts, private and public, illegal. In this context, it may not be surprising that the apparently content 'community of men' in Stevenson's remarkable novel are confronted with a frightening image of a double life. The characters are all middle-aged bachelors and presumably celibate; there are virtually no women at all in the novel, and certainly no central romantic interests (an 'abnormal' feature soon put to rights by subsequent film adaptations). In the midst of all this is unleashed a monstrous other, Mr Hyde – entering through the back door of 'Blackmail House' in 'Queer Street'. The murder of an 'aged and beautiful' man who approaches Hyde 'with a very pretty manner of politeness' in the street late in the evening – a man who is carrying no identifying papers and who turns out to be a Member of Parliament – is one of many events which allow for a reading of this troubled novel in the frame of what is sometimes called the Gay Gothic.

Sue-Ellen Case's extract comes from a special issue of the feminist cultural studies journal *differences* on queer theory. Case 'tracks' a queer 'counterdiscourse' in romantic poetry, leading to the lesbian vampire. Her piece is a panegyric to this figure, not as she is (in cinema and fiction) but as she might be. In this respect, she qualifies earlier tributes to the vampire-as-homosexual (Dyer: 1988), and anticipates later ones (e.g. Brown: 1997) – queer theory has certainly enjoyed the vampire as a figure capable of disturbing straight sexual relations. For Case, the normative equation of heterosexuality-as-fertile (life) and homosexuality-as-sterile (death) is undone by the lesbian vampire, which dwells at a place where the living and the dead meet. She looks at how this equation inhabits Freud's notion of the uncanny (as a returning of, or to, the mother), as well as feminist psychoanalytical film theory, particularly Linda Williams' (1984) account of the woman spectator's gaze in horror cinema. Several contributors to this Reader have already noted how the woman and monstrosity can be metaphorically drawn together; Williams, too, speaks of the 'shared identification' arising when the woman looks at the monster on screen. But the woman here is assumed to be heterosexual and is, as we've also seen, often maternalized. If she simply 'identifies' with the monster-as-woman, the possibility of same-sex desire is ruled out. The lesbian disappears from this relationship even as her spectre is raised.

The final extract in this section, by Patricia White, is in fact precisely about the 'lesbian spectre'. She examines Robert Wise's extraordinary film, *The Haunting* (1963) – all the more extraordinary since it comes midway between two very different movies directed by Wise at this time, *West Side Story* (1961) and *The Sound of Music* (1965). One of the striking things about *The Haunting* is its inclusion of an identifiably lesbian character, the sophisticated and telepathic Theodora. White, like Sue-Ellen Case, is critical of feminist work on horror and Gothic cinema that has seemed to 'retreat from the ghost of lesbian desire'. Yet *The Haunting* works in a similar way, unleashing the possibility of lesbian sexuality only to turn against it through the very fabric of the film. Events take place in Hill House under the diagnostic eye of Dr Markway, a Freudian father-figure who seems as interested in 'deviant femininity' as he is in the paranormal. Eleanor is the target of the haunting, set upon by ghosts that are heard but not seen. Their terrible noises drive Eleanor into Theodora's bed at one point, but they also work as a 'prohibition' to lesbian seduction – so that, although the lesbian is seen, lesbianism itself remains as invisible as the ghosts and seems capable of producing the same 'spine-chilling' reactions. Recalling Todorov's account in Chapter 1, we might say that the lesbian is thus rendered fantastic: the question, 'is she really there?' is one that haunts this film, and haunts feminist film theory, too.

Chapter 15

ELAINE SHOWALTER

DR JEKYLL'S CLOSET
(extract)

IN JANUARY 1886, THE SAME month that Robert Louis Stevenson published *The Strange Case of Dr. Jekyll and Mr. Hyde*, another strange case of 'multiple personality' was introduced to English readers in the pages of *The Journal of Mental Science*. It involved a male hysteric named 'Louis V.,' a patient at Rochefort Asylum in France whose case of 'morbid disintegration' had fascinated French doctors. Louis V.'s hysterical attacks had begun in adolescence, when he underwent a startling metamorphosis. Having been a 'quiet, well-behaved, and obedient' street urchin, he abruptly became 'violent, greedy, and quarrelsome,' a heavy drinker, a political radical, and an atheist. So far his 'symptoms' might be those of any teenage boy; but what seems to have upset his doctors particularly was that he tried to caress them. The French physicians attributed his condition to a shock he received from being frightened by a viper, and they cured him through hypnosis so effectively that he could not even remember what he had done (Myers: 1886, 648–66).

Stevenson (called 'Louis' by his friends) may well have read the case of Louis V.; it had been written up earlier in the *Archives de Neurologie*, and his wife recalled that he had been 'deeply impressed' by a 'paper he read in a French journal on sub-consciousness' while he was writing *Jekyll and Hyde* (Stevenson: 1924, V, xvi). He was also a friend of Frederic W. H. Myers, who discussed the case for English specialists. But male hysteria was a topic of considerable scientific interest in 1886. Berjon in France published his book, *La grande hystérie chez l'homme*; and in Austria Freud made his debut at the Vienna Medical Society with a controversial paper about male hysteria. While it was recognized in men, hysteria carried the stigma of being a humiliatingly female affliction. Another scholar of male hysteria, Charcot's disciple Emile Batault, observed that hysterical men in the Sâlpetrière's special ward were 'timid and fearful men, whose gaze is neither lively nor piercing, but rather, soft, poetic and langorous. Coquettish and eccentric, they prefer ribbons and scarves to hard manual labor' (Batault: 1885, author's translation). Later this view of the hysterical man as effeminate would be carried into psychoanalytic theory, where the male hysteric is seen as expressing his bisexuality or homosexuality through the language of the body.

Homosexuality was also a topic of considerable scientific and legal interest in 1886. In January, just as Stevenson published his novel, the Labouchère Amendment criminalizing homosexual acts went into effect, and Krafft-Ebing's *Psychopathia Sexualis* offered some of the first case studies of homosexual men (see Koestenbaum: 1988). By the 1880s, such scholars as Jeffrey Weeks and Richard Dellamore have shown, the Victorian homosexual world had evolved into a secret but active subculture, with its own language, styles, practices, and meeting places. For most middle-class inhabitants of this world, homosexuality represented a double life, in which a respectable daytime world often involving marriage and family, existed alongside a night world of homoeroticism. Indeed, the fin de siècle was the golden age of literary and sexual doubles. 'Late Victorian duality,' writes Karl Miller in *Doubles*, 'may be identified with the dilemmas, for males, of a choice between male and female roles, or of a possible union of such opposites. The Nineties School of Duality framed a dialect and a dialectic, for the love that dared not speak its name – for the vexed question of homosexuality and bisexuality' (Miller: 1987, 209). J. A. Symonds wrote poignantly in his journals of 'the dual life . . . which had been habitual' (Grosskurth: 1984, 122). In Oscar Wilde's *The Importance of Being Earnest*, leading a double life is called 'Bunburying' and represents, as one critic notes, 'the "posing" and "double lives" to which homosexuals were accustomed' (Gagnier: 1986, 98).

Stevenson was the fin-de-siècle laureate of the double life. In an essay on dreams, he described his passionate aim to 'find a body, a vehicle for that strong sense of man's double being' which he had felt as a student in Edinburgh when he dreamed of leading 'a double life – one of the day, one of the night' (Stevenson: 1924, XXX, 43). The double life of the day and the night is also the double life of the writer, the split between reality and the imagination. Nonetheless, biographers have long hinted that Stevenson's own double life was more than the standard round of brothels and nighttime bohemia, and have rattled such skeletons in Stevenson's closet as 'homosexuality, impotence, a passionate feeling for his stepson, submission to a wilful and predatory wife' (Miller: 1987, 213; see also Veeder: 1988, 159–60; Koestenbaum: 1989, 149–51). In particular, Stevenson was the object of extraordinary passion on the part of other men. According to Andrew Lang, he 'possessed, more than any man I ever met, the power of making other men fall in love with him' (Lang: 1903, 51). Among the group of friends, both homosexual and heterosexual, in Stevenson's large literary and bohemian circle, 'male appreciation of Stevenson was often intensely physical' (Calder: 1980, 65).

Some of this appreciation and sexual ambiguity is vividly conveyed in the portrait, *Robert Louis Stevenson and His Wife* (1885), by one of the artists in Stevenson's circle who led his own double life, John Singer Sargent. In the foreground, a slender and anxious-looking Stevenson stares out at the painter, elongated fingers nervously stroking his droopy mustache. On the right, on the very margins of the painting, her body cut off by the picture frame, is the shadowy figure of his wife Fanny reclining on a velvet sofa, wrapped from head to toe in a gilded veil. Between the two is a door in the background wall, opening into a dark closet. For Stevenson himself, the painting was 'too eccentric to be exhibited. I am at one extreme corner; my wife, in this wild dress, and looking like a ghost, is at the extreme other end . . . All this is touched in lovely, with that witty touch of Sargent's; but of course, it looks dam queer as a whole.' For Sargent, the painting showed Stevenson trapped by domesticity and femininity; it is, he said, 'the caged animal lecturing about the foreign specimen in the corner' (Olson: 1986, 115, 114). In his marriage to Fanny, Stevenson wrote to W. E. Henley, he had come out 'as limp as a lady's novel . . . the embers of the once gay R.L.S.' (Elwin: 1950, 198).

Stevenson's real sexuality is much less the issue in *Jekyll and Hyde*, however, than his sense of the fantasies beneath the surface of daylight decorum, the shadow of homosexuality that surrounded Clubland and the nearly hysterical terror of revealing forbidden emotions between men that constituted the dark side of patriarchy. In many respects, *The Strange Case of Dr. Jekyll and Mr. Hyde* is a case study of male hysteria, not only that of Henry J., but also of the men in the community around him. It can most persuasively be read as a fable of fin-de-siècle homosexual panic, the discovery and resistance of the homosexual self. In contrast to the way it has been represented in film and popular culture, *Jekyll and Hyde* is a story about communities of men. From the moment of its publication, many critics have remarked on the 'maleness,' even the monasticism, of the story (see, for example, Heath: 1986). The characters are all middle-aged bachelors who have no relationships with women except as servants. Furthermore, they are celibates whose major emotional contacts are with each other and with Henry Jekyll. A female reviewer of the book expressed her surprise that 'no woman's name occurs in the book, no romance is even suggested in it.' Mr. Stevenson, wrote the critic Alice Brown, 'is a boy who has no mind to play with girls' (see Koestenbaum: 1989, 45). The romance of Jekyll and Hyde is conveyed instead through men's names, men's bodies, and men's pysches.

Henry Jekyll is in a sense the odd man of fin-de-siècle literature. Unable to pair off with either a woman or another man, Jekyll divides himself, and finds his only mate in his double, Edward Hyde. Jekyll is thus both odd and even, both single and double. 'Man is not truly one, but truly two,' he observes, and his need to pursue illicit sexual pleasure and yet to live up to the exacting moral standards of his bleak professional community have committed him to 'a profound duplicity of life,' accompanied by 'an almost morbid sense of shame.' Coming to acknowledge his unutterable desires, Jekyll longs to separate his mind and his body: 'If each, I told myself, could be housed in separable identities, life would be relieved of all that was unbearable.'

Not only the personality of Jekyll, but everything else about the book seems divided and split; Stevenson wrote two drafts of the novel, the Notebook Draft and the Printer's Copy; the fragments or 'fractions' of the manuscript are scattered among four libraries (two would obviously be more poetically just, but I cannot tell a lie); and Longmans published two Jekyll-and-Hyde-like simultaneous editions, a paperback shilling shocker and a more respectable cloth-bound volume. Stevenson alludes obliquely to the composition process in the novel itself when

Dr. Lanyon discovers the notebook in which Jekyll has recorded his experiments: 'Here and there a brief remark was appended to a date, usually no more than a single word: "double" occurring perhaps six times in a total of several hundred entries; and once very early in the list and followed by several marks of exclamation, "total failure!"' Just as Jekyll searches for the proper dose to fight decomposition, Stevenson hints at his own frustration in composing the narrative of doubles.

Like the stories hysterical women told Freud, full of gaps, inconsistencies, and contradictions, Dr. Jekyll's story is composed of fragments and fractions, told through a series of narratives that the reader must organize into a coherent case history. The central narrator of the story is Gabriel John Utterson, who utters the tale, and eventually inherits Jekyll's estate. More than the others in their social circle, Utterson is a 'Jekyll manqué' (Twitchell: 1985, 236). Like many narrators in late-Victorian fiction, he is a lawyer, a spokesman for the Law of the Father and the social order, and 'a lover of the sane and customary sides of life.' His demeanor is muted and sober; 'scanty and embarrassed in discourse'; 'undemonstrative' and 'backward in sentiment,' austere and self-denying, he spends evenings alone drinking gin 'to mortify a taste for vintages,' or reading 'a volume of some dry divinity'; although he likes the theater, he has not 'crossed the doors of one for twenty years.' He has almost a dread of the fanciful, a fear of the realm of the anarchic imagination.

Yet like Jekyll, Utterson also has an unconventional side to keep down; indeed, his self-mortification seems like an effort to stay within the boundaries of masculine propriety. Utterson's fantasies take the form of vicarious identification with the high spirits and bad fortune of 'down-going men,' for whom he is often the last respectable friend. 'I incline to Cain's heresy,' he is wont to say; 'I let my brother go to the devil in his own way.' Utterson, too, has a particular male friend, the younger 'man about town' Richard Enfield, whom he sees every Sunday for an excursion that is the 'chief jewel of every week,' although 'it was a nut to crack for many, what these two could see in each other.' In another scene, he shares an intimate evening with his clerk Mr. Guest, his own confidant; at least 'there was no man from whom he kept fewer secrets.' Perhaps because his own life is so involved with repression and fantasy, Utterson becomes 'enslaved' to the mystery of Hyde: 'If he be Mr. Hyde . . . I shall be Mr. Seek.' He begins to haunt the 'by street' near Jekyll's house and to have rape fantasies of a faceless figure who opens the door to the room where Jekyll lies sleeping, pulls back the curtains of the bed, and forces Jekyll to rise and do his bidding.

Fin-de-siècle images of forced penetration through locked doors into private cabinets, rooms and closets permeate Utterson's narrative; as Stephen Heath notes, 'the organising image for this narrative is the breaking down of doors, learning the secret behind them' (Heath: 1986, 95). The narrators of Jekyll's secret attempt to open up the mystery of another man, not by understanding or secret sharing, but by force. 'Make a clean breast of this [to me] in confidence,' Utterson pleads with Jekyll, who rebuffs him: 'it isn't what you fancy; it is not so bad as that.' Jekyll cannot open his heart or his breast even to his dearest male friends. Thus they must spy on him to enter his mind, to get to the bottom of his secrets. The first chapter is called 'The Story of the Door,' and while Hyde, as the text repeatedly draws to our attention, has a key to Jekyll's house, Utterson makes violent entries, finally breaking down the door to Jekyll's private closet with an axe, as if into what Jekyll calls 'the very fortress of identity.'

One of the secrets behind these doors is that Jekyll has a mirror in his cabinet, a discovery almost as shocking to Utterson and the butler Poole as the existence of Hyde. 'This glass has seen some queer doings,' Poole exclaims in the manu-script (changed to 'strange things' in the text) (see Veeder and Hirsch: 1988, 55). The mirror testifies not only to Jekyll's scandalously unmanly narcissism, but also to the sense of the mask and the Other that has made the mirror an obsessive symbol in homosexual literature. Behind Jekyll's red baize door, Utterson sees his own mirrored face, the image of the painfully repressed desires that the cane and the axe cannot wholly shatter and destroy.

The agitation and anxiety felt by the bachelor friends of Jekyll's circle reflects their mutual, if tacit and unspoken, understanding of Jekyll's 'strange preference' for Edward Hyde. Utterson, Enfield, and Lanyon initially think that Jekyll is keeping Hyde. What they see is that their rich friend Harry Jekyll has willed his very considerable estate to a loutish younger man, who comes and goes as he pleases, has expensive paintings and other gifts from Jekyll in his Soho apartment, gives orders to the servants, and cashes large checks Jekyll has signed. However unsuit-able, this young man is Jekyll's 'favorite,' a term that, as Vladimir Nabokov noted in his lecture on the novel, 'sounds almost like *minion*' (Nabokov: 1980, 194). Even when Hyde is suspected of a crime, Jekyll attempts to shield him, and begs Utterson to protect him: 'I do sincerely take a great, a very great interest in that young man.'

Jekyll's apparent infatuation with Hyde reflects the late-nineteenth-century upper-middle-class eroticization of working-class men as the ideal homosexual objects. 'The moving across the class barrier,' Weeks points out, 'on the one hand the search for "rough trade," and on the other the reconciling effect of sex across class lines, was an important and recurrent theme in the homosexual world' (Weeks: 1981, 113). Edward Carpenter dreamed of being loved by 'the thick-thighed hot coarse-fleshed young bricklayer with the strap round his waist,' while E. M. Forster fantasized about 'a strong young man of the working-class' (ibid., 113). Furthermore, prostitution was 'an indispensable part of the male homosexual life . . . with participants beginning usually in their mid-teens and generally leaving the trade by their mid-twenties.' The 'kept boy' was as common as the rough trade picked up on the streets; when he is 'accosted' by the 'aged and beautiful' MP, Sir Danvers Carew, late at night in the dark streets by the river and beats him to death, Hyde both strikes at a father figure and suggests a male prostitute mugging a client on the docks.

Furthermore, Enfield calls Jekyll's abode 'Blackmail House' on 'Queer Street' and speculates that Jekyll is 'an honest man paying through the nose for some of the capers of his youth.' While Enfield explicitly does not want to pursue these implications – 'the more it looks like Queer Street, the less I ask' – the butler Poole has also noted 'something queer' about Hyde. As a number of scholars have noted, the homosexual significance of 'queer' had entered English slang by 1900 (Veeder: 1988, 159). '"Odd," "queer," "dark," "fit," "nervous,"' notes Karl Miller, 'these are the bricks which had built the house of the double' (Miller: 1987, 241). For contemporary readers of Stevenson's novel, moreover, the term 'blackmail' would have immediately suggested homosexual liaisons. Originating in sixteenth-century Scotland, it was generally associated with accusations of buggery (Welsh: 1985, 9). Furthermore, the vision of blackmail as the penalty for homosexual sin was intensified by the Labouchère Amendment. While homosexual men had long been vulnerable to blackmail, the new law, as Edward Carpenter noted, 'opened wider than ever before the door to a real, most serious social evil and crime – that of blackmailing' (Weeks: 1977, 21). Popularly known as the 'Blackmailer's Charter,' the Labouchère Amendment put closeted homosexual men like Wilde and J. A. Symonds at particular risk. It made a major contribution to that 'black-mailability' that Sedgwick sees as a crucial component of the 'leverage of homophobia' (Sedgwick: 1985, 88).

In his original draft of the manuscript, Stevenson was more explicit about the sexual practices that had driven Jekyll to a double life. Jekyll has become 'from an early age . . . the slave of certain appetites,' vices which are 'at once criminal in the sight of the law and abhorrent in themselves. They cut me off from the sympathy of those whom I otherwise respected' (Veeder and Hirsch: 1988, 34–5). While these passages were omitted in the published version, Stevenson retained the sense of abhorrence and dread that surrounds Hyde. The metaphors associated with Hyde are those of abnormality, criminality, disease, contagion, and death. The reaction of the male characters to Hyde is uniformly that of 'disgust, loathing, and fear,' suggestive of the almost hysterical homophobia of the late nineteenth century. In the most famous code word of Victorian homosexuality, they find something *unspeakable* about Hyde 'that gave a man a turn,' something 'surprising and revolting.' Indeed, the language surrounding Hyde is almost uniformly negative, although when Jekyll first takes the drug, he feels 'younger, lighter, happier in body.' Hyde is represented as apelike, pale, and inexpressibly deformed, echoing the imagery of syphilitic afflictions in nineteenth-century medical texts, and Utterson speculates that Jekyll may have contracted a disease from Hyde, 'one of those maladies that both torture and deform the sufferer,' for which he is seeking the drug as an antidote. Meditating on Jekyll's possible youthful crime, Utterson fears 'the cancer of some concealed disgrace; punishment coming, *pede claudo*.' Along with the imagery of disease and retribution, the Latin phrase (literally 'on halting foot') suggests a bilingual pun on 'pederasty.'

The male homosexual body is also represented in the narrative in a series of images suggestive of anality and anal intercourse. Hyde travels in the 'chocolate-brown fog' that beats about the 'back-end of the evening'; while the streets he traverses are invariably 'muddy' and 'dark,' Jekyll's house, with its two entrances, is the most vivid representation of the male body. Hyde always enters it through the blistered back door, which, in Stevenson's words, is 'equipped with neither bell nor knocker' and which bears the 'marks of prolonged and sordid negligence.'

Finally, the suicide which ends Jekyll's narrative is the only form of narrative closure thought appropriate to the Gay Gothic, where the protagonist's death is both martyrdom and retribution. To learn Jekyll-Hyde's secret leads to death; it destroys Dr. Lanyon, for example [. . .]. While Jekyll tries to convince himself that his desire is merely an addiction, a bad habit that he can overcome whenever he wants, he gradually comes to understand that Hyde is indeed part of him. In a final spasm of homophobic guilt, Jekyll slays his other 'hated personality.' Death is the only solution to the 'illness' of homosexuality. As A. E. Housman would write in *A Shropshire Lad* (1896):

> Shot? So quick, so clean an ending?
> Oh that was right, lad, that was brave:
> Yours was not an ill for mending,
> 'Twas best to take it to the grave.

Jekyll is a 'self-destroyer,' Utterson concludes, not only because he has killed himself, but because it is self-destructive to violate the sexual codes of one's society.

In the multiplication of narrative viewpoints that makes up the story, however, one voice is missing: that of Hyde himself. We never hear his account of the events, his memories of his strange birth, his pleasure and fear. Hyde's story would disturb the sexual economy of the text, the sense of panic at having liberated an uncontrollable desire. Hyde's hysterical narrative comes to us in two ways: in the representation of his feminine behavior, and in the body language of hysterical discourse. As William Veeder points out, 'despite all his "masculine" traits of preternatural strength and animal agility, Hyde is prey to what the nineteenth century associated primarily with women' (Veeder: 1988, 149). He is seen 'wrestling against the approaches of hysteria,' and heard 'weeping like a woman.' Hyde's reality breaks through Jekyll's body in the shape of his hand, the timbre of his voice, and the quality of his gait.

In representing the effects of splitting upon the male body, Stevenson drew upon the advanced medical science of his day. In the 1860s, the French neuro-anatomist Paul Broca had first established the concept of the double brain and of left cerebral dominance. Observing that language disorders resulted from left-brain injuries, he hypothesized that the left frontal brain lobes, which controlled the right side of the body, were the seat of the intellectual and motor skills. Thus the left brain was more important than the right and virtually defined the distinction between the animal and the human. The right frontal brain lobes, which controlled the left side of the body, were subordinate; they were the seat of lesser, non-verbal traits. Individuals in whom the right hemisphere predominated had to be low on the human evolutionary scale. In describing or imagining the operations of the double brain, European scientists were influenced by their cultural assump-tions about duality, including gender, race and class. They characterized one side of the brain and body as masculine, rational, civilized, European, and highly evolved, and the other as feminine, irrational, primitive, and backward. Many scientists argued that the intellectual inferiority and social subordination of women and blacks could be attributed to their weak left brains. Furthermore, when mental disturb-ances occurred, as one physician noted in 1887, there must be a terrible struggle 'between the left personality and the right personality, or in other more familiar terms, between the good and the bad side' (Harrington: 1987, 170).

These ideas about the brain were strongly related to late-nineteenth-century ideas about handedness, since handedness was usually inversely related to brain dominance; and considerable effort was made to get left-handed children to change. Freud's close friend Wilhelm Fliess, however, argued that all human beings were bisexual, with the dominant side the brain representing the dominant gender, and the other the repressed gender. Thus Fliess believed that normal, heterosexual people would be right-handed, while 'effeminate men and masculine women are entirely or partly left-handed' (ibid., 94).

The imagery of hands is conspicuous in the text of *Jekyll and Hyde* and has also been dramatically put to use in the various film versions, where Hyde's hands seem almost to have a life of their own. It draws upon ideas of the double brain and hand, as well as upon other social and sexual meanings. As a child, Jekyll recalls, he had 'walked with my father's hand,' suggesting that he had taken on the bodily symbols of the 'right' – or proper – hand of patriarchal respectability and constraint. Hyde seems to be the sinister left hand of Jekyll, the hand of the rebellious and immoral son. Suddenly Jekyll discovers that he cannot control the metamorphosis; he wakes up to find that his own hand, the hand of the father, the 'large, firm, white and comely' hand of the successful professional, has turned into the 'lean, corded, knuckly,' and hairy hand of Hyde. The implied phallic image here also suggests the difference between the properly socialized sexual desires of the dominant society and the twisted, sadistic, and animal desires of the other side. Jekyll's 'hand' also means his handwriting and signature, which Hyde can forge, although his own writing looks like Jekyll's with a different slant. As Frederic W. H. Myers wrote to Stevenson, 'Hyde's writing might look like Jekyll's, done *with the left hand*' (Maixner: 1981, 215). Finally, the image draws upon the Victorian homosexual trope of the left hand of illicit sexuality. Jekyll tells Lanyon that in the days of their Damon and Pythias friendship, he would have sacrificed 'my left hand to help you.' In his secret memoirs, Symonds, too, uses the figure of the useless hand 'clenched in the grip of an unconquerable love' to express his double life and the sublimation of his homosexual desires (see Craft: 1988, 91–2).

Some men, like Symonds and Wilde, may have read the book as a signing to the male community. 'Viewed as an allegory,' Symonds wrote to Stevenson, 'it touches upon one too closely. Most of us at some epoch of our lives have been upon the verge of developing a Mr. Hyde' (Schueller and Peters: 1968, 120–1). Wilde included an anecdote in 'The Decay of Lying' about 'a friend of mine, called Mr. Hyde' who finds himself eerily reliving the events in Stevenson's story. But most Victorian and modern readers ignored such messages or evaded them. While there have been over seventy films and television versions of *Dr. Jekyll and Mr. Hyde*, for example, not one tells the story as Stevenson wrote it – that is, as a story about men. [. . .]

Chapter 16

SUE-ELLEN CASE

TRACKING THE VAMPIRE
(extract)

IN MY TEENS, WHEN I experienced the beginnings of fierce desire and embracing love for other women, the only word I knew to describe my desire and my feelings was 'queer' – a painful term hurled as an insult against developing adolescents who were, somehow, found to be unable to ante up in the heterosexist economy of sexual and emotional trade. 'Queer' was the site in the discourse at which I felt both immediate identification and shame – a contradiction that both established my social identity and required me to render it somehow invisible. At the same time, I discovered a book on the life of Arthur Rimbaud. I was astounded to find someone who, at approximately my same age, embraced such an identity and even made it the root of his poetic language. Thus, while brimming with a desire and longing that forced me to remain socially silent, I found in Rimbaud an exquisite language – a new way for language to mean, based on reveling in an illegitimate, homosexual state of desire.

This adolescent phase in the construction of my social identity is still marked in the word 'queer' for me, with its plenitude and pain, its silence and poetry, and its cross-gender identification. For I became queer through my readerly identification with a male homosexual author. The collusion of the patriarchy and the canon made Rimbaud more available to me than the few lesbian authors who had managed to make it into print. Later, a multitude of other experiences and discourses continued to enhance my queer thinking. Most prominent among them was the subcultural discourse of camp which I learned primarily from old dykes and gay male friends I knew in San Francisco, when I lived in the ghetto of bars – before the rise of feminism. Then there was feminism, both the social movement and the critique, which became my social and theoretical milieu – after the bars. And finally, my young lesbian students and friends who have taught me how, in many ways, my life and my writing reflect a lesbian 'of a certain age.' My construction of the following queer theory, then, is historically and materially specific to my personal, social, and educational experience, and hopefully to others who have likewise suffered the scourge of dominant discourse and enjoyed these same strategies of resistance. It is in no way offered as a general truth or a generative model.

My adolescent experience still resonates through the following discursive strategies: the pain I felt upon encountering heterosexist discourse here becomes a critique of heterosexism within feminist theory – a way of deconstructing my own milieu to ease the pain of exclusion as well as to confront what we have long, on the street, called 'the recreational use of the lesbian'; the identification with the insult, the taking on of the transgressive, and the consequent flight into invisibility are inscribed in the figure of the vampire; the discovery of Rimbaud and camp enables a theory that reaches across lines of gender oppression to gay men and, along with feminist theory, prompts the writing itself – ironically distanced and flaunting through metaphor. By imploding this particular confluence of strategies, this queer theory strikes the blissful wound into ontology itself, to bleed the fast line between living and dead.

But I am rushing headlong into the pleasure of this wound, an acceleration instigated by the figure that haunts this introduction, the figure that appears and disappears – the vampire. Like the actor peeking out at the audience from the wings before the curtain rises, she rustles plodding, descriptive prose into metaphors whose veiled nature prompts her entrance. Her discursive retinue whets my desire to flaunt, to camp it up a bit, to trans-invest the tropes. But first, the necessary warm-up act of exposition.

The relationship between queer theory and lesbian theory: Or, 'Breaking Up's So Very Hard to Do'

Queer theory, unlike lesbian theory or gay male theory, is not gender specific. In fact, like the term 'homosexual,' queer foregrounds same-sex desire without designating which sex is desiring. As a feminist, I am aware of the problems that congregate at this site. These problems are both historical and theoretical. Gay male theory is inscribed with patriarchal privilege, which it sometimes deconstructs and sometimes does not. Lesbian theory is often more narrowly lesbian feminist theory, or lesbian theory arising, historically, from various alignments with feminist theory. Through its alliance with feminism, lesbian theory often proceeds from theories inscribed with heterosexism. I will deal at length with this problem later. But for now, I would contend that both gay male and lesbian theory reinscribe sexual difference, to some extent, in their gender-specific construction. In her article 'Sexual Indifference and Lesbian Representation' (1990), Teresa de Lauretis has already elucidated some of the problematic ways that sexual difference is marked within lesbian representation. For, while gender is an important site of struggle for women, the very notion reinscribes sexual difference in a way that makes it problematic for the lesbian, as de Lauretis configures it, 'to be seen.' This gender base also leads to problems for lesbians when a certain feminist theory defines the gaze itself, as will be illustrated later.

In contrast to the gender-based construction of the lesbian in representation, queer theory, as I will construct it here, works not at the site of gender, but at the site of ontology, to shift the ground of being itself, thus challenging the Platonic parameters of Being – the borders of life and death. Queer desire is constituted as a transgression of these boundaries and of the organicism which defines the living as the good. The Platonic construction of a life/death binary opposition at the base, with its attendant gender opposition above, is subverted by a queer desire which seeks the living dead, producing a slippage at the ontological base and seducing through a gender inversion above. [. . .]

The lethal offshoot of Plato's organicism has been its association with the natural. Life/death becomes the binary of the 'natural' limits of Being: the organic is the natural. In contrast, the queer has been historically constituted as unnatural. Queer desire, as unnatural, breaks with this life/death binary of Being through same-sex desire. The articulation of queer desire also breaks with the discourse that claims mimetically to represent that 'natural' world, by subverting its tropes. In queer discourse, as Oscar Wilde illustrated, 'the importance of being earnest' is a comedy. Employing the subversive power of the unnatural to unseat the Platonic world view, the queer, unlike the rather polite categories of gay and lesbian, revels in the discourse of the loathsome, the outcast, the idiomatically-proscribed position of same-sex desire. Unlike petitions for civil rights, queer revels constitute a kind of activism that attacks the dominant notion of the natural. The queer is the taboo-breaker, the monstrous, the uncanny. Like the Phantom of the Opera, the queer dwells underground, below the operatic overtones of the dominant; frightening to look at, desiring, as it plays its own organ, producing its own music.

This un-natural sense of the queer was, of course, first constituted as a negative category by dominant social practices, which homosexuals later embraced as a form of activism. Historically, the category of the unnatural was one of an aggregate of notions aimed at securing the right to life for a small minority of the world's population. This right to life was formulated through a legal, literary, and scientist discourse on blood, which stabilized privilege by affirming the right to life for those who could claim blood and further, pure blood, and the consequent death sentence, either metaphorically or literally, for those who could not. Against the homosexual, this right was formulated as the seeming contradiction between sterile homosexual sex and fertile heterosexual practice; that is, before recent technological 'advances,' heterosexuals may have babies because of their sexual practice and queers may not. From the heterosexist perspective, the sexual practice that produced babies was associated with giving life, or practicing a life-giving sexuality, and the living was established as the category of the natural. Thus, the right to life was a slogan not only for the unborn, but for those whose sexual practices could produce them. In contrast, homosexual sex was mandated as sterile – an unlive practice that was consequently unnatural, or queer, and, as that which was unlive, without the right to life.

Queer sexual practice, then, impels one out of the generational production of what has been called 'life' and history, and ultimately out of the category of the living. The equation of hetero=sex=life and homo=sex=unlife generated a queer discourse that reveled in proscribed desiring by imagining sexual objects and sexual practices within the realm of the other-than-natural, and the consequent other-than-living. In this discourse, new forms of being, or beings, are imagined through desire. And desire is that which wounds — a desire that breaks through the sheath of being as it has been imagined within a heterosexist society. Striking at its very core, queer desire punctures the life/death and generative/destructive bipolarities that enclose the heterosexist notion of being.

'Was it the taste of blood? Nay . . . the taste of love'

Although, as a queer theorist, I eschew generational models of history, I would like to perform the reading of certain texts, not as precursors, fathers or mothers of a youthful time, but as traces of she-who-would-not-be-seen, whose movement is discernible within certain discursive equations. The compound of wounding desire, gender inversion, and ontological shift is early configured in mystic writings. The mystic women authors, such as Hrotsvitha von Gandersheim, Teresa of Avila, or Hildegard von Bingen write of reveling in the wounding, ontological desire. Yet their precision in marking the social oppression in the feminine position of such desire makes the gendering of that desire mimetic — stable in its historical resonances. Gender slippage, performed through the ontological break, may be found in the writings of an early male mystic — marking both oppression in the feminine and liberation in the adoption of it.

The works of John of the Cross, although not literally queer, begin a tradition that will be taken up later as literal by Rimbaud, Wilde, and more recently Alexis DeVeaux. John's wounding desire is articulated in several ways, but often as a fire, as in his treatise, the *Living Flame of Love* (1584): 'had not God granted a favor to [the] flesh, and covered it with his right hand . . . it would have died at each touch of this flame, and its natural being would have been corrupted'; or, 'the healing of love is to hurt and wound once more that which has been hurt and wounded already, until the soul comes to be wholly dissolved in the wound of love' (St John of the Cross: 1962, 49, 61). The flame of this desire not only corrupts natural beings, but sears into a world where being is reconfigured. John, the mystic lover, desires a being of a different order — one who does not live or die as we know it. In order to 'know' this being, the senses and thus epistemology must be reconfigured. In his poem 'The Dark Night of the Soul,' John lyricizes this reconfiguring of the senses necessary for his tryst. Then, in 'The Spiritual Canticle,' where his love finds full expression in the trope of marriage, John inverts his gender, writing his desire as if he were the bride with the other being as the bridegroom. John, the bride, languishes for her lover, seeks him everywhere, finally reaching him: 'Our bed: in roses laid/patrols of lions ranging all around . . . There I gave all of me; put chariness aside: there I promised to become his bride'. And the bridegroom says to John: 'I took you tenderly hurt virgin, made you well' (St John of the Cross: 1959, 7–9, 15). The wound of love liberates the lover from the boundaries of being — the living, dying envelope of the organic. Ontology shifts through gender inversion and is expressed as same-sex desire. This is queer, indeed.

Historically, John's queer break-through from 'life' also signaled a break with a dominant discourse that legislated the right to life through pure blood. His works were written in Spain during the so-called Golden Age, with its literature and social practice of honor and pure blood: the dominant discourse was spattered with the blood of women and their illicit lovers, but ultimately aimed, in the subtext, against the impure blood of Jews and Moors (the figure for illicit lover's a cover for *conversos*). The Golden Age tragedies set the scene of desire in the context of the generational model, the family and the potential family, in a verse that conflates racial purity with sexual honor, and spilt blood with the protection of pure blood. Writing his poems in a cramped prison cell designed to torture, John defied the generational, heterosexual mandate by a counterdiscourse that set desire in gender inversion: he countered the conflation of race/love/life in a discourse that imagined and orgiastically embraced the un-dead. Blood, in the dominant discourse which was writing racial laws along with such tragedies, is genealogy, the blood right to money; and blood/money is the realm of racial purity and pure heterosexuality. Looking forward several centuries, one can see the actual tragic performance of this dominant equation in Hitler's death camps, where, among others, both Jews and homosexuals were put to death. More recently, one can see such tropes operating in the anti-AIDS discourse that conflates male homosexual desire with the contamination of blood.

I would like to read from this dominant discourse of blood, death, purity, and heterosexual generation in its most obscene form: Hitler's *Mein Kampf* (1933). I apologize for quoting such a text, for, on the one hand, I can understand the necessity of censoring it as they do in Germany; but, on the other hand, this text sets out the compound I am here addressing in its most succinct form – the horror story of the obscene notion of the right to life for racially pure heterosexuals and death for the others.

> The Jew . . . like the pernicious bacillus, spreads over wider and wider areas. . . . Wherever he establishes himself the people who grant him hospitality are bound to be bled to death sooner or later. . . . He poisons the blood of others but preserves his own blood unadulterated. . . . The black-haired Jewish youth lies in wait for hours on end, satanically glaring and spying on the inconspicuous girl whom he plans to seduce, adulterating her blood and removing her from the bosom of her own people. . . . The Jews were responsible for bringing Negroes into the Rhineland, with the ultimate idea of bastardizing the white race.
>
> (Cited in Polakov: 1974, 1)

Such discourse invented the vampiric position – the one who waits, strikes, and soils the living, pure blood; and it is against this bloody discourse that the queer vampire strikes, with her evacuating kiss that drains the blood out, transforming it into a food for the un-dead.

The dominant image of the vampire began to appear in Western Europe in the eighteenth century through tales and reports from small villages in the East. In literature, Mario Praz observes in *The Romantic Agony* (1954), the vampire appears in the nineteenth century as the Byronic hero who destroys not only himself but his lovers. Praz finds 'the love crime' to be essential to the figure, who early in the century was a man, but in the second half – what Praz calls 'the time of Decadence' – was a woman (Praz: 1954, 75–7). For the purposes of queer theory, the most important work in the dominant tradition is 'Carmilla' (1872) by Sheridan Le Fanu, the first lesbian vampire story, in which the lesbian, desiring and desired by her victim, slowly brings her closer through the killing kiss of blood. In the dominant discourse, this kiss of blood is a weakening device that played into male myths of menstruation, where women's monthly loss of blood was associated with their pale, weak image (see Dijkstra: 1986, 337–8).

In the counterdiscourse, Rimbaud builds on the elements in John, writing those revels into a more literally queer poetry. To the gender inversion Rimbaud adds a moral and metaphysical one. The ontological break remains, but heaven becomes hell, and the saint becomes the criminal. In his *Season in Hell* (1873) such desire once again makes the male lover into the bride, but Rimbaud's lover is now the 'infernal bridegroom.' His wounding love is more literally painful, and this pain, this love, this ontological shift, as in John, creates a new epistemology – a reorganization of the senses. Along with these inversions, Rimbaud also revels in the mythical impurities of blood and race. One example from *A Season in Hell*: 'It's very obvious to me I've always belonged to an inferior race. I can't figure out revolt. My race never rose up except to loot: like wolves after beasts they haven't killed' (Rimbaud: 1976, 3–4). His sepulchral, racially inferior, dangerous queer rises up to walk in *Illuminations* (1886):

> Your cheeks are hollow. Your fangs gleam. Your breast is like a lyre, tinklings circulate through your pale arms. Your heart beats in that belly where sleeps the double sex. Walk through the night, gently moving that thigh, that second thigh, and that left leg.
>
> (Rimbaud: 1957, 25)

This is a fanged creature, who promises the wound of love that pierces the ontological/societal sac.

But it is Oscar Wilde who wrote the queer kiss in *Salome* (1893). At the end of the play, Salome stands with the severed head of Iokanaan in her hand. Herod, who looks on in horror, commands that the moon and the stars, God's natural creation, go dark. They shall not illuminate the transgressive, unnatural kiss. Wilde has the moon and stars actually disappear, and in the vacuum, outside of natural creation, Salome says;

> Ah, I have kissed thy mouth, Iokanaan, I have kissed thy mouth. There was a bitter taste on thy lips. Was it the taste of blood? . . . Nay, but perchance it was the taste of love . . . They say that love hath a bitter taste . . . But what matter? What matter? I have kissed thy mouth, Iokanaan, I have kissed thy mouth.
>
> (Wilde: 1967, 66–7)

Wilde wrote these lines in 1892 – when they were first uttered on stage, after issues of censorship, Wilde was in prison. The immorality, or the taboo status of this desire, socially expressed in Wilde's incarceration, becomes a life/death break in his writing – the wound that decapitates the natural and delivers it into the hands of the queer who desires it.

Now, in the nineteenth century, this queer compound led by inverted brides and Oscar Wilde in drag as a dancing girl, the feminized gender that shifts onto-logies, was also represented as lesbian desire. Baudelaire's lesbians in 'Femmes Damnées Delphine et Hippolyte' (1857) lay in their chamber: 'Reclining at her feet, elated yet calm,/Delphine stared up at her with shining eyes/the way a lioness watches her prey once her fangs marked it for her own'. After their love-making, Baudelaire sends them down to hell, out of this life, dessicated by their dry desire, as he called it, the 'stérilité de votre jouissance' (Baudelaire: 1983, 304, 307). At least, in Baudelaire, *jouissance* belongs to the lesbian couple. Nevertheless, once again the fangs, the death, the other world of the living dead. But what was the metaphorical bride of inverted gender is represented here as lesbian desire – the gender trope of the double-feminized.

I read lesbian here, the two 'shes' together, as a trope. The term does not mimetically refer to a gender in the world. In queer discourse, 'she' is the wounding, desiring, transgressive position that weds, through sex, an unnatural being. 'She' is that bride. 'She' is the fanged lover who breaks the ontological sac – the pronominal Gommorrah of the queer. When two 'shes' are constructed, it is a double trope – a double masquerade. To read that desire as lesbian is not to reinscribe it with dominant, heterosexist categories of gender, for lesbian, in queer theory, is a particular dynamic in the system of representation: the doubled trope of 'shes,' constructed in the dominant discourse as the doubly inferior, the doubly impure, and recast in the queer as Wrigley chewing gum celebrates it: 'double your pleasure, double your fun.'

I realize that this seems to be a move away from the material, historical condition of lesbians. Yet the entry point of this theory rests upon my entrance, as an adolescent, into the speaking and hearing, reading and writing about my sexuality. Insofar as I am queer, or lesbian, this identity is in consonance with the discursive strategies that those words represent historically: my desire and my sexual practice are inscribed in these words and, conversely, these words – the historical practice of a discourse – are inscribed in my sexual practice. Take, for instance, my years of furtive pleasure between the sheets, or my years of promiscuous tweeking and twaddling. Both eras were performances of the double trope of the 'she,' either as the doubly inferior, marked by oppression, or as double pleasure, reveling in transgression. To ask 'will the real lesbian please stand up,' when she is em-bedded in the dominant discursive mandate to disappear, or in the subcultural subversion to flaunt her distance from the 'real,' is like asking the vampire to appear in the mirror. (She made me write that. For now is the time of her entrance on screen.) The double 'she,' in combination with the queer fanged creature, produces the vampire. The vampire is the queer in its lesbian mode.

The en-tranced take: the lesbian and the vampire

So finally, now, the vampire can make her appearance. But how does she appear? How can she appear, when the visible is not in the domain of the queer, when the apparatus of representation still belongs to the un-queer? Thus far, we've had the fun, fun, fun of imagining the liberating, creative powers of the queer in representation. Unfortunately, daddy always takes the T-Bird away and the vampire, those two 'shes' in the driver's seat, is left standing at the cross-roads of queer theory and dominant discourse. Although the 'she' is not mimetic of gender, 'she' is shaped, in part, by her pronominal history – that is, how 'she' is constructed elsewhere and previously in language. Along the metaphorical axis, 'she' is somehow the queer relative of the other girls. What this 'she' vampire flaunts is the cross – the crossing out of her seductive pleasure, the plenitude of proximity and the break. Thus, the dominant gaze constructs a vampire that serves only as a proscription – is perceived only as a transgression: interpolated between the viewer and the vampire is the cross – the crossing out of her image. Dominant representation has made of the vampire a horror story.

But this site/sight of proscription lingers in the theoretical construction of the gaze in feminist theory as well – specifically in the theories of the gaze proceeding from psychoanalytic presumptions. There, the vampire is subjected to the familiar mode of 'seduced and abandoned,' or 'the recreational use of the lesbian,' for while such heterosexist feminist discourse flirts with her, it ultimately double-crosses her with the hegemonic notion of 'woman,' reinscribing 'her' in the generational model and making horrible what must not be seductive. The vampire as the site or sight of the undead leads such feminist discourse back to the mother's right to life, where fruition becomes the counterdiscourse of exclusion. For example, taking [Julia] Kristeva's cue that the birthing mother is transgressive, flowing with the milk of semiosis, the cover photo of Jane Gallop's *Thinking Through the Body* (1988) fixes the gaze at the birthing vaginal canal of the author, suggesting that her head may be found inside the book. In other words, Mother Gallop's site of fruition counters discursive exclusion. But does not the feminist political privileging of this sight, designed to empower 'women,' re-enliven, as the shadowy 'other' of this fertile, feminist mother, the earlier categories of the 'unnatural' and 'sterile' queer, transposed here from dominant discourse to feminist troping on the body? Further, the melding of mother and desire into the hegemonic category of 'woman's' plenitude also masks the transgression at the very site of fruition by both the 'racially inferior' and the 'sexually sterile.' Because my desire is for the vampire to appear/disappear, guided by the pain of exclusion, I must now critically read the feminist theory of the gaze and of 'woman' in order to reclaim her (the vampire's) role in representation.

Popular lore tells us that if we look at the vampire without the proscriptions that expel her, our gaze will be hypnotically locked into hers and we will become her victims. The feminist theorists, aware of the seductive quality of the vampire's look, excavate the proscription to discover the desire below. For example, Linda Williams's ground-breaking article 'When the Woman Looks' (1984) constructs a certain dynamic of women looking at monsters. Williams notes that when the woman sees the monster, she falls into a trance-like fascination that 'fails to maintain the distance between observer and observed so essential to the "pleasure" of the voyeur.' As the woman looks at the monster, her 'look of horror paralyzes her in such a way that distance is overcome' (Williams: 1984, 86). Hers is an en-tranced look, and the fascination in it could be read as a response to lesbian desire.

However, Williams's notion of proximity in the look proceeds from the hegemonic notion of 'woman.' As Mary Ann Doane phrases it, woman is '[t]oo close to herself, entangled in her own enigma, she could not step back, could not achieve the necessary distance of a second look' (Doane: 1982, 75–6). Thus, Williams's reading of 'woman's trance-like lock into the gaze with the monster is an extension of 'woman's' condition in the gaze. How this 'woman' is locked in the gaze, or what constitutes her pleasurable proximity, figures Williams, is her identification with the monster – a shared identification between monster and woman in representation: since they both share the status of object, they have a special empathy between them. In other words, this entranced seeing and proximity in the vision, consonant with psychoanalytic theory, rests upon the special status of 'woman' as object of the viewer's scopophilia – and hence the shared identification of woman and monster. I want to come back to this premise later, but let us continue for a moment to see how Williams situates sexuality within this monstrous looking.

Within the horror genre, she observes, it is in the monster's body that the sexual interest resides, and not in the bland hero's. The monster's power is one of sexual difference from the normal male; thus, the monster functions like woman in representing the threat of castration. So, as Williams would have it, when the woman looks at the monster and when the cross is removed from before her gaze, they are totally proximate and contiguous, alike in sexual difference from the male and transfixed, outside of scopophilia, in the pleasures of shared sexual transgression. Desire is aroused in this gaze, but Williams quickly defers it to identification. In relegating the proximity and desire in the trance between woman and monster to (female) identification, Williams has securely locked any promise of lesbian sexuality into an Oedipal, heterosexual context.

This 'woman,' then, in Doane, Williams, and others, is really heterosexual woman. Though her desire is aroused vis-à-vis another woman (a monstrous occasion), and they are totally proximate, they identify with rather than desire one another. Their desire is still locked in the phallocractic order, and the same-sex taboo is still safely in place. What melds monster to woman is not lesbian desire – trance is not entranced – but finally daughter emulating mother in the Oedipal triangle with the absent male still at the apex. By inscribing in this configuration of looking a sexuality that is shared and not male, Williams both raises the possibility of the site of lesbian looking and simultaneously cancels it out. Like the image of the vampire in the currency of dominant discourse, this heterosexist configuration of the gaze seems to derive some power for its formulation by careening dangerously close to the abyss of same-sex desire, both invoking and revoking it. The critical pleasure resides in configuring the look by what it refuses to see. Thus, the revels of transgression enjoyed by the queer remain outside the boundaries of heterosexist proscription. You can hear the music, but you can't go to the party. Nevertheless, the site/sight of the monstrous is invoked and, though horrible, is sometimes negatively accurate and often quite seductive.

The hegemonic spread of the psychoanalytic does not allow for an imaginary of the queer. It simply reconfigures queer desire back into the heterosexual by deploying sexual difference through metaphors. [. . .]

But now I must once again register the vampire's perturbations in this discourse. She is perturbed by this lengthy encounter with heterosexism and is agitating for her return to the discourse. As far as she is concerned, the heterosexual overlay of the queer is just another version of *Guess Who's Coming to Dinner*. So allow me to return to the site where the vampire appears/disappears, that is, in the configuration of proximity. In vampire lore, proximity is a central organizing principle – not only in the look, but also in the mise en scène.

In his work on the supernatural, Tzvetan Todorov (1975) maintains that the central diegetic force in these tales is their atmosphere – an atmosphere of proximity. Settings in fog and gloom connect the disparate elements of the structure through a palpable, atmospheric 'touching.' Judith Mayne, writing on *Nosferatu* (1922), agrees, describing the twilight as a 'dangerous territory where opposing terms are not so easily distinguishable' (Mayne: 1986, 27). From the entranced look, through the mise en scène, to the narrative structure, proximity pervades the vampire lore. But why is this proximate potential represented as horror by the dominant culture? There is a supernatural tale that unlocks the code of the prohibition against this proximity – Freud's paper on the Uncanny (1919). Freud's entry, so to speak, into the uncanny is through the notion of the double and of doubling processes, such as the feeling that we have been somewhere before. Thus, the uncanny for Freud is a kind of haunting proximity. In fact, Freud's endpoint is in a haunted house.

> To many people the idea of being buried alive while appearing to be dead is the most uncanny thing of all. And yet psycho-analysis has taught us that this terrifying fantasy originally had nothing terrifying about it at all, but was filled with a certain lustful pleasure – the fantasy, I mean, of intra-uterine existence.
>
> (Freud: 1959a, 4, 397)

For in German *unheimlich* (uncanny) implies, on one level, un-homely. So, Freud continues, 'this *unheimlich* place, however, is the entrance to the former *Heim* [home] of all human beings [and] the prefix 'un' is the token of repression' (ibid., 4, 399).

So this proscribed proximity, the very world of vampires and of the 'entranced' women who view them, is the desire for what Freud calls intra-uterine existence. More than the fog, the gloom, the cobwebs, and the twilight, Freud's article serves as an exact description of the vampire's sleep in her coffin: toward the end of every night, she races back there, to her native soil, and enjoys the lustful pleasure of being buried alive and dead – her intra-uterine re-creation. However, while Freud unlocks one repressive code to liberate a certain pleasure, his notion of intra-uterine pleasure further defers the actual pleasure proscribed here. And the feminist psychoanalytic theorists carry on his tradition: his intra-uterine pleasure, this *jouissance*, can only be enjoyed as a pre-Oedipal *jouissance* with the mother.

If, for Lacan, sexuality is dominated by the phallus in a trench coat, for Kristeva and her ilk, it is the masked mother. The feminist allocation of this lascivious pleasure of proximity with the mother is simply a bad hangover from too much Freud – it shares his anxieties and proclivities. When Freud imagined this lustful recreation, he imagined the mise en scène as dirty and musty, with the sense of an old vampire who's about to exhibit her true wrinkled self. That's Freud's sexist anxiety about the wrinkled, musty vagina displaced onto an ageist fantasy of the old mother. Moreover, the idea of this pre-Oedipal *jouissance* with the mother reinscribes Freud's patriarchal obsession with genealogy and sexuality as generative – part of the nineteenth-century proscription against homosexuality. Locating *jouissance* in a mother keeps heterosexuality at the center of the picture – the son can insert himself into the site of *jouissance*. As Hamlet gleefully puts it in Müller's 'Hamletmaschine,' 'the mother's womb is not a one-way street' (Müller: 1978, 89–97).

Yet the history of anti-semitism is also marked in Freud's preoccupation with 'home' here; the founder of what the Nazis termed the 'Jewish science' locates a so-called primal desire in returning to the home – a desire that became painfully identificatory for the Jews in the following years, forced into exile, as even Freud himself. Similarly, the vampires, often from Eastern Europe as well, who sought their lustful sleep in dirt from their *Heimat* are marked as the wandering tribe and the despised. Thus, Freud's is both a dominant discourse and a counterdiscourse: while interpolating the heterosexual into the lesbian vampiric, it is also haunted by the outsider position of a myth of 'race' that violently denied the pleasure of 'home.' This intersection of racism and notions of *Heim* or more dangerously *Heimat* seems crucial once again, as the term and the danger reappear in this time of Germany's reunification.

On the brighter (or the darker) side of things, in tracking the vampire, we can here re-imagine her various strengths: celebrating the fact that she cannot see herself in the mirror and remains outside that door into the symbolic, her proximate vanishing appears as a political strategy; her bite pierces platonic metaphysics and subject/object positions; and her fanged kiss brings her the chosen one, trembling with ontological, orgasmic shifts, into the state of the undead. What the dominant discourse represents as an emptying out, a draining away, in contrast to the impregnating kiss of the heterosexual, becomes an activism in representation.

Now, if you watch some recent vampire films, it may seem that things are getting better. Surely, you offer, the confining nineteenth-century codes are liberalized in the late twentieth century. For example, if you watch some recent vampire films, you may note that the vampire is actually portrayed as a lesbian. But this move only reflects a kind of post-Watergate strategy of representation; that is, don't keep any secrets because they can be revealed, just reveal the repression and that will serve to confirm it. So the vampire is portrayed as lesbian, but costumed in all the same conventions, simply making the proscription literal. The strategic shift here is in revelation, not representation. Whether she is the upperclass, decadent, cruel Baroness in *Daughters of Darkness* (1971; played by the late Delphine Seyrig, who was marked in the subculture as a lesbian actor), whose coercive lesbian sex act is practiced behind closed doors and whose languorous body proscribes the lesbian as an oozing, French dessert cheese; or whether she is the rough-trade, breast-biting Austrian lesbian vampire in *Vampire Lovers* (1970), or even the late-capitalist, media-assimilated lesbian vampire in the independent film *Because the Dawn* (1988), her attraction is (in) her proscription. Only the proscription of the lesbian is literally portrayed – the occult becomes cult in the repression.

While the lesbian has become literalized in contemporary vampire films, the proscription against same-sex desire has also been reconfigured in a trope more consonant with late-twentieth-century conditions. For one thing, nature isn't what it used to be, and likewise, the undead have altered with it. In the nineteenth century, the stable notion of nature as natural and of the natural as good made it possible to configure same-sex desire as unnatural — thus monster — thus vampire. Beginning with horror films in the fifties, the binarism of natural/unnatural gives way. Nature is contaminated — it is a site of the unnatural. Metaphors of Romantic organiscism fail where technology has transformed. The agrarian dream gives way to the nuclear nightmare. The representation of nature, contaminated by nuclear testing in the desert, is a site for the production of monsters that transgress what was considered natural. Hollywood produced *Them* (1954), *Tarantula* (1955), *Crab Monsters* (1956), *Giant Grasshoppers* (1957), and *Killer Shrews* (1959). The urban replaces the agrarian as a haven. The humanist scientist, such as van Helsing, warring against the perverse isolated vampire gives way to the military-industrial complex warring against its own creations. The giant tarantula created by nuclear reaction is destroyed by napalm; another monster is killed by a shift in the ozone layer.

After the 50s, the lone vampire, or the family of vampires that threatened the human community, is replaced by a proliferation of the undead. Romero's trilogy illustrates the progression: in *Night of the Living Dead* (1968), a score of the undead threatens a family-unit-type group in a house; in the second film, *Dawn of the Dead* (1977), thousands of undead threaten a smaller, less-affiliated group in a shopping mall, one of the few places remaining; and in *Day of the Dead* (1985), the undead have successfully taken over the continent, finally threatening what dwindles down to the basic heterosexual-couple-unit in a military-industrial complex. Successively, the undead have eliminated the family unit, claimed commodity reification for their own in the shopping mall, and defeated the military-industrial complex. One hope remains in a kind of Adam and Eve ending of the final film, although it seems unlikely. The undead overrrun things, proliferate wildly, are like contamination, pollution, a virus, disease — AIDS. Not AIDS as just any disease, but AIDS as it is used socially as a metaphor for same-sex desire among men, AIDS as a construction that signifies the plague of their sexuality. But why is the taboo now lodged in proliferation? This is Freud's double gone wild, the square root of proximity. The continual displacements in the system have become like a cancer, spreading, devouring, and reproducing themselves. The oppressive politics of representation have cathected to displacement, settling their sites/sights there again and again and again. The taboo against same sex becomes like the Stepford wives when they break down, pouring coffee over and over and over again.

These neo-undead doubly configure away the lesbian position, since same-sex desire appears as gay male. The lesbian position is only the motor for multiple displacements. Where does this all leave the lesbian vampire, then? Outside of the mirror, collapsing subject/object relations into the proximate, double occupancy of the sign, abandoning the category of woman as heterosexist, and entering representation only in a guise that proscribes her. You still can only see her, in horror and fear, when you don't.

[. . .]

Chapter 17

PATRICIA WHITE

FEMALE SPECTATOR, LESBIAN SPECTER: *THE HAUNTING* (extract)

Genre and deviance

WHAT HAVE BEEN CONSIDERED the very best of 'serious' Holly-wood ghost movies – *Curse of the Cat People* (1944), *The Uninvited* (1944), *The Innocents* (1961), and Robert Wise's 1963 horror classic *The Haunting* to name a few – are also, by some uncanny coincidence, films with eerie lesbian overtones. Masquerading as family romance, these films unleash an excess of female sexuality which cannot be contained without recourse to the super-natural. To be more explicit, in the case of *The Haunting*, female homosexuality is mani-fested in the character of Claire Bloom. Regrettably though perhaps understand-ably eclipsed by two films Wise directed just before and after *The Haunting*, namely *West Side Story* (1961) and *The Sound of Music* (1965), the film will maintain its place in cinematic history for two reasons. First, it is one of the few Hollywood films that *has* a lesbian character. Claire Bloom appears as what is perhaps the least objectionable of sapphic stereotypes – the beautiful, sophisticated, and above all predatory lesbian. Although not herself a fashion designer, her wardrobe is by Mary Quant; she has ESP, and she shares top billing with Julie Harris, a star who from her film debut in *The Member of the Wedding* (1952) through her incongruous casting as James Dean's love interest in *East of Eden* (1955), to her one-woman-show as *The Belle of Amherst*, has insistently been coded 'eccentric.' The second reason for which *The Haunting* is remembered is its effectiveness as a horror film. Like its source, Shirley Jackson's *The Haunting of Hill House* (1959), the movie is adept in achieving in the spectator what Dorothy Parker on the book jacket calls 'quiet, cumulative shudders.' At least one reliable source pronounces *The Haunting* 'undoubtedly the scariest ghost movie ever made' (Weldon: 1983, 307). It is clear that reason number two is related to reason number one – for *The Haunting* is one of the screen's most spine-tingling representations of the disruptive force of lesbian desire.

Though the alliance of horror with lesbianism may leave one uneasy, it should be pointed out that the horror genre has been claimed by film criticism as a 'progressive' one on several grounds. Concerned with the problem of the normal, it activates the abnormal in the 'threat' or the figure of the monster. Linda Williams has noted a potentially empowering affinity between the woman and the monster in classic horror films, without exploring the trope of the monster as lesbian. The omission of any mention of lesbian desire is all the more striking given her thesis: 'it is a truism of the horror genre that sexual interest resides most often in the monster and not the bland ostensible heroes,' or 'clearly the monster's power is one of sexual difference from the normal male' (Williams: 1984, 87).

The horror genre manipulates codes specific to the cinema – camera angles that warp the legibility of the image and the object of the gaze; framing that evokes the terror of what-lies-beyond the frame; sound effects that are not diegetically motivated; unexplained point-of-view shots that align the spectator with the monster – for effect and affect.

In *The Haunting* the two female leads, both 'touched by the supernatural' (as it were), are invited to take part in a psychic experiment in a haunted New England mansion. As explicitly deviant women, they are asked to bear witness to an other power, an alternative reality. They join their host Dr. Markway (Richard Johnson), the pompous anthropologist turned ghost-buster, and the wisecracking future heir to the house, Luke (Russ Tamblyn), who is skeptical of any unusual 'goings-on'. A truly terrifying sojourn with the supernatural at Hill House leaves the Julie Harris character dead due to unnatural causes and the spectator thoroughly shaken.

Secret beyond theory's door

The lesbian specter can also be said to haunt feminist film theory, and in parti-cular to stalk the female spectator as she is posited and contested in that discourse. The 'problem' of female spectatorship has taken on a dominant and in a sense quite puzzling position in feminist film theory, which in some instances has denied its very possibility. Laura Mulvey herself, reading her widely read 'Visual Pleasure and Narrative Cinema,' in an essay called 'Afterthoughts on "Visual Pleasure and Narrative Cinema"' explains: 'At the time, I was interested in the relationship between the image of woman on the screen and the "masculinization" of the spec-tator position, regardless of the actual sex (or possible deviance) of any real live movie-goer' (Mulvey: 1981, 12). This parenthetical qualifier, '(or possible deviance),' is one of the few references to sexual orientation in the body of film theory. Yet within the binary stranglehold of sexual difference, lesbianism is so neatly assimilated to the 'masculinization of the spectator position' as to consti-tute an *impossible* deviance. In asserting the female spectator's narcissistic over-identification with the image; in describing her masculinization by an active relation to the gaze; or in claiming that the fantasy of the film text allows the spectator to circulate among identifications 'across' gender and sexuality, feminist film theory seems to enact what Freud poses as the very operation of paranoia:

the defense against homosexuality (see Freud: 1963, 29). Female spectatorship may well be a theoretical 'problem' only insofar as lesbian spectatorship is a real one.

In *The Desire to Desire: The Woman's Film of the 1940s* (1987) Mary Ann Doane addresses female spectatorship in relation to the film gothic, a (sub)genre which she aptly designates the 'paranoid woman's film.' Doane argues that the figuration of female subjectivity in the woman's film plays out the psychoanalytic description of femininity, characterized in particular by a deficiency in relation to the gaze, a metonymy for desire itself. Within this framework 'subjectivity can . . . only be attributed to the woman with some difficulty,' and 'female spectatorship . . . can only be understood as the confounding of desire' (Doane: 1987, 10, 13) — or at most as the desire to desire.

The gothic subgenre has a privileged status within Doane's book, corresponding to its ambiguous position within the woman's film genre. Related to the 'male' genres of film noir and horror 'in [its] sustained investigation of the woman's relation to the gaze,' the gothic is both an impure example of the woman's film and a 'metatextual' commentary on it (ibid., 125–6). The 'paranoid woman's film' is inadvertently privileged in another sense. For, via Freud's definition of paranoia, the specter of homosexuality makes a rare appearance in the text. The process by which it is exorcised is intimately bound up with Doane's definition of female spectatorship.

Paranoia and homosexuality

In *The Desire to Desire*, Doane devotes to the gothic two chapters entitled: 'Paranoia and the Specular' and 'Female Spectatorship and Machines of Projection,' offering a compelling analysis of the genre to which my reading of *The Haunting* is indebted. Yet despite a lengthy discussion of the psychoanalytic description of paranoia, she qualifies Freud's identification of paranoia with a defense against homosexuality as the 'technical' definition of the disorder (ibid., 129). Freud himself was 'driven by experience to attribute to the homosexual wish-phantasy an intimate (perhaps an invariable) relation to this particular form of disease' (Freud: 1963, 29). The relevance of homosexuality to the discussion of paranoia and to the content of film gothics returns as the 'repressed' of Doane's argument:

> Yet, there is a contradiction in Freud's formulation of the relationship between paranoia and homosexuality, because homosexuality presupposes a well-established and unquestionable subject/object relation. There is a sense in which the very idea of an object of desire is foreign to paranoia.
>
> (Doane: 1987, 129–30)

Homosexuality, it appears, is foreign to the definition of paranoia that Doane wishes to appropriate to describe the gothic fantasy: 'Because Freud defines a passive homosexual current as feminine, paranoia, whether male or female, involves the adoption of a feminine position.' This assimilation of homosexuality to the feminine effectively forecloses the question of the difference of lesbianism when Doane later turns to Freud's 'Case of Paranoia Running Counter to the Pyschoanalytical Theory of the Disease' (1915). In this case, which is said to run 'counter' to psychoanalytic theory on the point of homosexual desire, the fantasy which Freud ultimately uncovers as confirmation of his hypothesis (the homosexual wish betrayed by the discovery of a same-sex persecutor) is read by Doane as the female patient's 'total assimilation to the place of the mother.' Desire is elided by identification. Doane writes that

> the invocation of the opposition between subject and object in connection with the paranoid mechanism of projection indicates a precise difficulty in any conceptualization of female paranoia – one which Freud does not mention. For in his short case history, what the woman projects, what she throws away, is her sexual pleasure, a part of her bodily image.
>
> (ibid., 168)

In forming a delusion as defense against a man's sexual advances and breaking off relations with him (whether this shields a defense against a homosexual wish is here immaterial), the woman is seen to be throwing away her pleasure.

For Doane homosexuality is too locked into the subject/object dichotomy to have much to do with paranoia. Femininity represents a default in relation to the paranoid mechanism of projection – 'what [the woman spectator] lacks . . . is a "good throw"' (ibid., 168–9) – precisely because the woman cannot achieve subject/object differentiation. The 'contradiction' between homosexuality and paranoia, and the 'precise difficulty' inherent in female paranoia are related by a series of slippages around a central unspoken term, lesbianism.

'Homosexuality' appears in Doane's text only furtively; female subjectivity is its central focus. Yet, remarkably, it is an account of 'lesbian' desire that is used to summarize Doane's position on female spectatorship:

> The woman's sexuality, as spectator, must undergo a constant process of transformation. She must look, as if she were a man with the phallic power of the gaze, at a woman who would attract that gaze, in order to be that woman. . . . The convolutions involved here are analogous to those described by Julia Kristeva as 'the double or triple twists of what we commonly call female homosexuality': 'I am looking, as a man would, for a woman', or else, 'I submit myself, as if I were a man who thought he was a woman, to a woman who thinks she is a man.'
>
> (ibid., 157)

Doane has recourse to what only Kristeva could call 'female homosexuality' to support a definition of female spectatorship that disallows homoeroticism completely – lesbianism and female spectatorship are abolished at one 'twist.' Female subjectivity is analogous to female homosexuality which *is* sexuality only insofar as it is analogous to male sexuality. The chain of comparisons ultimately slides into actual delusion: 'a woman who thinks she is a man.' In what seems to me a profoundly disempowering proposition, the very possibility of female desire as well as spectatorship is relinquished, in the retreat from the ghost of lesbian desire. As we shall see, a similar path is traced in *The Haunting*.

A house is not her home

> An evil old house, the kind that some people call haunted, is like an undiscovered country waiting to be explored . . .

The male voice-over – Dr. Markway's – with which *The Haunting* opens, will have, for some viewers, an uncanny resonance with a description of woman as 'the dark continent.' This connection between signifiers of femininity and the domicile is unsurprising; in cinema it appears in genres from the western to the melodrama. Mary Ann Doane cites Norman Nolland and Leona Sherman's version of the gothic formula as, simply, 'the image of woman-plus-habitation' (Holland and Sherman: 1977, 279; Doane: 1987, 124). It is the uncanny house that the heroine is forced to inhabit – and to explore.

Freud's essay on the uncanny (1919) draws on the literary gothic, particularly the work of E. T. A. Hoffman. In it he associates the sensation with the etymological overlap between the definitions of the uncanny, *das Unheimliche*, and its apparent opposite *das Heimliche* (literally the homely, the familiar), ultimately identifying this convergence with 'the home of all humans,' the womb (Freud: 1985, 335–76). The woman provokes the uncanny; her experience of it remains a shadowy area.

[. . .]

Hill House reflects the obsessions of its builder, we are told. 'The man who built it was a misfit. . . . He built his house to suit his mind. . . . All the angles are slightly off; there isn't a square corner in the place.' Visitors become lost and disoriented, doors left ajar close unnoticed. The film's montage exploits this as well, disorienting the spectator with threatening details – a gargoyle, a door knob, a chandelier – and unexplained camera set-ups and trick shots. Yet as a house that is 'literally' haunted, Hill House [. . .] is 'uncanny' *for the woman*; it is a projection not only of the female body, but also of the female mind, a mind which, like the heavy oak doors, may or may not be unhinged. An ad slick for the film uses the image of a female figure trapped in a maze. Architectural elements are integrated into the title design. Thus the aspect of the house, its gaze, are crucial in the film, as they were even for the novelist who, Shirley Jackson's biographer tells us, 'plowed through architecture books and magazines' for a picture of the perfect house before writing her tale, only to find out that her great grandfather, an architect, had designed it' (Oppenheimer: 1988, 226).

[. . .] The relationship between the representation of woman and the space of the house is not, Teresa de Lauretis tells us in her reading of Jurij Lotman's work on plot typology, a coincidence or simply a generic requirement of the literary or film gothic. De Lauretis analyzes Lotman's reduction of plot types to a mere two narrative functions: the male hero's 'entry into a closed space, and emergence from it. . . .' Lotman concludes that

> inasmuch as closed space can be interpreted as 'a cave,' 'the grave,' 'a house,' 'woman' . . . entry into it is interpreted on various levels as 'death,' 'conception,' 'return home' and so on; moreover all these acts are thought of as mutually identical.
>
> (cited in de Lauretis: 1984, 118)

And de Lauretis sums up: 'the obstacle, whatever its personification, is morphologically female and indeed, simply, the womb' (ibid., 119). The sinister slippage in the chain of designations from grave to house to woman lends a narrative progression to Freud's uncanny. Given the collapse of 'woman' onto the space rather than the subject of narrative, and given the identification of heterosexuality *qua* conception with the very prototype of narrative progression, it is no wonder that the lesbian heroine (and her spectatorial counterpart) are so difficult to envisage.

Insofar as the cinema rewrites all stories according to an Oedipal plot, when the woman is the hero of a gothic such as *Rebecca* (1940), her story is told as the female Oedipus (see Modleski: 1988; de Lauretis: 1984, 51–5). Her conflicting desires for the mother and for the father are put into play only to be 'resolved' as the mirror image of man's desire. De Lauretis proposes that as the story unfolds the female spectator is asked to identify not only with the two poles of the axis of vision – feminist film theory's gaze and image – but with a second set of positions, what she calls the figure of narrative movement and the figure of narrative closure. Of this last, de Lauretis writes that

> The female position, produced as the end result of narrativization, is the figure of narrative closure, the narrative image in which the film, as [Stephen] Heath says, 'comes together.'
>
> (ibid., 140)

We can recognize the 'narrative image' as fundamentally an image of heterosexual closure, or, in Lotman's equation, death.

It is in relation to the narrative work of classical cinema defined as the playing out of space (the house, the grave, the womb) as the very image of femininity that I wish to situate the story of *The Haunting*. It is an exceptional Hollywood film that would frustrate the hero's 'entry into a closed space' and stage a story of deviant female subjectivity, of the *woman*'s return home as a struggle with the topos of the home. [. . .]

The Haunting tells not the story of Theodora (Claire Bloom's character) but of Eleanor (Julie Harris's character), a woman whose sexuality – like that of the heroine of *Rebecca* – is latent, not necessarily, not yet, lesbian. Her journey is articulated as female Oedipal drama almost against her will, and is resolved, with her death, as a victory of, exactly, the house and the grave (perhaps the womb). 'Now I know where I am going, I am disappearing inch by inch into this house', she finally recognizes. My reading of the film will attempt to trace the 'haunting' of Hill House as it shifts between homosexuality and homophobia.

The Haunting as ghost film dramatizes not the lesbian's 'deficiency in relation to vision' as feminist film theory would characterize femininity, but a deficiency in relation to visibility or visualization – in *The Haunting* we never see the ghost

Figure 17.1 Still from *The Haunting* (MGM 1963). Courtesy of the Ronald Grant Archive.

but we do see the lesbian. Which is not to say that we 'see' lesbian sexuality. *The Haunting* is not 'a film about lesbians'; it is (pretends to be) about something else. I would consider 'something else' to be a useful working definition of lesbianism in classical cinema. For it is precisely the fact that the 'haunting' is unseen, that there are no 'special effects,' that renders *The Haunting* the 'ultimate' ghost film.

[. . .]

'Scandal, murder, insanity, suicide'

Dr. Markway's voice-over resumes after the opening credits of *The Haunting*. The story of Hill House as Dr. Markway envisions it – literally en-visions it, for his narration is accompanied by a bizarre flashback/fantasy sequence – is the story of female death. The mansion, built by one Hugh Crain 'ninety-odd – very odd' years ago, is the site of the deaths of four women, which are enacted for us: his two wives, his daughter Abigail who lived to old age in the house, and her paid companion. This prologue sequence supplies us with a surplus of cinema's 'narrative image' – female scandal, suicide, murder, and insanity – *before* the drama even begins to unfold. It is as if all the visual power of cinema (surpassing even Dr. Markway as narrator) is amassed to contain the threat that 'whatever' it is that haunts Hill House poses.

Dr. Markway hides his interest in the supernatural under the guise of science; his true object of study, like that of Freud, another 'pseudo' scientist, is deviant femininity. [. . .] He rejects the word 'haunted' preferring 'diseased,' 'sick' and 'deranged,' pathologizing, anthropomorphizing and, I would argue, lesbianizing the haunted house.

When his version of the story of Hill House includes the proclamation: 'It is with the young companion that the evil reputation of Hill House really begins' we are prepared, indeed invited, to speculate what the scandal attached to the companion might be. It is onto the fates of the four female characters/ghosts, most crucially that of the companion who is extraneous (subordinate) to the nuclear family, that Eleanor Lance maps her 'Oedipal' journey, her crisis of desire and identification.

As narrativity would demand, she starts out in the place of the daughter. Yet she is a grown-up daughter, a spinster, who leaves her family home – her mother has recently died, and as the maiden aunt she lives in her sister's living room – to return home to Hill House. [. . .] In the internal monologue accompanying her journey to the house (a voice-over that recurs through the film, giving the spectator an often terrifying access to her interiority) Eleanor refers to herself as 'homeless.' She has never belonged within the patriarchal home and its family romance. Her 'dark, romantic secret' is her adult attachment to her mother, which she angrily defines as 'eleven years walled up alive on a desert island.' Eleanor is thrilled at the prospect of 'being expected' at her destination; for the first time something is happening to *her*. More is 'expected' of her than she dreams . . .

Things that go bump in the night

When Eleanor arrives at Hill House she is relieved to meet one of her companions. 'Theodora – just Theodora,' Claire Bloom's character introduces herself to Eleanor, immediately adding, 'The affectionate term for Theodora is Theo.' 'We are going to be great friends, Theo,' responds Eleanor, whose affectionate name 'Nell' Theo has already deduced by keen powers of extrasensory perception which are exercised most frequently in reading Eleanor's mind. 'Like sisters?', Theo responds sarcastically. Theo recommends that Eleanor put on something bright for dinner, sharing with her the impression that it is a good idea always to remain 'strictly visible' in Hill House. On their way downstairs, they encounter their first supernatural experience, with Eleanor shouting, 'Don't leave me, Theo,' and Theo observing, 'It wants you, Nell.' After they have joined the others Eleanor proposes a toast: 'I'd like to drink to companions.' Theo responds with obvious pleasure and the camera moves in to frame the two women. 'To my new companion,' replies Theo with inimitable, elegant lasciviousness. The toast, like their relationship, alas, remains unconsummated, for Eleanor continues – 'except I don't drink.'

Eleanor clearly is the 'main attraction' of both the house and Theo, each finding in her what Theo calls 'a kindred spirit.' The film, resisting the visualization of desire between women, displaces that desire onto the level of the supernatural, Theo's seduction of Eleanor onto the 'haunting.'

The process whereby the apparition of lesbian desire is deferred to the manifestation of supernatural phenomena is well illustrated by a sequence depicting the events of the first night spent by the company in Hill House. Theo accompanies Eleanor to the door of her bedroom, and invites herself in, under the pretext of arranging Eleanor's hair. Although Eleanor refuses Theo's advances, the women end up in bed together anyway, but not according to plan. Eleanor, realizing with a mixture of relief and anxiety that she is alone, locks her door ('Against what?,' she muses) and drifts off to sleep. A shot of the exterior of the house and a dissolve to a shot from the dark interior at the base of the main staircase are accompanied by a faint pounding which rises in volume. Eleanor stirs and, half-asleep, knocks in response on the wall above her bed: 'All right, mother, I'm coming.' When Theo calls out to her in fear, Eleanor realizes her mistake and rushes into Theo's adjoining room. Huddled together in Theo's bed throughout the protracted scene, the women face off an unbearably loud knocking which eventually comes to the door of the bedroom. Finally the sound fades away, and Eleanor runs to the door when she hears Luke and the doctor in the hall. The men enter, explain they had been outside chasing what appeared to be a dog, and ask whether anything has happened. The women burst into laughter, and after catching their breath, sarcastically explain that something knocked on the door with a cannonball. Luke remarks that there isn't a scratch on the woodwork – 'or anywhere else,' and the doctor soberly intones: 'When we are decoyed outside, and you two are bottled up inside, wouldn't you say that something is trying to separate us?' The sequence ends with ominous music and a close-up of Theo.

The knocking that terrorizes the women takes up an element of the film's prologue – the invalid Abigail pounds with her cane on the wall to call the companion who fails to come, sparking malicious town gossip that she had somehow or other murdered her mistress. At this point in the film we are already aware that Eleanor harbors guilt about her own mother's death; what this scene makes explicit is the exact parallel, down to the knocking on the wall that Eleanor later admits she fears she may have heard and ignored on the fatal night, which puts Eleanor in the position of 'companion' *vis-à-vis* her own mother.

> When a wife loses her husband, or a daughter her mother, it not infre-
> quently happens that the survivor is afflicted with tormenting scruples
> . . . which raise the question whether she herself has not been guilty
> through carelessness or neglect of the death of the beloved person. No
> recalling of the care with which she nursed the invalid, no direct refut-
> ation of the asserted guilt can put an end to the torture . . .
>
> (Freud: 1946, 80)

Freud concludes in *Totem and Taboo* (1913) that a repressed component of hostility toward the deceased is the explanation for these reproaches, and similarly for the 'primitive' belief in the malignancy of spirits of dead loved ones: the *projection* of that hostility is feared aggression from the dead. Projection is also a technique of those suffering from paranoia who are 'struggling against an intensification of their homosexual trends.' In paranoia, Freud tells us, 'the persecutor is in reality the loved person, past or present' (Freud: 1963, 99).

Eleanor's psychosexual history is similar to that of the subject of Freud's 'Case of Paranoia Running Counter to the Pyschoanalytical Theory of the Disease', a thirtyish woman living with her mother who forms a paranoic delusion to defend herself against the attentions of a man. In both cases, the loved person, then, the persecutor, is the mother. Much has been made in film theory of the form the patient's delusion took in this case: that of being photographed, sparked by an 'accidental knock or tick' which she hears while visiting the man in his apartment. The visual and the auditory, the camera and the click are the two registers of which the cinema is composed, rendering it analogous to paranoid projection (see Doane: 1987, 123). The noteworthy point of Freud's case history is his reading of the instigating cause of the delusion: 'I do not believe that the clock ever ticked or that any noise was to be heard at all. The woman's situation justified a sensa-tion of throbbing in the clitoris. . . . There had been a "knocking" of the clitoris.' 'In her subsequent rejection of the man,' Freud concludes, 'lack of satisfaction undoubtedly played a part' (Freud: 1963, 109).

The knock recurs in this scene from *The Haunting* with the force of a cannon-ball [. . .] and intervenes precisely at the moment of a prohibition against homosexual desire. It is a knocking which on the manifest level can be read as the ghost of Abigail looking for a companion, or on a latent level as the persecution of Eleanor by her own mother in conjunction with her taking of a new lover. [. . .] Like Freud, the men do not believe there had been any noise at all. Love between women is considered unspeakable; it is inaudible; and it doesn't leave a scratch. I do not contend that the laughter Theo and Eleanor share over the men's ignorance is irrecuperable; indeed the scene most literally transforms homosexu-ality into homophobia – replacing sexuality with fear. When the doctor pompously acknowledges that 'something' is separating the girls from the boys in Hill House, he resolves to take precautions. 'Against what?', Eleanor asks, naively, for the second time in this sequence. For the camera tells us it is Theo, someone, not some thing, who separates the doctor and Eleanor.

The next morning Eleanor awakens a little too excited by her first experi-ence of the 'supernatural.' Over breakfast, her hair arranged in a new style, she claims to be 'much more afraid of being abandoned or left behind than of things that go bump in the night.' This does not appear to be entirely true, for her feeling of excitement is accompanied by her turning away from Theo as a potential love object and towards the doctor, whose paternalistic interest in her Theo calls unfair. When asked what *she* is afraid of, Theo responds, 'of knowing what I really want.' Her words make Eleanor uncomfortable on several levels. Eleanor misreads her own desire, as I suspect some feminist film critics would, as desire for the man, i.e., the father. Theo's attitude toward her demeaning rival is manifested with knowing sarcasm, telling Eleanor she 'hasn't the ghost of a chance.' [. . .] Eleanor's turning towards the father smacks indeed of 'a defense against a homosexual wish,' and she literally begins to see Theo as a persecutor. The very forcefulness of this defense supports a reading of the night of knocking as a seduction scene.

More than meets the eye

[. . .] 'You're the monster of Hill House,' Eleanor finally shouts at Theo, several scenes later, coming closer to the truth than she knows. It is at the culmination of this scene: 'Life is full of inconsistencies, nature's mistakes – you for instance', that Mrs. Markway, consistently, makes her entrance. [. . .]

The materialization of the wife at this point in the film seems to be part of the process whereby cinema – like the house itself, which calls Eleanor home through literal writing on the wall – demands its tribute of the heroine. On this 'final' night of Eleanor's stay, she imagines she has killed off the wife/mother when Mrs. Markway, because of her skepticism, becomes 'deranged' by Hill House, and disappears from her room – the nursery, Abigail's room, 'the cold rotten heart of Hill House,' that had remained locked before opening spontaneously on the night of her arrival. Mrs. Markway then appears unexpectedly to scare Eleanor (ultimately to scare her to death) on two additional occasions.

First she interrupts Eleanor's intense identification with the place of the companion's suicide, the library. Eleanor's haunting by the wife is quite logically played out over the architecture of the house, which is fantasmatically inflected with Eleanor's own psychic history. Eleanor sums up her subjective crisis: 'So what if he does have a wife, I still have a place in this house. I belong.' As Eleanor runs through the house, she is frightened by her own reflection; we hear loud creaking and crashing, and the image rocks. She thinks, 'the house is destroying itself, it is coming down around me.' Eleanor had been unable to enter the library before, overpowered by a smell she associates with her mother, but tonight she seems to be called there; the *unheimlich* is transformed to the *heimlich*. Eleanor climbs the library's spiral staircase as if induced by the camera which makes the dreamlike ascent before her. The companion had hung herself from the top of the staircase, and the camera had prefigured these later ascents in the prologue's enactment of this death: 'I've broken the spell of Hill House. I'm home, I'm home', Eleanor senses. The doctor 'rescues' her when she reaches the top, yet just as she turns to descend, Mrs. Markway's head pops into the frame through a trap door above. Eleanor faints, and the screen fades to black.

It is now that the doctor, futilely, decides to send Eleanor away from Hill House. For he misrecognizes (as an hallucination) her recognition of the wife. Yet for once she has actually *seen* something that we, importantly, also see. She is terrorized, at the very moment of her identification with the companion, by the apparition of the heterosexual role model, the wife. Eleanor comprehends the displacement of her Oedipal drama (the substituting of herself for the mother) by the inverted drama of Hill House (the wife's substitution for Eleanor in relation to the house's desire). 'I'm the one who's supposed to stay. She's taken my place.' And Eleanor dies, ironically, literally in the wife's place.

For the 'narrative image' figured in the film's prologue – the death of Hugh

Crain's first wife – her lifeless hand falling into the frame, after her horse rears, 'for no apparent reason' – is now offered as the 'narrative image' of the film. The shot is repeated exactly after Eleanor's car crashes into the very same tree, her hand falling into the frame. The first wife died before rounding the corner that would have given her the gothic heroine's first glimpse of the house; Eleanor cannot leave the gaze of Hill House.

She crashes, apparently to avoid hitting Mrs. Markway, who, for the second time, suddenly runs across her path. Mrs. Markway appears as the agent of a deadly variant of heterosexual narrative closure. Eleanor is not allowed to live or die as the companion; incapable of living as the wife, she is tricked into dying in her place.

But, being a ghost film, *The Haunting* goes beyond the image of death. The final image is properly the house – the grave, woman? – accompanied by Eleanor's voice-over (or rather the voice of Eleanor's ghost) echoing these words from the opening narration: 'Whatever walked there, walked alone.' Prying the 'narrative image' from its Oedipal logic and usurping the authoritative male voice-over, Eleanor transforms the words: 'We who walk here, walk alone.' Eleanor finally belongs – to a 'we' that we know to be feminine and suspect might be lesbian, 'we who walk alone,' and the house belongs to her. The 'haunting' exceeds the drive of cinema to closure, actually using the material codes of cinema, the sound-track, to *suggest* something else.

The Haunting exceeds the woman's story as female Oedipal drama enacted, Tania Modleski demonstrates, in a gothic like *Rebecca*. In that genre the protagonist's search for the 'secret' of a dead woman is facilitated (or impeded) by a key figure, an older, sometimes sinister female character variously the 'housekeeper,' the 'nurse,' or in some other capacity a 'companion' to the dead woman. These roles are truly a gallery of the best of lesbian characters in classic cinematic history. Played by Judith Anderson (Mrs. Danvers in *Rebecca*) or Cornelia Otis Skinner (*The Uninvited* [1944]) they are a compelling reason for the young woman, recently married and suspecting it might have been a mistake, to realize that it *was* one. I have discussed the centrality of the companion in the psychic history of Hill House, and will venture that the companion function provides a mapping and an iconography of female homosexuality throughout the gothic genre. In *The Haunting* a crucial transformation has taken place with the manifest appearance of lesbianism. The representation of the dead woman, the object of the heroine's desire ('Rebecca' as precisely unrepresentable in that film), and the function of the companion, converge in the figure of Theodora, who is emphatically not the mother.

The canny lesbian

If the nameless heroine of *Rebecca* oscillates between the two poles of female Oedipal desire – desire for the mother and desire for the father – Mrs. Danvers sets the house on fire and dies with it, joining the ghost of Rebecca which, as Modleski reads it, 'haunts' her (Modleski: 1988, 51) And if Eleanor's trajectory sums up these two variants, Theo grows up – like Abigail, the daughter before her – and lives to tell of the terrors of Hill House. In developing a feminist film theory which would incorporate Theo, we might recall the model of spectatorship she offers in the film. Telepathy, to lesbians and gay men as historical readers and viewers, has always been an alternative to our own mode of paranoic spectatorship: 'Is it really there?' The experience of this second sight involves the identification of and with Theo as a lesbian. As for *The Haunting*, it's a very scary movie, even a threatening one. As the TV movie guide recommends, 'See it with a friend' (Maltin: 1989, 444).

Or, perhaps, a 'companion.'

Part Seven

ETHNIC MONSTERS

Introduction to Part Seven

■ Ken Gelder

W E H A V E A L R E A D Y E N C O U N T E R E D arguments for seeing some horror texts as an expression of specific racial anxieties – as in Stephen Arata's account of Dracula as an Eastern European migrating into the West, or Elizabeth Young's reading of James Whale's monster as a metaphor for the Negro in 1930s America. Elsewhere, Virginia Wright Wexman has given a similar reading of Rouben Mamoulian's 1932 Academy Award-winning film of *Dr Jekyll and Mr Hyde* – noting that 'racial overtones are inescapable in Mamoulian's conception of Hyde as a primitive man' (Wexman: 1988, 288) and arguing that the incarnation of 'Negro-like' characteristics in Hyde underpins the film's valorization of whiteness as the only colour capable of beauty. Horror and blackness, on the other hand, have often joined forces, producing monsters (like Whale's and Mamoulian's) that are thus seen, from the white point of view, as both threatening and persecuted. Not every 'primitive' monster is raced, but it is certainly true that horror has persistently endowed the primal forces it unleashes, and so often relishes, with racial undertones.

The narrative of 'reverse colonization' can indeed be one location for an anxious white encounter with a character whose ethnicity makes him or her (or it) appear monstrous. But the narratives attached to colonization itself also routinely work in this way. The journey into the 'heart of darkness' turns the colonial imperative into a Gothic horror adventure, as likely to be expressed in cinema and fiction as it is in the earnest reporting of foreign correspondents and scientific expeditions. The voodoo film is a good example, centred – as in Jacques Tourneur's *noir* masterpiece, *I Walked with a Zombie* (1943) – on the long, suspenseful trek to the source of the horror. This journey simulated routes already charted by anthropologists in the Caribbean (specifically, Haiti), becoming tangled up in turn with the voodoo visions of visiting French surrealists around this time and the lurid-but-sceptical accounts given by travel writers such as Patrick Leigh Fermor. Later on, the notorious Italian zombie and cannibal films of the 1970s and early 1980s turned the journey out to the Other (usually deep into the jungles of the Amazon, New Guinea or the Philippines) into a vicious display of primal revenge upon gold-diggers seeking fortunes or film-makers driven by the need — in the case of what Kim Newman calls 'the *ne plus ultra* of the cannibal movie' (Newman: 1988, 193), Ruggero Deodato's *Cannibal Holocaust* (1979) — to see natives perform their 'savagery' for the camera.

Fatimah Tobing Rony's contribution to this section is precisely about the intimate links between anthropology, photography and the production of horror. Taken from *The Third Eye: Race, Cinema, and Ethnographic Spectacle*, this extract is part of a long and fascinating examination of Merian C. Cooper and Ernest B. Schoedsack's classic film, *King Kong* (1933). The film presents the journey of a 'jungle film-maker' and his crew — along with the starlet Ann Darrow (Fay Wray) — to Skull Island, where they capture a huge prehistoric ape, Kong. Returning to Manhattan, Kong is turned into an ethnographic spectacle for paying audiences. Photography had been central to ethnographic classification since the latter part of the nineteenth century, of course. Rony's point is that the transformation of the ethnographic object into visual image is (to recall a term used in the introduction to Part Three) *teratogenic*: productive of monstrosity. Most obviously, it is a means of confirming (to 'civilized' audiences) the unbridgeable backwardness and 'savagery' of the object on display. Aspects of *King Kong* were in fact explicitly linked to ethnographic cinema; Carl Denham, the leader of the film crew expedition, was modelled on Frank Buck, who made films about capturing animals for zoos, such as *Bring 'Em Back Alive* (1932) (Rony: 1996, 171). Skull Island is given a referent in the real world, with the islanders speaking an actual language from an island off the coast of Sumatra. (Rony speaks of the film's 'curious obsession with authenticity', ibid., 177.) Bringing Kong to Manhattan pushes the prehistoric into the frame of modern technological advances, a moment made iconic with Kong atop the Empire State Building. In the meantime, the film produces another spectacle through the figure of Ann Darrow, linking the ape and the white woman in a signifying chain. The relations between gender (especially 'savage' white women), race and monstrosity in 1930s 'jungle horror' films is discussed by Rony, as well as by Rhona J. Berenstein (1996, 160–97).

Other kinds of monstrosities can be produced by travelling to places that might seem to be better known and closer to home. The extract from my book *Reading the Vampire* notes that Transylvania was by no means the only source for these creatures. The vampire fragments and stories produced by Lord Byron and John Polidori in the early part of nineteenth century are in fact set in Greece. Byron had travelled through Greece as part of his Grand Tour in 1809–10; he soon became committed to Greek independence from Turkish rule, implicating himself in a Hellenistic, classical-folk ideal of racial purity. Polidori's vampire story gives this ideal a certain feminine, vulnerable embodiment — vulnerable in this case to a lethal, visiting vampire who may well have some Byronic features.

Hellenistic Greeks, investing in the production of a folk-lore which privileged an authentic, original Greekness, felt equally vulnerable to foreign influences nearer their borders: Turks, Albanians, Macedonians, Slavs. The extract takes the vampire as a representation of foreign influences that have already made themselves at home in the nation – signifying the kind of ethnicity a nation feels it must expel, even as it requires it for self-definition.

Chapter 18

KEN GELDER

VAMPIRES IN GREECE
(extract)

T HE VAMPIRE'S IDENTIFICATION WITH Transylvania comes rather late in the day: was it associated with other places before this? In fact, it is difficult to pin the vampire down to one original place and moment – and it is equally difficult to avoid surrendering to the cliché (often utilised in vampire fiction) that it is as 'ancient' as the human race itself. Van Helsing's account in [Bram Stoker's] *Dracula* places no limits on the vampire's whereabouts and history:

> For, let me tell you, he is known everywhere that men have been. In old Greece, in old Rome; he flourish in Germany all over, in France, in India, even in the Chersones; and in China. . . . He have follow the wake of the beserker Icelander, the devil-begotten Hun, the Slav, the Saxon, the Magyar.
>
> (Stoker: 1988, 239)

Most histories of the vampire similarly gesture towards a multiplicity of origins, whereby the vampire's identity is thoroughly dispersed across history and across place. Radu Florescu and Raymond T. McNally's *In Search of Dracula* (1972) and Gabriel Ronay's *The Truth About Dracula* (1972) take up the kind of narrative outlined above, returning to 'sources' only to pluralise them so that one is as good as another – as if every country and every moment in history has had its vampires. [. . .] Florescu and McNally's *Dracula: Prince of Many Faces* (1990) confirms the multiplicity of origins – as does Brian J. Frost's *The Monster with a Thousand Faces* (1989), an inventory of stories featuring the 'vampire motif' which concludes at the outset that the vampire, evolving from 'obscure' conditions, 'is a polymorphic phenomenon with a host of disparate guises to its credit' (Frost: 1989, 1).

Montague Summers's two monumental histories, *The Vampire: His Kith and Kin* (1928) and *The Vampire in Europe* (1929), also show the vampire to be both 'ancient' and everywhere. Indeed, it is internationalised as a 'citizen of the world' – Summers takes this phrase from the title of Oliver Goldsmith's literary work of the same name (1760–2) (Summers: 1928, 22). His second history, however, focusses on those European countries in which vampirism is or had been most intensive. Interestingly, Hungary is not the only source: 'In no country has the Vampire tradition more strongly prevailed and more persistently maintained its hold upon the people than in modern Greece' (ibid., 217). Summers here reproduces an orthodoxy which folklore studies – a discipline which consolidated itself in the latter part of the nineteenth century – had maintained for some time. Indeed, there is even a case to be made for suggesting that folklore studies cohered as a discipline in the nineteenth century through its interest in popular Greek beliefs about vampires. This point will be taken up shortly in the development of an argument about the importance of folklore, with its enshrining of the folk as Other and its schematisation of their beliefs and practices, for vampire fiction. But in fact the connection between vampire fiction and Greece has itself been long-standing. The first English vampire story – Dr John William Polidori's 'The Vampyre' (1819) – has its hero Aubrey journey to Greece just as Jonathan Harker journeys to Transylvania in *Dracula*. And the 'Vampire tradition' seems even at this stage to have had a strong hold upon 'the people' there.

Greece and the grand tour

Polidori's story has a complicated history, but a brief outline can be given here. In 1816 Polidori accompanied Lord Byron – as his physician – on a Grand Tour of the Continent. In Geneva, Byron met Percy Shelley, Mary Godwin and Claire Clairmont (who he had already known), and they took accommodation near the shores of Lake Leman. Their stay together is now legendary and has been well documented by biographers and critics. One night in mid-June, after reading among other things J. B. B. Eyries's collection of horror stories *Fantasmagoriana* – published in English as *Tales of the Dead* (1813) – Byron suggested they each write a ghost story themselves. Mary Godwin worked on the narrative that became *Frankenstein* (1818); Byron wrote a fragment of a horror story which may or may not have been about a vampire, which he dated 17 June 1816 (but published in 1819, after Polidori's story); and Polidori, probably a short while after June, wrote 'The Vampyre'. It is usually claimed that Polidori, under Byron's influence, slavishly plagiarised Byron's fragment for his narrative. My own view is that, although Polidori certainly did draw on Byron's fragment as well as on an earlier vampire poem by Byron, 'The Giaour' (1813), he used this material creatively (even ironically) rather than slavishly. We should also note that, although Polidori had in fact never been to Greece (just as Stoker had never been to Transylvania), Byron had already travelled through Greece and Turkey during an earlier Grand Tour in 1809–10. 'The Giaour' and his 'vampire' fragment were no doubt shaped by his experiences there, and these and other 'Byronic' representations of Greece may certainly in turn have influenced Polidori.

Byron's support for Greek independence – Greece was under Turkish rule at this time – was, of course, shared by other Romantics with an Oxbridge education in the classics, including Shelley and Leigh Hunt. He had gone to Athens to engage in the 'purity' of classical Greece, with its antiquities and monuments; he found, however, that Athens was populated with Turks and Albanians, and that the Greeks were administered from Constantinople. A discourse of degeneration was already available to describe this ethnic mixture, in particular the 'barbarity' of the Turks whom Byron came increasingly to dislike. He noted sourly, 'The pines, eagles, vultures, and owls were descended from those Themistocles and Alexander had seen, and not degenerated like the humans' (Marchand: 1971, 77). After the first Grand Tour, Byron melodramatically lamented the 'fall' of Greece in *Childe Harold's Pilgrimage* (1812) – 'Fair Greece! sad relic of departed worth!' (Canto II, verse 73). His popularity helped to entrench such sentiments; indeed, as James Buzard has pointed out, this poem did much to establish certain perceptions about the Continent (the romance of one place, the decadence of another) for subsequent British travellers. Buzard looks at the democratisation of travel and tourism in the early part of the nineteenth century, when the Grand Tour was increasingly accessible for the British middle classes. But the numbers of tourists on the Continent (an 'unprecedented flood') made travel seem no longer special or 'individual'. What was needed was a mode of 'anti-tourism' which captured the romance of travel in the terms expressed by Hazlitt – 'to leave ourselves behind, much more to get rid of others' (cited in Buzard: 1991, 33). Byron's poems answered this yearning, providing a set of perceptions about countries such as Greece which 'held out the promise of making Continental experience "live", of saturating it anew with poetical evocations, and even the *frisson* of a sexual daring that was not for domestic consumption' (ibid., 35). The Byronic image of a solitary wanderer in a perpetual state of exile became, paradoxically enough, immensely popular as a touristic posture. Indeed, the poems laid the foundation for a tourist industry which thrived by marketing those perceptions, making them *available* for domestic consumption – so much so that abridged versions of them were incorporated into travel guides.

Byron's 'The Giaour'

Byron described Athens in *Childe Harold* as 'The city won for Allah from the Giaour' (Canto II, verse 77), *Giaour* being a derogatory term used by Turks to describe Christians. In his poem, 'The Giaour' – subtitled 'A Fragment of a Turkish Tale' – Byron produces a kind of revenge fantasy for Athens' occupation. The poem's events take place in the late 1770s – coinciding in particular with Hassan Ghazi's brutal campaign in the Morea. [. . .] Greece, now, is lost and overrun: the poem begins with an image of pastoral Greece 'trampled' by the Turkish colonisers and no longer 'alive':

> 'Tis Greece, but living Greece no more!
> So coldly sweet, so deadly fair,
> We start, for soul is wanting there.
> Hers is the loveliness in death,
> That parts not quite with parting breath . . .

(lines 91–5)

A hero appears who is neither Greek nor Turkish — the Giaour in this poem was once a Moslem ('Apostate from his own vile faith,' line 616), but is now 'Christian in his face' (line 811). His Venetian or Albanian identity is sometimes recognisable ('now array'd in Arnaut garb,' line 615) and sometimes not; indeed, by the end he appears suitably nationless, with no 'name or race' (line 1329) of his own. The Giaour has eloped with Leila; she in turn is murdered — thrown into the sea — by the Turk Hassan, to whom she was betrothed; and the Giaour takes his revenge by ambushing and killing Hassan. Clearly, Leila is made to stand for Greece itself: while alive, her 'Soul beam'd forth in every spark' (line 477) and was, for the Giaour, inspirational, like a muse. Byron had figured Greece in precisely this way: the 'air of Greece,' he claimed, had made him a poet (Marchand: 1971, 99). More specifically, the poem is based on Byron's intervention in the punishment of a Turkish woman who was caught fornicating (see ibid., 89–90). Byron's self-projection as the Giaour is typical of his self-monumentalisation, but it also articulates his sense of powerlessness in Greek affairs. The Giaour's revenge is localised as a minor skirmish in the mountains; the national struggle remains beyond him. He subsequently occupies a position – a posture – somewhere in between engagement and disengagement: aware of the struggle, but isolated from it; attracted to the nationalist cause, but in a permanent condition of exile – residing in Greece only for a short while, but figuring his engagement with the Greek struggle as eternal. In the poem, this posture is graphically represented by turning the Giaour into a vampire after his death [. . .]. The relevant passage is particularly purple and was subsequently lifted out of the poem to preface a number of vampire narratives – including Polidori's story (it is cited in the introduction – which may not have been written by Polidori – to the first edition of 'The Vampyre'), and the various popular stage melodramas which derived from that story:

> But first, on earth as Vampire sent,
> Thy corse shall from its tomb be rent:
> Then ghastly haunt thy native place,
> And suck the blood of all thy race;
> There from thy daughter, sister, wife,
> At midnight drain the streak of life;
> Yet loathe the banquet which perforce
> Must feed thy livid living corse:
> Thy victims ere they yet expire
> Shall know the demon for their sire,
> As cursing thee, thou cursing them,
> Thy flowers are wither'd on the stem.
> But one that for thy crime must fall,
> the youngest, most beloved of all,
> Shall bless thee with a *father's* name –
> That word shall wrap thy heart in flame!
> Yet must thou end thy task, and mark
> Her cheek's last tinge, her eye's last spark,
> And the last glassy glance must view
> Which freezes o'er its lifeless blue;
> Then with unhallow'd hand shalt tear

The tresses of her golden hair,
Of which in life a lock when shorn,
Affection's fondest pledge was worn,
But now is borne away by thee,
Memorial of thine agony!
Wet with thine own best blood shall drip
Thy gnashing tooth and haggard lip;
Then stalking to thy sullen grave,
Go — and with Gouls and Afrits rave;
Till these in horror shrink away
From spectre more accursed than they!

The melancholy self-projection is grounded here not so much in national as *familial* identity. Showing the vampire preying upon those women closest to him in familial terms, Byron juxtaposes a sentimental fantasy of fatherhood with a horror of infanticide and incest (he was, as it happens, embarking on an affair with his half-sister Augusta around the time of publication). But the vampire is in one sense only a Gothic intensification of a posture already well developed in this poem and in others. The figure in perpetual exile, condemned to wander the earth, never at peace, unable and unwilling — as Byron described it in *Childe Harold* — to 'herd with Man; with whom he held/Little in common' (Canto III, verse 12), a witness to rather than a participant in national struggles, and above all, *suffering*: this is the typical Byronic hero. Andrew M. Cooper has analysed this posture, noting the Byronic hero's flâneurian mode of traversing the earth 'invisible but gazing' [. . .]. The poems become, in effect, 'self-contained, animated system[s]' (cited in Cooper: 1988, 541), entirely divorced from the historicality of their sites. The extent of this divorce is, of course, debatable; certainly, by placing the poems in the context described by Buzard — the increasing democratisation of the Grand Tour, and the subsequent forging of a Romantic self-image through which the British traveller's individualism can be preserved — their historicality is restored at the level of representation. Moreover, the poem's idealist calls for a resurrected Greek nationhood are in tune with sentiments already in vogue at the time. Conversely, the Giaour is unable to realise this resurrection — indeed, he is himself presented as a degenerate figure who is more destructive than creative, more of a problem to national identity than a solution. At one level, the protean Byronic vampire becomes a figure for the utterly self-conscious 'citizen of the world' (Marchand uses this phrase to describe Byron: 1971, 93), drawing life out of each nation he visits; at another level, he is romantically involved with a Greece whose identity remains lost or unrealisable; at another level still, he symbolises the depths to which nationhood, with its mixture of 'races' and its lost classical heritage, has sunk. Like so many vampire narratives, the fantasy indulged in here is one of *incompletion*; the Giaour remains a vampire so long as national identity is unattainable.

Byron, Polidori and popular fiction

Byron's 'fragment of a novel' also describes the beginning of a Grand Tour, undertaken by the young narrator and a mysterious older man he greatly admires,

Augustus Darvell. Darvell 'had already travelled extensively' (Byron: 1988, 3): he is another of Byron's 'citizens of the world', a restless, protean figure who has no 'original' identity of his own. His physiognomy makes this fact particularly visible: 'the expressions of his features would vary so rapidly . . . it was useless to trace them to their sources . . . none could be fixed upon with accuracy' (ibid., 3). The narrator is pleased to accompany Darvell; as they journey towards the East, however, he is concerned to see Darvell appear 'daily more enfeebled' (ibid., 3), his health rapidly declining. In a Turkish cemetery somewhere between Smyrna and Ephesus, close to 'the broken columns of Diana – the roofless walls of expelled Christianity, and the still more recent but complete desolation of abandoned mosques' (ibid., 4), Darvell comes to rest at last. The journey, it seems, was planned from the beginning: Darvell has, he confesses, visited this empty, unin-habited place before. Dying, he arranges a solemn pact with the narrator – to 'conceal my death from every human being', to throw his seal ring ('on which there were some Arabic characters') into the Bay of Eleusis, and then 'repair to the ruins of the temple of Ceres' (ibid., 5) at a designated time. A stork appears on one of the tombstones, with a snake in its beak which it 'does not devour' (ibid., 6). The narrator watches it fly away; at which point Darvell expires, his face suddenly turning black. The narrator buries him in a Turkish grave, and the fragment closes with an uncertain response to the events, as if nothing so far lends itself to diagnosis: 'Between astonishment and grief, I was tearless' (ibid., 6).

It is difficult to read this fragment, since – as well as being unfinished – much of it (the image of the stork and the snake, for instance) *is* cryptic, functioning as 'unexplained ritual' (Skarda: 1989, 256n). Nevertheless, its ethnographics are reasonably clear: in his connection to the site, Darvell reaches back into an 'ori-ginal' classical antiquity, beyond Turkish occupation, beyond Christianity, to the temples of Diana or Ceres. There are no resurrected vampires in the fragment; however, Polidori had written an account of Byron's intentions for the remainder of the narrative:

> Two friends were to travel from England to Greece; while there one of them should die, but before his death, should obtain from his friend an oath of secrecy with regard to his decease. Some short time after, the remaining traveller returning to his native country, should be star-tled at perceiving his former companion moving about in society, and should be horrified at finding that he made love to his former friend's sister.
>
> (cited in ibid., 257)

Polidori's own vampire story is certainly close to this sketch of Byron's tale: his vampire, Lord Ruthven, does indeed resurrect himself to 'make love' to Aubrey's sister. Also, the travellers' destination – given here as Greece – is precisely the destination of Aubrey and Ruthven. But in Polidori's story, the travellers – Aubrey especially – find a very different kind of Greece. Byron's poem and his narrative fragment were solitary psychodramas, depopulated texts – the 'social' is missing from them. But the Byronic return to antiquity, to a 'source' that one can contemplate in solitude, is now ironically displaced by Polidori. Greece, now, is an *inhabited* country – where 'the people' are callously used and discarded by just such Byronic, vampire-like, 'citizens of the world'.

Critics like Skarda (1989) and Barbour (1992), who see 'The Vampyre' as a crude narrative written under the influence of a greater and more subtle talent, ignore the ironic mode of Polidori's story – and reproduce the usual academic prioritising of (great) literature over sensationalist fiction. It is, of course, certainly reasonable to read the relationship between Lord Ruthven and Aubrey as a projection of the relationship between Byron and Polidori – the latter under the former's spell, overshadowed by him, even haunted by him, but resolutely documenting his bad habits. In fact, Polidori had taken the name of his Byronic vampire from Clarence de Ruthven, Lord Glenarvon, the rakish villain modelled on Byron in Caroline Lamb's notorious novel, *Glenarvon* (1816) – which, when he read it, Byron considered libellous. 'The Vampyre' is in this sense a work transmitting 'gossip' through a Gothic mode; Polidori was both trading on Byron's already fictionalised reputation, and adding his own Gothic inflexion to it. This is hardly a passive writerly position: Skarda's claim, with its offensive simile – that 'Polidori, like a willing rape victim, sacrifices himself in life and Aubrey in his fiction to the father-god he found in Byron' (Skarda: 1989, 262) – comes from reading the story for its hysterics only.

The feminising and subordination of Polidori in relation to a masculine, assertive Byron perhaps recalls Andreas Huyssen's argument in his influential essay 'Mass Culture as Woman: Modernism's Other', which opens with a discussion of Flaubert's relationship to his character Madame Bovary. For Huyssen, the latter is positioned as a consumer of popular fiction – 'subjective, emotional, passive' – as opposed to the former, who is taken as a 'writer of genuine, authentic literature – objective, ironic, and in control of his aesthetic means' (Huyssen: 1986, 189–90). Polidori and Byron are conventionally figured in exactly these terms. The same configuration is at work in Polidori's story, too, through the relationship between Aubrey and Lord Ruthven – but it is treated ironically, rather than surrendered to wholesale. The story opens by *distancing* itself from Aubrey's attraction to 'high romantic feeling' (Polidori: 1988, 8). In fact, just like Madame Bovary, Aubrey's view of the world is shaped by the illusions of popular fiction, 'the romances of his solitary hours' (ibid., 8). At the moment of his *disillusion* – just as he is about to find that 'there was no foundation in real life for any of that congeries of pleasing pictures and descriptions contained in those volumes, from which he formed his study' (ibid., 8) – he meets Lord Ruthven. The prioritising of Byron/Lord Ruthven – as original or authentic – over Polidori/Aubrey – as plagiarising, inauthentic – is then playfully reversed. Aubrey in fact self-consciously *invents* Lord Ruthven: 'He soon formed this object into the hero of a romance, and determined to observe the offspring of his fancy, rather than the person before him' (ibid., 8). The story goes on to trace out the oscillation between illusion and disillusion. Aubrey finds that Ruthven's financial affairs 'were embarrassed', that he gambles and inhabits places of 'vice.' Aubrey's guardians beg him to leave such a 'dreadfully vicious' associate. Both in spite of this and because of it, Ruthven comes to assume for Aubrey's 'exalted imagination . . . the appearance of something supernatural' (ibid., 10). The discovery that Ruthven is a vampire folds illusion and disillusion into each other: it is impossible (only an 'exalted imagination' could conceive it) and yet it is true. The oath Aubrey swears to Ruthven operates in the same way: he must not tell anyone that Ruthven is a vampire – no one would believe him anyway – and yet the story itself brings this 'fact' to the public's attention. Polidori was commissioned by John Murray to keep a diary of his Grand Tour with Byron; it was not published until 1911, but 'The Vampyre' serves as a kind of substitute, relying as it does on the disclosure of a terrible knowledge that only a most intimate companion – someone who, like Aubrey, watches Ruthven's every move – can possess.

'The Vampyre', antiquity and the folk

[. . .] In 'The Giaour', Byron had feminised Greece, figuring it through the lost figure of Leila, who remains absent throughout the poem. In 'The Vampyre', Aubrey – having left Lord Ruthven after an argument – travels to Athens where he meets the beautiful Ianthe. [. . .] Aubrey had typically gone to Greece to contemplate the *inanimate* – 'tracing the fading records of ancient glory upon monuments that apparently, ashamed of chronicling the deeds of freemen only before slaves, had hidden themselves beneath the sheltering soil or many coloured lichen' (ibid., 11). But he is constantly distracted from his classical studies by Ianthe – and in particular, by the stories she tells him. In effect, two images of Greece, two kinds of texts with two very different effects, compete for Aubrey's attention: the classical and 'almost effaced' narratives of antiquity, patiently awaiting their 'proper interpretation', and Ianthe's tales of vampires, which are animated enough to 'excite' Aubrey and make his 'blood run cold' (ibid., 12). Although immersed in the 'romance' of popular fiction, Aubrey tries to disillusion Ianthe; but she implores him to believe that her stories are real:

> turning to subjects that had evidently made a greater impression upon her mind, [she] would tell him all the supernatural tales of her nurse. Her earnestness and apparent belief of what she narrated, excited the interest even of Aubrey; and often as she told him the tale of the living vampyre, who had passed years amidst his friends, and dearest ties, forced every year, by feeding upon the life of a lovely female to prolong his existence for the ensuing months, his blood would run cold, whilst he attempted to laugh her out of such idle and horrible fantasies; but Ianthe cited to him the names of old men, who had at last detected one living among themselves, after several of their near relatives and children had been found marked with the stamp of the fiend's appetite; and when she found him so incredulous, she begged of him to believe her, for it had been remarked, that those who had dared to question their existence, always had some proof given, which obliged them, with grief and heartbreaking, to confess it was true. She detailed to him the traditional appearance of these monsters, and its horror was increased, by hearing a pretty accurate description of Lord Ruthven; he, however, still persisted in persuading her, that there could be no truth in her

> fears, though at the same time he wondered at the many coincidences which had all tended to excite a belief in the supernatural power of Lord Ruthven.
>
> (ibid., 12–13)

The word 'excite' is repeated several times: these animated stories in turn animate Aubrey. The distinction is drawn between classical texts – which require contemplation and 'proper interpretation' – and what we might see here as popular fiction, which immediately realises its content through a direct stimulation of the reader's imagination. The former are dead texts, while the latter is very much alive – and seductive, too, for Aubrey's 'excitement' as he listens to Ianthe is surely also sexual. But Aubrey is by now the perfect reader of popular fiction: he is *easily* seduced: he comes to believe in the illusion of vampires because they are now already familiar to him. What triggers the belief in such 'foreign' creatures is Aubrey's recognition of Lord Ruthven – so that, in these terms, the story is close to Freud's account of 'The "Uncanny"' (1919): the source of one's anxiety about the unfamiliar lies much closer to home.

But [. . .] what is interesting about this passage – and what distinguishes it from Byron's depopulated vampire narratives, with their solitary, anti-social heroes – is that these beliefs, and the 'excitement' they generate, are shared by others, who readily communicate them to Aubrey. Ianthe and her nurse believe in vampires; various 'old men' do, too; later, Ianthe's parents 'affirmed their existence, pale with horror at the very name' (ibid., 13); and after her death, a group of villagers have no trouble identifying the cause, 'A Vampyre! A Vampyre!' (ibid., 15). In other words, this story grounds the vampire in the everyday life of 'the people' – the *folk*. The journey to Greece brings Aubrey into contact with the folk, which is where the origins of vampire superstitions are located. Whereas Byron's vampire narratives *remove* their characters from socialised contexts, Polidori's characters are immersed in them. Indeed, the distinction between classical texts and folk or popular narratives in 'The Vampyre' sits alongside a further distinction between the folk and 'society' itself – meaning the fashionable, leisured classes. Thus, Ianthe – an image for the folk, with her natural innocence and her love for stories – contrasts with Lady Mercer, a notorious socialite. Ianthe is 'unconscious' of love, while Lady Mercer is a wily seductress immersed in 'vice'. Lord Ruthven moves freely around in 'society', unnoticed, while in the forests of Greece he is immediately recognised and feared – and, of course, it is suggested, he murders Ianthe. Polidor's story seems to suggest that 'society' itself is vampirish; its aristocratic representatives prey upon 'the people' wherever they go.

Vampires, folklore and modern Greece

It would be possible to argue that vampire fiction consolidated itself because of (or, in relation to) the establishment in the nineteenth century of folklore as a modern discipline with an identifiable field of study: the folk, or 'the people'. Vampire fiction as it developed intermittently through the century – Polidori's story, J. Sheridan Le Fanu's 'Carmilla' (1872), R. L. Stevenson's 'Olalla' (1885),

Stoker's *Dracula* – usually required the existence of rumours or gossip or 'rustic' superstitions to enable the vampire to exist. A context of belief has to be established, but kept at a distance: 'the people' are shown to be both superstitious ('excitable', prone to exaggeration) and right. More literate, educated characters who speak up for the vampire – like Professor Van Helsing in *Dracula* – must operate in relation to this context. He is a scientist who mediates between folkish superstition and enlightened knowledge, 'the people' (subjective) and science (objective), equally at home in these otherwise contradictory spheres. Thus he is both rational and clear-headed, and yet given to 'regular fit[s] of hysterics' (Stoker: 1988, 174), behaving excessively, becoming excitable and highly animated by his subject. He never says, as scientists might, that the vampire is an illusion; his job is not to disillusion, but – quite the opposite – to make the illusion *real*.

[. . .]

In the early nineteenth century, the best-known chronicler of folk superstitions was Sir Walter Scott. Influenced by Goethe and German collectors of folk narratives – the Grimm brothers produced their major texts in the second decade of the nineteenth century – Scott folded folk superstitions into a mode of romance that unpacked itself as it went along, ending, precisely, with disillusion. His novels (*The Pirate* (1822) is a good example) inscribed the folk into the past – as archaic, unwilling to adapt (politically) to the present day, naive, marginal. At the same time, they laid the groundwork for a developing field of study and a particularly influential conception of the Scottish national identity. In fact the nineteenth century saw an increased commitment to the folk and 'folklore'. The term itself was not coined until 1846: in an article in *Athenaeum*, William John Thoms introduced the 'good Saxon compound, Folk-Lore' to replace the 'circumlocutions' in current usage at the time, 'Popular Antiquities' and 'Popular Literature' (cited in Herzfeld: 1982, 111–12). Certainly, the connections between 'folklore' as an emergent discipline of study and representations of the folk – rustic types, rural communities – in popular fiction (as well as ballads, street songs and so on) ought to be noticed. But it is also important to note the connection between the emergent discipline of 'folklore' and the formation of modern national identities. The term may have been coined in England, but it was already in circulation in other forms in other European countries – in particular, the two centres for folklore studies in the nineteenth century, Germany and Greece.

The Romantic investment in the Hellenic struggle has already been noted. Greece was identified as the origin of Europe itself, the most ancient of all European countries – and yet, under Turkish rule at the beginning of the nineteenth century and with an ethnically mixed population, its modern identity as a nation-state had not yet cohered. Observers at this time were nevertheless imagining a national identity: the aristocratic British traveller F.S.N. Douglas, in his *An Essay on Certain Points of Resemblance between the Ancient and Modern Greeks* (1813), saw the 'essential' Greeks as descended from the Hellenised *barbaroi* – thus explaining, as Michael Herzfeld notes, 'the features which to his mind bespoke decadence and superstition' (ibid., 77). The Greek war of independence galvanised Hellenism and received much sympathy from foreign observers – radical Romantics like Byron, who returned to Greece to take part, and died there in 1824. Indeed, Hellenism may have been more of a projected image than a self-image – a means of attracting the support of cautious nations like Britain. Nevertheless, it gave folklore studies in Greece its impetus. It enabled the formation of a discipline which saw the ancient become visible in the modern; with the realisation of Greece as a modern nation state, it brought the ancient back to life – it demonstrated the ability of antiquity to live again. Of course, folklore as it developed in other European countries during the nineteenth century also revived the ancient, showing its lingering influence in the present day – Jakob Grimm's *Deutsche Mythologien* (1835), for example, was important in this respect for the nationalisation of folklore, ancient and modern, in Germany. The debates in Britain between what Mary Douglas has called the progressionists (who saw the 'primitive' as almost vanished) and their opponents, such as W. Robertson Smith, who emphasised 'the common elements in modern and primitive experience' (Douglas: 1991, 14), have been well documented. But Greece had a particular investment in the latter position, precisely because of its projected image as the 'source' of Europe itself, its 'originality' – what Herzfeld calls its 'special ancestral status' (Herzfeld: 1982, 11).

Herzfeld's study, *Ours Once More: Folklore, Ideology, and the Making of Modern Greece*, emphasises the importance folklore studies had in the creation of an 'organic' national identity built around an 'originally' conceived Greek people. The folk were construed as a kind of muse upon which a cultivated culture could ground itself – a one-way relationship which Polidori's story both confirms and vampirises, showing Aubrey 'distracted' by a feminised folk-image, but also showing 'society' preying upon the folk for its own gratification. [. . .]. But in [Herzfeld's] account, the nationalisation of Greek identity – through a view of the modern as an animated realisation of the ancient – ran into trouble precisely when it turned *towards* the object of study, the folk, which was supposed to enable it to cohere. In the early part of the nineteenth century especially [. . .], the promotion of a Greek national identity was largely the work of foreigners and expatriate bodies. In contrast, Herzfeld notes,

> It is difficult to know what the rural population thought of these developments. Their scanty acquaintance with Classical culture made it easy for European enthusiasts and western-educated Greeks to promote the ideal of a regenerated Hellas over their heads. Some historians have argued that the rural folk preserved no knowledge or memory of the Classical past at all. The rural Greeks certainly seemed to have been puzzled by the expectations which the philhellenes entertained of them, to judge from the accounts of those non-Greeks who returned to tell the tale.
>
> (ibid., 15)

Polidori's arrangement in 'The Vampyre' would seem to be close to the truth here: the 'folk' seem oblivious to the classical antiquities around them – the latter being of interest only to foreigners like Aubrey. Moreover, as folklore studies moved closer to ethnography, the folk were by no means found to be the site of a pure and 'original' Greek identity. Greece was declared a nation-state in 1822, and the Turks were expelled by the end of that decade; but Turkish influences remained. The German nationalist J.P. Fallmerayer (1790–1861) outraged Hellenes by further corrupting Greek identity, claiming Slavish and Albanian influences. Ethnographic work carried out in the provinces and close to the borders only confirmed the extent of these corruptions: the folk identity seemed always already to be ethnically mixed. And intimately associated with this realisation – even, bringing this realisation into being, enabling it to be articulated – was the (re)discovery of the vampire.

Genuine vampires

Rennell Rodd's popular study, *The Customs and Lore of Modern Greece* (1892) – partly a late Victorian travelogue, and partly an ethnographic work with scientific pretensions – depended upon a distinction between the classical and the folk for its appeal. One arrives in Greece expecting to see and examine the former; but the latter slowly makes itself visible, the longer one stays:

> It is only after a long sojourn in this land of myth and fable, of art and inspiration, and after many wanderings, that one is able to learn how, in solitary islands, in sequestered valleys . . . there lives a people who seem to have preserved, in manner and in look, that old-world freshness of our dreams.
>
> (Rodd: 1968, x)

The folk keep the ancient 'fresh', 'preserved': this is where the real Greece – the Greece of 'our dreams' – resides. Although Rodd seems familiar with the texts of modern Greek folklore – he cites the work of Johann Georg von Hahn, Nikolaos G. Politis and Charles Fauriel's influential *Chants populaires de la Grèce moderne* (1825) – his own study is too 'leisurely' to engage in the various debates. Nevertheless, by focussing solely on the folk – in particular, those people living at the edges of the nation – Rodd presents a 'hitherto rather neglected' (ibid., xvi) account of the ethnically mixed nature of Greece. His remarks on the etymology of the vampire express this mixture – while wishing to maintain a sense of Greece itself as an authentic source:

> The genuine vampire is the Vourkolakas, of whom a number of stories are still current, though Colonel Leake [William Martin Leake, *Researches in Greece* (1814) and *Travels in Northern Greece* (1835)] more than fifty years ago expressed the opinion that it would be difficult in Greece to find any one who still believed in such a barbarous superstition. The Albanians call it Wurwolakas, and the name has a number of slightly varying forms in different parts of Greece. The word itself is undoubtedly of Slavonic origins, being found in Bohemia, Dalmatia, Montenegro, Servia, and Bulgaria; while it reappears as Vilkolak among the Poles, with the signification of weir-wolf (*sic*). The superstition itself is, however, of extreme antiquity, and the name only was introduced by the Slavonic immigrants.
>
> (ibid., 188)

In this account, the vampire seems to be simultaneously indigenous and introduced – 'genuinely' Greek, and yet 'undoubtedly' Slavonic, nationally identified and yet leaked across the border by immigrants from the north. In the context of Hellenism, these countries are in fact related to each other in terms of purity and corruption, the genuine and the derivative. John Cuthbert Lawson's *Modern Greek Folklore and Ancient Greek Religion* (1910) – influenced by Politis' *Modern Greek Mythology* (1871, 1874) – returns to this arrangement, consolidating it through ethnographic practices and an extensive knowledge of philology. For Lawson, Macedonia was an important source for the vampire, for here 'the Greek population lives in constant touch with Slavonic people' (Lawson: 1964, 378). He spends some time trying to sort out the vampire's etymological origins: 'Is the superstition a foreign importation, or is it only partly alien and partly native?' (ibid., 381). Finally he makes the following two claims:

> first, that the word *vrykolakas* was originally borrowed from the Greeks by the Slavs in the sense of 'were-wolf,' though it is now almost universally employed in the sense of 'vampire'; secondly, that whatever ideas concerning vampires the Greeks may have learnt from the Slavs, they did not adapt the Slavonic word 'vampire' but employed one of those native Greek words . . . which are still in local usage; whence it follows that some superstition anent re-animated corpses existed in Greece before the coming of the Slavs.
>
> (ibid., 383)

For Lawson, then, the Greek vampire is more original than the Slavonic vampire. And, underwriting the Hellenism at work in this study, the latter is presented as a *debasement* of the former: 'The Greeks had believed in reasonable human *revenants*; the Slavs taught them to believe in brutish, inhuman vampires' (ibid., 391). In fact, Lawson's project is to recuperate a Hellenic image of the vampire that is, in effect, Romantic. He had presented the familiar thesis that the revenant had been someone excommunicated by the Church. By sanctioning excommunication, the Church thus brought vampires into existence. For Lawson, the Church was as much to blame for the debasement of modern Greece as the Slavs:

> The Devil is a Christian conception, just as the vampire is Slavonic. Both must go, if the modern superstition is to be stripped of its accretions, and the genuinely Hellenic elements discovered. What then remains? Simply the belief that the bodies of certain classes of persons did not decay away in their graves but returned there-from, and the feeling that such persons were sufferers deserving of pity.
>
> (ibid., 407)

The vampire, essentially, 'suffers': this is close to the Byronic image of the vampire in 'The Giaour'. But what is interesting about this passage is that the 'modern superstition' does, finally, remain intact. Lawson does nothing to disillusion the belief: he is concerned only to establish its 'genuine' credentials. Indeed, to enable the discovery of the Hellenic ideal, the illusion of the vampire must be rendered *real*. The Turks have been driven out, the Slavish influences – along with Christianity – have been stripped away. All those Others which introduce or produce vampires have been expelled – and yet still the vampire remains. It would be tempting to say that the vampire has now come to stand for originality itself; at the same time, however, it signifies those very 'accretions' that Lawson is attempting to remove. As Rodd had noted, the vampire is both 'genuine' *and* introduced, pure and corrupted, nationally identified and alien, a 'foreign importation'. But, of course, the illusion here resides with the folk, 'the people': it is *their* originality which is being claimed and contested. The point is important for the kind of popular fiction – early vampire fiction, in this case – which depends on the one hand upon a representation of the folk or 'the people' and their lore or superstitions as original to the nation, while on the other hand moves its vampire nomadically through and across nations, letting it gather up 'accretions' as it goes. The vampire thus both enables a national identity to cohere, and ceaselessly disturbs that identity by showing it to be always at the same time foreign to itself.

Chapter 19

FATIMAH TOBING RONY

KING KONG AND THE MONSTER IN ETHNOGRAPHIC CINEMA
(extract)

King Kong and ethnographic spectacle

IN MERIAN C. COOPER AND Ernest B. Schoedsack's film *King Kong* (1933), the giant prehistoric gorilla Kong is captured and made into a lucrative Broadway attraction by the jungle picture filmmaker Carl Denham (Robert Montgomery). Kong then escapes, creating terror in the metropolis; he stalks the blonde heroine Ann Darrow (Fay Wray) and carries her off to the top of the Empire State Building where Kong is killed by an incessant barrage of bullets from fighter airplanes. The incredibly polysemous quality of *King Kong*, which has assured its continuing widespread popularity, has also led to a multitude of interpretations of the film – as dream, capitalist fairy tale, imperialist metaphor, allegory for the unconscious, and repressed spectacle for racial taboos. Its status as cinematic *fantasy*, as 'a modern, movie-born myth' without historical antecedents, remains, however, largely unquestioned (Telotte: 1988, 390). But *King Kong* is not merely a classic Hollywood film, it is a work which in significant respects builds on and redeploys themes borrowed from the scientific time machine of anthropology.

The lineage of *King Kong* should be obvious: the filming, capture, exhibition, photographing, and finally murder of Kong takes its cue from the historic exploitation of native peoples as freakish 'ethnographic' specimens by science, cinema, and popular culture. Critics has consistently passed lightly over the fact that, in the 1920s, Cooper and Schoedsack were well-known ethnographic filmmakers, producing and directing both *Grass* (1925) and *Chang* (1927). *King Kong*, moreover, begins with an expedition, fully equipped with film camera, to a remote tropical island: *King Kong* is literally a film about the making of an ethnographic film. As exaggerated and baroque as *King Kong* may appear [. . .], the film makes reference to many of the themes that characterized the construction of the 'ethnographic' in early cinema.

If, as Cooper had complained, there were no longer any remote, genuinely alien cultures left to be discovered, monsters still lurked in the imagination of inter-war ethnographic cinema. In the spectacular commercial cinema of this period, monstrosity was the mode of representation of the Ethnographic.

Pierre Leprohon writes that the cinema of exoticism – and under this rubric he includes both the research films of an anthropologist like Marcel Griaule and falsified documentaries like the film *Ingagi* (1933) – partakes at the same time of science and of dream: as scientific document, it furthers the pursuit of knowledge; as poetry, it is the food of dreams (Leprohon: 1945, 12–13). I will show how the monster is both the subject of scientific representation, as was the case with the Komodo dragon, the object of W. Douglas Burden's museum expedition in 1927, and of fantastic cinematic representation, as in Cooper and Schoedsack's *The Most Dangerous Game* (1932) and Erle C. Kenton's *The Island of Lost Souls* (1933), horror films which explore the notion of hybridity in teratological terms. Whether the monster was the object of science or fantasy, and whether shot with rifle or camera, it was a mode of representation inextricably linked with sex, power, and death.

[. . .] With the advent of sound technology in the early 1930s, the 'racial film' genre ironically lost one of the dimensions of its 'realism.' André F. Liotard, Samivel, and Jean Thévenot note, 'Even if it doesn't have dialogue, the exotic sound film always risks being betrayed by its noises, and especially by its music and its voiceover' (Liotard, Samivel and Thévenot: 1950, 61). What propels *King Kong* forward is not the voice-over or intertitles of the scientific research film or lyrical ethnographic film, but sound of a different sort – the blonde heroine's screams, the giant gorilla Kong's roar, the lush Wagnerian score of Max Steiner – and *movement* – the longboat rushes to Skull Island to save Ann, the crew runs through the jungle in order to save her, and later the heroes run through Manhattan in an attempt to save Ann from Kong again. *King Kong* is a film of [. . .] frenetic braggadocio, clunking the viewer over the head visually and aurally, a tone set by the very title of the film with its alliteration and rough-hewn rhythm. *King Kong* is the ultimate carnivalesque version of early ethnographic cinema.

Teratology and fantasy: the science expedition and the horror film

My notion that the mode of representation of the 'ethnographic' in spectacular commercial cinema takes the form of *teratology* – the study of monstrosity – derives from Stephen Bann's study of the rhetoric of history-writing in nineteenth-century France and Great Britain. Emphasizing the parallel between monstrosity and taxidermy, Bann points out that the monster is 'the composite, incongruous beast which . . . simulated the seamless integrity of organic life' (Bann: 1984, 22). [. . .] *King Kong* is not only a film about a monster – the film itself is a monster, a hybrid of the scientific expedition and fantasy genres.

[. . .] Teratology was an important aspect of early anthropology: the 'monster,' like the Primitive Other, was of keen interest because it could be used to study and define the normal. In *The Normal and the Pathological*, historian of science Georges Canguilhem describes how abnormality is necessary to constitute normality: 'The abnormal, as ab-normal, comes after the definition of the normal, it is its logical negation. . . . The normal is the effect obtained by the execution of the normative project, it is the norm exhibited in the fact. . . . It is not paradoxical to say that the abnormal, while logically second, is existentially first' (Canguilhem: 1991, 243).

The Ethnographic could be romanticized as authentic culture and/or as 'pathological' culture, as in Margaret Mead's representation of the Balinese as schizoid. But one need not seek out extreme examples: the notion of the 'ethnographic' as monster was only an exaggeration of the common propensity to see native peoples as strange, bizarre, and abhorrent. It is significant that anthropologist Bronislaw Malinowski's infamous invocation of *Heart of Darkness* – 'exterminate the brutes' – comes out of his exasperation at the refusal of the Trobrianders to sit still long enough to be photographed (Malinowski: 1989, 69). The Ethnographic becomes monstrous at the very moment of visual appropriation.

Noël Carroll has explained that, in the horror film, the two essential characteristics of the monster are its impurity and its dangerousness. Borrowing from Mary Douglas's analysis in *Purity and Danger* (1966), he explains that monsters are impure in that, as hybrids, they are not easily categorized, and thus cross the boundaries of cultural schemas. Monsters are, Carroll emphasizes, interstitial. Kong, neither human nor ape, is impure in this sense. Thus the monster is not just physically threatening, but also cognitively threatening: its existence threatens cultural boundaries. As Carroll suggests, this cultural dangerousness explains why the geography of horror often involves lost continents and outer space (Carroll: 1990, 31–4).

[. . .] Monstrosity is essentially visual, an aspect of 'seeing anthropology' that involves a search for visual evidence of the pathological, a theme made evident in both Paul Broca's and Franz Boas's recommendations that anthropologists observe the indigenous person as a patient (see Stocking: 1979, 243). Because the image in ethnographic film is taken as 'real,' footage of a person in trance frothing at the mouth and biting off a chicken head, or of a person slicing open a seal and eating raw meat, often is read by the intended viewer of ethnographic film, the Western viewer, as evidence of the essential savagery of the Ethnographic. As Wilson Martinez and Asen Balikci have explained and documented, cultures in ethnographic films are usually seen by students and other audiences as aberrant, bizarre, and even repulsive, unless the culture on display is similar to the culture of the audience (Martinez: 1990, 34–47; Balikci: 1989, 4–10). Such audience studies raise questions about the ethics of filming acts which were never meant to be seen by outsiders, and showing the films in contexts in which – even with extensive commentary from anthropologists – abhorrence is aroused. Brazilian ethnographic filmmaker Jorge Preloran explains:

> After seeing dozens of films on ethnographic subjects, one thing stands out clearly for me: the majority of [the films] create a gulf between us and the 'primitive' people they usually depict. This to me is a racist approach because unless we have a chance to listen firsthand to those

people, letting them explain to us WHY they act as they do, WHY they have those extraordinary rituals, those fantastic, colorful, exotic, disgusting, fascinating – you label it – ceremonies that are shown to us, we will only think of them as savages.

(Preloran: 1975, 105)

Several different tendencies converged to produce the image of the Ethnographic as monstrous. First, the great variety of indigenous societies continually destabilized the Modern/Primitive dichotomy. Second, the perception of indigenous peoples as a link between the ape and the white man, as in between animal and 'human' (white), made the Ethnographic always already monstrous. Third, the image betrays anthropology's obsession with hybridity. The concern with hybridity manifested itself both through an abhorrence of interracial intercourse and 'blood mixing,' reflected in Paul Broca's influential research purportedly establishing that the offspring of blacks and whites were infertile (Cohen: 1980, 234), and through notions of salvage ethnography, the belief that the 'ethnographic' as embodiment of an earlier, purer humanity, would spoil upon contact with the West, a conceit which was played out in the 'racial film' genre. [. . .]

Its literary counterpart to the spoils-upon-contact theme is exemplified in Lévi-Strauss's description of the society of Brazilian Indian rubber tappers in *Tristes Tropiques* (1955). He explains that if the Nambikwara had taken him to the Stone Age, and the Tupi-Kawahib to the sixteenth century, then the society of the *seringal* (rubber plantation) in the Brazilian Amazon brought him to the eighteenth century. It is worth quoting his description of the Indian women at length:

> Under a layer of rouge and powder they were hiding syphilis, tuberculosis and malaria. They came in high-heeled shoes from the *barracão*, where they lived with 'the man,' their *seringueiro*, and, although ragged and dishevelled all the rest of the year, for one evening they appeared spick and span; yet they had had to walk two or three kilometres in their evening dresses along muddy forest paths. And in order to get ready, they had washed in darkness in filthy *igarapés* (streams), and in the rain, since it had poured all day. There was a staggering contrast between these flimsy appearances of civilization and the monstrous reality which lay just outside the door.
>
> (Lévi-Strauss: 1981b, 371)

Although with great pathos, Lévi-Strauss mourns the passage of time: acculturation brings disease and despair, and indigenous culture cannot withstand the onslaught. Mixture, whether it takes the form of miscegenation or acculturation, produces monsters.

Stephen Neale's description of the monster in the horror film reveals a direct similarity between screen monsters and the Ethnographic rendered as monster. In both cases, the focus is on bodily disruption:

> The monster, and the disorder it initiates and concretises, is always that which disrupts and challenges the definitions and categories of the

'human' and the 'natural.' Generally speaking, it is in the monster's body which focuses the disruption. Either disfigured, or marked by a heterogeneity of human and animal features, or marked only by a 'non-human' gaze, the body is always in some way signalled as 'other,' signalled, precisely, as monstrous.

(Neale: 1980, 21)

Not surprisingly, the archetypal narrative of many forms of ethnographic cinema, but especially of the expedition film, mirrors that of the horror film. Carroll points out that the horror film uses variations on the 'complex discovery' plot: the monster first appears or is created (onset); it is then noticed by the human protagonists (discovery); its horrible existence is acknowledged (confirmation); and the film ends with a fight to the death between human and monster (confrontation) (Carroll: 1990, 99). As Neale explains, the narrative process in the horror film is 'marked by a search for that specialized form of knowledge which will enable human characters to comprehend and control that which simultaneously embodies and causes its "trouble"' (Neale: 1980, 22). Similarly, the plot of expedition films like *Grass* is structured around the discovery and confirmation of a being (whether zoological rarity or group of people) with incongruous features or habits.

The expedition film did not have to take native peoples as its subject matter in order for it to be informed by the obsession with race and fears of hybridity characteristic of ethnographic cinema. Perhaps the best example of an expedition film that contains 'ethnographic' elements without being explicitly about indigenous peoples is a film by W. Douglas Burden, on the 1927 American Museum of Natural History expedition to study the Komodo dragon lizard. Komodo, an island in what is now Indonesia, is the home of *Varanus komodensis*, the Komodo dragon lizard, described as the largest lizard in the world and the closest living relative of the dinosaur. Cooper would later claim that Burden's expedition was a direct inspiration for his film *King Kong*.

Burden's short film begins with a view of the American Museum of Natural History, followed by a map detailing the itinerary of the Burden voyage, and then scenes of the arrival of the expedition on Komodo Island, the hunting of animals for use as bait, the hunting and shooting of the lizard, and the capture of other live lizards. Although Carroll is discussing the plot of the horror film here, he might as well be discussing the Burden expedition film: 'An initial, contested discovery calls forth a project or expedition for the purpose of corroborating it, and closure is secured when the confirmation can be made to stick' (Carroll: 1990, 114). *King Kong*, labeled a fantasy horror film, was successfully modeled on the narrative of an expedition film. The fantasy of the movie draws its sustenance from the science of the museum expedition.

The title of Burden's book on his expedition even sounds like a horror film title: *Dragon Lizards of Komodo: The Expedition to the Lost World of the Dutch East Indies*. Burden, like Carl Denham, the fictional expedition filmmaker in *King Kong*, stressed the importance of maintaining secrecy in order to be assured of being the first white man to lay claim to the exotic beast. In Burden's book, Komodo Island is represented much as *King Kong's* Skull Island will be represented by Cooper and Schoedsack: Burden writes of the sound of 'tomtoms beating across the water;

incessant, monotonous, rhythmic beats, thrilling and barbarous,' evidence that the natives are 'child-like and superstitious' (Burden: 1927, 103). Burden's portrayal of the expedition's Chinese servant Chu as an amusing lackey prefigures *King Kong's* portrayal of the Chinese cook Charlie (ibid., 216–32).

Similarly, just as Kong and the dinosaurs of Skull Island are portrayed as riveting, prehistoric monsters, the Komodo dragon according to Burden is 'a perfectly marvelous sight, – a primeval monster in a primeval setting' (ibid., 112). Cooper later explained that the character of Ann Darrow was inspired by Burden's wife, Katherine Burden, a photographer on the museum expedition (Behlmer: 1976, 10). Burden himself extolled the spectacle of a monster attracted to a beautiful white woman, a theme repeated frequently in *King Kong* in Carl Denham's oft-repeated reference to Ann's relationship with Kong as 'Beauty and the Beast.' Burden comments, 'A fiery dragon in itself is a fascinating idea – so, also, is the thought of a beautiful white-skinned maiden. Link these two ideas together, in some way or other, and you have a story which by its very nature would survive through untold ages' (Burden: 1927, 90–2). Thus the narrative of the expedition was propelled forward by the figure of the white woman, a kind of lure for the monster-like beast.

Cooper, the creative mind behind Kong, was struck by Burden's account of the immediate death of the two Komodo dragons which Burden brought back and displayed at the Bronx Zoo. In a letter to Burden dated 22 June 1964, Cooper wrote,

> When you told me that the two Komodo Dragons you brought back to the Bronx Zoo, where they drew great crowds, were eventually killed by civilization, I immediately thought of doing the same thing with my Giant Gorilla. I had already established him in my mind on a prehistoric island with prehistoric monsters, and I now thought of having him destroyed by the most sophisticated thing I could think of in civilization, and in the most fantastic way. My very original concept was to place him on the top of the Empire State Building and have him killed by airplanes. I made considerable investigation on how this could be done technically with a live gorilla.
>
> (Behlmer: 1976, 10)

In the expedition film, Burden himself does the shooting. At one point, there is a shot of Katherine Burden cranking the camera juxtaposed to a shot of Douglas Burden shooting with his rifle. The positioning of the two makes it appear as if he is in fact shooting Katherine. This scene is followed by one in which a Komodo dragon is shot and killed. Shooting with a camera and shooting with a rifle are conjoined: the product will be the display of the stuffed dragon lizards together with film footage at the American Museum of Natural History. But the woman is also shot and captured on Burden's film: sex and the hunt are implicitly made parallel.

In *King Kong*, the monster Kong's attraction to Ann is transgressive: Kong, a hybrid figure, a manlike beast, threatens the taboo on interracial sex. Burden's obsession with racial difference – the Javanese are 'unfathomable,' the 'cannibals' of Wetar are 'Oceanic Negroids' – is exposed in his disgust for the Dutch colonials who do not enforce a caste system or color line:

> Where is this getting the world, this intermarriage between race and race, this breaking down of the barriers of race consciousness? In the long run, as intermarriage becomes more and more frequent, does it not lead inevitably to one grand hodge podge, one loathsome mixture of all races into a pigsty breed? An unattractive thought, perhaps, but sure of fulfillment, as long as racial intermarriage continues.
>
> (Burden: 1927, 57)

It is the body of the racially mixed hybrid which Burden finds loathsome, the hybrid body which defies the idealized polarization by science and modernity of the Ethnographic Other and Historical Same, nature and science, archaic and modern.

Islands of fantasy: *King Kong* and the horror film

King Kong borrowed not only from the scientific expedition film, but also from the Hollywood horror film. *The Most Dangerous Game* (1932), directed by Irving Pichel and Schoedsack and produced by Cooper, was started before but made concurrently with *King Kong*, with some of the same sets and actors (Robert Armstrong, Fay Wray, Noble Johnson, and Steve Clemente). As in *King Kong*, the hunt in *The Most Dangerous Game* is a means of playing out the survival of the fittest. Count Zaroff (Leslie Banks), the bored, effete big game hunter, lures Rainsford (Joel McCrea) and Eve Trowridge (a brunette Fay Wray) onto his island and then forces them to become game for his hunting pleasure. The plot again follows Carroll's model – onset/discovery/confirmation/confrontation. Here, however, the monster is the Count [. . .].

Zaroff violates cultural boundaries, but he also pushes certain notions to their logical limits, such as the link between sex and the hunt: 'We barbarians know that it is after the chase, and then only, that man revels. You know the saying of the Ogandi chieftains: "Hunt first the enemy, then the woman." It is the natural instinct. The blood is quickened by the kill. One passion builds upon another. Kill, then love! When you have known that, you have known ecstasy!'

The monster is thus the Count himself who crosses the boundary between Civilization and Savagery, and tellingly invokes the 'Ogandi chieftains.' Rainsford is the hunter who remains within 'proper' bounds: he hunts only animals and recognizes the value of expedition photography as evidence of 'having been there.' As Rainsford says to the Doctor, 'You didn't turn out so hot as a hunter, Doc, but oh what a photographer! Say, if we'd had you to take pictures on the Sumatran trip, they might have believed my book.' The Count, by contrast, takes the visual logic of the Great White Hunter to its logical extreme: his own desire to *see*, to visualize the hunted, is revealed in his collections of pickled human heads [. . .]. His pathological vision, embodied in his bulging, piercing eyes, in one scene fixes Eve, in the manner of a scientist gleefully pinning down a butterfly specimen.

According to film critic Claude Beylie, the very dry, nearly scientific style of the film mixes elements of the documentary with a touch of de Sade: *The Most Dangerous Game* utilizes 'the words of science, or of teratology, because it was about a prehistoric animal, or a phenomenon of a fair.' Thus the very tenor of the film betrays a fascination with teratology. Watching the film, Beylie asserts, is like watching animals at a zoological preserve (Beylie: 1982, 4–5). In his intriguing analysis of *The Most Dangerous Game*, Thierry Kuntzel sees the film as revealing a relationship between dreams and cinema, because the viewer must believe a little, but not too much; he or she is drawn into viewing not only from the point of view of normality, that is, of the hunter hero, Rainsford, but also from the point of view of abnormality, that is, that of Zaroff (Kuntzel: 1980, 22). The horror film thus makes the viewer complicit not only with the protagonists, but with the monster as well.

The Most Dangerous Game is an exploration of the relationship between the hunted and the hunter, between Savagery and Civilization, a theme signified by the recurrent image of the centaur. The centaur, half-beast and half-man, emblazons the film as both mythical and fantastic. Kuntzel has pointed out that all the men in the film figure for the centaur, especially Ivan, the Cossack servant (Noble Johnson) (ibid., 14). The same fascination with hybridity betrayed in Burden's account of his expedition is made explicit in this fantasy horror film in the image of the centaur.

If *The Most Dangerous Game* is a meditation on Savagery and Progress, unlike the 'racial film' which purported to offer a peephole into the past, the film also looks to the future, envisioning a 'monster' of overcivilization. Another horror film that presents a vision of deviant evolution is Erle C. Kenton's *Island of Lost Souls* (1933) based on H. G. Wells's *The Island of Dr. Moreau* (1896). The island of Dr. Moreau is described as 'an experimental station for bioanthropological research.' The narrative is again one of onset/discovery/confirmation/confrontation: the shipwrecked Edward Parker (Richard Arlen) is lured by the oily, odd-looking Moreau (Charles Laughton) to the latter's island station, where Moreau has caused evolution to be speeded up hundreds of thousands of years, producing not only giant plants, but also a new breed of 'humans' from the sadistic vivisection of live animals. The doctor hopes that Parker will mate with his most prized creation, the beautiful Lota, the Panther Woman (Kathleen Burke).

The monsters in the film, Moreau's creatures, are neither fully animal nor human. The racialist and imperialist underpinnings of the film are quite explicit, for the monsters are coded in racial terms. Ourlan, an ape-man, is coded as the lusty and bestial dark Savage. M'ling, Moreau's faithful dog-man, is coded as East Asian – servile and bestial – slightly higher in status than some of Moreau's other beasts who have become his slaves and perform hard physical labor. Lota passes as a Polynesian: with her heavily made-up eyes, rouged lips, long black curly hair, and skimpy bandeau and sarong, she is a typical 'South Seas' screen siren. When they kiss, Parker discovers that her fingernails are really claws, and he confronts Moreau with his knowledge. Moreau is merely perturbed, because this fact is evidence that the animal nature of his 'human' creatures reverts back and cannot be suppressed. Interbreeding fails (nineteenth-century anthropologist Paul Broca might have approved), and the monster is thus necessarily impure, no longer animal but not capable of becoming fully human.

The danger of miscegenation appears again when Parker's virtuous blonde fiancée, Ruth Thomas (Leila Hyams), comes to rescue Parker only to be nearly raped by Ourlan, the hairy ape-man, mirroring Ann Darrow in the paws of Kong. Parker saves her from this fate, but is warned not to do the same for Lota, the Panther Woman. Later, Ourlan pursues Lota: when he grabs her, they maul each other to death, as natural selection takes its toll on the unfit.

In the end of the film, Moreau's society of hybrid Savages rebels in a perfect enactment of the colonialist nightmare. Although forced to worship Moreau as a God, and as keeper of the Law, they revolt and torture Moreau with instruments from his own laboratory, called the House of Pain. In both films, the true monster is the insane white male who desires to manipulate nature and is willing to upset the boundaries separating man from beast. In *Island of Lost Souls* as in *The Most Dangerous Game*, the viewer takes his or her cue as to how to react to what is happening from the human protagonists on the screen, but since the viewer at times sees the action from the point of view of Moreau or of the island's other 'humans,' the viewer is made into a monster as well. Like Moreau, a doctor obsessed with knowledge, with destroying the limits between the biological and the fantastic, the viewer is simultaneously fascinated and horrified by the transgression of boundaries. The revolt of Moreau's hybrid experimental subjects is signaled cinematographically by the reverse of a zoom: one by one, the beasts rush up to the camera lens, their hairy faces filling the lens as they peer up at the camera.

In his discussion of *King Kong*, J. P. Telotte has argued that an effective horror film draws the viewer into its world of excitement and terror through its manipulation of boundaries: 'The horror film can play most effectively on its boundary position; monsterlike, it can simply reach into our world and make us part of its nightmarish realm, forcing us to complete horrific sequences' (Telotte: 1988, 395). Similarly, citing Tzvetan Todorov, Noël Carroll explains that the fantastic in cinema is produced by allowing for a vacillation between supernatural and naturalistic explanations. Many horror stories begin as narratives purporting to offer rational explanations for the fantastic, but then build up to a confrontation with the monster, a supernatural being that cannot be explained by science (Carroll: 1990, 145). Above all, Carroll adds, the horror film demands proof, proof of the monster's existence and a clear explanation of why it exists. The horror film genre works because the audience is fascinated by the monster's impurity, its hybridity, and because it is curious to get at the heart of this unknowable: the audience follows the narrative until it discloses all the secrets of the monster (ibid., 157, 182–93). This knowledge is arrived at only by observation. It is this desire for proof by observation that links the ethnographic film to the horror film: from its inception, the efficacy of ethnographic film was believed to derive from its status as pure observation, pure inscription, evidence for the archive. But this logic linking vision to knowledge, producing an incessant desire to see, is not without its attendant dangers.

[. . .]

Part Eight

AMERICAN GOTHIC

Introduction to Part Eight

■   Ken Gelder

T HE UNITED STATES IS the great modern centre of horror production, a place that has made a whole range of horrific texts, practices and rhetorics seem perversely representative of the national character: an institutionalized 'enemy within' mode of paranoia, mass murders at fast food joints and high schools, alien abductee testimonies, sanctioned forms of racial hatred and segregation, the normalization of spectacular violence on television and in cinema, and so on. It is as if the most powerful country in the world is ceaselessly condemned to encounter forms of its own Otherness. Not surprisingly, the kind of criticism best suited to reading American horror has been psycho-social: using horror as a way of diagnosing the nation's (ill-)health, its vulnerability to (recalling Baudrillard again) 'viral attacks'. Stephen King, the bestselling horror novelist of all time, provides a lucid instance of this kind of diagnosis for his particular generation in his book, *Danse Macabre*:

> We were fertile ground for the seeds of terror, we war babies; we had been raised in a strange circus atmosphere of paranoia, patriotism, and national *hubris*. We were told that we were the greatest nation on earth ... but we were also told exactly what to keep in our fallout shelters and how long we would have to stay in there after we won the war. We had more to eat than any nation in the history of the world, but there were traces of Strontium-90 in our milk from nuclear testing.
>
> (King: 1981, 23)

For King, the 'real terror' begins for Americans in 1957, when the 'Russians had beaten us into space' (ibid., 22) – that is, at a moment of America's global humiliation. For Gregory A. Waller, however, modern American horror comes into the world a little over ten years later and is more caught up with problems at home. The extract here is from his introduction to a ground-breaking collection of essays titled *American Horrors*, a critical acknowledgement of the huge number of horror films coming out of the United States around this time. Waller takes 1968 as the moment of modern horror's inception, with the release of George A. Romero's low-budget *Night of the Living Dead* and Roman Polanski's New York, apartment-dwelling, urban paranoia film, *Rosemary's Baby*. These films may not have captured the revolutionary spirit of the times, but Waller does at least inscribe them – and the films from the 1970s that followed in their wake – with a 'critical' function. This is an important step to take: it recovers a marginal, derided form and makes it speak for the nation. Horror thus participates in America's 'public debate'. It 'engages' with current events: Watergate, the prolonged withdrawal from Vietnam, the rise of the Moral Majority.

The sheer amount of horror films being produced at this time means, however, that 'no simple formula' can account for them. They divide themselves up into subgenres (the stalker film, the slasher film, the paranoia film), each requiring its own analytical approach; and they entwine themselves with other genres such as the family melodrama and science fiction. The family in particular became an identifiable point of reference for the modern American horror film. Tony Williams' study *Hearths of Darkness* (1996) gives us an example of the psycho-social approach to the horror film's representation of American family life, drawing liberally on Freud and the concept of repression. Williams had studied under film critic Robin Wood, whose co-edited 1979 collection *American Nightmare* laid out some of the groundwork for both Williams' book and Waller's later anthology. Wood was also responding to the proliferation of American horror in the 1960s and 1970s. Drawing on Marxian-influenced ideology critique, and especially on Freud, he famously saw the American horror film as an enactment of 'the return of the repressed', an exposure of the primal underbelly of the most civilized nation on earth – Tobe Hooper's *The Texas Chainsaw Massacre* (1974) being exemplary in this regard and achieving, for Wood, the 'force of authentic art' (Wood *et al.*: 1979, 22). But the critical function of the modern American horror film could not always be taken for granted. For Waller and others, horror could both illuminate and obscure cultural contradictions, unleashing forces which may have radical or reactionary effects, depending on the case. Vivian Sobchack has in fact taken *Rosemary's Baby* as the first of a number of American horror films about a conservatively-articulated crisis over fatherhood, showing 'patriarchy simultaneously terrified and terrorising in the face of its increasing impotence' (Sobchack: 1987, 185) – in which case, the 'repressed' that returns to the scene works ambivalently as a reminder of why the family has became dysfunctional in the first place.

Waller begins his extract by defining the 'everyday', contemporary settings of modern American horror against British horror cinema at the time, especially the stagy, period films produced by Hammer. Teresa A. Goddu begins her extract, the introduction to her book *Gothic America*, in the same vein, distinguishing American Gothic from its creakier eighteenth century British counterparts. 'American Gothic' has been an evocative term for the New World for some time now – its own moment of inception perhaps arriving with the title of Grant Wood's famous 1930 painting of that stern, midwestern preacher, pitchfork in hand, standing rigidly beside his daughter. The use of the Gothic in America has mostly had regional application: the unleashed perversities of the Southern Gothic, for example. But it may also have an originating force in the nation, linked in some studies to the carving out of the American frontier (see, for example, Mogen *et al.*: 1993). Goddu's task is to make the term speak for a national malaise, and in particular, to 'resurrect' it in the field of American literary studies. Certainly there is an early American Gothic literary tradition which has increasingly attracted critical attention – beginning with Charles Brockden Brown and, later, Edgar Allan Poe. Looking at these and other writers in her study, Goddu aims to inscribe the Gothic with the potential for social critique. American literary critics in the past, she notes, have mostly kept the Gothic minor and 'otherworldly', reading literary examples of it solely in psychological or theological terms. For Goddu, however, the Gothic speaks directly to American history, and especially a history of race and black slavery. Like Waller, Goddu thus endows her horror texts with a critical function: to unsettle America's myth of 'new world innocence'. But like Waller again, she remains ambivalent about Gothic, noting that it can also work conservatively to strengthen an 'idealized national identity'. Both the modern American horror film and the American Gothic thus seem to pendulate back and forth between a world of nightmare and (the American) dream.

Chapter 20

GREGORY A. WALLER

INTRODUCTION TO
AMERICAN HORRORS
(extract)

W**HAT I REFER TO AS** the modern era of the American horror film began in 1968 – the year George A. Romero's *Night of the Living Dead* and Roman Polanski's *Rosemary's Baby* were released (and perhaps not coincidentally, the year of the National Commission on the Causes and Prevention of Violence and the election of Richard M. Nixon as president). Through the 1970s and into the 1980s the horror film remained on the whole commercially viable (unlike the western, for example) and repeatedly proved its affinity for the topical and the novel, and thereby affirmed its place as a type of storytelling particularly apt and relevant to post-1968 America. At the same time, however, the genre became increasingly reflexive and allusive, flaunting its own generic inheritance and its own identity as horror and as film. Thus, as Noël Carroll and others have argued (Carroll: 1981; Twitchell: 1985), contemporary horror demands to be seen in the context not only of American life in the 1970s and 1980s but also of those classic texts that it quotes, parodies, imitates, and remakes – films like *Frankenstein* (1931), *Dracula* (1931), *King Kong* (1933), *Cat People* (1942), *The Thing* (1951), and *Invasion of the Body Snatchers* (1956). These films are horror's collective memory, acknowledged by filmmakers and fans alike, yet what of modern horror's more immediate precursors in the years before *Night of the Living Dead* and *Rosemary's Baby*?

The 1960s provided a number of noteworthy horror films – still disturbing oddities like *What Ever Happened to Baby Jane?* (1962) and *Lady in a Cage* (1964); *The Haunting* (1964), with its restrained 'adult' (i.e., major studio, quasi-Victorian) terror; *Two Thousand Maniacs* (1964) and Herschell Gordon Lewis's other notoriously violent drive-in movies; and from outside of America, Michael Powell's *Peeping Tom* (1960), Roman Polanski's *Repulsion* (1965), Mario Bava's baroque tales of witchcraft and repression (like *Black Sunday* [1960]), and Masaki Kobayashi's cinematic rendering of Japanese ghost stories (*Kwaidan* [1965]). Most important, the 1960s saw the release of two of the most accomplished American horror films,

Alfred Hitchcock's *Psycho* (1960) and *The Birds* (1963), both of which would greatly influence the shape the genre would take in the 1970s and 1980s. The presence of *Psycho*, for example, haunts innumerable films, from *Sisters* (1973), *Halloween* (1978), and *Psycho II* (1983) to made-for-television movies like *Scream Pretty Peggy* (1973), which features an apparently harmless young man who assumes the identity of his dead sister and murders attractive women. And *The Birds* lies behind *Night of the Living Dead* and virtually all post-1968 films of apocalyptic horror, as well as films like *Day of the Animals* (1977), *The Swarm* (1978), and *Savage Harvest* (1981).

Hitchcock also had his imitators in the 1960s (William Castle in *Homicidal* [1961], for one), but the decade was dominated by horror films much safer and more formulaic than *Psycho* and *The Birds*, films like American International Pictures' adaptations of Edgar Allan Poe stories and Hammer Studio's series of British-made monster movies that pit humankind against familiar antagonists like Count Dracula, the Mummy, and Frankenstein's creature. In different ways, Hammer and AIP both transformed the horror film into a colorful period piece (usually set in the nineteenth century) peopled by inspired, grandly theatrical, often middle-aged villains; well-meaning, innocuous, young male heroes; and buxom young women waiting to be ravished or rescued.

Hammer films like *The Reptile* (1965), *Dracula, Prince of Darkness* (1966), and *Dracula Has Risen from the Grave* (1968) place a premium on unobtrusive, nonde-script cinematography, stylized performances, special attention to decor and set design as bearers of meaning, and utterly straightforward plotting involving perfectly legible scenes of exposition, confrontation, and resolution that announce the film's system of values. Blending an unambiguous style with easily decoded themes and 'messages,' these films are often small-scale social fables that reveal certain correctable flaws in the nineteenth-century worlds they depict. For example, *The Reptile*, a representative Hammer production, pictures the danger to a rural community as emanating from an upper-class manor whose owner, a forbidding and stern 'Doctor of Theology,' has looked too deeply into the mysteries of the East and so must eventually suffer for his sins (and so must the rest of this community, since the doctor's sins have social consequences). In the film's finale a fire of purification destroys the manor house, killing both the overreaching scholar and his victimized daughter who has been transformed by a 'primitive' religious cult into a murderous, reptilian monster. As a result of this sacrificial destruction – in the guise of self-defense – the rural world is once again safe from imported evil, and the middle-class newlyweds who were the real targets of the monster can proceed with the all-important task of setting up a household and beginning a family. What virtually all Hammer's horror films of the 1960s – particularly Hammer's extremely popular vampire films – offer the viewer is a world in which religious faith, ritualized violence, and individual heroism defeat a powerful but easily identified threat. Thus quite unlike *Psycho* and *The Birds*, Hammer's films reafffirm what are assumed to be the 'normal' values of heterosexual romance, clearly defined sexual roles, and the middle-class family and testify to the importance and the relevance of social stability and traditional sources of authority and wisdom.

In vastly different ways, *Night of the Living Dead* and *Rosemary's Baby*, the two films that could be said to have ushered in the modern era of horror, challenge the moral-social-political assumptions, production values, and narrative strategies of Hammer and AIP films. Though there were zombielike creatures and satanic cults in the movies before 1968, Romero and Polanski redefine the monstrous – thereby redefining the role of the hero and the victim as well – and situate horror in the everyday world of contemporary America. [. . .] Looking backward, we can now see how these two innovative, much-imitated, commercially and critically successful films helped to map out certain directions the American horror film would take in the 1970s and 1980s.

Romero's *Night of the Living Dead*, independently produced on a budget of $114,000 in the wilds of Pennsylvania, is a graphically violent and darkly ironic treatment of catastrophic yet fully 'natural' horror. In its images of invasion and social breakdown, it follows in the tradition of *The Birds* and Don Siegel's 1956 *Invasion of the Body Snatchers*. And like later films such as *The Texas Chain Saw Massacre* (1974), *It's Alive* (1973), *Carrie* (1976), and *The Hills Have Eyes* (1977), *Night of the Living Dead* offers a thoroughgoing critique of American institutions and values. It depicts the failure of the nuclear family, the private home, the teenage couple, and the resourceful individual hero; and it reveals the flaws inherent in the media, local and federal government agencies, and the entire mechanism of civil defense. Romero's first feature also is a prototype of the low-budget, money-making horror film produced outside the established industry. Following *Night of the Living Dead* come, on the one hand, cut-rate, utterly derivative exploitation films (including most of the so-called teenie-kill or slice-and-dice movies released in the wake of *Halloween* and *Friday the 13th*) and, on the other hand, idiosyncratic independent productions like the films of David Cronenberg, Michael Laughlin, and Larry Cohen – imaginative, disturbing, often outrageous films like *Rabid* (1977), *Strange Behavior* (1981), and *Q – The Winged Serpent* (1982).

In contrast to *Night of the Living Dead*, Polanski's *Rosemary's Baby* was produced and distributed by a major Hollywood studio and adapted from a best-selling novel. *Rosemary's Baby*, we might say, gave birth to highly professional, much-publicized, mainstream (and so somehow acceptable and authorized) horror films like *The Exorcist* (1973), *The Omen* (1976), and *Poltergeist* (1982). *Rosemary's Baby* also has a different lineage than *Night of the Living Dead*, for it has ties to previous films about female madness, conspiratorial evil, and sexual repression, including certain of Val Lewton's atmospheric productions of the 1940s (like *Cat People*). If *Night of the Living Dead* draws upon age-old fears associated with invasion and the end of the world (and on what Sigmund Freud calls our fear of the dead as malevolent enemy), *Rosemary's Baby* brings up to date the theme of humankind's weakness and complicity with supernatural satanic evil. Furthermore, like countless subsequent makers of horror films, Polanski takes as his focal point an apparently defenseless young woman. With Rosemary we discover the terror that lurks in the heart of the familiar, the evil in the mundane and the banal. *Rosemary's Baby* tells us of an isolated, justifiably paranoid woman who attempts to become independent from traditional (which is to say, male, paternalistic, socially validated) sources of protection and strength. From *Rosemary's Baby* to *Demon Seed* (1977), *Eyes of Laura Mars* (1978), *Alien* (1979), and *Visiting Hours* (1982), horror films have proven to be among the most significant documents in America's public debate over the status of the independent woman in a society still dominated by men.

If 1968 could be said to inaugurate the modern era of horror, it is not simply because this year saw the release of *Night of the Living Dead* and *Rosemary's Baby*. More important, in 1968 the Motion Picture Association of America (MPAA) instituted its 'Industry Code of Self-Regulation' as a response to (and an attempt to sidestep) public concern over the role of censorship in the media. From the late 1960s into the 1980s, the MPAA's Code and Rating Administration (CARA) has grappled with the status of the horror film – refusing to grant an R-rating to Romero's *Dawn of the Dead* in 1979, for example, and making a concerted effort in the early 1980s to restrain the tendency toward graphic violence in films like *Halloween II* (1981). With few exceptions, the modern horror film has been an R-rated genre, and the MPAA R-rating has allowed for and perhaps even legitimized the presentation of explicit violence – the violence of decapitation and dismemberment, of needles to the eyeball, and of scissors, kitchen appliances, handtools, and shish kabob skewers as deadly weapons. Such violence, undertaken with an air of 'top that!' ingenuity and lovingly explicit detail, is perhaps the single defining characteristic of gore movies like *Maniac* (1980). (It is equally important to note that the R-rating also allows these and all other horror films much more freedom than pre-1968 films in the explicit treatment of sex, nudity, profanity, and what are euphemistically called 'adult' themes like incest, necrophilia, rape, and cannibalism.) By continually pressing the boundaries of both PG- and R-ratings, the modern horror film has violated taboos with a monsterlike ferocity unprecedented in the contemporary American cinema, and in the process horror has increased freedom of expression and affected the codes of commercial television as well as the motion-picture industry. Without *Night of the Living Dead* and *The Exorcist*, we would have had to wait much longer for made-for-television movies to bring child pornography and nuclear holocaust into our homes during primetime viewing hours.

There are any number of valuable and critically defensible generalizations to be drawn about the horror film – including, for example, James B. Twitchell's distinction between terror and horror ('the etiology of horror is *always* in dreams, while the basis of terror is in actuality', ibid., 19), Robin Wood's definition of the horror film as a collective nightmare in which 'normality is threatened by the Monster' (Wood *et al.*: 1979, 14), and Dennis Giles's contention that 'central to the strategy of horror' is 'delayed, blocked or partial vision' (Giles: 1984, 41). Yet given the diversity of the genre since 1968, it is impossible, I think, to define once and for all the essence of modern horror (or, for that matter, of the Hollywood musical, the post-World War II western, or the hardboiled detective story). Nonetheless, there is no question that violence is a major element in the genre, as it is in virtually all dreams and all narratives of fact or fiction that we would label as horror stories. The motion-picture industry's often predictable advertising campaigns for horror movies entice with the promise of escalating body counts and elevators filled with blood, the same blood and gore that lead the genre's many detractors to deem horror dismissible or damn it as dangerous. Like the characters on screen, the viewer cannot ignore the violence in these films, which is linked, as Philip Brophy argues, to a 'graphic sense of physicality' and 'Body-horror' (Brophy: 1986, 8–10). How, then, should we face up to or master or make sense of modern horror's violence?

Although it is essential to acknowledge the role of the individual viewer and the collective audience as elements of and in the filmic text, studies of the quantifiable behavioral effects of violence on the movie or television viewer seem to me to be beside the point. What horror films offer, after all, is the representation of violence – violence embedded in a generic, narrative, fictional, often highly stylized, and oddly playful context. Only by ignoring the precise terms of the context and the codes and conventions of representation (and of perception) can we categorically group, say, *The Texas Chain Saw Massacre*, *The Omen*, *The Burning* (1981), *Scanners* (1981), and *Slumber Party Massacre* (1982) together as interchangeable exercises in dehumanizing ultraviolence. Rather than validating our safe oversimplifications – about horror, genre films, and popular culture in general – these and other horror films insist on offering (and at times unsettling and interrogating) us with what Stephen Neale calls the 'conjunction' of images of violence with 'images and definitions of the monstrous' (Neale: 1980, 21). What is most significant, psychologically and ideologically, is the precise way each horror film displays this 'conjunction' and speaks about the nature and function of aggression and conflict. Taken as a whole, the entire genre is an unsystematic, unresolved exploration of violence in virtually all its forms and guises. Thus recent horror films return again and again to questions concerning the meaning of self-defense, vengeance, and justified violence, to myths of uncommon 'masculine' valor and all-too-common female victimization, and to images of violation, sacrifice, ritual, and of life reduced to a struggle for survival. This much-maligned genre undoubtedly has its share of forgettable demonstrations of the fine art of murder, like *Happy Birthday To Me* (1981) and *The Prowler* (1981), but it also includes films like George A. Romero's *Martin* (1976) and *Dawn of the Dead* (1979), Stanley Kubrick's *The Shining* (1980), and David Cronenberg's *Videodrome* (1983), which are among the most noteworthy recent examinations of the role and the representation of violence in American culture.

One common response to the violence in modern horror is to praise or damn the genre simply on the basis of its preoccupation with state-of-the-art make up and special effects work. ('Fanzines' like *Cinéfantastique* and *Fangoria* are given over almost exclusively to articles and interviews that focus on production information and special effects.) More telling is the contention – voiced by Chicago movie reviewers Roger Ebert and Gene Siskel, among others – that modern horror has become what Morris Dickstein calls a reductive 'hard-core pornography of violence made possible by the virtual elimination of censorship' (Dickstein: 1980, 33).

The equation of explicitly violent horror with pornographic gore is often based on the assumption that truly effective horror is always indirect and suggestive, leaving the horrific primarily to the viewer's imagination. This assumption informs histories of the genre like Ivan Butler's *Horror in the Cinema* (1970) and Carlos Clarens's *An Illustrated History of the Horror Film* (1967), as well as S. S. Prawer's 1980 study, *Caligari's Children: The Film as Tale of Terror*. These critics follow H. P. Lovecraft's distinction in *Supernatural Horror in Literature* (1945) between the 'true weird tale', which offers 'a certain atmosphere of breathless and unexplainable dread of outer, unknown forces' and the story that is merely 'mundanely gruesome' (Lovecraft: 1973, 15). The prescriptive call for films of suggestive horror – and implicitly for films that valorize an unseeable, transcendent signifier

– is generally linked with a nostalgic longing for the 'golden age' of horror, from *Nosferatu, A Symphony of Horror* (1922) and *Vampyr* (1932) to Universal's politically and socially conservative classics of the 1930s and 1940s. (A reviewing of *Frankenstein* [1931] and *King Kong* [1933], however, reveals that these films quite clearly rely on images of explicit violence – as close to gore as was possible in 1930s Hollywood.) This approach to the genre unjustly serves the past as well as the present. We would do better, I think, to pay attention to films like *Dracula* (1979), *An American Werewolf in London* (1981), *The Funhouse* (1981), and *Re-Animator* (1985), which in modernizing and commenting on classic monster movies prove that the relationship between contemporary and golden age horror involves much more than simply the distinction between the graphically direct and the atmospherically suggestive. (*Invasion of the Body Snatchers* [1978] and *The Thing* [1982] perform a similar function for 1950s horror.)

The most important criticism of modern horror's so-called pornography of violence is directed more explicitly toward ideological rather than stylistic questions. For example, what are we to make of the genre's propensity for depicting sexually active teenagers and independent women as victims and for suggesting that the (male) monster is something of a superego figure, reaffirming through vicious murder the mechanics of repression so necessary for a patriarchal society? Seen in this light, certain horror films [. . .] could be read as being of a piece with X-rated pornographic displays of rape and other male fantasies of sadism and exploitation. The question of how we are to assess the horror film's representation of violence against women is further complicated because the genre includes texts (like *The Velvet Vampire* [1971], *Friday the 13th*, and *The Hunger*) that picture the threat to normality as a female or that offer a narrative in which the besieged female victim is alone capable of destroying her psychopathic assailant. Through her independent actions, the woman in *Eyes of a Stranger* (1981) and *Visiting Hours* (and in *Alien* and *Aliens* [1986] as well) proves her capacity for self-reliance and self-defense, but has she simply switched roles in the ongoing patriarchal drama? [. . .]

Examining modern horror in terms of what I have called its exploration of violence is but one – albeit important – way of defining lines of continuity and areas of emphasis within the varied field of modern horror. We can, for example, construct a typology of the monstrous; after all, without the disequilibrium caused by the monster, there is no story to be told. No doubt it is true, as Rudolf Arnheim declared in 1949, that 'the monster has become a portrait of ourselves and of the kind of life we have chosen to lead' (Arnheim: 1972, 257) and that, in Frank McConnell's words, 'each era chooses the monster it deserves and projects' (McConnell: 1975, 137). There is, however, no simple formula that can explain the many shapes the monster takes in recent horror – not all monsters are embodiments of our repressed fears and sexual desires or personifications of social ills or adolescent anxieties. Yet certain distinctions should be drawn between, for instance, the monster as willfully, irredeemably Evil (*The Exorcist*, *Halloween*, *Damien – Omen II* [1978], *Christine* [1983]) and the monster as somehow beyond or beneath good and evil (*Carrie*, *It Lives Again* [1978], *Of Unknown Origin* [1983]). Overlapping these categories is the distinction between the singular threat – Count Dracula, the shark in *Jaws*, the extraterrestrial being in *Alien*, the psychopathic killer in *Friday the 13th* – and the multiple threat – Romero's living dead, the Manson Family in *Helter Skelter* (1976), the ghostly avengers in *The Fog* (1980), the werewolf colony in *The Howling* (1981), and the corporate Machiavels in *The Stuff*. While it would run the risk of reducing the horror film to a wax museum or catalogue of creatures, a fully developed typology of monsters would offer a valuable means of delineating the paradigmatic possibilities open to this genre and the sort of fears that it feels will suitably trouble its audience.

Furthermore, since modern horror – like virtually all popular art – tends to run in sequels and cycles or sets of texts (call this the principle of exploitation or imitation or safe investment strategy), a necessary critical task is to chart the course of specific cycles or subgenres or formulae. [. . .] To write the history of modern horror we would need to place the stalker film and the modern vampire story in the context of other overlapping cycles and subgenres, including, for instance, films that come in the wake of *Frogs* (1972) and *Jaws*, which pit humankind against a threat from the natural world; stories of hauntings (*The Amityville Horror* [1979], *Poltergeist*) and possession (*The Possession of Joel Delaney* [1982], *Ruby* [1977], *Amityville II: The Possession* [1982]); ecological nightmares like *Prophecy* (1979) and *Humanoids from the Deep* (1980); and films of visionaries and dreamers from *Deadly Dream* (1971) to *The Sender* (1982) and *A Nightmare on Elm Street* (1984).

Since such subgenres find expression in novels as well as movies, one unquestionably important context for the contemporary horror film is mass-market horror fiction of the 1970s and 1980s. From *Rosemary's Baby* and *The Other* (1972) to the spate of adaptations of Stephen King novels in 1983 (*The Dead Zone*, *Cujo*, *Christine*) and 1984 (*Firestarter*, *Children of the Corn*), the major studios have approached horror principally as a matter of adapting best-sellers for the screen. (The countless paperback novelizations of films are of no intrinsic interest, though they surely attest to the popularity of horror in the 1970s and 1980s and to the interdependence of the entertainment industries.) Like horror fiction, the made-for-television horror movie also provides an important corollary and counterpoint to films released since the late 1960s, both because filmmakers like Steven Spielberg, John Carpenter, Wes Craven, and Tobe Hooper have all directed telefilms, and also [. . .] because horror takes a vastly different shape when it is tailored for prime-time network television. In addition, 'subliterary' comic books and, in the 1980s, 'subcinematic' rock music videos have served as host for as well as parasite of horror films.

Paying due attention to the subgenres and cycles within the horror film and to the intermedia relationships within the larger field of horror underscores the variety and adaptability as well as the continuity of modern horror. When we place horror within the broader continuum of popular culture, which is in a perpetual state of realignment and renovation, ideologically as well as formally, the boundaries demarcating this genre become hazy at best. Spurred by the demands of the marketplace, the interests of the audience, the cultural and political climate, and the contribution of the individual artist, popular genres mingle, influence each other, and evolve through a cumulative process of repetition and variation. One result of this process is a film like *Mommie Dearest* (1981), a blend of family melodrama, investigative exposé, and old-fashioned 'bio-pic' that derives a good deal of its imagery and its thematic preoccupations from the horror film. Or consider the case of *Prom Night* (1980) and *Terror Train* (1980), which were unambiguously advertised as horror movies in the manner of *Halloween* and *Friday the 13th*. Though they do feature psychopathic killers, both of these stalker films are structured very much like classical whodunits, complete with a plethora of mysterious clues and a cast of likely suspects. *Prom Night* and *Terror Train*, in turn, have their analogues in the many recent detective films, including *Sharky's Machine* (1981), *I, The Jury* (1982), *Endangered Species* (1982), and *Tightrope* (1984), which match the detective against the monstrous opponent who seems to be an interloper from the realm of horror. As Leo Braudy puts it, 'Understanding the appeal of horror films these days is crucial to understanding films in general because the motifs and themes of the horror film have so permeated films of quite different sorts' (Braudy: 1985, 10).

Finally, to situate horror in the context of contemporary popular culture, we have to take into account not only questions of adaptation, imitation, and 'permeation,' but also the relationship between horror and the other popular movie genres of the 1970s and 1980s. For example, the rise of the modern horror film should be seen in relation to the decline of the disaster story and the early 1980s reemergence of the story of nuclear war, both of which – like horror – dramatize a sense of vulnerability and the capacity for survival. And the many horror films that picture teenagers as survivors and monsters, but preeminently as victims, find their doubles in *Porky's* (1981) and other R-rated comedies of sexual misadventures and adolescent highjinks. So, too, the highly traditional dream of heroic valor and selfless sacrifice in a universe of absolute values and transcendent Forces, a dream embodied in *Star Wars* (1977), *Raiders of the Lost Ark* (1981), and any number of fantasy adventure films and space operas, is answered and undercut in different ways by the many horror films like *It's Alive* and *Dawn of the Dead* that refuse to present us with situations in which moral, political, and spiritual distinctions are perfectly clear. And as Vivian Sobchack so effectively proves (Sobchack: 1987, 175–96), the many horror films since *Rosemary's Baby* that focus on the child and the family are best read as companion pieces to family melodramas like *Ordinary People* (1980) and science fiction films from *Close Encounters of the Third Kind* (1977) to *Starman* (1984). Taking the horror film as our guide we can and should begin to rethink the nature of 'influence' and 'imitation' and the meaning of 'genre' and 'formula' in contemporary popular culture – in so doing we will inevitably rethink our own understanding of horror as well.

[. . .]

While modern horror can be understood as but the latest manifestation of broad-based, post-Romantic archetypes and psychosexual myths (Twitchell [1985] makes the best case for such a reading), it is at least equally important to keep in mind that the horror film has engaged in a sort of extended dramatization of and response to the major public events and newsworthy topics in American history since 1968: fluctuations in 'key economic indicators' and attempts to redirect domestic and foreign policy; Watergate and the slow withdrawal from Vietnam; oil shortages and the Iranian hostage crisis; the rise of the New Right and the Moral Majority; and the continuing debate over abortion, military spending, and women's rights. Further, contemporary horror can and has been interpreted as an index to and commentary on what have often been identified as the more general cultural conditions of our age: its 'crisis of bourgeois patriarchy,' to borrow

Sobchack's phrase; its narcissism, postmodernism, and sense of the apocalyptic; and its attitude toward technology, death, and childhood.

As much as any branch of contemporary popular art, modern horror mirrors our changing fashions and tastes, our shifting fears and aspirations, and our sense of what constitutes the prime moral, social, and political problems facing us individually and collectively. But 'mirrors' is too limited a concept, for just as horror can run the gamut from the reactionary to the radical, so it can alternately underscore, challenge, over-simplify, cloud, and explain the facts, styles, and contradictions of American culture. If nothing else, this genre is ambitious – not least of all because, in Kawin's words, horror films 'represent a unique juncture of personal, social, and mythic structure' (Kawin: 1981, 292). Horror defines and redefines, clarifies and obscures the relationship between the human and the monstrous, the normal and the aberrant, the sane and the mad, the natural and the supernatural, the conscious and the unconscious, the daydream and the nightmare, the civilized and the primitive – slippery categories and tenuous oppositions indeed, but the very oppositions and categories that are so essential to our sense of life.

Chapter 21

TERESA A. GODDU

INTRODUCTION TO
AMERICAN GOTHIC
(extract)

Defining the American Gothic

WHEN MODIFIED BY *AMERICAN*, the gothic loses its usual referents. [. . .] As a critical category, the American gothic lacks the self-evident validity of its British counterpart.

Several factors contribute to the uncertain status of the American gothic. Unlike the British gothic, which developed during a definable time period (usually marked as beginning with Walpole's *The Castle of Otranto* [1764] and continuing through the 1820s) and has a recognized coterie of authors (Walpole, Radcliffe, Monk Lewis, Godwin, Hogg, Maturin, Mary Shelley), the American gothic, one of several forms that played a role in the development of the early American novel, is less easily specified in terms of a particular time period or group of authors. There was no founding period of gothic literature in America, and given the critical preference for the term *romance*, few authors were designated as gothicists. Even when authors such as Edgar Allan Poe or periods such as the twentieth-century Southern Renaissance are associated with the gothic, they reveal the difficulty of defining the genre in national terms: the American gothic is most recognizable as a regional form. Identified with gothic doom and gloom, the American South serves as the nation's 'other,' becoming the repository for everything from which the nation wants to disassociate itself. The benighted South is able to support the irrational impulses of the gothic that the nation as a whole, born of Enlightenment ideals, cannot. America's self-mythologization as a nation of hope and harmony directly contradicts the gothic's most basic impulses. The American gothic, as Leslie Fiedler points out, is 'a literature of darkness and the grotesque in a land of light and affirmation' (Fiedler: 1982, 29).

If the American gothic is difficult to understand due to its seemingly antagonistic relationship to America's national identity, it is equally difficult to classify in generic terms. Just as *gothic* unsettles the idea of America, the modifier *American* destabilizes understandings of the gothic. Once imported to America, the gothic's key elements were translated into American terms, and its formulas were also unfixed. As Charles Brockden Brown, one of America's first novelists to use the gothic, argues in his preface to *Edgar Huntly* (1799), 'the field of investigation, opened to us by our own country, should differ essentially from those which exist in Europe' (Brown: 1984, 3). 'Puerile superstition and exploded manners; Gothic castles and chimeras' might be the materials usually employed in this genre, Brown continues, but the 'incidents of Indian hostility, and the perils of the western wilderness, are far more suitable; and, for a native of America to overlook these, would admit of no apology' (ibid., 3). To be sure, some authors, such as Isaac Mitchell in *The Asylum; or, Alonzo and Melissa* (1811), imported castles to America, but most American authors transformed and hence dislocated British models of the gothic. Combined with other literary forms and adapted to native themes, the American gothic consists of a less coherent set of conventions. Its more flexible form challenges the critically unified gothic genre and demands a reassessment of the gothic's parameters. As a result, a definition of the American gothic depends less on the particular set of conventions it establishes than on those it disrupts. Any attempt to define it without showing how the terms 'American' and 'gothic' complicate and critique each other curtails the challenge to both terms.

Even the British gothic, against which the American gothic is defined, has proven oddly elusive. From early works such as Edith Birkhead's *The Tale of Terror: A Study of the Gothic Romance* (1921), to more recent studies such as Eve Sedgwick's *The Coherence of Gothic Conventions* (1980), an effort to demarcate the conventions of this genre has been at the heart of criticism of the gothic. The debate between Robert Hume and Robert Platzner in *PMLA* highlights the critical need to define the 'essence' of the gothic and the difficulty of doing so. While the two disagree on the central traits, they are 'agreed that the "generic character" of the Gothic novel is hard to deal with' (Hume and Platzner: 1971, 268). Despite its formulaic and conventional nature, despite its easily listed elements and effects – haunted houses, evil villains, ghosts, gloomy landscapes, madness, terror, suspense, horror – the gothic's parameters and 'essence' remain unclear. While easy classification seems to imply a definitional stability, the gothic genre is extremely mutable. Cobbled together of many different forms and obsessed with transgressing boundaries, it represents itself not as stable but as generically impure. As Maggie Kilgour writes, 'one of the factors that makes the gothic so shadowy and nebulous a genre, as difficult to define as any gothic ghost, is that it cannot be seen in abstraction from the other literary forms from whose graves it arises. . . . The form is thus itself a Frankenstein's monster, assembled out of the bits and pieces of the past' (Kilgour: 1995, 3–4).

Though the gothic foregrounds its generic instability, critics still insist on categorizing it. The tendency toward 'generic essentializing' (Hart: 1973) in criticism on the gothic has to do with where this genre ranks in the canon's hierarchy. The drive to order and identify the gothic stems less from a critical desire to discover its particular essence than from a need to differentiate it from other, 'higher' literary forms. As Jacques Derrida suggests in his essay 'The Law of Genre,' the critical desire for generic classification and clarity signals a fear of contagion: the law of genre depends upon the principle of impurity. Categorical generic distinctions aim to ensure the purity of certain individual works or the stature of related genres. Associated with the hackneyed, the feminine, and the popular, the gothic lacks respectability and hence must be quarantined from other literary forms. Elizabeth Napier, for instance, would 'delimit the genre with greater strictness,' arguing that

> it is essential to make such distinctions in the case of the Gothic because of its peculiar likeness to many of the more searching works that it in part inspired. The Gothic does, in fact, exhibit many of the procedures of fragmentation and disjunction that the romantics . . . would elevate to art, but they seldom at this early stage lead to the profound realizations about human consciousness that some critics have asserted that they do. It is with this systematic failure that the present study is concerned.
>
> (Napier: 1987, xiii, 7)

Seeing the gothic as a 'systematic failure' and arguing that it is a cruder anticipation of Romanticism and hence easily distinguishable from it, Napier polices the difference between the two forms. Ironically, the likeness between the gothic and the romantic necessitates that the gothic's boundaries be located and limited. Whether establishing a distinction between the romantic and the gothic or between the popular gothic and the more serious works it inspired, the critical aim is a clean canon.

The desire to quarantine the gothic from higher literary forms is especially prevalent in the scholarship devoted to American literature. Given its historical belatedness, critics are particularly anxious to provide the American literary canon with a respectable foundation. American literature might be 'embarrassingly, a gothic fiction,' as Leslie Fiedler argues, but critics have made every effort to hide this fact (Fiedler: 1982, 29). Despite the origins of the American romance in the gothic and historical romance, critics such as Richard Chase in his foundational work *The American Novel and Its Tradition* (1957) have followed Hawthorne's idiosyncratic use of the term in order to define a respectable canon. As Nina Baym has pointed out, before 1860 the term *romance* in America connoted characteristics now associated with the gothic: *romance* designated 'pre-modern types of novels . . . which depended on supernatural and marvelous events to resolve their plots and to achieve their effects,' along with works of sensational fiction or fictions associated with the 'highly wrought, the heavily plotted, the ornately rhetorical, the tremendously exciting and the relentlessly exterior' (Baym: 1984, 437, 438). In American literary criticism, however, the romance has come to be elevated above and separated from its modifier, gothic, rather than recognized as sharing gothic characteristics.

The category of romance dominates the critical discourse within American literature while the term *gothic* is almost fully repressed. For instance, in *The American Novel and Its Tradition*, Richard Chase subsumes gothic under the heading of melodrama:

> The term has taken on a general meaning beyond the Mrs. Radcliffe kind of thing and is often used rather loosely to suggest violence, mysteries, improbabilities, morbid passions, inflated and complex language of any sort. It is a useful word but since, in its general reference, it becomes confused with 'melodrama,' it seems sensible to use 'melodrama' for the general category and reserve 'Gothic' for its more limited meaning.
>
> (Chase: 1980, 37)

By making the gothic a 'subdivision' of melodrama, Chase limits its application. More recently, in *Beneath the American Renaissance* (1988), David Reynolds uses the heading 'Dark Adventure' to describe gothic works. In both cases, *gothic* is replaced by a broader generic term. This displacement also occurs when *dark* is substituted for *gothic* as the modifier of romance. Chase follows Malcolm Cowley in identifying Charles Brockden Brown as the 'originator of that strand of dark romance that runs through the tradition' (ibid., 31); Reynolds argues that the roots of Dark Adventure are in 'European Dark Romanticism' (Reynolds: 1989, 190). Whether the term *gothic* is displaced in favor of another generic category or the broader, less-specific modifier *dark*, it disappears and is securely segregated from the romance. In American literary criticism, then, there is no need to police the boundaries between romantic and gothic, high and low, since the gothic is erased from the equation altogether.

The replacement of *gothic* with *dark* signifies the critical displacement of the category from discussions of American literature. While the adjective *dark* conjures the atmospheric associations of the gothic, it does not carry the same generic baggage. Unlike the term *gothic*, which connotes 'popular,' *dark* has come to signify 'profound' in American literary criticism. Beginning with Herman Melville's famous discourse on Hawthorne's soul, which is 'shrouded in blackness, ten times black,' American literature's 'power of blackness' has been defined as mystical and metaphysical: the 'deep far-away things' in Hawthorne are also the 'flashings-forth of the intuitive Truth in him,' claims Melville (Melville: 1987, 243, 244). In *The Power of Blackness*, Harry Levin also reads American literature's blackness in weighty symbolic terms. The vision of evil it represents is that of the introspective mind, not some staged fright: the 'symbolic character of our greatest fiction,' Levin argues, is linked to the 'dark wisdom of our deeper minds' (Levin: 1958, xii). In distinguishing between the 'palatable' gothic novels that translate gothic decor into a symbol for the 'hidden blackness of the human soul and human society' and those gothic novels that fail to make their 'cheapjack machinery' symbolic, Leslie Fiedler's work exemplifies the way that *blackness* is critically weighted: the gothic's superficial, dark spectacles are transformed into the more meaningful symbolism of psychological and moral blackness (Fiedler: 1982, 28, 27). American literature's *darkness*, then, becomes associated with depth rather than surface, a psychological and metaphysical symbolism rather than cheap tricks.

However, at the same time that the term *blackness* displaces the gothic's unpalatable associations, it is stripped of its racial connotations. By evacuating *darkness* of racial meaning, critics can claim that the blackness that typifies the American romance is, for the most part, symbolic and not societal, a sign of an inner darkness or moral truth. This conjunction between the displacement of the gothic as a critical term and the abstraction of the American romance's blackness is hardly coincidental. [But] the American gothic is haunted by race: resurrecting the term *gothic* reasserts the racial roots of the romance's blackness. Significantly, when race is restored to the *darkness* of American literature, the gothic reappears as a viable category. In *Playing in the Dark* (1992), Toni Morrison not only insists upon restoring race to the *blackness* of American literature, but also reconstructs the American literary canon in terms of the *gothic* romance. Remarking on 'how troubled, how frightened and haunted our early and founding literature truly is,' Morrison argues that one of the words we have for this haunting is *gothic* (Morrison: 1992, 35, 36). Looking at disturbances within the American romance, Morrison reveals how race haunts American literature. Once specified in historical rather than symbolic terms, *darkness* emblematizes the gothic's disruptive potential instead of replacing the term as a more palatable modifier.

[. . .]

Historicizing the American gothic

When Cathy Davidson poses the question, 'Does America have enough of a history to sustain the Gothic's generic challenge to history, its rewriting and unwriting of history?' she exposes the American gothic's problematic status: it is an historical mode operating in what appears to be an historical vacuum (Davidson: 1986, 231). The gothic's connection to American history is difficult to identify precisely because of the national and critical myths that America and its literature *have* no history. [. . .] Views of the American gothic rely upon the traditional misreading of American literature as representing, in Richard Poirier's term, 'a world elsewhere.' Through critical readings of the romance as otherworldly, American literature's exceptionality came to be located in its ahistoricism. As Nina Baym points out, '[m]ost specialists in American literature have accepted the idea that in the absence of history (or a sense of history) as well as a social field, our literature has consistently taken an ahistorical, mythical shape for which the term "romance" is formally and historically appropriate' (Baym: 1984, 427). Despite the significant body of criticism that situates the British gothic within its cultural context, critics of the American gothic continue to resist historical readings. If the British gothic is read in social terms, the American gothic is viewed within psychological and theological rubrics. Because of America's seeming lack of history and its Puritan heritage, the American gothic, it has been argued, takes a turn inward, away from society and toward the psyche and the hidden blackness of the American soul. As Joseph Bodziock asserts, 'the American gothic replaced the social struggle of the European with a Manichean struggle between the moral forces of personal and communal order and the howling wilderness of chaos and moral depravity' (Bodziock: 1988, 33). Leslie Fiedler, the first critic to discuss the American gothic's peculiarity and to recognize its social impulse, sees the American gothic as 'a Calvinist exposé of natural human corruption' (Fiedler: 1982, 160). For Fiedler, as for many others, the American gothic remains first and foremost an expression of psychological states.

Cathy Davidson and Lawrence Buell are two notable exceptions to this rule. Both argue that the American gothic has a social referent: Davidson sees the early American gothic as a critique of individualism and Buell notes in his study of the 'provincial gothic' the 'potential inherent in gothic, from the start, to give this irrationalist vision a social ground' (Buell: 1986, 352). Moreover, Karen Halttunen's work (1993) on how the 'cult of horror' emerged during the late eighteenth century in America and how nineteenth-century gothic literature illuminates redefinitions of pain provides historical frameworks in which to view the development of the American gothic and suggests that it responded to and reinforced certain historical movements. Halttunen's historicizing of the American gothic also reflects a movement toward reading the American gothic in social, not psychological, terms.

Arguing that America does have enough history to sustain the gothic's challenge, the American gothic [can be situated] within specific sites of historical haunting, most notably slavery. American gothic literature criticizes America's national myth of new-world innocence by voicing the cultural contradictions that undermine the nation's claim to purity and equality. Showing how these contradictions contest and constitute national identity even as they are denied, the gothic tells of the historical horrors that make national identity possible yet must be repressed in order to sustain it.

I [would] use the term 'abject' to signify these historical horrors. The nation's narratives – its foundational fictions and self-mythologizations – are created through a process of displacement: their coherence depends on exclusion. By resurrecting what these narratives repress, the gothic disrupts the dream world of national myth with the nightmares of history. Moreover, in its narrative incoherence, the gothic discloses the instability of America's self-representations; its highly wrought form exposes the artificial foundations of national identity. However, while the gothic reveals what haunts the nation's narratives, it can also work to coalesce those narratives. Like the abject, the gothic serves as the ghost that both helps to run the machine of national identity and disrupts it. The gothic can strengthen as well as critique an idealized national identity.

[. . .] Although the gothic is not the only form that articulates abjection, it serves as a primary means of speaking the unspeakable in American literature.

Part Nine

READING SPLATTER/ SLASHER CINEMA

Introduction to Part Nine

■   Ken Gelder

S TALKER AND SLASHER FILMS make up two striking and related subgenres in modern American horror cinema, both attracting much critical attention. They each had their 'peak' moments, a time when the genre seemed at the height of its (sometimes quite awesome) powers. For Vera Dika, the stalker 'cycle' began with John Carpenter's *Halloween* (1978) and ran for about three years (Dika: 1990). These films were usually low-budget and independently-produced, characterized by a shadowy, resurrected killer who was identified on screen primarily through a set of 'visual and aural markers' (ibid., 123). They were sometimes set at a time of ritualistic teenage celebration (Prom Night, graduation day, and so on), unfolding in the frame of an insular, small-town community – to which the killer was once intimately linked. The killings themselves are brutal and dispassionate, graphically presented, and generally without sexual motivation. Dika also argues that the stalker films are both derivative and repetitive, borrowing liberally from previous horror cinema and producing a surprisingly large number of sequels. This is what she means by the stalker 'cycle' – which, by repeating what it does over and over, turns these films into a kind of 'game' in which audiences can increasingly participate.

The slasher film is sometimes traced back to Herschell Gordon Lewis's *Blood Feast* (1963) – an early example of the 'gore' films of the 1960s, revolving around grisly slaughters depicted in 'realistic' detail. But the point of origin of the slasher genre itself is usually taken to be Tobe Hooper's *The Texas Chainsaw Massacre* (1974), another low-budget film which fairly lays claim to the 'longest solid scream-track ever to shake out darkened American movie houses' (Hooper, cited in Carson: 1986, 9). Shown at Cannes and the London Film Festival, this film takes its travelling teenage victims to a cannibal family's charnel-house that is also laid out like a work of art – complete with mobiles and mini-installations of intricately-woven bones and feathers. It is the film that Carol J. Clover, once familiar only with 'quality' horror and horror classics, was 'dared to see' by friend in 1985 – resulting in her influential book, *Men, Women and Chainsaws*, an extract of which is in this section (Clover: 1992, 19).

The stalker and slasher films were received enthusiastically by horror *aficionados*, no doubt in part because of this cinema's out-of-the-mainstream location. The first contribution to this section from Philip Brophy – taken from a special issue of *Screen* devoted to horror – sees this 'displaced audience' identity as a virtue, bridging the conventional gulf between academic analysis and a fan's excitement. Far from being 'dared to see' these films, Brophy relishes their visual features – in particular, the spectacular destruction of the body. Turning to the early films of David Cronenberg as well as De Palma's *The Fury* (1978) and Carpenter's *The Thing* (1982), Brophy identifies a cinema that is only interested in 'results', a cinema which throws its excesses onto the screen's surface to provoke both shock and laughter, fear and pleasure. He coins a keyword for this unique blend of 'horror, textuality, morality, hilarity': horrality. The term comes to speak for the heady moment of the body-horror film of the early 1980s, a saturated genre which 'mimics itself mercilessly' – announcing in the process the horror film's new identity as a *postmodern* form.

Tania Modleski's extract, from her edited collection, *Studies in Entertainment*, is also a celebration (with reservations) of the slasher film, mostly because of its adversarial position in the cultural field. The critical theorists of the Frankfurt School and, more recently, the high priests of postmodernism had dismissed mass culture on the grounds that it produced conformity and complacency amongst its audiences. The pleasure to be found in mass cultural forms reconciled consumers to what used to be called 'dominant ideology'. High art, on the other hand, was said to refuse the straightforward offer of pleasure and was thus privileged as an oppositional form; it relayed instead the loftier experience of what Roland Barthes had called *jouissance*. But, as Modleski points out, the slasher film *also* refuses to give straightforward pleasures to its audience. Its teen victims are themselves characterized as complacent, pleasure-seeking, indifferent consumers: all the more reason to ruthlessly dispose of them. It ruptures rather than reconciles, launching 'an assault on all that bourgeois culture is supposed to cherish', thus producing what Modleski calls an 'anti-narcissistic identification' on behalf of the audience – a point that perhaps recalls Bertolt Brecht's alienation effect. The slasher film is closer to postmodernism than might first be realized, producing the kind of ultra-proximity and 'schizophrenia' that Jean Baudrillard had seen as characteristic of the postmodern condition.

But although she sees the slasher film as an interesting problem for the cultural field, Modleski doesn't wish to recover it wholesale – mostly because the 'sustained terror' it produces relies on the gendering of its victims as women. More than other kinds of horror cinema, the slasher film has certainly been difficult for feminist critics to come to grips with – a point worked through elsewhere by Elizabeth Young in her analysis of a much later big-budget slasher-psychological thriller, Jonathan Demme's *The Silence of the Lambs* (1991) (Young: 1991b). Nevertheless, there are features of the slasher film that refuse to let issues of gender and heterosexist identification settle. The contribution by Carol J. Clover to this section is an extract from her provocative chapter, 'Her Body, Himself', an analysis of what she calls the slasher film's 'female victim-hero'. In these films, it can be difficult for male audiences to identify with males on screen. Boyfriends are usually killed early on, fathers are usually absent, and no man rushes in at the end to save the day. The killer is shadowy enough, or deranged enough, to obstruct identification; in Sean S. Cunningham's *Friday the 13th* (1980), the killer is in fact a woman anyway. So, it seems, is the sole survivor in these slasher holocausts: what Clover calls the Final Girl. The slasher film certainly continues the heterosexist gendering of 'abject terror' as feminine, but it also 'regenders' femininity by giving the Final Girl herself a heroic role. Drawing connections with Victorian flagellation literature, Clover thus sees a certain 'theatricalization of gender' at work in the slasher film – with the Final Girl as victim and hero simultaneously, a 'feminine male'. Audiences might well participate in this crossing of gender, male audiences especially being 'feminized' both through their own terror and through a protagonist whose heroism is 'no longer strictly gendered masculine'. The slasher film in this respect may or may not be a progressive cinematic form, but it can at least produce what Clover calls a 'loosening of the categories'.

Chapter 22

PHILIP BROPHY

HORRALITY – THE TEXTUALITY OF CONTEMPORARY HORROR FILMS

'HORRALITY' WAS WRITTEN IN mid-'83 during what appears to have been (on reflection) the peak of a small 'golden period' of the contemporary horror film. The article serves as a general introduction to certain characteristics of the contemporary horror film which distinguish this particular phase of horror from previous ones. The act of showing over the act of telling; the photographic image versus the realistic scene; the destruction of the family, the body, etc; and a perverse sense of humour all go toward qualifying these films as contemporary, both in terms of social entertainment and cinematic form.

The following two and a half years has seen many new developments, from the hysteria surrounding 'video nasties' to the maturing of many horror auteurs. Serious discussion is then needed on, respectively, the politics of taste (what makes one able to/not able to watch a horror movie?) and personal tonalities of the genre (how does one film-maker sustain thematic continuity within a genre *about genre*?). And even that would be pruning our problematics. The horror film could very well hold many keys to problems which the cinema will be addressing (or avoiding) for some time to come: How does one qualify genre *now*? What effects have the dichotomies of horror/terror and telling/showing had on the development of cinematic language? What are the relationships between certain aspects of pornography and certain aspects of the cinema? What defines our notion of *special* effects in the cinema? How does one provide a *critical* voice for exploitation in the writing of the history of the cinema?

'Horrality' does not even get to ask these questions, but rather points out that something *different* is happening in these films. We're only on the front porch of a monstrous mansion full of critical zombies waiting to be awakened and engaged. Soon enough – we'll be in the basement. . . .

Philip Brophy, September 1985

The word

Phrases are coined; terms are invented; metaphors are employed. The invention of language always carries a blasphemous tone, be it comical, opportunistic or hypothetical. The invention is devoid of linguistic validation though the effect is unavoidably semantic. The neologism exercises language as the utility that its design describes. It is said that there has already been a word invented for everything that needs to be said. By the same token, some new things that need to be said need new words invented for them.

In August 1979, the first issue of the American magazine *Fangoria* was released. It is a bi-monthly magazine devoted to horror movies. The title speaks volumes: gore, fantasy, phantasmagoria, fans. It simultaneously expands a multiplicity of cross-references and contracts them into a referential construct. This semantic effect strangely echoes the relationship between the emergence of *Fangoria* and the development of the contemporary horror film, whereby an ever-growing cult journal expands and contracts a critical voice for a mutant market – that of the contemporary film: a genre about genre; a displaced audience; a short-circuiting entertainment.

Another word is invented. More pretentious in tone and more theoretical in intention: 'Horrality' – horror, textuality, morality, hilarity. In the same way that *Fangoria* celebrates the re-birth of the Horror genre, 'Horrality' celebrates the precise nature of what constitutes the films of this re-birth as texts. As neologisms, both words do not so much 'mean' something as they do describe a specific historical juncture, a cultural phase that is as fixed as the semantic accuracy of the words.

The object

The modern horror film is a strange animal. A camouflaged creature, it has generally been accorded a less than prominent place in the institution of the Cinema, due mainly to the level at which its difference (its specificity, its textuality) is articulated. It is a genre which mimics itself mercilessly – because its statement is coded within its very mimicry.

Increasingly throughout the first half of the Seventies, the Horror film defied itself, distancing itself immensely from what historically had been defined as the genre, incorporating the hey-days of the Universal, Hammer and Toho studios and the legacy of Roger Corman and Herschell Gordon Lewis. To make a broad distinction, the Seventies have heralded a double death for Genre in general, as critically and theoretically it became a problematic which more and more could not bear its own weight, and, in terms of audiences and commerciality, it was diffused, absorbed and consumed by that decade's gulping, belching plug-hole: Realism.

Nonetheless, Horror films were always being made, though their attraction was usually minor, punctuated by mainstream successes that provided well-crafted Horror: *The Abominable Doctor Phibes* (1971); *Last House on the Left* (1972); *The Exorcist* and *Sisters* (1973); and *Carrie* (1976), for example. However, it was the transition period between 1978 and 1979 that clearly announced the rebirth (at least popularly if not also critically) of the Horror film, culminating in (i) the mainstream successes of *Halloween* (1978), an independent production made by newcomer John Carpenter, and *Alien* (1979), a big-budget production by another newcomer, Ridley Scott; and (ii) the cementing of the underground status of George Romero with *Dawn of the Dead* (1979) and David Cronenberg with *The Brood* (1979). The historical door of the Horror genre was reopened, allowing discovery of Romero's *Martin* (1978), *The Crazies* (1973) and the classic *Night of the Living Dead* (1968), as well as Cronenberg's *Rabid* (1977) and *Shivers* (1976).

In 1983 the contemporary Horror film is definitely a felt presence, with the never-ending onslaught of Horror films reaching large audiences, a rejuvenation of the Drive-In circuit, the rise in video libraries and the increasing value and relevance that the genre currently holds not only for mainstream film audiences but also for rock culture and film culture. A major problem still exists, though, in the domain of mainstream film criticism (i.e. taste arbitration for those who would 'benefit' from it) and film distribution, where the former has no critical language to encompass the contemporary Horror film while the latter is ignorant of the marketing potential that these films have. Thus, the bulk of my horror film viewing over the past four-five years has consisted of Drive-In doubles, Dusk-to-Dawns and hired video cassettes. [. . .] It is this state of affairs that constitutes the displaced audience of the contemporary Horror film.

The text

My first problem (among many) in speaking of the textuality of the contemporary Horror film is in dislocating it from its more traditional generic overtones. It is a strategy that involves handling the films themselves like freshly severed limbs: objects both on their own and obviously fragmented. A history of generic study already clothes the Horror genre, encompassing the politics of (films like) *The Invasion of the Body Snatchers* (1956); the philosophy of (films like) *The Incredible Shrinking Man* (1957); the sexuality of *Dracula* (1931); and the morality of *Frankenstein* (1931). The fantasy film in general has provided a morphology of the metaphor, an endless commentary on humanity in its aspirations, implications and complications. At its most conventional, the genre is worked as being a formalist catalogue of mythological writings that organically and historically form the growth of the genre. It is such a growth that critically lays down the notions of origins (from Mary Shelley to Transylvania to Witchcraft); actors (from Karloff and Lugosi to Cushing and Leé); auteurs (from Roger Corman to Terence Fisher); and sub-genres (Vampires, Created Life Forms, Ghosts, Mummies, Zombies, Monsters, Aliens, Demons, Werewolves, etc).

It is not so much that the modern Horror film refutes or ignores the conventions of genre, but it is involved in a violent awareness of itself as a saturated genre. Its rebirth as such is qualified by *how* it states itself as genre. The historical blue-prints have faded, and the new (post-1975) films recklessly copy and re-draw their generic sketching. In this wild tracing, there are two major areas that affect the modern Horror film: (i) the growth of special effects with cinematic realism and sophisticated technology, and (ii) an historical over-exposure of the genre's iconography, mechanics and effects. The textuality of the modern horror film is integrally and intricately bound up in the dilemma of a saturated fiction whose primary aim in its telling is to generate suspense, shock and horror. It is a mode of fiction, a type of writing that in the fullest sense 'plays' with its reader, engaging the reader in a dialogue of textual manipulation that has no time for the critical ordinances of social realism, cultural enlightenment or emotional humanism. The gratification of the contemporary Horror film is based upon tension, fear, anxiety, sadism and masochism – a disposition that is overall both tasteless and morbid. The pleasure of the text is, in fact, getting the shit scared out of you – and loving it; an exchange mediated by adrenalin.

'Horrality' involves the construction, employment and manipulation of horror – in all its various guises – as a textual mode. The effect of its fiction is not unlike a death-defying carnival ride: the subject is a willing target that both constructs the terror and is terrorised by its construction. 'Horrality' is too blunt to bother with psychology – traditionally the voice of articulation behind horror – because what is of prime importance is the textual effect, the game that one plays *with* the text, a game that is impervious to any knowledge of its workings. The contemporary Horror film *knows* that you've seen it before; it *knows* that you know what is about to happen; and it knows that you know it knows you know. And none of it means a thing, as the cheapest trick in the book will still tense your muscles, quicken your heart and jangle your nerves. It is the *present* – the precise point of speech, of utterance, of plot, of event – that is ever of any value. Its effect disappears with the gulping breath, the gasping shriek, swallowed up by the fascistic continuum of the fiction. A nervous giggle of amoral delight as you prepare yourself in a totally self-deluding way for the next shock. Too late. Freeze. Crunch. Chill. Scream. Laugh.

The effect

When the 'R' certificate was first introduced to Australia, one particular movie that was strongly linked to the titilation caused by this moralistic parental censorship was *The Exorcist* (1973). Swamped with gore, it was what has now come to be the ultimate Drive-In movie: an opiate of adrenalin. Historically, its controversy was, among other things, due to it being one of the first instances of the whole family being subjected to graphic gore, unadulterated horror and fantastic violence. But none of it was gratuitous. *The Exorcist* was a tale of Catholic moralism (Good vs. Evil) that utilised state-of-the-art gore techniques to produce a work which thrust its audience into a vertigo of realism – the real of its depiction and the real of its fiction. It was a film that was culturally situated in a time when demonic possession was one of those mysteries that threatened the social parameters of the real, of the truthful. One entered into the cinema not for a fiction, but for a direction on that particular social debate. One left confused by the initial vertigo, a two-pronged dilemma – not only 'how did they do *that?*' but 'do such things exist?' The fiction undercut itself, impregnating its effect with plausible existence.

In 1980, *The Amityville Horror* was released. It ironically (but dumbly) copied the currency of *The Exorcist* but went one step further: where *The Exorcist* was founded on a plausibility mediated by our (inherently religious) fears, *The Amityville Horror* purported to be a dramatisation of an actual event. This time, yes: it really did happen. Still, the film was as interesting as the News, a type of telling that performs a journalistic dance around its factual base, creating a dull gap between fiction and fact, neither one nor the other. *The Amityville Horror* occupied such a space, devoid of any perversity in its telling and full of golly-gosh realism.

Some years after, the whole thing was proved a fraud – and out came *Amityville 2: The Possession* (1982). To counter both *The Exorcist* and *The Amityville Horror*, *Amityville 2* revelled in itself as fiction and went all out to make a horror movie, marking a commercial peak in a growing trend in Horror films, namely the destruction of the Family. Whereas suspense was traditionally hinged on individual identification (the victim, the possessed, the pursued, etc), it was now shifted onto not a family identification, but a pleasure in witnessing the Family being destroyed – it being the object of the horror and us being the subject of their demise. *The Hills Have Eyes* (1977) clearly delineated this by positing two totally opposite families against one another in a battle of horror and fight for survival. An all-white all-blond middle-class American family (mom, dad, two teenage kids, grandma, elder brother and his wife) set out on a camper holiday in the mid-west desert. While camped, they encounter an inbred family of cannibals (papa, mamma, son, daughter, grandma and other animals) who kill off the 'white bread' family (director Wes Craven's description) one by one in the most gory ways possible. While *The Hills Have Eyes* is an unabashed horror-comedy, *Amityville 2* situates its horror in a social-realist frame, making it like *The Exorcist* meets *Ordinary People* (1980). Continually the family in *Amityville 2* is pictorially framed within the screen frame – through doors, by windows, in mirrors, on tables – forever reinforcing the Family as a pathetic polaroid of complacency, ripe for the total destruction that eventually befalls it. At the film's end, the fully possessed son methodically shoots all the members of the family. A strange suspense is generated here: not only is one wondering 'is he or she going to get it?' but also 'how far is this movie going to go?' The film takes pleasure in actually killing off *everybody*. Hitchcock once regretted having the young boy with the bomb parcel blow himself up on a packed double-decker bus in *Sabotage* (1936) because the audience (then) was not relieved of the tension created in wondering whether the boy would survive. *Amityville 2* – like most contemporary Horror films – has no such regrets.

Perhaps what has been an even more prolific trend is the destruction of the Body. The contemporary Horror film tends to play not so much on the broad fear of Death, but more precisely on the fear of one's own body, of how one controls and relates to it. In 1976, an Italian movie *Deep Red* made an impact not by portraying graphic violence – a trademark of Herschell Gordon Lewis in the '60s with films like *Blood Feast*, *Color Me Blood Red* and *She Devils on Wheels* – but by conveying to the viewer a graphic sense of physicality, accentuating the very presence of the body on the screen, e.g. scenes where a person gets rammed into a marble slab, mouth wide open in a scream, crushing the teeth on impact. *Deep Red* is cinematic scraping of chalk on a blackboard. Suspense is set up by knowing that the next scene of violence is going to be uncomfortably physical, due to the graphic feel effected by a very exact and acute cinematic construction of sound, image, framing and editing. But the contemporary Horror film often discards the sophistication of such a traditionally well-crafted handling of cinematic language. *Deep Red* in fact functions as a mid-way point between the Hitchcock debt (carried on by De Palma and Carpenter) and the Lewis debt (carried on by the likes of Paul Morrissey, John Waters, Steve Cuningham, Tobe Hooper and Sam Raimi), incorporating a mode that both 'tells' you the horror and 'shows' it.

It is this mode of *showing* as opposed to *telling* that is strongly connected to the destruction of the Body. David Cronenberg has consolidated himself as a director who almost exclusively works in this field, with films about an artificially created sex-parasite that transfers itself from body to body during intercourse, causing a wild sex epidemic (*Shivers*, 1976); a mutant cancer growth resultant from a plastic surgery experiment (*Rabid*, 1977); the birth of a mutant brood by a psychologically unstable mother receiving treatment by a special psychiatrist who promotes the physicalisation of his patients' problems *through* their bodies (*The Brood*, 1979); and the awesome physical power that the mind has over its own body and other bodies through parapsychology (*Scanners*, 1981). *Scanners*, alone, could rest as the penultimate Body movie, with an opening shot where a 'scanner' – through the pure power of thought – blows another scanner's head apart. And you see it happen. The *ending* of the movie is something that defies literary description. The horror for such films' subjects is the matter-of-fact nature of the films' plots, as they are slight twists on the fear of getting cancer or even rabies itself. *Scanners* goes further and incorporates a fear of what amounts to mental mugging, translating the liberal fear of having someone read your mind into someone exploding your head through reading your mind.

Ironically, one of the original exploding-head scenes appeared in Brian De Palma's *The Fury* (1978) to which *Scanners* perhaps owes a debt due to both movies dealing with thought-reading more as a *physical* phenomenon than a spiritual, ethereal experience. The difference between the two films is the incredible sense of theatre used in *The Fury*; dramatic intercutting between a man violently shaking and a slow zoom in on the girl with the incredible power of ultra-parapsychology is coupled with an equally dramatic orchestral score, bellowing out its crescendo. Cut. Kaboom! Right on cue as the tonality of the symphony resolves itself, the whole body of the man explodes. A true opera of violence, the ending is a stirring cathartic experience that is emotionally charged by its classical construction. On the other hand, the end scene of *Scanners* is *photographic*. It, too, has cuts, pans and zooms coupled with an appropriately physical soundtrack of synthesised music, but it centres on what is more of a transition period of the physique: a metamorphosis of the body. Veins ripple up the arm, eyes turn white and pop out, hair stands on end, blood trickles from all facial cavities, heads swell and contract. *An American Werewolf in London* (1981) (despite it being a black comedy that uses its *comedy* to affect the audience more than its horror) employs the same photographic sensibility to actually show you the transition from Man to Werewolf in *real time*, as opposed to the ellipse-time of the dissolves of Lon Chaney Jr's face with different stages of make-up to signify his mutation. It's not unlike being on a tram and somebody has an epileptic fit – you're there right next to the person, you can't get away and you can't do anything. *The Beast Within* (1982) sets the stage for such an event as the boy undergoes an agonising transformation on his hospital bed, where a mutated cicada-like creature erupts *out* of his body, in full view of his mother, 'presumed' father, a doctor, and us. The doctor exclaims 'My God!' (*the* catch-phrase of the modern horror film) and the mother cries 'My Son!?' The boy not only goes through a transformation, but his body is discarded, shed to make way for the 'beast' within. The horror is conveyed through torture and agony of havoc wrought upon a body devoid of control. The identification is then levelled at that loss of control – the fictional body is as helpless as its viewing subject.

The Thing (1982) took to its logical limit the Body-horror that was initiated in *Alien* (1979) with that infamous scene where the alien bursts out of a crew member's stomach. Both films deal with the notion of an alien purely as a biological life force, whose blind motivation for survival is its only existence. Not just a parasite but a total consumer of *any* life form, a biological black-hole. Each film nonetheless generates a different mode of suspense with a similar form of horror. John Carpenter's graphically 'realistic' suspense horror is a world away from Howard Hawks' B-Grade classic, showing *everything* that the original only alluded to. The essential horror of *The Thing* was in the Thing's total disregard for and ignorance of the human body. To it, the human body is merely protein – no more. A central scene in the film is when the doctor attempts to revive what is presumed a dead officer but which is in fact the Thing in a dormant phase. The doctor goes to push on the officer's chest but his hands go crashing through the chest like an egg-shell, getting his hands torn off by the Thing's 'jaws' within the chest. The awakened Thing then mobilises the dead body, sprouting tentacles through its flesh and limbs through its muscles in an orgy of gore. But what must be remembered is that the 'original' person has actually died, so that pain and agony is *absent*. Stan Brakhage's underground art film *The Act of Seeing with One's Own Eyes* (1973) deals with a similar effect. Silent and lasting only about 20 minutes, all the footage is shot in a morgue, detailing every method that is used in autopsies in full view for the camera. Lacking any conventional narrative structure, the film starts and ends, a blur of flesh, bone, muscle and tissue that presents the human body in every way except its recognisable forms. Both in terms of its subject matter and its fictional structure, *The Act of Seeing with One's Own Eyes* does not *recognise* the human body. Likewise, *The Thing* does not honour any of our beliefs or perceptions of what the human body is.

The Thing is a violently self-conscious movie. In the aforementioned central scene, the biological nightmare that explodes on the doctor's table is shot down in flames – a difficult task as *any* part of the Thing is a whole lifeform by itself. After all the flesh, blood and guts have been incinerated, the head officer's head lying underneath the table is latched onto by a small bloody tentacle. In what is perhaps the single most technically stunning scene in special effects, the tentacle lashes out of the head onto a door, and drags itself on its side. Just as it reaches the doorway, the crew see it and are transfixed by it. The head slowly turns upside down and, suddenly, eight insect-like legs rip through the head using it like a body. The sight is of an upside-down severed human head out of which have grown insect feet. As it 'walks' out the door, a crew member says *the* line of the film: 'You've got to be fucking kidding!' Quite obviously, this exclamation operates as a two-fold commentary – (i) the scene portrays the lack of limits that the Thing has in its emasculation of the human body; and (ii) the scene presents to the audience the mind-boggling state that special-effects make-up is in at the moment. Later, the film then presents its most physically effective scene: in *extreme* close-up, a thumb is slit by a razor for a blood sample. The audience might gasp and scream in the other scene, but in this scene, one's body is queasily affected not by fear or horror, but by the precision that the photographic image is able to exact upon us. *The Thing* perversely plays with these extensions of cinematic realism, presenting them as a dumbfounding magical spectacle in total knowledge of the irreducible effect that is generated by their manipulation.

The contemporary Horror film in general plays with the contradiction that it is only a movie, but nonetheless a movie that can work upon its audience with immediate results. As such, it is only the result that counts. A film like *Ghost Story* (1982) even names itself – its design and function – in its very title. Within the fiction, four old men form a 'chowder society' as a regular social occasion to tell each other stories for the sole purpose of scaring one another. Out of this unfolds the central story, which is designed to scare the viewer. All stories engulf one another in a whirlpool of fright generated by the act of telling. The opening of *The Fog* (1980) sets a similarly quaint scene: an old fisherman is camped out on the beach at night with a group of kids aged between seven and ten, their awe-filled faces lit by the flickering camp fire. In this Norman Rockwell setting, the fisherman tells the local folklore tale about the curse put on the town by pirates who were killed by the prominent townsfolk a hundred years ago to the day. On come the film's credits, and then the movie starts – which is the story about what the curse originally promised, the revenge of the pirates. The introductory scene is dense in stereotypography. But rather than smash the cliché or undermine it, it is totally played out and fully lived. The contemporary Horror film rarely denies its clichés, but instead accepts them, often causing an undercurrent by overplaying them.

Another twist on the emphasis of the tale as a basic narrative form for the Horror film is the cinematic realisation of the textual organisation of the comic book. The most famous of Horror comics were the E.C. comics from the early 1950s, the style and form of which have influenced the contemporary Horror film to a large degree. Although Hammer Horror films were mainly derived from gothic literature and imagery, the 1971 film *The Abominable Doctor Phibes* is perhaps the first cinematic version of an E.C. comic. Amounting to not much more than a speedy revenge tale full of truly inventive and gory deaths, *The Abominable Doctor Phibes* combines the macabre with the hilarious in a way that was picked up in Milton Subotsky's Amicus films *Tales from the Crypt* (1972), and *Vault of Horror* (1973) and carried on in the outlandish Paul Morrissey films *Blood for Dracula* and *Flesh for Frankenstein* (both made in 1974), culminating in George Romero's exacting homage to E.C., *Creepshow* (1983). *Creepshow* in particular is notable not only for how it puts cinematic language at the service of the comic-strip (the reverse is usually the case in nearly all comic adaptations) but also for the incredible variation in tone of each of the five stories, ranging from the farcical to the horrific.

Still, it is humour that remains one of the major features of the contemporary Horror film, especially if used as an undercutting agent to counter-balance its more horrific moments. The humour is not usually well-crafted but mostly perverse and/or tasteless, so much so that often the humour might be horrific while the horror might be humorous. Furthermore, the joke or punchline is embedded *in* the film text and does not function separate from the film. As such, the humour in a gory scene is the result of the contemporary Horror film's saturation of all its codes and conventions – a punchline that can only be got when one fully acknowledges this saturation as the departure point for viewing pleasure. *The* film that most clearly illustrates this is *The Evil Dead* (1982) which is a gore movie beyond belief that has one simultaneously screaming with terror and laughter (as opposed to the jarring effect attempted in *American Werewolf in London*). After almost deliberately setting itself up as a boring cheap horror flick, it suddenly pulls out all the stops when a possessed girl thrusts a sharp lead pencil into the ankle of a girl and swirls it around making mince meat out of her ankle – in real time and full close-up. A similar effect is used in the now seminal (though not as funny as *The Evil Dead*) *Friday the 13th* where the girl who appears to be the main star suddenly gets her throat slit in a totally non-eventful way, causing a dull thud with its awkward and messy depiction of her death.

And I could go on – having not yet even mentioned the classical construction of *Alien* (the most flawless suspense text I've yet encountered); the meeting of a Disneyland sentimentality with traditional avant-garde technical experimentation in *Poltergeist* (1982), or the Slasher sub-genre initiated most forcibly by *Halloween*. But the contemporary Horror film is always changing as each new film sets new precedents and new commentaries on special effects, plot, realism, horror, suspense, humour and subject matter, which affect whatever films are to follow. 'Horrality' is thus a mode of textuality that is dictated by trends within both the Horror genre and cinematic realism. But what amounts to an awkward problematic in analysis and writing in fact works very productively in the viewing of the films, and it is at this point in film history that one is able to experience the speed of this genre about genre.

Chapter 23

TANIA MODLESKI

THE TERROR OF PLEASURE

The contemporary horror film
and postmodern theory

IN THE *GRUNDRISSE* (1857–8), Karl Marx's description of the capitalist as a werewolf turns into an enthusiastic endorsement of that creature's
activities. Marx tells us that the capitalist's 'werewolf hunger,' which drives him
continually to replace 'living labour' with 'dead labour' (that is, human beings
with machines), will lead to a mode of production in which 'labour time is no
longer the sole measure and source of wealth' (Marx: 1973, 706). Thus, in the
words of one commentator, 'capitalism furnishes the material basis for the eventual realization of an age-old dream of humankind: the liberation from burdensome
toil' (Balbus: 1982, 41). Marx's critics have tended to place him in the role of
mad scientist, with his vision of the miracles to be wrought by feeding the werewolf's insatiable appetite. Writers from Jacques Ellul to Isaac Balbus have argued
(to mix narratives here) that allowing the capitalist his unhindered experimentation in the 'workshops of filthy creation' – his accumulation of more and more
specimens of dead labor – cannot possibly provide a blessing to humankind.

These critics claim that rather than truly liberating humanity by freeing it from
burdensome toil, the proliferation of dead labor – of technology – has resulted in
the invasion of people's mental, moral, and emotional lives, and thus has rendered
them incapable of desiring social change. To quote Jacques Ellul, who has traced the
intrusion of technique into all aspects of human existence, 'as big city life became
for the most part intolerable, techniques of amusement were developed. It
became indispensable to make urban suffering acceptable by furnishing amusements,
a necessity which was to assure the rise, for example, of a monstrous motion picture
industry' (Ellul: 1964, 113–14). In advanced capitalism, the narrative shifts, though
the genre remains the same: physical freedom – that is, increased leisure time – is
bought at the price of spiritual zombieism. The masses, it is said, are offered various
forms of easy, false pleasure as a way of keeping them unaware of their own desperate
vacuity. And so, apparently, we are caught in the toils of the great monster, mass

culture, which certain critics, including some of the members of the Frankfurt School and their followers, have equated with ideology. For the Frankfurt School, in fact, mass culture effected a major transformation in the nature of ideology from Marx's time: once 'socially necessary illusion,' it has now become 'manipulative contrivance,' and its power is such that, in the sinister view of T. W. Adorno, 'conformity has replaced consciousness' (Adorno: 1975, 17).

Today many people tend to believe that other, more sophisticated approaches to the issue have superseded the Frankfurt School's conception of mass culture as a monstrous and monolithic ideological machine. The work of Roland Barthes is often cited as an example of such an advance. But when Barthes offers the converse of the proposition that mass culture (for example, the cinema) is ideology and contends rather that 'ideology is the Cinema of society,' we are entitled, I think, to question just how far this removes us from many of the premises we think we have rejected (Barthes: 1979, 3). Isn't Barthes here implying that both cinema and ideology, being seamless and without gaps or contradictions, create what the Frankfurt School called the 'spurious harmony' of a conformist mass society?

According to many of the members of the Frankfurt School, high art was a subversive force capable of opposing spurious harmony. On this point especially, certain contemporary theorists have disagreed. In *The Anti-Aesthetic*, a recent collection of essays on postmodern culture, the editor, Hal Foster, suggests the need to go beyond the idea of the aesthetic as a negative category, claiming that the critical importance of the notion of the aesthetic as subversive is now 'largely illusory' (Foster: 1983, xv). However, despite such pronouncements, which are common enough in the literature of postmodernism, I believe it can be shown that many postmodernists do in fact engage in the same kind of oppositional thinking about mass culture that characterized the work of the Frankfurt School. Take, for example, Barthes' writings on pleasure. Although it is inaccurate to maintain, as critics sometimes do, that Barthes always draws a sharp distinction between pleasure and jouissance (since in *The Pleasure of the Text* [1975] Barthes straightaway denies any such strenuous opposition), whenever Barthes touches on the subject of mass culture, he is apt to draw a fairly strict line – placing pleasure on the side of the consumer, and jouissance in contrast to pleasure. Here is a remarkable passage from *The Pleasure of the Text*, in which Barthes begins by discussing the superiority of a textual reading based on disavowal and ends by casually condemning mass culture:

> Many readings are perverse, implying a split, a cleavage. Just as the child knows its mother has no penis and simultaneously believes she has one . . . so the reader can keep saying: *I know these are only words, but all the same.* . . . Of all readings that of tragedy is the most perverse: I take pleasure in hearing myself tell a story *whose end I know*: I know and I don't know, I act toward myself as though I did not know: I know perfectly well Oedipus will be unmasked, that Danton will be guillotined, *but all the same.* . . . Compared to a dramatic story, which is one whose outcome is unknown, there is here an effacement of pleasure and a progression of *jouissance* (today, in mass culture, there is an enormous consumption of 'dramatics' and little *jouissance*).
>
> (Barthes: 1975, 47–8)

Anyone who has read Christian Metz's persuasive argument that disavowal is *constitutive* of the spectator's pleasure at the cinema will find it difficult to give ready assent to Barthes' contention that mass culture deprives the consumer of this 'perverse' experience (Metz: 1982, 99–148). And anyone who is acquainted with the standardized art products – the genre and formula stories – which proliferate in a mass society will have to admit that their import depends precisely upon our suspending our certain knowledge of their outcome – for example, the knowledge that, as the critics say, the gangster 'will eventually lie dead in the streets.' Barthes' remarks are illuminating, then, not for any direct light they shed on the high/mass culture debate, but because they vividly exemplify the tendency of critics and theorists to make mass culture into the 'other' of whatever, at any given moment, they happen to be championing – and, moreover, to denigrate that other primarily because it allegedly provides pleasure to the consumer.

While Barthes' *The Pleasure of the Text* has become one of the canonical works of postmodernism, in this respect it remains caught up in older modernist ideas about art. In an essay entitled 'The Fate of Pleasure,' written in 1963, the modernist critic Lionel Trilling speculated that high art had dedicated itself to an attack on pleasure in part because pleasure was the province of mass art: 'we are repelled by the idea of an art that is consumer-oriented and comfortable, let alone luxurious' (Trilling: 1963, 178). He went on to argue that, for the modernist, pleasure is associated with the 'specious good' – with bourgeois habits, manners, and morals – and he noted, 'the destruction of what is considered to be specious good is surely one of the chief literary enterprises of our age' (ibid., 182). Hence, Trilling has famously declared, aesthetic modernity is primarily adversarial in impulse.

The 'specious good,' or 'bourgeois taste,' remains an important target of contemporary thinkers, and postmodernism continues to be theorized as its adversary. Indeed, it might be argued that postmodernism is valued by many of its proponents insofar as it is considered *more* adversarial than modernism, and is seen to wage war on a greatly expanded category of the 'specious good,' which presently includes meaning (Barthes speaks of the 'regime of meaning') and even form (Barthes: 1977, 167). For example, in an essay entitled 'Answering the Question: What is Postmodernism?' Jean-François Lyotard explicitly contrasts postmodernism to modernism in terms of their relation to 'pleasure.' For Lyotard, modernism's preoccupation with form meant that it was still capable of affording the reader or viewer 'matter for solace and pleasure, [whereas the postmodern is] that which denies itself the solace of good forms, the consensus of a taste which would make it possible to share collectively the nostalgia for the unattainable' (Lyotard: 1983, 340). It is important to recognize the extent to which Lyotard shares the same animus as the Frankfurt School, although his concern is not merely to denounce *spurious* harmony, but to attack *all* harmony – consensus, collectivity – as spurious, that is, on the side of 'cultural policy,' the aim of which is to offer the public 'well-made' and 'comforting' works of art (ibid., 335).

Although Lyotard has elsewhere informed us that 'thinking by means of oppositions does not correspond to the liveliest modes of postmodern knowledge,' he does not seem to have extricated himself entirely from this mode (Lyotard: 1979, 29). Pleasure (or 'comfort' or 'solace') remains the enemy for the postmodernist thinker because it is judged to be the means by which the consumer is reconciled to the prevailing cultural policy, or the 'dominant ideology.' While this view may well provide the critic with 'matter for solace and pleasure,' it is at least debatable that mass culture today is on the side of the specious good, that it offers, in the words of Matei Calinescu, 'an ideologically manipulated illusion of taste,' that it lures its audience to a false complacency with the promise of equally false and insipid pleasures (Calinescu: 1977, 240). Indeed, the contemporary horror film – the so-called exploitation film or slasher film – provides an interesting counter-example to such theses. Many of these films are engaged in an unprecedented assault on all that bourgeois culture is supposed to cherish – like the ideological apparatuses of the family and the school. Consider Leonard Maltin's capsule summary of an exemplary film in the genre, *The Brood* (1979), directed by David Cronenberg and starring Samantha Eggar: 'Eggar eats her own afterbirth while midget clones beat grandparents and lovely young school teachers to death with mallets' (Maltin: 1981–2, 95). A few of the films, like *The Texas Chainsaw Massacre* (1974), have actually been celebrated for their adversarial relation to contemporary culture and society. In this film, a family of men, driven out of the slaughterhouse business by advanced technology, turns to cannibalism. The film deals with the slaughter of a group of young people travelling in a van and dwells at great length on the pursuit of the last survivor of the group, Sally, by the man named Leatherface, who hacks his victims to death with a chainsaw. Robin Wood has analyzed the film as embodying a critique of capitalism, since the film shows the horror both of people quite literally living off other people, and of the institution of the family, since it implies that the monster is the family (Wood *et al.*: 1979, 20–22).

In some of the films the attack on contemporary life strikingly recapitulates the very terms adopted by many culture critics. In George Romero's *Dawn of the Dead* (1979), the plot involves zombies taking over a shopping center, a scenario depicting the worst fears of the culture critics who have long envisioned the will-less, soul-less masses as zombie-like beings possessed by the alienating imperative to consume. And in David Cronenberg's *Videodrome* (1982), video itself becomes the monster. The film concerns a plot, emanating from Pittsburgh, to subject human beings to massive doses of a video signal which renders its victims incapable of distinguishing hallucination from reality. One of the effects of this signal on the film's hero is to cause a gaping, vagina-like wound to open in the middle of his stomach, so that the villains can program him by inserting a video cassette into his body. The hero's situation becomes that of the new schizophrenic described by Jean Baudrillard in his discussion of the effects of mass communication:

> No more hysteria, no more projective paranoia, properly speaking, but this state of terror proper to the schizophrenic: too great a proximity of everything, the unclean promiscuity of everything which touches, invests, and penetrates without resistance, with no halo of private protection, not even his own body, to protect him anymore. . . . The schizo is bereft of every scene, open to everything in spite of himself, living in the greatest confusion.
>
> (Baudrillard: 1983, 132–3)

'You must open yourself completely to us,' says one of *Videodrome*'s villains, as he plunges the cassette into the gaping wound. It would seem that we are here very far from the realm of what is traditionally called 'pleasure' and much nearer to so-called *jouissance*, discussions of which privilege terms like 'gaps,' 'wounds,' 'fissures,' 'splits,' 'cleavages,' and so forth.

Moreover, if the text is 'an anagram for our body,' as Roland Barthes maintains (Barthes: 1975, 17), the contemporary text of horror could aptly be considered an anagram for the schizophrenic's body, which is so vividly imaged in Cronenberg's film. It is a ruptured body, lacking the kind of integrity commonly attributed to popular narrative cinema. For just as Baudrillard makes us aware that terms like 'paranoia' and 'hysteria,' which film critics have used to analyze both film characters and textual mechanisms, are no longer as applicable in mass culture today as they once were, so the much more global term 'narrative pleasure' is similarly becoming outmoded.

What is always at stake in discussions of 'narrative pleasure' is what many think of as the ultimate 'spurious harmony,' the supreme ideological construct – the 'bourgeois ego.' Contemporary film theorists insist that pleasure is 'ego-reinforcing' and that narrative is the primary means by which mass culture supplies and regulates this pleasure. For Stephen Heath, Hollywood narratives are versions of the nineteenth-century 'novelistic,' or 'family romance,' and their function is to 'remember the history of the individual subject' through processes of identification, through narrative continuity, and through the mechanism of closure (Heath: 1981, 157). Julia Kristeva condemns popular cinema in similar terms in her essay on terror in film, 'Ellipsis on Dread and the Specular Seduction':

> [The] terror/seduction node . . . becomes, through cinematic commerce, a kind of cut-rate seduction. One quickly pulls the veil over the terror, and only the cathartic relief remains; in mediocre potboilers, for example, in order to remain within the range of petty bourgeois taste, film plays up to narcissistic identification, and the viewer is satisfied with 'three-buck seduction.'
>
> (Kristeva: 1979, 46)

But just as the individual and the family are *dis*-membered in the most gruesomely literal way in many of these films, so the novelistic as family romance is also in the process of being dismantled.

First, not only do the films tend to be increasingly open-ended in order to allow for the possibility of countless sequels, but they also often delight in thwarting the audiences' expectations of closure. The most famous examples of this tendency are the surprise codas of Brian De Palma's films – for instance, the hand reaching out from the grave in *Carrie* (1976). And in *The Evil Dead*, *Halloween*, and *Friday the 13th*, the monsters and slashers rise and attempt to kill over and over again each time they are presumed dead. At the end of *The Evil Dead* (1983), the monsters, after defying myriad attempts to destroy them, appear finally to be annihilated as they are burned to death in an amazing lengthy sequence. But in the last shot of the film, when the hero steps outside into the light of day, the camera rushes toward him, and he turns and faces it with an expression of horror.

In the final sequence of *Halloween* (1978), the babysitter looks at the spot where the killer was apparently slain and, finding it vacant, says, 'It really was the bogey man.'

Secondly — and this is the aspect most commonly discussed and deplored by popular journalists — these films tend to dispense with or drastically minimize the plot and character development that is thought to be essential to the construction of the novelistic. In Cronenberg's *Rabid* (1977), the porn star Marilyn Chambers plays a woman who receives a skin transplant and begins to infect everyone around her with a kind of rabies. The symptom of her disease is a vagina-like wound in her armpit out of which a phallic-shaped weapon springs to slash and mutilate its victims. While the film does have some semblance of a plot, most of it comprises disparate scenes showing Marilyn, or her victims, or her victims' victims, on the attack. Interestingly, although metonymy has been considered to be the principle by which narrative is constructed, metonymy in this film (the contagion signified by the title) becomes the means by which narrative is *disordered*, revealing a view of a world in which the center no longer holds. Films like *Maniac* and *Friday the 13th* and its sequels go even further in the reduction of plot and character. In *Friday the 13th* (1980), a group of young people are brought together to staff a summer camp and are randomly murdered whenever they go off to make love. The people in the film are practically interchangeable, since we learn nothing about them as individuals, and there is virtually no building of a climax — only variations on the theme of slashing, creating a pattern that is more or less reversible.

Finally, it should scarcely need pointing out that when villains and victims are such shadowy, undeveloped characters and are portrayed equally unsympathetically, narcissistic identification on the part of the audience becomes increasingly difficult. Indeed, it could be said that some of the films elicit a kind of *anti-narcissistic* identification, which the audience delights in indulging just as it delights in having its expectations of closure frustrated. Of *The Texas Chainsaw Massacre*, Robin Wood writes, 'Watching it recently with a large, half-stoned youth audience who cheered and applauded every one of Leatherface's outrages against their representatives on the screen was a terrifying experience' (Wood *et al.*: 1979, 22). The same might be said of films like *Halloween* and *Friday the 13th*, which adopt the point of view of the slasher, placing the spectator in the position of an unseen nameless presence which, to the audiences' great glee, annihilates one by one their screen surrogates. This kind of joyful self-destructiveness on the part of the masses has been discussed by Jean Baudrillard in another context — in his analysis of the Georges Pompidou Center in Paris to which tourists flock by the millions, ostensibly to consume culture, but also to hasten the collapse of the structurally flawed building (Baudrillard: 1977, 23–5). There is a similar paradox in the fact that *Dawn of the Dead* (1979), the film about zombies taking over a shopping center, has become a midnight favorite at shopping malls all over the United States. In both cases the masses are revelling in the demise of the very culture they appear most enthusiastically to support. Here, it would seem, we have another variant of the split, 'perverse' response favored by Roland Barthes.

The contemporary horror film thus comes very close to being 'the other film' that Thierry Kuntzel says the classic narrative film must always work to conceal: 'a film in which the initial figure would not find a place in the flow of a narrative, in which the configuration of events contained in the formal matrix would not form a progressive order, in which the spectator/subject would never be reassured . . . within the dominant system of production and consumption, this would be a film of sustained *terror*' (Kuntzel: 1980, 24–5). Both in form and in content, the genre confounds the theories of those critics who adopt an adversarial attitude toward mass culture. The type of mass art I have been discussing – the kind of films which play at drive-ins and shabby downtown theaters, and are discussed on the pages of newsletters named *Trashola* and *Sleazoid Express* – is as apocalyptic and nihilistic, as hostile to meaning, form, pleasure, and the specious good as many types of high art. This is surely not accidental. Since Jean-François Lyotard insists that postmodernism is an 'aesthetic of the sublime,' as Immanuel Kant theorized the concept, it is interesting to note that Kant saw an intimate connection between the literature of the sublime and the literature of terror, and moreover saw the difference as in part a matter of audience education: 'In fact, without the development of moral ideas, that which, thanks to preparatory culture, we call sublime, merely strikes the untutored man as terrifying' (Kant: 1952, 115). And there is certainly evidence to suggest that the converse of Kant's statement has some truth as well, since a film like *The Texas Chainsaw Massacre*, which might seem designed principally to terrify the untutored man, strikes a critic like Robin Wood as sublime – or at least as 'authentic art.' Wood writes, 'The Texas Chainsaw Massacre . . . achieves the force of authentic art. . . . As a "collective nightmare," it brings to a focus a spirit of negativity, an undifferentiated lust for destruction that seems to lie not far below the surface of the modern collective consciousness' (Wood *et al.*: 1979, 22). It is indeed possible for the tutored critic versed in preparatory film culture to make a convincing case for the artistic merit of a film like *The Texas Chainsaw Massacre*, as long as art continues to be theorized in terms of negation, as long as we demand that it be uncompromisingly oppositional.

However, instead of endorsing Wood's view, we might wish to consider what these films have to teach us about the *limits* of an adversarial position which makes a virtue of 'sustained terror.' Certainly women have important reasons for doing so. In Trilling's essay, 'The Fate of Pleasure,' he notes almost parenthetically that, according to the *Oxford English Dictionary*, 'Pleasure in the pejorative sense is sometimes personified as a female deity' (Trilling: 1963, 168). Now, when pleasure has become an almost wholly pejorative term, we might expect to see an increasing tendency to incarnate it as a woman. And, indeed, in the contemporary horror film it is personified as a lovely young school teacher beaten to death by midget clones (*The Brood*), as a pretty blond teenager threatened by a maniac wielding a chainsaw (*The Texas Chainsaw Massacre*), or as a pleasant and attractive babysitter terrorized throughout the film *Halloween* by a grown-up version of the little boy killer revealed in the opening sequence. Importantly, in many of the films the female is attacked not only because, as has often been claimed, she embodies sexual pleasure, but also because she represents a great many aspects of the specious good – just as the babysitter, for example, quite literally represents familial authority. The point needs to be stressed, since feminism has occasionally made common cause with the adversarial critics on the grounds that we too have been oppressed by the specious good. But this is to overlook the fact that in some profound sense we have also been historically and physically identified with it.

Further, just as Linda Williams has argued that in the horror film woman is usually placed on the side of the monster even when she is its pre-eminent victim, so too in the scenario I outlined at the beginning woman is frequently associated with the monster mass culture (Williams: 1984, 85–8). This is hardly surprising since, as we have seen, mass culture has typically been theorized as the realm of cheap and easy pleasure – 'pleasure in the pejorative sense.' Thus, in Ann Douglas's account, the 'feminization of American culture' is synonymous with the rise of mass culture (Douglas: 1977). And in David Cronenberg's view, mass culture – at least the video portion of it – is terrifying because of the way it feminizes its audience. In *Videodrome*, the openness and vulnerability of the media recipient are made to seem loathsome and fearful through the use of feminine imagery (the vaginal wound in the stomach) and feminine positioning: the hero is raped with a video cassette. As Baudrillard puts it, 'no halo of private protection, not even his own body . . . protect[s] him anymore' (Baudrillard: 1983, 132). Baudrillard himself describes mass-mediated experience in terms of rape, as when he speaks of 'the unclean promiscuity of everything which touches, invests and penetrates without resistance' (ibid., 132). No resistance, no protection, no mastery. Or so it might seem. And yet the mastery that these popular texts no longer permit through effecting closure or eliciting narcissistic identification is often reasserted through projecting the experience of submission and defenselessness onto the female body. In this way the texts enable the male spectator to distance himself some-what from the terror. And, as usual, it is the female spectator who is *truly* deprived of 'solace and pleasure.' Having been denied access to pleasure, while simultane-ously being scapegoated for seeming to represent it, women are perhaps in the best position to call into question an aesthetics wholly opposed to it. At the very least, we might like to experience more of it before deciding to denounce it.

Beyond this, it remains for the postmodernist to ponder the irony of the fact that when critics condemn a 'monstrous motion picture industry' they are to a certain extent repeating the gestures of texts they repudiate. And the question then becomes: How can an adversarial attitude be maintained toward an art that is itself increasingly adversarial? In *The Anti-Aesthetic*, Hal Foster considers modernism to be postmodernism's other, and he pointedly asks, 'how can we exceed the modern? How can we break with a program that makes a value of crisis . . . or progress beyond the era of Progress . . . or *transgress the ideology of the transgressive?*' (Foster: 1983, ix, my italics). Foster does not acknowledge the extent to which mass culture has also served as postmodernism's other, but his question is pertinent here too.

Part of the answer may lie in the fact that for many artists, transgression is not as important a value as it is for many theorists. A host of contemporary artistic endeavors may be cited as proof of this, despite the efforts of some critics to make these works conform to an oppositional practice. In literature, the most famous and current example of the changed, friendly attitude toward popular art is Umberto Eco's *The Name of the Rose* (1980), which draws on the Sherlock Holmes mystery tale. Manuel Puig's novels (his *Kiss of the Spider Woman* [1979], for example) have consistently explored the pleasures of popular movies. In the visual arts, Cindy Sherman's self-portraiture involves the artist's masquerading as figures from old Hollywood films. The 'Still Life' exhibition organized by Marvin Heiferman and Diane Keaton consists of publicity stills from the files of Hollywood movie studios. In film, Rainer Werner Fassbinder continually paid homage to Hollywood melodramas; Wim Wenders and Betty Gordon return to *film noir*; Mulvey and Wollen to the fantastic; Valie Export to science fiction; and so on.

A few theorists have begun to acknowledge these developments, but usually only to denounce them. In a recent article entitled 'Post-modernism and Consumer Society,' Fredric Jameson concludes by deploring the fact that art is no longer 'explosive and subversive,' no longer 'critical, negative, contestatory, . . . oppositional, and the like' (Jameson: 1983, 125). Instead, says Jameson, much recent art appears to incorporate images and stereotypes garnered from our pop cultural past. However, instead of sharing Jameson's pessimistic view of this tendency, I would like to end on a small note of comfort and solace. Perhaps the contemporary artist continues to be subversive by being nonadversarial in the modernist sense, and has returned to our pop cultural past partly in order to explore the site where pleasure was last observed, before it was stoned by the gentry and the mob alike, and recreated as a monster.

Chapter 24

CAROL J. CLOVER

HER BODY, HIMSELF
(extract)

O N T H E F A C E O F I T, the relation between the sexes in slasher films could hardly be clearer. The killer is with few exceptions recognizably human and distinctly male; his fury is unmistakably sexual in both roots and expression; his victims are mostly women, often sexually free and always young and beautiful. Just how essential this victim is to horror is suggested by her historical durability. If the killer has over time been variously figured as shark, fog, gorilla, birds, and slime, the victim is eternally and prototypically the damsel. Cinema hardly invented the pattern. It has simply given visual expression to the abiding proposition that, in Poe's famous formulation, the death of a beautiful woman is the 'most poetical topic in the world' (Poe: 1970, 55). As horror director Dario Argento puts it, 'I like women, especially beautiful ones. If they have a good face and figure, I would much prefer to watch them being murdered than an ugly girl or man' (Schoell: 1985, 54). Brian De Palma elaborates: 'Women in peril work better in the suspense genre. It all goes back to the *Perils of Pauline*. . . . If you have a haunted house and you have a woman walking around with a candelabrum, you fear more for her than you would for a husky man' (ibid., 41). Or Hitchcock, during the filming of *The Birds* (1963): 'I always believe in following the advice of the playwright Sardou. He said, "Torture the women!" The trouble today is that we don't torture women enough' (Spoto: 1983, 483). What the directors do not say, but show, is that 'Pauline' is at her very most effective in a state of undress, borne down upon by a blatantly phallic murderer, even gurgling orgasmically as she dies. The case could be made that the slasher films available at a given neighborhood video rental outlet recommend themselves to censorship under the Dworkin-MacKinnon guidelines at least as readily as do the hard-core films the next section over, at which that legislation aimed; for if some of the victims are men, the argument goes, most are women, and the women are brutalized in ways that come too close to real life for comfort. But what this line of reasoning does not take into account is the figure of the Final Girl. Because slashers lie for all practical purposes beyond the purview of legitimate criticism, and to the extent that they have been reviewed at all have been reviewed on an individual basis, the phenomenon of the female victim-hero has scarcely been acknowledged.

It is, of course, 'on the face of it' that most of the public discussion of film takes place – from the Dworkin-MacKinnon legislation to Siskel and Ebert's reviews to our own talks with friends on leaving the movie house. Underlying that discussion is the assumption that the sexes are what they seem; that screen males represent the Male and screen females the Female; that this identification along gender lines authorizes impulses toward violence in males and encourages impulses toward victimization in females. In part because of the massive authority cinema by nature accords the image, even academic film criticism has been slow – slower than literary criticism – to get beyond appearances. Film may not appropriate the mind's eye, but it certainly encroaches on it; the gender characteristics of a screen figure are a visible and audible given for the duration of the film. To the extent that the possibility of cross-gender identification has been entertained, it has been that of the female with the male. Thus some critics have wondered whether the female viewer, faced with the screen image of a masochistic/narcissistic female, might not rather elect to 'betray her sex and identify with the masculine point of view.' The reverse question – whether men might not also, on occasion, elect to betray their sex and identify with screen females – has scarcely been asked, presumably on the assumption that men's interests are well served by the traditional patterns of cinematic representation. For there is the matter of the 'male gaze.' As E. Ann Kaplan sums it up, 'within the film text itself, men gaze at women, who become objects of the gaze; the spectator, in turn, is made to identify with this male gaze, and to objectify the woman on the screen; and the camera's original "gaze" comes into play in the very act of filming' (Kaplan: 1983, 15; Bovenschen: 1977, 114; see also Doane: 1980). But if it is so that all of us, male and female alike, are by these processes 'made to' identify with men and 'against' women, how are we then to explain the appeal to a largely male audience of a film genre that features a female victim-hero? The slasher film brings us squarely up against fundamental questions of film analysis: where does the literal end and the figurative begin? how do the two levels interact and what is the significance of the interaction? and to which, in arriving at a political judgment (as we are inclined to do in the case of low horror and pornography in particular), do we assign priority?

A figurative or functional analysis of the slasher begins with the processes of point of view and identification. The male viewer seeking a male character, even a vicious one, with whom to identify in a sustained way has little to hang onto in the standard example. On the good side, the only viable candidates are the boyfriends or schoolmates of the girls. They are for the most part marginal, unde-veloped characters. More to the point, they tend to die early in the film. If the traditional horror plot gave the male spectator a last-minute hero with whom to identify, thereby 'indulging his vanity as protector of the helpless female' (Wood: 1983, 64), the slasher eliminates or attenuates that role beyond any such function; indeed, would-be rescuers are not infrequently blown away for their trouble, leaving the girl to fight her own fight. Policemen, fathers, and sheriffs appear only

Figure 24.1   Still from *The Texas Chainsaw Massacre* (Vortex 1974). Courtesy BFI Films: Stills, Posters and Designs, and Blue Dolphin.

long enough to demonstrate risible incomprehension and incompetence. On the bad side, there is the killer. The killer is often unseen or barely glimpsed, during the first part of the film, and what we do see, when we finally get a good look, hardly invites immediate or conscious empathy. He is commonly masked, fat, deformed, or dressed as a woman. Or 'he' is a woman: woe to the viewer of *Friday the Thirteenth I* (1980) who identifies with the male killer only to discover, in the film's final sequences, that he was not a man at all but a middle-aged mother. In either case, the killer is himself eventually killed or otherwise evacuated from the narrative. No male character of any stature lives to tell the tale.

The one character of stature who does live to tell the tale is in fact the Final Girl. She is introduced at the beginning and is the only character to be developed in any psychological detail. We understand immediately from the attention paid it that hers is the main story line. She is intelligent, watchful, levelheaded; the first character to sense something amiss and the only one to deduce from the accumulating evidence the pattern and extent of the threat; the only one, in other words, whose perspective approaches our own privileged understanding of the situation. We register her horror as she stumbles on the corpses of her friends. Her momentary paralysis in the face of death duplicates those moments of the universal nightmare experience – in which she is the undisputed 'I' – on which horror frankly trades. When she downs the killer, we are triumphant. She is by any measure the slasher film's hero. This is not to say that our attachment to her is exclusive and unremitting, only that it adds up, and that in the closing sequence (which can be quite prolonged) it is very close to absolute.

[. . .] For the moment, let us accept this equation: point of view = identification. We are linked, in this way, with the killer in the early part of the film, usually before we have seen him directly and before we have come to know the Final Girl in any detail. Our closeness to him wanes as our closeness to the Final Girl waxes – a shift underwritten by story line as well as camera position. By the end, point of view is hers: we are in the closet with her, watching with her eyes the knife blade pierce the door; in the room with her as the killer breaks through the window and grabs at her; in the car with her as the killer stabs through the convertible top, and so on. And with her, we become if not the killer of the killer then the agent of his expulsion from the narrative vision. If, during the film's course, we shifted our sympathies back and forth and dealt them out to other characters along the way, we belong in the end to the Final Girl; there is no alternative. When Stretch eviscerates Chop Top at the end of *Texas Chain Saw II* (1986), she is literally the only character left alive, on either side.

Audience response ratifies this design. Observers unanimously stress the readiness of the 'live' audience to switch sympathies in midstream, siding now with the killer and now, and finally, with the Final Girl. As Schoell, whose book on shocker films wrestles with its own monster, 'the feminists,' puts it:

> Social critics make much of the fact that male audience members cheer on the misogynous misfits in these movies as they rape, plunder, and murder their screaming, writhing female victims. Since these same critics walk out of the moviehouse in disgust long before the movie is over, they don't realize that these same men cheer on (with renewed enthusiasm, in fact) the heroines, who are often as strong, sexy, and independent as the [earlier] victims, as they blow away the killer with a shotgun or get him between the eyes with a machete. All of these men are said to be identifying with the maniac, but they enjoy *his* death throes the most of all, and applaud the heroine with admiration.
>
> (Schoell: 1985, 55)

What filmmakers seem to know better than film critics is that gender is less a wall than a permeable membrane.

No one who has read 'Red Riding Hood' to a small boy or attended a viewing of, say, *Deliverance* (1972) (an all-male story that women find as gripping as men do) – or, more recently, *Alien* (1979) and *Aliens* (1986), with whose space-age female Rambo, herself a Final Girl, male viewers seem to engage with ease – can doubt the phenomenon of cross-gender identification. This fluidity of engaged perspective is in keeping with the universal claims of the psychoanalytic model: the threat function and the victim function coexist in the same unconscious, regardless of anatomical sex. But why, if viewers can identify across gender lines and if the root experience of horror is sex blind, are the screen sexes not interchangeable? Why not more and better female killers, and why (in light of the maleness of the majority audience) not Pauls as well as Paulines? The fact that horror film so stubbornly figures the killer as male and the principal as female would seem to suggest that representation itself is at issue – that the sensation of bodily fright derives not exclusively from repressed content, as Freud insisted, but also from the bodily manifestations of that content.

Nor is the gender of the principals as straightforward as it first seems. The killer's phallic purpose, as he thrusts his drill or knife into the trembling bodies of young women, is unmistakable. At the same time, however, his masculinity is severely qualified: he ranges from the virginal or sexually inert to the transvestite or transsexual, and is spiritually divided ('the mother half of his mind') or even equipped with vulva and vagina. Although the killer of *God Told Me To* (1976) is represented and taken as a male in the film text, he is revealed, by the doctor who delivered him, to have been sexually ambiguous from birth: 'I truly could not tell whether that child was male or female; it was as if the sexual gender had not been determined . . . as if it were being developed.' In this respect, slasher killers have much in common with the monsters of classic horror – monsters who, in Linda Williams's formulation, represent not just 'an eruption of the normally repressed animal sexual energy of the civilized male' but also the 'power and potency of a *non-phallic* sexuality' (Williams: 1984, 90). To the extent that the monster is constructed as feminine, the horror film thus expresses female desire only to show how monstrous it is. The intention is manifest in *Aliens*, in which the Final Girl, Ripley, is pitted in the climactic scene against the most terrifying 'alien' of all: an egg-laying Mother.

[. . .]

The gender of the Final Girl is likewise compromised from the outset by her masculine interests, her inevitable sexual reluctance, her apartness from other girls, sometimes her name. At the level of the cinematic apparatus, her unfemininity is signaled clearly by her exercise of the 'active investigating gaze' normally reserved for males and punished in females when they assume it themselves; tentatively at first and then aggressively, the Final Girl looks *for* the killer, even tracking him to his forest hut or his underground labyrinth, and then *at* him, therewith bringing him, often for the first time, into our vision as well. When, in the final scene, she stops screaming, faces the killer, and reaches for the knife (sledge hammer, scalpel, gun, machete, hanger, knitting needle, chain saw), she addresses the monster on his own terms. To the critics' objection that *Halloween* (1978) in effect punished female sexuality, director John Carpenter responded: 'They [the critics] completely missed the boat there, I think. Because if you turn it around, the one girl who is the most sexually uptight just keeps stabbing this guy with a long knife. She's the most sexually frustrated. She's the one that killed him. Not because she's a virgin, but because all that repressed energy starts coming out. She uses all those phallic symbols on the guy. . . . She and the killer have a certain link: sexual repression' (McCarthy: 1980, 17–24). For all its perversity, Carpenter's remark does underscore the sense of affinity, even recognition, that attends the final encounter. But the 'certain link' that puts killer and Final Girl on terms, at least briefly, is more than 'sexual repression.' It is also a shared masculinity, material-ized in 'all those phallic symbols' – and it is also a shared femininity, materialized in what comes next (and what Carpenter, perhaps significantly, fails to mention): the castration, literal or symbolic, of the killer at her hands. The Final Girl has not just manned herself; she specifically unmans an oppressor whose masculinity was in question to begin with. By the time the drama has played itself out, darkness yields to light (typically as day breaks) and the close quarters of the barn (closet, elevator, attic, basement) give way to the open expanse of the yard (field, road, lakescape, cliff). With the Final Girl's appropriation of 'all those phallic symbols' comes the dispelling of the 'uterine' threat as well. Consider again the paradigmatic ending of *Texas Chain Saw II*. From the underground labyrinth, murky and bloody, in which she faced saw, knife, and hammer, Stretch escapes through a culvert into the open air. She clambers up the jutting rock and with a chain saw takes her stand. When her last assailant comes at her, she slashes open his lower abdomen – the sexual symbolism is all too clear – and flings him off the cliff. Again, the final scene shows her in extreme long shot, standing on the ledge of a pinnacle, drenched in sunlight, buzzing chain saw held overhead.

The tale would indeed seem to be one of sex and parents. The patently erotic threat is easily seen as the materialized projection of the viewer's own incestuous fears and desires. It is this disabling cathexis to one's parents that must be killed and rekilled in the service of sexual autonomy. When the Final Girl stands at last in the light of day with the knife in her hand, she has delivered herself into the adult world. Carpenter's equation of the Final Girl with the killer has more than a grain of truth. The killers of *Psycho* (1960), *The Eyes of Laura Mars* (1978), *Friday the 13th II–VI* (1981–6), and *Cruising* (1980) among others, are explicitly figured as sons in the psychosexual grip of their mothers (or fathers, in the case of *Cruising*). The difference is between past and present and between failure and success. The Final Girl enacts in the present, and successfully, the parenticidal struggle that the killer himself enacted unsuccessfully in his own past – a past that constitutes the film's backstory. She is what the killer once was; he is what she could become should she fail in her battle for sexual selfhood. 'You got the choice, boy,' says the tyrannical father of Leatherface in *Texas Chain Saw II*, 'sex or the saw; you never know about sex, but the saw – the saw is the family.'

The tale is no less one of maleness. If the experience of childhood can be – is perhaps ideally – enacted in female form, the breaking away requires the assumption of the phallus. The helpless child is gendered feminine; the autonomous adult or subject is gendered masculine; the passage from childhood to adulthood entails a shift from feminine to masculine. It is the male killer's tragedy that his incipient femininity is not reversed but completed (castration) and the Final Girl's victory that her incipient masculinity is not thwarted but realized (phallicization). When De Palma says that female frailty is a predicate of the suspense genre, he proposes, in effect, that the lack of the phallus, for Lacan the privileged signifier of the symbolic order, is itself simply horrifying, at least in the mind of the male observer. Where pornography (the argument goes) resolves that lack through a process of fetishization that allows a breast or leg or whole body to stand in for the missing member, the slasher film resolves it either through eliminating the woman (earlier victims) or reconstituting her as masculine (Final Girl). The moment at which the Final Girl is effectively phallicized is the moment that the plot halts and horror ceases. Day breaks, and the community returns to its normal order.

Casting psychoanalytic verities in female form has a venerable cinematic history. Ingmar Bergman, for one, has made a career of it. One immediate practical advantage, by now presumably unconscious on the part of makers as well as viewers, has to do with a preestablished cinematic 'language' for capturing the moves and moods of the female body and face. The cinematic gaze, we are told, is male, and just as that gaze 'knows' how to fetishize the female form in pornography (in a way that it does not 'know' how to fetishize the male form), so it 'knows', in horror, how to track a woman ascending a staircase in a scary house and how to study her face from an angle above as she first hears the killer's footfall. A set of conventions we now take for granted simply 'sees' males and females differently.

To this cinematic habit may be added the broader range of emotional expression traditionally allowed women. Angry displays of force may belong to the male, but crying, cowering, screaming, fainting, trembling, begging for mercy belong to the female. Abject terror, in short, is gendered feminine, and the more concerned a given film is with that condition – and it is the essence of modern horror – the more likely the femaleness of the victim. It is no accident that male victims in slasher films are killed swiftly or offscreen, and that prolonged struggles, in which the victim has time to contemplate her imminent destruction, inevitably figure females. Only when one encounters the rare expression of abject terror on the part of a male (as in *I Spit on Your Grave* [1977]) does one apprehend the full extent of the cinematic double standard in such matters.

It is also the case that gender displacement can provide a kind of identificatory buffer, an emotional remove that permits the majority audience to explore taboo subjects in the relative safety of vicariousness. Just as Bergman came to realize that he could explore castration anxiety more freely via depictions of hurt female bodies (witness the genital mutilation of Karin in *Cries and Whispers* [1972]), so the makers of slasher films seem to know that sadomasochistic incest fantasies sit more easily with the male viewer when the visible player is female. It is one thing for that viewer to hear the psychiatrist intone at the end of *Psycho* that Norman as a boy (in the backstory) was abnormally attached to his mother; it would be quite another to see that attachment dramatized in the present, to experience in nightmare form the elaboration of Norman's (the viewer's own) fears and desires. If the former is playable in male form, the latter, it seems, is not.

The Final Girl is, on reflection, a congenial double for the adolescent male. She is feminine enough to act out in a gratifying way, a way unapproved for adult males, the terrors and masochistic pleasures of the underlying fantasy, but not so feminine as to disturb the structures of male competence and sexuality. The question then arises whether the Final Girls of slasher films – Stretch, Stevie, Marti, Will, Terry, Laurie, and Ripley – are not boyish for the same reason that female 'victims' in Victorian flagellation literature – 'Georgy,' 'Willy' – are boyish: because they are transformed males. The transformation, Steven Marcus writes, 'is itself both a defense against and a disavowal of the fantasy it is simultaneously expressing – namely, that a *boy* is being beaten – that is, loved – by another man' (Marcus: 1964, 260–1). What is represented as male-on-female violence, in short, is figuratively speaking male-on-male sex. For Marcus, the literary picture of flagellation, in which *girls* are beaten, is utterly belied by the descriptions (in *My Secret Life*) of real-life episodes in which the persons being beaten are not girls at all but 'gentlemen' dressed in women's clothes ('He had a woman's dress on tucked up to his waist, showing his naked rump and thighs. . . . On his head was a woman's cap tied carefully round his face to hide whiskers') and whipped by prostitutes. Reality, Marcus writes, 'puts the literature of flagellation out of the running . . . by showing how that literature is a completely distorted and idealized version of what actually happens' (ibid., 125–7). Applied to the slasher film, this logic reads the femaleness of the Final Girl (at least up to the point of her transformation) and indeed of the woman victims in general as only apparent, the artifact of heterosexual deflection. It may be through the female body that the body of the audience is sensationalized, but the sensation is an entirely male affair.

At least one director, Hitchcock, explicitly located thrill in the equation victim = audience. So we judge from his marginal jottings in the shooting instructions for the shower scene in *Psycho*: 'The slashing. An impression of a knife slashing, as if tearing at the very screen, ripping the film' (Spoto: 1983, 431). Not just the body of Marion is to be ruptured, but also the body on the other side of the film and screen: our witnessing body. As Marion is to Norman, the audience of *Psycho* is to Hitchcock; as the audiences of horror film in general are to the directors of those films, female is to male. Hitchcock's 'torture the women' then means, simply, torture the audience. De Palma's remarks about female frailty ('Women in peril work better in the suspense genre. . . . you fear more for her than you would for a husky man') likewise contemplate a male-on-'female' relationship between director and viewer. Cinefantastic horror, in short, succeeds in incorporating its spectators as 'feminine' and then violating that body – which recoils, shudders, cries out collectively – in ways otherwise imaginable, for males, only in nightmare. The equation is nowhere more plainly put than in David Cronenberg's *Videodrome* (1982). Here the threat is a mind-destroying video signal; the victims, television viewers. Despite the (male) hero's efforts to defend his mental and physical integrity, a deep, vagina-like gash appears on his lower abdomen. Says the media conspirator as he thrusts a videocassette into the victim's gaping wound, 'You must open yourself completely to this.'

If the slasher film is 'on the face of it' a genre with at least a strong female presence, it is in these figurative readings a thoroughly male exercise, one that finally has very little to do with femaleness and very much to do with phallocentrism. Figuratively seen, the Final Girl is a male surrogate in things oedipal, a homoerotic stand-in, the audience incorporate; to the extent she means 'girl' at all, it is only for purposes of signifying male lack, and even that meaning is nullified in the final scenes. Our initial question – how to square a female victim-hero with a largely male audience – is not so much answered as it is obviated in these readings. The Final Girl is (apparently) female not despite the maleness of the audience, but precisely because of it. The discourse is wholly masculine, and females figure in it only insofar as they 'read' some aspect of male experience. To applaud the Final Girl as a feminist development, as some reviews of *Aliens* have done with Ripley, is, in light of her figurative meaning, a particularly grotesque expression of wishful thinking. She is simply an agreed-upon fiction and the male viewer's use of her as a vehicle for his own sadomasochistic fantasies an act of perhaps timeless dishonesty.

For all their immediate appeal, these figurative readings loosen as many ends as they tie together. The audience, we have said, is predominantly male; but what about the women in it? Do we dismiss them as male-identified and account for their experience as an 'immasculated' (see Fetterley: 1978) act of collusion with the oppressor? This is a strong judgment to apply to large numbers of women; for while it may be that the audience for slasher films is mainly male, this does not mean that there are not also many female viewers who actively like such films, and of course there are also women, however few, who script, direct, and produce them. These facts alone oblige us at least to consider the possibility that female fans find a meaning in the text and image of these films that is less inimical to their own interests than the figurative analysis would have us believe. Or should we conclude that males and females read these films differently in some fundamental sense? Do females respond to the text (the literal) and males the subtext (the figurative)?

Some such notion of differential understanding underlies the homoerotic reading. The silent presupposition of that reading is that male identification with the female cannot be, and that the male viewer/reader who adjoins feminine experience does so only by homosexual conversion. But does female identification with male experience then similarly indicate a lesbian conversion? Or are the processes of patriarchy so one-way that the female can identify with the male directly, but the male can identify with the female only by transsexualizing her? Does the Final Girl mean 'girl' to her female viewers and 'boy' to her male viewers? If her masculine features qualify her as a transformed boy, do not the feminine features of the killer qualify him as a transformed woman (in which case the homoerotic reading can be maintained only by defining that 'woman' as phallic and retransforming her into a male)? Striking though it is, the analogy between the Victorian flagellation story's Georgy and the slasher film's Stretch falters at the moment that Stretch turns on her assailant and unmans him. Are we to suppose that a homoerotic beating fantasy suddenly yields to what folklorists call a lack-liquidated fantasy? Further: is it simply coincidence that this combination tale – trials, then triumph – bears such a marked resemblance to the classic (male) hero story? Does the standard hero story featuring an anatomical female 'mean' differently from one featuring an anatomical male?

As Marcus perceived, the relationship between the Georgy stories of flagellation literature and the real-life anecdote of the Victorian gentlemen is a marvelously telling one. In his view, the maleness of the latter must prove the essential or functional maleness of the former. What his analysis does not come to full grips with, however, is the clothing the gentleman wears – not that of a child, as Marcus's 'childish' reading of the scene contemplates, but explicitly that of a woman. These women's clothes can of course be understood, within the terms of the homoerotic interpretation, as a last-ditch effort on the part of the gentleman to dissociate himself from the (incestuous) homosexuality implicit in his favored sexual practice. But can they not just as well, and far more economically, be explained as part and parcel of a fantasy of literal femaleness? By the same token, cannot the femaleness of the gentleman's literary representatives – the girls of the flagellation stories – be understood as the obvious, even necessary, extension of that man's dress and cap? The same dress and cap, I suggest, haunt the margins of the slasher film. This is not to deny the deflective convenience, for the male spectator (and filmmaker), of a female victim-hero in a context so fraught with taboo; it is only to suggest that the femaleness of this character is also conditioned by a kind of imaginative curiosity about the feminine in and of itself.

So too the psychoanalytic case. These films do indeed seem to pit the child in a struggle, at once terrifying and attractive, with the parental Other, and it is a rare example that does not directly thematize parent-child relations. But if Freud stressed the maternal source of the *Unheimlich*, the Other of our films is decidedly androgynous: female/feminine in aspects of character and place (the 'intrauterine' locale) but male in anatomy. Conventional logic may interpret the killer as the phallic mother of the transformed boy (the Final Girl), but the text itself does not compel such a reading. On the contrary, the text at every level presents us with hermaphroditic constructions — constructions that draw attention to themselves and demand to be taken on their own terms.

For if we define the Final Girl as nothing more than a figurative male, what do we then make of the context of the spectacular gender play in which she is emphatically situated? In his essay on the uncanny, Freud rejected out of hand Jentsch's theory that the experience of horror proceeds from intellectual uncertainty (curiosity?) — feelings of confusion, induced by an author or a coincidence, about who, what, and where one is (Freud: 1955b, 219–21, 226–7). One wonders, however, whether Freud would have been quite so dismissive if, instead of the mixed materials he used as evidence, he were presented with a coherent story corpus — forty slashers, say — in which the themes of incest and separation were relentlessly played out by a female character, and further in which gender identity was repeatedly thematized as an issue in and of itself. For although the factors we have considered thus far — the conventions of the male gaze, the feminine constitution of abject terror, the value for the male viewer of emotional distance from the taboos in question, the special horror that may inhere, for the male audience, in phallic lack, the homoerotic deflection — go a long way in explaining why it is we have Pauline rather than Paul as our victim-hero, they do not finally account for our strong sense that gender is simply being fooled with, and that part of the thrill lies precisely in the resulting 'intellectual uncertainty' of sexual identity.

The 'play of pronoun function' that underlies and defines the cinefantastic is nowhere more richly manifested than in the slasher; if the genre has an aesthetic base, it is exactly that of a visual identity game. Consider, for example, the now-standard habit of letting us view the action in the first person long before revealing who or what the first person *is*. In the opening sequence of *Halloween I*, 'we' are belatedly revealed to ourselves, after committing a murder in the cinematic first person, as a six-year-old boy. The surprise is often within gender, but it is also, in a striking number of cases, across it. Again, *Friday the 13th I*, in which 'we' stalk and kill a number of teenagers over the course of an hour of movie time without even knowing who 'we' are; we are uninvited, by conventional expectation and by glimpses of 'our' own bodily parts — a heavily booted foot, a roughly gloved hand — to suppose that 'we' are male, but 'we' are revealed, at film's end, as a woman. If this is the most dramatic case of pulling out the gender rug, it is by no means the only one. In *Dressed to Kill* (1980), we are led to believe, again by means of glimpses, that 'we' are female — only to discover, in the denouement, that 'we' are a male in drag. In *Psycho*, the dame we glimpse holding the knife with a 'visible virility quite obscene in an old lady' is later revealed, after additional gender teasing, to be Norman in his mother's clothes. *Psycho II* (1983) plays much the same game. *Cruising* (in which, not accidentally, transvestites play a prominent role) adjusts the terms along heterosexual/homosexual lines. The tease here is whether the originally straight detective assigned to the string of murders in a gay community does or does not succumb to his assumed homo-sexual identity; the camerawork leaves us increasingly uncertain as to his (our) sexual inclinations, not to speak of his (our) complicity in the crimes. Even at film's end we are not sure who 'we' were during several of the first-person sequences.

The gender-identity game, in short, is too patterned and too pervasive in the slasher film to be dismissed as supervenient. It would seem instead to be an integral element of the particular brand of bodily sensation in which the genre trades. Nor is it exclusive to horror. It is directly thematized in comic terms in the 'gender-benders' *Tootsie* (1982) (in which a man passes himself off as a woman), *All of Me* (1984) (in which a woman is literally introjected into a man and affects his speech, movement, and thought), and *Switch* (1975). It is also directly thematized, in the form of bisexual and androgynous figures and relations, in such cult films as *Pink Flamingos* (1972) and *The Rocky Horror Picture Show* (1975). (Some version of it is indeed repeatedly enacted on MTV.) It is further thematized (predictably enough, given their bodily concerns) in such pornographic films as *Every Woman Has a Fantasy* (1984), in which a man, in order to gain access to a women's group in which sexual fantasies are discussed, dresses and passes himself off as a woman. (The degree to which 'male' pornography in general relies for its effect on cross-gender identification remains an open question; the proposition makes a certain sense of the obligatory lesbian sequences and the phenomenal success of *Behind the Green Door* (1972), to pick just two examples.) All of these films, and others like them, seem to be asking some version of the question: what would it be like to be, or to seem to be, if only temporarily, a woman? Taking exception to the reception of *Tootsie* as a feminist film, Elaine Showalter argues that the success of 'Dorothy Michaels' (the Dustin Hoffman character), as far as both plot and audience are concerned, lies in the veiling of masculine power in feminine costume. *Tootsie*'s cross-dressing, she writes,

> is a way of promoting the notion of masculine power while masking it. In psychoanalytic theory, the male transvestite is not a powerless man; according to the psychiatrist Robert Stoller, in *Sex and Gender*, he is a 'phallic woman' who can tell himself that 'he is, or with practice will become, a better woman than a biological female if he chooses to do so.' When it is safe or necessary, the transvestite 'gets great pleas-ure in revealing that he is a male-woman. . . . The pleasure in tricking the unsuspecting into thinking that he is a woman, and then revealing his maleness (e.g., by suddenly dropping his voice) is not so much erotic as it is proof that there is such a thing as a woman with a penis.' Dorothy's effectiveness is the literal equivalent of speaking softly and carrying a big stick.
>
> (Showalter: 1983, 138)

By the same literalistic token, then, Stretch's success must lie in the fact that in the end, at least, she 'speaks loudly' *even though* she carries *no* 'stick.' Just as 'Dorothy's' voice slips serve to remind us that her character really is male, so the Final Girl's 'tits and scream' serve more or less continuously to remind us that she really is female – even as, and despite the fact that, she in the end acquits herself 'like a man.' Her chain saw is thus what 'Dorothy Michael's' skirt is: a figuration of what she *does* and what she *seems*, as opposed to – and the films turn on the opposition – what she *is*. The idea that appearance and behavior do not necessarily indicate sex – indeed, can misindicate sex – is predicated on the understanding that sex is one thing and gender another; in practice, that sex is life, a less-than-interesting given, but that gender is theater. Whatever else it may be, Stretch's waving of the chain saw is a moment of high drag. Its purpose is not to make us forget that she is a girl but to thrust that fact on us. The moment, it should be added, is also one that openly mocks the literary/cinematic conventions of symbolic representation.

It may be just this theatricalization of gender that makes possible the willingness of the male viewer to submit himself to a brand of spectator experience that Hitchcock designated as 'feminine' in 1960 and that has become only more so since then. In classic horror, the 'feminization' of the audience is intermittent and ceases early. Our relationship with Marion's body in *Psycho* halts abruptly at the moment of its greatest intensity (slashing, ripping, tearing). The considerable remainder of the film distributes our bruised sympathies among several lesser figures, male and female, in such a way and at such length as to ameliorate the Marion experience and leave us, in the end, more or less recuperated in our presumed masculinity. Like Marion, the Final Girl is the designated victim, the audience incorporate, the slashing, ripping, and tearing of whose body will cause us to flinch and scream out in our seats. But unlike Marion, she does not die. If *Psycho*, like other classic horror films, solves the femininity problem by obliterating the female and replacing her with representatives of the masculine order (mostly but not inevitably males), the modern slasher solves it by regendering the woman. We are, as an audience, in the end 'masculinized' by and through the very figure by and through whom we were earlier 'feminized.' The same body does for both, and that body is female.

The last point is the crucial one: the same *female* body does for both. The Final Girl (1) undergoes agonizing trials, and (2) virtually or actually destroys the antagonist and saves herself. By the lights of folk tradition, she is not a heroine, for whom phase 1 consists in being saved by someone else, but a hero, who rises to the occasion and defeats the adversary with his own wit and hands. Part 1 of the story sits well on the female; it is the heart of heroine stories in general (Red Riding Hood, Pauline), and in some figurative sense, in ways I have elaborated in some detail, it is gendered feminine even when played by a male. Odysseus's position, trapped in the cave of the Cyclops, is not after all so different from Pauline's lashed to the tracks or Sally's tied to a chair in the dining room of the slaughterhouse family. The decisive moment, as far as the fixing of gender is concerned, lies in what happens next: those who save themselves are male, and those who are saved by others are female. No matter how 'feminine' his experience in phase 1, the traditional hero, if he rises against his adversary and saves himself in phase 2, will be male.

What is remarkable about the slasher film is how close it comes to reversing the priorities. Presumably for the various functional or figurative reasons I have considered in this chapter, phase 1 wants a female: on that point all slashers from *Psycho* on are agreed. Abject fear is still gendered feminine, and the taboo anxieties in which slashers trade are still explored more easily via Pauline than Paul. The slippage comes in phase 2. As if in mute deference to a cultural imperative, slasher films from the seventies bring in a last-minute male, even when he is rendered supernumerary by the Final Girl's sturdy defense. By 1980, however, the male rescuer is either dismissably marginal or dispensed with altogether; not a few films have him rush to the rescue only to be hacked to bits, leaving the Final Girl to save herself after all. At the moment that the Final Girl becomes her own savior, she becomes a hero; and the moment that she becomes a hero is the moment that the male viewer gives up the last pretense of male identification. Abject terror may still be gendered feminine, but the willingness of one immensely popular current genre to re-represent the hero as an anatomical female would seem to suggest that at least one of the traditional marks of heroism, triumphant self-rescue, is no longer strictly gendered masculine.

[. . .]

The slasher is hardly the first genre in the literary and visual arts to invite identification with the female; one cannot help wondering more generally whether the historical maintenance of images of women in fear and pain does not have more to do with male vicarism than is commonly acknowledged. What distinguishes the slasher, however, is the absence or untenability of alternative perspectives and hence the exposed quality of the invitation. As a survey of the tradition shows, this has not always been the case. The stages of the Final Girl's evolution – her piecemeal absorption of functions previously represented in males – can be located in the years following 1978. The fact that the typical patrons of these films are the sons of marriages contracted in the sixties or even early seventies leads me to speculate that the dire claims of that era – that the women's movement, the entry of women into the workplace, and the rise of divorce and woman-headed families would yield massive gender confusion in the next generation – were not entirely wrong. We preferred, in the eighties, to speak of the cult of androgyny, but the point is roughly the same. The fact that we have in the killer a feminine male and in the main character a masculine female – parent and everyteen, respectively – would seem, especially in the latter case, to suggest a loosening of the categories, or at least of the category of the feminine. It is not that these films show us gender and sex in free variation; it is that they fix on the irregular combinations, of which the combination masculine female repeatedly prevails over the combination feminine male. The fact that masculine males (boyfriends, fathers, would-be rescuers) are regularly dismissed through ridicule or death or both would seem to suggest that it is not masculinity per se that is being privileged, but masculinity in conjunction with a female body – indeed, as the term victim-hero contemplates, masculinity in conjunction with femininity. For if 'masculine' describes the Final Girl some of the time, and in some of her more theatrical moments, it does not do justice to the sense of her character as a whole. She alternates between registers from the outset; before her final struggle she endures the deepest throes of 'femininity'; and even during the final struggle she is now weak and now strong, now flees the killer and now charges him, now stabs and is stabbed, now cries out in fear and now shouts in anger. She is a physical female and a characterological androgyne: like her name, not masculine but either/or, both, ambiguous.

Robin Wood speaks of the sense that horror, for him the by-product of cultural crisis and disintegration, is 'currently the most important of all American [film] genres and perhaps even the most progressive, even in its overt nihilism' (Wood: 1978, 28). Likewise Vale and Juno say of the 'incredibly strange films,' mostly low-budget horror, that their volume surveys, 'They often present unpopular – even radical – views addressing the social, political, racial, or sexual inequities, hypocrisy in religion or government' (Vale and Juno: 1986, 5). And Tania Modleski rests her case against the Frankfurt School-derived critique of mass culture on the evidence of the slasher, which does *not* propose a spurious harmony; does *not* promote the 'specious good' (but indeed often exposes and attacks it); does *not* ply the mechanisms of identification, narrative continuity, and closure to provide the sort of narrative pleasure constitutive of the dominant ideology (Modleski: 1986, 155–66). One is deeply reluctant to make progressive claims for a body of cinema as spectacularly nasty toward women as the slasher film is, but the fact is that the slasher does, in its own perverse way and for better or worse, constitute a visible adjustment in the terms of gender representations. That it is an adjustment largely on the male side, appearing at the furthest possible remove from the quarters of theory and showing signs of trickling upward, is of no small interest in the study of popular culture.

Part Ten

LOWBROW/LOW-BUDGET HORROR

Introduction to Part Ten

■   Ken Gelder

IT HAS BEEN FASHIONABLE to observe, in these postmodern times, that the once-definitive boundary between high culture and low culture has been well and truly breached. The art world now routinely borrows from low culture; and many low cultural forms have in turn been 'recovered' and given some kind of social approval. This is certainly true for horror, as we have seen – where even the slasher film can attract something close to a 'progressive' reading. As one descends deeper into the cultural field, however, the obstacles to this kind of recovery can at times seem insurmountable. Lowbrow, low-budget horror cinema has a long history, of course, developing in the United States through the 1930s and 1940s with a variety of horror melodramas, spoofs and quickie monster flicks – like the 'Poverty Row' cheapies mostly produced during the Second World War by Monogram, PRC and Republic, with their raunchy mixtures of zombies, vampires, gangsters, secret societies and mad monsters (see Weaver: 1993). The form did in fact gain some respectability at this time with Val Lewton's B-grade 'chillers', several of which have since become classics. By the late 1950s, however, the agendas of low-budget horror had changed markedly. Reaching its heyday in the late 1960s and early 1970s and then lingering in the late 1980s in the form of 'video nasties', this kind of film often relished its marginal, derided position in the cultural field. Through its flaunting of 'bad taste', its low-level, gross-out special effects and lurid colouration, its gratuitous and exaggerated acts of violence and dismemberment and its willing embrace of exploitation and 'sexploitation' tags, modern low-budget, lowbrow horror cinema made sure it remained at the bottom end of the market and on the fringes of cultural analysis.

The best resources for students of low-budget horror are thus still the genre guides and the fanzines: venues that make themselves utterly at home with the form, defiantly parading their encyclopedic knowledges of films, directors, actors, make-up artists and a range of other paraphernalia. Stefan Jaworzyn's *Shock Express* and *Shock* book collections, from the early 1990s onwards, provide a wealth of information about horror exploitation films – while Kim Newman's *Nightmare Movies* (1988), John McCarthy's *The Official Splatter Movie Guide* (1989) and Welch Everman's *Cult Horror Films* (1993), amongst others, try to sort through the unruly mass of sub-aesthetic 'trash' horror cinema. The first contribution to this section, a piece by David Sanjek first published in *Literature/Film Quarterly*, looks at horror fanzines and notes that they, too, are 'guaranteed to offend'. Their facetious mode of delivery nevertheless sits along-side a serious appreciation of 'the marginalia of the horror genre'. They know the material *they* recover will never receive broad social approval: all the more reason to pay tribute to it. Yet these fanzines (like *Samhain*, Britain's longest-running horror film magazine) are not indiscriminate. As Sanjek suggests, the attraction to a 'uniqueness of vision' in low-budget horror films allows fanzines to distinguish them from commercial film production, which is generally despised. Low-budget horror is fetishised as real and authentic, a point made apparent more recently with the success of Daniel Myrick and Eduardo Sanchez's *The Blair Witch Project* (1999). Commercial horror, by contrast, is 'crap'.

The fannish interest in low-budget horror can thus develop into an archival search for original, uncut, uncensored prints – a process undertaken through the 1990s by Nigel Wingrove's Redemption Films, sometimes with mixed results. Samuel Z. Arkoff's American International Pictures (AIP) did not help matters: in the late 1950s, Arkoff and his partner James H. Nicholson began to buy Italian low-budget horror films, cutting and splicing and dubbing over them for matinee American audiences. Sanjek notes that horror fanzines in fact had often cham-pioned Italian horror films, especially the work of Dario Argento, Riccardo Freda and Mario Bava – directors mostly ignored in standard histories of Italian cinema. Bava's directorial debut was *La maschera del demonio* (1960), cut down to size by AIP for its US release in 1961 as *The Mask of Satan* – and banned in Britain until 1968. His second film, *Blood and Black Lace* (1964), is nevertheless credited as the influential source of the *giallo* films, developed by Argento later on – baroque tales of psychopaths, murder and madness that take their name from the lurid yellow covers of earlier Italian pulp fiction. Bava had also featured Barbara Steele in *The Mask of Satan*, an actress who went on to become 'queen of the horror films' for the fanzines, moving to the US to star in Roger Corman's *The Pit and the Pendulum* (1961) and then returning to Italy for more films by Bava and Freda.

These and no doubt many other features turned Italian horror from the 1960s and early 1970s into a zone of fanzine and genre guide fascination – with other low-budget directors of note including Lucio Fulci (the 'king of spaghetti splatter') and Massimo Pupillo. Indeed, Euro-trash horror has itself been lovingly archived in these venues (see, for example, Tohill and Tombs, 1995): the erotic vampire films of French director Jean Rollin, the work of Spanish directors Jesus Franco and Amando de Ossorio, and so on. Leon Hunt's extract, from the film journal,

The Velvet Light Trap, is one of the few academic appreciations of the form, however. He wonders how it is possible to write seriously and critically about low-budget, lowbrow Italian horror cinema outside of the frame of the fanzines and genre guides. These films are 'bad objects', graphic and perverse, often shifting 'deliriously' into sexploitation. They also shamelessly plunder *other* films for their ideas. Looking closely at Argento's films, however, Hunt also traces connections to arthouse cinema, noting the influence of Michelangelo Antonioni, the moments of hesitation akin to the fantastic, and the creation of a high fashion 'bourgeois world'. At the same time, these films stage scenes of sadistic violence that – as Linda Williams (1990) has said of pornography – produce a 'frenzy of the visible'. For Hunt, Argento's cinema draws the slasher/exploitation film and the art film together, sliding back and forth between lowbrow and highbrow, and raising 'provocative issues in horror spectatorship' in the process.

Sexploitation horror cinema may find its counterpart in the low-budget 'rape-and-revenge' film, a point elaborated by Carol J. Clover through her analysis of Meir Zarchi's *I Spit on Your Grave* (1977) – which, in a manner recalling the fanzines, she values over mainstream equivalents like *The Accused* (1988) because of its confrontational, no-nonsense simplicity (see Clover: 1992, 114–65). The third extract in this section from Vivian Sobchack, taken from the collection, *Uncontrollable Bodies*, is also about low-budget horror films that show women 'getting even'. Here, however, the women are middle-aged, increasingly excluded from the sexual economy even though their own sexual desires have not diminished. Looking at Nathan Juran's *Attack of the 50 Ft. Woman* (1958), Roger Corman's *The Wasp Woman* (1960) and Edward Dein's *The Leech Woman* (1960), Sobchack's courageously self-reflexive chapter identifies an image of monstrousness built around the aging woman's humiliation and subsequent fury at what ageing (and the responses it elicits from others) has done to her. She becomes both terrified and terrifying, driven to feelings of 'self-contempt' – leading (in two of the films) to experiments with mysterious youth-restoring potions – and then unleashing her own form of revenge on the men around her. Like Clover, Sobchack values the explicitness of these low-budget horror films, their refusal to conceal or dilute their subject-matter. Indeed, she uses them as a medium through which a real predicament can be made apparent: their very literalness is what enables, or encourages, her to speak plainly.

Chapter 25

DAVID SANJEK

FANS' NOTES: THE HORROR
FILM FANZINE

The man who insists on high and serious pleasures is depriving himself
of pleasure; he continually restricts what he can enjoy; in the constant
exercise of his good taste he will eventually price himself out of the
market, so to speak.

(Sontag: 1969, 242–3)

'film buff': that species who collect movies the way others collect stamps
or butterflies, thereby depriving them of their contextual significance.

(Robin Wood in Wood *et al.*: 1979, 29)

SLIMETIME, GRIND, TRASHOLA, *The Gore Gazette*. The titles reflect an
unseemly juvenile fascination with unrespectable and illicit imagery, the domain
of the horror film. For most adults horror films are the junk food of the imagination, trivially dispensable cultural artifacts undeserving of critical attention and
devoid of artistic or intellectual sophistication. Even defenders of the genre, like
Stephen King, admit that 'good horror movies operate most powerfully on this
"wanna-look-at-my-chewed-up-food?" level,' a primitively childish consciousness
'sometimes also known as the "Oh my God, was that gross!" factor' (King: 1983,
189). Sophisticated critics may speak of a typology of the monstrous or the genre's
reflection of personal, social or mythic structures, but it is some undeniable, primitive, precritical instinct that compels successive generations willingly to pay good
money to be made extremely uncomfortable and thereby answer 'an invitation to
indulge in deviant, antisocial behavior by proxy – to commit gratuitous acts of
violence, indulge our puerile dreams of power, to give in to our most craven
fears' (ibid., 31).

Among the willing participants in this sometimes unsavory process are the editors of horror film and video fanzines: independent, non-commercial, amateur publications compulsively produced by individuals who have fallen prey to what Stephen King called 'the siren song of crap.' Either mimeographed or off-set printed, available only by mail and unpredictable in their publication, the fanzines are suffused with that juvenile fascination with grue and gore, most evident in their frequent inclusion of illustrations appealing to the lowest kind of prurient interest and guaranteed to offend: a policeman's severed head laid out on a kitchen table like some grisly hors d'oeuvre; ravenous zombies about to satisfy their appetites upon an unwilling victim.

Connoisseurs of the bad film, trash and gore, the fanzine editors insist upon the pleasures to be found in the consumption of such raw, undiluted imagery. Their enthusiasm may seem to lack irony or finesse; however, at its source the fanzine perspective is 'such a deadly serious undertaking that its seriousness can never be openly acknowledged. The gross-out afficionado savors his sense of complicity when the values of a smug social stratum, from which he feels himself excluded, are systematically trashed and ridiculed' (Chute: 1983, 13–14). What may seem to some a sophomoric interest in putatively indefensible outrage for outrage's sake is to the fanzine editor a healthy interest in forms of expression that call into question social and cultural norms. This perspective is best summarized by V. Vale and Andrea Juno in the introduction to their seminal publication, *Research #10: Incredibly Strange Films*:

> This is a functional guide to territory largely neglected by the film-criticism establishment – encompassing tens of thousands of films. Most of the films discussed test the limits of contemporary [middle-class] cultural acceptability, mainly because they don't meet certain 'standards' utilized in evaluating direction, cinematography, etc. Many of the films are overtly 'lower-class' or 'low-brow' in content and art direction. However, a high percentage of these works disdained by the would-be dictators of public opinion are sources of pure enjoyment and delight, despite improbable plots, 'bad' acting, or ragged film technique. At issue is the notion of 'good taste,' which functions as a filter to block out entire areas of experience judged – and damned – as unworthy of investigation.
>
> The concepts of 'good taste' are intricately woven into society's control process and class structure. Aesthetics are not an objective body of laws suspended above us like Plato's supreme 'Ideas'; they are rooted in the fundamental mechanics of how to control the population and control the status quo.
>
> (Vale and Juno: 1986, 4)

Clearly, these publications cannot be dismissed in the pejorative tone employed by Robin Wood as merely the sophomoric ramblings of overgrown adolescents, cinephiliacs who lack the skill or the desire to distinguish between the work of Edward D. Wood Jr. and David Cronenberg. Instead, their editors are acutely in touch with what David Chute has called those 'rock-bottom truths about movies [which] precede the operation of criticism,' including 'the plain fact that some of the things movies do for us can easily be done without finesse or imagination or wit' (Chute: 1983, 12–13). The fanzines constitute an alternative brand of film criticism, a school with its own set of values and virtues. They aim not only to *épater le bourgeois* but also to root out obscure marginalia of the horror genre and revel in the private consumption of outrage for outrage's sake.

What values, then, do these publications hold and what use can they be to the film scholar? Once the reader gets beyond the often alienating nature of their format, the fanzines provide a valuable resource for examination of the horror and other genres, albeit at times in a sophomoric manner, as well as embody a distinct though disturbing element of the contemporary sensibility: that which identifies with the monstrous in a nihilistic manner.

Fanzines typically are amateur publications, which by form and content distinguish themselves from 'prozines': the commercial, mainstream magazine, typified in the horror field by *Cinefantastique* (1970–) and *Fangoria* (1979–). Both widely distributed publications focus almost exclusively on current films, previewing them before release in a sycophantic manner fanzine editors condemn as little more than unpaid publicity. Too often the articles resemble press kits, replete with interviews of cast and crew and premature praise of the unfinished product. True, both prozines have incorporated retrospective analyses of major figures and films in the genre or coverage of the European horror market, but for the most part their emphases are exclusively Anglo-American and predictable in the attention paid to the 'hot' figures in the genre. Craig Ledbetter, editor of *Hi-Tech Terror*, caused a sympathetic stir in fanzine circles when he wrote [in issue 33]:

> I don't give a shit A) What Larry Cohen is doing, B) How Sam Raimi plans on remaking *Evil Dead* for the rest of his life, or C) The fact there are hundreds of straight-to-video American made Junk waiting to find a home in someone's VCR. *I JUST DON'T CARE* . . . We Americans refuse to recognize the tremendous amount of superlative work taking place overseas. We'd rather fawn over Tobe Hooper Abortions from Cannon (next up is Empire), thank Charles Band for resurrecting the drive-in double-bill so we can see two turds for the price of one and interview Herschell Gordon Lewis for the 50th time. C'mon folks, show some originality.

[. . .]

The fanzines' point of view, on the other hand, owes a great deal to two defunct prozines: Forest J. Ackerman's *Famous Monsters of Filmland* and Calvin Beck's *Castle of Frankenstein*. *Famous Monsters of Filmland*, which began publishing in the 1950s, projected a jocular tone, indulging at times in wearisome punning, and a predilection for the horror classics of Karloff, Lugosi, and the Chaneys Jr. and Sr. as well as the archetypical horror figures, particularly the vampire and Frankenstein's monster. For all its affability and good humour, *Famous Monsters of Filmland* seemed singularly devoted to what James Twitchell calls 'artificial horror': 'what an audience searches for in a verbal or visual text when it wants a particular kind of frisson without much intellectual explanation or sophistication' (Twitchell: 1985,

8). *Castle of Frankenstein*, on the other hand, displayed a greater affinity for 'real horror,' those images which often are repellent in actuality and deliberately violate our sensibilities (ibid., 9). Beck's prozine, which was published twenty-five times between 1962 and 1975, furthermore avoided *Famous Monsters of Filmland*'s Anglo-American exclusivity by covering European and Asian efforts in the genre as well as horror and fantasy literature, art, and theatre. It also provided valuable research materials, as one of *Castle of Frankenstein*'s editors, director Joe Dante, then only a teenager, contributed an astute and extensive capsule dictionary of film reviews, thereby introducing many readers to the wealth of material in the genre. Fanzines ever since have incorporated both publications' perspectives, treating the horror genre in a jocular or synoptic manner.

As a result of their independent, amateur status, fanzine editors feel obliged to no one, save, perhaps, their subscribers. They lack the indiscriminate, slavish devotion of prozine editors, who bow to commercial producers for interviews, access to sets, and provocative and grotesque publicity photos to attract or offend their readers. If anything, fanzines seem most attracted to uniqueness of vision. Their editors have so immersed themselves in the genre about which they write that they have little interest in and no patience for the slavish devotion to accepted formulae and conventions of the mainstream Hollywood product. Few fanzines therefore praise the ritualized carnage of the recent instalments of the *Friday the 13th* or *Nightmare on Elm Street* series, for as a reviewer in *Samhain* (13, Feb–March 1989) asks, 'how can anything like *Friday the 13th Part 7* be original in *any* aspect?' The degree to which these films now border on self-parody is underscored by their exploitation as syndicated television series which bowdlerize whatever frisson they may once have possessed. Therefore, if to the outsider fanzines appear to be obsessed with the most turgid forms of exploitation fodder, it must be remembered that 'Bad films may sometimes be amusing, sometimes even successful, but their only real usefulness is to form that basis of comparison: to define positive values in terms of their own negative charm' (King: 1983, 217). At the same time, the fanzines' exhaustive research often uncovers 'the sort of interesting, untouted, "discovery" movies that crop up whenever devotees of the genre write' (Newman: 1988–9, 68). Fanzine editors and writers may well be drawn by 'the siren song of crap,' but they just as well know crap when they see it.

This devotion to uniqueness of vision has led the fanzines to value most works which bear the mark of an uninhibited visionary sensibility, one which pushes the boundaries of social, sexual, and aesthetic assumptions. The fanzine writers were among the first to praise the work of such now mainstream directors as George Romero, David Lynch, Wes Craven and David Cronenberg. It has also led them to be attentive to censorship of the genre, practiced in the United States by the MPAA ratings board and abroad by state bodies of social control, such as those in England which in the early 1980s legislated against 'video nasties.' The British fanzines in particular regularly editorialize against the powers of the state: *Samhain* has included a column, 'Police 55: Banned!,' which describes in detail those films the law has made unavailable to the public, while *Cold Sweat* discusses the effect of censorship laws upon the availability of films in European markets. In an environment where the censor's hand has been so indiscriminate, even summarizing a restricted film's plot can be a subversive action.

Furthermore, those fanzines which have begun to market videotapes, including not only titles in the public domain but also others sometimes surreptitiously obtained from foreign sources, underscore their devotion to authenticity of expression by emphasizing that their copies are *uncut* or recorded in the proper letterboxed, widescreen format. Such factors are of particular importance in the case of foreign films, as students of the genre are aware of the extent to which non-domestic horror films are routinely released in any number of versions, their continuity undermined by unconscionable tampering. For example, Dario Argento's *Phenomena* (1985) was domestically released by New Line Cinema with twenty-two minutes excised; the fanzines alone carry a complete print, taken from a Japanese laser disk. The perplexing proliferation of running times listed for many films in Phil Hardy's *Encyclopedia of Horror Films* underscores this point. Fanzines have rectified the dilemma by obtaining the most complete prints by legal or clandestine means.

While many fanzines employ a studious tone, others revel in a smart aleck, supercilious approach to the genre, best typified by John Bloom a.k.a. Joe Bob Briggs's 1982–85 columns in the 'Dallas Times Herald.' Adopting the persona of a redneck drive-in aficionado, Bloom sarcastically covered such fare as *The Grim Reaper* and *Pieces* until his journalistic tenure was terminated by the publication of a facetiously offensive parody of the popular anthem against world hunger 'We Are the World.' The final paragraphs of Joe Bob's reviews always enumerated how much blood was spilled, how many breasts were bared and beasts were featured in the given film, ending more often than not with the admonition, 'Joe Bob says check it out.' His analysis of Tobe Hooper's *Texas Chainsaw Massacre* aptly represents Bloom's style:

> But, of course, the most brilliant thing about *Chainsaw* is that it can scare the bejabbers out of you to the point where you think it was made by a cannibal. A lot of people say *Psycho* is the scariest movie ever made. Bullstuff. *Chainsaw* is the only movie ever made in which anybody can die at any moment. It's also the only movie with *three* psychos who are buddies working shifts, so as soon as Sally and Franklyn veer off that main highway, they're potential meals. Think about *that* the next time you stop for gas in a strange place.
>
> (Bloom: 1987, 51–2)

Any number of fanzines feature a similar sarcastic perspective, including *Temple of Schlock*, *Exploitation Retrospect*, and *Gore Gazette*, which featured the following review in issue 93:

> *Feel the Heat* – Another example of a 'free' feature being offered to theatres to satisfy a video presale, this wacky exploitationer features sultry slopehead karatress Tianna Alexandra as an LA narcotics detective sent to Buenos Aires to break up has-been Rod Steiger's international heroin ring. It seems that the old Roadster is posing as a South American talent agent scouting for dancers to come to New York. When he finds prospective bimbo candidates, he gets them to submit to silicone beef-ups, and unbeknownst to the girls he fills up

their hooters with heroin instead of silicone and subsequently offs them by having goons tear off their tits when they reach the U.S. This radical plot premise could have been handled a lot grislier by restrained director Joel Silberg as its blood count is quite anemic, but *Feel the Heat* still packs enough double-entendres, killings, assorted vulgarities and groin crunchings by Alexandra to elicit a bunch of chuckles from fans of Grade B depravity. Well worth a look!

As is evident in this review, the sarcastic fanzines' jocular tone is often laced with self-conscious misogyny, racism and sexism, the very qualities which led Bloom to lose his newspaper column. The editors of the *Gore Gazette* explain their irreverence [in issue 98] as 'meant merely to inform, entertain and expose those wormbags who may be trying to take advantage of genre fans' hardearned greenbacks and nothing more.' A recent *Washington Times* article (12 January 1989) on fanzines written by David Mills stressed this perspective, much to [the] defensive dismay of a number of editors who felt the author missed the point that this intentionally juvenile hard-boiled tone goes hand in hand with the fanzines' belief that only the most hardened sensibilities can bear the assault of offensive imagery. Charles Kilgore, editor of *Ecco*, provided one of the most intelligent responses to the controversy:

> Though they vary somewhat in content, the angry editorials both employ a 'fuck 'em if they can't take a joke' rationale. Both suggest that Mills didn't 'get' the gag; that only his hyper-sensitivity, and not his color (yes, Mills is Black), excludes him from appreciating their ethnic humor. One even tries the long-dead 'But some of my best friends are . . .' routine. When Mills interviewed me by phone, the subject of racism in one of the 'zines was inadvertently raised. I defended the fanzine, explaining that what he found offensive was not racism but rather a nihilistic form of humor based on sarcasm and irony.
>
> I should have also reminded him of Jonathon Swift's essay 'A Modest Proposal,' in which Swift outlines the absurdity of a position by pretending to adopt it. Or pointed to the independent music scene of the late seventies, when bands tired of baiting born-again conservatives turned their aim on fresh quarry: complacent liberals. *Kill The Poor*, *Crippled Children Suck*, *Holiday in Cambodia*. Titles designed to make fair-minded people squirm . . . if they don't get it.
>
> The trouble is, what if they don't? Mills apparently didn't. What about the reader who misunderstands, nodding in agreement instead of laughing? In case you haven't noticed, racism is back with a vengeance. Some of its newest manifestations, such as the skinhead branch of the Aryan Nation, veer uncomfortably close to ideological home. If Morton Downey Jr. lied about his attack by young neo-Nazis, his populist grandstanding will have trivialized a serious issue.

For the most part, fanzine editors lack Kilgore's deliberate and thoughtful consideration of this issue, and their frat-boy sensibility proves wearisome unless taken in small doses.

On the other hand, a number of fanzine editors are anything but facetious in their interest in exploitation films and use their fanzines as a forum to fill black holes in the analysis of commercial cinema by their encyclopedic knowledge of internationally produced exploitation material. Steve Puchalski, editor of *Slimetime*, has published exhaustive overviews of the blaxploitation and biker genres in the British fanzine *Shock Express*, while Craig Ledbetter contributed a lengthy study of the Italian zombie and cannibal cycles that followed the release of George Romero's *Dawn of the Dead* to the fanzine *Wet Paint*. However, most studies, serious and otherwise, of the horror genre are unashamedly Anglo-American in their bias and rarely consider non-English material. Many fanzines form an exception to this rule, Bill Connolly's *Spaghetti Cinema* being the work of a capable archivist of Italian commercial film, having included analyses of the peplum, giallo, spaghetti western and other genres. His conclusive legwork helps illuminate the hazy material conditions in which international exploitation filmmaking is conducted. Such work can only help answer questions of production and consumption, thereby adding to the 'transdisciplinary' approach to the analysis of 'formula cinema' proposed by Christopher Frayling in his study *Spaghetti Westerns* (1981). As Frayling indicates, adequate assessment of 'formula cinema' must not be reduced to any simple ideological or theoretic grid which excludes 'questions about production ("How did this film come to be made?" "What process did the film go through, to become the finished product?") or about reception ("Why did audiences choose this film or this genre as opposed to that one?", "What was particularly exciting about this director's work?")' (Frayling: 1981, xiii). The work of archivists like Connelly helps to 'incorporate the act of film-making [and] the act of looking at films into [our] theoretical model, factors which are typically unexamined in analyses of foreign commercial film' (ibid., xii).

Other fanzines also have taken on the role of archivist. There has been of late considerable reevaluation of the British Gothic horror film, particularly the work of the Hammer Studio; Dick Klemenson's *Little Shoppe of Horrors* devotes itself exclusively to that studio, and other zines, *Samhain* in particular, have assessed the virtues of Hammer's premiere director, Terence Fisher, both adding to the landmark study of the English horror film, David Pirie's *A Heritage of Horror* (1973). However, it is the work of certain Italian horror stylists which has received the most considerable and detailed attention and begun to indicate the degree of European influence upon Anglo-American filmmakers. Three directors in particular – Riccardo Freda, Mario Bava, and Dario Argento – appropriately have been singled out for attention.

Freda, whose two delirious, Gothic melodramas starring horror icon Barbara Steele, *The Horrible Doctor Hitchcock* (1962) and *The Ghost* (1963), have been praised by Phil Hardy as deploying 'perfect control of colour, rhythm, and atmosphere' (Hardy: 1986, 149), receives extensive analysis in issues of *Shock Express* (Winter 1987) and *Spaghetti Cinema* (issues 18, 19, 20). The dark, exotic romanticism of his visually lush style reanimated the gothic stereotypes of the Hammer films by underscoring the form's sexual morbidity while engaging in an obsessive fascination with Steele's physically striking features.

Of even greater importance and influence is the work of Mario Bava, originally a cinematographer, whose work in the horror genre stretches from 1956, when he photographed Freda's *I Vampiri*, to 1977's *Shock* a.k.a. *Beyond the Door II*. Even those critics conscious of his faults – indifferent scripting and acting as well as a tendency to overuse shock cuts and zoom lenses – readily admit 'Bava is a superb painter on celluloid, electrifying otherwise routine films by his color and compositions' (Milne: 1981, 235). More specifically, a number of Bava's films initiated stylistic and thematic trends in the genre: *Black Sunday* (1960), his first and in the mind of many critics best film, starring Barbara Steele, stylishly combined elegant and loathsome imagery while reinvigorating, like Freda, gothic stereotypes; *Blood and Black Lace* (1964) initiated the *giallo* genre as well as laid the visual and thematic seeds for the slasher film, albeit with greater style and psychological complexity than any of its successors; *Planet of the Vampires* (1965) integrated the science fiction and horror genres and incorporated imagery foreshadowing later similar works, including *Alien* (1979); and *Kill Baby Kill* (1966), a film of genuine poetic power and visual ingenuity, successfully inverted gothic stereotypes of good and evil by having the power of good embodied by a dark-haired witch while evil is represented by an angelic, blonde young girl. Bava's erratic but fascinating work has been discussed by any number of fanzines, including *Shock Express*, *Ecco*, and *Spaghetti Cinema*, which has helped increase interest in and awareness of his influential landmark films.

Finally, the fanzines have been instrumental in seriously analyzing the visually excessive, rhapsodically violent *giallo* thrillers of Dario Argento, whose work is critically and commercially honored in Europe and dismissed as grindhouse fodder in the United States. Save for Maitland McDonagh's recent *Film Quarterly* article, the fanzines alone have accorded the Italian director the attention he deserves for 'eight horror films whose visual density is extraordinary; their intricate storylines – improbable and deceptive – are systematically sublimated to a mise en scène whose escalating complexity . . . [conspires] to delineate a diegetic world gone mad' (McDonagh: 1987–8, 3; see also McDonagh: 1991). Appraisal of Argento's work has appeared in *Wet Paint*, *Photon*, *Blood Times*, and *Samhain*, which published John Martin's three-part 'Magic All Around Us,' the only analysis of substance other than McDonagh's (see issues 6, 7, and 8).

In addition to these sarcastic or archivist fanzines, others, including *Subhuman*, *Trash Compactor*, *Cold Sweat*, and *Sheer Filth*, nihilistically identify with repulsive imagery. They propose that good taste acts as a repressive safety valve, filtering out entire areas of experience and expression, and relish the deliberate breaking of social and aesthetic taboos. The structural principle of the films they most appreciate seems to be one of deliberate visual and thematic aggression whereby 'an almost musical interaction [exists] between moments of tension and moments of respite, in the form of more or less closely spaced and more or less pronounced crossings of the pain threshold' (Burch: 1981, 126). And yet, these fanzines all too infrequently raise or address questions proposed by *Ecco* editor Charles Kilgore: 'Where in the nether-world of exploitation does freedom of expression end and the necessity for social responsibility begin . . . is it possible to advocate cinematic celebrations of human depravity and cruelty in a socially responsible manner?' (issue 8).

Liberation of the unfettered imagination and the crossing of social taboos can result in films imbued with frightening negativity, such as Tobe Hooper's *Texas*

Chainsaw Massacre (1974), which redeem their unrelenting horror through a 'degraded but impressive creativity . . . a kind of hideous aesthetic beauty' (Wood *et al.*: 1979, 21). A striking, though less well-known example of this phenomenon is Michael Reeves' *The Conqueror Worm* a.k.a. *The Witchfinder General* (1968). In this film, detailing the horrendous behavior of a putative hunter of witches (Vincent Price) during Cromwell's struggle for power, 'evil is inextricably intertwined with good, the [characters'] violence is circular, and ambiguous' (Pirie: 1973, 148). No one escapes the taint of inherent depravity, yet while Reeves never minimizes the narrative's brutality, he refuses to titillate the audience or allow them respite from the 'theme of the morally outraged seeking a revenge that ultimately degrades them to the level of their quarry' (Wood: 1969–70, 7). Clearly, our empathy for the film's hero must acknowledge his sadistic extermination of Price's character and therefore force us to question our voyeuristic involvement with the narrative.

However, Reeves' film is an exception, and all too often liberation of the unfettered imagination gives birth to grisly works of art which transgress the 'greyland between art and porno-exhibitionism' (King: 1983, 130). Many filmmakers have descended to the base level of unredeemable splatter and gore typified by the cycle of Italian cannibal and zombie films, the spawn of directors like Lucio Fulci and Ruggere Deodato, which followed in the wake of George Romero's infinitely superior *Dawn of the Dead* (1979). Films such as Fulci's *The Gates of Hell* (1980) and Deodato's *Cannibal Holocaust* (1979) not only deny us any protection or distance from their effects but endorse a kind of obscene literalism, defying their audiences to dismiss the undeniable gruesomeness of their imagery.

The nihilistic fanzines fecklessly address this sub-aesthetic realm, seemingly oblivious to its unregenerate nihilism. What is even more disturbing is that the films' conservative point of view, particularly their misogynistic dismissal of female sexuality, is believed to undermine the status quo. The editors of these zines rarely address the reactionary elements of the splatter genre or the disturbing assertion made by Robin Wood: 'One important aspect of what the horror film has come to signify [is] the sense of a civilization condemning itself, through its popular culture, to ultimate disintegration, and ambivalently (with the simultaneous horror/wish-fulfillment of nightmare) celebrating the fact' (Wood *et al.*: 1979, 22).

One fanzine, Bill Landis's *Sleazoid Express*, faced this dilemma and as a result ruled itself out of existence. Its five-year run (1980–85) began typically, as Landis staked out 42nd Street and its environs as his territory. He reviewed the requisite exploitation fare, albeit with a discriminating eye that took in the work of underground filmmakers, including Kenneth Anger, Curt McDowell, and Stan Brakhage. Quite quickly, however, Landis's tone grew more acerbic and biting; much of the exploitation fare now seemed to him witless and indefensible. His comments on the April 1983 issue on films he selected for a Sleaze Festival are instructive. He points to the 'emotional brutality' pervading the work of Andy Milligan, a New York splatter filmmaker. All his characters, Landis states, are 'completely hateful,' providing us with 'the most unflattering portraits of humanity ever to reach a movie screen.'

Increasingly, Landis had little patience with commercial exploitation films, including those often praised by the mass of fanzine editors. In an article titled

'Exploitation Cancer' in the March 1983 issue, he lambasts Sam Raimi's *Evil Dead* (1983) as

> just the latest model in the invasion of exploitation by a nerd brained, stamp collector mentality which has particularly involved itself in gore. Obsession with special effects, blockheadedly judging laughability without comprehending its aesthetic basis, and praising gore for gore's sake are all examples of this. It's just these type of fans [that] are now picking up cameras.

Bored and angered by such triviality, Landis turns his attention to the consumers of sleaze, for whom he has even more considerable contempt. To Landis, they are self-indulgent voyeurs, living out repressed, juvenile fantasies, using the stock phrase 'so bad it's good' to rationalize their debased appetites. He designates the habitues of adult theaters 'popeyes' and those muscle-bound pontificators over the virtues of sleaze 'blockheads.' Landis's loathing for both groups is obvious and unremitting.

In the end, Landis leaves commercial exploitation movies behind, and the final issues of *Sleazoid Express* anatomize the culture and preoccupations of the denizens of 42nd Street, most memorably, as Jack Barth has said, 'an entire Summer 1984 issue sketching the ambience of The Deuce that comes across like Joyce describing Dublin' (Barth: 1985, 25). As virtually all films, exploitation and otherwise, bore Landis, he increasingly turns his attention to hard core pornography, which he feels at least has the honesty to lack any pretense of social redemption or pseudo-artistic self-consciousness. *Sleazoid Express* holds a mirror up to an element of the audience that the fanzines represents and illustrates that, as Roland Barthes has written, 'What's terrible about the cinema is that it makes the monstrous viable' (cited in Haberman and Rosenbaum: 1983, 304). If Landis has given attraction to the monstrous a human face, few of us would wish to share its features.

The range of fanzines is wide, from the sophomoric to the archival to the nihilistic. They define and dissect a territory of expression that can fascinate as easily as it can repulse. Furthermore, they widen our knowledge of the range of human expression and reanimate those primal urges which drew us in the dark to the screen. Much as we [may] not wish to admit, to deny the pleasures they address will only price us out of the market.

Chapter 26

LEON HUNT

A (SADISTIC) NIGHT
AT THE *OPERA*
Notes on the Italian horror film

Dario Argento, *Terror at the Opera* (1987):

> Take a good look. If you try to close your eyes, you'll tear them apart.
> So you'll just have to watch everything!

IN THE ENTRY FOR MARIO BAVA'S *Antefatto* (1971, also known under the titles *Ecologia del Delitto*, *Twitch of the Death Nerve*, *Bloodbath*, *Bay of Blood*, and even *Last House on the Left 2*), *The Aurum Film Encyclopedia* is largely appreciative, describing its scenario as '13 murders like so many stanzas in a funeral chant' (Hardy: 1985, 233). It does, however, have one important reservation: 'Unfortunately, Bava doesn't quite manage to get rid of all vestiges of characterization or "psychological realism" so the film falls short of being the symphony of violence it might have been in a non-commercial context' (ibid., 233). Allowing for its willful perversity (and 'perverse', after all, is the *Aurum*'s favorite adjective for Bava), this passage points to some of the problems of writing 'seriously' about Italian horror. Is it legitimate to aestheticize their perverse pleasures (funeral chants, symphonies of violence, morbidity, sadism) at the expense of questions of gender and power? Are these films marginalized art or exotic exploitation? Not surprisingly, fanzines rather than critical/academic texts have done most of the work on film-makers like Mario Bava, Dario Argento, and Lucio Fulci and have expressed in less complicated terms where their pleasures reside. In a promotional piece on Fulci's gory *Paura nella Città dei Morti Viventi* (1980, *Gates of Hell*), *Fangoria* makes the following promise: 'scenes of a young man getting his head drilled and a young woman vomiting her guts are sure to please *Fango* readers who demand nothing but the grossest' (Schlockoff and Everitt: 1983, 9).

Two factors, in particular, problematize the satisfactory cultural location and critical analysis of Italian horror. First of all, as Carol Jenks has suggested, the

Italian horror film 'gives . . . the impression of having suddenly sprung from nowhere, whereas the epic spectacles and male and female figures who inhabit mythological and *peplum* fantasies date back to the pre-World War I Italian cinema' (Jenks: 1989, 2). Second, this problem is compounded by the fact that postwar Italian genre cinema has a history of making cheap imitations of successes in America and Britain. Over the years, James Bond, Hammer films, *The Exorcist* (1973), and George Romero zombie movies have 'inspired' low-budget Cinecitta copies, leading Kim Newman to claim that 'Rome has become the Taiwan of the international film industry' (Newman: 1988, 187). More engagingly, director Luigi Cozzi has said, 'In Italy, when you bring a script to a producer, the first question he asks is not "what is your film like?" but "what *film* is your film like?" That's the way it is, we can only make *Zombie 2*, never *Zombie 1*' (Newman: 1986b, 92). On the other hand, both Newman and Maitland McDonagh have argued for comparisons to be made between certain privileged films (mainly those of Bava and Argento) and the most critically respectable Italian 'ripoff' genre, the spaghetti western. 'While it is undoubtedly true that many Italian genre films are simply worthless carbon copies with a few baroque trimmings, the best examples of most cycles are surprisingly sophisticated mixes of imitation, pastiche, parody, deconstruction, reinterpretation and operatic inflation' (Newman: 1986a, 20).

I want to situate the often complex and heterogeneous texts of Italian horror under four headings: horror as 'bad object,' exploitation/art cinema, the gothic and *Giallo* cycles, and pornography/sadism/masochism. I am also interested in Italian horror's characteristic concern with gender and a specific set of images of women. In terms of stardom alone, it's worth remembering that while the British horror film seemed inconceivable without Peter Cushing and Christopher Lee, and the American horror film has produced such icons as Boris Karloff and Vincent Price, Italy's most enduring cult figure in the 1960s was Barbara Steele, an icon who seemed to exist simply to torture and be tortured, to terrify and be terrified.

Indeed, one 'history' of Italian horror might be charted as the ground covered between two very charged images. The first is the opening scene of Mario Bava's *La Maschera del Demonio* (1960, *Black Sunday*), in which Steele, as the witch/vampire/succubus Asa, has a spiked mask hammered into her face in an attempt to eliminate the threat of female sexuality and desire that she embodies. The second scene is from Argento's *Terror at the Opera*, described by its director as 'an aria of violence beyond imagination' (Jones: 1986, 27). The heroine of *Opera*, the young opera singer Betty (played by model Cristina Marsillach), is tied and gagged and has needles taped under her eyes so that she cannot close them without tearing her eyelids. From this position, she is forced to watch a particularly graphic murder (an ordeal repeated later in the film). Both scenes seem to confirm everyone's worst fears about the horror film as a sadistic and misogynist treatment of violence rendered into ultrachic spectacle. Also important, however, is the relationship between the gaze of the woman in the text, the gaze of the spectator, and the violence committed against both. If these films are sadistic and/or masochistic, then for whom and under what conditions? As Carol Jenks has noted, the violence committed against Steele/Asa in *Black Sunday* is also directed 'towards the audience, a desire to aggress against the very site of vision, the eye . . . the spiked mask of Satan is carried forward into the camera to pierce the gaze of the spectator' (Jenks:

1989, 5). In Argento's film, violated spectatorship is presented even more self-consciously, all within the context of a convoluted sexual-sadistic scenario. The nature of what Jenks terms 'textual sadism' has been spelled out by Argento himself: 'For years I've been annoyed by people covering their eyes during the unspooling of the gorier moments in my films. I film these images because I want people to see them and not avoid the positive confrontation of their fears by looking away. So I thought to myself, "How would it be possible to achieve this and force someone to watch the most gruesome murder and make sure they can't avert their eyes?" The answer I came up with is the core of what *Opera* is all about' (ibid., 5). While the case of *Terror at the Opera* supports Carol J. Clover's assertion that 'abject terror . . . is gendered feminine' in the slasher movie (Clover: 1989, 117), this does raise the question of where the spectator is placed in such texts and what pleasures seem to be available.

Horror as 'bad object'

Progressive accounts of horror have emphasized the genre's notoriety as an oppositional/subcultural form. But if Italian horror has been an extreme case of the genre's outlaw status, it is also difficult to imagine a 'progressive' reading of Dario Argento's films. Yet this critical 'unacceptability' is worth charting. *Psycho* (1960), *Peeping Tom* (1960), and early Hammer each prompted cries of outrage from critics when first released, a sense that things were going too far. But by the early 1960s Hitchcock had his apologists and British critics had turned to ignoring Hammer rather than loudly deploring their excesses. Yet Mario Bava's *Black Sunday* was banned in Britain for eight years (apart from two National Film Theatre performances) before finally being released as *Revenge of the Vampire* (1968) in a heavily cut version. One year earlier, Carlos Clarens published his seminal and comparatively early study of the genre, *An Illustrated History of the Horror Film* (1967). Seemingly mindful of the genre's dubious reputation, Clarens's book epitomizes longstanding critical orthodoxy – 'good' horror movies do not show much actual horror (Universal, Lewton, Tourneur), but 'bad' ones do (Hammer, the Italians) because they lack imagination, taste, and restraint. Specifically, such an agenda could not help but react strongly against the 'new gothic' that emerged in Britain, Italy, and, to a lesser extent, America, where it was largely confined to Corman's Poe films. These gothic cycles were more overtly about sex (or perverse sexuality) than horror had ever been before. They were more graphic, less tied to the big studios' 'good' taste, and more eager to indulge in excess. A range of literary sources gave these films their central themes – torture, necrophilia, incest, premature burial, violent sexuality. The *Hollywood Reporter* expressed concern that in *Black Sunday* 'some shots of the dead are considerably too imaginative for the very young, bordering on necrophilia' (Fleming: 1978, 24). Riccardo Freda's *L'Orribile Segreto del Dr Hitchcock* (1962, *The Horrible Dr. Hitchcock*) does nothing so prosaic as to 'border' on necrophilia – it plunges, unapologetically, into filming Barbara Steele in induced deathlike paralysis amidst ornate set designs and vibrant reds and greens. These films are marked by what Carol Jenks calls 'a new element, overt images of sadism and bodily corruption' (Jenks: 1989, 4). As William K. Everson states, 'Italy's horror films . . . have always had a rather unhealthy tendency towards the excesses of *Grand Guignol*, to dwelling on the detailed unpleasantries of death or torture. There has been an especial obsession with facial disfigurement, and an almost clinical attention to the methods by which it was achieved (a girl's head enclosed in a cage of live rats being quite typical)' (Everson: 1974, 207–8). Hammer was also criticized for dwelling on sadism. One British reviewer suggested a new certificate for *The Curse of Frankenstein* (1957), 'S.O. . . . for Sadists Only' (Pirie: 1980, n.p.). But if critics soon felt inoculated against the British gothic, it may have been because the comparatively soft-pedaled sexuality in Hammer's films was located in a strong patriarchal-Christian moral framework. While the excesses of England's Dracula were punishable acts of sexual perversity, Italy's Dr. Hitchcock seemed to make the most of his sexual conquests on the slab, not so much in spite of but because of his status as a respectable Victorian patriarch. More important, the Italian horror film located its sadism more in a sexual-oneiric landscape than a narrative-classic realist one. By the time of Britain's 'video nasty' debate in the early 1980s, this particular treatment of violence distinguished Italian horror. Some of the most notorious 'nasties' were Italian – *Cannibal Holocaust*, *Cannibal Ferox*, and *S.S. Experiment Camp*. Certainly, there was some sense that once again something 'new' and disturbingly 'Other' had infected an already suspect form of entertainment: 'All too many people believe that a nasty is something like a hotted up Hammer horror movie. It isn't; it's something entirely different' (Petley: 1984, 351).

Exploitation/art cinema

During a scene in Argento's *Inferno* (1980), a character is pursued by the forces of darkness. She meets a sportswriter in an elevator and persuades him to stay with her for a few hours. She puts on Verdi's 'Va Pensiero' from *Nabucco*, its opening chords accompanied, ominously, by shots of the full moon. As she sits nervously, we see the following sequence. Black-gloved hands hold a row of paper dollies cut out of black paper. The hands take a pair of scissors and cut off one of the heads. There follows a shot of a lizard eating a still struggling butterfly. We cut back to the gloved hands as they snip off another doll's head. The next shot shows a girl twitching at the end of a noose, which leads to another shot of the gloved hand cutting off a head. The sequence ends with a shot of a house in New York as the camera zooms in.

Three of these shots deploy a spatial dislocation in a game of cat and mouse with the audience. We infer that the killer is nearby and thus 'know' something that Sara does not. But we do not know where he/she is (in an adjacent room? scheming in another part of Rome?) or when the attack will take place. The lizard, the hanging girl, and the house are also impossible to place temporally, and the film never illuminates the meaning of these images. In *Tenebrae* (1982, *Unsane*), as two women in an apartment block are about to be killed, the camera crawls giddyingly over the outside of the building in a single gyroscopic take that is as close to Michael Snow as to Welles' *Touch of Evil* (1958). *The Aurum Encyclopedia* is clearly looking for this 'symphony of violence' (and, significantly, not quite finding it) in

Bava's *Twitch of the Death Nerve*. As these sequences illustrate, Argento's films often embody features of the art film as described by David Bordwell. Argento's work frequently displays 'patterned violations of the classical norm . . . an unusual angle, a stressed bit of cutting, a prohibited camera movement . . . [a] failure to motivate cinematic space and time by cause-effect logic.' Prominent as well are enigmas of narration –' Who is telling the story? How is this story being told? Why tell the story this way?' (Bordwell *et al*.: 1985, 374).

While Argento is virtually unique as an 'art' horror director who has transcended the cyclic, production-line, spin-off genre system (his family are well placed in the film industry and he now owns his own company, Dac films), his generic origins may lie partly in films made under more impoverished production conditions. As Christopher Frayling has shown in his extensive study of spaghetti westerns, Italy's mass-appeal genre films tended toward a cyclic, rapid, production-line mode after the war. Frayling lists such major cycles as the 'film fumetto' (tear-jerkers, 1948–1954), farcical comedies (1958–1964), the peplum films (1958–1964), horror (1959–1963), the 'sexy' documentaries spawned by *Mondo Cane* (1961–1964), and a series of sub-James Bonds (1964–1967) (Frayling: 1981, 70–71). Frayling has suggested that the formal eccentricities of many of these films, made cheaply at Cinecitta and often on recycled sets, can be attributed both to their mixing and matching of elements from different cycles (the spaghettis taking the unstoppable hero from the peplum, the gadgetry of the Bond films, and even gothic elements in films like Sergio Corbucci's extraordinary *Django* [1966]), as well as their efforts to outdo each other in sheer audacity. Often one ends up with engaging hybrids like Bava's *Planet of the Vampires* (1965, *Terrore nello Spazio*), with its fetchingly camp fake leather spacesuits, a spaceship called the *Argos*, spacemen returning from the dead in polythene shrouds, and a giant skeleton and wrecked spaceship that predate [Ridley Scott's] *Alien* (1979).

At times the result of a fortuitous hybridization, the art/exploitation link in Italian cinema is in some instances even more explicit. Bava's *Kill Baby Kill* (1966, *Operazione Paura*) has been fairly widely acknowledged as an influence on Fellini's 'Toby Dammit' episode for the portmanteau Poe film, *Histoires extraordinaires* (1968). Argento collaborated with Bertolucci on *Once Upon a Time in the West* (1969), and while Bertolucci planned a 'straight' adaptation of Frederic Brown's pulp thriller *The Screaming Mimi* (1958), a major influence on the Italian horror film, Argento mutated it into his first film, *The Bird with the Crystal Plumage* (1969, *L'Uccello dalle Piume di Cristallo*).

But as Kim Newman has noted, the major art movie link to Italian horror is Antonioni's *Blow Up* (1966). Not only does Argento cast David Hemmings in *Deep Red/Profondo Rosso* (1975), but he has returned repeatedly to *Blow Up*'s device of the ambiguous 'scene' that needs decoding. Newman defines the 'difference between art and commerce' in the use of this similar device as 'the fact that, in Antonioni, the solution to the mystery is important but unknowable while in the mainstream *giallo*, it is negligible but has to be gone into' (Newman: 1986a, 24). What this ignores, however, is what the Italian horror film actually takes from *Blow Up*. What gets emphasized is less the notion of the unsolvable puzzle than the fact that, amongst other things, Antonioni constructs an elaborate primal scene, one in which the 'mother' is the aggressor. What Thomas gradually uncovers (in the sense that the film's effect is partly uncanny) is that the woman he has spied on is in some way 'guilty' and the 'father' already dead. In *The Bird with the Crystal Plumage*, all of the enigmas hinge on gender, misrecognition/misidentification, on recognizing who is the aggressor in the primal scene – in Argento's anxiously phallocentric scenarios, it is always the mother. While trapped between two sliding glass doors, Sam Dalmas, the hero of *Bird*, witnesses a struggle between a mysterious figure and a woman, Monica Ranieri. Monica is wounded and the 'killer' escapes, presumably to continue the chain of killings that structures the film. Sam continually 'replays' the scene – something is missing, something does not add up. As it turns out, Monica is the killer (*The Screaming Mimi's* plot twist) and Sam has 'misread' the scene. But Monica's motivation, in turn, rests on another misrecognition – of her 'correct' identification with another primal scene. Having been traumatized years earlier by an attack in a park, the supposedly recovered Monica sees a painting depicting a similar attack which triggers another breakdown. But she identifies not with her 'correct' counterpart (herself as violated mother) but with the attacker, reconstituting herself as violent and phallic. Thus, *Bird* is haunted by violent castration anxieties organized around art cinema's characteristic fascination with ambiguity, perception, and memory.

Argento's killers are generally constructed as perverse in their reluctance or inability to undergo 'correct' heterosexual Oedipal trajectories. *Deep Red* opens with the primal scene – a children's lullaby accompanies a violent stabbing depicted as a shadowplay on a wall (it is replayed later as a child's drawing). A child in white socks picks the knife up. This time, Mommy is literally killing Daddy, as witnessed by the hero's gay friend, Carlo. The film, full of nervous jokes about heterosexual male inadequacy, is more than anything else about 'solving' Carlo's homosexuality. (His mother is the psychopathic killer; her murder of Carlo's father is presented as being motivelessly insane while structurally 'explaining' her son's sexuality.) The homophobia of the film's solution is indicative of the relentless Oedipality of the *giallo*, one of the subgenres to dominate the history of Italian horror, from Bava, via Argento, to a younger generation of directors like Michele Soavi.

The gothic and the *giallo*

Prior to 1956, less than a handful of Italian films could by any stretch of the imagination be classified as horror movies. The most likely suspects would include *Satana* (1912), a three-episode film about the devil; *L'Atketa Fantasma* (1919), featuring a masked fighter of evil; a 'lost' Frankenstein film, *Il Mostro di Frankenstein* (1920); and a Toto comedy featuring the devil, *Toto all'Inferno* (Camillo Mastrocinque, 1954). When Freda's *I Vampiri* (1956, *The Devil's Commandment*), photographed and partly directed by Bava, and Bava's *Black Sunday* initiated the Italian horror film proper, it was as part of a three-headed gothic attack. The style of Italian horror was radically different from the British tradition's relatively restrained, comparatively realist, and male-centered focus. Corman's perverse languor and knowing pop-Freud mediates between the two but is stylistically closer to Bava and Freda. For example, Corman made very Bava-like use of Barbara

Steele in *Pit and the Pendulum* (1961). If one image of Hammer is of Lee and Cushing locked in (im)mortal combat, and if Corman's female protagonists capture the desire/fear axis of male masochism, the Italians shift the genre even more deliriously to the terrain of women.

If the gothic constitutes one tradition in Italian horror, the *giallo* might usefully be seen as the missing link between the protoserial killer narratives of Frederic Brown and Cornell Woolrich and the American slasher film of the late 1970s/early 1980s. The term is derived from the yellow covers of Italian hardboiled thrillers, but in its cinematic form it becomes 'the peculiarly Italian mixture of thriller, sexploitation and horror/terror conventions initiated by Mario Bava's *La Ragazza che Sapeva Troppo*' (1962) and elaborated into a major formula by Dario Argento (Hardy: 1985, 294). But perhaps *the* seminal *giallo* is *Blood and Black Lace* (1964), which puts most of the subgenre's features in place. Amongst these features are elements such as black gloves and masks, which function in several ways. The mask can conceal gender and point as well in a quite reflexive way to the killer as a function within the text. For example, the white, featureless mask of *Blood and Black Lace* is worn by two different characters and can thus perpetrate a seemingly impossible chain of killings. Even so, the murders are gendered – the male killer (Cameron Mitchell) scars, burns, and disfigures his victims, the female killer (Eva Bartok) suffocates them.

The choice of murder weapon is also distinctive in the cinematic *giallo*. Carole J. Clover observes that killing instruments in the American slasher film are 'pretechnological . . . knives, hammers, axes, icepicks, hypodermic needles, red hot pokers, pitchforks, and the like' (Clover: 1989, 103). While several of these weapons do turn up in Italian slashers, the choice here seems to be made more on the basis of their aesthetic merits and capacity for disfigurement. While guns are rare in American slashers, for example, one of *Terror at the Opera*'s set pieces follows the trajectory of a bullet in slow motion through the barrel, through Daria Nicolodi's eye, and into a television set at the far end of the hallway. In this case, the weapon is made subservient to the film's aesthetic organization around injury-to-the-eye motifs. More outlandish examples include an electronic voice box which throttles its owner (*Inferno* [1980]), an attic full of barbed wire (*Suspiria* [1977]), and even guide dogs who turn on their blind owners (*Suspiria*, *The Beyond* [1980]). Most tellingly, Argento favors glass and mirrors on a fairly consistent basis, scarring and dispatching his actresses in an assault on the 'narcissism' the films so fetishistically construct.

While the *giallo* may occasionally use shock effects similar to the American slasher (the killer emerges from an unexpected place, the victim strays into a dangerous place), it most often favors an elaborately choreographed and protracted set piece that draws on the full resources of baroque set design, lighting (the flashing reds, blues, and greens used by both Bava and Argento), and music (the numbingly hypnotic scores of Ennio Morricone and the rock group Goblin, whose 'prog-rock' mantras and sinister lullabies are crucial to *Deep Red* and *Suspiria*). More than one account has noted the radical split in *Blood and Black Lace* between its prosaic scenes used to advance the plot and the murders, which literally arrest the narrative and are filmed in a totally different style. The film has two agendas, one narrative and one visual. The motive for the killings is tied up with an elaborate and inconsequential blackmail plot, but the murders are performed as though something more fundamentally sadosexual is taking place.

Argento's set pieces have inspired comparisons with Sergio Leone (the elaborate, prolonged confrontations in his westerns) and even Vincente Minnelli (the murder set piece as production number) (see Newman: 1988, 107). But in many ways, Argento's murders perhaps more closely resemble the fashion shots taken by Faye Dunaway in *The Eyes of Laura Mars* (1978), in which 'women's bodies are fetishized and the connection made between female sexuality and violence' (Fischer and Landis: 1987, 65). In *Laura Mars*, as well as in collections like *World without Men*, fashion photographer Helmut Newton's photographs place his elaborately coiffured models in scenarios which play on androgyny, fetishism (guns, panthers, and orthopedic corsets), aggression, and punishment. While the violence inherent in these photographs is often condensed into their extreme objectification, some display a more overtly sadistic voyeurism. Examples include Catherine Deneuve in red menaced by a large black gun, two models alongside a car, one lying in a pool of blood, the substitution of dummies for models in elaborate poses (*Blood and Black Lace* puts a similar substitution to murderous effect). *Unsane* (1982), in particular, is like Newton's *World without Men* brought to life and to its logical conclusion (Newton: 1984). The female victims are made up to look as similar as possible, giving a sense of the same woman being killed over and over again. When the first of the two killers photographs the corpses, the images even resemble Newtonesque fashion shots.

In the *giallos* of Bava and Argento, the link is repeatedly made between 'high fashion' and 'high violence' as two aggressive mediations of sexual difference. *Blood and Black Lace* is actually set in a fashion house, where the preparation for a catwalk show is filmed like a killer stalking his prey with the voyeuristic camera prowling relentlessly. Another moment in *Unsane* conflates most succinctly the woman-as-fashion-object and the woman-as-object-of-violence. Placed against one of the film's chic white interiors, one character has her arm severed with an axe and turns to spray blood against the wall like an ultraviolent action painting. The fashion link is found as well in *Creepers* (1985), where the costumes were designed by Giorgio Armani (who 'discovered' *Terror at the Opera*'s star Cristina Marsillach on the catwalk).

While the gothic horror cycle employed a female archetype epitomized by the erotic ambivalence of Barbara Steele, the *giallo* centers on a chic fetishistic object who embodies the implicit logic of this much-quoted statement by Dario Argento: 'I like women, especially beautiful ones. If they have a good face and figure, I would much prefer to watch them being murdered than an ugly girl or a man' (Jones: 1983, 20). This aesthetic led to one of Argento's most notorious projects, a 1986 video for the Trussardi fashion show which reenacted the opening scene of *Suspiria* on a catwalk, with models dragged off in see-through body bags.

Finally, if the American slasher film emphasizes the 'bad place,' the old houses of *Psycho* and *The Texas Chainsaw Massacre*, or the woodlands of *Friday the 13th*, the *giallo* belongs more to a setting that is ornately baroque (*Suspiria*'s school, just about everywhere in *Inferno*) or intensely modern/postmodern, bright and hi-tech (*Unsane*, *Terror at the Opera*). More important, it is a world which suggests wealth, an haute bourgeois world that leads Kim Newman to dub these movies '*telefono rosso*' films, a gory mutation of the fascist era 'white telephone' comedies (Newman: 1988, 107).

If this partly explains Argento's odd assertion that *Unsane* is set in a future 'inhabited by fewer people with the result that the remainder are wealthier and less crowded' (Jones: 1983, 20), it also accounts for some of the misogyny in these films, a scenario in which the 'softness' of the spoiled rich is characterized as feminine. In one of *Terror at the Opera*'s climactic scenes, for example, ravens are let loose in a crowded theater and identify the killer by removing one of his eyes. In the process, the ravens terrify the wealthy patrons. As one of the birds settles to consume the eyeball, a frame reveals with some relish the array of beads, necklaces, and jewelry left on the plush red carpet during the evacuation.

The gothic cycle of Italian horror virtually fizzled out in 1966. It was three years before Bava made another horror film. A second cycle, initiated by Argento's *Bird with the Crystal Plumage*, emphasized the *giallo* almost exclusively. However, the gothic and the *giallo* are not necessarily totally separate. Argento's two super-natural films, *Suspiria* and *Inferno*, often referred to as the 'Three Mothers' films, mix gothic and *giallo* elements (ghosts and witches, but also black-gloved killers), and the latter in particular deals with three mother figures who function as a kind of transmutation of the Italian gothic female. The Mother of Sighs (Mater Suspiriorum), the Mother of Tears (Mater Lachrymarum), and the Mother of Darkness or Mother of Shadows (Mater Tenebrarum) are drawn from De Quincey's *Suspiria de Profundis* (1845), a sequel to *Confessions of an English Opium Eater* (1821) and a hymn to male powerlessness.

If Argento's version is less drowsily romantic than the typical gothic, it does envision a displacement of the father by these archaic figures. The wheelchair-bound Varelli, whose 'building has become my body' (a building inhabited and controlled by the Mother of Darkness), writes the book guiding the protagonist but states ultimately, 'I'm not the master . . . I am just a slave.' The Mother of Darkness ('the cruellest of them all') rearticulates some of the (male) masochism of the late 1960s gothic, the desire for the woman fused and synonymous with death. She tells the hero triumphantly: 'You were looking for me, just like your sister . . . This is what you wanted. I'm coming to get you . . . The Three Mothers. Haven't you understood? Mater Tenebrarum, Mater Lachrymarum, Mater Suspiriorum. But men call us by a single name, a name that strikes fear into everyone's heart. They call us . . . Death!'

Pornography/sadism/masochism

Talking about the relationship between the heroine of *Terror at the Opera* and the killer who ties her up and forces her to watch his murders, Dario Argento said, 'The murderer needs her to see it all as her enforced restraint will bring the ulti-mate orgasm – the perpetration of death being the clearest act of love' (Jones: 1983, 31). Such a statement does much to support Carol J. Clover's claim that, in horror, 'violence and sex are not concomitants but alternatives, the one as much a substi-tute for and a prelude to the other as the teenage horror film is a substitute for and a prelude to the "adult" film (or the meat movie a substitute for and prelude to the skin flick)' (Clover: 1989, 100).

'Like pornography,' Linda Williams writes, 'the slasher film pries open the fleshy secrets of normally hidden things' (Williams: 1990, 191). In this respect, Italian horror is particularly extreme and symptomatic, from the sexually charged scene when Asa's rotting body is 'revealed' in *Black Sunday* to the disgust registered in Lucio Fulci's films. A film like *The New York Ripper/Lo Squartore di New York* (1982) displays its fear of the hostility toward the female body with a violent, numbing realism that would be difficult to equal (all signs of 'difference' are the targets of razors, knives, and, in one scene, a broken bottle). Williams links hardcore with two agendas concerned with seeing and knowing. On the one hand, there is the tradition of *scientia sexualis*, the construction of 'body knowledge' through the relentless surveillance of the workings of (largely female) bodily pleasures, increasingly by means of elaborate optical apparatuses. At the same time, Williams notes that the invention of the cinema is tied to this pursuit of body knowledge and an accurate recording of its 'secrets.'

Paradoxically, the films of Argento and Fulci deploy special effects in this documentary exploration of the body's hidden and involuntary responses. Significantly, Argento has more than once used medical camera equipment to 'capture' impossible places and movements – the inside of someone's mouth as they scream, someone beheaded in slow motion by a shattered car windscreen. In *Suspiria*, during a stabbing, the camera 'enters' the body to show the beating of a heart as it is penetrated by a knife. A similar shot in *Terror at the Opera* occurs as a character is stabbed through the jaw, making visible the entry of the knife into his mouth. This is a kind of 'realism' which many would characterize as 'pornographic,' an ultraviolent 'frenzy of the visible,' to use Williams' term.

Terror at the Opera presents an entire film devoted almost exclusively to issues of visibility, spectatorship, and horror. The film is set around a hi-tech production of Verdi's *Macbeth*, directed by Marco (Ian Charleson), a specialist in horror movies. When the female lead is run over, she is replaced by a younger singer, Betty (Cristina Marsillach), who immediately arouses the interest of a mysterious figure. A series of flashbacks, apparently the killer's memories, show young women being tormented, watched by another woman who is tied up but apparently sexually excited. After the first show, Betty attempts unsuccessfully to make love to a young stagehand. He is murdered, and Betty is forced to watch with needles taped under her eyes. Two more murders take place; the second under similar conditions to the first. Betty dreams about her mother, who turns out to be the woman in the flashbacks (Betty witnessed this scene as a child). Marco decides that the ravens used in the production can identify the killer and lets them loose during the next performance. The killer is Santini (Urbano Barberini), the young police inspector investigating the case. He loses an eye but kidnaps Betty, explaining that he was her mother's lover and that she forced him to torture and murder women for her pleasure. He ties and blindfolds Betty and begs her to shoot him, assuring her that she is 'just like your mother.' He is only apparently killed and turns up for a coda in which Betty reassures him that she is like her mother, stalling him long enough for the police to capture him. As they take him away, she shouts at him, 'It's not true! I'm not like my mother! Nothing like her! Nothing at all!'

As a study in spectatorial sadism, *Terror at the Opera* offers three types of violent 'scenes.' First of all, there is the chain of acts of violence against the eye. Myra, Betty's agent (Daria Nicolodi), is shot through the eye. The inspector has his eye removed and eaten by a raven. Most important, Betty has needles taped under her eyes to force her to watch. As Argento's comments suggest, this is also a sadistic assault on the spectator. Not only does the camera look through those needles and provide an even more painfully close view of the murders than the one forced on Betty, but several other shots visually evoke the needles (by framing a scene through a ventilator grill, for example). The spectator is placed as the object of sadistic instruction. This is corroborated by Argento's explanation of the scene (teaching us not to look away, a punishment for all those gory horror movies we did look away from). Clearly, this type of scene is the exact opposite of the one Kaja Silverman is thinking of when she says that 'the fascination of the sadistic point of view is merely that it provides the best vantage point from which to watch the masochistic story unfold' (Silverman: 1988, 5).

The second 'scene,' linked to the first, is the demonstration of Betty's power-lessness, both to her and the spectator. After the second murder, while Betty is still tied up, the killer moves the knife between her stomach and groin and tells her, 'I can take you wherever and whenever I want.' In the following scene, she tells Inspector Santini, who is not yet identified as the killer, 'He ties me up . . . touches me . . . makes me watch. But he never lets me see his face.' In the third type of scene, which is embodied in the revelation of Santini as the killer, Betty is educated into the role of the cold, cruel mother of the masochistic scenario. 'You're just like your mother . . . she taught me a cruel little game, killing and torturing. Only then could I have her – I was her slave.'

In his influential account of masochism, Gilles Deleuze identifies the sadist and the masochist not as the interlocking parts of a practice known as 'sadomasochism' (a term he dismisses) but as mutually exclusive scenarios. Linda Williams observes that Deleuze's sadists and masochists are exclusively male and argues for some provisional use of the term *sadomasochistic*. 'While still problematic, the term at least keeps in play the oscillation between active and passive and male and female subject positions, rather than fixing one pole or the other as the essence of the viewer's experience' (Williams: 1990, 217). Carol J. Clover's account of identi-fication in the slasher film, meanwhile, proposes a bisexual oscillation between male and female, active and passive, victim and aggressor. 'The makers of slasher films seem to know that sadomasochistic incest fantasies sit more easily with the male viewer when the visible player is female' (Clover: 1989, 117). The viewer identifies with the girl's vulnerability but then recognizes a surrogate male as she picks up the phallus/knife to defeat the killer.

Betty, on the other hand, defeats the killer not by adopting the phallus but by oscillating between being and not being the cruel mother. This is complicated by the fact that the killer, too, adopts a number of guises – the 'fake' policeman who tries to enter Betty's apartment, the sadistic father who symbolically rapes her, and finally the son who wants to educate her into a specific role (just as Marco is now to direct her in *La Traviata* – 'How do you want to play her? Tender? Timid? Sensual?'). Betty asserts that she is and then denies that she is 'like my mother,' but her performance implies more of the former. However one reads this scene, the film does at least allow her a way out of the woman's usual choice between victim and phallicized woman.

Deleuze argues that masochism is based on fetishism/disavowal, postponement of pleasure, waiting, suspense — 'the art of suspense always places us on the side of the victim and forces us to identify with him, whereas the gathering momentum of repetition tends to force us onto the side of the torturer and make us identify with the sadistic hero' (Deleuze: 1989, 34). What makes *Terror at the Opera* so remarkable is its extreme play with such vacillating positions of identification. *Terror at the Opera* violates the spectator but at the same time aestheticizes sadistic violence as spectacle. It combines the Oedipal violence of the *giallo* with the pre-Oedipal masochism of the gothic. It joins the narrative of the American slasher film with the extremely self-conscious narrational strategies characteristic of art cinema. Thus, in many ways, *Terror at the Opera* stands as a summary moment in the hybrid tradition of Italian horror, an aestheticized 'bad' object that vacillates between strategies of art cinema and exploitation while also raising provocative issues in horror spectatorship. If the history of the Italian horror film takes place between two violated 'looks,' those of *Black Sunday* and *Terror at the Opera*, then this trajectory hints at the problems these often marginalized and dismissed yet extremely complex films raise for studies of the horror genre.

Chapter 27

VIVIAN SOBCHACK

REVENGE OF *THE LEECH WOMAN*
On the dread of aging in a low-budget horror film

O N SATURDAYS IN BROOKLYN, when I was a child, my younger sister and I used to go to the movies, where we'd sit all day watching the cartoons, coming attractions, and double feature loop themselves several times over until it was almost dark outside and we knew our mother was just starting to get anxious. I loved science fiction films, tolerated westerns, was indifferent to musicals and melodramas, and – like all the kids around me – squirmed whenever a couple kissed on screen. Both my sister and I loved horror films especially – at that time, before Psycho (1960), often set in the Carpathians, or at least not in Brooklyn, and remote from our quotidian life. Nonetheless, they still seemed close enough to fire our imaginations and make the walk home in the darkening twilight titillating and perilous. Insofar as my mother confirms my recollection, the wolf men, the Frankenstein monster and his bride, Dracula and his daughters, never invaded my dreams, but my more susceptible sister almost always had nightmares on Saturday nights. In contrast, I never found those early horror films all that horrible or really scary, although I did find them incredibly poetic, and I almost always identified with the monsters, whatever their gender (assuming they had one). Now, a grown woman and film scholar, I am surrounded by the intellectual discourse on horror, a discourse that is thoughtful but never quite gets to a description of my experiences – either then when I was very young and gloried in a sense of my own difference and its power, or now when I am middle-aged and often surprised by moments of fear and horror – both at the movies and in my life.

The horror film has been seen by many contemporary, psychoanalytically oriented, feminist scholars as a misogynist scenario elaborated within a patriarchal and heterosexual social formation and based on the male fear of female sexuality. To put it simply and reductively, on the one hand, male fear is generated by male desire – and the power women have over its satisfaction. On the other hand, male fear is generated by female desire – the desire of the Other, which provokes the specter of male 'lack' in the face of sexual difference and manifests itself in castration anxiety (an anxiety justified recently by Lorena Bobbitt's castration of her husband and revealed in his testimony that she was angry not because he repeatedly abused and raped her, but because he hadn't been able to satisfy her sexually). The elaboration of this male dread of women is played out in horror films at both manifest and latent levels, and all of us, whether practiced in psychoanalytic readings of popular culture or not, are certainly familiar with the genre's dual articulation of women as both 'scared' and 'scary.' Generally speaking, these two 'female conditions' are intimately and systemically related – not only to each other but also to the regulation of heterosexual desire and biological reproduction in patriarchal Western culture. Indeed, it is nearly impossible to think about the threat of 'scary women' in horror films without recognizing that threat as emerging from a woman who, first, was scared. Nonetheless, perhaps because it's more interesting and certainly more empowering, feminist scholarly emphasis has been on the 'scary' rather than 'scared' women of the horror film and on describing the relation between the psychic dread they cinematographically engender and their sexual and reproductive potency.

Here, however, I want to talk about another sort of 'scary woman' in the horror film – one whose scariness, while related to her sexuality, has less to do with power than with powerlessness, and whose scariness to men has less to do with sexual desire and castration anxiety than with abjection and death. Here I want to talk about the middle-aged woman who is both scared and scary – the woman who is neither lover nor mother, the woman who becomes excessive by virtue of her being regarded as excess. This is a woman who can't be dealt with as either the object or the subject of the gaze. Indeed, up until very recently and under the pressure of changing demographics and actuarial tables, in films (whether horror films or not) and in culture, she has been so threatening and disgusting a sight that the gaze slides quickly over her and disavows her visibility. Not yet static and frozen in time as a feisty but safe Jessica Tandy in *Driving Miss Daisy* (1990) and *Fried Green Tomatoes* (1991), not yet clearly physically and peacefully 'old' (as if there were such stasis, as if it would be sweet), this woman evokes in herself and to others the horror and fear of an inappropriate and transgressive sexual desire that lingers through the very process of aging, physical degradation, and decay.

Myself a fifty-three-year-old woman, this scary woman scares not only men but also me – although I am ashamed to admit it. Much as I attempt to counter my fear of aging with intellectual rationalization, cultural critique, or humor, I find myself unable to laugh off a recurrent image that truly horrifies me even as I joke about it. The image? It's me and yet her, on Other – and, as her subjective object of a face has aged, the blusher I've worn every morning since I was a teenager has migrated and condensed itself into two distinct and ridiculous red circles in the middle of her cheeks. This image – which correspondingly brings a subjective flush of shame and humiliation to my cheeks for the pity and unwilling horror and contempt with which I objectively regard hers – is that of an aging woman who not only deceives herself into thinking she is still young enough to wear makeup and poorly applies it, but who also inscribes upon her face the caricature both of her own desire and of all that was once (at least to some) desirable.

This, to me, is the image of a *really* scary woman – and all my demystified knowledge of the cultural practices that posit her as such do little to demystify or rob her of her negative-affective power to scare me. Subjectively felt, she engenders humiliation and its ancillary horrors. Objectively viewed, she is ludicrous, grotesque. Subjectively felt, she is an *excess woman* – desperately afraid of invis-ibility, uselessness, lovelessness, sexual and social isolation and abandonment, but also deeply furious at both the double standard of aging in a patriarchal culture and her acquiescence to male heterosexist values and the self-contempt they engender. Objectively viewed, she is sloppy, self-pitying, and abjectly needy or she is angry, vengeful, powerful, and scary. Indeed, she is an *excessive woman*, a woman in masquerade, in whiteface. She is the Leech Woman, the Wasp Woman, the 50 Foot Woman. She is Norma Desmond and whatever happened to Baby Jane.

This quasi-autobiographical confession is meant to point to the doubled nature and complex phenomenological affect of the cinematic figuration I want to address here – namely, the explicit engendering of the cultural fear, loathing, and anger directed at the mortal fact and process of physical aging in the scared and scary women of a number of low-budget horror/science fiction films made in the American context, primarily from the late 1950s through the mid-1960s. In chrono-logical order of release these are *Attack of the 50 Ft. Woman* (1958), *The Wasp Woman* (1960), and *The Leech Woman* (1960), this last providing my primary or 'tutor' text for its explicit and sustained focus on the process and horrors of aging. Indeed, in their variations on a theme, all three films are explicit.

Yet explicitness is relative. I first saw these films while still in my teens and yet I must not have seen them at all. I do remember the nameless pleasure I felt when each of the female characters – 'transformed' from scared to scary by extraterrestrial contact or special serum – was suddenly empowered to carry out excessive acts of vengeance. I don't recall, however, thinking specifically about the reasons for this vengeance; nor, even though I was female, do I remember feeling uncomfortable with the way these women were figured in their scared, pre-scary, state. The boys in the audience – in all likelihood simultaneously disgusted, titillated, and scared by the sight of someone the age of their mothers still radiating desire – were intending toward the moment when their fear and desire would take visible shape to prove its monstrousness. However, I, a girl still in my teens, was also directed toward that moment. Not only did I, too, find it disgusting to think that my mother still 'did it,' but what did such an alien state as middle age have to do with me? Thus, as I watched these women, like the boys, my highly conventionalized disgust and fear was of them, not for them. Nonetheless, unlike the boys, I think I sensed the pleasure of their revenge.

Attack of the 50 Ft. Woman tells the story of Nancy, a wealthy, childless, middle-aged woman unhappily married to a philanderer and prone to sloppy drinking. (We're told she's been in a private sanitarium for treatment.) After a close encounter with a (please don't laugh) 'space ball' and the giant alien man within it, she collapses and is taken home to eventually – impossibly – awaken 50 feet tall in a bedroom too small to hold her. Using her bedclothes as a bra and sarong, she strides off to town and the roadhouse where her husband is romancing a younger woman (generically named 'Honey'). As one shocked male bystander says to another as she passes: 'She'll tear up the whole town till she finds Harry . . . and then she'll tear up Harry.' Calling her husband's name, she pulls off the roof of the roadhouse and plucks him out, only to be killed (and to kill him) by elec-trocution from felled power lines. However hysterical both the 50 Foot Woman and the special effects, there is a sober side to this tale of a woman's humiliation and revenge. Toward the beginning of the film, as Nancy lies in her bedroom after her close encounter but before her transformation, downstairs her doctor speaks to the concerned family butler about her 'wild story' and strange behavior and says: 'When women reach the age of maturity, Mother Nature sometimes over-works their frustration to a point of irrationalism. Like the middle-aged man of our age who finds himself looking longingly at a girl in her early twenties.' If this non-sequitur analysis makes us raise our eyebrows, consider the following from Freud, writing on obsessional neurosis in 1913:

> It is well known, and has been a matter for much complaint, that women often alter strangely in character after they have abandoned their genital functions. They become quarrelsome, peevish, and argu-mentative, petty and miserly; in fact, they display sadistic and analerotic traits which were not theirs in the era of womanliness.
>
> (Freud: 1959a, 2, 130)

There is a half-truth hidden somewhere here, but it has nothing to do with some inherent postgenital transformation and everything to do with a sense of lovelessness, a sense of being invisible and untouchable. There was a period in my middle age when I felt dried up and experienced an aridity that had nothing to do with a postmenopausal lack of vaginal lubri-cation. Rather, the phenomenological truth of this sense of desiccation, this 'dry spell' in my affective and sexual life, was grounded in what seemed a forced exclusion from the sexual economy, from the sensual, a deprivation of the caresses from another that make one sensi-tive to one's own skin. Peevish, argumentative, sadistic? You bet. The desire to assert one's bodily and desiring existence knows no bounds, and is indeed 50 feet tall.

The Wasp Woman is a much simpler film; Roger Corman, who made it, went straight to the surface of the matter. The film essentially begins in an executive boardroom with a severely dressed and bespectacled middle-aged woman execu-tive coldly chewing out what appear to be her male subordinates for the company's poor sales. We find out that she is Janet Starlin, a single woman of forty, who heads a now fading cosmetics empire. The reason for its recent failures? A daring male executive tells her, 'It's because of you.' He explains that people were used to seeing her picture in the advertisements, which read, 'Return to Youth with Janet Starlin,' but now that she's aged and her picture no longer appears in the ads, the consumer no longer feels any product identification. Fixed on remedying her situation in all ways, Janet speaks to her chemists about the royal bee jelly they've been using and inquires whether wasp jelly might have a more dramatic effect on forestalling the aging process. They're not buying any; as one puts it, 'Socially, the queen wasp is on a par with the black widow.' Janet, however, looks to her own devices and finds a scientist willing to experiment with wasps. Eventually he finds a serum that not only reduces but also reverses the aging process. Watching the rejuvenation of lab animals, Janet does not want to wait for FDA approval, first offering herself as a human guinea pig and then – after she does begin to look younger – stealing into the lab to administer more and larger injections. She looks twenty-two and gorgeous for her stated forty years, but there are side effects: Overdosed with the royal wasp jelly serum, she regularly turns into a Wasp Woman – that is, a woman in a sheath dress and heels, with the head of a wasp and the urge to kill. Eventually, of course, after the non-gender-specific murders of a number of people, she is killed herself. *The Wasp Woman*, then, is a simple but paradoxical little cautionary tale: 'There are some things that woman is not meant to *know*,' i.e., the secret of rejuvenation; and yet there are some things she must always *be*, i.e. 'young.' What is most interesting about the film is that, watching it, one gets the feeling that Janet Starlin's monstrousness has less to do with the fact that she is a single, independent, and powerful corporate executive than it has to do with her age. As one psychotherapist wrote in a revisionist 'self-help' book several decades after the film was made: 'Ageism is, in fact, the last bastion of sexism. . . . The last mental barrier to equality is the almost visceral disgust for the older woman as a physical being' (Melamed: 1983, 30). This same psychotherapist relates that, perhaps unaware of *The Wasp Woman*, a friend told her: 'I'm prepared to die, but not to look lousy for the next forty years' (ibid., 42).

Now, fifty-three, in front of the mirror, I look at my face and contemplate – with desire and fear – cosmetic, plastic, surgery. My skin is still good for those who never saw it before (when I was young). But my eyelids are wrinkled, and a crease runs downward from the right side of my mouth and makes me look less happy than I am. I pull my facial skin up taut and I do see myself again rather than my mother when she was middle-aged. But I am also afraid that if I do it, if I really do it, they'll go for the broad stroke and I'll emerge with a face I don't recognize as mine. Which is ironic, because right now, looking in the mirror, the face I see is also a face I never quite recognize as mine. I am, of course, appalled more by my desire than by my fear. I'm an intellectual, a feminist, and supposed to know better. But still I care. I, too, am prepared to die but not to look lousy for the next forty years.

The Leech Woman, as I've said, is the most complex of the three films in bringing together the self-abjection and drunken sloppiness of the despised and neglected middle-aged wife with the science fictional rejuvenation fantasies that will supposedly – and superficially – do away with the need to resolve social problems that are far more than skin deep. The plot deserves a somewhat detailed recounting not only for its explicit and ongoing address of the humiliation and abjection suffered by middle-aged women, and the justified rage they feel and often express in excessive acts, but also for its recurrent dramatization of the disgust and dread their physical presence engenders in men.

June Talbot is forty-something and a self-pitying yet self-aware drunk. (Drinking in these films, for middle-aged women, is clearly coded to connote disgusting and excessive behavior and physical sloppiness.) At the film's beginning, a nasty confrontation with her endocrinologist husband at his office convinces her to give him the divorce he wants. He is visited, however, by a wizened, mysterious African woman named Mala, who proves to him that she has the secret to an age-retarding powder and a rejuvenating serum. She persuades him to finance her journey back to the Nandos tribe from which she was taken over 140 years before by slavers. Greedy for wealth and knowledge, the doctor cancels his divorce plans, professes his need for June (which goes only as far as his need for a human guinea pig), and, guided by a local hunter, they both take off after Mala into the wilds of a stock-footage African jungle. During the trek, June wonders why her husband is so cold toward her, only to be reassured rather easily by a cursory, contemptuous, and momentary display of affection. Soon, however, June realizes his intentions to use her as an experimental subject and runs off into the jungle, to be saved and brought back by the handsome white hunter. Shortly after, the three are captured and brought to the Nandos village, where Mala tells them that they will learn her secret but must die when she dies the next morning.

That night the three outsiders watch a ritual ceremony with Mala at its center. The scene and the speech that prefaces it are extraordinary. In the midst of this low-budget and ridiculously colonial vision of 'primitive' African tribal life, the words of old and wizened Mala lose none of their resonance, righteousness, and power. She says to those who watch:

> For a man, old age has rewards. If he is wise, his gray hairs bring dignity and he is treated with honor and respect. But for the aged woman, there is nothing. At best, she's pitied. More often, her lot is of contempt and neglect. What woman lives who has passed the prime of her life who would not give her remaining years to reclaim even a few moments of joy and happiness and know the worship of men. For the end of life should be its moment of triumph. So it is with the aged women of Nandos, a last flowering of love, beauty — before death.

The secret of Mala's rejuvenation is revealed. *Nipe* (the pollen from a rare jungle orchid) is mixed with the pineal hormones of a male victim, who must be stabbed fatally at the base of his neck with a special ring that extracts the fluid. The now youthful (and lighter-skinned) Mala rises beautiful, proud, and imperious and tells them that while they must die with her the next morning, the night is theirs, and she offers June her youth again. Morally horrified by the murder necessary for rejuvenation, June refuses, but her husband urges her to accept as a cover for his and the guide's escape. Cursorily, he tells her that, of course, he will return and rescue her. June now clearly grasps her situation, and she agrees. And when she is told that she may pick any male to supply the pineal hormone, she surveys the village men, then wheels around and chooses her husband. (Mala says, 'You have made an excellent choice. You will have beauty and revenge at the same time.')

June is transformed into a gorgeous young woman, and the guide is entranced. He finds a way for them to escape, bringing with them the pouch containing the *nipe* and the lethal ring. They make love in the bush. June, however, starts to age, as the effect of the serum is temporary, and each time it wears off it leaves the user older than before. The amorous guide not only proves fickle but is also horrified and disgusted. He withholds the *nipe* from June and tries to leave her. In the process, he becomes trapped in quicksand, and June — extracting the pouch as the price of his rescue — coolly leaves him to die. She returns to America as her own niece, although she resumes her own persona when she ages and must find a new victim. As her niece, she romances the young family lawyer, whose fiancée, Sally, is determined not to let the intruding sexpot interfere with her marital future. As herself, out to find a source of pineal hormone, June dresses in widow's weeds adorned with expensive, visible jewelry, frequents the seamy side of town, and picks up a man who takes her to a secluded spot, admires her jewels, asks, 'You dig young guys, honey?' and if she has any relatives, and then attempts to strangle her. Instead, she murders him. The film's denouement occurs after Sally, brandishing a gun, visits the 'niece' (now clad in lamé lounge pajamas, and icing champagne for a tryst) and warns her to stay away from the lawyer. June scuffles with Sally, knocks her out, extracts the girl's pineal hormones for future use, and then begins a romantic evening with the young lawyer. The police arrive – apparently some of June's identification was found near her previous victim's body – and during the questioning, June begins to age. She excuses herself and mixes the *nipe* with Sally's hormones, but the female pineal fluid doesn't work. 'I killed Sally for nothing,' she says in horror. Downstairs the police hear a crash and a scream and break into June's bedroom. From the open window, they see her body – dead and incredibly decrepit on the ground below.

The Leech Woman and its companions are extraordinary texts – no less for their explicit address of the horrors of female aging in a patriarchal society than for an awe-inspiring obviousness that threatens to strike the film exegete dumb. Indeed, insofar as *The Leech Woman* lets its real cultural fears 'all hang out,' it thwarts the scholarly elaboration of psychic processes of displacement and condensation, of poetic processes of metaphor and metonymy. The hermeneutic challenge of the film and its earlier companions comes not from their breathtaking literalness, their astonishing demonic prosody, but rather from the complex allegories of reading they suggest. That is, the figuration of such excessive and excess women prompts us, as James Clifford writes of ethnographic allegory, to say of these films 'not "this represents, or symbolizes, that" but rather, "this is a (morally charged) *story* about that"' (Clifford: 1986, 100). The story here is about aging, desire, and the body, and its moral charge is derived from the double standard of which Mala speaks, a standard that elicits a complex of engendered emotions from both the women and the men who bear it: fear, humiliation, abjection, shame, power, rage, and guilt. Furthermore, this story and its moral and emotional charge have not changed very much since the 1950s and 1960s; it can be read across the history of American film, beginning perhaps with the breakdown of the extended family (an effect of the rise of urban centers), but coming to the foreground in the post-World War II period, which marked the cultural repression of a great many working and independent wartime women back into the patriarchal home, now dislocated to the featureless, cultureless suburbs. This period seems marked by the phenomenological awareness that many middle-class women, barring motherhood, had nothing to do, an awareness that war brides were aging, possibly unfulfilled and 'frustrated.' Coincidentally, this period also saw the proliferation of high technologies developed during the war throughout the public sphere, where they intersected with, among other institutions, medicine and the biological sciences to create a science fictional milieu that gave rise not only to the generic emergence of science fiction feature films but also to a notion of a technologized and, ultimately, perfectible human body.

Indeed, although it is true that women have 'come a long way, baby' since the end of World War II, the increasingly technologized quotidian life of our culture since the war suggests that a phenomenology of contemporary body consciousness would reveal that the 'progress' of coming 'a long way, *baby*' is intimately tied to fantasies of rejuvenation and agelessness. With 'advances' in electronic and medical technologies and new aerobicized forms of Taylorism come the promise of bodily overhauls, replacement parts, and a fulfilled, if rigidly disciplined, existence as an ageless 'lean, mean machine.' Hence, for heterosexual women, there has been an increasing emphasis on looking – if not staying – young and an increasing contempt for those 'undisciplined' bodies unable or unwilling to 'pull themselves together,' 'stay in shape,' or regularly avail themselves of cosmetic surgery. *Death Becomes Her* (1992) says it all. Hence also, for both hetero-sexual and homosexual men, the current ideal is the ageless 'hard body' of the 'cyborg' (whose pecs – Donna Haraway notwithstanding [see Haraway: 1985, 65–107] – are certainly not those of a liberated woman). Despite the sacrificial ending of *Terminator 2* (1990), the Terminator is never terminal; what resonates is the immortal promise: 'I'll be back.'

I, too, am about to become a cyborg, although what I value about the experience has less to do with cheating death than with rejuvenation. My leg having been amputated recently because of recurrent cancer, and a number of operations having forced me into increasing physical inactivity, I now find myself learning to use a prosthesis. I look forward not only to being enabled again but also to wearing high heels. And, after months of extreme and rigorous exercise, all the clothes I never gave away fit me again. In anger at its built-in self-criticism, I gave up dieting years ago and, hardly a glutton, worked on accepting myself 'as I was.' Nonetheless, slim has always gone with young, and now I'm overjoyed at my weight loss and do feel younger. There is something truly perverse at work here: I feel less the loss of the leg than the loss of weight. I feel more attractive and younger now that there is less of me. And I didn't have to diet. This is the power of the cyborg woman – and, although ironical, hardly the irony out of which liberation is wrested.

Today – even more than in the decades in which films like *The Leech Woman* or *Whatever Happened to Baby Jane?* (1962) were made – the visibly aging body represents a challenge to the self-deluding fantasies of immortality that mark the dominant technoculture. Furthermore, in a sexist as well as ageist technoculture, the visibly aging body of a woman has been and still is especially terrifying – not only to the woman who experiences self-revulsion and anger, invisibility and aban-donment, but also to the men who find her presence so unbearable that they must – quite literally – 'disavow' her and divorce her. As one psychologist dealing with aging relates: 'I once heard a man say to his gray-haired wife, without rancor: "I only feel old when I look at you"' (Rosenthal: 1990, 38). And another writes:

> There are male archetypes of death – the grim reaper, the skeleton. Perhaps it would be more accurate to say that they are neutral, because of their impersonal quality. They symbolize abstract mortality. But aging with its catalog of fleshly indignities is the human face of death, and it is a woman's face. There is no male counterpart to the witch or hag . . . [and here I would add the Wasp Woman and the Leech Woman] or any male figure who rivals the horror and loathing she inspires. She is the scapegoat par excellence for our fear of aging.
>
> (Melamed: 1983, 54)

Julia Kristeva, in dealing with the phenomenon of abjection and its relation to horror, suggests that abjection has various forms. Particular to the exploration of the issues of female aging I've dealt with here is her distinction between the abject that comes from without and the abject that comes from within. The abject that comes from without includes 'excrement and its equivalents (decay, infection, disease, corpse, etc.),' which 'stand for the danger to identity that comes from without: the ego threatened by the non-ego, society threatened by its outside, life by death' (Kristeva: 1982, 71). These excess middle-aged women of low-budget horror films, these visibly decaying bodies that reach out to touch a man who recoils in horror, these 'non-egos' who threaten society less by their rage than by their presence, certainly engender this form of the abject.

In contrast, the abject that comes from within is described thus:

> Cells fuse, split, and proliferate; volumes grow, tissues stretch, and body fluids change rhythm, speeding up or slowing down. Within the body, growing as a graft, indomitable, there is an other. And no one is present, within that simultaneously dual and alien space, to signify what is going on.
>
> (Kristeva: 1980, 11)

While Kristeva makes reference to pregnancy and cancer as possible forms of inner abjection, her description also holds for the bodily changes in the 50 Foot Woman, the Wasp Woman and the Leech Woman. Within the transformed, monstrous, and visible bodies of these women divided against themselves in desperation, anger, and self-loathing, there is indeed an 'other.' As psychotherapist Elissa Melamed suggests in her book *Mirror, Mirror: The Terror of Not Being Young*: 'We often experience the changes of aging as somehow alien to us, as if the "real self" is frozen in time, imprisoned somewhere within the aging body' (Melamed: 1983, 47). Thus, abjection suffered by the women aging in the horror film is doubled. Is it any wonder that they cannot possibly survive?

It is now a commonplace to acknowledge the complicity of ageism and sexism in white heterosexist culture in the United States. Professionals and academics across a range of disciplinary areas have pointed to the social and economic problems consequent to the cultural practice of regarding the growing number of older women in our society 'like guests who have tactlessly worn out their welcome,' who are seen 'not as a resource, but as a "problem"' (ibid., 25). The opening image I presented as 'my' scary woman belongs not only to me but also to others. Along with the 'bag lady' or the 'cat lady,' she exists as the abject, excess, excessive figure of a great many women in our culture – including the psychotherapist I just quoted above, who recalls a woman she saw at a hairdresser's: 'her skin . . . plastered with a tannish coating, further overlaid with spots of pinkish color. Only her eyeballs and the inside of her mouth were recognizably human tissue' (ibid., 9). She continues:

> As I look back, I am not proud of what I felt: a mixture of pity, scorn, and above all, denial that [she] could have anything to do with me. . . . Why couldn't she see herself? And I told myself loudly that this could never happen to me. . . . Yet one day, the memory . . . came back to haunt me. Somehow or other, I too was now over forty. I didn't really like it – even worse, I was ashamed to admit that I really didn't like it. . . .

As a psychotherapist, I realized that I was obviously dealing with something deeper than some wrinkles and gray hairs. I was feeling divided . . . against myself: a changeless person trapped inside a changing body; a centered person at odds with a needy person; an honest person ashamed of the 'me' who wanted to play the youth game.

(ibid., 10–11)

The prose here might seem simple, but the phenomenology of the experience of this process of change is complex and alien – however much we are now intellectually aware of the self-displacing, decentered, constantly mutable subject. At least in our fantasies, many of us would still rather be the scary woman that is the beautiful, frozen mask of Catherine Deneuve in *The Hunger* (1983) than the chilling whiteface of the self-deluded Baby Jane.

And yet, there is a passion that speaks to me in Bette Davis's grotesque performance as the child star who never grew up but did grow old in Whatever Happened to Baby Jane?. *That painted face, expressing glee and spite, pleases and excites me in its outrageousness and its outrage. Ludicrous, grotesque, overpowdered and rouged, mascara and lipstick bleeding into and around her wrinkled eyes and mouth, Davis's Jane is a manic proclamation of an energy that does not want containment, that refuses invisibility and contempt. I feel her somewhere deep within me even as I want to avert my eyes and not look upon my possible future.*

At the post office this week, I – a middle-aged woman in good clothes and great shape (but for want of a leg) – stood in line in front of an old woman in mismatched clothes who had padded toward me on flat feet. Acutely aware of her because of this essay, I wondered how scared and scary she was and why. I saw no transgressive desire on her face – only a misshapen package in her arms. And if she had a rage to live, it certainly wasn't evident in her comportment. I could not tell if she was scared, but what scared me was her clothing. She wasn't in rags, but the colors and patterns clashed, had not been in any way coordinated, and her clothing seemed merely a bodily covering, put on as an afterthought. The dread she elicited from me was, on the one hand, economic. Like the 'bag lady' and the more genteel 'cat lady,' she embodied my fear of not being able to 'take care of myself,' and her ragtag clothing marked the social reality of an increasing number of elderly women living on impossibly inadequate incomes who are lucky to merely 'make do.' On the other hand, however, the dread was existential, if certainly also acculturated. Not being able to 'take care of myself' presaged a slide into 'not caring' – not caring how I looked, not caring whether or not I 'pulled myself together,' not even caring about the sensual pleasures I used to get from color or from silk on my skin. This was a not caring that was hardly liberating, merely defeating. I think (although I'm not absolutely sure) I would rather inappropriately, transgressively, gleefully tap dance (prosthesis and all), wear makeup and a bow in my hair, and spite the world around me when I am really old – particularly if it remains the world it is. This would be the real revenge: to insist that I am alive and in the world and ever full of desire.

Part Eleven

NEW REGIONAL HORROR

Introduction to Part Eleven

■ Ken Gelder

THE FOCUS THUS FAR IN THIS Reader has been on British, European and North American horror forms. It has indeed been true that these regions have attracted almost all the attention of horror analysts over the last twenty years, whether they be academic or media commentators, genre buffs or contributors to the fanzines – or any combination of these. But what about other locations for horror? In the field of cinema, for instance, we might move down to South and Central America to look at Brazilian horror master José Mojica Marins' film, *Awakening of the Beast* (1969), or Guillermo del Toro's Mexican vampire film, *Cronos* (1993). On the other side of the Pacific, in the Philippines, we might examine Peque Gallaga and Lore Reyes' *Shake, Rattle and Roll* horror series from the 1980s to the early 1990s, as well as their film, *Aswang* (1992), built around an indigenous threatening female monster (see Lim: 1997). Japan has produced a tremendous amount of SF-horror cinema and SF-horror *anime* (animation) over the last forty years, from the early *Godzilla* films to Shinya Tsukamoto's confrontational 'body hammer' film *Tetsuo* (1989) and demon-invasion cartoons like the graphic *Urotsukidoji: Legend of the Overfiend* series – not to mention a range of sex-horror and other hybrid variations, mostly at the low-budget end of horror film production (see Weisser and Weisser: 1997). Korean horror has seen a revival in recent times, following in the wake of earlier films by Kim Ki-Young, such as *The Insect Woman* (1972). Modern Indian horror films, although few in number, may have their beginnings in the Ramsey Brothers' demon-from-the-past musical, *Purana Mandir* (*The Old Temple*) (1985). Peter Jackson's earlier splatter horror-comedies chronicle a 1950s settler New Zealand, culturally conservative and yet highly impressionable. To the west, Australia has a ghost story tradition which gives expression to colonial and postcolonial anxieties; two contemporary films which take up these spectral themes are Tracey Moffat's *BeDevil* (1993) and Margot Nash's *Vacant Possession* (1996) (see Mellencamp: 1995, 258–75; and Gelder and Jacobs: 1998, 23–42).

In outlying regions subjected to colonialism, the ghost story may very well become an appropriate medium through which to chart contemporary anxieties – and reactivate old traumas. Colonizers can find themselves preoccupied by the indigenous peoples they dispossess, especially when land, compensation and recognition are called for. The sense that the land is 'haunted' by its original inhabitants thus functions both as a romantic literary trope and a political reality. Graham Huggan's contribution to this section, from a collection titled *Cannibalism and the Colonial World*, sees the Caribbean in precisely this way, as a place 'haunted by ghostly presences' which stand as reminders of loss, defeat and grief – explaining why the ghost story is one of its 'most prolific forms'. Drawing on two local works of literature – Edgar Mittelholzer's *My Bones and My Flute* (1955) and Wilson Harris's *Palace of the Peacock* (1960) – Huggan reads the creolized ghost story as providing an 'occluded' alternative to the European colonial record in the Caribbean. Here, ghosts forecast crisis, signalling the return of colonialism's repressed. But they can also have muse-like, creative qualities, leading Huggan to attribute them with two contradictory roles: as 'countermemory' (which fractures colonialism and produces difference) and as 'collective memory' (which positively transforms, moving towards reconciliation).

The ghost story has flourished in other regional formations outside of the Euro-American hegemony: notably, and most spectacularly, in Chinese Hong Kong cinema. Along with Japan, Hong Kong has been one of the most prolific locations for horror film production outside Europe and the US, building the genre around ancient Chinese legends on the one hand, and outrageous recastings of Western horror cinematic tropes (possession, vampirism, splatter, serial killing, etc.) on the other. In 1973, the British Hammer Studios teamed up with Hong Kong's Shaw Brothers to co-produce an early East-meets-West horror outing, *Legend of the Seven Golden Vampires* – with martial arts sequences directed by Chang Cheh. But the Shaw Brothers, who were responsible for hundreds of Hong Kong films from the 1960s to the 1980s, had themselves produced a great deal of graphic action-horror, notably those directed by Chang Cheh and Yang Chuan, as well as (to single out one above many others) Lu Chin Ku's more recent and renowned martial arts horror romp, *Holy Flame of the Martial World* (1983). The 'epic' fusion of martial arts, fantasy, ghosts and slapstick comedy may have had its beginnings in Sammo Hung's *Encounters of the Spooky Kind* (1980). Interestingly, the time-lapse between this film and its follow-up – nine years – is unusual for Hong Kong horror cinema, where sequels can come thick and fast. The many 'spin-off' *Mr Vampire* films are an example (see Dannen and Long: 1997, 223); so are Ronny Yu's *The Bride With White Hair* (1993) and *The Bride With White Hair II* (1993); and so are the three *A Chinese Ghost Story* films, directed by Ching Siu-tung in 1987, 1990 and 1991.

The other contribution to this section by Audrey Yue, published here for the first time, turns to the first *A Chinese Ghost Story*, as well as another ghost film released during the same year, Stanley Kwan's *Rouge*. Like Huggan, Yue sees both works of horror as speaking to real historical conditions: this is one of the significances attributed to an otherwise marginal form. But Hong Kong's condition is very different to the Caribbean's. As a postmodern, global city that is also colonial, in 1997 Hong Kong found itself in the strange position of being handed over to its old master (or mistress), China: its movement forwards was thus also a kind of belated return. Yue herself returns to the word 'preposterous' (often used to dismiss the trashiest or most unbelievable kinds of horror cinema) as an expression of this predicament, drawing out its implicit conflation of 'pre-' and 'post-' : before and after. *Rouge*, for example, develops a 'preposterous' form of nostalgia as its female ghost returns to contemporary Hong Kong seeking reunification with her lost lover. *A Chinese Ghost Story* is much more *visually* preposterous, spinning 'a love story from a cyclone of fantastic action' (Hammond and Wilkins: 1996, 17): ridiculous, absurd, and saturated with flamboyant special effects. But the term 'preposterous' is given further potential, also signifying queerness – where the conflation of before and after is also a confusion over front and back. Yue's reading of the young hero in *A Chinese Ghost Story* – as he is spectacularly 'rimmed' by a tree monster's 'sticky, creamy' and very phallic tongue – thus compares with Carol J. Clover's claim that some American rape-and-revenge films open up a 'world of one-sex-reasoning' in which 'the (male) anus and the vagina are . . . one and the same thing' (Clover: 1992, 157–8). For Yue, however, this and other back-to-front situations enable even the most bewildering works of Hong Kong horror to speak – however 'preposterously' – to that place's modern identity crisis.

Chapter 28

GRAHAM HUGGAN

GHOST STORIES, BONE FLUTES, CANNIBAL COUNTERMEMORY

The Ghost is the fiction of our relationship to death.

(Cixous: 1976, 542)

Face to face with the white man, the Negro has a past to legitimate, a vengeance to exact; face to face with the Negro, the contemporary white man feels the need to recall the times of cannibalism.

(Fanon: 1967, 225)

MOVING BETWEEN LITERATURE and history, this [chapter] has three objectives. First, it seeks to forge an unholy alliance between the cannibal and the ghost, and to explore their interworkings in the context of revisionist Caribbean history. Second, it examines the cannibal and the ghost as textual mediators, as means by which Caribbean writers reimagine their European literary ancestry. And third, it charts the attempt through the shape-shifting cannibal/ghost alliance to transform the orthodox, largely negative, perception of Caribbean history, and to set up a countermemory to the hegemonic European record. The primary texts are the creolised ghost stories of two modern Guyanese writers: Edgar Mittelholzer's *My Bones and My Flute* (1955) and Wilson Harris's *Palace of the Peacock* (1960). In both of these stories the ghost – the 'uncanny cannibal' – has a dual function, reasserting the presence of a past (or pasts) that had previously been repressed while estranging that past and converting it into forms that sublimate material exploitation.

Uncanny cannibals

It is little wonder that Derek Walcott, the Caribbean's best-known poet, begins an essay on the region's past by citing Joyce's familiar epigraph, 'History is the nightmare from which I am trying to awake.' For the Caribbean region is haunted by ghostly presences, reminders of a history seen as loss, distress, defeat. Walcott takes as his artistic task the deliverance from this collective trauma:

> The New World originated in hypocrisy and genocide, so it is not a question for us of returning to an Eden or of creating Utopia; out of the sordid and degraded beginning of the West Indies, we could only go further in indecency and regret. Poets and satirists are afflicted with the superior stupidity which believes that societies can be renewed, and one of the most nourishing sites for such a renewal, however visionary it may seem, is the American archipelago.
>
> (Walcott: 1974, 13)

Walcott drives out the ghosts that crowd in upon ancestral memory, clearing the space for history to direct its gaze toward the future. Other writers, however, from the Caribbean region – a region defined as much by discursive ties as by history or climate – have found themselves repeatedly, even obsessively, drawn back to the past. Kamau Brathwaite, Edouard Glissant, Alejo Carpentier, Wilson Harris: all of these writers have explored the hidden recesses of Caribbean history, rejecting the Eurocentric claim that the region has no past to speak of, and uncovering instead the 'traces of historical experience [that have been] erased from the collective memory of an oppressed and exploited people' (Webb: 1992, 7).

Caribbean literature, in this context, enacts a struggle over origins. Where does the past begin? What might be seen as the region's heritage? And can this heritage – acknowledged as multiple, fluid, and syncretistic – be reinvented to suit the purposes of emancipation and renewal? (Caribbean cultural origins clearly predate the European record, stretching back beyond 'discovery' and the history of slavery to engage with folk mythologies that have survived in adapted forms despite the decimation of both the islands' and the mainland's indigenous peoples.) Modern Caribbean writing participates in a process of perceptual transformation: it submits itself to its own haunting but with a view to overcoming it, and with an aim to convert a spectral past into a speculative future.

It seems appropriate, then, that among the region's most prolific forms is the ghost story, or a hybrid variant of it, at least, derived both from African/Amerindian oral sources and from the repository of Western (Euroamerican) literary fantasy. This [chapter] deals with two novel-length ghost stories set in 'ancestral' Guyana: an area of the Caribbean whose complex racial intermixture owes both to 'mestizo' (Euro/Amerindian) and 'mulatto' (Euro/African) forms of cultural creolisation. Before turning to the works themselves, however, a few prefatory remarks seem necessary, both on the properties of the genre and its ambivalent stance to history.

Ghost stories, according to Gillian Beer, 'elide the distance between the actual and the imagined': they speak, literally and figuratively, of an intrusion into the everyday world. In ghost stories, says Beer, 'the fictional takes place in the everyday:

it takes space, and it is this usurpation of space by the immaterial which is one of the deepest terrors released by the ghost story . . . [G]host stories are to do with the insurrection, not the resurrection of the dead' (Beer: 1978, 260).

The return of the undead may act as a trigger for personal memories; for the ghost, as Hélène Cixous reminds us, is 'the direct figure of the uncanny' (Cixous: 1976, 542). Ghosts are uncanny in the Freudian sense that they register the familiar: they belong, as Freud puts it in his essay on 'The "Uncanny"' (1919), to 'that class of the terrifying which leads us back to something long known to us' (Freud: 1959a, 369–70). Yet the ghost, and its ambiguous return, also have far-reaching social consequences. History is reintroduced into the arena of the present, but in such a way that it threatens the fixity of existing social structures. Ghosts bring with them a knowledge other than that ratified by social charter: they make a mockery of the institutional respects we pay to satisfy the dead. [. . .] They walk through historical walls, co-existing with the present, and literalising the memories we consecrate in metaphor in order to contain them. [. . .] Ghosts bring the past into our midst, that we might recognise it. But they also estrange the past: their relationship to the history that they reinstate is inherently uncertain. What renders the ghost intolerable, according to Cixous, is not so much that it is an announcement of death nor even the proof that death exists, since it 'announces and proves nothing more than [its] return. What is intolerable is that the [g]host erases the limit which exists between the two states, neither alive nor dead; passing through, the dead man returns in the manner of the Repressed. It is his coming back which makes the ghost what he is, just as it is the return of the Repressed that inscribes the repression' (Cixous: 1976, 543).

Ghosts are the unwelcome carriers of an occluded history; they show us how we screen, and thus protect ourselves from, the past. They function, to be sure, as agents for the reconstruction of historical memory. But they are double agents: they are working for the 'other' side. They make us recognise another past to the one we might have chosen: they transform, not the past itself but our 'normal,' socialised perception of it.

This set of preliminary observations on the disruptive properties of ghosts suggests that ghost stories might be effective as vehicles of historical revisionism, or as means by which repressed histories can be brought back to the surface. It also suggests that ghost stories might help construct a kind of countermemory, in [Michel] Foucault's sense of the transformation of (linear) history into a different form of time. In the Caribbean context, this need to transform the past becomes an urgent imperative. Denis Williams states the dilemma well:

> We are all shaped by our past; the imperatives of a contemporary culture are predominantly those of a relationship to this past. Yet in the Caribbean and in Guyana we think and behave as though we have no past, no history, no culture. And where we do come to take notice of our history it is often in the light of biases adopted from one [racially] thoroughbred culture or another, of the Old World. We permit ourselves the luxury . . . of racial dialectics in our interpretation of Caribbean and Guyanese history and culture. In the light of what we are this is a destructive thing to do, since at best it perpetuates what

we might call a filialistic dependence on the cultures of our several racial origins, while simultaneously inhibiting us from facing up to the facts of what we uniquely are.

(quoted in Harris: 1970, 13)

Ghost stories in the Caribbean thus often have a dual purpose: they revive in order to dispel the ghosts of a past conceived by Europe, a history couched in the paralysing terms of dispossession and defeat. At the same time, they reclaim a past anterior to European conquest, a history whose outlines blend with those of originary myth, and whose ghosts are not horrifying apparitions from another, unwanted era but welcome catalysts for the recovery of a buried ancestral consciousness. Ghost stories, like ghosts themselves, shift the shape of the past(s) that they engage with; they are co-opted, in the Caribbean, into a discourse of conversion, whereby a history of exploitation is estranged even as it is confronted, and a pattern is established for the transformation of individual trauma into the inspiring recollective force that bonds a whole community.

This discourse of conversion goes by many names. It might refer, for instance, to Kamau Brathwaite's project of cultural creolisation, whereby the appeal to ancestors other than the European (such as the African and Amerindian) involves the writer in a 'journey into the past and hinterland which is at the same time a movement of possession into present and future' (Brathwaite: 1974a, 42). Or then again it might take in Denis Williams's model of catalysis, whereby an interaction between the region's racial groups qualifies each other's self-image, and a history of race-based conflict is turned into a valuable source of artistic creativity. For Wilson Harris, too, adversarial contexts can be productive. Harris's experimental fictions are exercises in what he calls a 'dialectic of alteration': historical antagonisms are converted into a volatile symbiosis, with the Old World and the New nurturing each other's creativity; meanwhile, history itself is turned into a set of 'architectural complexes,' spatial frameworks offering alternatives to a linear vision of time and to a 'block' perspective on the past that blindly serves self-interest – the obsessive pursuit of material goals that only strengthen social divisions; the obstinate refusal to acknowledge 'visionary' schemes other than one's own (Harris: 1970, 32). There is an ethical dimension, then, to all of these projects of conversion, which present a challenge to the teleology of imperial conquest, asserting in its place a dialectical or processual view of (cross-)cultural interchange. In proposing what Harris calls 'a treaty of sensibility between alien cultures' (ibid., 19), each writer recognises the need for continuing self-critique. Caribbean counter-discourses (in Helen Tiffin's useful gloss on Harris) 'evolve textual strategies which continually 'consume their own biases' [Harris's term] at the same time as they expose and erode those of the dominant discourse' (Tiffin: 1987, 18). Harris's arrresting metaphor of "consuming one's own biases" is linked throughout his work to the symbolic practice of cannibalism. Cannibals, according to Harris, do not merely feed on the dead; they absorb the dead into themselves, drawing on their enemies' strength but suggesting, at the same time, that the declaration of material hostilities might eventually give way to an uneasy metaphysical truce. Harris explains this process further in his preface to *The Guyana Quartet* (1960). Here he refers the reader to the Carib/cannibal bone flute, an instrument traditionally made from the hollowed-out bones of the Caribs' war-victims and whose music, in releasing the ghosts of victories past, works to sublimate them. The relevant passage is as follows:

> The Carib bone flute was hollowed out from the bone of an enemy in time of war. Flesh was plucked and consumed and in the process secrets were digested. Spectres arose from, or reposed in, the flute. [The anthropologist Michael] Swan identifies this flute of soul with 'transubstantiation in reverse.' In parallel with an obvious violation ran therefore, it seems to me, another subtle force resembling yet differing from terror in that the flute became the home or curiously *mutual* fortress of spirit between enemy and other, an organ of self-knowledge suffused with enemy bias so close to native greed for victory.
>
> (Harris: 1985, 9–10)

Harris's language is characteristically metaphor-laden and oracular. Peggy Sanday's anthropological analysis helps put it in perspective: 'When projected onto enemies, cannibalism . . . becomes the means by which powerful threats to social life are dissipated. By consuming enemy flesh one assimilates the animus of another group's hostile power into one's own' (Sanday: 1986, 6). Harris's description of the bone flute also reflects on Dean MacCannell's more speculative distinction (derived from Montaigne) between economic and symbolic cannibalism: the former motivated by the selfish desire for material gain; the latter, paradoxically, by the mutual need for human kinship (see MacCannell: 1992, 17–73).

The flute, which Harris seems to see as an organising metaphor for his work, integrates the cannibal and the ghost – the phobic creatures of a paralysed unconscious – into an alchemical process where they act in tandem as catalysts of transformation. The flute works to sublimate the physical violence it embodies; its spectral music provides both for the rehearsal of cannibal urges and for their translation into an ephemeral form that dematerialises the act of conquest. The flute functions as a mnemonic device whose range is atavistic – to play it is to summon the ghosts of an ancestral past into the present, submitting oneself to one's primal fears and fantasies of the 'other.' It embodies the cannibal act but then converts it into ghostly music; in the process the threat of cannibal destruction is not diminished, but is dispersed in the re-enactments of former cannibal confrontations, dismemberments now re-membered in a disembodied form. The flute transforms the cannibal, the West's irreducible 'other,' into a free-floating manifestation of the Freudian uncanny. This cannibal ghost is a blueprint for fantastic liminality: neither alive nor dead, both physical and spiritual, it absorbs the 'other' only to reassert it as a powerful 'absent presence.' By trading on the interplay between containment and dispersal – between the incorporated body and the unassailable ghost – the bone flute records and regulates the violence of the past while acknowledging that this violence can never be fully controlled.

Letting in the demons

In Mittelholzer's *My Bones and My Flute* (1955), the eponymous flute and its ghostly music are associated with the Dutch planter Jan Peter Voorman, victim of a slave revolt in mid eighteenth-century (British) Guyana. Voorman's ghost still roams abroad, it seems, hounded by demonic spirits – spirits whose presence his magic flute had originally summoned, but who now leave him, and all those who associate with him, no rest. A parchment he leaves for posterity draws its readers into a pact: either they must find his bones and flute and give them a Christian burial or they, too, will be lured by the flute's nefarious music to their death. Enter the novel's protagonists, the aristocratic mill-owner and part-time antiquarian Ralph Nevinson, and the narrator Milton Woodsley, an aspiring writer and painter and, like the Nevinsons, from old Coloured – and thus respectable – Guyanese stock. Billed both as a 'good thrilling sort of old-fashioned ghost story, with the mystery solved at the end' and as a 'true record, including nothing that might be attributed to [its narrator's] imagination' (Mittelholzer: 1955, 5–6), *My Bones and My Flute* tells the story of Woodsley's and the Nevinsons' quest to lay Voorman to rest. At the same time, the novel reads as an allegory of Guyana's mixed racial ancestry and as an attempt to come to terms with the country's violent colonial past.

From the outset, Mittelholzer's ghost story acquires racial dimensions. 'I curse these black wretches,' Voorman says of the slaves who work for him, 'even as I curse the Blacker Ones,' the demons his flute has summoned (ibid., 29). These demons turn out to be a cross between neanderthals and extra-terrestrials; they shift in shape and form: now ghosts, now beasts, now cannibal vampires. They are, in short, a composite of the white man's racial phobias, phobias linked in Voorman's case to the justified fear of insubordination, and in Woodsley's to the guilt instilled by a puritanical religious education. (The Day of Judgement, says Woodsley's grandmother, might come at any moment, with 'the Righteous lifted as they sleep and transported up to Heaven while the Unrighteous are cast into Eternal Flames with Satan and his *Black Angels*' (ibid., 57–8, my italics).)

The Blacker Ones also have another, literary, ancestry. In recalling the ghostly predators of Poe's and M. R. James's fictions, they remind us of the paranoid racial myths endemic in Western fantasy. James's *Ghost-Stories of an Antiquary* (1904) is cited as an intertext, as is, almost inevitably, Poe's *Tales of Mystery and Imagination* (1845). And another text of Poe's appears to lie beneath the surface: *The Narrative of Arthur Gordon Pym* (1838), with its spectral visions of Blackness and its projections of the writer's pathological fears of Southern slave rebellion (see Rowe: 1992, 117–40). *My Bones and My Flute* locates itself squarely within this dubious tradition; but it does so not to reinforce the white man's racial fantasies but to reassess their function within a specific historical context. And the context here is that of British Guyana's colonial history – a record of the drudgery, cruelty, and violence of the plantations, but also of the hybrid cultural forms thrown up by that encounter.

Kamau Brathwaite distinguishes usefully here between two forms of New World creolisation: 'A mestizo-creolization, the interculturation of Amerindian and European (mostly Iberian) and located primarily in Central and South America; and a mulatto-creolization, the interculturation of Negro-African and European (mainly Western European) and located primarily in the West Indies and the slave areas of the North American continent' (Brathwaite: 1974b, 30). Guyana's history intersects these two different forms of cultural creolisation. In *My Bones and My Flute*, Woodsley and the Nevinsons are the 'olive-coloured' products of racial inter-mixture: their ancestors, Woodsley tells us, go back to the late eighteenth century, after which time they acquired the 'strain of Negro slave blood that runs in them today' (Mittelholzer: 1955, 8). It is significant, though, that each of them down-plays this aspect of their cultural ancestry, choosing instead to emulate their (white) European forebears and accepting their 'superior' status within a (post)colonial pigmentocracy.

It is tempting, in this context, to read the novel as an allegory of accultura-tion and of the 'lactification complex' that afflicts Caribbean societies (see Fanon: 1967, 30). Such a reading might account for the Nevinsons' condescension toward their black and/or Indian workers; it might also help explain Mr. Nevinson's and Woodsley's taste for European art. Most importantly, it might rationalise their joint decision to save the planter from perdition: for Voorman's blood is in their veins – theirs is a common history. Woodsley and the Nevinsons stake their claim on a European ancestry; yet as they stave off Voorman's demons, other ghosts come into their midst. These are their 'other' ancestors, the enslaved blacks on the plantations, and their 'absent presence' within the text signals a return of the Repressed. By the end of the novel, Woodsley and the Nevinsons are confronted with a subaltern history; they are made to recognise the past they had disclaimed as being their own.

Voorman ends his diary, which also ends the novel, with a premonition of slave rebellion. Still haunted by demons – the Blacker Ones – Voorman becomes increasingly desperate:

> Last night I heard them speaking in varied languages – languages I know not and yet which I myself spoke. I heard French and German and English and Italian and other tongues I could not identify . . . They babbled about me in a clamour too deafening to describe. They fumed and wreathed [*sic*] and turned in spirals . . . and the air thundered about me . . . A catastrophe threatens. I sense it in the air. I am a thwarted, craven soul, a human tottering on the edge of ultimate darkness. To whom, to what, must I turn for salvation?
>
> (Mittelholzer: 1955, 174)

Voorman's demons speak in European tongues: they ape the coloniser's language. Yet they also foreshadow an imminent end to white planter autocracy – they usher in, like Poe's Madeline, the downfall of an era, as the white man's fears of violent black revenge are reconfirmed. For Voorman's necromancy converges with the Berbice Slave Rebellion – an uprising that results in his own death and the slaughter of other white families. The white man's spell is broken; the other-worldly Blacker Ones – the emanations of a troubled unconscious – bring with them the ghostly tidings of a decisive break in history. (The date listed for the rebellion – 1763 – is all the more ironic in that it coincides with the year of the post-Seven Years War Caribbean Peace Treaty. Thus, at the very apex of British mercantile achievement comes a revolt that prefigures the fall of their, among other white, fortunes in Guyana.)

Mittelholzer's ghost story, then, seems to clear the space for an emancipatory history. It drives out one kind of demon in order to let in another; but these latter 'demons' are not just the incubi of white colonial history, they are the catalytic agents of revolutionary change. In laying Voorman's bones to rest and relieving themselves of the White Planter's Burden, Woodsley and the Nevinsons are forced to recognise a history they had previously suppressed. Mittelholzer, similarly, delivers himself from his white literary ancestors, acknowledging the influence of Poe and James but taking possession of them, either to turn their ghosts against themselves and render them insubstantial or to redeploy their racial fears as a means of reclaiming black agency.

My Bones and My Flute turns the tables on its literary predecessors. Rather than submitting to a Western (Euroamerican) 'anxiety of influence,' Caribbean texts such as Mittelholzer's use the conventions of the ghost story to expose the West to the anxieties of its own imposed authority. The flute – a Prosperan wand – is a generator of illusion; but it is equally deceptive for the person who controls it. Its primary function in the novel seems to be as a conductor for Voorman's evil thoughts and intentions; turning against him, it eventually becomes the instrument of his perdition. The flute also provides the means, however, for Voorman's own salvation and for the reconciliation of his followers to an 'inconceivable' past. Its function is therefore similar to that of the Carib/cannibal bone flute, even though Voorman's flute is made of metal and has no obvious 'tribal' affiliation. (Its closest symbolic connection, perhaps, is to the slave-owner's branding-iron – on more than one occasion, the invisible flute sears its victim's flesh.) The bone flute remains peripheral to Mittelholzer's text: it is a spectral presence hovering around the novel's title credits. Nonetheless, the flute (like Mozart's, to which it more obviously alludes) works a generalised kind of intertextual/cultural alchemy. It releases the collective ghosts of Guyana's ancestral past; not all of these ghosts are a figment of the white imagination. *My Bones and My Flute* is, after all, a creolised form of the Western ghost story: it owes as much to Amerindian as to European sources. It is precisely in the syncretism of its forms that Mittelholzer's novel works its magic: in the weaving together of disparate, nominally hostile creative traditions, and in the production of a countermemory to Caribbean material history – one which willingly rehearses the traumas of a brutal past, but then transmutes them into a vision of change that moves beyond catastrophe.

Transubstantiating hostility

In *My Bones and My Flute*, Woodsley's and the Nevinsons' quest is eventually cathartic: it allows them to confront and accept a hidden aspect of their past by staging the in/resurrection of their ghostly slave ancestors. In Harris's *Palace of the Peacock*, ancestral memory stretches back further, taking in the European myth of the New World El Dorado and uncovering behind it a rich array of different 'sources.' Ostensibly, Harris's novel recounts the quest for El Dorado within the context of a latter-day journey to (and beyond) an Amerindian Mission. The plot, however, like the journey, is impossibly convoluted, not least because Harris's novel oscillates between past and present. The journey takes place in a dreamtime where history merges with myth and legend, and where the fated expeditions of de Berrio, de Vera, and Raleigh are interlaced with creation myths from both Amerindian and Judaeo-Christian traditions. El Dorado is the meeting-place, the Source of all these sources. But the City of Gold remains, as of course it must, just out of reach; and each successive quest to find it is condemned to re-enact defeat. V.S. Naipaul has captured well the compulsiveness of the delusion, as the 'original' story passed from mouth to mouth, leaving more deaths in its wake:

> There had been a golden man, el dorado, the gilded one, in what is now Colombia: a chief who once a year rolled in turpentine, was covered in gold dust and then dived into a lake. But the tribe of the golden man had been conquered a generation before Columbus came to the New World. It was an Indian memory that the Spaniards pursued; and the memory was confused with the legend, among jungle Indians, of the Peru the Spaniards had already conquered.
>
> (Naipaul: 1984, 18)

For Naipaul, El Dorado presents a cautionary tale of repeated New World failure. The story outruns, outlasts, and eventually engulfs its actors, revealing the spiritual vacuum behind their dreams of material wealth. Harris's view of El Dorado is, however, somewhat different. He sees an 'instinctive idealism' associated with the adventure, even though he recognises that these ideals usually give way to greed and cruelty. El Dorado represents a chain of contradictory correspondences; in uncovering these correspondences in *Palace of the Peacock*, Harris gestures toward the reversal 'of the "given" conditions of the past, freeing oneself from catastrophic idolatry and blindness to one's own historical and philosophical conceptions and misconceptions which may bind one within a statuesque present or a false future' (Harris: 1967, 36).

The ghost is a primary instrument of this historical reversal; for the mixed-race crew that sets up-river in search of the Mariella Mission are ghosts returned from the dead to confront, once more, their own mortality. Mariella, the expedition leader Donne's former Amerindian mistress, now pursued by him to the secluded jungle Mission that bears her name, is herself described as a phantom, a ghostly object of desire. Mariella, at once executioner and victim, pursuer and pursued, becomes a symbol in the novel for the circularity of desire. Her presence, restored in the figure of the ancient Arawak woman, is a reminder to the crew not of what they might gain but of what they have already lost. For as they move beyond the Mission into increasingly dangerous territory, they condemn themselves to a 'second death,' as inevitable as the first:

> It was all well and good they reasoned as inspired madmen would to strain themselves to gain that elastic frontier where a spirit might rise from the dead and rule the material past world. All well and good was the resurgence and reconnoitre they reasoned. But it was doomed again from the start to meet endless catastrophe: even the ghost one dreams

of and restores must be embalmed and featured in the old lineaments of empty and meaningless desire.

(Harris: 1985, 80)

The ghost is the lack inscribed in their material ambitions; and it is the talisman that presages their own repeated destruction. It reminds them, too, that the past returns to batten on the present; that there is no escape from the phantoms (re)produced by a guilty conscience. [. . .]

The ghost – that which returns – reinscribes a legacy of shame and fear: a legacy associated elsewhere with the involuntary memory of cannibalism. The cannibal act is linked most closely to the expedition leader Donne, whose relentless greed and cruelty amount in the novel to 'an incalculable devouring principle' (ibid., 79). Yet Donne draws others, too, into a blasphemous communion: the fish the narrator eats becomes 'a morsel of recollection,' a 'memory spring[ing] from nowhere into [his] belly and experience' (ibid., 48); while Donne, the spectre released from a history of cannibal savagery, becomes 'an apparition stoop[ing] before him and cloth[ing] him with the frightful nature of the jungle,' striking him dumb with the knowledge that he has swallowed 'a morsel of terror' (ibid., 52). Donne, here, is the uncanny cannibal, forcing the past into the present, bringing with him unwanted memories and previously ingested secrets. The terror that he induces owes to the yoking of two forces: the all-devouring incorporative principle of the ferocious cannibal and the uncontainable mnemonic power of the surreptitious ghost. Violent assimilation, inexorable repetition: these are the forces that propel the crew toward renewed destruction. And they are also the forces that lock them in an incestuous alliance. For the crew are all related: they are, quite literally, 'one spiritual family' (ibid., 39) – and cannibalism, as resurrected through the figure of the predatory ghost, is, as Lévi-Strauss reminds us, 'the alimentary form of incest' (Lévi-Strauss: 1981a, 141). Cannibalism, like incest, is a rudimentary form of violation: it transgresses the social boundaries that separate us from kith and kin. And yet, as Harris suggests, it is also born of the need for kinship: cannibalism, again like incest, is a disallowed form of symbiosis. It is this conjunctive aspect to the cannibal infraction that Harris draws upon and absorbs, in turn, into his own 'cannibalistic' text. Thus, whereas in *My Bones and My Flute* the 'cannibal ghost' is a primarily phobic entity, a manifestation of the white man's racial fears and paranoid fantasies, in *Palace of the Peacock* it provides the reminder of a productive violation, displaying the incestuous ties that bond together a Creole (Caribbean) people.

Over and against the Donnean principle of cannibal devoration, Harris asserts a counter-principle of alchemical transformation. The cannibal/ghost alliance – a Donnean conceit if there ever was one – forms the bonding agent that produces an unlikely metamorphosis. This metamorphosis, as Michael Gilkes has suggested, is best seen in alchemical terms as a process of psychic reintegration. Here it is Jung, rather than Freud or Lévi-Strauss, who captures best the nature of Harris's project. Historically, says Jung,

[Alchemy] was a work of reconciliation between two apparently incompatible opposites which, characteristically, were understood not merely

as the natural hostility of the physical elements but at the same time
as a moral conflict. Since the object of the endeavour was seen outside
as well as inside, as both physical and psychic, the work extended as
it were through the whole of nature, and its goal consisted in a symbol
which had an empirical and at the same time a transcendental aspect.

(Jung: 1970, 554)

The relevance of Jung's quotation to Harris's novel need hardly be stressed; it
might serve, indeed, as an epitaph to the novel's final, epiphanic sequence, where
the crew-members, meeting their second deaths, consumed by their own will-to-
consumption, realise that 'the wall that had divided [them] from their true
otherness' is nothing other than 'a web of dreams' (Harris: 1985, 114). The recognition of 'otherness,' and of the 'otherness' in themselves, allows them to cancel
the 'forgotten fear of strangeness and catastrophe in a destitute world' (ibid., 116)
and to free themselves from their obsessive desire for material possession. Reborn
to themselves, they are reawakened to the world which they see now in its unity;
their need for each other fades into the vision of 'one muse and one undying soul'
(ibid., 117). This vision seems to hold as well for the novel's intertextual project:
its integration of Western writers working within the Symbolic tradition (the
Metaphysicals; Hopkins; Eliot, Yeats, and Conrad) into a unifying pattern of regen-
erative myth. What is interesting in Harris's case, however, is the attention he
pays to context: the violent New World encounters that act as a backdrop to
Donne's devotionals; the 'savagery' that Conrad locates at the heart of modern
European civilisation. Like Mittelholzer, then, Harris plays on the fears of his
European ancestors, 'inhabiting' their texts, preying upon them like a ghost; but
also transforming them into actors in a New World spiritual drama, a kind of
passion play which moves beyond the Manichaean categories of Good and Evil. So
whereas Mittelholzer releases the racialised spectres that lurk behind the Western
ghost story, giving them material form as agents of revolutionary vengeance, Harris
invites the cannibal and the ghost to link their other-worldly fingers and to perform
together the alchemical work of transubstantiation.

In *Palace of the Peacock*, the cannibal ghost is an inspiring, muse-like figure; it
is transformed from a source of terror into a vehicle of reconciliation. This transformation both resubstantiates the immateriality of memory and dematerialises the
act of conquest by giving it a spectral form. The cannibal and the ghost are, in
this sense, collaborators in paradox: the one breaks down divisions between the
eater and the eaten, 'creat[ing] a total identity between [them] while insisting on
the unreciprocal and yet ultimately total control – the literal consumption – of the
latter by the former' (Kilgour: 1990, 7); the other bridges the gap between
the actual and the imaginary, producing a hybrid entity that straddles ontological
realms. The cannibal ghost, along with the instrument that brings it into being,
the Carib bone flute, produces an uneasy harmony from apparently incompatible
elements. At the same time, it is a symbol of radical discontinuity (the internal-
isation of the fragmented body; the defiance of solid form). In this second sense,
it features as an agent of countermemory, disrupting a view of history that insists
on continuous progress. Countermemory, in Michel Foucault's formulation,
consists of three components: 'The first of these is parodic, directed against reality,

and opposes the theme of history as reminiscence or recognition; the second is dissociative, directed against identity, and opposes history given as continuity or representative of a tradition; the third is sacrificial, directed against truth, and opposes history as knowledge' (Foucault: 1984, 93).

The cannibal ghost inhabits the interstices of the recognisable past; its discontinuous form eludes attempts at historical identification. The countermemory it instantiates functions on a principle of uncontrollable heterogeneity; the history it perceives 'will not discover a forgotten identity . . . but a complex system of . . . multiple elements, unable to be mastered by the powers of synthesis' (ibid., 94). For Harris, cannibal countermemory opposes European history: it fragments the vision of time that underpins an ideology of conquest. The cannibal ghost, however, reinstitutes a form of collective remembrance; it absorbs and synthesises, if in a new substantive form. Here, then, are the two conflicting aspects of Harris's 'dialectic of alteration': on the one hand, a countermemory that challenges reminiscence, and that delivers itself from the 'origins' that Europe has imposed upon it; on the other, an equal and opposite move toward mythic transcendence, restoring collective memory but elevating it to a higher form. This dialectic remains unresolved. The cannibal absorbs the 'other'; the 'other' returns – as a ghost. Yet this cycle of repetition, this pattern of what Harris calls 'infinite rehearsal,' need not be seen in terms of alienation or imprisonment; instead, it asserts the principle of creole transmutation, as Caribbean writers, inspired by the bone flute, reinvent their region – and themselves.

[. . .]

Chapter 29

AUDREY YUE

PREPOSTEROUS HONG KONG HORROR

Rouge's (be)hindsight and *A* (sodomitical) *Chinese Ghost Story*

A NALYSES OF HONG KONG cinema are a recent phenomenon, prompted by Hong Kong's 1984–1997 period of transition from capitalist British colonial rule to communist Chinese sovereignty, as well as the current success of the industry in Hollywood and elsewhere. These analyses generally prioritise two dominant genres: the arthouse, auteur cinema of Stanley Kwan, Wong Kar-wai, Ann Hui and Clara Law, and the martial arts and high octane styles of Jackie Chan, Jet Li, John Woo, Ringo Lam and Tsui Hark. Converging on either the filmmaker or the male action hero, they highlight the mainstreaming of Hong Kong cinema in the international, indigenous and cult arenas. This chapter seeks to break away from the global dominance of such analyses, however, by focussing instead on the marginal tropes of horror and queer. *Rouge* (1987), a romance melodrama, and *A Chinese Ghost Story* (1987), a martial arts period comedy, deploy a queer practice that I shall call 'preposterous' – a practice which may lend support to the claim that horror occupies a central logic in Hong Kong's modern identity crisis.

The term *praeposterus* is a Latin derivative, from *prae*, in the front, followed by *posterus*, at the back. Contrary to nature, reason or sense, the 'preposterous' functions as a site for cinema to articulate both the absurd and the belated. This positional logic resonates with Hong Kong's identity crisis during the transitional years. The signing of the Sino-British Joint Declaration in 1984, which authorised Hong Kong's return to China, produced 1997 as a form of consciousness which anticipated loss, separation and reunification. But the direction forward was also a movement back to where it had already been: as a British colony in cessation, Hong Kong was to be reunited with China, its 'motherland.' 1997 was thus marked as a turning point involving a paradox of time and space: the movement towards this moment finds itself on the other side (post-), but at the same point that it was before (pre-). Such a positional logic exemplifies the preposterous and expresses Hong Kong's pre-post-1997 identity.

This identity can also be queer because it emphasises the discourse of what Lee Edelman calls '(be)hindsight,' where the posterior is privileged in order to destabilise normative positionality. '(Be)hindsight,' he says, is a 'rhetorical substitution of cause for effect or effect for cause, a substitution that disturbs the relationship of early and late, or before and behind' (Edelman: 1991, 96). It is a kind of curved movement, synchronicising the past (pre-) and the future (post-) in such a way that in the movement forward, a destination is reached through a turning point that is the same as the point of departure, but *on the other side*. This movement underpins the foundational logic of Hong Kong's identity crisis which, like the moebius loop, was marked by its inability to distinguish the 'pre-' from the 'post-' or the front from the back. Characterised by an absurd set of representations which see front and back, pre- and post-, before and after, as undifferentiated, this movement also finds articulation in the preposterous horror of two films made a decade earlier, *Rouge* and *A Chinese Ghost Story*.

The emergence of Hong Kong horror in the late 1980s came in the midst of this spectre of return, unleashing a phantasmagoria of moods, attitudes and beliefs. From the symbolic to the imaginary, the material to the metaphysical, the real to the unconscious, East-West dilemmas found themselves processed and contested in this genre through competing postcolonial and postmodern chronotopes. The genre itself was many-faceted, marked by vampire movies (*Mr Vampire* [1985], *Vampire's Breakfast* [1987], *New Mr Vampire* [1986], *Doctor Vampire* [1990]), ghost stories (*A Chinese Ghost Story*, *Picture of a Nymph* [1988], *My Cousin the Ghost* [1987]), reincarnation themes (*Rouge*, *Reincarnation of the Golden Lotus* [1989], *Spiritual Love* [1987], *Dream Lovers* [1986]) and Category 111 slasher-styled blaxploitation films (*Doctor Lamb* [1992], *The Untold Story* [1993], *Remains of a Woman* [1993]).

Hong Kong horror has indeed been seen as a hybrid amalgamation of Eastern and Western imaginings: this is, at least, the perspective of Hong Kong International Film Festival elites, who produce local retrospectives alongside this annual international event. In *Phantoms of the Hong Kong Cinema* (1989), festival curator and editor Li Cheuk-to describes Hong Kong horror as 'a heterodoxy of genre combinations,' where horror incorporates other elements borrowed from kung-fu, comedy, thrillers, science fiction, melodrama and the opera film (Li Cheuk-to: 1989, 9). Mobilising indigenous sources from legends, folklore and the supernatural and mixing them with different Western devices of narrativity, this heterodoxy makes the genre a showcase for Hong Kong cinema's East-West identity. Sek Kei, another contributor to this volume, claims that the significant feature of horror films in the 1980s is its 'active mingling of Chinese and foreign spooks' (Sek Kei: 1989, 14). Hong Kong vampire movies certainly show off this feature, with a formula comprising Manchu-costumed vampires, Daoist priests and the bloodsucking contagious qualities of the Western Dracula. They produce an ambivalent milieu where ghosts are modernized in a modernity that nevertheless longs for traditionalism. Stephen Teo argues that the central presence of Daoism in these films reveals an ideology that resonates with postmodern Hong Kong's renegotiation of its East-West liminality – by 'betraying the stubborn survival of premodern ways of thinking beyond the historical moment where they ought to have died, just like the cadavers' (Teo: 1997, 224). He suggests that horror cinema's reincarnation themes, through their recognition of old forms persisting in the new, express Hong Kong's fundamental hybridity, caught between Western capitalism and Chinese communism.

Both *Rouge* and *A Chinese Ghost Story* are certainly hybrid forms. Like most period horror films, their narratives are loosely based on aspects of Pu Songling's classical text, *Laozhai Zhiyi* (*Strange Tales from a Chinese Studio*). *Laozhai Zhiyi*'s canonic status has inspired a diverse range of Chinese and Asian cultural productions: Japanese filmmaker Kenji Mizoguchi's horror classic, *Ugetsu Monogatari* (1953), and popular Hong Kong writer Li Bihua's novella, *Yanzhi kou* (1986), are two examples. Drawing directly on *Yanzhi kou*, *Rouge* was co-adapted into a screenplay by Li Bihua and Yau Dai On-ping. Its filmic aesthetics can in turn be traced back to *Ugetsu Monogatari*. Similarly, *A Chinese Ghost Story* is a cinematic remake of Li Hanxing's 1966 film, *The Enchanting Shadow*, another horror film enabled by *Laozhai Zhiyi*. Stephen Teo thus rightly describes *A Chinese Ghost Story* as a film situated within 'the Chinese literary tradition,' as well as 'a costumed adventure, a Hollywood-style special effects extravaganza. . . .' (ibid., 219). Occidental film reviewer Alan Stanbrook, in an article commissioned by the Hong Kong International Film Festival committee, hails *Rouge* as a 'masterpiece' because it also resembles the arthouse styles of Michelangelo Antonioni and Max Ophuls (Stanbrook: 1991, 50). These allegiances to European, Japanese, Cantonese and Mandarin cinematic and literary sources reflect a position that emphasises hybridity both in form and content – and highlight what is literally a Hong Kong pre-occupation with the question of 1997.

Both *Rouge* and *A Chinese Ghost Story* were produced a decade earlier, during a year that witnessed the heightened effect of Hong Kong's panic consciousness when British National Overseas passports were replaced by British Dependent Territories passports, the Hang Seng Index fell 1000 points in a single day, and the Hong Kong Stock Exchange was forced to close for almost a week. They use horror to express this culture by employing three similar tropes. Firstly, they both deploy the figure of the female ghost, usually as noir-like *femme fatale* prostitutes and seductresses. In an industry stereotypically dominated by the male action hero, from Bruce Lee and Jackie Chan to John Woo and Chow Yun-Fatt, the use of the female ghost as a main protagonist marks the emergence of issues of gender and sexual difference in contemporary Hong Kong cinema. This is especially pertinent when such a figure is both sexually desirable and desiring, characterised by her preposterous narrative function as a feminised *yin* energy serving to emplot and trap the masculinised *yang* energy. In both films, the female ghost must either lure or seek out the male protagonist to resolve the narratives' reincarnation quests. Ng Ho writes that the use of the breath of *yang* to signify life is one of the defining characteristics of the Hong Kong horror genre (Ng Ho: 1989, 31). Clearly, gender and sexual differences function in this absurdly spectacular performance as sites for the articulation of a cinema's increasing self-awareness – a feature which broadly resonates with Hong Kong's heightened panic consciousness as it confronts its own difference from both one (British capitalist) system and the other (Chinese communist) system.

Secondly, the wandering ghost captures the transitional theme of reincarnation. Both films focus on the Buddhist themes of transmigration as a metaphor for Hong Kong's own changing predicament. Caught between the boundaries of the past and the present, life and death, the real and the virtual, the netherworld in these films symbolises the passage of Hong Kong-in-transition, where the narrative of the homeless female ghost becomes a narrative about the quest for home. But the act of transmigration takes the theme of reincarnation to another level: home is (re)inscribed within the trope of homelessness, in-between the frontiers of 'here' and 'there,' 'inside' and 'outside,' and 'home' and 'host.' These Hong Kong horror films thus present the question of 1997 as an allegory inhabited by authoritative demons, unappeased ghosts and wandering spirits that reflect the territory's resignation to the destiny of its fate. Unable to speak directly to the Sino-British Joint Declaration which authorised Hong Kong's return, they present the dilemma of homelessness as both doom and dissent.

Thirdly, *Rouge* and *A Chinese Ghost Story* are period films which evoke nostalgic sensibilities. *Rouge* uses a ghost from the 1930s who returns to Hong Kong in 1987 to induce a narrative commentary about the present and its longing for the past. Like the Hong Kong vampire movies, *A Chinese Ghost Story* deploys the traditions of the supernatural, Daoism and Buddhism to ward off the evil spirits of wandering ghosts. These nostalgic sensibilities parallel the territory's sudden and heightened belief (panic consciousness) in destiny and the supernatural. Expressing a simultaneous interest in the past, present and the future, they take us into a second perspective on Hong Kong cinema seminally presented through the work of Ackbar Abbas, who argues that Hong Kong horror exemplifies what he terms a 'culture of disappearance' (Abbas: 1997).

Underpinning the 'culture of disappearance' in Hong Kong is the effect of *déjà disparu*. Abbas describes this as 'the feeling that what is new and unique about the situation is always already gone, and we are left with holding a handful of clichés, or a cluster of memories of what has never been' (ibid., 25) – and he illustrates it through the figure of the ghost in *Rouge*. This film juxtaposes two temporalities and mobilises the device of flashback from the point-of-view of the female protagonist. The story revolves around Fleur, a courtesan in a brothel from the 1930s who returns as a ghost in contemporary Hong Kong to search for her lover, Twelve Master Chan. Since the only feature that distinguishes Fleur from her contemporary counterpart Ah Chor is her attire and her formal make-up, Abbas argues that the film challenges the ghost genre by suspending the supernatural in favour of the uncanny. This uncanniness, where absolute otherness gives way to an inability to distinguish the familiar from the unfamiliar, the present from the past, the old from the new, relates the figure of the ghost to what he calls 'the cinematization of space' (ibid., 41). In this space, the ghost and its uncanny cinematic image are dialectically reversible through replacement and substitution. Abbas's view that disappearance is a consequence of 'reverse hallucination' supports this argument. He suggests that Fleur's ghost evokes David Harvey's 'time-space compression' (ibid., 41), encapsulating Hong Kong as a cinematic image because it expresses a spectral presence elucidated by the authority of the electronic simulation. Abbas refers here to the turbo-capitalism of Hong Kong, where the speed of the circulation of information and technology has resulted in the collapse of the analogue. This collapse has produced a city mediated by technological and digital reproduction – where representational visibility has given way to informational visuality. The ghost as a simulated image thus provides a means of identification for Hong

Kong. Abbas also argues that *Rouge* is a nostalgia film that recodes the expression
of decadence. Looking at moments when the narrative juxtaposes and confuses
emotions from the 1930s world of baroque, theatre, opera and leisure with the
1980s milieu of urbanity, emotional inertia and alienation, Abbas points to the
production of nostalgia as a dis-location that mutates the old and the new and blurs
the boundaries between what might otherwise be different.

While Abbas's arguments are critically insightful, his concept of disappearance
is theoretically problematic. The production of 'reverse hallucination' sees the
figure of the ghost and its cinematic simulation exemplify the culture of disappearance as an entirely negative operation. Appearance is condemned to refer back
to disappearance, reinforcing or hiding behind it under a modernist logic of transparency and opacity. Equating the figure of the simulated ghost with the time-space
compression of global capitalism, Abbas conceptualises Hong Kong in a temporality that leaves no space for its *spatiality*. By arguing that the ghost and its
simulation are metonymically substituted for one another, Abbas fixes space through
an abstraction defined only by its relation to technological forces of (re)produc-
tion. This logic fetishises and feminises time as an other, consumed and exhausted
in the service of the ephemerality of commodity, information and capital – a view
which thus reifies the alienation it wishes to describe. Finally, Abbas's use of the
apparition of 1997 to theorise Hong Kong as a cultural formation that has *already*
disappeared in fact echoes the perspective of the Hong Kong film festival elites
discussed earlier. Stephen Teo, for example, concludes his 1997 British Film
Institute book, *Hong Kong Cinema: The Extra Dimensions*, with a portentous chapter
entitled 'Postmodernism and the End of Hong Kong Cinema' (Teo: 1997, 243–56).
Here, Hong Kong cinema is reposed romantically, celebrated as emanating from
a culture that is either vanishing or has already perished. This episteme is premised
on the splitting of 1997 into two distinct stages. It suggests that, by separating the
'pre-' from the 'post-,' Hong Kong cinema can be periodised so as to protect it
from post-1997 hegemonic subsumption. It is recovered here as a form of 'national'
culture, one that does not allow for the complexities and ambivalence of its place
within the transnational contradictions of modernity. Inadvertently, it runs the risk
of leaving Hong Kong cinema suspended, to be locked, lost and effaced in 1997
time.

The cultural critic Rey Chow offers a rethinking of nostalgia as a way of coming
to terms with identity crisis in the postcolonial space of Hong Kong. Her own
reading of *Rouge* suggests a reversed form of nostalgia, where nostalgia's structure
of feeling is experienced as a temporal displacement. The flashback images of Fleur
evoke 'the *filmic-image-as-nostalgia*' and embody 'nostalgia's ambivalence between
dream and reality . . . [and] insistence on seeing "concrete" things in fantasy and
memory' (Chow: 1993, 64). The nostalgic film image registers as a 'movement
of temporality' which imagines identity not as an attempt to retrieve the past, but
as an effect of dislocation in time (ibid., 74). For Chow, nostalgia expresses itself
in 'compressed forms' where 'the fantasies of time' are indexed through 'a loop,
a throw, a network of chance, rather than a straight line' (ibid., 61). Positioning
Fleur as a character in a story supposedly told by herself, Chow sees her as an
image rather than, say, a voice or a gaze. Because the temporal effect of Fleur's
flashbacks visualises the character as a 'larger-than-life "other" with strong, moral

beliefs that are out-of-sync with contemporary times,' Chow also suggests that this image offers a way of imagining an alternative, albeit mythical, identity and community. This temporal dislocation thus expresses an aesthetic that idealises the past alongside 'a submission to chance, fate, physiognomy, *feng shui* (geomancy), and other varieties of *shushu* (techniques of calculating the unknown)' (ibid., 74).

Such an aesthetic is exemplified in her reading of the film's opening sequence, the first encounter between the two lovers, Fleur and Chan. The sequence begins with Fleur dressed as a male impersonator, performing Cantonese opera in front of her patrons. It is intercut with stylised shots of Chan ascending the brothel stairs, following Fleur's seductive voice as she sings to the 1920s southern tune of Bai Jurong's well-known and highly-acclaimed opera classic, *Ke tu qiu hen*. As Chan enters the room and discovers Fleur, the music stops. Interrupted by each other for a moment, Fleur then resumes her song: 'Look at the pair of swallows against the setting sun.' For Chow this visual encounter, when inserted alongside Fleur's performance, relays the object of the song – the melancholy pining of a scholar for a courtesan-songstress – as a site underscored by the agency of chance: 'it was as if the song were flowing down the stairs looking for an object, and it found [Chan]' (ibid., 71). The meeting between the two lovers and the historical text of the song expresses the film's nostalgia for 'older tales, legends and romances' with the lovers becoming the song's 'actualization and self-fulfillment' (ibid., 72).

However, nostalgia here is a belated construction marked by what I would call the preposterous logic of (be)hindsight. Although the lovers clearly do function as the song's self-actualisation, Chow does not say what makes both the song's foreplay and its consequent fulfillment possible. Is it 'a submission to chance' that sees Fleur dressed as a man? Is it chance that Fleur, played by Anita Mui – one of Cantopop's top-billing singers and actors (a.k.a. the 'Hong Kong Madonna') – is renowned for her handsome, definitive facial features and deep sultry voice? Is it chance that Chan, played by Leslie Cheung Kwok-wing, is portrayed as a stereotypical dandy, ineffectual and delicate – and that, as another of Cantopop's top-billing stars, Cheung is a recently 'out' homosexual? Is it chance that director Stanley Kwan himself enounces a half-in, half-out gay identity in his film *Yang-Yin* (1996)? If we consider how chance encounters are queered in *Rouge*, can this romantic encounter be recast as a moment in the meeting of same-sex desire? Although she notices that Fleur is dressed as a man, Chow ignores this to focus on the narrative of the song, thus maintaining the love story's heterosexual matrix. But if the narrative of melancholic loss involves 'a feeling looking for an object' (Chow: 1993, 61), what has nostalgia found in the object that is Chan? As an object caught by nostalgia, Chan may indeed embody the compressed images of melancholia which speak to the temporal form of displacement characteristic of Hong Kong's identity crisis. If so, then what loop or deviation from the straight line does Chan narrate *in addition* to Chow's discussion of temporal displacement? In other words, how does the object that is Chan signify the preposterous?

At the other end of *Rouge*, in the final scene, Fleur encounters an aged Chan at a film studio. As the only moment in the narrative when the two lovers are reunited, it functions as a narrative loop that synchronises two disjunctive temporalities: 1937 and 1987. This loop thus represents '1987' as the preposterous moment that enables the narrative of 'post-1937' to come in the time of 'pre-

1937.' Fleur and Chan's previous encounter was in fact *in* 1937, when their joint suicide pact failed and the lovers were prevented from union in the afterlife because one survived and the other did not. The final scene thus stages the lovers' reunion as a belated event. As a preposterous way of constituting reunification, it exposes the contemporaneous 'truth' underpinning Fleur's apparitional quest. When Fleur meets Chan in 1987 and realises that Chan was never serious about their suicide pact, Fleur's (be)hindsight enables the narratives of pre-1937 and post-1937 Chan to emerge. Separated by Fleur's death but synchronised in the loop of 1987, Chan – as both quest and truth – thus expresses the preposterous as a belated apparitional event. Their contemporary meeting disrupts the straightforward narrative quest by staging the reunion as a preposterous encounter that is at once constitutive and destructive, a belated event that happens only through a life-after-death. Seen allegorically, it expresses a self-consciousness surrounding the fifty years of transition underpinning post-1997 Hong Kong's one country-two system reunification. The benefit of our own (be)hindsight thus enables this preposterous horror film to be read as destabilising its normative narrative by simultaneously articulating same-sex desire and the myth of reunification, as well as – given the background set in this final scene, comprising flying swordsmen with ropes visibly tied to their waists, showing off (equally preposterously) the film's expertise in choreographed action, special effects and self-consciously revealed optical illusions – the globally popular status of Hong Kong action cinema.

It also reflects the cultural capital of its star phenomenon. Stars are shifting signifiers, reflecting the signs and times of their society both within and without its own indigenous codes (see Dyer: 1980, 1986, 1992; Gledhill: 1991). During the transition years, cultural desires invested in Hong Kong Cantopop stars highlighted the cinema as a site for negotiating anxiety surrounding reunification. The immense popularity of Stephen Chow Sing Chi, for example, illustrates this star phenomenon clearly. Creating *molaytau* nonsensical dialogues by linguistically hybridising Cantonese, English and Mandarin, Chow generated a *nonsense* genre of his very own, promoted, circulated and consumed in the mainstream as 'a Stephen Chow film.' Represented in films such as *Fight Back to School* (1991) and *A Chinese Odyssey* (1995), this nonsensical unsettlement of linguistic normativity is also reflected in the consumption and codification of other stars who engender different modes of destabilisation. We can see this in the deployment of Cheung as the leading male protagonist in both *Rouge* and *A Chinese Ghost Story*. Prior to coming out in 1993, Cheung had performed only straight roles – in which case, again with the benefit of (be)hindsight, the paradigm of queerness can be used to read *A Chinese Ghost Story* as narrating a destabilising discourse that similarly disrupts normative positionalities.

In this period fantasy martial arts thriller-cum-cult-classic, horror is staged both as a preposterous and a sodomitical encounter. Cheung plays a poverty-stricken, clumsy, travelling debt-collector who seeks refuge in a deserted and haunted temple. The temple is surrounded by hungry female ghosts who roam the nights seducing men, trapping their 'masculine' *yang* energy to appease their boss, Lord Black of Hell. Cheung falls in love with a ghost who is betrothed as a concubine in hell to Lord Black, and tries to save her. The story revolves around Cheung's rescue missions and his encounters with the dominatrix mistress who is the ghosts' pimp. Using quick cuts, close-ups, music videos, Cantopop songs and science fiction laser beams, infused with the traditions of martial arts, sorcery, sword play and Daoist ghost-busting rap chants, *A Chinese Ghost Story* is Hong Kong's first post-modern pastiche. English-language feminist film theorists Pam Cook, Barbara Creed and Linda Williams, appropriating the traditional narrative logics underpinning psychoanalysis and film, have written about the relationship between the horror film and women, and the repression of the feminine that is in turn unleashed when the woman-as-monster-vampire-ghost returns the gaze (Cook, 1985; Williams, 1984; Creed, 1993). Creed, for example, reconceptualises the status of the feminine through what she terms the 'monstrous-feminine's' seven 'faces,' represented as archaic mother, monstrous womb, vampire, witch, possessed body, monstrous woman and castrator. She argues that man fears woman *as* castrator, rather than as castrated. Perhaps comparing with Creed's mobilisation of the monstrous-feminine around the trope of *the vagina dentata* in her reading of the *Alien* trilogy (Creed: 1993, 16–30), the dominatrix pimp-tree-monster in *A Chinese Ghost Story*, with its fifty-foot tongue that wraps and coils like a serpent, bears the image of a phallic tongue. Assuming both female and male voices that switch with the enunciation of each sentence, the phallic tongue is also represented in the film as bisexual. Indeed, with its place of origin stemming from the roots of a tree, it assumes the guise of a hermaphrodite tree monster, with elongated branches and roots sensually protruding like tongues, penises and arms.

A Chinese Ghost Story is not solely an articulation of the monstrous-feminine, however; the encounters between Cheung and the phallic tongue can also be seen as homoerotic, sodomitical moments which reenact Lee Edelman's metalepsis of (be)hindsight, discussed earlier. Their specular pleasures in fact recall Edelman's reading of Sigmund Freud's Wolf Man analysis, in which the radical indeterminacy of sexual identity cathects at the moment where the primal scene is centered around the Wolf Man's 'identification with the pleasure derived from (what he took to be) the penetration of the anus' (Edelman: 1991, 102–3). Freud suggested that three formulations surrounding castration anxiety, anal penetration and sexual identity could be generated from the child's observation of parental intercourse (Freud: 1955c, 1–122). Firstly, the child views this act as aggression on the part of the father. Secondly, the child is sexually excited and this excitement forms the basis for castration anxiety. Thirdly, the child interprets this act as anal penetration. These three formulations are based on Freud's stress on the deferred reading of the event, where meaning (the preoedipal child's interpretation) is attributed after the fact (of seeing sexually indeterminate parents). Edelman suggests that Freud's emphasis on anal penetration allows the primal scene to be 'perceived as sodomitical,' shaped as 'a sodomitical scene between sexually undifferentiated partners, both of whom, phantasmatically at least, are believed to possess the phallus' (Edelman: 1991, 101). In such a scenario, 'penetration' is 'both the act of penetrating and the act of being penetrated' (ibid., 103).

A Chinese Ghost Story's numerous extended scenes, where the pimp-tree-monster-phallic tongue's snapper-like jaws and sharp metallic incisors drip sticky, creamy, semen-like froth and frantically rim Cheung's gaping mouth, can easily be construed as sodomitical. This is particularly so in the film's fantastically visualised homoerotic encounters of thrusting forward and recoiling backward, where

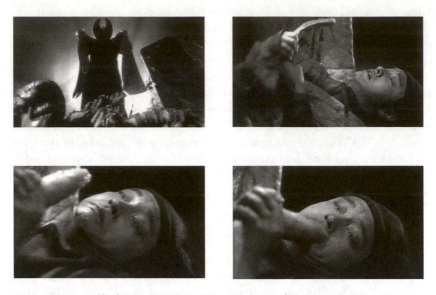

Figure 29.1 Stills from *A Chinese Ghost Story* (Media Asia 1987).

both Cheung and the tree monster are active and passive, top and bottom, dominant and submissive, penetrator and penetratee, all at the same time. In its desire
to penetrate Cheung from the front, the tree monster is also at the same time
surreptitiously desiring to be taken from the back. In this instance, the penis-
tongue tree monster disturbs Cheung's phallic positioning such that his anus-mouth
represents the posterior endowment of the castration complex which accompanies
the emergence of female sexuality. Cheung's anus-mouth is metaphorically equated
to the mother's vagina, so that Cheung is just like the man described by Edelman
– who 'from the front, is like his father from the front, is also, from the back,
like his mother *from the front*' (ibid., 105; original italics). As sexually undifferentiated and possessing the phallus, both Cheung and the monster specularise and
sodomise, taking from the front and from the back. Clearly, both the bisexual tree
monster and Cheung, in their double identification of the phantasmatic possession
of the phallus, incorporate the signs of castration as both desire and rejection.
Indeed, stemming from the film's generic hybrid of western, action, horror and
martial arts narrative plots, the *fabula* is constructed so that Cheung and the
tree monster must evidently both take each other on first in order to kill each
other. In this reconstitution from Cheung's (be)hindsight, heterosexual phallic
masculinity is worked upon to enable – literally – an opening for a homosexual
subjectivity.

Edelman suggests that the sodomite is himself like the moebius loop, enacting
'a troubling resistance to the binary logic of before and behind, constituting himself
as a single-sided surface whose front and back are never completely indistinguishable as such' (ibid., 105). Cheung's homosexual destabilisation of the film's narrative
may in this respect reflect or allegorise the positional logic of pre-post-1997 Hong
Kong. Underpinning the British colony's return to China is a crisis of identity and
certainty. Marked by its inability to distinguish the 'pre-' from the 'post-,' the

front from the back, this crisis — characterised by a destabilising episteme — constitutes modern Hong Kong's foundational logic. As in *Rouge*, instability in *A Chinese Ghost Story* is signified by the discourse of (be)hindsight, which privileges the posterior in order to destabilise normative positionality. This discourse, as we've seen, is 'preposterous,' visually fantastic and ridiculous; it is also queer because it signifies 'the disturbance of positionality that is located in and effected by the sodomitical scene; sodomy, that is, gets figured as the literalization of the "preposterous" precisely insofar as it is interpreted as the practice of giving precedence to the posterior and thus as confounding the stability or determinacy of linguistic or erotic positioning' (ibid., 104–5). It speaks in turn to the emergence of pre-post-1997 Hong Kong as a belated panic culture distinguished by foreboding, by the anticipation of loss, separation and reunification — as well as by an obsession with 1997 as a turning point marked by paradox, because the movement forward has already found itself on the other side that it was before. These otherwise marginal forms of preposterous horror cinema clearly function as exemplary models for articulating Hong Kong's identity crisis.

Notes on contributors

Stephen D. Arata is an Associate Professor of English at the University of Virginia. He is author of *Fictions of Loss in the Victorian Fin de Siècle*, and has written various articles on late-Victorian and modernist literature and culture. His Broadview Literary Texts edition of William Morris's *News from Nowhere* is forthcoming.

Philip Brophy teaches in Audio Visual Concepts in Media Arts at the RMIT University, Melbourne. He has published articles on horror cinema and Japanese manga and organises the annual CINESONIC conferences. He blew up well-known Australian actor Lisa McCune's womb in his horror film, *Body Melt*.

Sue-Ellen Case is a Professor of Theater and Dance at the University of California, Davis. She is author of *Feminism and Theatre* and *The Domain-Matrix: Performing Lesbian at the End of Print Culture*. She has edited *Performing Feminisms: Feminist Critical Theory and Theatre* and *Split Britches: Lesbian Practice/Feminist Performance*, and is co-editor of *Cruising the Performative*.

Terry Castle is a Professor of English at Stanford University, California. Her books include *Clarissa's Ciphers: Meaning & Disruption In Richardson's 'Clarissa'*, *Masquerade and Civilisation: The Carnivalesque in Eighteenth-Century English Culture and Fiction*, *The Female Thermometer: Eighteenth-Century Culture and the Invention of the Uncanny*, *The Apparitional Lesbian: Female Homosexuality and Modern Culture* and *Noël Coward & Radclyffe Hall: Kindred Spirits*.

Carol J. Clover is a Professor of Rhetoric at the University of California, Berkeley. She is author of *The Medieval Saga* and *Men, Women and Chainsaws: Gender in* *the Modern Horror Film*, and is co-author of a book on Stan Douglas, a Canadian cinematic artist. She is also co-editor of *Old Norse-Icelandic Literature: A Critical Guide*.

Joan Copjec teaches in English, Media Study and Comparative Literature at the University of Buffalo, New York, where she is also Director of the Center for the Study of Psychoanalysis and Culture. She is author of *Read My Desire: Lacan against the Historicists*, and *The Ethics of the Absolute All: Sex, Sublimation, and the Body* (forthcoming). She has edited numerous books, including *Jacques Lacan's Television*, *Shades of Noir* and *Radical Evil*.

Barbara Creed is an Associate Professor in Cinema Studies at the University of Melbourne. She is author of *The Monstrous-Feminine: Film, Feminism, Psychoanalysis*, and co-editor of *Don't Shoot Darling! Women's Independent Filmmaking in Australia*.

Ken Gelder is a Reader in English at the University of Melbourne. He is author of *Reading the Vampire* and *Atomic Fiction: The Novels of David Ireland*, and is co-author of *The New Diversity: Australian Fiction 1970–1988* and *Uncanny Australia: Sacredness and Identity in a Postcolonial Nation*. He has edited *R. L. Stevenson: The Scottish Stories and Essays* and *The Oxford Book of Australian Ghost Stories* and is co-editor of *The Subcultures Reader*.

Teresa A. Goddu teaches in the English Department at Vanderbilt University, Nashville, Tennessee. She is author of *Gothic America: Narrative, History and Nation*.

Marie-Hélène Huet is M. Taylor Pyne Professor of French at Princeton University. She is author of *Rehearsing the Revolution: The Staging of Marat's Death, 1793–1797*, *Monstrous Imagination*, and most recently, *Mourning Glory: The Will of the French Revolution*.

Graham Huggan is a Professor of English at the University of Munich. He is author of *A Tale of Two Parrots: Walcott, Rhys, and the Uses of Colonial Mimicry*, *Peter Carey*, *Territorial Disputes: Maps and Mapping Strategies in Contemporary Canadian and Australian Fiction*, and *Critical Perspectives on J.M. Coetzee*.

Leon Hunt lectures in Film and Television Studies at Brunel University, Middlesex, England. He is author of *British Low Culture: From Safari Suits to Sexploitation* and has published work in *You Tarzan: Masculinity, Movies and Men*, *British Crime Cinema* and *Framework*.

Tania Modleski is a Professor of English at the University of Southern California, Los Angeles. She is author of *Loving with a Vengeance: Mass-Produced Fantasies for Women*, *The Women Who Knew Too Much: Hitchcock and Feminist Theory*,

Feminism Without Women: Culture and Criticism in a 'Postfeminist' Age, and *Old Wives' Tales, and Other Women's Stories*. She has edited *Studies in Entertainment: Critical Approaches to Mass Culture*.

José B. Monleon is a Professor of Spanish and Portuguese at the University of California, Los Angeles. He is the author of *A Specter is Haunting Europe: A Sociological Approach to the Fantastic*, and has produced an annotated edition of Becquer's *Leyendas*. He has published articles on vampires and the fantastic, as well as on various Spanish authors, modernism and postmodernism.

Franco Moretti is a Professor of Comparative Literature at Columbia University in New York. He is the author of *Signs Taken for Wonders: Essays in the Sociology of Literary Forms, The Way of the World: The Bildungsroman in European Culture, Modern Epic: The World-System from Goethe to Garcia Marquez*, and most recently, *Atlas of the European Novel 1800–1900*.

Paul O'Flinn is Chair of the Department of English Studies at Oxford Brookes University, England. He is author of *How to Study Romantic Poetry* and *Them and Us in Literature* and has recently published work in *Writing and Radicalism* and *Aliens: Across the Film/Fiction Divide*.

Fatimah Tobing Rony teaches in the Program in Film Studies at the University of California, Irvine. She is author of *The Third Eye: Race, Camera, and Ethnographic Spectacle*, and is writer and director of the film, *On Cannibalism*.

Mary Russo is a Professor in Humanities at Hampshire College, Amherst, Massachussetts. She is author of *The Female Grotesque: Risk, Excess, and Modernity*, and co-editor of *Revisioning Italy: National Identity and Global Culture*.

David Sanjek is the Director of the BMI Archives, New York City. He has published work in *Literature/Film Quarterly, Film Criticism, Cineaste* and *Cinema Journal*, and has chapters in *Sights on the Sixties, Re-Viewing British Cinema 1900–1992, The Films of Oliver Stone, CINESONIC: The World of Sound on Film, Film Genre 2000: New Critical Essays* and *The Trash Film Reader: Essays on Disreputable Film*.

Mark Seltzer is a Professor of English at Cornell University, Ithaca, New York. He is the author of *Bodies and Machines, Henry James and the Art of Power*, and *Serial Killers: Death and Life in American Wound Culture*.

Elaine Showalter is a Professor of English at Princeton University. She is author of *A Literature of Their Own: British Women Writers from Brontë to Lessing, The Female Malady: Women, Madness and English Culture, Sexual Anarchy: Gender and Culture in the Fin de Siècle, Sister's Choice: Tradition and Change in American Women's Writing* and *Hystories: Hysterical Epidemics and Modern*

Culture. She is co-author of *Hysteria Beyond Freud* and has edited a number of books, including *Speaking of Gender* and *Daughters of Decadence*.

Vivian Sobchack is an Associate Dean and Professor of Film and Television Studies at the School of Theatre, Film and Television, University of California, Los Angeles. The first woman elected president of the Society for Cinema Studies, she is now on the Board of Trustees of the American Film Institute. Her books include *Screening Space: The American Science Fiction Film, The Address of the Eye: A Phenomenology of Film Experience*, and *Carnal Thoughts: Bodies, Texts, Scenes and Screens* (forthcoming). She has edited *The Persistence of History: Cinema, Television and the Modern Event*, and *Meta-Morphing: Visual Transformation in the Culture of Quick Change*.

Tzvetan Todorov is a Director at the Centre de Recherches sur les Arts et le Langage in Paris. He is the author of many books; those available in English include *The Fantastic: A Structural Approach to a Literary Genre, The Poetics of Prose, Introduction to Poetics, Genres in Discourse, Mikhail Bakhtin: The Dialogical Principle, Symbolism and Interpretation, The Conquest of America: The Question of the Other* and most recently, *Facing the Extreme: Moral Life in the Concentration Camps*.

Elizabeth Young is Associate Professor of English and Chair of Film Studies at Mount Holyoke College. She has published essays on horror in *Camera Obscura* and *Feminist Studies* and is the author of *Disarming the Nation: Women's Writing and the American Civil War*.

Audrey Yue teaches in Cultural Studies at the University of Melbourne. Her doctoral research was on postcolonial Hong Kong cinema. She has published articles in *New Formations, Asian Journal of Communication, Meanjin* and *Journal of Homosexuality*.

Gregory A. Waller is a Professor of English at the University of Kentucky. He is author of *The Stage/Screen Debate: A Study in Popular Aesthetics, The Living and the Undead: From Stoker's Dracula to Romero's Dawn of the Dead*, and *Main Street Amusements: Movies and Commercial Entertainment in a Southern City, 1896–1930*. He has edited *American Horrors: Essays on the Modern American Horror Film*.

Patricia White is an Assistant Professor in English and Film Studies at Swarthmore College, Pennsylvania. She is author of *Uninvited: Classical Hollywood Cinema and Lesbian Representability*, and has published widely on issues of feminism and film.

Jennifer Wicke is a Professor of English at the University of Virginia. She is author of *Advertising Fictions: Literature, Advertisement and Social Reading*, and co-editor of *Feminism and Postmodernism*. She has published chapters in *Marketing Modernisms, Centuries' Ends, Narrative Means* and *Dirty Looks: Women, Pornography, Power,* and articles in a number of journals including *South Atlantic Quarterly, Boundary 2, The Yale Journal of Criticism, Critical Quarterly* and *Novel*.

Slavoj Žižek is a Researcher at the Institute for Sociology, Ljubljana, Slovenia. He is the author of numerous books, including *The Sublime Object of Ideology, For They Know Not What They Do: Enjoyment as a Political Factor, Looking Awry: An Introduction to Jacques Lacan Through Popular Culture, The Metastases of Enjoyment: Six Essays on Women and Casuality, The Plague of Fantasies, The Ticklish Subject* and *Tarrying with the Negative*. He is also editor of *Everything You Wanted to Know About Lacan (But Were Afraid to Ask Hitchcock)*. He now has his own Reader, devoted entirely to his work.

Bibliography

'A Mere Phantom' (1866) *The Magic Lantern: How to Buy, and How to Use It*, London: Houlston and Wright.

Abbas, Ackbar (1997) *Hong Kong: Culture and the Politics of Disappearance*, Minneapolis: University of Minnesota Press.

Abrams, M.H. (1958) *The Mirror and the Lamp: Romantic Theory and the Critical Tradition*, New York: W.W. Norton.

Adorno, Theodor W. (1975) 'Culture Industry Revisited,' trans. Anson G. Rabinbach, *New German Critique*, 6 (Fall).

Adorno, Theodor (1991) *The Culture Industry: Selected Essays on Mass Culture*, London: Routledge.

Aguirre, Manuel (1990) *The Closed Space: Horror Literature and Western Symbolism*, Manchester: Manchester University Press.

Altick, Richard D. (1978) *The Shows of London*, Cambridge, MA: Harvard University Press.

Ames, Jessie Daniel (1973) *The Changing Character of Lynching*, New York: AMS Press.

Anon. (1818) 'Phantasmagoriana', *Blackwood's Magazine*, 3 (August).

Appadurai, Arjun (1990) 'Disjuncture and Difference in the Global Cultural Economy,' *Public Culture* 2: 2.

Arata, Stephen D. (1990) 'The Occidental Tourist: *Dracula* and the Anxiety of Reverse Colonisation,' *Victorian Studies*, 33.

Arata, Stephen D. (1996) *Fictions of Loss in the Victorian Fin de Siècle*, Cambridge: Cambridge University Press.

Archer, Leonard (1973) *Black Images in the American Theater: NAACP Protest Campaigns – Stage, Screen, Radio and Television*, Brooklyn: Pageant-Poseidon.

Aristotle (1963) *Generation of Animals*, trans. A.L. Peck, Cambridge, MA: Harvard University Press.

Arnheim, Rudolf (1972) 'A Note on Monsters,' in Rudolf Arnheim (ed.), *Toward a Psychology of Art*, Berkeley: University of California Press.

Astle, Richard (1977) 'Structures of Ideology in the English Gothic Novel,' Ph.D., University of California, San Diego.

Auerbach, Nina (1982) *Woman and the Demon: The Life of a Victorian Myth*, Cambridge, MA: Harvard University Press.

Bablot, Benjamin (1788) *Dissertation sur le pouvoir de l'imagination des femmes enceintes*, Paris: Croulleboy and Royez.

Bacon, Wendy (1995) *States of Injury: Power and Freedom in Late Modernity*, Princeton: Princeton University Press.

Badley, Linda (1995) *Film, Horror and the Body Fantastic*, Westport, Conn.: Greenwood Press.

Badley, Linda (1996) *Writing Horror and the Body: The Fiction of Stephen King, Clive Barker, and Anne Rice*, Westport, Conn.: Greenwood Press.

Bakhtin, Mikhail (1984) *Rabelais and His World*, trans. Helene Iswolsky, Bloomington: Indiana University Press.

Balbus, Isaac (1982) *Marxism and Domination*, Princeton: Princeton University Press.

Baldick, Chris (1987) *In Frankenstein's Shadow: Myth, Monstrosity, and Nineteenth-Century Writing*, Oxford: Clarendon Press.

Balikci, Asen (1989) 'Anthropology, Film and the Arctic Peoples,' *Anthropology Today*, 5: 2 (April).

Bann, Stephen (1984) *The Clothing of Clio: A Study of the Representation of History in Nineteenth-Century Britain and France*, Cambridge: Cambridge University Press.

Barbour, Judith (1992) 'Dr John William Polidori, Author of The Vampyre,' in Dierdre Coleman and Peter Otto (eds), *Imagining Romanticism*, West Cornwall, CN: Locust Hill Press.

Barkan, Elazar and Bush, Ronald (eds) (1995) *Prehistories of the Future: The Primitivist Project and the Culture of Modernism*, Stanford, CA: Stanford University Press.

Baronian, Jean Baptiste (1978) *Panorama de la littérature fantastique de langue française*, Paris: Editions Stock.

Barth, Jack (1985) 'Fanzines,' *Film Comment*, 21: 2.

Barthes, Roland (1975) *The Pleasure of the Text*, trans. Richard Miller, New York: Hill and Wang.

Barthes, Roland (1977) *Image-Music-Text*, trans. Stephen Heath, London: Fontana Press.

Barthes, Roland (1979) 'Upon Leaving the Movie Theater,' trans. Bertrand Augst and Susan White, *University Publishing*, 6 (Winter).

Bataille, Georges (1997) *Literature and Evil: Essays by Georges Bataille*, trans. Alastair Hamilton, London: Boyars.

Batault, Emile (1885) *Contribution a l'étude de l'hystérie chez l'homme*, Paris: Steinheil.

Bates, Jean Victor (n.d.) *Our Allies and Enemies in the Near East*, New York: E.P. Dutton & Co.

Baudelaire, Charles (1983) *Les Fleurs du Mal*, trans. Richard Howard, Boston: Godine.

Baudrillard, Jean (1977) *L'Effet beaubourg: implosion et dissuasion*, Paris: Galilée.

Baudrillard, Jean (1983) 'The Ecstasy of Communication,' in Hal Foster (ed.), *The Anti-Aesthetic: Essays on Postmodern Culture*, Port Townsend, WA: Bay Press.

Baudrillard, Jean (1993) *The Transparency of Evil: Essays on Extreme Phenomena*, trans. James Benedict, London and New York: Verso.

Baym, Nina (1984) 'Concepts of the Romance in Hawthorne's America,' *Nineteenth-Century Fiction*, 38.

Becker, Carol (1975) 'Edgar Allan Poe: The Madness of the Method,' Ph.D., University of California, San Diego.

Beer, Gillian (1978) 'Ghosts,' *Essays in Criticism*, 28: 3.

Behlmer, Rudy (1976) 'Foreword,' in Ronald Gottesman and Harry Geduld (eds), *The Girl in the Hairy Paw*, New York: Avon Books.

Bell, Daniel (1976) *The Cultural Contradictions of Capitalism*, New York: Basic Books.

Belsey, Catherine (1980) *Critical Practice*, London: Methuen.

Benjamin, Walter (1969) 'The Work of Art in an Age of Mechanical Reproduction,' in *Illuminations*, trans. Harry Zohn, New York: Schocken.

Bennett, Betty T. (ed.) (1980) *The Letters of Mary Wollstonescraft Shelley, Vol. 1: A Part of the Elect*, Baltimore: Johns Hopkins University Press.

Bennett, Tony (1979) *Formalism and Marxism*, London: Methuen.

Benshoff, Harry M. (1997) *Monsters in the Closet: Homosexuality and the Horror Film*, Manchester and New York: Manchester University Press.

Berenstein, Rhona J. (1996) *Attack of the Leading Ladies: Gender, Sexuality, and Spectatorship in Classic Horror Cinema*, New York: Columbia University Press.

Bergonzi, Bernard (1961) *The Early H.G. Wells: A Study of the Scientific Romances*, Manchester: Manchester University Press.

Beylie, Claude (1982) 'La chasse du Comte Zaroff: la bête humaine,' *L'Avant-scene*, 1–15 November.

Bierman, Joseph (1977) 'The Genesis and Dating of *Dracula* from Bram Stoker's Working Notes,' *Notes and Queries*, 24.

Birken, Lawrence (1988) *Consuming Desire: Sexual Science and the Emergence of a Culture of Abundance, 1871–1914*, Ithaca, NY: Cornell University Press.

Bloom, John (1987) *Joe Bob Briggs Goes to the Drive-In*, New York: Delcatore Press.

Bodziock, Joseph (1988) 'Richard Wright and Afro-American Gothic,' in C. James Trotman (ed.), *Richard Wright: Myths and Realities*, New York: Garland.

Bogdan, Robert (1988) *Freak Show: Presenting Human Oddities for Amusement and Profit*, Chicago: University of Chicago Press.

Bogle, Donald F. (1989) *Toms, Coons, Mulattoes, Mammies, and Bucks: An Interpretive History of Blacks in American Films*, New York: Continuum.

Bonaparte, Marie (1949) *The Life and Works of Edgar Allen Poe: A Psychoanalytic Interpretation*, London: Imago.

Boner, Charles (1865) *Transylvania: Its Products and Its People*, London: Longmans.

Bordwell, David, Staiger, Janet and Thompson, Kristen (1985) *The Classical Hollywood Cinema: Film Style and Mode of Production to 1960*, New York: Columbia University Press.

Bosworth, Patricia (1985) *Diane Arbus: a Biography*, New York: Avon Books.

Botting, Fred (1991) *Making Monstrous: Frankenstein, Criticism, Theory*, Manchester: Manchester University Press.

Bourdieu, Pierre (1993) *The Field of Cultural Production: Essays on Art and Literature*, edited and introduction by Randal Johnson, Cambridge: Polity Press.

Bovenschen, Silvia (1977) 'Is There a Feminine Aesthetic?', *New German Critique*, 10.

Brantlinger, Patrick (1988) *Rule of Darkness: British Literature and Imperialism, 1830–1914*, Ithaca, NY: Cornell University Press.

Brathwaite, Kamau (1974a) 'Timehri,' in Orde Coombs (ed.), *Is Massa Day Dead?* New York: Anchor.

Brathwaite, Kamau (1974b) *The Development of Creole Society in Jamaica 1770–1820*, Oxford: Clarendon Press.

Braudy, Leo (1985) *Shadows of the Magic Lamp: Fantasy and Science Fiction in Film*, Carbondale: Southern Illinois University Press.

Breines, Wini (1982) *Community and Organisation in the New Left: 1962–1968*, New York: Praeger.

Brewster, David (1833) *Letters on Natural Magic*, J.A. Smith (ed.), London: J. Murray.

Bronfen, Elisabeth (1998) *The Knotted Subject: Hysteria and its Discontents*, Princeton, NJ: Princeton University Press.

Brophy, Philip (1986) 'Horrality – The Textuality of Contemporary Horror Films,' *Screen*, 27: 1.

Brown, Carolyn (1997) 'Figuring the Vampire: Death, Desire and the Image,' in Sue Golding (ed), *The Eight Technologies of Otherness*, London and New York: Routledge.

Brown, Charles Brockden (1984) *Edgar Huntly; or, Memoirs of a Sleep-walker*, S.J. Krause and S.W. Reid (eds), Kent, OH: Kent State University Press.

Brunas, Michael, Brunas, John and Weaver, Tom (1990) *Universal Horrors: The Studio's Classic Films, 1931–46*, Jefferson, NC, and London: McFarland & Co.

Buell, Lawrence (1986) *New England Literary Culture: From Revolution Through Renaissance*, New York: Cambridge University Press.

Bulwer-Lytton, Edward (1862) *A Strange Story*, London: S. Low.

Burch, Noel (1981) *Theory of Film Practice*, Princeton: Princeton University Press.

Burden, Douglas (1927) *Dragon Lizards of Komodo: The Expedition to the Lost World of the Dutch East Indies*, New York and London: G.P. Putnam's Sons.

Butler, Judith (1990) *Gender Trouble: Feminism and the Subversion of Identity*, London and New York: Routledge.

Buzard, James (1991) 'The Uses of Romanticism: Byron and the Victorian Continental Tour,' *Victorian Studies*, 35.

Byron, Lord George Gordon (1986) *Byron*, Jerome J. McGann (ed.), Oxford: Oxford University Press.

Byron, Lord George Gordon (1988) 'Fragment of a Novel,' in Alan Ryan (ed.), *The Penguin Books of Vampire Stories*, Harmondsworth: Penguin.

Calder, Jenni (1980) *Robert Louis Stevenson: A Life Study*, New York: Oxford University Press.

Calinescu, Matei (1977) *Faces of Modernity: Avant-Garde, Decadence, Kitsch*, Bloomington: Indiana University Press.

Canguilhem, Georges (1991) *The Normal and the Pathological*, trans. Carolyn R. Fawcett, New York: Zone Books.

Carlyle, Thomas (1837) *The French Revolution*, 3 Vols, London: James Fraser.

Carlyle, Thomas (1973) *Sartor Resartus*, London: J.M. Dent.

Carroll, Noël (1981) 'Nightmare and the Horror Film: The Symbolic Biology of Fantastic Beings,' *Film Quarterly*, 34 (Spring).

Carroll, Noël (1990) *The Philosophy of Horror, or, Paradoxes of the Heart*, London and New York: Routledge.

Carson, L.M. Kit (1986) ''Saw Thru,' *Film Comment*, 22: 8.

Carter, Margaret (ed.) (1988) *Dracula: the Vampire and the Critics*, Ann Arbor, MI: UMI Research Press.

Case, Sue-Ellen (1991) 'Tracking the Vampire,' *Differences*, 3.

Castle, Terry (1995) *The Female Thermometer: 18th Century Culture and the Invention of the Uncanny*, Oxford: Oxford University Press.

Céard, Jean (1977) *La nature et les prodiges, l'insolite au XVIe siècle, en France*, Geneva: Droz.

Chase, Richard (1980) *The American Novel and Its Tradition*, Baltimore: Johns Hopkins University Press.

Chevalier, Louis (1973) *Labouring Classes and Dangerous Classes*, New York: Howard Fertig.

Chion, Michel (1992) 'The Impossible Embodiment,' in Slavoj Žižek (ed.), *Everything You Always Wanted to Know about Lacan (But Were Afraid to Ask Hitchcock)*, London and New York: Verso.

Chow, Rey (1993) 'A Souvenir of Love,' *Modern Chinese Literature*, 7:2.

Chute, David (1983) 'Outlaw Cinema, Its Rise and Fall,' *Film Comment*, 19: 5.

Cixous, Hélène (1976) 'Fiction and Its Phantoms: A Reading of Freud's "Das Unheimliche",' *New Literary History*, 7: 3.

Clarke, I.F. (1966) *Voices Prophesying War 1763–1914*, London: Oxford University Press.

Clifford, James (1986) 'On Ethnographic Allegory,' in James Clifford and George E. Marcus (eds), *The Poetics and Politics of Ethnography*, Berkeley: University of California Press.

Clover, Carol J. (1989) 'Her Body, Himself: Gender in the Slasher Film,' in James Donald (ed.), *Fantasy and the Cinema*, London: BFI Publishing.

Clover, Carol J. (1992) *Men, Women and Chainsaws: Gender in the Modern Horror Film*, London: BFI Publishing.

Coe, Jonathan (1996) 'Hammer's Cosy Violence,' *Sight and Sound*, August.

Cohen, Jeffrey Jerome (1996) *Monster Theory: Reading Culture*, Minneapolis and London: University of Minnesota Press.

Cohen, William B. (1980) *The French Encounter with Africans: White Responses to Blacks, 1530–1880*, Bloomington: Indiana University Press.

Colonna, François-Marie-Pompée (1731) *Les principes de la nature, ou de la génération des choses*, Paris.

Conrad, Joseph (1921) *Notes on Life and Letters*, London and Toronto: J.M. Dent & Sons Ltd.

Cook, David (1984) 'American Horror: The Shining,' *Literature/Film Quarterly*, 12: 1.

Cook, Pam (ed.) (1985) *The Cinema Book*, London: BFI Publishing.

Cooper, Andrew M. (1988) 'Chains, Pains, and Tentative Gains: The Byronic Prometheus in the Summer of 1816,' *Studies in Romanticism*, 27.

Copjec, Joan (1991) 'Vampires, Breast-Feeding, and Anxiety,' *October*, 58.

Copjec, Joan (1994) *Read My Desire: Lacan Against the Historicists*, Cambridge, MA: MIT Press.

Copjec, Joan (ed.) (1996) *Radical Evil*, New York: Verso.

Cornwall, Neil (1990) *The Literary Fantastic: From Gothic to Postmodernism*, New York: Harvester Wheatsheaf.

Craft, Christopher (1984) '"Kiss Me With Those Red Lips": Gender and Inversion in Bram Stoker's *Dracula*,' *Representations*, 8.

Craft, Christopher (1988) '"Descend and Touch and Enter": Tennyson's Strange Manner of Address,' *Genders*, 1 (Spring).

Crane, Jonathan Lake (1994) *Terror and Everyday Life: Singular Moments in the History of the Horror Film*, Thousand Oaks: Sage Publications.

Creed, Barbara (1989) 'Horror and the Monstrous-Feminine – An Imaginary Abjection,' *Screen*, 27 (January-February).

Creed, Barbara (1993) *The Monstrous-Feminine: Film, Feminism, Psychoanalysis*, London and New York: Routledge.

Cripps, Thomas (1977) *Slow Fade to Black: The Negro in American Film, 1900–1942*, New York: Oxford University Press.

Crosse, Andrew W. (1878) *Round About the Carpathians*, Edinburgh and London: William Blackwood & Sons.

Cullen, Robert (1993) *The Killer Department*, New York: Ivy Books.

D'Emilio, John and Freedman, Estelle (1988) *Intimate Matters: A History of Sexuality in America*, New York: Harper & Row.

Dannen, Fredric and Long, Barry (1997) *Hong Kong Babylon: An Insider's Guide to the Hollywood of the East*, London: Faber and Faber.

Darmon, Pierre (1981) *Le mythe de la procréation à l'age baroque*, Paris: Seuil.

Davidson, Cathy (1986) *Revolution and the Word: The Rise of the Novel in America*, New York: Oxford University Press.

Davis, Angela Y. (1981) 'Rape, Racism, and the Myth of the Black Rapist,' in *Women, Race, and Class*, New York: Random House.

de Boismont, Alexandre Brierre (1855) *A History of Dreams, Visions, Apparitions, Ecstasy, Magnetism, and Somnambulism*, Philadelphia: Lindsay and Blakiston.

de Lauretis, Teresa (1984) *Alice Doesn't: Feminism, Semiotics, Cinema*, Bloomington: Indiana University Press.

de Lauretis, Teresa (1990) 'Sexual Indifference and Lesbian Representation,' in Sue-Ellen Case (ed.), *Performing Feminisms: Feminist Critical Theory and Theater*, Baltimore: Johns Hopkins University Press.

Debord, Guy (1983) *Society of the Spectacle*, Detroit: Black and Red.

Deleuze, Gilles (1989) *Masochism*, New York: Zone Books.

Dendy, Walter Cooper (1841) *The Philosophy of Mystery*, London: Longman, Orme, Brown, Green and Longmans.

Dickstein, Morris (1980) 'The Aesthetics of Fright,' *American Film*, 5 (September).

Dijkstra, Bram (1986) *Idols of Perversity: Fantasies of Feminine Evil in Fin-de-siecle Culture*, Oxford: Oxford University Press.

Dika, Vera (1990) *Games of Terror: Halloween, Friday the 13th, and the Films of the Stalker Cycle*, Rutherford: Fairleigh Dickinson University Press.

Doane, Mary Ann (1980) 'Misrecognition and Identity,' *Ciné-Tracts*, 11.

Doane, Mary Ann (1982) 'Film and the Masquerade: Theorising the Female Spectator,' *Screen*, 23: 3–4.

Doane, Mary Ann (1987) *The Desire to Desire: The Woman's Film of the 1940s*, Bloomington: Indiana University Press.

Dolar, Mladen (1991) '"I Shall be with You on Your Wedding Night": Lacan and the Uncanny,' *October*, 58.

Donald, James (ed.) (1989) *Fantasy and the Cinema*, London: BFI Publishing.

Douglas, Ann (1977) *The Feminisation of American Culture*, New York: Avon.

Douglas, Mary (1966) *Purity and Danger: An Analysis of Concepts of Pollution and Taboo*, London: Ark.

Douglas, Mary (1991) *Purity and Danger: An Analysis of Concepts of Pollution and Taboo*, London and New York: Routledge.

Drew, William A. (1852) *Voyage and Visit to London and the Great Exhibition in the Summer of 1851*, Boston: Homan and Manley.

Dunn, Jane (1978) *Moon in Eclipse: A Life of Mary Shelley*, New York: St Martin's Press.

Dyer, Richard (1980) *Stars*, London: British Film Institute.

Dyer, Richard (1986) *Heavenly Bodies: Film Stars and Society*, London: Macmillan.

Dyer, Richard (1988) 'Children of the Night: Vampirism as Homosexuality, Homosexuality as Vampirism,' in Susannah Radstone (ed), *Sweet Dreams: Sexuality, Gender and Popular Fiction*, London: Lawrence & Wishart.

Dyer, Richard (1992) *Only Entertainment*, London and New York: Routledge.

Dyson, Jeremy (1997) *Bright Darkness: The Lost Art of the Supernatural Horror Film*, London and Washington: Cassell.

Eagleton, Terry (1981) *Walter Benjamin: Or, Towards a Revolutionary Criticism*, London: Verso.

Ebert, Roger (1981) 'Why Movie Audiences aren't Safe Any More,' *American Film*, vi, 5: 54–6.

Edelman, Lee (1991) 'Seeing Things,' in Diana Fuss (ed.), *Inside/Out: Gay and Lesbian Theories*, London and New York: Routledge.

Edmundson, Mark (1997) *Nightmare on Main Street: Angels, Sadomasochism, and the Culture of Gothic*, Cambridge, MA: Harvard University Press.

Ehrenreich, Barbara (1983) *The Hearts of Men: American Dreams and the Flight from Commitment*, New York: Anchor.

Ellis, Kate (1979) 'Monsters in the Garden: Mary Shelley and the Bourgeois Family,' in George Levine and U.C. Knoepflmacher (eds), *The Endurance of Frankenstein: Essays on Mary Shelley's Novel*, Berkeley: University of California Press.

Ellul, Jacques (1964) *The Technological Society*, trans. John Wilkinson, New York: Vintage.

Elwin, Malcolm (1950) *The Strange Case of Robert Louis Stevenson*, London: MacDonald.

Everson, William K. (1974) *Classics of the Horror Film*, Secaucus, NJ: Citadel Press.

Eyles, Allan, Adkinson, Robert and Fry, Nicholas (eds) (1973) *The House of Horror: The Story of Hammer Films*, San Diego: Barnes.

Fanon, Frantz (1967) *Black Skin, White Masks*, trans. Charles Markmann, New York: Grove Weidenfeld.

Ferguson, Otis (1935) review of *'Bride of Frankenstein,'* *The New Republic*, 29 May.

Ferriar, John (1813) *An Essay Towards a Theory of Apparitions*, London: Cadell and Davies.

Fetterley, Judith (1978) *The Resisting Reader: A Feminist Approach to American Fiction*, Bloomington: University of Indiana Press.

Fiedler, Leslie (1978) *Freaks: Myths and Images of the Secret Self*, New York: Simon and Schuster.

Fiedler, Leslie (1982) *Love and Death in the American Novel*, New York: Stein and Day.

Fischer, Lucy and Landis, Marcia (1987) in Gregory A. Waller (ed.), *American Horrors: Essays on the Modern American Horror Film*, Urbana and Chicago: University of Illinois Press.

Fleming, John (1978) 'Flashback: *Revenge of the Vampire*,' *Halls of Horror*, 2: 10 (July).

Florescu, Radu N. (1975) *In Search of Frankenstein*, Boston: New York Graphic Society.

Forry, Steven Earl (1990) *Hideous Progenies: Dramatisations of Frankenstein from Mary Shelley to the Present Day*, Philadelphia: University of Pennsylvania Press.

Foster, Hal (1983) 'Postmodernism: A Preface,' in Hal Foster (ed.), *The Anti-Aesthetic: Essays on Postmodern Culture*, Port Townsend, WA: Bay Press.

Foucault, Michel (1984) 'Nietzsche, Genealogy, History,' in Paul Rabinow (ed.), *The Foucault Reader*, New York: Pantheon.

Francke, Lizzie (1993) 'Seeing in the Dark,' *Sight and Sound*, June, 12.

Frayling, Christopher (1981) *Spaghetti Westerns: Cowboys and Europeans from Karl May to Sergio Leone*, London: Routledge & Kegan Paul.

Freud, Sigmund (1946) *Totem and Taboo*, New York: Vintage Books.

Freud, Sigmund (1955a) 'Totem and Taboo,' *The Standard Edition of the Complete Psychological Works of Sigmund Freud, Vol.XIII*, London: The Hogarth Press.

Freud, Sigmund (1955b) 'The "Uncanny",' *The Standard Edition of the Complete Psychological Works of Sigmund Freud, Vol.XVII*, London: The Hogarth Press.

Freud, Sigmund (1955c) 'From the History of an Infantile Neurosis,' *The Standard Edition of the Complete Psychological Works of Sigmund Freud. Vols X, XVII*, London: The Hogarth Press.

Freud, Sigmund (1959a) 'The "Uncanny",' in Ernest Jones (ed.), *Collected Papers*, Vol. 4, New York: Basic Books.

Freud, Sigmund (1959b) 'The Predisposition to Obsessional Neurosis,' in James Strachey, (ed), *Collected Papers*, Vol. 2, New York: Basic Books.

Freud, Sigmund (1963) 'On the Mechanism of Paranoia,' in *General Psychological Theory*, New York: Collier Books.

Freud, Sigmund (1985) *Art and Literature*, (ed.) Albert Dickson, Harmondsworth: Penguin.

Frost, Brian J. (1989) *The Monster with a Thousand Faces: Guises of the Vampire in Myth and Literature*, Bowling Green, OH: Bowling Green State University Popular Press.

Frost, Thomas (1881) *The Lives of the Conjurers*, London: Chatto & Windus.

Fuss, Diana (1991) *Inside/Out: Lesbian Theories, Gay Theories*, London and New York: Routledge.

Gagnier, Regenia (1986) *Idylls of the Marketplace: Oscar Wilde and the Victorian Public*, Stanford: Stanford University Press.

Gallagher, Catherine and Young, Elizabeth (1991) 'Feminism and *Frankenstein*: A Short History of American Feminist Criticism,' *Journal of Contemporary Thought*, 1: 1.

Gaskell, Elizabeth (1970) *Mary Barton*, Hardmondsworth: Penguin.

Gelder, Ken (1994) *Reading the Vampire*, London and New York: Routledge.

Gelder, Ken and Jacobs, Jane M. (1998) *Uncanny Australia: Sacredness and Identity in a Postcolonial Nation*, Melbourne: Melbourne University Press.

Gerard, Emily (1888) *The Land Beyond the Forest: Facts, Figures, and Fancies from Transylvania*, 2 Vols, Edinburgh and London: William Blackwood & Sons.

Giddens, Anthony (1992) *The Transformation of Intimacy: Sexuality, Love and Eroticism in Modern Societies*, Stanford: Stanford University Press.

Gilbert, Sandra and Gubar, Susan (1979) *The Madwoman in the Attic: The Woman Writer and the Nineteenth-Century Literary Imagination*, New Haven: Yale University Press.

Giles, Dennis (1984) 'Conditions of Pleasure in Horror Cinema,' in Barry Keith Grant (ed), *Planks of Reason: Essays on the Horror Film*, Metuchen, NJ: Scarecrow Press.

Gilkes, Michael (1975) *Wilson Harris and the Caribbean Novel*, London: Longman.

Ginzburg, Ralph (1962) *100 Years of Lynchings*, Baltimore: Black Classic Press.

Gledhill, Christine (ed.) (1991) *Stardom: The Industry of Desire*, London and New York: Routledge.

Glover, David (1992) 'Bram Stoker and the Crisis of the Liberal Subject,' *New Literary History*, 23.

Glut, Donald F. (1973) *The Frankenstein Legend*, Metuchen, NJ: Scarecrow Press.

Glut, Donald F. (1984) *The Frankenstein Catalog*, Jefferson, NC: McFarland & Co.

Goddu, Teresa A. (1997) *Gothic America: Narrative, History, and Nation*, New York: Columbia University Press.

Goethe, Johann Wolfgang von (1962) *Eclective Affinities*, trans. J.A. Froude and R.D. Boylan, New York: Frederick Ungar.

Goethe, Johann Wolfgang von (1971) *The Sorrows of Young Werther*, trans. Elizabeth Mayer and Louise Bogan, New York: Random House.

Golden, Christopher (ed.) (1992) *Cut! Horror Writers on Horror Film*, New York: Berkley Books.

Gould, Stephen Jay (1981) *The Mismeasure of Man*, New York: Norton.

Grant, Barry Keith (ed.) (1984) *Planks of Reason: Essays on the Horror Film*, Metuchen, NJ: Scarecrow Press.

Grant, Barry Keith (ed.) (1996) *Dread of Difference: Gender and the Horror Film*, Austin: University of Texas Press.

Greenspun, Roger (1977) 'Carrie, and Sally and Leatherface among the Film Buffs,' *Film Comment*, January-February.

Greenway, John L. (1986) 'Seward's Folly: *Dracula* as a Critique of "Normal Science",' *Stanford Literature Review*, 3 (Fall).

Grixti, Joseph (1989) *Terrors of Uncertainty: The Cultural Contexts of Horror Fiction*, London and New York: Routledge.

Grosskurth, Phyllis (ed.) (1984) *The Memoirs of John Addington Symonds: The Secret Homosexual Life of a Leading Nineteenth-Century Man of Letters*, Chicago: University of Chicago Press.

Grunenberg, Christoph (1997) *Gothic: Transmutations of Horror in Late Twentieth Century Art*, Cambridge, MA: The MIT Press.

Gunning, Tom (1989) 'An Aesthetic of Astonishment: Early Film and the (In)credulous Spectator,' *Art and Text*, 34.

Haberman, J. and Rosenbaum, Jonathon (1983) *Midnight Movies*, New York: Harper & Row.

Hacking, Ian (1995) *Rewriting the Soul: Multiple Personality and the Sciences of Memory*, Princeton, NJ: Princeton University Press.

Halberstam, Judith (1995) *Skin Shows: Gothic Horror and the Technology of Monsters*, Durham, NC: Duke University Press.

Hall, Jacqueline Dowd (1983) '"The Mind That Burns in Each Body": Women, Rape, and Racial Violence,' in Ann Snitow *et al.* (eds), *Powers of Desire: The Politics of Sexuality*, New York: Monthly Review Press.

Halttunen, Karen (1993) 'Early American Murder Narratives: The Birth of Horror,' in R.W. Fox and T.J. Jackson Lears (eds), *The Power of Culture: Critical Essays in American History*, Chicago: University of Chicago Press.

Hammond, Stefan and Wilkins, Mike (1996) *Sex and Zen & A Bullet in the Head: The Essential Guide to Hong Kong's Mind-Bending Films*, New York: Fireside.

Hanke, Ken (1991) *A Critical Guide to Horror Film Stories*, New York and London: Garland Publishing, Inc.

Haraway, Donna (1985) 'A Manifesto for Cyborgs,' *Socialist Review*, 80.

Harding, D.W. (1957) 'The Character of Literature from Blake to Byron,' in Borid Ford (ed), *The Pelican Guide to English Literature, Vol. 5: From Blake to Byron*, Harmondsworth: Penguin.

Hardy, Phil (1985) *The Aurum Film Encyclopedia, Vol. 3: Horror*, London: Aurum Press.

Hardy, Phil (ed.) (1986) *The Encyclopedia of Horror Film*, New York: Harper & Row.

Harrington, Anne (1987) *Medicine, Mind, and the Double Brain*, Princeton: Princeton University Press.

Harris, Wilson (1967) *Tradition, the Writer, and Society*, London: New Beacon.

Harris, Wilson (1970) 'History, Fable and Myth in the Caribbean and Guianas,' *Caribbean Quarterly*, 16: 1.

Harris, Wilson (1985) *The Guyana Quartet*, London: Faber and Faber.

Hart, Francis R. (1973) 'Limits of the Gothic: The Scottish Example,' in H.E. Pagliaro (ed.), *Studies in Eighteenth-Century Culture: Racism in the Eighteenth Century*, Cleveland: The Press of Case Western Reserve University.

Hasselbach, Ingo (with Tom Reiss) (1996) 'How Nazis are Made,' *New Yorker*, 8 January.

Hayes, Carlton (1963) *A Generation of Materialism 1871–1900*, New York: Harper & Row.

Heath, Stephen (1981) *Questions of Cinema*, Bloomington: Indiana University Press.

Heath, Stephen (1986) 'Psychopathia Sexualis: Stevenson's *Strange Case*,' *Critical Quarterly*, 28.

Heath, Stephen (1988) 'Psychopathia Sexualis: Stevenson's *Strange Case*,' in Colin McCabe (ed.), *Futures for English*, Manchester: Manchester University Press.

Herman, Ellen (1995) *The Romance of American Psychology: Political Culture in the Age of Experts*, Berkeley: University of California Press.

Herzfeld, Michael (1982) *Ours Once More: Folklore, Ideology, and the Making of Modern Greece*, Austin: University of Texas Press.

Hibbert, Samuel (1825) *Sketches of the Philosophy of Apparitions*, Edinburgh: Oliver & Boyd.

Himmelfarb, Gertrude (1985) *The Idea of Poverty: England in the Early Industrial Age*, New York: Vintage Books.

Hobsbawm, E.J. (1962) *The Age of Revolution 1789–1848*, New York, New American Library.

Hobsbawm, E.J. (1975) *The Age of Capital 1848–1875*, New York: New American Library.

Hoffmann, E.T.A. (1982) *Tales of Hoffmann*, trans. Sally Hayward, Harmondsworth: Penguin.

Hoile, Christopher (1984) 'The Uncanny and the Fairy Tale in Kubrick's *The Shining*,' *Literature/Film Quarterly*, 12: 1.

Holland, Norman N. and Sherman, Leona F. (1977) 'Gothic Possibilities,' *New Literary History*, 8: 2 (Winter).

Hollinger, Karen F. (1989) 'The Monster as Woman: Two Generations of Cat People,' *Film Comment*, 13 (Winter).

Holmes, Oliver Wendell (1861) *Elsie Venner*, Boston and New York: Houghton, Mifflin.

Holmes, Ronald M. and De Burger, James (1988) *Serial Murder*, Newbury Park, CA: Sage.

Homans, Margaret (1986) *Bearing the World: Language and Female Experience in Nineteenth-Century Women's Writing*, Chicago: Chicago University Press.

Huet, Marie-Hélene (1993) *Monstrous Imagination*, Cambridge, MA: and London: Harvard University Press.

Huggan, Graham (1998) 'Ghost Stories, Bone Flutes, Cannibal Countermemory,' in Peter Hulme *et al.* (eds), *Cannibalism and the Colonial World*, Cambridge: Cambridge University Press.

Hume, Robert D. and Platzner, Robert L. (1971) 'Gothic versus Romantic: A Rejoinder,' *PMLA*, 86.

Hunt, Leon (1992) 'A (Sadistic) Night at the Opera: Notes on the Italian Horror Film,' *The Velvet Light Trap: Review of Cinema*, 30.

Hutchings, Peter (1993) *Hammer and Beyond: The British Horror Film*, Manchester: Manchester University Press.

Huyssen, Andreas (1986) 'Mass Culture as Woman: Modernism's Other,' in Tania Modleski (ed.), *Studies in Entertainment*, Bloomington and Indianapolis: Indiana University Press.

Huyssen, Andreas (1987) *After the Great Divide: Modernism and Mass Culture*, New York: Columbia University Press.

Ingpen, Roger and Peck, Walter E. (1965) *The Complete Works of Percy Bysshe Shelley, Vol. VI*, London: Benn.

Irigaray, Luce (1985) *This Sex Which Is Not One*, trans. Catherine Porter, Ithaca, NY: Cornell University Press.

Iser, Wolfgang (1974) *The Implied Reader*, Baltimore: Johns Hopkins University Press.

Jackson, Rosemary (1981) *Fantasy: the Literature of Subversion*, London: Methuen.

Jacobus, Mary (1982) 'Is There a Woman in This Text?', *New Literary History*, 14 (Autumn).

Jacoby, Russell (1977) *Social Amnesia: A Critique of Conformist Psychology from Adler to Laing*, Brighton: Harvester.

Jameson, Fredric (1981) '*The Shining*,' *Social Text*, 4.

Jameson, Fredric (1983) 'Postmodernism and Consumer Society,' in Hal Foster (ed.), *The Anti-Aesthetic: Essays on Postmodern Culture*, Port Townsend, WA: Bay Press.

Jancovich, Mark (1992) *Horror*, London: B.T. Batsford Ltd.

Jenkins, Philip (1994) *Using Murder: The Social Construction of Serial Homicide*, New York: de Gruyter.

Jenks, Carol (1989) 'The Other Face of Death: Barbara Steele, *Black Sunday* and the Beginnings of the Italian Horror Film,' unpublished paper, conference on Popular European Cinema, Warwick University, UK.

Jensen, Paul M. (1974) *Boris Karloff and His Films*, San Diego: Barnes.

Johnson, C. (1885) *On the Track of the Crescent*, London: Hurst & Blackett.

Jones, Alan (1983) 'Argento,' *Cinefantastique*, 18 (March).

Jones, Alan (1986) 'Interview with Dario Argento,' *Cinefantastique*, 16 (May).

Jones, Ernest (1931) *On the Nightmare*, London: The Hogarth Press.

Jones, Frederick L. (ed.) (1964) *The Letters of Percy Bysshe Shelley, Vol. 1: Shelley in England*, Oxford: Oxford University Press.

Jung, C.G. (1970) *Mysterium Coniunctionis: An Inquiry into the Separation and Synthesis of Psychic Opposites in Alchemy*, Princeton: Princeton University Press.

Kahane, Claire (1980) 'Gothic Mirrors and Feminine Identity,' *The Centennial Review*, 24: 1.

Kant, Immanuel (1952) *Critique of Judgment*, trans. James Creed, Oxford: Clarendon.

Kaplan, E. Ann (1983) *Women and Film: Both Sides of the Camera*, London: Methuen.

Kawin, Bruce F. (1981) 'The Mummy's Pool,' *Dreamworks*, 1.

Kermode, Mark (1998) 'Lucifer Rising,' *Sight and Sound*, July.

Kilgour, Maggie (1990) *From Communion to Cannibalism: An Anatomy of Metaphors of Incorporation*, Princeton: Princeton University Press.

Kilgour, Maggie (1995) *The Rise of the Gothic Novel*, London: Routledge.

King, Stephen (1981) *Danse Macabre: The Anatomy of Horror*, London: Futura.

King, Stephen (1983) *Danse Macabre*, New York: Berkley Books.

Kipling, Rudyard (1987) *Plain Tales from the Hills*, Oxford: Oxford University Press.

Kittler, Friedrich (1989) 'Dracula's Legacy,' *Stanford Humanities Review*, 1.

Kittler, Friedrich (1990) *Discourse Networks 1800/1900*, trans. Michael Metteer, with Chris Cullens, Stanford, CA: Stanford University Press.

Koestenbaum, Wayne (1988) 'The Shadow Under the Bed: Dr Jekyll, Mr Hyde, and the Labouchere Amendment,' *Critical Matrix*, 1 (Spring).

Koestenbaum, Wayne (1989) *Double Talk: The Erotics of Male Literary Collaboration*, London and New York: Routledge.

Kristeva, Julia (1979) 'Ellipsis on Dread and the Specular Seduction,' trans. Dolores Burdick, *Wide Angle*, 3: 3.

Kristeva, Julia (1980) *Desire in Language*, Oxford: Basil Blackwell.

Kristeva, Julia (1982) *Powers of Horror: An Essay on Abjection*, trans. Leon S. Roudiez, New York: Columbia University Press.

Kuntzel, Thierry (1980) 'The Film-Work, 2,' trans. Nancy Huston, *Camera Obscura*, 5 (Spring).

Lacan, Jacques (1986) *L'ethique de la psychoanalyse*, Paris: Editions du Seuil.

Lacan, Jacques (1988) *The Ego in Freud's Theory and in the Technique of Psychoanalysis, 1954–1955*, Jacques-Alain Miller (ed.), New York and London: Norton.

Lacan, Jacques (1990) *Television: A Challenge to the Psychoanalytic Establishment*, New York and London: Norton.

Lang, Andrew (1903) 'Recollections of Robert Louis Stevenson,' in *Adventures Among Books*, London: Longmans, Green and Co.

Laplanche, Jean (1976) *Life and Death in Psychoanalysis*, trans. Jeffrey Mehlmen, Baltimore: Johns Hopkins University Press.

Laufer, Peter (1995) *Inside Talk Radio*, New York: Birch Lane Press.

Laurens, André du (1634) *Oeuvres*, trans. Théophile Gelée, Paris.

LaValley, Albert J. (1979) 'The Stage and Film Children of *Frankenstein*: A Survey,' in George Levine and U.C. Knoepflmacher (eds), *The Endurance of Frankenstein*, Berkeley: University of California Press.

Lawrence, D.H. (1924) *Studies in Classic American Literature*, London: Martin Secker.

Lawson, John Cuthbert (1964) *Modern Greek Folklore and Ancient Greek Religion*, New York: University Books.

Leab, Daniel J. (1975) *From Sambo to Superspade: The Black Experience in Motion Pictures*, Boston: Houghton Mifflin.

Lears, T.L. Jackson (1983) 'From Salvation to Self-Realisation: Advertising and the Therapeutic Roots of the Consumer Culture, 1880–1930,' in R.W. Fox and T.L. Jackson Lears (eds), *The Culture of Consumption: Critical Essays in American History, 1880–1980*, New York: Pantheon.

Lefebvre, Henri (1991) *The Production of Space*, Malden, MA: Basil Blackwell.

Leprohon, Pierre (1945) *L'exotisme et le cinéma*, Paris: J. Susse.

Levin, Harry (1958) *The Power of Blackness: Hawthorne, Poe, Melville*, New York: Knopf.

Levine, George and Knoepflmacher, U.C. (eds) (1979) *The Endurance of Frankenstein*, Berkeley: University of California Press.

Lévi-Strauss, Claude (1981a) *The Naked Man*, trans. J. and D. Weightman, London: Harper & Row.

Lévi-Strauss, Claude (1981b) *Tristes Tropiques*, trans. John and Doreen Weightman, New York: Penguin.

Li Bihua (1986) *Yanzhi kou*, Hong Kong: Cosmos Books.

Liceti, Fortunii (1708) *De la nature, des causes et des différences des monstres*, Leyden: Bastiaan Schouten.

Li Cheuk-to (ed.) (1989) *The 13th Hong Kong International Film Festival Retrospective: Phantoms of the Hong Kong Cinema*, Hong Kong: Urban Council Press.

Lim, Felicidad C. (1997) 'The Politics of Horror: the *Aswang* in Film,' *Asian Cinema* (Fall).

Liotard, André F., Samivel, P. and Thévenot, Jean (1950) *Cinéma d'exploration, cinéma au long cours*, Paris: P.-A. Chavane.

Lovecraft, H.P. (1973) *Supernatural Horror in Literature*, introduction E.F. Bleiler, New York: Dover Publications, Inc.

Lyotard, Jean-François (1979) *La Condition postmoderne*, Paris: Minuit.

Lyotard, Jean-Francois (1983) 'Answering the Question: What is Postmodernism?' in Ihab Hassan and Sally Hassan (eds), *Innovation/Renovation: New Perspectives on the Humanities*, Madison: The University of Wisconsin Press.

MacCannell, Dean (1992) *Empty Meeting Grounds: The Tourist Papers*, London: Routledge.

McCarthy, John 1989) *The Official Splatter Movie Guide*, New York: St Martin's Press.

McCarthy, Todd (1980) 'Trick or Treat,' *Film Comment*, 16.

McConnell, Frank D. (1975) *The Spoken Seen: Film and the Romantic Imagination*, Baltimore: Johns Hopkins University Press.

McDonagh, Maitland (1987) 'Broken Mirrors/Broken Minds: The Dark Dreams of Dario Argento,' *Film Quarterly*, 41: 2.

McDonagh, Maitland (1991) *Broken Mirrors/Broken Minds: The Dark Dreams of Dario Argento*, London: Sun Tavern Fields.

McWhir, Anne (1987) 'Pollution and Redemption in *Dracula*,' *Modern Language Studies*, 17 (Summer).

Maixner, Paul (1981) *Robert Louis Stevenson: The Critical Heritage*, London: Routledge & Kegan Paul.

Malinowski, Bronislow (1989) *A Diary in the Strict Sense of the Term*, Stanford: Stanford University Press.

Maltin, Leonard (1981–2) *T.V. Movies*, rev. edn, New York: Signet.

Manguel, Alberto (1998) *The Bride of Frankenstein*, London: BFI Publishing.

Marchand, Leslie A. (1971) *Byron: A Portrait*, London: John Murray.

Marcus, Steven (1964) *The Other Victorians: A Study of Sexuality and Pornography in Mid-Nineteenth-Century England*, New York: Basic Books.

Marsh, Joss Lutz (1995) 'In a Glass Darkly: Photography, the Premodern, and Victorian Horror,' in Elazar Barkan and Ronald Bush (eds), *Prehistories of the Future: The Primitivist Project and the Culture of Modernism*, Stanford: Stanford University Press.

Martinez, Wilson (1990) 'Critical Studies and Visual Anthropology: Aberrant vs. Anticipated Readings of Ethnographic Film,' *CVA Review* (Spring).

Marx, Karl (1973) *Grundrisse: Foundations of the Critique of Political Economy*, trans. Martin Nicolaus, Harmondsworth: Penguin.

Marx, Karl (1976a) *Capital*, Vol. 1, Harmondsworth: Penguin.

Marx, Karl (1976b) 'The Property of Philosophy,' in Karl Marx and Friedrich Engels, *Collected Works*, Vol. 6, London: Lawrence & Wishart.

Marx, Karl and Engels, Frederick (1968) *Selected Works*, New York: International Publishers.

Masters, Brian (1993) *Killing for Company: The Story of a Man Addicted to Murder*, New York: Random House.

Mayes, Stanley (1959) *The Great Belzoni*, London: Walker.

Mayne, Judith (1986) 'Dracula in the Twilight: Murnau's *Nosferatu* (1922),' in Eric Rentschler (ed), *German Film and Literature: Adaptations and Transformations*, New York: Methuen.

Medovoi, Leerom (1998) 'Theorising Historicity, or, The Many Meanings of *Blacula*,' *Screen*, 39: 1.

Melamed, Elissa (1983) *Mirror, Mirror: The Terror of Not Being Young*, New York: Linden Press/Simon & Schuster.

Mellencamp, Patricia (1995) *A Fine Romance: Five Ages of Film Feminism*, Philadelphia: Temple University Press.

Mellor, Anne (1988) *Mary Shelley: Her Life, Her Fiction, Her Monsters*, London: Methuen.

Melville, Herman (1987) *The Piazza Tales and Other Prose Pieces 1839–1860*, Evanston, IL: Northwestern University Press.

Methvin, Eugene H. (1995) 'The Face of Evil,' *National Review*, 23 January.

Metz, Christian (1982) *The Imaginary Signifier: Psychoanalysis and the Cinema*, trans. Celia Britton *et al.*, Bloomington: Indiana University Press.

Metz, Walter (1997) 'Towards a Post-Structural Influence in Film Genre Study: Intertextuality and *The Shining*,' *Film Criticism*, 22: 1.

Michaud, Stephen G. and Aynesworth, Hugh (1989) *Ted Bundy: Conversations with a Killer*, New York: Signet.

Miller, D.A. (1986) 'Cage aux folles: Sensation and Gender in *The Woman in White*,' *Representations*, 14.

Miller, Karl (1987) *Doubles: Studies in Literary History*, London: Oxford University Press.

Mills, C. Wright (1951) *White Collar: The American Middle Class*, New York: Oxford University Press.

Milne, Tom (1981) 'Vittorio Cottafavi, Riccardo Freda and Mario Bava,' in Richard Roud (ed.), *Cinema: A Biographical Dictionary*, New York: Viking.

Mittelholzer, Edgar (1955) *My Bones and My Flute*, London: Longman.

Modleski, Tania (1986) 'The Terror of Pleasure: The Contemporary Horror Film and Postmodern Theory,' in Tania Modleski (ed.), *Studies in Entertainment: Critical Approaches to Mass Culture*, Bloomington and Indianapolis: Indiana University Press.

Modleski, Tania (1988) *The Woman Who Knew Too Much: Hitchcock and Feminist Theory*, New York and London: Methuen.

Modleski, Tania (1991) 'Femininity and Mas(s)querade,' in *Feminism Without Women: Culture and Criticism in a 'Post Feminist' Age*, New York: Routledge.

Moers, Ellen (1974) *Literary Women*, New York: Doubleday.

Mogen, David, Sanders, Scott P. and Karpinski, Joanne B. (1993) *Frontier Gothic: Terror and Wonder at the Frontier in American Literature*, Rutherford, NJ: Fairleigh Dickinson University Press.

Monleon, José B. (1990) *A Specter is Haunting Europe: A Sociohistorical Approach to the Fantastic*, Princeton: Princeton University Press.

Moretti, Franco (1983) 'Dialectic of Fear,' *Signs Taken for Wonders*, trans. Susan Fischer *et al.*, London and New York: Verso.

Morrison, Toni (1992) *Playing the Dark: Whiteness and the Literary Imagination*, Cambridge: Harvard University Press.

Müller, Heiner (1978) 'Die Hamletmaschine,' in *Mauser*, Berlin: Rotbuch.

Mulvey, Laura (1981) 'Afterthoughts on "Visual Pleasure and Narrative Cinema" Inspired by *Duel in the Sun* (King Vidor, 1946),' *Framework*, 15/16/17.

Myers, Frederic (1886) 'Multiplex Personality,' *The Nineteenth Century* (November).

Nabokov, Vladimir (1980) 'The Strange Case of Dr. Jekyll and Mr. Hyde,' in *Lectures on Literature*, New York: Harcourt Brace Jovanovich.

Naipaul, V.S. (1984) *The Loss of El Dorado*, New York: Vintage.

Napier, Elizabeth R. (1987) *The Failure of Gothic: Problems of Disjunction in an Eighteenth-Century Literary Form*, Oxford: Clarendon Press.

Neale, Stephen (1980) *Genre*, London: British Film Institute.

Newman, Kim (1986a) 'Thirty Years in Another Town: The History of Italian Exploitation Part 1,' *Monthly Film Bulletin*, 53 (January).

Newman, Kim (1986b) 'Review of Contamination,' *Monthly Film Bulletin*, 53 (March).

Newman, Kim (1988) *Nightmare Movies: A Critical History of the Horror Movie from 1968*, London: Bloomsbury.

Newman, Kim (1988–9) 'Horrors,' *Sight and Sound*, 58 (January).

Newnham, William (1830) *Essay on Superstition*, London: J. Hatchard & Son.

Newton, Helmut (1984) *World Without Men*, London: Quartet.

Newton, Michael (1990) *Hunting Humans: The Encyclopedia of Serial Killers*, New York: Avon.

Newton, Michael (1992) *Serial Slaughter: What's Behind America's Murder Epidemic?*, Port Townsend, WA: Loompanics Unlimited.

Ng Ho (1989) 'Abracadaver,' in Li Cheuk-to (ed.), *The 13th Hong Kong International Film Festival Retrospective: Phantoms of the Hong Kong Cinema*, Hong Kong: Urban Council Press.

Nietzsche, Friedrich (1969) *On the Genealogy of Morals*, trans. W. Kaufmann and R.J. Hollindale, New York: Vintage.

Nitchie, Elizabeth (1953) *Mary Shelley, Author of Frankenstein*, New Brunswick, NJ: Rutgers University Press.

Norden, Martin F. (1986) 'Sexual References in James Whale's *Bride of Frankenstein*,' in Donald F. Palumbo (ed.), *Eros in the Mind's Eye: Sexuality and the Fantastic in Art and Film,* Westport, CT: Greenwood Press.

Norris, Joel (1988) *Serial Killers*, New York: Anchor.

Noyes, James O. (1857) *Roumania*, New York: Rudd & Carlton.

O'Flinn, Paul (1986) 'Production and Reproduction: The Case of *Frankenstein*,' in Peter Humm *et al.* (eds), *Popular Fictions: Essays in Literature and History*, London and New York: Methuen.

Olsen, Jack (1994) *Charmer*, New York: William Morrow.

Olson, Stanley (1986) *John Singer Sargent*, New York: St Martin's Press.

Oppenheimer, Judy (1988) *Private Demons: The Life of Shirley Jackson*, New York: Ballantine.

O'Reilly-Fleming, Thomas (1992) 'Serial Murder: Towards Integrated Theorising,' *The Critical Criminologist*, 4: 3/4 (Autumn/Winter).

Orlando, Francesco (1978) *Toward a Freudian Theory of Literature*, Baltimore: Johns Hopkins University Press.

Pagel, Walter (1958) *Paracelsus: An Introduction to Philosophical Medicine in the Era of the Renaissance*, New York: S. Karger.

Paget, John (1855) *Hungary and Transylvania*, London: Murray.

Paul, William (1994) *Laughing Screaming: Modern Hollywood Horror and Comedy*, New York: Columbia University Press.

Peithman, Stephen (ed.) (1981) *The Annotated Tales of Edgar Allan Poe*, Garden City, NY: Doubleday and Co.

Petley, Julian (1984) 'Two or Three Things I Know About Video Nasties,' *Monthly Film Bulletin*, 51 (November).

Pick, Daniel (1988) ' "Terrors of the Night": *Dracula* and "Degeneration",' *Critical Quarterly*, 30 (Winter).

Pick, Daniel (1989) *Faces of Degeneration: A European Disorder, c.1848–c.1918*, Cambridge: Cambridge University Press.

Pirie, David (1973) *A Heritage of Horror: The English Gothic Cinema 1946–1972*, London: Gordon Fraser/New York: Avon.

Pirie, David (1977) *The Vampire Cinema*, London: Paul Hamlyn.

Pirie, David (1980) *Hammer: A Cinema Case Study*, London: BFI Publishing.

Poe, Edgar Allan (1970) 'The Philosophy of Composition,' in G.R. Thompson (ed.), *Great Short Works of Edgar Allan Poe*, New York: Literary Classics of the United States.

Poe, Edgar Allan (1978) *Collected Works of Edgar Allan Poe, Tales and Sketches 1831–1842*, 3 Vols, T.O. Mabbott (ed.), Cambridge, MA: Harvard University Press.

Polan, Dana (1997) 'Eros and Syphilization: The Contemporary Horror Film,' in Peter Gibian (ed.), *Mass Culture and Everyday Life*, New York and London: Routledge.

Poliakov, Leon (1974) *The Aryan Myth*, trans. Edmund Howard, New York: Basic Books.

Polidori, John (1988) 'The Vampyre,' in Alan Ryan (ed.), *The Penguin Books of Vampire Stories*, Harmondsworth: Penguin.

Polidori, John (1997) *The Vampyre and Other Tales of the Macabre*, Robert Morrison and Chris Baldick (eds), Oxford: Oxford University Press.

Poovey, Mary (1984) *The Proper Lady and the Woman Writer: Ideology as Style in the Works of Mary Wollstonecraft, Mary Shelley and Jane Austen*, Chicago: University of Chicago Press.

Prawer, S.S. (1980) *Caligari's Children: The Film as Tale of Terror*, Oxford: Oxford University Press.

Praz, Mario (1954) *The Romantic Agony*, trans. Angus Davidson, London: Oxford University Press.

Preloran, Jorge (1975) 'Documenting the Human Condition,' in Paul Hockings (ed.), *Principles of Visual Anthropology*, The Hague: Mouton.

Proust, Marcel (1981) *Remembrance of Things Past, Vol. 1: Swann's Way*, trans. C.K. Scott Moncrieff and Terence Kilmartin, New York: Random House.

Punter, David (1980) *The Literature of Terror*, London and New York: Longman.

Quigley, Martin, Jr (1948) *Magic Shadows: The Story of the Origin of Motion Pictures*, Washington, DC: Georgetown University Press.

Rabinowitz, Paula (1990) 'Seeing Through the Gendered I: Feminist Film Theory,' *Feminist Studies*, 16 (Spring).

Rebello, Stephen (1980) *Alfred Hitchcock and the Making of 'Psycho,'* New York: Dembner.

Reddick, Lawrence (1975) 'Of Motion Pictures,' in Lindsay Patterson (ed.), *Black Films and Filmmakers*, New York: Dodd, Mead.

Reynolds, David (1989) *Beneath the American Renaissance: The Subversive Imagination in the Age of Emerson and Melville*, Cambridge: Harvard University Press.

Rieger, James (1963) 'Dr Polidori and the genesis of *Frankenstein*,' *Studies in English Literature*, 3 (Autumn).

Riesman, David (1989) *The Lonely Crowd: A Study of the Changing American Character*, New Haven, CN: Yale University Press.

Rimbaud, Arthur (1957) *Illuminations*, trans. Louise Varese, New York: New Directions.

Rimbaud, Arthur (1976) *A Season in Hell*, trans. Bertrand Mathieu, Cambridge: Pomegranate.

Robertson, Étienne-Gaspard (1885) *Mémoires récréatifs, scientifiques, et anecdotiques d'un physicien-aéronaute*, 2 Vols, introduction Philippe Blon, Langres: Clima.

Robinson, Henry Crabb (1966) *The London Theatre 1811–1866: Selections from the Diary of Henry Crabb Robinson*, Eluned Brown (ed.), London: Society for Theatre Research.

Rodd, Rennell (1968) *The Customs and Lore of Modern Greece*, Chicago: Argonaut.

Rony, Fatimah Tobing (1996) *The Third Eye: Race, Cinema, and Ethnographic Spectacle*, Durham, NC: Duke University Press.

Rosenthal, Evelyn R. (1990) 'On Gray Hair and Oppressed Brains,' in Evelyn R. Rosenthal (ed.), *Women, Aging and Ageism*, New York: The Haworth Press.

Rostand, Jean (1930) *La formation de l'etre, histoire des idées sur la génération*, Paris: Hachette.

Rousseau, Jean-Jacques (1979) *Emile, or On Education*, Allan Bloom (ed.), New York: Basic Books.

Rowbotham, Sheila (1973) *Women's Consciousness, Man's World*, Harmondsworth: Penguin.

Rowe, John Carlos (1992) 'Poe, Antebellum Slavery, and Modern Criticism,' in R. Kopley (ed.), *Poe's Pym: Critical Explorations*, Durham, NC: Duke University Press.

Rubin, Gayle (1975) 'The Traffic in Women: Notes Toward a "Political Economy" of Sex,' in R.R. Reiter (ed.), *Toward an Anthropology of Women*, New York: Monthly Review Press.

Rule, Ann (1980) *The Stranger Beside Me*, New York: Signet.

Russo, Mary J. (1995) *The Female Grotesque: Risk, Excess and Modernity*, New York and London: Routledge.

Russo, Vito (1981) *The Celluloid Closet: Homosexuality in the Movies*, New York: Harper & Row.

Samuel, Raphael (1981) *East End Underworld: Chapters in the Life of Arthur Harding*, London: Routledge & Kegan Paul.

Sanday, Peggy Reeves (1986) *Divine Hunger: Cannibalism as a Cultural System*, Cambridge: Cambridge University Press.

Sanjek, David (1990) 'Fans' Notes: the Horror Film Fanzine,' *Literature/Film Quarterly*, 18: 3.

Sappington, Rodney and Stallings, Tyler (eds) (1994) *Uncontrollable Bodies: Testimonies of Identity and Culture*, Seattle: Bay Press.

Schiller, Daniel (1981) *Objectivity and the News: The Public and the Rise of Commercial Journalism*, Philadelphia: University of Pennsylvania Press.

Schlockoff, Robert and Everitt, David (1983) 'Attention Gorehounds! The Gates of Hell Are Open,' *Fangoria*, 29 (September).

Schoell, William (1985) *Stay Out of the Shower: Twenty-five Years of Shocker Films Beginning with Psycho*, New York: Dembner.

Schueller, Herbert M. and Peters, Robert L. (eds) (1968) *Letters of J.A. Symonds*, Detroit: Wayne State University Press.

Sconce, Jeffrey (1993) 'Spectacles of Death: Identification, Reflexivity, and Contemporary Horror,' in Jim Collins *et al.* (eds), *Film Theory Goes to the Movies*, London and New York: Routledge.

Scott, Sir Walter (1831) *Letters on Demonology and Witchcraft*, London: J. Murray.

Sedgwick, Eve Kosofsky (1985) *Between Men: English Literature and Male Homosocial Desire*, New York: Columbia University Press.

Seed, David (1985) 'The Narrative Method of *Dracula*,' *Nineteenth Century Fiction*, 40 (June).

Seesslen, Georg (1980) *Kino der Angst*, Hamburg: Rowohlt.

Sek Kei (1989) 'The Wandering Spook: A Decade of Horror Films in the Hong Kong Cinema,' in Li Cheuk-to (ed.), *The 13th Hong Kong International Film Festival Retrospective: Phantoms of the Hong Kong Cinema*, Hong Kong: Urban Council Press.

Seltzer, Mark (1998) *Serial Killers: Death and Life in America's Wound Culture*, New York and London: Routledge.

Sharrett, Christopher (1993) 'The Horror Film in Neoconservative Culture,' *Journal of Popular Film and Television*, 21: 3.

Shelley, Mary (1965) *Frankenstein*, New York: New American Library.

Shelley, Mary (1969) *Frankenstein, or The Modern Prometheus*, M.K. Joseph (ed.), London: Oxford University Press.

Showalter, Elaine (1983) 'Critical Cross-Dressing: Male Feminists and the Woman of the Year,' *Raritan*, 3.

Showalter, Elaine (1990) *Sexual Anarchy: Gender and Culture at the Fin de Siecle*, Harmondsworth: Penguin Books.

Silverman, Kaja (1988) 'Masochism and Male Subjectivity,' *camera obscura*, 17.

Skal, David J. (1993) *The Monster Show: A Cultural History of Horror*, New York and London: W.W. Norton.

Skarda, Patricia L. (1989) 'Vampirism and Plagiarism: Byron's Influence and Polidori's Practice,' *Studies in Romanticism*, 28.

Small, Christopher (1972) *Ariel Like a Harpy: Shelley, Mary and Frankenstein*, London: Gollancz.

Smith, Valerie (1990) 'Split Affinities: The Case of Interracial Rape,' in M. Hirsch and E.F. Keller (eds), *Conflicts in Feminism*, New York: Routledge.

Sobchack, Vivian (1987) 'Bringing It All Back Home: Family Economy and Generic Exchange,' in Gregory A. Waller (ed.), *American Horrors: Essays on the Modern American Horror Film*, Urbana and Chicago: University of Illinois Press.

Sobchack, Vivian (1994) 'Revenge of *The Leech Woman*: On the Dread of Aging in a Low-Budget Horror Film,' in Rodney Sappington and Tyler Stallings (eds), *Uncontrollable Bodies: Testimonies of Identity and Culture*, Seattle: Bay Press.

Sontag, Susan (1969) *Against Interpretation*, New York: Dell/Laurel.

Spark, Muriel (1951) *Child of Light: A Reassessment of Mary Wollstonecraft Shelley*, Hadleigh: Tower Bridge Publications Ltd.

Spivak, Gayatri Chakravorty (1985) 'Three Women's Texts and a Critique of Imperialism,' *Critical Inquiry*, 12 (Autumn).

Spoto, Donald (1983) *The Dark Side of Genius: The Life of Alfred Hitchcock*, New York: Ballantine.

St John of the Cross (1959) *The Poems of St. John of the Cross*, trans. John Frederick Nims, New York: Grove Press.

St John of the Cross (1962) *Living Flame of Love*, trans. and ed. E. Allison Peers, Garden City, NY: Image.

Stanbrook, Alan (1991) 'Under Western Eyes,' *The 15th Hong Kong International Film Festival Retrospective: Hong Kong Cinema in the Eighties*, Hong Kong: Urban Council Press.

Steinbrunner, Chris and Goldblatt, Burt (1972) *Cinema of the Fantastic*, New York: Saturday Review Press.

Stendhal (1957) *De L'Amour*, Paris: Le Divan.

Sterrenburg, Lee (1979) 'Mary Shelley's Monster: Politics and Psyche in *Frankenstein*,' in George Levine and U.C. Knoepflmacher (eds), *The Endurance of Frankenstein*, Berkeley: University of California Press.

Stevenson, John Allen (1988) 'A Vampire in the Mirror: The Sexuality of *Dracula*,' *PMLA*, 103.

Stevenson, R.L. (1924) *The Works of Robert Louis Stevenson*, Tusitala Edition, London: William Heinemann, Ltd.

Stewart, Susan (1993) *On Longing: Narratives of the Miniature, the Gigantic, the Souvenir, the Collection*, Durham, NC and London: Duke University Press.

Stocking, George W. Jr (1987) *Victorian Anthropology*, New York: Free Press.

Stoker, Bram (1981) *Dracula*, New York: Bantam.

Stoker, Bram (1984) *Dracula*, Harmondsworth: Penguin.

Stoker, Bram (1988) *Dracula*: Oxford: Oxford University Press.

Sulivan, Lawrence (1802) 'Epilogue to Julius Caesar, performed at Mr Newcome's School, Hackney, in May 1802,' *Gentleman's Magazine* (June).

Summers, Montague (1928) *The Vampire: His Kith and Kin*, London: Kegan Paul, Trench, Trubner & Co.

Telotte, J.P. (1985) *Dreams of Darkness: Fantasy and the Films of Val Lewton*, Urbana and Chicago: University of Illinois Press.

Telotte, J.P. (1988) 'The Movies as Monster: Seeing in King Kong,' *Georgia Review*, 42: 2 (Summer).

Teo, Stephen (1997) *Hong Kong Cinema: The Extra Dimensions*, London: British Film Institute.

Theweleit, Klaus (1989) *Male Fantasies*, trans. Erica Carter and Chris Turner, Minneapolis: University of Minnesota Press.

Thomis, Malcolm I. (1970) *The Luddites: Machine-Breaking in Regency England*, Newton Abbot: David & Charles.

Thompson, E.P. (1968) *The Making of the English Working Class*, Harmondsworth: Penguin.

Tiffin, Helen (1987) 'Post-Colonial Literatures and Counter-Discourses,' *Kunapipi*, 9: 3.

Todorov, Tzvetan (1975) *The Fantastic: A Structural Approach to a Literary Genre*, trans. Richard Howard, Ithaca, NY: Cornell University Press.

Tohill, Cathal and Tombs, Pete (1995) *Immoral Tales: Sex and Horror Cinema in Europe, 1956–1984*, London: Titan Books.

Trilling, Lionel (1963) 'The Fate of Pleasure: Wordsworth to Dostoevsky,' *Partisan Review* (Summer).

Tropp, Martin (1974) *Mary Shelley's Monster*, Boston: Houghton Mifflin.

Tudor, Andrew (1997) 'Why Horror? The Peculiar Pleasures of a Popular Genre,' *Cultural Studies*, 11: 3.

Twitchell, James (1985) *Dreadful Pleasures: An Anatomy of Modern Horror*, New York: Oxford University Press.

Vale, V. and Juno, Andrea (1986) *Incredibly Strange Films*, San Francisco: Re/Search.

Varnado, S.L. (1981) 'The Idea of the Numinous in Gothic Literature,' in Peter B. Messent (ed.), *Literature of the Occult*, Englewood Cliffs, NJ: Prentice Hall.

Veeder, William (1988) 'Children of the Night: Stevenson and Patriarchy,' in William Veeder and Gordon Hirsch (eds), *Dr Jekyll and Mr Hyde After One Hundred Years*, Chicago: University of Chicago Press.

Veeder, William and Hirsch, Gordon (eds) (1988) *Dr Jekyll and Mr Hyde After One Hundred Years*, Chicago: University of Chicago Press.

Walcott, Derek (1974) 'The Caribbean: Culture or Mimicry?', *Journal of Interamerican Studies*, 16: 3.

Waller, Gregory A. (ed.) (1987) *American Horrors: Essays on the Modern American Horror Film*, Urbana and Chicago: University of Illinois Press.

Ware, Susan (1982) *Holding Their Own: American Women in the 1930s*, Boston: Twayne.

Weaver, James B. and Tamborini, Ron (1996) *Horror Films: Current Research on Audience Preferences and Reactions*, Mahwah, NJ: Lawrence Erlbaum Associates.

Weaver, Tom (1988) *Interviews with B Science Fiction and Horror Movie Makers*, Jefferson, NC, and London: McFarland & Company, Inc., Publishers.

Weaver, Tom (1993) *Poverty Row Horrors! Monogram, PRC and Republic Horror Films of the Forties*, Jefferson, NC, and London: McFarland & Company, Inc., Publishers.

Webb, Barbara (1992) *Myth and History in Caribbean Fiction*, Amherst: University of Massachussetts Press.

Weeks, Jeffrey (1977) *Coming Out: Homosexual Politics in Britain from the Nineteenth Century to the Present*, London: Quartet Books.

Weeks, Jeffrey (1981) *Sex, Politics, and Society*, New York and London: Longman.

Weiss, Allen S. (1995) *Phantasmic Radio*, Durham, NC: Duke University Press.

Weisser, Thomas and Weisser, Yuko Mihara (1997) *Japanese Cinema Encyclopedia: Horror, Fantasy, Science Fiction*, Miama, FL: Vital Books.

Weldon, Michael (1983) *The Psychotronic Encyclopedia of Film*, New York: Ballantine.

Welsh, Alexander (1985) *George Eliot and Blackmail*, Cambridge, MA: Harvard University Press.

Wexman, Virginia Wright (1988) 'Horrors of the Body: Hollywood's Discourse on Beauty and Rouben Mamoulian's *Dr Jekyll and Mr Hyde*,' in William Veeder and Gordon Hirsch (eds), *Dr Jekyll and Mr Hyde After One Hundred Years*, Chicago: University of Chicago Press.

White, Patricia (1991) 'Female Spectator, Lesbian Specter: The Haunting,' in Diana Fuss (ed.), *Inside/Out: Lesbian Theories, Gay Theories*, London and New York: Routledge.

Wicke, Jennifer (1992) 'Vampiric Typewriting: *Dracula* and its Media,' *ELH*, 59.

Wilde, Oscar (1967) *Salome*, trans. Lord Alfred Douglas, New York: Dover.

Williams, Linda (1984) 'When the Woman Looks,' in Mary Ann Doane *et al.* (eds), *Re-Vision: Essays in Feminist Film Criticism*, Frederick, MD: University Publications of America.

Williams, Linda (1990) *Hardcore: Power, Pleasure and the 'Frenzy of the Visible'*, London: Pandora Press.

Williams, Linda (1993) 'A Virus is Only Doing Its Job,' *Sight and Sound*, May.

Williams, Linda (1994) 'Learning to Scream,' *Sight and Sound*, December.

Williams, Tony (1983) 'Haitian Horror: *White Zombie*,' *Jump Cut*, 28.

Williams, Tony (1996) *Hearths of Darkness: the Family in the American Horror Film*, Madison, NJ: Fairleigh Dickinson University Press.

Wollstonecraft, Mary (1972) *Thoughts on the Education of Daughters with Reflections on Female Conduct in the more important Duties of Life*, Clifton, NJ: Augustus M. Kelley Publ.

Wood, Robin (1969–70) 'In Memorium Michael Reeves,' *Movie*, 17 (Winter).

Wood, Robin (1976) 'The Shadow Worlds of Jacques Tourneur,' *Personal Views: Explorations in Film*, London: Gordon Fraser.

Wood, Robin (1977) *Hitchcock's Films*, New York: A.S. Barnes.

Wood, Robin (1978) 'Gods and Monsters,' *Film Comment*, 14.

Wood, Robin (1983) 'Beauty Bests the Beast,' *American Film*, 8.

Wood, Robin (1984) 'An Introduction to the American Horror Film,' in Barry Keith Grant (ed.), *Planks of Reason: Essays on the Horror Film*, Metuchen, NJ: Scarecrow Press.

Wood, Robin (1985) 'An Introduction to the American Horror Film,' in Bill Nicholls (ed.), *Movies and Methods*, Vol. II, Berkeley: University of California Press.

Wood, Robin *et al.* (eds) (1979) *American Nightmare: Essays on the Horror Film*, Toronto: Festival of Festivals.

Yeats, William Butler (1961) 'A General Introduction for My Work,' *Essays and Introductions*, New York: Macmillan.

Young, Elizabeth (1991a) 'Here Comes the Bride: Wedding, Gender and Race in *Bride of Frankenstein*,' *Feminist Studies*, 17: 3.

Young, Elizabeth (1991b) '*The Silence of the Lambs* and the Flaying of Feminist Theory,' *camera obscura*, 27 (September).

Yuzna, Brian (1994) 'Spiralling Fear,' *Sight and Sound*, February.

Zanger, Jules (1991) 'A Sympathetic Vibration: Dracula and the Jews,' *English Literature in Transition, 1880–1920*, 34: 1.

Zangrando, Robert L. (1980) *The NAACP Crusade Against Lynching*, Philadelphia: Temple University Press.

Žižek, Slavoj (1992) 'In His Bold Gaze My Ruin is Writ Large,' in Slavoj Žižek (ed.) (1995) *Everything You Wanted to Know about Lacan (But Were Afraid to Ask Hitchcock)*, London: Verso.

Žižek, Slavoj (1994) *The Metastases of Enjoyment: Six Essays on Women and Causality*, London: Verso.

Index